CIMA
PUBLISHING

CIMA's Official
Learning System

Managerial Level

Management Accounting – Performance Evaluation

Bob Scarlett

ELSEVIER

AMSTERDAM   BOSTON   HEIDELBERG   LONDON   NEW YORK   OXFORD
PARIS   SAN DIEGO   SAN FRANCISCO   SINGAPORE   SYDNEY   TOKYO

CIMA Publishing is an imprint of Elsevier
Linacre House, Jordan Hill, Oxford OX2 8DP, UK
30 Corporate Drive, Suite 400, Burlington, MA 01803, USA

First edition 2008

British Library Cataloguing in Publication Data
A catalogue record for this book is available from the British Library

978-0-7506-8688-4

For information on all CIMA publications
visit our website at www.elsevierdirect.com

Typeset by Charon Tec Ltd., A Macmillan Company. (www.macmillansolutions.com)

Printed and bound in Italy

08 09 10   10 9 8 7 6 5 4 3 2 1

Contents

CONTENTS

CONTENTS

CONTENTS

CONTENTS

The CIMA
Learning System

Acknowledgements

Every effort has been made to contact the holders of copyright material, but if any here have been inadvertently overlooked the publishers will be pleased to make the necessary arrangements at the first opportunity.

How to use your CIMA *Learning System*

This *Performance Evaluation Learning System* has been devised as a resource for students attempting to pass their CIMA exams and provides:

- a detailed explanation of all syllabus areas;
- extensive 'practical' materials, including readings from relevant journals;
- generous question practice, together with full solutions;
- an exam preparation section, complete with exam standard questions and solutions.

This Learning System has been designed with the needs of home-study and distance-learning candidates in mind. Such students require very full coverage of the syllabus topics, and also the facility to undertake extensive question practice. However, the Learning System is also ideal for fully taught courses.

The main body of the text is divided into a number of chapters, each of which is organised on the following pattern:

- *Detailed learning outcomes.* This is expected after your studies of the chapter are complete. You should assimilate these before beginning detailed work on the chapter, so that you can appreciate where your studies are leading.
- *Step-by-step topic coverage.* This is the heart of each chapter, containing detailed explanatory text supported where appropriate by worked examples and exercises. You should work carefully through this section, ensuring that you understand the material being explained and can tackle the examples and exercises successfully. Remember that in many cases knowledge is cumulative: if you fail to digest earlier material thoroughly, you may struggle to understand later chapters.
- *Readings and activities.* Most chapters are illustrated by more practical elements, such as relevant journal articles or other readings, together with comments and questions designed to stimulate discussion.

THE CIMA *LEARNING SYSTEM*

- *Question practice*. The test of how well you have learned the material is your ability to tackle exam-standard questions. Make a serious attempt at producing your own answers, but at this stage do not be too concerned about attempting the questions in exam conditions. In particular, it is more important to absorb the material thoroughly by completing a full solution than to observe the time limits that would apply in the actual exam.
- *Solutions*. Avoid the temptation merely to 'audit' the solutions provided. It is an illusion to think that this provides the same benefits as you would gain from a serious attempt of your own. However, if you are struggling to get started on a question you should read the introductory guidance provided at the beginning of the solution, and then make your own attempt before referring back to the full solution.

Having worked through the chapters you are ready to begin your final preparations for the examination. The final section of this CIMA *Learning System* provides you with the guidance you need. It includes the following features:

- A brief guide to revision technique.
- A note on the format of the examination. You should know what to expect when you tackle the real exam, and in particular the number of questions to attempt, which questions are compulsory and which optional and so on.
- Guidance on how to tackle the examination itself.
- A table mapping revision questions to the syllabus learning outcomes allowing you to quickly identify questions by subject area.
- Revision questions. These are of exam standard and should be tackled in exam conditions, especially as regards the time allocation.
- Solutions to the revision questions. As before, these indicate the length and the quality of solution that would be expected of a well-prepared candidate.

If you work conscientiously through this CIMA *Learning System* according to the guidelines above you will be giving yourself an excellent chance of exam success. Good luck with your studies!

Guide to the Icons used within this Text

 Key term or definition

 Equation to learn

 Exam tip to topic likely to appear in the exam

 Exercise

 Question

 Solution

 Comment or Note

Study technique

Passing exams is partly a matter of intellectual ability, but however accomplished you are in that respect you can improve your chances significantly by the use of appropriate study and revision techniques. In this section we briefly outline some tips for effective study during the earlier stages of your approach to the exam. Later in the text we mention some techniques that you will find useful at the revision stage.

Planning

To begin with, formal planning is essential to get the best return from the time you spend studying.

Estimate how much time in total you are going to need for each subject that you face. Remember that you need to allow time for revision as well as for initial study of the material. The amount of notional study time for any subject is the minimum estimated time that students will need to achieve the specified learning outcomes set out earlier in this chapter. This time includes all appropriate learning activities, for example, face-to-face tuition, private study, directed home study, learning in the workplace, revision time and so on. You may find it helpful to read *Better Exam Results* by Sam Malone, CIMA Publishing, ISBN: 05066357X. This book will provide you with proven study techniques. Chapter by chapter it covers the building blocks of successful learning and examination techniques.

The notional study time for *Managerial level Performance Evaluation* is 200 hours. Note that the standard amount of notional learning hours attributed to one full-time academic year of approximately 30 weeks is 1,200 hours.

By way of example, the notional study time might be made up as follows:

	Hours
Face-to-face study: up to	60
Personal study: up to	100
'Other' study – e.g. learning in the workplace, revision, etc.: up to	40
	200

Note that all study and learning-time recommendations should be used only as a guideline and are intended as minimum amounts. The amount of time recommended for face-to-face tuition, personal study and/or additional learning will vary according to the type of course undertaken, prior learning of the student, and the pace at which different students learn.

Now split your total time requirement over the weeks between now and the examination. This will give you an idea of how much time you need to devote to study each week. Remember to allow for holidays or other periods during which you will not be able to study (e.g. because of seasonal workloads).

With your study material before you, decide which chapters you are going to study in each week, and which weeks you will devote to revision and final question practice.

Prepare a written schedule summarising the above – and stick to it!

The amount of space allocated to a topic in the study material is not a very good guide as to how long it will take you. For example, 'Summarising and Analysing Data' has a weight of 25 per cent in the syllabus and this is the best guide as to how long you should spend on it. It occupies 45 per cent of the main body of the text because it includes many tables and charts.

It is essential to know your syllabus. As your course progresses you will become more familiar with how long it takes to cover topics in sufficient depth. Your timetable may need to be adapted to allocate enough time for the whole syllabus.

Tips for effective studying

(1) Aim to find a quiet and undisturbed location for your study, and plan as far as possible to use the same period of time each day. Getting into a routine helps to avoid wasting time. Make sure that you have all the materials you need before you begin so as to minimise interruptions.

(2) Store all your materials in one place, so that you do not waste time searching for items around the house. If you have to pack everything away after each study period, keep them in a box, or even a suitcase, which will not be disturbed until the next time.

(3) Limit distractions. To make the most effective use of your study periods you should be able to apply total concentration, so turn off the TV, set your phones to message mode and put up your 'do not disturb' sign.

(4) Your timetable will tell you which topic to study. However, before diving in and becoming engrossed in the finer points, make sure you have an overall picture of all the areas that need to be covered by the end of that session. After an hour, allow yourself a short break and move away from your books. With experience, you will learn to assess the pace you need to work at. You should also allow enough time to read relevant articles from newspapers and journals, which will supplement your knowledge and demonstrate a wider perspective.

(5) Work carefully through a chapter, making notes as you go. When you have covered a suitable amount of material, vary the pattern by attempting a practice question. Preparing an answer plan is a good habit to get into, while you are both studying and revising, and also in the examination room. It helps to impose a structure on your solutions, and avoids rambling. When you have finished your attempt, make notes of any mistakes you made or any areas that you failed to cover or covered only skimpily.

(6) Make notes as you study, and discover the techniques that work best for you. Your notes may be in the form of lists, bullet points, diagrams, summaries, 'mind maps' or the written word, but remember that you will need to refer back to them at a later date, so they must be intelligible. If you are on a taught course, make sure you highlight any issues you would like to follow up with your lecturer.

(7) Organise your paperwork. There are now numerous paper storage systems available to ensure that all your notes, calculations and articles can be effectively filed and easily retrieved later.

The Performance Evaluation syllabus

Examined for the first time in May 2005

Syllabus outline

The syllabus comprises:

Topic	Study Weighting
A Cost Accounting Systems	25%
B Standard Costing	25%
C Budgeting	30%
D Control and Performance Measurement of Responsibility Centres	20%

Learning aims

Students should be able to:

- apply both traditional and contemporary approaches to cost accounting in a variety of contexts and evaluate the impact of 'modern' data processing and processing technologies, such as MRP, ERP and JIT;
- explain and apply the principles of standard costing, calculate variances in a variety of contexts and critically evaluate the worth of standard costing in the light of contemporary criticisms;
- develop budgets using both traditional and contemporary techniques, evaluate both interactive and diagnostic uses of budgets in a variety of contexts and discuss the issues raised by those that advocate techniques 'beyond budgeting';
- prepare appropriate financial statements for cost, profit and investment centre managers, calculate appropriate financial performance indicators, assess the impact of alternative transfer pricing policies and discuss the behavioural consequences of management control systems based on responsibility accounting, decentralisation and delegation.

Assessment strategy

There will be a written examination paper of 3 hours, with the following sections.

Section A – 40 marks

A variety of compulsory objective test questions, each worth between 2 and 4 marks. Mini-scenarios may be given, to which a group of questions relate.

Section B – 30 marks

Six compulsory short answer questions, each worth 5 marks. A short scenario may be given, to which some or all questions relate.

Section C – 30 marks

One question, from a choice of two, worth 20 marks. Short scenarios may be given, to which questions relate.

Learning outcomes and syllabus content

A – Cost Accounting Systems – 25%
Learning outcomes

On completion of their studies students should be able to:

(i) compare and contrast marginal and absorption costing methods in respect of profit reporting and stock valuation;

(ii) apply marginal and absorption costing approaches in job, batch and process environments;

(iii) prepare ledger accounts according to context: marginal or absorption based in job, batch or process environments, including work in progress and related accounts, such as production overhead control account and abnormal loss account;

(iv) explain the origins of throughput accounting as 'super variable costing' and its application as a variant of marginal or variable cost accounting;

(v) apply standard costing methods within costing systems and demonstrate the reconciliation of budgeted and actual profit margins;

(vi) compare activity-based costing with traditional marginal and absorption costing methods and evaluate its potential as a system of cost accounting;

(vii) explain the role of MRP and ERP systems in supporting standard costing systems, calculating variances and facilitating the posting of ledger entries;

(viii) evaluate the impact of just-in-time manufacturing methods on cost accounting and the use of 'backflush accounting' when work-in-progress stock is minimal.

Syllabus Content

- Marginal (or variable) costing as a system of profit reporting and stock valuation.
- Absorption costing as a system of profit reporting and stock valuation.
- Throughput accounting as a system of profit reporting and stock valuation.
- Activity-based costing as a potential system of profit reporting and stock valuation.
- The integration of standard costing with marginal cost accounting, absorption cost accounting and throughput accounting.
- Process accounting, including establishment of equivalent units in stock, work in progress and abnormal loss accounts and the use of first in, first out, average cost and standard cost methods of stock valuation.
- MRP and ERP systems for resource planning and the integration of accounting functions with other systems, such as purchase ordering and production planning.
- Backflush accounting in just-in-time production environments. The benefits of just-in-time production, total quality management and theory of constraints and the possible impacts of these methods on cost accounting and performance measurement.

B – Standard Costing – 25%

Learning outcomes

On completion of their studies students should be able to:

(i) explain why and how standards are set in manufacturing and in service industries with particular reference to the maximisation of efficiency and minimisation of waste.

(ii) calculate and interpret material, labour, variable overhead, fixed overhead and sales variances;

(iii) prepare and discuss a report which reconciles budget and actual profit using absorption and/or marginal costing principles;

(iv) calculate and explain planning and operational variances;

(v) prepare reports using a range of internal and external benchmarks and interpret the results;

(vi) discuss the behavioural implications of setting standard costs.

Syllabus content

- Manufacturing standards for material, labour, variable overhead and fixed overhead.
- Price/rate and usage/efficiency variances for materials, labour and variable overhead. Further subdivision of total usage/efficiency variances into mix and yield components. (Note: The calculation of mix variances on both individual and average valuation bases is required.)

- Fixed overhead expenditure and volume variances. (Note: The subdivision of fixed overhead volume variance into capacity and efficiency elements will not be examined.)
- Planning and operational variances.
- Standards and variances in service industries, (including the phenomenon of 'McDonaldisation'), public services (e.g. Health) (including the use of 'diagnostic related' or 'reference' groups) and the professions (e.g. labour mix variances in audit work). Criticisms of standard costing in general and in advanced manufacturing environments in particular.
- Sales price and sales revenue/margin volume variances (calculation of the latter on a unit basis related to revenue, gross margin and contribution margin). Application of these variances to all sectors, including professional services and retail analysis.
- Interpretation of variances: interrelationship, significance.
- Benchmarking.
- Behavioural implications of setting standard costs.

C – Budgeting – 30%

Learning outcomes

On completion of their studies students should be able to:

  (i) explain why organisations prepare forecasts and plans;
 (ii) calculate projected product/service volumes employing appropriate forecasting techniques;
(iii) calculate projected revenues and costs based on product/service volumes, pricing strategies and cost structures;
 (iv) evaluate projected performance by calculating key metrics including profitability, liquidity and asset turnover ratios;
  (v) describe and explain the possible purposes of budgets, including planning, communication, co-ordination, motivation, authorisation, control and evaluation;
 (vi) evaluate and apply alternative approaches to budgeting;
(vii) calculate the consequences of 'what if' scenarios and evaluate their impact on master profit and loss account and balance sheet;
(viii) explain the concept of responsibility accounting and its importance in the construction of functional budgets that support the overall master budget;
 (ix) identify controllable and uncontrollable costs in the context of responsibility accounting and explain why 'uncontrollable' costs may or may not be allocated to responsibility centres;
  (x) explain the ideas of feedback and feedforward control and their application in the use of budgets for control;
 (xi) evaluate performance using fixed and flexible budget reports;
(xii) discuss the role of non-financial performance indicators and compare and contrast traditional approaches to budgeting with recommendations based on the 'balanced scorecard';
(xiii) evaluate the impact of budgetary control systems on human behaviour;
(xiv) evaluate the criticisms of budgeting particularly from the advocates of techniques that are 'beyond budgeting'.

Syllabus content

- Time series analysis including moving totals and averages, treatment of seasonality, trend analysis using regression analysis and the application of these techniques in forecasting product and service volumes.
- Fixed, variable, semi-variable and activity-based categorisations of cost and their application in projecting financial results.
- 'What-if' analysis based on alternate projections of volumes, prices and cost structures and the use of spreadsheets in facilitating these analyses.
- The purposes of budgets and conflicts that can arise (e.g. between budgets for realistic planning and budgets based on 'hard to achieve' targets for motivation).
- The creation of budgets, including incremental approaches, zero-based budgeting and activity-based budgets.
- The use of budgets in planning: 'rolling budgets' for adaptive planning.
- The use of budgets for control: controllable costs and variances based on 'fixed' and 'flexed' budgets. The conceptual link between standard costing and budget flexing.
- Behavioural issues in budgeting: participation in budgeting and its possible beneficial consequences for ownership and motivation; participation in budgeting and its possible adverse consequences for 'budget padding' and manipulation; setting budget targets for motivation and so on.
- Criticisms of budgeting and the recommendations of the advocates of the balanced scorecard and 'beyond budgeting'.

D – Control and Performance Measurement of Responsibility Centres – 20%

Learning outcomes

On completion of their studies students should be able to:

(i) discuss the use of cost, revenue, profit and investment centres in devising organisation structure and in management control;

(ii) prepare cost information in appropriate formats for cost centre managers, taking due account of controllable/uncontrollable costs and the importance of budget flexing;

(iii) prepare revenue and cost information in appropriate formats for profit and investment centre managers, taking due account of cost variability, attributable costs, controllable costs and identification of appropriate measures of profit centre 'contribution';

(iv) calculate and apply measures of performance for investment centres (often 'strategic business units' or divisions of larger groups);

(v) discuss the likely behavioural consequences of the use of performance metrics in managing cost, profit and investment centres;

(vi) explain the typical consequences of a divisional structure for performance measurement as divisions compete or trade with each other;

(vii) identify the likely consequences of different approaches to transfer pricing for divisional decision-making, divisional and group profitability, the motivation of divisional management and the autonomy of individual divisions.

Syllabus content

- Organisation structure and its implications for responsibility accounting.
- Presentation of financial information, including issues of controllable/uncontrollable costs, variable/fixed costs and tracing revenues and costs to particular cost objects.
- Return on investment and its deficiencies; the emergence of residual income and economic value added to address these.
- Behavioural issues in the application of performance measures in cost, profit and investment centres.
- The theory of transfer pricing, including perfect, imperfect and no market for the intermediate good.
- Use of negotiated, market, cost-plus and variable cost–based transfer prices. 'Dual' transfer prices and lump sum payments as means of addressing some of the issues that arise.
- The interaction of transfer pricing and tax liabilities in international operations and implications for currency management and possible distortion of internal company operations in order to comply with Tax Authority directives.

1

Basic Aspects of
Management Accounting

Basic Aspects of Management Accounting

1

LEARNING OUTCOMES

The contents of this chapter provides the theory that underpins material in subsequent chapters. As such it contributes to the Learning Outcomes of those chapters. However, none of the Learning Outcomes for Performance Evaluation draw wholly on material from this chapter.

1.1 Introduction

You should have encountered the basic principles of cost and revenue behaviour in your Foundation (or equivalent) studies. The major part of this chapter amounts to a revision of those basic principles.

You are reminded, once again, that the CIMA examination scheme is cumulative and Performance Evaluation examination questions may draw heavily on material taken from Foundation studies. This may be a critical issue for students who were exempted from or only narrowly passed Foundation examinations, or who passed Foundation examinations some time ago.

Much of the content of this chapter is 'assumed prior knowledge' for Performance Evaluation studies and for material covered in subsequent chapters of this text. If you are entirely familiar with the basic aspects of management accounting, then you may prefer just to skim-read this chapter. However, you are advised not to ignore it completely – particularly the sections on relevant costs and limiting factor analysis.

1.2 Cost behaviour

Many factors affect the level of costs incurred; for instance, inflation will cause costs to increase over a period of time. In management accounting, when we talk about cost behaviour we are referring to the way in which costs are affected by fluctuations in the level of activity.

The level of activity can be measured in many different ways. For example, we can record the number of units produced, miles travelled, hours worked, percentage of capacity utilised and so on.

An understanding of cost behaviour patterns is essential for many management tasks, particularly in the areas of planning, decision-making and control. It would be impossible for managers to forecast and control costs without at least a basic knowledge of the way in which costs behave in relation to the level of activity.

In this section, we will look at the most common cost behaviour patterns and we will consider some examples of each.

1.2.1 Fixed cost

> The CIMA *Terminology* defines a fixed cost as 'a cost which is incurred for an accounting period, and which, within certain output or turnover limits, tends to be unaffected by fluctuations in the levels of activity (output or turnover)'.

Another term which can be used to refer to a fixed cost is 'period cost'. This highlights the fact that a fixed cost is incurred according to the time elapsed, rather than according to the level of activity.

A fixed cost can be depicted graphically as shown in Figure 1.1.

Examples of fixed costs are rent, rates, insurance and executive salaries.

The graph shows that the cost is constant (in this case at £5,000 for all levels of activity). However, it is important to note that this is only true for the relevant range of activity. Consider, for example, the behaviour of the rent cost. Within the relevant range it is possible to expand activity without needing extra premises and therefore the rent cost remains constant. However, if activity is expanded to the critical point where further premises are needed, then the rent cost will increase to a new, higher level.

This cost behaviour pattern can be described as a stepped fixed cost (Figure 1.2).

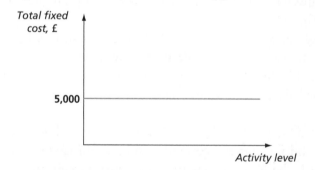

Figure 1.1 Fixed cost

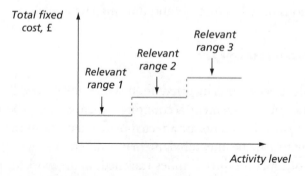

Figure 1.2 Stepped fixed cost

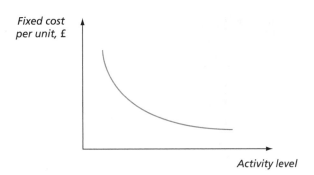

Figure 1.3 Fixed cost per unit

The cost is constant within the relevant range for each activity level but when a critical level of activity is reached, the total cost incurred increases to the next step.

The possibility of changes occurring in cost behaviour patterns means that it is unreliable to predict costs for activity levels which are outside the relevant range. For example, out records might show the cost incurred at various activity levels between 100 and 5,000 units. We should therefore try to avoid using this information as the basis for forecasting the level of cost which would be incurred at an activity of, say, 6,000 units, which is outside the relevant range.

> This warning does not only apply to fixed costs: it is never wise to attempt to predict costs for activity levels outside the range for which cost behaviour patterns have been established.

When you are drawing or interpreting graphs of cost behaviour patterns, it is important that you pay great attention to the label on the vertical axis. In Figures 1.1 and 1.2 the graphs depicted the total cost incurred. If the vertical axis had been used to represent the fixed cost per unit, then it would look as shown Figure 1.3.

The fixed cost per unit reduces as the activity level is increased. This is because the same amount of fixed cost is being spread over an increasing number of units.

1.2.2 Variable cost

> The CIMA *Terminology* defines a variable cost as 'a cost which varies with a measure of activity'.

Examples of variable costs are direct material, direct labour and variable overheads.

Exercise 1.1

Figure 1.4 depicts the total variable cost at each activity level. Can you draw a sketch graph of the variable cost per unit?

Figure 1.4 depicts a linear variable cost. It is a straight line through the origin which means that the cost is nil at zero activity level. When activity increases, the total variable cost increases in direct proportion, that is if activity goes up by 10%, then the total variable cost also increases by 10%, as long as the activity level is still within the relevant range.

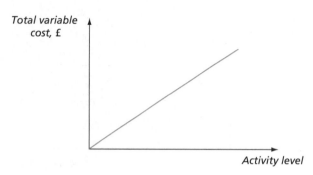

Figure 1.4 Linear variable cost

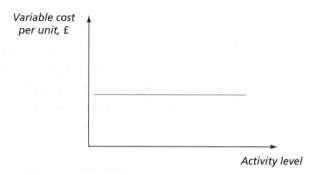

Figure 1.5 Variable cost per unit

The gradient of the line will depend on the amount of variable cost per unit.

If you attempted Exercise 1.4, then your graph of variable cost per unit should look like Figure 1.5.

The straight line parallel to the horizontal axis depicts a constant variable cost per unit, within the relevant range.

In most examination situations, and very often in practice, variable costs are assumed to be linear. Although many variable costs do approximate to a linear function, this assumption may not always be realistic. A variable cost may be non-linear as depicted in either of the diagrams in Figure 1.6.

These costs are sometimes called curvilinear variable costs.

The graph of cost A becomes steeper as the activity level increases. This indicates that each successive unit of activity is adding more to the total variable cost than the previous unit. An example of a variable cost which follows this pattern could be the cost of direct labour where employees are paid an accelerating bonus for achieving higher levels of output. The graph of cost B becomes less steep as the activity level increases. Each successive unit of activity adds less to total variable cost than the previous unit. An example of a variable cost which follows this pattern could be the cost of direct material where quantity discounts are available.

 Exercise 1.2

Can you think of other variable costs which might follow the behaviour patterns depicted in Figure 1.6?

The important point is that managers should be aware of any assumptions that have been made in estimating cost behaviour patterns. They can then use the information which is based on these assumptions with a full awareness of its possible limitations.

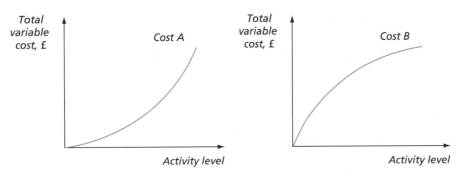

Figure 1.6 Non-linear variable costs

1.2.3 Semi-variable cost

> A semi-variable cost is also referred to as a semi-fixed, hybrid, or mixed cost. The CIMA *Terminology* defines it as 'a cost containing both fixed and variable components and which is thus partly affected by a change in the level of activity'.

A graph of a semi-variable cost might look like Figure 1.7.

Examples of semi-variable costs are gas and electricity. Both of these expenditures consist of a fixed amount payable for the period, with a further variable amount which is related to the consumption of gas or electricity.

Alternatively a semi-variable cost behaviour pattern might look like Figure 1.8.

This cost remains constant up to a certain level of activity and then increases as the variable cost element is incurred. An example of such a cost might be the rental cost of a photocopier where a fixed rental is paid and no extra charge is made for copies up to a certain number. Once this number of copies is exceeded, a constant charge is levied for each copy taken.

Exercise 1.3

Can you think of other examples of semi-variable costs with behaviour patterns like those indicated in Figures 1.7 and 1.8?

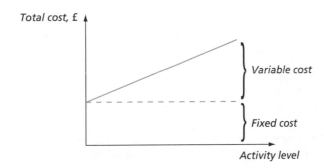

Figure 1.7 Semi-variable cost

BASIC ASPECTS OF MANAGEMENT ACCOUNTING

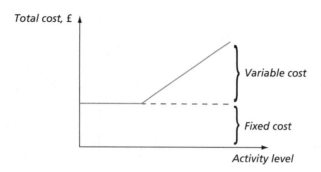

Figure 1.8 Semi-variable cost

1.2.4 Analysing semi-variable costs

The semi-variable cost behaviour pattern depicted in Figure 1.7 is most common in practice and in examination situations.

When managers have identified a semi-variable cost they will need to know how much of it is fixed and how much is variable. Only when they have determined this will they be able to estimate the cost to be incurred at relevant activity levels. Past records of costs and their associated activity levels are usually used to carry out the analysis. The three most common methods used to separate the fixed and variable elements are as follows:

(a) The high–low method.
(b) The scattergraph method.
(c) The least squares method of regression analysis.

You will be learning about the least squares method in your studies of *Business Mathematics.* In this text we will look at methods (a) and (b) in more depth.

The high–low method

This method picks out the highest and lowest activity levels from the available data and investigates the change in cost which has occurred between them. The highest and lowest points are selected to try to use the greatest possible range of data. This improves the accuracy of the result.

Example: the high-low method

A company has recorded the following data for a semi-variable cost:

Month	Activity level units	Cost incurred £
January	1,800	36,600
February	2,450	41,150
March	2,100	38,700
April	2,000	38,000
May	1,750	36,250
June	1,950	37,650

The highest activity level occurred in February and the lowest in May. Since the amount of fixed cost incurred in each month is constant, the extra cost resulting from the activity increase must be the variable cost.

	Activity level units	£
February	2,450	41,150
May	1,750	36,250
Increase	700	4,900

The extra variable cost for 700 units is £4,900. We can now calculate the variable cost per unit:

$$\text{Variable cost} = \frac{4,900}{700} = £7 \text{ per unit}$$

Substituting back in the data for February, we can determine the amount of fixed cost:

February		£
Total cost		41,150
Variable cost (2,450 units × £7)		17,150
Therefore, fixed cost per month		24,000

Now that the fixed and variable cost elements have been identified, it is possible to estimate the total cost for any activity level within the range 1,750 units to 2,450 units.

The scattergraph method

This method takes account of all available historical data and it is very simple to use. However, it is very prone to inaccuracies that arise due to subjectivity and the likelihood of human error.

1. First a scattergraph is drawn which plots all available pairs of data on a graph.
2. Then a line of best fit is drawn by eye. This is the line which, in the judgement of the user, appears to be the best representation of the gradient of the sets of points on the graph. This is demonstrated in Figure 1.9.

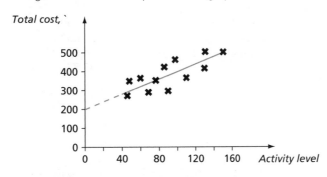

Figure 1.9 Scattergraph

 The inaccuracies involved in drawing the line of best fit should be obvious to you. If you had been presented with this set of data, your own line of best fit might have been slightly different from ours.

3. The point where the extrapolation of this line cuts the vertical axis (the intercept) is then read off as the total fixed cost element. The variable cost per unit is given by the gradient of the line.
   From Figure 1.9, the fixed cost contained within this set of data is adjudged to be £200.
   The variable cost is calculated as follows:

Cost for zero units = £200
Cost for 150 units = £500

$$\text{Gradient (i.e. variable cost)} = \frac{500 - 200}{150 - 0} = £2 \text{ per unit.}$$

1.2.5 Using historical data

The main problem which arises in the determination of cost behaviour is that the estimates are usually based on data collected in the past. Events in the past may not be representative of the future and managers should be aware of this if they are using the information for planning and decision-making purposes.

1.3 Costs and activity-based techniques

Since the mid-1980s, activity-based techniques (ABTs) have been at the forefront of developments in management accounting. The use of ABTs will be explored in some depth later in this text.

The general background to ABTs is discussed in 'Activity-Based Techniques', in Section 8.9.1. This article should be accessible to you at this point and you may care to read forward to it if the topic interests you.

The key point to note for now is that costs can be collected and reported in various different ways. One way is to report them according to the activities that they contribute to. For example, the overhead costs associated with the stores operation of a manufacturing business for period X can be reported as follows:

(1) Chart of accounts view

	£
Indirect wages	50,000
Rent of premises	25,000
Maintenance of equipment	5,000
Total	80,000

And/or:

(2) Activity-based view

	£	Activities	£ per Activity
Placing orders	40,000	2,000 orders	20
Receipt of deliveries	30,000	3,000 receipts	10
Issues of supplies	10,000	10,000 issues	1
Total	80,000		

The traditional management accounting treatment of these costs would be to treat them as fixed overheads and absorb them into product costs using some arbitrary overhead absorption base such as direct labour hours. This logic follows the chart of accounts view shown above.

In fact, few costs are truly fixed if you take a long enough time horizon, consider a wide enough span of activity levels and study the costs carefully to determine what activities they vary with. If costs are reported according to the activities they relate to, then one obtains the activity-based view shown above. This provides a sensitive view of costs that can be used for a variety of management purposes. We will explore those purposes as we progress through this text and consider ABTs such as activity-based costing (ABC), activity-based budgeting (ABB) and activity-based management (ABM).

1.4 Breakeven or cost-volume-profit analysis

> *Cost–volume–profit* (CVP) analysis is defined in CIMA's *Official Terminology* as 'the study of the effects on future profit of changes in fixed cost, variable cost, sales price, quantity and mix'.

A more common term used for this type of analysis is 'breakeven analysis'. However, this is somewhat misleading, since it implies that the focus of the analysis is the *breakeven point*, that is the level of activity that produces neither profit nor loss. the scope of CVP analysis is much wider than this, as indicated in the definition. However, you should be aware that the terms 'breakeven analysis' and 'CVP analysis' tend to be used interchangeably.

1.4.1 Calculating the breakeven point

Contribution is so called because it literally does contribute towards fixed costs and profit. As sales revenues grow from zero, the contribution also grows until it just covers the fixed costs. This is the breakeven point where neither profits nor losses are made.

It follows that to break even the amount of contribution must exactly match the amount of fixed costs. If we know how much contribution is earned from each unit sold, then we can calculate the number of units required to break even as follows:

$$\text{Breakeven point in units} = \frac{\text{Fixed costs}}{\text{Contribution per unit}}$$

For example, suppose that an organisation manufactures a single product, incurring variable costs of £30 per unit and fixed costs of £20,000 per month. If the product sells for £50 per unit, then the breakeven point can be calculated as follows:

$$\text{Breakeven point in units} = \frac{£20,000}{£50 - £30} = 1{,}000 \text{ units per month.}$$

1.5 The margin of safety

The margin of safety is the difference between the expected level of sales and the breakeven point. The larger the margin of safety, the more likely it is that a profit will be made, that is if sales start to fall there is more leeway before the organisation begins to incur losses. (Obviously, this statement is made on the assumption that projected sales volumes are above the breakeven point.)

In the above example, if forecast sales are 1,700 units per month, the margin of safety can be easily calculated.

$$\begin{aligned}\text{Margin of safety} &= \text{projected sales} - \text{breakeven point}\\ &= 1{,}700 \text{ units} - 1{,}000 \text{ units}\\ &= 700 \text{ units per month, or } 41\% \text{ of sales } (700/1{,}700 \times 100\%)\end{aligned}$$

The margin of safety should be expressed as a percentage of projected sales to put it in perspective. To quote a margin of safety of 700 units without relating it to the projected sales figure is not giving the full picture.

The margin of safety might also be expressed as a percentage of the breakeven value, that is 70 per cent of the breakeven value in this case.

The margin of safety can also be used as one route to profit calculation. We have seen that the contribution goes towards fixed costs and profit. Once breakeven point is reached the fixed costs have been covered. After the breakeven point there are no more fixed costs to be covered and all of the contribution goes towards making profits grow.

In our example the monthly profit from sales of 1,700 units would be £14,000.

$$\text{Margin of safety} = 700 \text{ units per month}$$
$$\text{Monthly profit} = 700 \times \text{contribution per unit}$$
$$= 700 \times £20$$
$$= £14,000.$$

1.6 The contribution to sales (C/S) ratio

The contribution to sales ratio is usually expressed as a percentage. It can be calculated for the product in our example as follows:

$$\text{Contribution to sales ratio (C/S ratio)} = £20 / £50 \times 100\%$$
$$= 40\%$$

A higher contribution to sales ratio means that contribution grows more quickly as sales levels increase. Once the breakeven point has been passed, profits will accumulate more quickly than for a product with a lower contribution to sales ratio.

You might sometimes see this ratio referred to as the profit–volume (P/V) ratio.

If we can assume that a unit's variable cost and selling price remain constant, then the C/S ratio will also remain constant. It can be used to calculate the breakeven point as follows (using the data from the earlier example):

$$\text{Breakeven point in sales value} = \frac{\text{Fixed costs}}{\text{C/S ratio}} = \frac{£20,000}{0.40} = £50,000$$

This can be converted to 1,000 units as before by dividing by the selling price of £50 per unit.

 Exercise

A company manufactures and sells a single product that has the following cost and selling price structure:

	£/unit	£/unit
Selling price		120
Direct material	22	
Direct labour	36	
Variable overhead	14	
Fixed overhead	12	
		84
Profit per unit		36

The fixed overhead absorption rate is based on the normal capacity of 2,000 units per month. Assume that the same amount is spent each month on fixed overheads.

Budgeted sales for next month are 2,200 units.
You are required to calculate

 (i) the breakeven point, in sales units per month;
 (ii) the margin of safety for next month;
(iii) the budgeted profit for next month;
(iv) the sales required to achieve a profit of £96,000 in a month.

 **Solution**

 (i) The key to calculating the breakeven point is to determine the contribution per unit.

Contribution per unit $= £120 - (£22 + £36 + £14) = £48$

$$\text{Breakeven point} = \frac{\text{Fixed overhead}}{\text{Contribution per unit}}$$

$$= \frac{£12 \times 2,000}{£48} = 500 \text{ units}$$

 (ii) Margin of safety = budgeted sales − breakeven point
     = 2,200 − 500
     = 1,700 units (or, 1,700/2,200 × 100% = 77% of budgeted sales)

(iii) Once breakeven point has been reached, all of the contribution goes towards profits because all of the fixed costs have been covered.

Budgeted profit = 1,700 units margin of safety × £48 contribution per unit
              = £81,600

(iv) To achieve the desired level of profit, sufficient units must be sold to earn a contribution that covers the fixed costs and leaves the desired profit for the month.

$$\text{Number of sales units required} = \frac{\text{Fixed overhead + desired profit}}{\text{Contribution per unit}}$$

$$= \frac{(£12 \times 2,000) + £96,000}{£48} = 2,500 \text{ units}$$

1.7 Drawing a basic breakeven chart

A basic breakeven chart records costs and revenues on the vertical axis and the level of activity on the horizontal axis. Lines are drawn on the chart to represent costs and sales revenue. The breakeven point can be read off where the sales revenue line cuts the total cost line.

We shall use our basic example to demonstrate how to draw a breakeven chart. The data is

Selling price	£50 per unit
Variable cost	£30 per unit
Fixed costs	£20,000 per month
Forecast sales	1,700 units per month

> You must be able to prepare breakeven charts to scale using data provided. To give yourself some practice it would be a good idea to follow the step-by-step guide that follows to produce your own chart on a piece of graph paper.

- *Step 1. Select appropriate scales for the axes and draw and label them.* Your graph should fill as much of the page as possible. This will make it clearer and easier to read. You can make sure that you do this by putting the extremes of the axes right at the end of the available space.

  The furthest point on the vertical axis will be the monthly sales revenue, that is,

  1,700 units × £50 = £85,000

  The furthest point on the horizontal axis will be monthly sales volume of 1,700 units. Make sure that you do not need to read data for volumes higher than 1,700 units before you set these extremes for your scales.

- *Step 2. Draw the fixed cost line and label it.* This will be a straight line parallel to the horizontal axis at the £20,000 level.

  The £20,000 fixed costs are incurred in the short term even with zero activity.

- *Step 3. Draw the total cost line and label it.* The best way to do this is to calculate the total costs for the maximum sales level, which is 1,700 units in our example. Mark this point on the graph and join it to the cost incurred at zero activity, that is £20,000

		£
Variable costs of 1,700 units		
(1,700 × £30)		51,000
Fixed costs		20,000
Total cost for 1,700 units		71,000

- *Step 4. Draw the revenue line and label it.* Once again, the best way is to plot the extreme points. The revenue at maximum activity in our example is 1,700 × £50 = £85,000. This point can be joined to the origin, since at zero activity there will be no sales revenue.

- *Step 5. Mark any required information on the chart and read off solutions as required.* Check that your chart is accurate by reading off the measures that we have already calculated in this chapter: the breakeven point, the margin of safety, the profit for sales of 1,700 units.

- *Step 6. Check the accuracy of your readings using arithmetic.* We already have the solutions calculated arithmetically for our example. However, it is always good examination practice to check the accuracy of your answers and make adjustments for any errors in your chart (if you have time!).

The completed graph is shown in Figure 1.10.

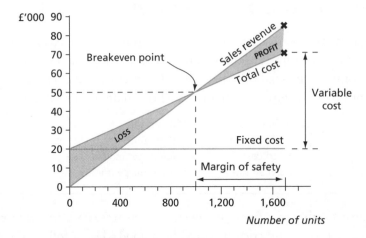

Figure 1.10 Basic breakeven chart

Your own graph should be considerably larger than this: a full A4 graph-ruled sheet is recommended to facilitate ease of interpretation.

1.8   The contribution breakeven chart

One of the problems with the conventional or basic breakeven chart is that it is not possible to read contribution directly from the chart. A contribution breakeven chart is based on the same principles but it shows the variable cost line instead of the fixed cost line (Figure 1.11). The same lines for total cost and sales revenue are shown so the breakeven point and profit can be read off in the same way as with a conventional chart. However, it is also possible to read the contribution for any level of activity.

Using the same basic example as for the conventional chart, the total variable cost for an output of 1,700 units is 1,700 × £30 = £51,000. This point can be joined to the origin since the variable cost is nil at zero activity.

The contribution can be read as the difference between the sales revenue line and the variable cost line.

This form of presentation might be used when it is desirable to highlight the importance of contribution and to focus attention on the variable costs.

1.9   The PV chart

Another form of breakeven chart is the PV chart. This chart plots a single line depicting the profit or loss at each level of activity. The breakeven point is where this line cuts the horizontal axis. A PV graph for our example will look like Figure 1.12.

The vertical axis shows profits and losses and the horizontal axis is drawn at zero profit or loss.

At zero activity the loss is equal to £20,000, that is the amount of fixed costs. The second point used to draw the line could be the calculated breakeven point or the calculated profit for sales of 1,700 units.

The PV graph is also called a profit graph or a contribution–volume graph.

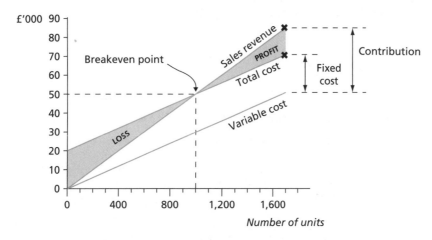

Figure 1.11   Contribution breakeven chart

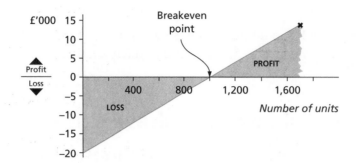

Figure 1.12 Profit–volume chart

 Exercise

Make sure that you are clear about the extremes of the chart axes. Practise drawing this chart to scale on a piece of graph paper.

1.9.1 The advantage of the PV chart

The main advantage of the PV chart is that it is capable of depicting clearly the effect on profit and breakeven point of any changes in the variables. An example will show how this can be done.

Example

A company manufactures a single product that incurs fixed costs of £30,000 per annum. Annual sales are budgeted to be 70,000 units at a sales price of £30 per unit. Variable costs are £28.50 per unit.

(a) Draw a PV graph, and use it to determine the breakeven point.

The company is now considering improving the quality of the product and increasing the selling price to £35 per unit. Sales volume will be unaffected, but fixed costs will increase to £45,000 per annum and variable costs to £33 per unit.

(b) Draw, on the same graph as for part (a), a second PV graph and comment on the results.

Solution

The PV chart is shown in Figure 1.13.
The two lines have been drawn as follows:

- *Situation (a).* The profit for sales of 70,000 units is £75,000.

	£'000
Contribution 70,000 × £(30 − 28.50)	105
Fixed costs	30
Profit	75

This point is joined to the loss at zero activity, £30,000, that is the fixed costs.

- *Situation (b).* The profit for sales of 70,000 units is £95,000.

	£'000
Contribution 70,000 × £(35 − 33)	140
Fixed costs	45
Profit	95

This point is joined to the loss at zero activity, £45,000, that is the fixed costs.

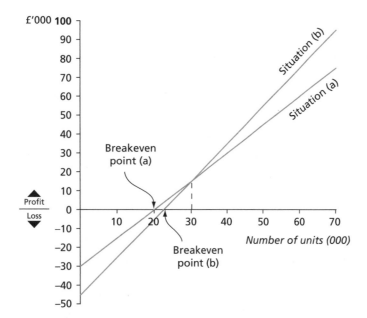

Figure 1.13   Showing changes with a PV chart

Comment on the results

The graph depicts clearly the larger profits available from option (b). It also shows that the breakeven point increases from 20,000 to 22,500 units but that this is not a large increase when viewed in the context of the projected sales volume. It is also possible to see that for sales volumes above 30,000 units the profit achieved will be higher with option (b). For sales volumes below 30,000 units option (a) will yield higher profits (or lower losses).

The PV graph is the clearest way of presenting information like this. If we attempted to draw two conventional breakeven charts on one set of axes, the result would be a jumble that would be very difficult to interpret.

1.10   The limitations of breakeven (or CVP) analysis

The limitations of the practical applicability of breakeven analysis and breakeven charts stem mostly from the assumptions that underline the analysis:

(a) Costs are assumed to behave in a linear fashion. Unit variable costs are assumed to remain constant and fixed costs are assumed to be unaffected by changes in activity levels. The charts can in fact be adjusted to cope with non-linear variable costs or steps in fixed costs, but too many changes in behaviour patterns can make the charts very cluttered and difficult to use.

(b) Sales revenues are assumed to be constant for each unit sold. This may be unrealistic because of the necessity to reduce the selling price to achieve higher sales volumes. Once again, the analysis can be adapted for some changes in selling price but too many changes can make the charts unwieldy.

(c) There is assumed to be no change in stocks. Reported profits can vary if absorption costing is used and there are changes in stock levels.

(d) It is assumed that activity is the only factor affecting costs, and factors such as inflation are ignored. This is one of the reasons why the analysis is limited to being essentially a short-term decision aid.

(e) Apart from the unrealistic situation described above of a constant product mix, the charts can only be applied to a single product or service. Not many organisations have a single product or service, and if there is more than one then the apportionment of fixed costs between them becomes arbitrary.

(f) The analysis seems to suggest that as long as the activity level is above the breakeven point, then a profit will be achieved. In reality certain changes in the cost and revenue patterns may result in a second breakeven point after which losses are made. This situation will be depicted in the next section of this chapter.

1.11 The economist's breakeven chart

An economist would probably depict a breakeven chart as shown in Figure 1.14.

The total cost line is not a straight line that climbs at a constant rate as in the accountant's breakeven chart. Instead, its slope increases moving from left to right because marginal costs are likely to increase with output – given short-term capacity constraints.

The revenue line is not a straight line as in the accountant's chart. The line becomes less steep to depict the need to reduce unit selling prices in order to achieve higher sales volumes.

However, you will see that within the middle range the economist's chart does look very similar to the accountant's breakeven chart. This area is marked as the relevant range in Figure 1.14.

For this reason it is unreliable to assume that the CVP relationships depicted in breakeven analysis are relevant across a wide range of activity. In particular, Figure 1.14 shows that the constant cost and price assumptions are likely to be unreliable at very high or very low levels of activity. Managers should therefore ensure that they work within the relevant range for the available data, that is within the range over which the depicted cost and revenue relationships are more reliable.

1.12 Using costs for decision-making

Most management decisions involve a change in the level, method or mix of activities in order to maximise profits. The only costs that should be considered in decision-making are

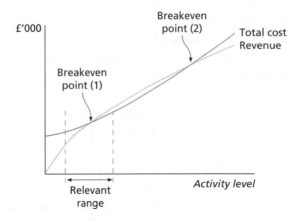

Figure 1.14 The economist's breakeven chart

those that will be altered as a result of the decision. Those costs that will be affected by the decision may be referred to as *relevant costs,* while others are non-relevant and should be ignored in the analysis.

It is often the case that variable costs are relevant whereas fixed costs are not, unless the decision affects the cost structure of the organisation. Thus, information for decision-making should always be based on marginal costing principles, since marginal costing focuses on the variable costs and is not concerned with arbitrary apportionment of fixed costs that will be incurred anyway.

1.12.1 Short-term decision-making

An important point that you should appreciate for all of the decision-making techniques that you learn about in this chapter is that they are usually most relevant to short-term, one-off decisions. Furthermore, as you will see with the example of the minimum-price quotation, the analysis provides only a starting point for management decisions. The financial figures are only part of the information needed for a fully informed decision. It is also important to consider the non-financial factors which might be relevant to the decision.

 You must get into the habit of considering non-financial and qualitative factors in any decision. Many exam questions will specifically ask you to do so.

1.13 Evaluating proposals

As an introduction to using cost information to evaluate proposals, use your understanding of breakeven analysis and cost behaviour patterns to evaluate the proposals in the following exercise.

 Exercise

A summary of a manufacturing company's budgeted profit statement for its next financial year, when it expects to be operating at 75% of capacity, is given below.

	£	£
Sales 9,000 units at £32		288,000
Less		
Direct materials	54,000	
Direct wages	72,000	
Production overhead – fixed	42,000	
– variable	18,000	
		186,000
Gross profit		102,000
Less admin., selling and dist'n costs		
Fixed	36,000	
Varying with sales volume	27,000	
		63,000
Net profit		39,000

It has been estimated that

(i) if the selling price per unit were reduced to £28, the increased demand would utilise 90% of the company's capacity without any additional advertising expenditure;

(ii) to attract sufficient demand to utilise full capacity would require a 15% reduction in the current selling price and a £5,000 special advertising campaign.

You are required to

(a) calculate the breakeven point in units, based on the original budget;
(b) calculate the profits and breakeven points that would result from each of the two alternatives and compare them with the original budget.

 Solution

(a) First calculate the current contribution per unit.

	£'000	£'000
Sales revenue		288
Direct materials	54	
Direct wages	72	
Variable production overhead	18	
Variable administration, etc.	27	
		171
Contribution		117
Contribution per unit (÷9,000 units)		£13

Now you can use the formula to calculate the breakeven point.

$$\text{Breakeven point} = \frac{\text{Fixed costs}}{\text{Contribution per unit}} = \frac{£42,000 + £36,000}{£13} = 6,000 \text{ units}$$

(b) Alternative (i)

Budgeted contribution per unit	£13
Reduction in selling price (£32 − £28)	£4
Revised contribution per unit	£9
Revised breakeven point = $\dfrac{£78,000}{£9}$	8,667 units
Revised sales volume = 9,000 × 90/75	10,800 units
Revised contribution = 10,800 × £9	£97,200
Less fixed costs	£78,000
Revised profit	£19,200

Alternative (ii)

Budgeted contribution per unit	£13.00
Reduction in selling price (15% × £32)	£4.80
Revised contribution per unit	£8.20
Revised breakeven point = $\dfrac{£78,000 + £5,000}{£8.20}$	10,122 units
Revised sales volume = 9,000 units × 100/75	12,000 units
Revised contribution = 12,000 × £8.20	£98,400
Less fixed costs	£83,000
Revised profit	£15,400

Neither of the two alternative proposals is worthwhile. They both result in lower forecast profits. In addition, they will both increase the breakeven point and will therefore increase the risk associated with the company's operations. This exercise has shown you how an understanding of cost behaviour patterns and the manipulation of contribution can enable the rapid evaluation of the financial effects of a proposal. We can now expand it to demonstrate another aspect of the application of marginal costing techniques to short-term decision-making

 Exercise

The manufacturing company decided to proceed with the original budget and has asked you to determine how many units must be sold to achieve a profit of £45,500.

 Solution

Once again, the key is the required contribution. This time the contribution must be sufficient to cover both the fixed costs and the required profit. If we then divide this amount by the contribution earned from each unit, we can determine the required sales volume.

$$\text{Required sales} = \frac{\text{Fixed costs} + \text{required profit}}{\text{Contribution per unit}}$$

$$= \frac{(£42,000 + £36,000) + £45,500}{£13} = 9,500 \text{ units.}$$

Now we shall move from this very basic analysis to consider specific types of cost that may assist management decision-making.

1.14   Relevant costs

Relevant costs are those which will be affected by the decision being taken. All relevant costs should be considered in management decision-making If a cost will remain unaltered regardless of the decision being taken, then it is called a non-relevant cost.

1.14.1   Non-relevant costs

Costs that are not usually relevant in management decisions include the following:

(a) Sunk or past costs, that is money already spent that cannot now be recovered. An example of a sunk cost is expenditure that has been incurred in developing a new product. The money cannot be recovered even if a decision is taken to abandon further development of the new product. The cost is therefore not relevant to future decisions concerning the product.

(b) Absorbed fixed overheads that will not increase or decrease as a result of the decision being taken. The amount of overhead to be absorbed by a particular cost unit might alter because of the decision; however, this is a result of the company's cost accounting procedures for overheads. If the actual amount of overhead incurred by the company will not alter, then the overhead is not a relevant cost.

(c) Expenditure that will be incurred in the future, but as a result of decisions taken in the past that cannot now be changed. These are known as committed costs. They can sometimes cause confusion because they are future costs. However, a committed cost will be incurred regardless of the decision being taken and therefore it is not relevant.

An example of this type of cost could be expenditure on special packaging for a new product, where the packaging has been ordered and delivered but not yet paid for. The company is obliged to pay for the packaging even if they decide not to proceed with the product; therefore it is not a relevant cost.

(d) Historical cost depreciation that has been calculated in the conventional manner. Such depreciation calculations do not result in any future cash flows. They are merely the book entries that are designed to spread the original cost of an asset over its useful life.

(e) Notional costs such as notional rent and notional interest. These are only relevant if they represent an identified lost opportunity to use the premises or the finance for some alternative purpose.

In these circumstances, the notional costs would be opportunity costs. This explanation will become clearer when you learn more about opportunity costs later in this chapter.

 ## Exercise

Test your understanding of relevant and non-relevant costs by seeing if you can identify which of the following costs are relevant:

(a) The salary to be paid to a market researcher who will oversee the development of a new product. This is a new post to be created specially for the new product but the £12,000 salary will be a fixed cost. Is this cost relevant to the decision to proceed with the development of the product?

(b) The £2,500 additional monthly running costs of a new machine to be purchased to manufacture an established product. Since the new machine will save on labour time, the fixed overhead to be absorbed by the product will reduce by £100 per month. Are these costs relevant to the decision to purchase the new machine?

(c) Office cleaning expenses of £125 for next month. The office is cleaned by contractors and the contract can be cancelled by giving 1 month's notice. Is this cost relevant to a decision to close the office?

(d) Expenses of £75 paid to the marketing manager. This was to reimburse the manager for the cost of travelling to meet a client with whom the company is currently negotiating a major contract. Is this cost relevant to the decision to continue negotiations?

 ## Solution

(a) The salary is a relevant cost of £12,000. Do not be fooled by the fact that it is a fixed cost. The cost may be fixed in total but it is definitely a cost that is relevant to the decision to proceed with the future development of the new product. This is an example of a directly attributable fixed cost.

   A directly attributable fixed cost may also be called product-specific fixed cost.

(b) The £2,500 additional running costs are relevant to the decision to purchase the new machine. The saving in overhead absorption is not relevant since we are not told that the *total* overhead expenditure will be altered. The saving in labour cost would be relevant but we shall assume that this has been accounted for in determining the additional monthly running costs.

(c) This is not a relevant cost for next month since it will be incurred even if the contract is cancelled today. If a decision is being made to close the office, this cost cannot be included as a saving to be made next month. However, it will be saved in the months after that so it will become a relevant cost saving from month 2 onwards.

(d) This is not a relevant cost of the decision to continue with the contract. The £75 is sunk and cannot be recovered even if the company does not proceed with the negotiations.

Conclusion

It is essential to look to the future when deciding which costs are relevant to a decision. Costs that have already been incurred or that will not be altered in the future as a result of the decision being taken are not relevant costs.

1.15   Opportunity costs

An opportunity cost is a special type of relevant cost. It is defined in the CIMA *Terminology* as 'the value of the benefit sacrificed when one course of action is chosen, in preference to an alternative. The opportunity cost is represented by the forgone potential benefit from the best rejected course of action.'

With opportunity costs we are concerned with identifying the value of any benefit forgone as the result of choosing one course of action in preference to another.

1.15.1   Examples of opportunity costs

The best way to demonstrate opportunity costs is to consider some examples.

(a) A company has some obsolete material in stock that it is considering to use for a special contract. If the material is not used on the contract it can either be sold back to the supplier for £2 per tonne or it can be used on another contract in place of a different material that would usually cost £2.20 per tonne.

The opportunity cost of using the material on the special contract is £2.20 per tonne. This is the value of the next best alternative use for the material, or the benefit forgone by not using it for the other contract.

(b) Chris is deciding whether or not to take a skiing holiday this year. The travel agent is quoting an all-inclusive holiday cost of £675 for a week. Chris will lose the chance to earn £200 for a part-time job during the week that the holiday would be taken.

The relevant cost of taking the holiday in £875. This is made up of the out-of-pocket cost of £675, plus the £200 opportunity cost, that is the part-time wages forgone.

1.15.2   Notional costs and opportunity costs

Notional costs and opportunity costs are in fact very similar. This is particularly noticeable in the case of notional rent. The notional rent could be the rental that the company is forgoing by occupying the premises itself, that is it could be an opportunity cost. However, it is only a true opportunity cost if the company can actually identify a forgone opportunity to rent the premises. If nobody is willing to pay the rent, then it is not an opportunity cost.

> If an examination question on relevant costs includes information about notional costs, read the question carefully and state your assumptions concerning the relevance of the notional cost.

1.16 Avoidable, differential and incremental costs

There are two other types of relevant cost that you will need to know about: avoidable costs and differential/incremental costs.

1.16.1 Avoidable costs

CIMA defines avoidable costs as 'the specific costs of an activity or sector of a business which would be avoided if that activity or sector did not exist'.

For example, if a company is considering shutting down a department, then the avoidable costs are those that would be saved as a result of the shutdown. Such costs might include the labour costs of those employed in the department and the rental cost of the space occupied by the department. The latter is an example of an attributable or specific fixed cost. Costs such as apportioned head office costs that would not be saved as a result of the shutdown are unavoidable costs. They are not relevant to the decision.

1.16.2 Differential/incremental costs

CIMA defines a differential/incremental cost as 'the difference in total cost between alternatives; calculated to assist decision-making'.

For example, if the relevant cost of contract X is £5,700 and the relevant cost of contract Y is £6,200, we would say that the differential or incremental cost is £500, that is the extra cost of contract Y is £500.

1.16.3 Using incremental costs

Incremental costs can be useful if the cost accountant wishes to highlight the consequences of taking sequential steps in a decision. For example, the accountant might be providing cost information for a decision about whether to increase the number of employees in a department. Instead of quoting several different total-cost figures, it might be more useful to say 'the incremental cost per five employees will be £5,800 per month'.

Remember that only relevant costs should be used in the calculations.

1.16.4 Incremental revenues

Just as incremental costs are the differences in cost between alternatives, so incremental revenues are the differences in revenues between the alternatives. Matching the incremental costs against the incremental revenue will produce a figure for the incremental gain or loss between the alternatives.

 Exercise

To consolidate the material so far on relevant costs and opportunity costs, work through the following exercise to identify the relevant costs of the decision. Try to work out the relevant cost of each item before you look at the solution.

ABC Ltd is deciding whether or not to proceed with a special order. Use the details below to determine the relevant cost of the order.

(a) Materials P and Q will be used for the contract. 100 tonnes of material P will be needed and sufficient material is in stock because the material is in common use in the company. The original cost of the material in stock is £1 per tonne but it would cost £1.20 per tonne to replace if it is used for this contract. The material Q required is in stock as a result of previous over-purchasing This material originally cost £500 but it has no other use. The material is toxic and if it is not used on this contract, then ABC must pay £280 to have it disposed of.

(b) The contract requires 200 hours of labour at £5 per hour. Employees possessing the necessary skills are currently employed by the company but they are idle at present due to a lull in the company's normal business.

(c) Overhead will be absorbed by the contract at a rate of £10 per labour hour, which consists of £7 for fixed overhead and £3 for variable.

(d) The contract will require the use of a storage unit for 3 months. ABC is committed to rent the unit for 1 year at a rental of £50 per month. The unit is not in use at present. A neighbouring business has recently approached ABC offering to rent the unit from them for £70 per month.

(e) Total fixed overheads are not expected to increase as a result of the contract.

 Solution

(a) The relevant cost of a material that is used regularly is its replacement cost. This will ensure that the business profits are unaffected by the use of the material for this contract. The relevant cost of material P is therefore £1.20 per tonne.

   Material Q has a 'negative' cost if used for the contract. This is the saving that will be made through not having to pay the disposal cost of £280.

(b) The relevant cost of labour is zero. The labour cost is being paid anyway and no extra cost will be incurred as a result of this contract.

(c) The fixed overhead is not relevant because we are told that fixed overheads are not expected to increase. The relevant variable overhead cost is £3 per hour × 200 hours = £600.

   Even if you are not specifically told that fixed overheads will remain unaltered, it is usual to assume that they will not increase, stating the assumption clearly.

(d) The rental cost £50 per month is not relevant because it will not be affected by the contract. The relevant cost of using the storage unit is the forgone rental income of £70 per month.

Summary of relevant costs

		£
(i)	Material P	120
	Material Q	(280)
(ii)	Labour	–
(iii)	Variable overhead	600
(iv)	Rent forgone	210
	Total relevant cost	650

1.17 Limiting factor decision-making

A limiting factor is any factor that is in scarce supply and that stops the organisation from expanding its activities further, that is it limits the organisation's activities.

The limiting factor for many trading organisations is sales volume because they cannot sell as much as they would like. However, other factors may also be limited, especially in the short term. For example, machine capacity or the supply of skilled labour may be limited for one or two periods until some action can be taken to alleviate the shortage.

1.17.1 Decisions involving a single limiting factor

If an organisation is faced with a single limiting factor, for example machine capacity, then it must ensure that a production plan is established that maximises the profit from the use of the available capacity. Assuming that fixed costs remain constant, this is same as saying that the contribution must be maximised from the use of the available capacity. The machine capacity must be allocated to those products that earn the most contribution per machine hour.

This decision rule can be stated as 'maximising the contribution per unit of limiting factor'.

Example

LMN Ltd manufactures three products, L, M and N. The company that supplies the two raw materials that are used in all three products has informed LMN that their employees are refusing to work overtime. This means that supply of the materials is limited to the following quantities for the next period:

Material A   1,030 kg
Material B   1,220 kg

No other source of supply can be found for the next period.
Information relating to the three products manufactured by LMN Ltd is as follows:

	L	M	N
Quantity of material used per unit manufactured			
Material A (kg)	2	1	4
Material B (kg)	5	3	7
Maximum sales demand (units)	120	160	110
Contribution per unit sold	£15	£12	£17.50

Owing to the perishable nature of the products, no finished goods stocks are held.

Requirements

(a) Recommend a production mix that will maximise the profits of LMN Ltd for the forthcoming period.
(b) LMN Ltd has a valued customer to whom they wish to guarantee the supply of 50 units of each product next period. Would this alter your recommended production plan?

Solution

(a) The first step is to check whether the supply of each material is adequate or whether either or both of them represent a limiting factor.

	L	M	N	Total
Maximum sales demand (units)	120	160	110	
Material A required per unit (kg)	2	1	4	
Total material A required (kg)	240	160	440	840
Material B required per unit (kg)	5	3	7	
Total material B required (kg)	600	480	770	1,850

There will be sufficient material A to satisfy the maximum demand for the products but material B will be a limiting factor.

The next step is to rank the products in order of their contribution per unit of limiting factor. The available material B can then be allocated according to this ranking.

	L	M	N
Contribution per unit sold	£15	£12	£17.50
Material B consumed (kg)	5	3	7
Contribution per kg of material B	£3	£4	£2.50
Ranking	2	1	3

The available material B will be allocated to the products according to this ranking, to give the optimum production plan for the next period.

Product	Recommended production (units)	Material B utilized (kg)	
M	160 (maximum)	480	
L	120 (maximum)	600	
N	20	140	(balance)
		1,220	

The available material B is allocated to satisfy the maximum market demand for products M and L. The balance of available material is allocated to the last product in the ranking, product N.

(b) The recommended production plan in part (a) does not include sufficient product N to satisfy the requirement of 50 units for the valued customer. Some of the material allocated to product L (second in the ranking) must be allocated to product N. The recommended production plan will now be as follows:

Product	Recommended production (units)	Material B utilised (kg)	
N	50	350	
M	160	480	
L	78	390	(balance)
		1,220	

This recommendation makes the best use of the available material B within the restriction of the market requirements for each product.

 # Exercise

Gill Ltd manufactures three products, E, F and G. The products are all finished on the same machine. This is the only mechanised part of the process. During the next period the production manager is planning an essential major maintenance overhaul of the machine. This will restrict the available machine hours to 1,400 hours for the next period. Data for the three products is

	Product E £ per unit	Product F £ per unit	Product G £ per unit
Selling price	30	17	21.00
Variable cost	13	6	9.00
Fixed production cost	10	8	6.00
Other fixed cost	2	1	3.50
Profit	5	2	2.50
Maximum demand (units/period)	250	140	130

No stocks are held.

Fixed production costs are absorbed using a machine hour rate of £2 per machine hour.

You are required to determine the production plan that will maximise profit for the forthcoming period.

Solution

The first step is to calculate how many machine hours are required for each product. We can then determine whether machine hours are really a limiting factor.

	Product E	*Product F*	*Product G*	*Total*
Fixed production costs per unit @ £2 per hour	£10	£8	£6	
Machine hours per unit	5	4	3	
Maximum demand (units)	250	140	130	
Maximum hours required	1,250	560	390	2,200

1.18 Summary

In this chapter we have explored the basic ideas behind and cost and revenue behaviour that are used by management accountants in the design and operation of product costing, budgetary planning and financial control systems. These ideas are fundamental to much of what follows in this text, so you should have a clear understanding of them.

Self-test quiz

(1) Explain the term 'fixed cost' (Section 1.2.1).
(2) Explain the term 'variable cost' (Section 1.2.2).
(3) Explain the term 'semi-variable cost' (Section 1.2.3).
(4) Explain the 'high-low' method for analysing cost structures (Section 1.2.4).
(5) Distinguish between the 'chart of accounts' view and the 'activity view' of a set of costs (Section 1.3).
(6) State the possible uses of the 'margin of safety' measure (Section 1.5).
(7) Distinguish between the CVP chart and the PV chart (Sections 1.4 and 1.9).
(8) What makes a cost 'relevant' in a decision making situation (Section 1.14)?
(9) In a decision making situation, what is an 'opportunity cost' (Section 1.15)?
(10) Explain the term 'limiting factor' in the context of decision making where there is a constraint (Section 1.17).

Revision Questions

1

? Question 1

GHI manufactures three products – X, Y and Z. GHI's factory is highly automated and labour can be quickly recruited to support any level of production. However, machine capacity is limited to 18,000 hours. GHI's goods dispatch department is equipped in a manner which makes it impossible to send out more than 1,000 units of any one product to customers in a single period.

Details concerning production in the coming period are as follows:

	X	Y	Z
Market demand, units	900	1,000	1,200
Variable cost per unit, £	21	28	9
Selling price per unit, £	38	52	29
Machine hours per unit	8.5	10.0	5.0

Fixed costs are £ 35,000 per period.

Requirements

(a) Calculate the mix of X, Y and Z production that will achieve the maximum possible profit in the current period. Prepare a statement showing how that maximum profit is made up. **(9 marks)**

(b) Advise GHI's management on whether or not it should hire new equipment (rental per period £ 1,100) for the dispatch department in order to allow its handling capacity to be increased from 1,000 units of any one product to 1,200 units. **(9 marks)**

(c) Explain the full range of things that can be limiting factors in a business situation. Explain why these things might be only 'short-term' problems. **(7 marks)**

(Total marks = 25)

? Question 2

2.1 GA is the Project Manager of X Ltd where he earns an annual salary of $60,000. He has just identified an unexpected opportunity to undertake an extra project that he could supervise within his existing workload. The project would take 1 month to complete.

The project would also need a Marketing Manager, but the Marketing Manager of X Ltd, who earns an annual salary of $36,000, is extremely busy and she does not have any spare time. However, it would be possible to hire a temporary manager for $3,700 to cover her regular duties for the duration of the project. Alternatively, a marketing consultant could be hired for the project for $4,500.

The total relevant cost of the Project Manager and a Marketing Manager for the extra project would be

(A) $3,700
(B) $4,500
(C) $8,000
(D) $9,500.

[handwritten: P.M already employed, able to do additional work within workload ∴ no cost. M M – Temp Cover for 3700]

2.2 A company provides three services that use the same machine, M1. The budgeted details per service are as follows:

	Service X £ per unit	Service Y £ per unit	Service Z £ per unit
Selling price	12	14	24
Variable costs	6	4	13
Fixed cost	2	5	8
Profit	4	5	3
Number of M1 machine hours	2	3	6

[handwritten annotations: 6/2 = 6/m/cho; =3; 4/5 = 10; =3.3; 13/8 = 11; =1.3; rank 2, 1, 3]

The fixed costs are general fixed costs that have been absorbed by the services by their direct labour content.

If M1 hours are scarce, the most and least profitable services are

	Most profitable	Least profitable
(A)	Y	Z
(B)	Z	X
(C)	Y	X
(D)	X	Z

? Question 3 Objective test questions

3.1 OT Ltd plans to produce and sell 4,000 units of product C each month, at a selling price of £18 per unit. The unit cost of product C is as follows:

	£ per unit
Variable cost	8
Fixed cost	4
	12

Calculate (to the nearest whole number) the monthly margin of safety, as a percentage of planned sales.

3.2 Is the following statement *true* or *false*?
The P/V ratio is the ratio of profit generated to the volume of sales.

3.3 Product J generates a contribution to sales ratio of 30%. Fixed costs directly attributable to product J amount to £75,000 per month. Calculate the sales revenue required to achieve a monthly profit of £15,000.

3.4 Match the following terms with the labels **a** to **d** on the graph:

- Margin of safety
- Fixed cost
- Contribution
- Profit.

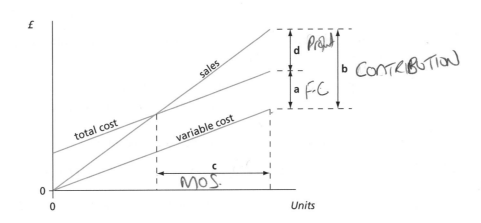

3.5 Which of the following statements about a PV chart are *true*?

(a) The profit line passes through the origin.
(b) Other things being equal, the angle of the profit line becomes steeper when the selling price increases.
(c) Contribution cannot be read directly from the chart.
(d) The point where the profit line crosses the vertical axis is the breakeven point.
(e) Fixed costs are shown as a line parallel to the horizontal axis.

3.6 (a) Printing costs of £30 are incurred in putting together a proposal for a new client. Is this cost relevant to the decision to continue negotiating to obtain the client's business? — Sunk Cost ∴ NO.
(b) In order to carry out a contract, additional premises will have to be rented at a cost of £2,000 per month. It is company policy to allocate rental costs to general fixed overheads. Is this rental cost relevant to the decision to accept the contract? incremental cost. YES
(c) Some material held in stock can be used on a particular job. The material has no other use but it could be sold for scrap for £1 per kg. Is the scrap value of the material a relevant cost of this job? — Relevant — job must return profit > £1/kg of material

3.7 PH Ltd has spare capacity in its factory. A supermarket chain has offered to buy a number of units of product XZ each month, and this would utilise the spare capacity. The supermarket is offering a price of £8 per unit and the cost structure of XZ is as follows:

	£ per unit
Direct material	3
Direct labour	2
Variable overhead	1
Fixed overhead	3
	9

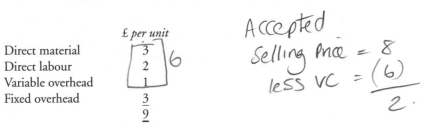

Accepted
Selling Price = 8
less VC = (6)
        2.

Fixed costs would not be affected.
On a purely financial basis, should the supermarket's offer be accepted or rejected?

BASIC ASPECTS OF MANAGEMENT ACCOUNTING

3.8 *Delete as appropriate.*

(a) If a material stock item is regularly used in a business, the relevant cost of using the item for a particular job is its ~~original purchase price~~/replacement price.

(b) If a material stock item is not regularly used in a business, and would not be replaced if it were used for a particular job, the relevant cost of using the item is the higher/~~lower~~ of its resale value and its value from an alternative use.

3.9 Put the following tasks in the correct sequence for deciding on the optimum production plan when a limiting factor exists.

- Rank the products according to the contribution per unit of limiting factor used.
- Calculate each product's contribution per unit of limiting factor used.
- Identify the limiting factor.
- Allocate the limited resource according to the ranking.

3.10 The following details relate to three services provided by JHN plc.

	Service J £	Service H £	Service N £
Fee charged to customers	84	122	145
Unit service costs			
Direct materials	12	23	22
Direct labour	15	20	25
Variable overhead	12	16	20
Fixed overhead	20	42	40

All three services use the same type of direct labour which is paid £30 per hour.

The fixed overheads are general fixed overheads that have been absorbed on the basis of machine hours.

If direct labour is a scarce resource, the most and least profitable uses of it are

	Most profitable	Least profitable
A	H	J
B	H	N
C	N	J
D	N	H

(2 marks)

? **Question 4** Profit statements and decision-making

BSE Veterinary Services is a specialist laboratory carrying out tests on cattle to ascertain whether the cattle have any infection. At present, the laboratory carries out 12,000 tests each period but, because of current difficulties with the beef herd, demand is expected to increase to 18,000 tests a period, which would require an additional shift to be worked.

The current cost of carrying out a full test is

	£ per test
Materials	115
Technicians' wages	30
Variable overhead	12
Fixed overhead	50

Working the additional shift would

(i) require a shift premium of 50% to be paid to the technicians on the additional shift;
(ii) enable a quantity discount of 20% to be obtained for all materials if an order was placed to cover 18,000 tests;
(iii) increase fixed costs by £700,000 per period.

The current fee per test is £300.

Requirements

(a) Prepare a profit statement for the current 12,000 capacity.
(b) Prepare a profit statement if the additional shift was worked and 18,000 tests were carried out.
(c) Comment on three other factors that should be considered before any decision is taken.

Question 5 PV graphs

(a) MC Ltd manufacturers one product only, and for the last accounting period has produced the simplified profit and loss statement below:

	£	£
Sales		300,000
Costs		
Direct materials	60,000	
Direct wages	40,000	
Prime cost	100,000	
Variable production overhead	10,000	
Fixed production overhead	40,000	
Fixed administration overhead	60,000	
Variable selling overhead	40,000	
Fixed selling overhead	20,000	
		270,000
Net profit		30,000

You are required to construct a PV graph from which you should state the breakeven point and the margin of safety.

(b) Based on the above, draw separate PV graph to indicate the effect on profit of each of the following:

(i) an increase in fixed cost;
(ii) a decrease in variable cost;
(iii) an increase in sales price;
(iv) a decrease in sales volume.

Question 6 Decision-making, limiting factor

ABC Limited makes three products, all of which use the same machine, which is available for 50,000 hours per period.

BASIC ASPECTS OF MANAGEMENT ACCOUNTING

50,000 hrs / period

The standard costs of the product, per unit, are

	Product A	Product B	Product C
	£	£	£
Direct materials	70	40	80
Direct labour			
Machinists (£8/hour) —4	48 6hrs	32 4hrs	56 7hrs
Assemblers (£6/hour)	36 6hrs	40 6.66hrs	42 7.
Total variable cost	154	112	178
Selling price per unit	200	158	224
Maximum demand (units)	3,000	2,500	5,000

Contrib 46   46   46

Fixed costs are £300,000 per period.

C/LF   7.6   11.5   6.57

Rank   ②   ①   ③

Requirements
(a) Calculate the deficiency in machine hours for the next period.
(b) Determine the production plan that will maximise ABC Ltd's profit for the next period.
(c) Calculate the profit that will result from your recommended production plan.

Ⓐ
A
3000 × 6 = 18,000hrs

B
2500 × 4 = 10,000hrs

C
5,000 × 7 = 35,000hrs

63,000
(50,000)
13,000 deficit.

Ⓑ
Prod B   2500 × 4hrs = 10,000
Prod A   3000 × 6hrs = 18,000
                        28,000
            (50,000) Available hrs
3142 × 7   7 ÷ 22,000 hrs left for Prod C

Ⓒ
Profit = Prod B   46 × 2500 =   115,000
            A   46 × 3000 =   138,000
            C   46 × 3142 =   144 532
                              397 532
                            (300,000)
FC
Profit   97,532

Solutions to Revision Questions

✓ Solution 1

(a) The products are ranked according to the contribution they offer in regard to the primary limiting factor (machine hours). This is so because maximum production allowed by both market demand and handing capacity cannot be achieved because of the machine hour constraint. Resources are then allocated according to this ranking and the secondary limiting factor (handling capability). The results are

	X	Y	Z	Total
Selling price p.u. (£)	38	52	29	
Variable cost p.u. (£)	21	28	9	
Contribution p.u. (£)	17	24	20	
Mac. Hrs. p.u.	8.5	10	5	
Cont. per mac. hr. (£)	2	2.4	4	
Rank	3	2	1	
Units	353	1,000	1,000	
Contribution (£)	6,001	24,000	20,000	50,001
Fixed costs (£)				−35,000
Profit (£)				15,001

(b) Increasing the handling capability from 1,000 units of any one product to 1,200 units of any one product has the following results:

Units	235	1,000	1,200	
Contribution (£)	3,995	24,000	24,000	51,995
Fixed costs (£)				−36,100
Profit (£)				15,895

Since the new arrangement increases profit, it should be adopted.

(c) Machine hours, skilled labour hours, material availability and transport capacity are all factors that are capable of being limiting factors. They are usually only short-term factors because in a dynamic economy some means can usually be found to evade them. A new source of materials may be opened up, new skilled labour may be trained and products may be redesigned to have a lower machine hour requirement.

For example, one of the key limiting factors in the Second World War for UK armaments industry was availability of aluminium. So, aircraft were designed that could be built with wood rather than aluminium. These did not have the same performance, service life or reliability as metal built aircraft – but they were available in numbers that a metal building programme would not have allowed.

However, it is often found that as soon as one limiting factor is eliminated or avoided, then another one tends to appear. For example, there is no point in producing more aircraft if there are no spare pilots to fly them.

Solution 2

2.1   Answer: (A)

2.2

Service type	X	Y	Z
	£	£	£
Selling price	12	14	24
Variable costs	6	4	13
Contribution/unit	6	10	11
	Hours	Hours	Hours
Type M1 machine hours/unit	2	3	6
	£	£	£
Contribution/unit	3.00	3.30	1.83

Therefore the answer is (A), as the smallest additional cost.

Solution 3

3.1   Monthly fixed costs = 4,000 units × £4 = £16,000.

$$\text{Breakeven point} = \frac{\text{Fixed costs}}{\text{Contribution per unit}} = \frac{£16,000}{£18 - £8} = 1,600 \text{ units}$$

$$\text{Margin of safety\%} = \frac{\text{Planned sales} - \text{breakeven sales}}{\text{Planned sales}} \times 100\%$$

$$= \frac{4,000 - 1,600}{4,000} \times 100\% = 60\%$$

3.2   *False.* The P/V ratio is another term for the C/S ratio. It measures the ratio of the contribution to sales.

3.3   Required sales value $= \dfrac{\text{Required contribution}}{\text{C/S ratio}} = \dfrac{£75,000 + £15,000}{0.30} = £300,000.$

3.4   (a) Fixed cost
       (b) Contribution
       (c) Margin of safety
       (d) Profit.

3.5   (a) *False.* The profit line passes through the breakeven point on the horizontal axis, and cuts the vertical axis at the point where the loss is equal to the fixed costs.
       (b) *True.* Profits increase at a faster rate if the selling price is higher.
       (c) *True.* A contribution breakeven chart is needed for this.
       (d) *False.* The breakeven point is where the profit line cuts the horizontal axis.
       (e) *False.* No fixed cost line is shown on a PV chart.

3.6 (a) *Not relevant.* This is a sunk cost that will not be affected by a decision to continue negotiations.

(b) *Relevant.* Although the rental cost will be treated as a general fixed overhead, it is an incremental cost that will be incurred if the contract is accepted.

(c) *Relevant.* The opportunity cost of using the material on the contract is the scrap value forgone of £1 per kg.

3.7 *Accepted.* On a purely financial basis, the price of £8 per unit exceeds the incremental variable cost of £6 per unit.

3.8 (a) If a material stock item is regularly used in a business, the relevant cost of using the item for a particular job is its *replacement* price (The original purchase price is a sunk or past cost).

(b) If a material stock item is not regularly used in a business, and would not be replaced if it were used for a particular job, the relevant cost of using the item is the *higher* of its resale value and its value from an alternative use (This is the opportunity of using the stock item on this job.)

3.9 1. Identify the limiting factor.
2. Calculate each product's contribution per unit of limiting factor used.
3. Rank the products according to the contribution per unit of limiting factor used.
4. Allocate the limited resource according to the ranking.

3.10

	J	H	N
Contribution/unit	£45	£63	£78
Direct labour/unit	£15	£20	£25
Contribution/ £1 of direct labour	£3.00	£3.15	£3.12

Therefore the answer is (A).

☑ Solution 4

- In part (b) do not be tempted to use unit rates to calculate the new level of fixed costs. The current level of fixed costs is £600,000 *per period*. This will increase by £700,000.
- Also in part (b), notice that the shift premium applies only to the technicians working on the additional shift. It does not apply to all technicians' wages.
- In part (c) you may have thought of other, equally valid, factors to be considered. In an examination, if you are asked for three factors do not waste valuable time by suggesting more than three.

(a) Profit statement for current 12,000 capacity:

		£'000
Sales	12,000 tests @ £300/test	3,600
Direct materials	12,000 tests @ £115/test	(1,380)
Direct labour	12,000 tests @ £30/test	(360)
Variable overhead	12,000 tests @ £12/test	(144)
Contribution		1,716
Fixed costs	12,000 tests @ £50/test	(600)
Profit		1,116

(b) Profit statement for 18,000 capacity, with additional shift:

		£000	£000
Sales	18,000 tests @ £300/test		5,400
Direct materials	18,000 tests @ £92/test		(1,656)
Direct labour	12,000 tests @ £30/test	(360)	
	6,000 tests @ £45/test	(270)	
			(630)
Variable overhead	18,000 tests @ £12/test		(216)
Contribution			2,898
Fixed costs			(1,300)
Profit			1,598

(c) Three other factors that should be considered are

1. Will the increase in demand continue in the long run, or is it short-lived? If it is thought that it will continue in the long run, management should consider expanding its permanent workforce so that shift premiums can be avoided.
2. Will the quality of the test decrease if more tests are carried out in the same time period? Also purchasing materials at a 20% discount may indicate a decrease in the quality of the materials.
3. The elasticity of demand for the test. If demand is relatively inelastic, it may be more economic to increase the price of the test.

 Solution 5

- Try to obtain a piece of graph paper and practise drawing your graphs to scale. Remember to use the whole of the paper – do not produce a tiny graph in the corner of the sheet.
- Remember that the graph in part (a) will cut the vertical axis at the point equal to the fixed costs, that is, the loss when no sales are made.
- Practise good exam technique: check your breakeven point arithmetically to verify that your graph is accurate.

(a)

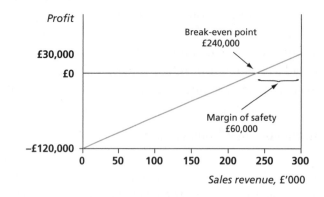

(b) These graphs show increase or decrease in profit by $+x$ or $-x$.

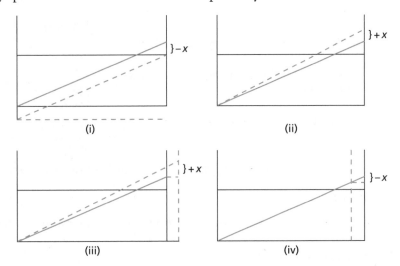

(i) An increase in fixed cost   (iii) An increase in sales price

(ii) A decrease in variable cost   (iv) A decrease in sales volume.

 ## Solution 6

- In part (b) remember to rank the products according to their contribution per machine hour. Then allocate the available machine hours according to this ranking.
- Do not attempt to apportion the fixed costs to the individual products. When you are calculating the profit in part (c), simply deduct the total fixed costs from your calculated contribution.

(a) Deficiency in machine hours for next period:

	Product A	Product B	Product C	Total
Machine hours required per unit	48/8 = 6	32/8 = 4	56/8 = 7	
Maximum demand (units)	3,000	2,500	5,000	
Total machine hours to meet maximum demand	18,000	10,000	35,000	63,000
Machine hours available				50,000
Deficiency of machine hours				13,000

(b)

	Product A	Product B	Product C
	£	£	£
Selling price per unit	200	158	224
Variable cost per unit	(154)	(112)	(178)
Contribution per unit	46	46	46
Machine hours required per unit	6	4	7
Contribution per machine hour	£7.67	£11.50	£6.57
Order of production	2	1	3

Therefore, make

	M/C hours
2,500 units of product B, using machine hours of (4 × 2,500)	10,000
3,000 units of product A, using machine hours of (6 × 3,000)	18,000
	28,000
Machine hours left to make product C	22,000
	50,000

Therefore, the company should make 3,142 i.e. (22,000/7) units of product C.

(b) Profit for the next period:

	Total £	Product A £	Product B £	Product C £
Contribution from recommended production:				
£46 × 3,000		138,000		
£46 × 2,500			115,000	
£46 × 3,142				144,532
	397,532	138,000	115,000	144,532
Fixed costs	(300,000)			
Profit for the period	97,532			

2

Cost Accounting
Systems

Cost Accounting Systems

2

LEARNING OUTCOMES

After completing this chapter, you should be able to

▸ compare and contrast marginal and absorption costing methods in respect of profit reporting and stock valuation;

▸ apply marginal and absorption costing approaches in job, batch and process environments;

▸ prepare ledger accounts according to context: marginal or absorption based in job, batch or process environments, including work in progress and related accounts, such as production overhead control account and abnormal loss account.

2.1 Introduction

In your certificate studies (or equivalent) you should have already encountered the basic principles and concepts involved in cost accounting. Specifically, you should be familiar with the manner in which the costs of objects and activities are determined through an exercise of cost allocation, apportionment and absorption. You should also be familiar with basic cost accounting practices such as stock valuation (LIFO, FIFO and average), profit determination (using marginal and absorption costing conventions), accounting in particular types of production environment (job, batch and process) and the principles of cost behaviour (fixed and variable). Be aware that the CIMA examination scheme is a cumulative one and you should refer back to your earlier studies if you are unfamiliar with any of the topics referred to.

In this chapter we will revisit these basic principles and develop our understanding of their use into more advanced areas. The content of this chapter will lead into an exploration of modern innovations in management accounting systems in Chapter 8.

2.2 The difference between marginal costing and absorption costing

You should already be aware that the difference between marginal costing and absorption costing lies in their treatment of fixed production overhead.

You are reminded that direct costs are expenditures on materials, labour and expenses that relate strictly to individual products. Indirect or overhead costs are expenditures incurred in running a factory that do not relate specifically to individual products.

With absorption costing, the fixed production overhead cost is absorbed into the cost of units and all stock items are valued at their full production cost.

Example

ABC Ltd manufactures units. Relevant forecast details for the current period are:

Budget fixed overheads	€10,000
Budget production	500 units
Variable production cost	€10 per unit

The predetermined overhead absorption rate is therefore €20 per unit (€10,000/500) giving a unit cost of €30 (€20 fixed plus €10 variable).

Predetermined OARs are commonly used in cost accounting systems in order to minimise the vulnerability of product costs to random movements in output levels and overhead costs. The production overhead cost of a unit is determined in advance of the current period and nothing that happens in the period will alter that.

Relevant actual details for the period are as follows:

Actual production	520 units
Actual sales	480 units (at €40 per unit)

The profit for the period, calculated on the absorption costing principal, is:

		€
Sales		19,200 (480 × €40)
Production costs	15,600 (520 × €30)	
Closing stock	1,200 (40 × €30)	
Cost of sales		14,400
Gross profit		4,800
Overhead over absorption		400 (20 × €20)
Profit		5,200

By producing 520 units and charging €20 fixed overheads each, then we have charged €10,400 against profit. But only €10,000 fixed overheads have been incurred so we must credit €400 back to profit. This is the overhead over absorption figures referred to above.

Note that only production overheads are normally attributed to unit costs. Selling and administration overheads are not usually attributed to unit costs, although there may be circumstances when this is appropriate.

In contrast, marginal costing values all stock items at their variable or marginal cost only. Fixed costs are treated as period costs and are written off in full against the profit for the period.

Example

Given the details stated in the previous example, the profit calculated on the marginal costing principal is:

		€
Sales		19,200
Production costs	5,200 (520 × €10)	
Closing stock	400 (40 × €10)	
Cost of sales		4,800
Contribution		14,400
Fixed overheads		10,000
Profit		4,400

Since the two systems value stock differently, it follows that each will report a different profit figure for the period if stock levels alter.

The €800 (€5,200 − €4,400) difference between profits calculated above according to absorption and marginal costing principles is essentially a stock valuation thing. Absorption costing values stock at €1,200 while marginal costing values it at €400.

2.3 Preparing profit statements using each method

The best way to demonstrate how profit statements are prepared for each of the methods is to look at a worked example.

Example

Using the information below, prepare profit statements for June and July using (a) marginal costing and (b) absorption costing.

A company produces and sells one product only which sells for £50 per unit. There were no stocks at the end of May and other information is as follows:

	£
Standard cost per unit	
Direct material	18
Direct wages	4
Variable production overhead	3
Budgeted and actual costs per month	
Fixed production overhead	99,000
Fixed selling expenses	14,000
Fixed administration expenses	26,000
Variable selling expenses	10% of sales value

Normal capacity is 11,000 units per month.
The number of units produced and sold was:

	June units	July units
Sales	12,800	11,000
Production	14,000	10,200

2.3.1 Profit statements using marginal costing

A marginal costing will value all units at the variable production cost of £25 per unit (£18 + £4 + £3).

Profit statements using marginal costing

	June £'000	June £'000	July £'000	July £'000
Sales revenue		640		550
Less: variable cost of sales				
Opening stock	–		30	
Variable production cost				
(14,000 × £25)	350			
(10,200 × £25)			255	
	350		285	
Closing stock				
(1,200 × £25)	(30)			
(400 × £25)			(10)	
Variable production of sales	320		275	
Variable selling expenses	64		55	
Variable cost of sales		(384)		(330)
Contribution		256		220
Less: fixed overhead				
Fixed production overhead	99		99	
Fixed selling expenses	14		14	
Fixed administration expenses	26		26	
		(139)		(139)
Profit		117		81

2.3.2 Profit statements using absorption costing

Fixed production overheads are absorbed on the basis of normal capacity which is often the same as budgeted capacity. You should recall that predetermined rates are used partly to avoid the fluctuations in unit cost rates which arise if production levels fluctuate.

$$\text{Fixed production overhead per unit} = \frac{£99,000}{11,000} = £9 \text{ per unit}$$

$$\text{Full production cost per unit} = £25 \text{ variable cost} + £9 \text{ fixed cost} = £34 \text{ per unit}$$

This full production cost of £34 per unit will be used to value all units under absorption costing.

Since the production level is not equal to the normal capacity in either June or July there will be under- or over-absorbed fixed production overhead in both months. It is probably easier to calculate this before commencing on the profit statements.

	June £'000	July £'000
Fixed production overhead absorbed		
(14,000 × £9)	126	
(10,200 × £9)		91.8
Fixed production overhead incurred	(99)	(99.0)
Over/(under) absorption	27	(7.2)

Profit statements using absorption costing

	June		July	
	£'000	£'000	£'000	£'000
Sales revenue		640.0		550.0
Less: full production cost of sales				
Opening stock	–		40.8	
Full production cost				
(14,000 × £34)	476.0			
(10,200 × £34)			346.8	
	476.0		387.6	
Closing stock				
(1,200 × £34)	(40.8)			
(400 × £34)			(13.6)	
	435.2		374.0	
(Over-)/under-absorbed fixed				
production overhead*	(27.0)		7.2	
Full production cost of sales		408.2		381.2
Gross profit		231.8		168.8
Less: selling/admin. expenses				
Variable selling expenses	64.0		55.0	
Fixed selling expenses	14.0		14.0	
Fixed administration expenses	26.0		26.0	
		(104.0)		(95.0)
Net profit		127.8		73.8

*If overheads have been over-absorbed then too much has been charged as a cost of production. This amount is, therefore, deducted to derive the full production cost of sales. If overheads are under-absorbed, the amount is added to increase the production cost of sales.

2.4 Reconciling the profit figures

In addition to preparing profit statements using absorption costing and marginal costing, you should also recall how to reconcile the profits given by each method for the same period and by the same method for different periods.

2.4.1 Reconciling the profits given by the different methods

The profit differences are caused by the different valuations given to the closing stocks in each period. With absorption costing, an amount of fixed production overhead is carried forward in stock to be charged against sales of later periods.

If stocks increase, then absorption costing profits will be higher than marginal costing profits. This is because some of the fixed overhead is carried forward in stock instead of being written off against sales for the period.

If stocks reduce, then marginal costing profits will be higher than absorption costing profits. This is because the fixed overhead which had been carried forward in stock with absorption costing is now being released to be charged against the sales for the period.

A profit reconciliation for the previous example might look like this:

	June	July
	£'000	£'000
Marginal costing profit	117.0	81.0
Adjust for fixed overhead in stock		
Stock increase (1,200 × £9)	10.8	
Stock decrease (800 × £9)		(7.2)
Absorption costing profit	127.8	73.8

2.4.2 Reconciling the profits for different periods

You should also recall how to reconcile the profits for different periods using the same method.

(a) For marginal costing, the unit rates and the amount of fixed costs charged each period are constant. Therefore, the only thing which could have caused the profit difference was the change in sales volume. The lower sales volume in July resulted in a lower contribution and therefore a lower profit (since the amount of fixed cost remained constant).

The contribution per unit is £20 as follows:

	£per unit
Selling price	50
Variable production cost	(25)
Variable selling cost	(5)
Contribution	20

The marginal costing profit figures can be reconciled as follows:

	£'000
Marginal costing profit for June	117
Decrease in sales volume for July	
1,800 units × £20 contribution	(36)
Marginal costing profit for July	81

(b) For absorption costing the major part of the profit difference is caused by the change in sales volume. However, a further difference is caused by the adjustments for under- and over-absorbed fixed production overhead in each of the two periods.

The profit per unit with absorption costing is £11 as follows:

	£per unit
Selling price	50
Total production cost	(34)
Variable selling cost	(5)
Profit	11

The absorption costing profit figures can be reconciled as follows:

	£'000
Absorption costing profit for June	127.8
Decrease in sales volume for July	
1,800 units × £11 profit	(19.8)
Adjustments for under-/over-absorption	
June	(27.0)
July	(7.2)
Absorption costing profit for July	73.8

This may look confusing because both the under- and the over-absorption are deducted. This is because the over-absorption for June made profit for that month higher, therefore it must be deducted to arrive at July's profit. Similarly, the under-absorption in July made July's profit lower than June's, therefore it must also be deducted in the reconciliation.

2.4.3 Profit differences in the long term

The two different costing methods produce profit differences only in the short term when stocks fluctuate. If stocks remain constant then there will be no profit differences between the two methods.

In the long term the total reported profit will be the same whichever method is used. This is because all of the costs incurred will eventually be charged against sales; it is merely the timing of the sales that causes the profit differences from period to period.

2.5 Marginal costing or absorption costing?

There is no absolutely correct answer to when marginal costing or absorption costing is preferable. However, it is generally accepted that marginal costing statements provide the best information for the purposes of management decision-making.

Supporters of absorption costing argue that fixed production overheads are a necessary cost of production and they should therefore be included in the unit cost used for stock valuation. SSAP 9 requires the use of absorption costing for external reporting purposes.

If stocks are built up for sale in a future period – for example in distilling – then absorption costing smoothes out profit by carrying forward the fixed production overheads to be matched against the sales as they are made.

Supporters of marginal costing argue that management attention is concentrated on the more controllable measure of contribution. They say that the apportionment of fixed production overhead to individual units is carried out on a purely arbitrary basis, is of little use for decision-making and can be misleading.

However, it is widely accepted that for general accounting purposes (as opposed to business decision-making purposes) both fixed and variable overhead costs should be attributed to cost units in some meaningful way. Absorption costing is therefore in wide use. The problem lies in adopting an appropriate method of attributing overhead costs to cost units.

Modern thinking in this regard is that most costs are actually variable if you take a long enough view of them and understand what they vary with. This issue is pursued further in Chapter 4.

We will now move to a consideration of cost accounting practices in specific business environments. A theme which runs through this is the manner in which overhead costs are absorbed. Be aware that the adoption of absorption costing is implicit in this. For some decision-making purposes, the accountant may wish to exclude some or all of the absorbed overheads from reported product costs, and concentrate his/her attention on variable costs only. Revision Questions 2 and 3 involve particular consideration of this issue.

2.6 Specific order costing

Every organisation will have its own costing system with characteristics which are unique to that particular system. However, the basic costing system is likely to depend on the type of activity that the organisation is engaged in. The system would have the same basic characteristics as the systems of other organisations which are engaged in similar activities.

Specific order costing systems are appropriate for organisations which produce cost units which are separately identifiable from one another. Job costing and batch costing are types of specific order costing. In organisations which use these costing methods, each cost unit is different from all others and each has its own unique characteristics.

2.7 Job costing

Job costing applies where work is undertaken according to specific orders from customers to meet their own special requirements. Each order is of relatively short duration. For example, a customer may request the manufacture of a single machine to the customer's own specification. Other examples might be the repair of a vehicle or the preparation of a set of accounts for a client, that is, job costing can also be applied to services.

2.7.1 Job cost cards and databases

The main feature of a job costing system is the use of a job cost card or job card which is used to collect the costs of each job. In practice, this would probably be a file in a computerised system (using appropriate coding for each entry) but the essential feature is that each job would be given a specific job number which identifies it from all other jobs. Costs would be allocated to this number as they are incurred on behalf of the job. Since the sales value of each job can also be separately identified, it is then possible to determine the profit or loss on each job.

The job card would record details of the job as it proceeds. The items recorded would include

- job number;
- description of the job; specifications and so on;
- customer details;
- estimated cost, analysed by cost element;
- selling price, and hence estimated profit;
- delivery date promised;
- actual costs to date, analysed by cost element;
- actual delivery date, once the job is completed;
- sales details, for example, delivery note number, invoice number.

2.7.2 Collecting the direct costs of each job

Direct labour

The correct analysis of labour costs and their attribution to specific jobs depends on the existence of an efficient time-recording and booking system. For example, time sheets may be used to record how each employee's time is spent, using job numbers where appropriate to indicate the time spent on each job. The wages cost can then be charged to specific job numbers (or to overhead costs, if the employee was engaged on indirect tasks).

Direct material

All documentation used to record movements of material within the organisation should indicate the job number to which it relates. For example, a material requisition note should have a space to record the number of the job for which the material is being requisitioned. If any of this material is returned to stores, then the material returned note should indicate the original job number which is to be credited with the cost of the returned material.

Direct expenses

Although direct expenses are not as common as direct material and direct labour costs, it is still essential to analyse them and ensure that they are charged against the correct job number. For example, if a machine is hired to complete a particular job, then this is a direct expense of the job. The purchase invoice should be coded to ensure that it is charged to the job. Alternatively, if cash is paid, then the cash book analysis will show the job number which is to be charged with the cost.

2.7.3 Attributing overhead costs to jobs

(a) Production overheads

The successful attribution of production overhead costs to cost units depends on the existence of well-defined cost centres and appropriate absorption bases for the overhead costs of each cost centre. It must be possible to record accurately the units of the absorption base which are applicable to each job. For example, if machine hours are to be used as the absorption base, then the number of machine hours spent on each job must be recorded on the job cost card. The relevant cost centre absorption rate can then be applied to produce a fair overhead charge for the job.

Indirect costs are first apportioned between cost centres (or production departments) on an appropriate basis.

Example

A factory incurs €600 security costs. It has three departments, details as follows:

A – 1,000 m² floor space and 80 staff
B – 2,000 m² floor space and 120 staff
C – 3,000 m² floor space and 100 staff

[handwritten annotations:]
Based on floor space: = 600/6000 × 1000 = 100; 200; 300; total 600
Based on staff numbers: 600/300 × 80 = 160; 240; 200; total 600

If the security costs relate to excluding intruders then floor space is the appropriate apportionment basis – giving a charge split of €100 to A, €200 to B and €300 to C. But if security costs relate to preventing theft by staff then staff numbers is the appropriate apportionment basis – giving a charge split of €160 to A, €240 to B and €200 to C. Each type of overhead should be apportioned between cost centres using the most appropriate basis.

Where an indirect cost relates to a specific cost centre (A, B or C in the above case), then it may be allocated direct to that centre, without any apportionment.

Once all indirect costs have been apportioned and allocated to cost centres, then the resultant cost centre overhead figures may be absorbed into product costs (or 'cost units').

Example

[handwritten annotations:]
$1000/(50+150) = £5/labour hr.$
Prod 1: 50 hrs × 5 = 250
Prod 2: 150 hrs × 5 = 750

If cost centre X incurs €1,000 overheads and spends 50 direct labour hours on product 1 and 150 direct labour hours on product 2 then the obvious overhead absorption base will be direct labour hours and the overhead absorption rate will be €5 per direct labour hour – with €250 absorbed into 1 and €750 into 2. But what constitutes an appropriate absorption rate depends on circumstances. If most cost centre overheads relate to the employment of labour then labour hours may be the appropriate overhead absorption basis. But, if overheads mainly relate to machine usage then machine hours might be the appropriate overhead absorption basis.

Note that the choice of overhead absorption base impacts on reported product costs. A reported product cost is only meaningful if the overhead absorption base is appropriate.

(b) Non-production overheads

The level of accuracy achieved in attributing costs such as selling, distribution and administration overheads to jobs will depend on the level of cost analysis which an organisation uses.

Many organisations use a predetermined percentage (see earlier discussion of absorption costing) to absorb such costs, based on estimated or budgeted levels of activity for the forthcoming period. The following example will demonstrate how this works.

Example

A company uses a predetermined percentage of production cost to absorb distribution costs into the total cost of its jobs. Based on historical records and an estimate of activity and expenditure levels in the forthcoming period, they have produced the following estimates:

Estimated distribution costs to be incurred £13,300
Estimated production costs to be incurred on all jobs £190,000

$$\text{Therefore, predetermined overhead absorption rate of distribution costs} = \frac{£13,300}{£190,000} \times 100\%$$

$$= 7\% \text{ of production costs}$$

The use of predetermined rates will lead to the problems of under- or over-absorbed overhead which we discussed in the previous section. The rates should therefore be carefully monitored throughout the period to check that they do not require adjusting to more accurately reflect recent trends in costs and activity.

It may not always be considered appropriate to attribute non-production overheads to individual products. Some categories of administration and management costs relate to a whole production facility and it is meaningless to try and split them between products. In such cases, the overhead costs concerned are simply charged to the profit account without any attempt to absorb them into individual products.

2.7.4 A worked example

The following example will help you to practise presenting a cost analysis for a specific job.

Example

Jobbing Limited manufactures precision tools to its customers' own specifications. The manufacturing operations are divided into three cost centres: A, B and C.

An extract from the company's budget for the forthcoming period shows the following data:

Cost centre	Budgeted production overhead	Basis of production overhead absorption
A	£38,500	22,000 machine hours
B	£75,088	19,760 machine hours
C	£40,964	41,800 labour hours

Job number 427 was manufactured during the period and its job cost card reveals the following information relating to the job:

Direct material requisitioned	£6,780.10
Direct material returned to stores	£39.60
Direct labour recorded against job number 427	
Cost centre A	146 hours at £4.80 per hour
Cost centre B	39 hours at £5.70 per hour
Cost centre C	279 hours at £6.10 per hour
Special machine hired for this job: hire cost	£59.00
Machine hours recorded against job number 427	
Cost centre A	411 hours
Cost centre B	657 hours
Price quoted and charged to customer, including delivery	£17,200

Jobbing Limited absorbs non-production overhead using the following predetermined overhead absorption rates:

Administration and general overhead	10% of production cost
Selling and distribution overhead	12% of selling price

You are required to present an analysis of the total cost and profit or loss attributable to job number 427.

Solution

First, we need to calculate the predetermined overhead absorption rates for each of the cost centres, using the basis indicated.

$$Costcentre\ A = \frac{£38,500}{£22,000} = £1.75\ per\ machine\ hour$$

$$Costcentre\ B = \frac{£75,088}{£19,760} = £3.80\ per\ machine\ hour$$

$$Costcentre\ C = \frac{£40,964}{£41,800} = £0.98\ per\ labour\ hour$$

Now we can prepare the cost and profit analysis, presenting the data as clearly as possible.

Cost and profit analysis: job number 427

	£	£
Direct material*		6,740.50
Direct labour		
Cost centre A (146 hours × £4.80)	700.80	
Cost centre B (39 hours × £5.70)	222.30	
Cost centre C (279 hours × £6.10)	1,701.90	
		2,625.00
Direct expenses: hire of jig		59.00
Prime cost		9,424.50
Production overhead absorbed		
Cost centre A (411 hours × £1.75)	719.25	
Cost centre B (657 hours × £3.80)	2,496.60	
Cost centre C (279 hours × £0.98)	273.42	
		3,489.27
Total production cost		12,913.77
Administration and general overhead		1,291.38
(10% × £12,913.77)		
Selling and distribution overhead		2,064.00
(12% × £17,200)		
Total cost		16,269.15
Profit		930.85
Selling price		17,200.00

* The figure for material requisitioned has been reduced by the amount of returns to give the correct value of the materials actually used for the job.

2.7.5 Other applications for job costing

So far we have discussed the use of job costing in the context of jobs carried out on the organisation's own premises for customers external to the business.

The job costing method can also be applied to monitor the costs of internal work done for the organisation's own benefit. For example, job cost cards can be used to collect the costs of property repairs carried out by the organisation's own employees, or they may be used in the costing of internal capital expenditure jobs.

The job costing method can also be applied to services carried out on the customer's own premises. For example, it may be used in the costing of plumbing or cleaning services, where the objective of the costing system is to collect and monitor the cost of each job.

2.8 Batch costing

The CIMA *Terminology* defines a batch as 'a group of similar articles which maintains its identity throughout one or more stages of production and is treated as a cost unit'. You can probably see that a batch is very similar in nature to the jobs which we have been studying so far in this chapter. It is a separately identifiable cost unit for which it is possible to collect and monitor the costs.

The job costing method can therefore be applied in costing batches. The only difference is that a number of items are being costed together, instead of a single item or service. Once the cost of the batch has been determined, the cost per item within the batch can be calculated by dividing the total cost by the number of items produced.

Batch costing can be applied in many situations, including the manufacture of furniture, clothing and components. It can also be applied when manufacturing is carried out for the organisation's own internal purposes, for example in the production of a batch of components to be used in production.

2.9 Process costing

The basic costing model has to be adapted a little to accommodate accounting for a process operation. The latter produces a homogenous product on a continuous basis. An oil refinery is a process operation. The basic concepts involved are introduced in this section and these concepts are explored in more depth in subsequent sections.

The core issue is to determine what the production cost per unit is for the process in a given period. Let us say that a process incurs €20,000 costs in the period and its output is 5,000 units. Then the cost per unit of output is €4. Product would be credited to the process account and charged to the stock account at €4 per unit.

WIP

The matter may be complicated by allowing for the possibility of closing work-in-progress (WIP). Let us take the previous example but consider the possibility of there being output of 4,000 units plus 800 units 50% complete at the end of the period. The equivalent units output for the period is now $4,000 + (800 \times 50\%) = 4,400$. The cost per unit is now €4.545 (i.e. €20,000/4,400). We would credit the product to the process account at a value of €18,180 (i.e. $4,000 \times €4.545$) and carry forward €1,820 WIP (i.e. $800 \times 50\% \times €4.545$) on the process account.

A further refinement is where there are different categories of cost charged to the process account and WIP is complete to a different degree as regards each category of cost. Let us take our previous example and consider the possibility that costs are €10,000 labour and €10,000 materials. The 800 units of closing WIP are 100% complete as regards material and 60% complete as regards labour. The calculation of production cost per unit now requires a little more thought.

Effective units of production and unit costs are:

As regards		Materials	Labour
Output		4,000	4,000
WIP		800	480
Total		4,800	4,480
Total costs	(€)	10,000	10,000
Cost per unit		2.083	2.232

Output would be therefore be valued at €17,260 (i.e. 4,000 × (2.083 + 2.232)). This last amount would be credited to the process account and charged to stock. The WIP would be valued at €2,740 (i.e. is (800 × 2.083) + (800 × 2.232 × 60%)). This last amount would be carried forward on the process account.

Process losses

Another complication altogether is the issue of process losses. Let us say that we are operating a process that involves refining a fluid. Five per cent process losses are 'normal' meaning that if we input 100 litres of raw material then we expect to achieve an output of 95 litres of refined product. If we input 100 litres material (cost €200), incur €150 process costs and achieve 95 litres output then the process cost per unit is €3.684 (i.e. €350/95).

But what happens if we only obtain 92 litres of output from the process? This means we have experienced 5 litres of normal losses and 3 litres of 'abnormal losses'. The idea is that we should isolate the cost impact of the abnormal losses from the product valuation. This is important because we do not want our reported product costs (and hence stock valuation) to be distorted as the result of some random process defect. So, we would retain €3.684 as the process cost per litre output; €339 (i.e. 92 × €3.684) would be credited to the process account and charged to stock; and €11 (i.e. 3 × €3.684) would be credited to the process account and charged to a special abnormal losses account.

The situation can be complicated further by consideration of scrap sales. Let us say that process losses in the above case are in the form of a waste liquid, which can be sold at €0.20 per litre. Operating at normal efficiency would result in 5 litres of waste sales giving rise to miscellaneous income of €1 which would be credited to the process account. The net cost per unit of output at normal efficiency is now €3.674 (i.e. (€350 − 1)/95). The process account would appear as follows when arranged in traditional T account form with debits on the left and credits on the right:

Process account

Inputs	200	Waste sales	1
Process	150	Stock	349
	350		350

Let us return to the situation where actual output is 92 litres as a result of 3 litres abnormal losses. We want to retain a situation where the full cost impact of the abnormal losses are isolated in order not to influence stock valuation. The result appears as follows:

Process account

Inputs	200	Waste sales	1
Process	150	Stock	338
		Abnormal losses	11
	350		350

Only the sale proceeds of normal losses are credited to the process account. The output is valued at €338 (92 × €3.674) while the abnormal losses are valued at €11 (3 × 3.674).

Abnormal losses account			
Process	11.00	Waste sales	0.60
		Profit and loss	10.40
	11.00		11.00

The income from sale of the abnormal losses (3 × €0.20) is credited to the Abnormal losses account. The net cost impact of the abnormal losses is €10.40 and this has been isolated.

Before you read further, attempt the following Activity. It is simple enough but requires a good grasp of the basic concepts involved in process costing. A model answer is given at the end of this Chapter.

Activity

Rexine plc produces a single product which undergoes three processes in sequence. The following details relate to the period immediately ended:

		Process	
	A	**B**	**C**
Raw materials (60,000 units) (€)	80,000		
Materials introduced (€)	23,500	18,750	22,100
Direct wages (€)	15,600	12,000	13,400
Process overheads (€)	3,800	4,600	3,200
Output (units)	55,200	53,800	49,600
Scrap sales value, € per unit	Nil	1.00	1.80

In addition, €27,000 general overheads are to be apportioned between processes on the basis of direct wages. There is no WIP.

You are required to prepare ledger accounts for the operation using normal process accounting conventions.

See model answer at end of chapter

The following example is simple in concept, although elaborate. It incorporates both WIP and process losses. The reader is advised to spend some time working through it to ensure that the basic principles involved are fully understood.

Example: Basic process costing

Data concerning Process 2 last month was as follows:

Transfer from Process 1	400 kg at a cost of	£2,150
Materials added	3,000 kg	£6,120
Conversion costs		£2,344
Output to finished goods		2,800 kg
Output scrapped		400 kg
Normal loss		10% of materials added in the period

The scrapped units were complete in materials added but only 50% complete in respect of conversion costs. All scrapped units have a value of £2 each.

There was no opening work in progress, but 200 kg were in progress at the end of the month, at the following stages of completion:

80% complete in materials added
40% complete in conversion costs.

You are required to write up the accounts for the process.

Solution

The first step is to produce an input/output reconciliation. Notice that the losses are not complete. You will need to take account of this in the equivalent units columns. And remember that the normal loss units do not absorb any of the process costs. They are valued at their scrap value only, so they must not be included as part of the output to absorb costs.

| | | | | Equivalent kg to absorb cost | | |
| | | | | Process 1 | Materials | Conversion |
Input	kg	Output	kg	transfer	added	costs
Process 1 transfer	400	Finished goods	2,800	2,800	2,800	2,800
Material added	3,000	Normal loss	300	–	–	–
		Abnormal loss[1]	100	100	100	50
		Work in progress	200	200	160	80
	3,400		3,400	3,100	3,060	2,930
		Costs		£	£	£
		Incurred in period		2,150	6,120	2,344
		Scrap value of normal loss[2]		(600)		
				1,550	6,120	2,344
		Cost per unit	£3.30	0.50	2.00	0.80

Notes:
1. The abnormal loss is inserted in the output column as a balancing figure. Losses are 50% complete in conversion costs. Therefore, the 100 kg of abnormal loss represents 50 equivalent complete kg.
2. By convention, the scrap value of normal loss is usually deducted from the first cost element.

For each cost element the costs incurred are divided by the figure for equivalent kg produced. For example, the cost per kg for materials added = £6,120/3,060 = £2 per kg.

The unit rates can now be used to value each part of the output. For example, the 160 equivalent kg of materials added in the WIP are valued at 160 × £2 = £320. The 80 equivalent kg of conversion costs in work in progress are valued at 80 kg × £0.80 = £64.

| | | Process 1 | Materials | Conversion |
| | Total | transfer | added | costs |
Valuation	£	£	£	£
Finished goods	9,240	1,400	5,600	2,240
Abnormal loss	290	50	200	40
Work in progress	484	100	320	64

It is now possible to draw up the relevant accounts using these valuations of each part of the process output. Remember that the normal loss is valued at its scarp value.

Process 2 account					
	kg	£		kg	£
Process 1	400	2,150	Finished goods	2,800	9,240
Materials added	3,000	6,120	Normal loss	300	600
Conversion costs		2,344	Abnormal loss	100	290
			Work in progress	200	484
	3,400	10,614		3,400	10,614

Abnormal loss account			
	£		£
Process 2	290	Scrap stock	200
		Profit and loss	90
	290		290

Scrap account			
	£		£
Process 2	600	Bank/debtors:	800
Abnormal loss account	200	(300 + 100) × £2	
	800		800

If you had any difficulty in understanding the workings of this example, you should return now to your study material for *Management Accounting Fundamentals*. You need a thorough understanding of the basics before continuing to study the more advanced aspects of process costing.

2.9.1 Previous process costs

A common problem which students experience when studying process costing is understanding how to deal with previous process costs. An important point that you should understand is that production passes through a number of sequential processes. Unless the process is the last in the series, the output of one process becomes the input of the next. A common mistake is to forget to include the previous process cost as an input cost in the subsequent process.

You should also realise that all of the costs of the previous process (materials, labour and overhead) are combined together as a single cost of 'input material' or 'previous process costs' in the subsequent process.

In the workings for the last example, we assumed that the work in progress must be 100 per cent complete in respect of Process 1 costs. This is also an important point to grasp. Even if the Process 2 work had only just begun on these units, there cannot now be any mote cost to add in respect of Process 1. Otherwise the units would not yet have been transferred out of Process 1 into Process 2.

In the next section, we will be going on to see how to account for opening work in progress using the average cost and FIFO methods. For FIFO, you will need to determine the amount of work to be done to complete the opening work in progress. If you have grasped the fact that work in progress is complete in respect of previous process costs, then you should understand that no more cost is to be added to this cost element to complete the work in progress. There may still be more materials to be added in this process, but these are treated separately from previous process costs.

2.9.2 Opening work in progress

There are two ways in which opening work in progress (WIP) can be accounted for in process costing: average cost and FIFO.

With the average cost method, the cost of the opening WIP is added to the costs incurred in the period. This total cost is then averaged out over all of the units worked on in the period, including the closing work in progress.

With the FIFO method, the opening WIP is dealt with on a strict first in, first out basis. It is assumed that the opening WIP is completed first, before other units are started in the period. The cost of the opening WIP is analysed separately from the cost of the units which are started during the period. The closing WIP is therefore valued at the unit cost rate incurred during this period. It is not affected by the costs of the previous period which are brought forward in the opening WIP.

The best way to make this difference clear is to work through some examples. The next two examples in this chapter include some opening WIP. Work through them carefully, referring back to these paragraphs to help you to understand the differences between the FIFO and the average cost methods.

Example 1: Opening work in progress

The following information is available for Process 3 in June:

| | | | | Degree of completion and cost | | | | |
| | | | Process 2 input | | Materials added in Process 3 | | Conversion costs | |
	Units	Cost £	%	£	%	£	%	£
Opening stock	100	692	100	176	60	300	30	216
Closing stock	80		100		70		55	
Input costs								
Input from Process 2	900	1,600						
Materials added in Process 3		3,294						
Conversion costs		4,190						

Normal loss is 10% of input from Process 2; 70 units were scrapped in the month, and all scrap units realise £0.20 each.

Output to the next process was 850 units.

You are required to complete the account for Process 3 in June.

Solution using the average price method

As before, the first step is to complete an input/output reconciliation and then to extend this to calculate the number of equivalent units for each cost element.

| | | | | | Equivalent units absorb cost | | |
| | | | | | Process 2 input | Materials added | Conversion costs |
Input	Units		Output	Units			
Opening stock[1]	100		To Process 4	850	850	850	850
Process 2[2]	900		Normal loss	90	–	–	–
			Abnormal gain[3]	(20)	(20)	(20)	(20)
			Closing stock[4]	80	80	56	44
	1,000			1,000	910	886	874
			Costs	£	£	£	£
			Opening stock[5]		176	300	216
			Input costs		1,600	3,294	4,190
			Normal loss value		(18)		
					1,758	3,594	4,406
				£	£	£	£
			Cost per unit	11.029	1.932	4.056	5.041
			Evaluation[6]				
			To Process 4	9,375	1,642	3,448	4,285
			Abnormal gain	(221)	(39)	(81)	(101)
			Closing stock	604	155	227	222

Notes:
1. The opening stock is included as part of the input in the input/output reconciliation. The degree of completion of the opening stock is not relevant, because we are going to average its cost over all units produced in the period.
2. Note that we are not told the quantity of material added because it does not affect the number of basic units processed.
3. The number of units scrapped is less then the normal loss. There is thus an abnormal gain.
4. The equivalent units of closing stock takes account of the degree of completion for each cost element.
5. The opening stock is included in the statement of costs, so that its value is averaged over the equivalent units produced in the period.
6. In the evaluation section, the unit rate for each cost element is multiplied by the number of equivalent units in each part of the output. These values can then be used to complete the process account.

	Units	£		Units	£
			Process 3 account		
Opening stock	100	692	Process 4	850	9,375
Process 2	900	1,600	Normal loss	90	18
Materials added		3,294	Closing stock	80	604
Conversion costs		4,190			
Abnormal gain	20	221			
	1,020	9,997		1,020	9,997

 Exercise

To give yourself some extra practice, draw up the abnormal gain account and the scrap account.

 Solution

	£		£
		Abnormal gain account	
Scrap stock (20 × £0.20)	4	Process 3	221
Profit and loss account	217		
	221		221

	£		£
		Scrap account	
Normal loss	18	Bank/debtor: ((90 – 20) × £0.20)	14
		Abnormal gain	4
	18		18

2.9.3 Solution to Example 1 using the FIFO method

The FIFO method assumes that the opening stock is completed before work is begun on the new input during the period. The input/output reconciliation therefore analyses the 850 units completed to show how much work was done in finishing off the opening stock brought forward.

The 100 units brought forward were complete in Process 2 input, therefore no equivalent units were produced in this period for this cost element. They were 60 per cent complete in material added therefore the remaining 40 per cent (40 units) was completed in this period. They were 30 per cent complete in conversion costs therefore the remaining 70 per cent (70 units) was completed in this period.

Input	Units	Output	Units	Process 2 input	Material added	Conversion cost
				Equivalent units to absorb cost		
Opening stock	100	O.stock completed	100	–	40	70
Process 2	900	CPDP[1]	750	750	750	750
		Normal loss	90	–	–	–
		Abnormal gain	(20)	(20)	(20)	(20)
		Closing stock	80	80	56	44
	1,000		1,000	810	826	844
		Costs	£	£	£	£
		Input costs[2]		1,600	3,294	4,190
		Normal loss value		(18)		
				1,582	3,294	4,190
		Cost per unit	10.905	1.953	3.988	4.964
		Evaluation				
		O.stock completed	507	–	160	347
		CPDP	8,179	1,465	2,991	3,723
		Abnormal gain	(218)	(39)	(80)	(99)
		Closing stock	598	156	223	219

Notes:
1. CPDP is an abbreviation for Completely Processed During the Period. These are the 750 units that were both started and finished this month (850 units transferred less 100 units of opening stock finished off).
2. Since the statement of equivalent units includes only the work done in this period, the cost statement must exclude the value of work done in the last period, that is the value of the opening WIP must not be included.
3. The value of the Process 4 transfer must be built up from three pieces of information:

	£
Cost of work done on 100 units of opening stock:	
last period b/f	692
completed in this period*	507
Cost of 750 units completely processed during this period*	8,179
	9,378

* These two values are taken from the evaluation statement.

Process 3 account					
	units	£		units	£
Opening stock	100	692	Process 4	850	9,378
Process 2	900	1,600	Normal loss	90	18
Materials added		3,294	Closing stock	80	598
Conversion costs		4,190			
Abnormal gain	20	218			
	1,020	9,994		1,020	9,994

2.9.4 Discussion of Example 1

You can see that with the average cost method the units to value the process output were higher than with the FIFO method.

This is because the previous costs were higher than the costs for this period. These higher costs were contained in the opening WIP valuation, and with the average price method this is averaged over all units. Therefore the unit costs are higher than with the FIFO method, which analyses the opening work in process separately. Obviously if the previous period costs had been lower, then this would have had the opposite effect on the relative valuations.

In our example the differences are not large because costs are not very different between the two periods. However, if costs do fluctuate, then the choice of method can have a greater effect on the valuation of output.

If it is important for managers to be able to compare the unit costs from one period to the next, then FIFO might be the best method to use. This will mean that the costs for each period are analysed separately and no averaging takes place. However, if costs fluctuate dramatically from one period to the next and managers wish to even out the effect of these fluctuations, then the average price method may be preferable.

2.9.5 Choice of methods and standard costing

Both the practitioner and the student may be required to determine which method of stock valuation (Average or FIFO) is most appropriate in a particular process costing exercise. Be aware that under all but extreme or contrived circumstances it makes little difference to the outcome which method is adopted. Note that in Example 1, Average gives a charge to Process 4 of £9,375 while FIFO gives a charge of £9,378 – a trivial difference.

However, both methods involve relatively intricate calculations.

These calculations can be avoided by valuing stock at 'standard cost' rather than actual cost. Standard costs will be explored in some depth in the next two chapters and you should have already encountered the concept in your foundation studies. Let us take an example to illustrate the manner in which standard cost stock valuation might be used.

Example 2

Process B takes units from Process A and passes them on to Process C. Relevant operating details for Process B in the current period are

Opening stock	– 80 units, 60% complete as regards B processing
Closing stock	– 100 units, 40% complete as regards B processing
Transfers from Process A	– 900 units at £4.75 (standard) per unit
Process B costs	– £8,400

Additional information:
Normal process losses are 5% of units input (complete at time of loss)
Process losses generate £1.90 scrap income per unit
The standard cost per unit output from process B is

	£
Process A costs	5.00
Process B costs	10.00
Scrap sales	(0.10)
	14.90

Note: Never mind how that standard cost figure has been arrived at, but appreciate its consistency with other information given. 5% of input process losses means that scrap sales from 5 units (£9.50) are absorbed by 95 units of output (£0.10 per unit). 100 units input from A (at £4.75 per unit) are absorbed by 95 units of output (£5.00 per unit).

Requirement
Prepare the process account for the current period.

Solution

	Units	£		Units	£
			Process B account		
Opening stock	80	872.00	Process C	830	12,367.00
Process A	900	4,275.00	Normal loss	45	85.50
Process B		8,400.00	Abnormal loss	5	74.50
			Closing stock	100	890.00
			Cost variances		130.00
	980	13,547.00		980	13,547.00

Workings for most of the above figures are fairly obvious. For example, £the transfers to Process C are 830 units × £14.90. The closing stock is 100 units × (£4.90 + (£10 × 40%)).

However, note the £130 transfer to 'cost variances'. The use of standard cost for stock valuation means that there is an under-absorption of costs charged to the Process B account. The process account has to be cleared and this is done by crediting that account with a balancing figure of £130 and charging that amount to a cost variance account.

The cost variances may be used as an instrument of control. This will be explored fully in Chapters 2 and 3.
Note: In practice, minor variations on the above workings might be acceptable on the basis of alternative treatment of detail.

2.9.6   Process costing with opening work in progress

You must try to get as much practice as possible in preparing process cost accounts and you will find it much easier if you use a standard format for the working papers.

Work carefully through the next example – or better still try it for yourself before looking at the suggested solution. Notice that the scrapped units are not complete. You will need to take account of this in the equivalent units calculations.

Example 3

The following information is available for Process 2 in October:

			Process 1 input		*Degree of completion and cost — Materials added in Process 2*		*Conversion costs*	
	Units	Cost £	%	£	%	£	%	£
Opening stock	600	1,480	100	810	80	450	40	220
Closing stock	350		100		90		30	
Input cost:								
Input from Process 1	4,000	6,280						
Materials added in Process 2		3,109						
Conversion costs		4,698						

Normal loss is 5% of input from Process 1.
300 units were scrapped in the month. The scrapped units had reached the following degrees of completion.

Materials added	90%
Conversion costs	60%

All scrapped units realised £1 each.
Output to the next process was 3,950 units.
You are required to complete the account for Process 2 and for the abnormal loss or gain in October.

Solution to Example 3 using the average cost method

The first step is to prepare an input/output reconciliation to see if there was an abnormal loss or abnormal gain. This is found as a balancing figure in the output column.

| | | | | | Equivalent units to absorb cost | | |
| | | | | | Process 1 | Materials | Conversion |
Input	Units		Output	Units	input	added	costs
Opening stock	600		To process 3	3,950	3,950	3,950	3,950
Process 1	4,000		Normal loss	200	–	–	–
			Abnormal loss	100	100	90	60
			Closing stock	350	350	315	105
	4,600			4,600	4,400	4,355	4,115
			Costs	£	£	£	£
			Opening stock		810	450	220
			Input costs		6,280	3,109	4,698
			Normal loss value		(200)		
					6,890	3,559	4,918
			Cost per unit	3.578	1.566	0.817	1.195
			Evaluation				
			To process 3	14,133	6,186	3,227	4,720
			Abnormal loss	303	157	74	72
			Closing stock	931	548	257	126

Process 2 account

	units	£		units	£
Opening stock	600	1,480	Process 3	3,950	14,133
Process 1	4,000	6,280	Normal loss	200	200
Materials added		3,109	Abnormal loss	100	303
Conversion costs		4,698	Closing stock	350	931
	4,600	15,567		4,600	15,567

Abnormal loss account

	£		£
Process 2	303	Scrap stock	100
		Profit and loss	203
	303		303

Scrap account

	£		£
Normal loss	200	Bank/debtors: (200 + 100) × £1	300
Abnormal loss	100		
	300		300

2.9.7 Solution to Example 2 using the FIFO method

The statement of equivalent units must separately identify the units completely processed in this period, from those which were started during the last period.

Input	Units	Output	Units	Process 1 input	Material added	Conversion cost
				Equivalent units to absorb cost		
Opening stock	600	O.S completed[1]	600	–	120	360
Process 1	4,000	CPDP	3,350	3,350	3,350	3,350
		Normal loss	200	–	–	–
		Abnormal loss	100	100	90	60
		Closing stock	350	350	315	105
	4,600		4,600	3,800	3,875	3,875
		Costs	£	£	£	£
		Input costs[2]		6,280	3,109	4,698
		Normal loss value		(200)		
				6,080	3,109	4,698
		Cost per unit	3.614	1.600	0.802	1.212
		Evaluation				
		O.stock completed	532	–	96	436
		CPDP	12,107	5,360	2,687	4,060
		Abnormal loss	305	160	72	73
		Closing stock	940	560	253	127

Notes:
1. To complete the opening stock there was a further 20% of work to be done in material added (600 × 20% = 120) and 60% of work to be done in conversion cost (600 × 60% = 360). Remember that the opening work in process must always be 100% complete as regards the previous process cost – otherwise it would not be in this process yet!
2. The work done last period on the opening stock has been excluded from the statement of production. Therefore the costs of the opening stock must be excluded from the statement of costs.

Process 2 account

	Units	£		Units	£
Opening stock	600	1,480	Process 3*	3,950	14,122
Process 1	4,000	6,280	Normal loss	200	200
Materials added		3,109	Abnormal loss	100	305
Conversion costs		4,698	Closing stock	350	940
	4,600	15,567		4,600	15,567

Abnormal loss account

	£		£
Process 2	305	Scrap stock	100
		Profit and loss	205
	305		305

*The amount of £14,122 for the transfer to process 3 has been inserted as a balancing figure. It can be checked as in the last FIFO example:

	£
Work done on opening stock	
last period	1,480
this period	532
Completely processed this period	12,107
	14,119

The difference of £3 is caused by rounding.

2.9.8 Process losses

In all of the examples we have considered so far, the losses have had a scrap value. You may also come across situations where losses have no value (in which case they are defined as waste) or where losses have a disposal cost. We will now look at how the process accounts are prepared in these situations.

Example: Losses in process costing

Process 1 has a normal loss of 10% of input, due to quality control rejections at the end of the process. Output from the process is transferred to Process 2.

Process costs in the month were

Input materials – 1,000 units at a total cost of	£2,000
Conversion costs	£3,000

There were no opening or closing stocks.
Output to Process 2 was 850 units.

Requirement

Prepare the relevant accounts in the following separate situations;

(a) All rejected units are waste and have no value.
(b) All rejected units must be disposed of at a cost of £0.50 per unit.

Solution

(a) An input/output reconciliation can be prepared as in previous examples, but the process costs would not be reduced by the scrap value of the normal loss.

Input	Units	Output	Units	Units to absorb Process costs
Input material	1,000	Process 2 transfer	850	850
		Normal loss	100	–
		Abnormal loss	50	50
	1,000		1,000	900

Cost per unit = £(2,000 + 3,000)/900
= £5.556 per unit

This unit rate is used to value the good output and the abnormal loss. The normal loss would be given no value in the process account.
The relevant accounts would look like this:

	Units	£		Units	£
			Process 1 account		
Input material	1,000	2,000	Process 2	850	4,722
Conversion costs		3,000	Normal loss	100	–
			Abnormal loss	50	278
	1,000	5,000		1,000	5,000

	£		£
		Abnormal loss account	
Process 1	278	Profit and loss	278

The total costs of the abnormal loss is transferred to the profit and loss account. These is no scrap value to offset against it.

(b) The input/output reconciliation would remain unaltered and the number of units to absorb process costs would still be 900. However, the process costs would be increased by the disposal cost of the normal loss and the cost per unit would be calculated as follows:

$$Cost\ per\ unit = \frac{£5,000 + (£0.50 \times 100)}{900} = £5.61$$

This unit rate would be used to value the good output and the abnormal loss.
The relevant accounts would look like this:

Process 1 account

	Units	£		Units	£
Input material	1,000	2,000	Process 2	850	4,769
Conversion costs		3,000	Normal loss	100	–
Disposal cost of			Abnormal loss	50	281
normal loss		50			
	1,000	5,050		1,000	5,050

There is no scrap value of normal loss to credit to the process account. Instead there is a debit for the cost of disposing of the normal loss.

Abnormal loss account

	£		£
Process 1	281	Profit and loss	306
Disposal cost (50 × £0.50)	25		
	306		306

The total cost of the abnormal loss is transferred to the profit and loss account. This is made up of its disposal cost as well as its cost of production.

The main points that you should notice concerning the treatment of losses in all of these examples are as follows:

(a) The normal loss does not absorb any of the production costs.
(b) Abnormal losses and gains are valued at the same unit cost as the good units.
(c) If losses have a scrap value, only the value of the normal loss is credited to the process account. The scrap values of any abnormal losses or gains are offset against their production costs in the abnormal loss or gain account.
(d) If losses have no value, they are known as waste and the normal loss has zero value.
(e) If losses must be disposed of at a cost, only the cost of disposing of the normal loss is debited to the process account. The normal loss will have zero value. The disposal costs of any abnormal losses or gains are debited or credited in the abnormal loss or gain account respectively.

2.10 Joint products and by-products

Joint products are defined by the CIMA *Official Terminology* as 'two or more products produced by the same process and separated in processing, each having a sufficiently high saleable value to merit recognition as a main product'.

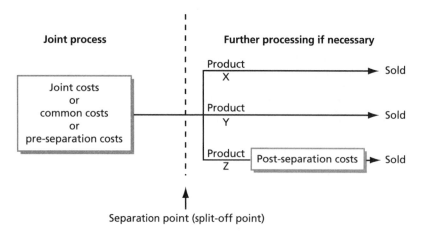

Three joint products are produced, only one of which (product Z) requires further processing before it is sold.

Figure 2.1 Common costs

Examples of joint products could be the output from oil refining: the various grades of petrol, diesel, paraffin and so on. Each of these products has a significant value compared with the others.

In contrast, a by-product is defined as 'output of some value produced incidentally in manufacturing something else (main product)'.

The key word in this definition is probably 'incidentally'. The by-product has some value but the process was not set up primarily for its manufacture. Its value is small and incidental when compared with that of the main product or products.

An example of a by-product could be the sawdust which is produced in a sawmill when timber is being processed. This has a small sales value compared with the value of the main product – the timber.

2.10.1 Joint product costing

Joint products are produced together in one or more processes. The point at which they become separately identifiable is known as the separation point or split-off point Any costs incurred in processing the products after this point are called post-separation point costs or subsequent processing costs. Costs incurred prior to the separation point are called common costs, joint costs or pre-separation point costs. Figure 2.1 demonstrates a possible situation.

The problem with costing joint products is that a basis must be found for apportioning the common costs to the various products. Common costs must be apportioned so that a total cost is available for each product. This total cost can then be used for stock valuation purposes.

2.10.2 Apportioning common costs to joint products

The two methods most commonly used to apportion common costs to joint products are

1. The quantity basis, where common costs are apportioned according to the weight or volume of each product at the separation point.
2. The sales value basis, where common costs are apportioned according to the sales value of each product at the separation point.

The following example will demonstrate how these methods work.

Products A, B and C are produced in a single process. The costs for this process during the last period amounted to £27,200. Data concerning the output is as follows:

Product	Output kg	Sales value at separation point £ per kg
A	1,600	7
B	3,890	4
C	1,870	5

(a) Using the quantity basis:

Product	Output kg		Common cost apportioned £
A	1,600	1,600/7,360 × £27,200	5,913
B	3,890	3,890/7,360 × £27,200	14,376
C	1,870	1,870/7,360 × £27,200	6,911
	7,360		27,200

 Exercise

As a separate exercise, calculate the gross margin percentage for each of the products if this method of apportionment is used. You should arrive at the following results: Product A – 47.2%, Product B – 7.6%, Product C – 26.1%.

(b) Using the sales value basis:

Product	Output kg	Price per kg £	Sales value £		Common cost apportioned £
A	1,600	7	11,200	11,200/36,110 × £27,200	8,436
B	3,890	4	15,560	15,560/36,110 × £27,200	11,721
C	1,870	5	9,350	9,350/36,110 × £27,200	7,043
			36,110		27,200

There is no correct way of apportioning common costs to join products because it is a purely arbitrary exercise. The sales value method has the advantage that it produces the same gross margin percentage for all products. Also it can be applied if the outputs are in different forms, for example solids, liquids and gases.

 Exercise

You can check for yourself that all three products in our example would produce a gross margin percentage of 24.7% with the sales value method. Contrast this with the widely differing percentages obtained with the quantity basis.

2.10.3 Using notional or proxy sales values for common cost apportionment

If you look back to the situation depicted in Figure 2.1, you will see that product Z was not saleable at the separation point. It required further processing to put it into a saleable state.

If management wished to use the sales value method of apportionment it would be necessary to determine a notional or proxy sales value for Product Z at the separation point. An example will demonstrate how this could be accomplished.

Assume that the final sales prices for Products X, Y and Z in Figure 2.1 are as follows: Product X £5 per litre, Product Y £3 per litre, Product Z £6.50 per litre.

The following data is available for the latest period:

Costs incurred in common process:	£41,000
Post-separation point costs incurred on product Z:	£11,730

Product	Output (litres)
X	4,000
Y	5,700
Z	5,100

There were no stocks at the beginning or end of the period.

If common costs are to be apportioned based on the sales value at the separation point, we need to determine a notional sales price for Product Z before further processing:

Post-separation point costs incurred per litre of Z = £11,730/5,100 = £2.30
Notional sales price of Z at separation point = £6.50 final price − £2.30 = £4.20 per litre

The common costs can now be apportioned.
At separation point:

Product	Output litres	Actual or notional sales price £	Actual or notional sales value £		Common costs apportioned £
X	4,000	5.00	20,000	20,000/58,520 × £41,000	14,012
Y	5,700	3.00	17,100	17,100/58,520 × £41,000	11,981
Z	5,100	4.20	21,420	21,420/58,520 × £41,000	15,007
			58,520		41,000

2.10.4 The final sales value method of common cost apportionment

Another cost apportionment method that you may encounter is the final sales value method. This method apportions common costs according to the sales values of the products after any further processing, but ignoring the costs of this further processing.

Using the data from Section 2.10.3 the costs would be apportioned as follows based on this method:

Product	Output litres	Actual final sales price £	Actual final sales value £		Common costs apportioned £
X	4,000	5.00	20,000	20,000/70,250 × £41,000	11,673
Y	5,700	3.00	17,100	17,100/70,250 × £41,000	9,980
Z	5,100	6.50	33,150	33,150/70,250 × £41,000	19,347
			70,250		41,000

Part of the justification for using any sales value basis of apportionment is to charge high-value products with a high share of the costs – a 'what the market will bear' approach to cost allocation. However, if post-separation costs are significant, the use of the final sales value method can cause serious anomalies in the resulting product cost figures.

2.10.5   Using joint product costs for decision-making

As stated earlier, common cost apportionment is necessary so that a total product cost is available for stock valuation purposes. However, the unit product cost obtained is of little use for decision-making purposes because of the arbitrary basis from which it is obtained.

For example, we saw how the apparent profitability of a product could be changed by simply altering the basis of apportionment from a quantity basis to a sales value basis.

As long as the process is undertaken, all of the products will be produced and their relative profitability is irrelevant. What is relevant is what managers decide to do with the products after the separation point, that is attention should be focused on post-separation point costs and whether or not they should be incurred. For example, managers may have to decide whether to subject products to further processing instead of selling them at the separation point.

2.10.6   Joint products and the further processing decision: an example

---

Example

A company manufactures three joint products – Exe, Wye, Zed. Each of the products is processed further after the separation point, although they are all saleable without further processing. Relevant data for the latest period is as follows:

	Exe	Wye	Zed
Sales price per kg			
After further processing	£15	£22	£18
At separation point	£10	£17	£12
Total product cost per kg, including			
apportionment of joint costs	£11	£10	£16
Output in kilograms	6,000	3,000	2,000

Joint costs of £77,000 have been apportioned according to the weight of the joint products. There was no work in progress in any process.

Requirement

Which of the products should be sold at the separation point, and not processed further?

Solution

First we need to determine how much of each product's total cost is joint or common costs. This is simply £7 per kg (£77,000/11,000 kg). The balance of the cost must be post-separation point costs:

	Exe	Wye	Zed
	£ per kg	£ per kg	£ per kg
Total cost	11	10	16
Joint cost apportioned	7	7	7
Post-separation point cost	4	3	9
Incremental sales value from further processing	5	5	6
Gain/(loss) From further processing	1	2	(3)

Product Zed should be sold at the separation point and not processed further. Its sales value increased by only £6 per kg (£18–£12) compared with an incremental processing cost of £9 per kg.

2.10.7 Costing by-products

The most common method of costing by-products is to deduct the net realisable value of the by-product from the main process costs. The by-product does not absorb any of the main process costs.

In effect a by-product is treated in the same way as a normal loss. It is valued at net realisable value and does not carry any of the process costs.

An example will show the workings of this method.

Example

A chemical is made in a single process, out of which a by-product, Z, also arises. Information for this process last month is as follows:

Material input = 4,200 units at a cost of	£94,500
Process cost	£58,111
Output of main product	3,800 units
Normal loss	5% of input
Scrap value of all losses	£5 per unit

There was also an output of 100 units of by-product, Z, which, after further processing at a cost of £6 per unit, were sold for £8.40 each.

There were no opening or closing process stocks.

Requirement

Prepare the account for the process for the month.

Solution

We can begin by preparing a simple input/output reconciliation. Since there is no work in process there is no need to perform an equivalent units calculation.

Input	Units	Output	Units	Units to absorb process costs
Material input	4,200	Main product	3,800	3,800
		Normal loss	210	–
		By-product	100	–
		Abnormal loss	90	90
	4,200		4,200	3,890

Costs	£
Material input	94,500
Process cost	58,111
Normal loss value	(1,050)
Net realisable value of by-product	(240)
	151,321

Cost per kg = £151,321/3,890 = £38.90 per kg

This rate is used to value the main product and the abnormal loss.
The net realisable value of the by-product is:

100 units × £(8.40 – 6.00)
= £240

Process account					
	Units	£		*Units*	£
Material input	4,200	94,500	Finished goods	3,800	147,820
Process cost		58,111	Normal loss	210	1,050
			By-product	100	240
			Abnormal loss	90	3,501
	4,200	152,611		4,200	152,611

If you look back over the workings of the example, you will see that the treatment of a by-product is very similar to that of a normal loss.

The costs of producing a by-product are borne by the main product, but the process costs are reduced by the net realisable value of the by-product.

2.10.8   Joint and by-products: an example

The last example in this chapter combines joint and by-products. Try it for yourself before looking at the solution.

Example

Products L, M and N are produced together in process 1. A by-product, B, also arises in this process. By-product B can be sold for £4 per kg after further processing and packing at a cost of £2.50 per kg. Products L and N are saleable without further processing, for £6 and £10 per kg respectively. Product M requires further processing in Process 2 at a cost of £2 per kg, before being sold for £16 per kg.

Information concerning process 1 for last month is as follows:

Material input		5,600 kg @ £4 per kg
Conversion costs		£14,020
Output:	Product L	2,450 kg
	Product M	990 kg
	Product N	1,960 kg
	Product B	200 kg
		5,600 kg

There were no losses in the process, and no opening or closing WIP. Common costs are apportioned on the basis of sales value at the separation point.

Requirement
Prepare the account for Process 1 for last month.

Solution

Since Product M is not saleable at the separation point (the end of Process 1) we need to use a notional price of £(16 − 2) per kg = £14 per kg.

The common costs are as follows:

	£
Material input 5,600 kg × £4	22,400
Conversion costs	14,020
Less: net realisable value of	
by-product 200 kg × £(4 − 2.50)	(300)
	36,120

This cost is to be apportioned to Products L, M and N on the basis of sales value at the separation point.

		Sales value £	Cost apportioned £
Product L	2,450 × £6	14,700	11,025
Product M	990 × £14	13,860	10,395
Product N	1,960 × £10	19,600	14,700
		48,160	36,120

Now the process account can be completed.

Process account					
	kg	£		kg	£
Material input	5,600	22,400	Finished goods:		
Conversion costs		14,020	product L	2,450	11,025
			product N	1,960	14,700
			By-product B	200	300
			Process 2: product M	990	10,395
	5,600	36,420		5,600	36,420

2.11 Summary

In this chapter, we have explored the basic principles that are used in the design and operation of cost accounting systems. In particular, we have considered the extent to which it is appropriate to attribute fixed and variable costs to products, the manner in which product costs may be determined in several different forms of production environment and the manner in which an associated system of ledger accounts is operated.

Self-test quiz

(1) State the factors that distinguish profit calculated according to (a) marginal costing and (b) absorption costing principles (Section 2.3).
(2) What are the respective uses for profit figures calculated using the two alternative principles? (Section 2.5)
(3) Explain the term 'overhead absorption rate' (Section 2.7.3).
(4) What is an 'over or under-absorption' of overheads? (Section 2.3.2)
(5) In the context of process costing, what is the meaning of the term 'equivalent production' for a particular period? (Section 2.9.2)
(6) In the context of process costing, what is the meaning of the term 'abnormal gain or loss'? (Section 2.9.8).
(7) Explain the differences between FIFO, Average and Standard cost methods for the valuation of stock in the context of process costing (Section 2.9.5).
(8) Explain and distinguish between the terms 'joint product', 'by- product' and 'waste product' in the context of process costing (Section 2.10).
(9) Explain the concept of cost apportionment between joint products (Section 2.10.2).
(10) What is the most common cost accounting treatment for the revenues generated through sales of a by-product? (Section 2.10.7)

Answer to Activity

Apportionment of general overheads

	A	B	C	Total
Direct wages (€)	15,600	12,000	13,400	41,000
General overheads (€)	10,273	7,902	8,824	27,000

Process A account

Charges:	
Costs allocated	122,900
Overheads apportioned	10,273
Total	133,173
Credits:	
Transfer to process B	128,968
Abnormal loss	4,205
Total	133,173

In the above case, the cost per unit output with normal efficiency is €133,173/ (60,0000 × 95%) = €2.3364. This gives a value for actual output of €128,968 (i.e., 55,200 × €2.3364) and €4,205 for the abnormal loss of 1,800 litres.

Process B account

Charges:	
Transfer from process A	128,968
Costs allocated	35,350
Overheads apportioned	7,902
Total	172,220
Credits:	
Transfer to process C	173,855
Normal loss	2,760
Abnormal gain	−4,395
Total	172,220

In the above case, there is a normal output of 52,440 litres and an actual output of 53,800 litres. So, there is an 'abnormal gain' of 1,360 litres. The logic used for handling this follows that where there is an abnormal loss. The cost impact of the abnormal gain has to be isolated.

The cost per unit output with normal efficiency is €3.2315 (i.e. (€172,220 costs − €2,760 normal waste scrap sales)/(55,200 × 95%)). This gives a value for the actual output and the abnormal gain. The value of the abnormal gain is a negative to the process account and a credit to the abnormal loss and gain account.

The €2,760 entry for the normal loss scrap sales is comprised of €1,400 cash for actual losses and an adjustment of €1,360 for the abnormal gain. This adjustment is matched by a contra entry on the Abnormal loss/gain account (see below).

Process C account

Charges:

Transfer from process B	173,855
Costs allocated	38,700
Overheads apportioned	8,824
Total	221,379
Transfer to stock	210,140
Normal loss	4,842
Abnormal loss	6,397
Total	221,379

In the above case there is a normal output of 51,110 litres and an actual output of 49,600 litres, giving an abnormal loss of 1,510 litres. The cost per unit output with normal efficiency is €4.2367 and this figure is used to value both the actual output and the abnormal loss.

Abnormal Loss/Gain account

Charges:

Process A	4,205
Process C	6,397
Lost scrap sales from process B	1,360
Total	11,963

Credits:

Process B	4,395
Scrap sales from process C	2,718
To profit and loss	4,850
Total	11,963

The above is an accumulation of the various entries made on the process accounts. The net balance of €4,850 is a write off to profit and loss.

Revision Questions

2

? Question 1

1.1 The marginal costing convention of profit is more relevant to decision-making than the absorption costing convention because

(A) So long as stock levels are rising, marginal costing gives a more conservative impression of profit than does absorption costing.

(B) When stock levels are falling, the profit disclosed by marginal costing is less influenced by costs from the previous period than is the case with absorption costing.

(C) Marginal costing provides a version of profit that relates only to those costs the level of which are influenced by the matters being decided upon.

(D) Marginal costing provides a valuation of stock that conforms with current accounting standards relevant to the preparation of published accounts.

1.2 The use of predetermined overhead absorption rates is generally favoured by management accountants because

(A) It allows product costs to be determined before the end of a given accounting period.

(B) It avoids the over-or under-absorption of overheads.

(C) It provides a more conservative version of product costs.

(D) It relates more to the activities that give rise to overhead costs than do more traditional methods of overhead absorption.

Scenario common to Questions 1.3 – 1.6

Details of Process 67 for August were

Materials transferred from Process 57 were 10,000 kg valued at £40,500.
Labour/overhead costs were £8,424.
Output transferred to finished goods was 8,000 kg.
Closing WIP was 900 kg.

Normal process losses are 10% of material input, 100% complete as to labour/overheads at the time of loss and losses have nil scrap value. Closing WIP is 100% complete as regards materials and 75% complete as regards labour/overheads.

1.3 The process cost per unit for Process 67 in August was

(A) £5.23

(B) £4.67

(C) £5.46

(D) £5.68

1.4 The entry on the abnormal gain/loss account in respect of Process 67 for August is

(A) £nil

(B) £546 debit

(C) £467 credit

(D) £546 credit

1.5 The amount credited to the Process 67 account for completions in August is

(A) £39,139

(B) £43,488

(C) £43,680

(D) £43,977

8000kg complete × 5.46 = 43,680

1.6 The value of closing WIP carried forward on the Process 67 account at end August is

(A) £4,403

(B) £4,698

(C) £4,892

(D) £4,947

9000kg ∂ 10% = 900kg × 4.50 = 4050·00
∂ 40.50
4·50
900kg ∂ 75% = 675kg ∂ 0.96 648·00
4698·00

1.7 The following details have been extracted from the budget papers of LK plc for June 2003:

Selling price per unit	£124
Variable production costs per unit	£54
Fixed production costs per unit	£36
Other variable costs per unit	£12
Sales volume	12,500 units
Production volume	13,250 units
Opening stock of finished items	980 units

If budgeted profit statements were prepared by using absorption costing and then by using marginal costing,

(A) Marginal costing profits would be higher by £27,000.

(B) Absorption costing profits would be higher £27,000.

(C) Absorption costing profits would be higher £35,000.

(D) Absorption costng profits would be higher £62,000.

1.8 Q Plc operates a process that converts a mix of chemicals into paint. A normal process loss equal to 15% of material input is expected in the process. The following data relates to April.

Opening work in process	4,050 litres, completes as to materials but only 60% converted
Materials input	45,600 litres
Output	39,460 litres
Closing work in process	7,630 litres, complete as to materials but only 35% converted

The total number of equivalent material units to be used to calculate the cost per unit using a FIFO basis of valuation is

(A) 36,760
(B) 38,760
(C) 40,810
(D) 42,810

1.9 In a period when finished stock levels increase, the profit and closing stock valuations shown under marginal costing and absorption costing would be

	Profit	Closing stock valuations
(A)	Marginal higher than absorption costing	Marginal lower than absorption costing
(B)	Marginal lower than absorption costing	Marginal higher than absorption costing
(C)	Marginal higher than absorption costing	Marginal higher than absorption costing
(D)	Marginal lower than absorption costing	Marginal lower than absorption costing

? Question 2

The following budgeted profit statement has been prepared using absorption costing principles:

	January–June		July–December	
	£'000	£'000	£'000	£'000
Sales		540		360
Opening stock	100		160	
Production costs				
Direct materials	108		36	
Direct labour	162		54	
Overhead	90		30	
	460		280	
Closing stock	160		80	
		300		200
GROSS PROFIT		240		160
Production overhead				
(Over-)/under-absorption	(12)		12	
Selling costs	50		50	
Distribution costs	45		40	
Administration costs	80		80	
		163		182
Net profit/(loss)		77		(22)
Sales units		15,000		10,000
Production units		18,000		6,000

The members of the management team are concerned by the significant change in profitability between the two 6-month periods. As management accountant, you have analysed the data upon which the above budget statement has been produced, with the following results:

1. The production overhead cost comprised both a fixed and a variable element, the latter appears to be dependent on the number of units produced. The fixed element of the cost is expected to be incurred at a constant rate throughout the year.
2. The selling costs are fixed.

3. The distribution cost comprises both fixed and variable elements, the latter appears to be dependent on the number of units sold. The fixed element of the cost is expected to be incurred at a constant rate throughout the year.
4. The administration costs are fixed.

Requirements

(a) Present the above budgeted profit statement in marginal costing format.   **(10 marks)**
(b) Reconcile each of the 6-monthly profit/loss values reported respectively under marginal and absorption costing.   **(4 marks)**
(c) Reconcile the 6-monthly profit for January to June from the absorption costing statement with the 6-monthly loss for July to December from the absorption costing statement   **(4 marks)**
(d) Calculate the annual number of units required to break even.   **(3 marks)**
(e) Explain briefly the advantages of using marginal costing as the basis of providing managers with information for decision-making   **(4 marks)**

(Total marks = 25)

 ## Question 3

XYZ Inc has scheduled production of 20,000 Units (a new product) in the coming period and has budgeted for £200,000 of production costs (50% fixed). XYZ executives TW (Management Accountant), IS (Financial Accountant) and HF (Sales Manager) meet to consider the following market research data for the coming period:

Unit selling price (£)	Sales volume (Units)
15	20,000
20	16,000
25	11,500

TW advocates adopting a Unit selling price of £20 because this will maximise contribution. IS advocates a Unit selling price of £25 because this will maximise of profit calculated according to normal accounting practice. HF advocates a Unit selling price of £15 because this will result in all output being sole and maximise market share.

Requirement

Explain each of these three points of view with supporting figures. Having regard to whatever facts you consider relevant, state which of the three points of view you consider to be correct.   **(25 marks)**

 ## Question 4

A company manufactures four products that form an input of a raw material to Process 1. Following this process, Product A is processed in Process 2, Product B in Process 3, Product C in Process 4 and Product D in Process 5.

The normal loss in Process 1 is 10% of input and normal losses in all the other Processes are nil. Scrap value in Process 1 is £0.50 per litre. The costs incurred in Process 1 are apportioned to each product according to the volume of output of each product. Production overhead is absorbed as a percentage of direct wages.

Data in respect of the month of October is as follows:

Process £'000	1	2	3	4	5	Total
Direct materials @ £1.25 per litre	100					
Direct wages	48	12	8	4	16	88
Production overhead						66

Product	A	B	C	D
Output ('000 litres)	22	20	10	18
Selling price per litre (£)	4.00	3.00	2.00	5.00
Estimated sales value at end of process 1 (£)	2.50	2.80	1.20	3.00

Requirements

(a) Calculate the profit or loss for each product and for the company in total in October assuming all output is sold at the normal selling price. **(9 marks)**

(b) Suggest and evaluate an alternative production strategy which would maximise profit for the month, assuming Process 1 output is fixed. State and comment on any critical assumptions included in your supporting evaluation. **(11 marks)**

(c) Suggest what management should devote its attention to, if it is to achieve the alternative strategy indicated in (b). **(5 marks)**

Question 5

PQR plc is a chemical processing company. The company produces a range of solvents passing materials through a series of processes. The company uses the First In First Out (FIFO) valuation method.

In Process 2, the output from Process 1 (XP1) is blended with two other materials (P2A and P2B) to form XP2. It is expected that 10% of any new input to Process 2 (i.e. transfers from Process 1 plus Process 2 materials added) will be immediately lost and that this loss will have no resale value. It is also expected that in addition to the loss, 5% of any new input will from a by-product, Z, which can be sold without additional processing for $2.00 per litre.

Data from Process 2 for April 2003 was as follows:

Opening work in process

Process 2 had 1,200 litres of opening work in process. The value and degree of completion of this was as follows:

	$	% degree of completion
XP1	1,560	100
P2A	1,540	100
P2B	750	100
Conversion costs	3,790	40
	7,640	

Input

During April, the inputs to Process 2 were

		$
XP1	5,000 litres	15,679
P2A	1,200 litres	6,000
P2B	3,000 litres	4,500
Conversion costs		22,800

Closing work in process

At the end of April, the work in process was 1,450 litres. This was fully complete in respect of all materials but only 30% complete for conversion costs.

Output

The output from Process 2 during April was

Z	460 litres
XP2	7,850 litres

Requirement

(a) Prepare the Process 2 account for April 2003.   **(16 marks)**

The output from Process 2 (XP2) is readily identifiable as three different grades of solvent (P, Q and R). For reporting purposes, the costs of Process 2 are apportioned to the three products in the ratio of their output volumes. The output volumes for April were

Product P	2,700 litres
Product Q	3,300 litres
Product R	1,850 litres

The Managers of PQR plc are currently deciding, for each individual product, whether they should sell it at the end of Process 2 or refine it further. The respective selling prices and further processing costs per litre are as follows:

Product	Selling price per litre at the end of Process 2 $	Selling price per litre after further processing $	Further processing costs per litre $
P	11.20	14.90	1.60
Q	9.20	12.60	2.40
R	6.50	8.60	1.20

The further processing costs are purely variable and they vary directly with the input volume. They are stated before any adjustment for revenue from further processing losses.

Further processing losses

When Product P is processed further, there is an expected loss of 15% of input. This loss can be sold for $8.00 per litre.

When Product Q is processed further, there is an expected loss of 20% of input. This loss has no scrap value.

There is no loss expected when Product R is processed further.

Requirement

(b) Prepare a numerical statement that shows whether each of the products should be further processed. State clearly your conclusion in respect of each product.   **(10 marks)**

The standard input mix of materials XP1, P2A and P2B and their standard costs per litre are as follows:

	% mix	Cost per litre
XP1	50	$2.75
P2A	20	$6.00
P2B	30	$1.40

At this point you may also care to attempt Question 4 from the MAPE Pilot Paper.

Solutions to Revision Questions

2

✓ Solution 1

1.1 Answer: (C)

(A), (B) and (C) are all correct statements under most circumstances, but it is (C) that explains why the marginal costing convention is most applicable to decision-making (D) is a false statement since it is absorption costing that is consistent with current accounting standards.

1.2 Answer: (A)

(B), (C) and (D) are all false statements.

1.3 Answer: (C)

Normal output from 10,000 kg input is 9,000 kg, giving a material cost per unit of £4.50 (i.e. £40,500/9,000 kg) and a labour cost of £0.96 (i.e. £8,424/8,000 kg completed + 100 kg abnormal losses + 675 equivalent kg WIP). This gives a cost per unit for the period of £5.46.

1.4 Answer: (B)

The abnormal loss for the period is 100 kg (being 10,000 kg × 90% normal output minus 8,000 kg completions minus 900 kg closing WIP). Hence the abnormal loss is valued at £546 (£5.46 × 100 kg) which is a debit to the abnormal gain/loss account.

1.5 Answer: (C)

That is, 8,000 kg × £5.46.

1.6 Answer: (B)

WIP is (900 kg × 4.50) + (675 equivalent kg × £0.96), = £4,698.

1.7 Finished goods stock increases during the period by 750 unit.
Fixed overhead absorbed per unit = £36
Difference in profits = 750 units × Fixed overhead absorbed per unit
Difference in profits = £27,000
When stock levels increase higher profits are reported under absorption costing. Therefore the answer is (B).

1.8

Output – started and finished	35,410
Closing work in process	7,630
Abnormal gain	(4,280)
Total	38,760

Opening work in process	4,050	Output	39,460
Materials input	45,600	Closing work in process	7,630
Abnormal gain	4,280	Normal loss	6,840
Totals	53,930		53,930

Therefore the answer is (B)

1.9   Answer: (D)

 ## Solution 2

- The emphasis in your MAPE syllabus is on the use of marginal costing information for performance evaluation. Ensure that you can produce a clear and complete answer to part (e).
- A common mistake is to include selling and distribution costs in stock valuations. Remember that stocks are valued at production cost only: variable production cost with marginal costing and total production cost with absorption costing, including absorbed fixed production overhead.

(a) The unit cost structure is the same in each 6-month period.

	£	£
Selling price		36
Direct materials	6	
Direct labour	9	
Variable overhead[2]	3	
Distribution cost[3]	1	
		19
Contribution		17

Notes:
1. Overhead January–June:
   £90,000 – £12,000 over-absorbed = £78,000
   Overhead July–December:
   £30,000 + £12,000 under-absorbed = £42,000

2. (£78,000 – £42,000)/12,000 = £3 variable
   £78,000 − (18,000 × £3) = £24,000 fixed

3. (£45,000 − £40,000)/5,000 = £1 variable
   £45,000 − (15,000 × £1) = £30,000 fixed

	January–June		July–December	
	£'000	£'000	£'000	£'000
Sales		540		360
Variable costs		285		190
Contribution		255		170

Fixed costs

Production overhead	24	24
Selling costs	50	50
Distribution costs	30	30
Administration	80	80
	184	184
Profit	71	(14)

(b) Distribution costs are not included in stock valuation. Therefore, marginal cost unit stock valuation = £19 − £1 = £18 per unit.

	£
Marginal cost unit stock valuation	18
Absorption cost unit stock valuation	20

	January–June £'000	July–December £'000
Absorption profit	77	(22)
c/fwd of fixed overhead in stock:		
(3,000 3 £2)	6	
(4,000 3 £2)		(8)
Marginal profit	71	(14)

(c) Absorption-based gross profit per unit is £400,000/25,000 = £16

	£'000
Profit from January–June	77
Reduction in sales volume (5,000 × £16)	(80)
Difference in overhead recovery (12,000 × £2)	(24)
Reduction in distribution cost	5
Profit/(loss) from July–December	(22)

(d) Fixed costs per annum £184,000 × 2 = £368,000

Contribution per unit £17
Annual breakeven sales in units £368,000/17 = 21,647 units

(e) Marginal costing is based on an understanding of cost behaviour, and attempts to model the real cash flows which will be the consequence of using resources and generating income. It can be represented graphically, giving simple, flexible and clear models of different scenarios. Marginal costing is closely associated with incremental costing and opportunity costing, which form a powerful grouping of financial modelling techniques which have common roots in the understanding of cost behaviour.

 Solution 3

Profit can be calculated according to two alternative conventions. The first of these is the marginal costing convention being advocated by TW

XYZ profit – marginal costing convention

£			
Unit sp	15	20	25
Sales	300,000	320,000	287,500
Variable costs	100,000	100,000	100,000
Stock	0	20,000	42,500
Cost of Sales	100,000	80,000	57,500
Contribution	200,000	240,000	230,000
Fixed costs	100,000	100,000	100,000
Profit	100,000	140,000	130,000

The second is the absorption costing convention advocated by IS.

XYZ profit – absorption costing convention

£

	15	20	25
Unit sp			
Sales	300,000	320,000	287,500
Costs	200,000	200,000	200,000
Stock	0	40,000	85,000
Cost of Sales	200,000	160,000	115,000
Profit	100,000	160,000	172,500

The two are distinguished by their treatment of fixed production costs in the stock valuation. The marginal costing convention adopts a stock valuation based on variable cost only – £5 per unit. The absorption costing convention adopts a stock variation based on full cost (including absorbed fixed costs) – £10 per unit. This latter method effectively allows a part of the fixed costs incurred in the current period to be carried forward into a subsequent period.

The absorption costing convention does give a maximum profit with a Unit selling price of £25. However, this involves carrying £42,500 of current period fixed costs forward into a subsequent period where they will have no impact on costs actually to be incurred. Those fixed costs are therefore 'decision relevant' to the current period and cannot be simply excluded from the decision before us.

The marginal costing convention charges all fixed costs to profit in the period in which they are incurred. Variable costs can be carried forward in the stock valuation – however, those variable costs will impact on the costs to be incurred in the subsequent period. Units produced in Period 1 and sold in Period 2 will allow production in Period 2 to be reduced and associated variable costs avoided.

Both sets of calculations given above assume that the stock will be marketable in the subsequent period. Were this not the case then the closing stock would have nil value and it would it would be appropriate to adopt a revenue maximising strategy. That would suggest a Unit selling price of £20. So, the Unit sales maximising strategy advocated by HF is unlikely to be appropriate – unless one wishes to maximising market share as part of some long term marketing concept.

The contribution maximising Unit selling price of £20 is therefore probably most appropriate in all the circumstances.

Solution 4

(a) General workings:

Process 1 Account

	Litres	Cpu (£)	£	Notes
Inputs				
Direct materials	80,000	1.25	100,000	
Direct wages			48,000	
Production overhead			36,000	(a)
Total	80,000		184,000	
Outputs				
A	22,000	2.50	55,000	(b)
B	20,000	2.50	50,000	(b)
C	10,000	2.50	25,000	(b)
D	18,000	2.50	45,000	(b)
Normal loss (scrap)	8,000	0.50	4,000	(b)
Abnormal loss	2,000	2.50	5,000	(b), (c)
Total	80,000		184,000	

Notes:
(a) Production o/h   £66000 × (48/88)
(b) cpu   (£184000 − £4000)/72000 litres
(c) Abn. Loss scrap   £1000, credited to Abn. Loss Account

Profit & Loss Statement
Product

£	A	B	C	D	Total
Sales	88,000	60,000	20,000	90,000	
Joint costs apportioned	55,000	50,000	25,000	45,000	
Post separation costs	21,000	14,000	7,000	28,000	
Product profit/loss	12,000	−4,000	−12,000	17,000	13,000
Abnormal Losses					4,000
Profit					9,000

(b) Assuming the 'post-separation costs' are wholly variable, the position may be analysed as follows:

Production Analysis
Product

£	A	B	C	D
Sales (with processing)	88,000	60,000	20,000	90,000
Sales (no processing)	55,000	56,000	12,000	54,000
Difference	33,000	4,000	8,000	36,000
Post separation costs	21,000	14,000	7,000	28,000
Gain from processing	12,000	−10,000	1,000	8,000

On this basis, the further processing of B should be ended. However, the critical assumptions in this analysis are that (i) the post-separation costs are wholly variable and avoidable and (ii) the absorption basis used for production overheads is meaningful.

(c) The critical issues relate to the cost structure of the operation. How far does the accounting treatment of the various costs reflect the way in which costs are actually incurred?

The analysis shown above suggests that C processing should be continued even though it is a loss-making product. This is correct, provided that all the costs in Process 1 are fixed and will be incurred regardless of whether of not C is produced. Further, the absorption of process costs on the basis of litre volumes may not be entirely meaningful.

The possible limitations of the analysis in regard to B production are discussed above.

The company might wish to review the accounting treatment of its costs and, perhaps, adopt a more sophisticated system such as ABC.

 Solution 5

(a)

Process 2 Account

	litres	$		litres	$
Opening work in process	1,200	7,640	Waste	920	nil
XP1	5,000	15,679	By-product Z	460	920
P2A	1,200	6,000	XP2	7,850	51,450
P2B	3,000	4,500			
Conversion cost		22,800			
Abnormal gain	280	1,753	Closing work in process	1,450	6,002
	10,680	58,372		10,680	58,372

COST ACCOUNTING SYSTEMS

Workings:

Equivalent Units Table

	Process 1 and materials added	Conversion
Output:		
Started & finished this period	6,650	6,650
Completion of opening work in process	nil	720
Abnormal Gain	(280)	(280)
Closing work in process	1,450	435
	7,820	7,525
	$	$
Period costs	26,179	22,800
By product value	(920)	
	25,259	22,800
Cost per equivalent unit	$3.23	$3.03

Valuation Statement

Finished joint product output:

		$
Started and finished 6,650 litres × ($3.23 + $3.03)	=	41,629
Opening work in process:		
Cost brought forward	=	7,640
Cost of completion 720 litres × $3.03	=	2,181
		51,450

Abnormal Gain

280 litres × ($3.23 + $3.03) = $1,753

Closing work in process:
1,450 litres × $3.23   = $4,684
435 litres × $3.03   = $1,318
                                                   $6,002

(b) *Product*

	P	Q	R
	$	$	$
Revenue per litre at the end of Process 2	11.20	9.20	6.50
Gross revenue per litre input at the end of further processing	12.66	10.08	8.60
Scrap revenue per litre input at the end of further processing	1.20*	0.00	0.00
	13.86	10.08	8.60
Incremental processing cost per litre input	1.60	2.40	1.20
Net revenue per litre input after further processing	12.26	7.68	7.40
Further processing Decision (Yes/No)	Yes	No	Yes

*$8.00 × 0.15 litres

3

The Theory and Practice
of Standard Costing

The Theory and Practice of Standard Costing

3

LEARNING OUTCOMES

After completing this chapter, you will be able to

► explain why and how standards are set in manufacturing and service industries with particular reference to the maximisation of efficiency and minimisation of waste;

► calculate and interpret material, labour, variable overhead, fixed overhead and sales variances;

► prepare and discuss a report which reconciles budget and actual profit using absorption and/or marginal costing principles.

3.1 Introduction

You should be familiar with the basic principles of standard costing and variance analysis from your foundation (or equivalent) studies. The initial content of this chapter amounts to a revision of these basic principles. You are advised to devote adequate time to this revision. The CIMA examination scheme is cumulative and MAPE examination questions in this particular area may draw heavily on material from foundation studies.

Standard costing and variance analysis represent a particular approach to performance evaluation. The concept that underpins them is that efficiency can be monitored by periodically comparing actual costs incurred with standard costs for output achieved. This concept is not valid under all circumstances. In subsequent chapters, the text goes on to explore both the practice and the limitations of standard costing.

3.2 The theory and practice of standard costing

CIMA's *Terminology* defines standard costing as follows:

 Standard costing: Control technique that reports variances by comparing actual costs to pre-set standards so facilitating action through management by exception.

You will see from this definition that there are very close relationships between standard costing and budgetary control (the practice of making continuous comparison between budget and actual results). They both compare the actual results with the expected performance to identify any variances. The difference is that with standard costing the comparison is usually made at a unit level, that is, the actual cost per unit is compared with the standard cost per unit. The resulting variances may be analysed to show their causes and we will see how this is done later in this chapter.

In order to be able to apply standard costing it must be possible to identify a measurable cost unit. This can be a unit of product or service but it must be capable of standardising: for example, standardised tasks must be involved in its creation. The cost units themselves do not necessarily have to be identical: for example, standard costing can be applied in some job costing situations where every cost unit is unique. However, the jobs must include standardised tasks for which a standard time and cost can be determined for monitoring purposes.

3.3 What is a standard cost?

A standard cost is a carefully predetermined unit cost which is prepared for each cost unit. It contains details of the standard amount and price of each resource that will be utilised in providing the service or manufacturing the product.

The standard cost may be stored on a standard cost card like the one shown below, but nowadays it is more likely to be stored on a computer, perhaps in a database. Alternatively, it may be stored as part of a spreadsheet so that it can be used in the calculation of variances.

The standard cost may be prepared using either absorption costing principles or marginal costing principles. The example which follows is based on absorption costing.

Example: Standard cost card: product 176

		£ per unit
Direct materials	40 kg @ £5.30	212.00
Direct wages		
Bonding	48 hours @ £2.50	120.00
Finishing	30 hours @ £1.90	57.00
Prime cost		389.00
Variable production overhead		
Bonding	48 hours @ £0.75	36.00
Finishing	30 hours @ £0.50	15.00
Variable production cost		440.00
Fixed production overhead		40.00
Total production cost		480.00
Selling and distribution overhead		20.00
Administration overhead		10.00
Total cost		510.00

For every variable cost the standard amount of resource to be used is stated, as well as the standard price of the resource. This standard data provides the information for a detailed variance analysis, as long as the actual data is collected in the same level of detail.

Standard costs and standard prices provide the basic unit information which is needed for valuing budgets and for determining total expenditures and revenues.

3.4 Performance levels

3.4.1 A standard

CIMA's *Terminology* defines a standard:

> *Standard:* A benchmark measurement of resource usage, set in defined conditions. The definition goes on to describe a number of bases which can be used to set the standard, including

- a prior period level of performance by the same organisation;
- the level of performance achieved by comparable organisations;
- the level of performance required to meet organisational objectives.

Use of the first basis indicates that management feels that performance levels in a prior period have been acceptable. They will then use this performance level as a target and control level for the forthcoming period.

When using the second basis management is being more outward looking, perhaps attempting to monitor their organisation's performance against 'the best of the rest'.

The third basis sets a performance level which will be sufficient to achieve the objectives which the organisation has set for itself.

3.4.2 Ideal standard

Standards may be set at ideal levels, which make no allowance for normal losses, waste and machine downtime. This type of ideal standard can be used if managers wish to highlight and monitor the full cost of factors such as waste, and so on; however, this type of standard will almost always result in adverse variances since a certain amount of waste and so on is usually unavoidable. This can be very demotivating for individuals who feel that an adverse variance suggests that have performed badly.

3.4.3 Attainable standard

Standards may also be set at attainable levels which assume efficient levels of operation, but which include allowances for factors such as normal loss, waste and machine downtime. This type of standard does not have the negative motivational impact that can arise with an ideal standard because it makes some allowance for unavoidable inefficiencies. Adverse variances will reveal whether inefficiencies have exceeded this unavoidable amount.

3.4.4 Basic standard

A basic standard is one which is kept unchanged over a period of time. It is used as the basis for preparing more up-to-date standards for control purposes. A basic standard may be used to show the trend in costs over a period of time.

3.5 Setting standard costs

You have already seen that each element of a unit's standard cost has details of the price and quantity of the resources to be used. In this section we shall list some of the sources of information that may be used in setting the standard costs.

3.5.1 Standard material price

The sources of information include the following:

(a) Quotations and estimates received from potential suppliers.
(b) Trend information obtained from past data on material prices.
(c) Details of any bulk discounts which may be available.
(d) Information on any charges which will be made for packaging and carriage inwards.
(e) The quality of material to be used: this may affect the price to be paid.
(f) For internally manufactured components: the predetermined standard cost for the component will be used as the standard price.

3.5.2 Standard material usage

The sources of information include the following:

(a) The basis to be used for the level of performance.
(b) If an attainable standard is to be used, the allowance to be made for losses, wastage and so on. Work study techniques may be used to determine this.
(c) Technical specifications of the material to be used.

3.5.3 Standard labour rate

The sources of information include the following:

(a) The personnel department for the wage rates for employees of the required grades with the required skills.
(b) Forecasts of the likely outcome of any trades union negotiations currently in progress.
(c) Details of any bonus schemes in operation.

3.5.4 Standard labour times

The sources of information include the following:

(a) The basis to be used for the level of performance.
(b) If an attainable standard is to be used, the allowance to be made for downtime, and so on.

(c) Technical specifications of the tasks required to manufacture the product or provide the service.

(d) The results of work study exercises which are set up to determine the standard time to perform the required tasks and the grades of labour to be employed.

The determination of standard labour hour requirements has a significant history and theoretical basis.

Extract from 'What is a fair day's work?'

Gene Gagnon, *Transport & Distribution,* **29:12, November 1998**
Full Text © Penton Media Inc. 1998

In 1884, Frederick Winslow Taylor, a foreman with Bethlehem Steel, was in charge of a system that brought coal and coke to the furnace. He determined that there were three things needed to maximise warehouse productivity: a definite task, proper method, and a time for completion of the task. He made observations about the proper size shovel and wheelbarrows in order to develop the best method. He was primarily interested in the information so he could establish the right crew size and not have to send anyone home, but the whole area of 'working smarter, not harder' sparked his interest. He expanded the concept to include what we now call Work Simplification. In 1911, he wrote Scientific Management which discussed management's role in dealing with workers.

In the early 1900s, Frank Gilbreth was watching bricklayers and determined that their task was, in reality, a conglomeration of small motions. He installed a number of methods improvements and reduced the tasks of the bricklayer from 18 to 5. He called each of these small tasks a 'therblig' which became the first scientific classification of motions. In 1920, he used a movie camera to document the time that certain motions took. By counting the frames he could estimate a length of time for each motion.

The expansion of the ideas of these measurement pioneers resulted in what we know today as 'predetermined times', tables that have predetermined time values for a given body motion or combinations of motions. This is the basis of the standard costing techniques now widely used in manufacturing industries.

In the early 1940s, the Westinghouse Electric Corporation sponsored a series of studies into sensitive drill press work. These duties yielded a predetermined time value system known as MTM (Methods Time Measurement). This system was much too detailed for long-cycled or non-repetitive operations so it was simplified.

The simplification was named the Master Standard Data (MSD) and is applicable to any type of work. It can measure work that has never before been considered measurable from an economic standpoint. MSD clearly identifies the exact work content of each element of an activity. The engineers stated 'in literally thousands of instances, it was accurate well within the accepted work measurement consistency limits of plus or minus five per cent'.

3.5.5 Production overhead costs

Overhead absorption rates represent the standard hourly rates for overhead in each cost centre. They can be applied to the standard labour hours or machine hours for each cost unit.

The overheads will usually be analysed into their fixed and variable components so that a separate rate is available for fixed production overhead and for variable production overhead.

3.6 Updating standards

The main purpose of standard costs is to provide a yardstick against which actual performance can be monitored. If the comparison between actual and standard cost is to be meaningful, then the standard must be valid and relevant. It follows that the standard cost should be kept as up to date as possible. This may necessitate frequent updating of standards to ensure that they fairly represent the latest methods and operations, and the latest prices which must be paid for the resources being used.

3.7 Standard costing in the modern industrial environment

There has recently been some criticism of the appropriateness of standard costing in the modern industrial environment. The main criticisms include the following:

(a) Standard costing was developed when the business environment was more stable and operating conditions were less prone to change. In the present dynamic environment, such stable conditions cannot be assumed.
(b) Performance to standard used to be judged as satisfactory, but in today's climate constant improvement must be aimed for in order to remain competitive.
(c) The emphasis on labour variances is no longer appropriate with the increasing use of automated production methods.

An organisation's decision to use standard costing depends on its effectiveness in helping managers to make the correct decisions.

Standard costing may still be useful even where the final output is not standardised. It may be possible to identify a number of standard components and activities for which standards may be set and used effectively for planning and control purposes. In addition, the use of demanding performance levels in standard costs may help to encourage continuous improvement.

3.8 What is variance analysis?

A variance is the difference between the expected standard cost and the actual cost incurred. A unit standard cost contains detail concerning both the usage of resources and the price to be paid for the resources. Variance analysis involves breaking down the total variance to explain how much of it is caused by the usage of resources being different from the standard, and how much of it is caused by the price of resources being different from the standard.

These variances can be combined to reconcile the total cost difference revealed by the comparison of the actual and standard cost.

A variance is said to be favourable if it causes actual profit to be greater than budget; it is said to be adverse if it causes actual profit to be less than budget.

3.9   Variable cost variances

We will use a simple example to demonstrate how the variances are calculated for direct material, direct labour and variable overhead.

 Exercise

A company manufactures a single product for which the standard variable cost is as follows.

		£ per unit
Direct material	81 kg × £7 per kg	567
Direct labour	97 hours × £4 per hour	388
Variable overhead	97 hours × £3 per hour	291
		1,246

During January, 530 units were produced and the costs incurred were as follows.

Direct material	42,845 kg purchased and used; cost £308,484	£7·20
Direct labour	51,380 hours worked; cost £200,382	£3·90/hr
Variable overhead	cost £156,709	

Calculate the variable cost variances for January.

3.9.1   Direct material cost variances

 Solution

(a) Direct material total variance

[handwritten margin note: Std – 567 × 530 = 300510 / 308484 / 7974 Adv / Actu]

	£
530 units should cost (× £567)	300,510
But did cost	308,484
Total direct material cost variance	7,974 Adverse

Note that this is an adverse variance because actual cost exceeds standard, hence causing actual profit to be less than budget.

This variance can now be analysed into its 'price' and 'quantity' elements.

(b) Direct material price variance

The direct material price variance reveals how much of the direct material total variance was caused by paying a different price for the materials used.

[handwritten margin note: (Act price − Std price) × Act Quantity; (£7·20 − 7·00) × 42845 = £8569 Adv.]

	£
42,845 kg purchased should have cost (× £7)	299,915
But did cost	308,484
Direct material price variance	8,569 Adverse

The adverse price variance indicates that expenditure was £8,569 more than standard because a higher than standard price was paid for each kilogram of material.

π *Material price variance:*   (Actual quantity of material purchased × standard price) − actual cost of material purchased.

(c) Direct material usage variance

The direct material usage variance reveals how much of the direct material total variance was caused by using a different quantity of material, compared with the standard allowance for the production achieved.

$$\left(Act\ usge - std\ use \right) \times std\ cost$$
$$81 \times 530$$
$$(42845 - 42930) \times 7 =$$
$$£595\ fav.$$

	kg	
530 units produced should have used (× 81 kg)	42,930	
But did use	42,845	
Variance	85	Favourable
× standard price per kg (£7)		
Direct material usage variance	£595	Favourable

42845⁄530
= 80·83

The favourable usage variance indicates that expenditure was £595 less than standard. This was because a lower amount of material was used compared with the standard expected for this level of output.

π   *Material usage variance:*   (Actual production × standard material cost per unit) − (actual material used × standard cost per unit of materials).

Check: £8,569 adverse + £595 favourable = £7,974 adverse (the correct total variance).

3.9.2 The direct material price variance and stock valuation

One slight complication sometimes arises with the calculation of the direct material price variance. In this example the problem did not arise because the amount of material purchased was equal to the amount used.

However, when the two amounts are not equal then the direct material price variance could be based either on the material purchased or on the material used. In the example, we used the following formula (we will call it method A):

(A) Direct material price variance:

	£
Material *Purchased* should have cost	X
But did cost	X
Direct material price variance	X

Alternatively we could have calculated the variance as follows (we will call it method B):

(B) Direct material price variance:

	£
Material *used* should have cost	X
But did cost	X
Direct material price variance	X

Obviously if the purchase quantity is different from the usage quantity, then the two formulae will give different results. So how do you know which formula to use? The answer lies in the stock valuation method.

If stock is valued at standard cost, then method A is used. This will ensure that all of the variance is eliminated as soon as purchases are made and the stock will be held at standard cost.

If stock is valued at actual cost, then method B is used. This means that the variance is calculated and eliminated on each bit of stock as it is used up. The remainder of the stock will then be held at actual price, with its price variance still 'attached', until it is used and the price variance is calculated.

3.9.3 Direct labour cost variances

 Exercise

Using the data from the previous exercise, calculate the direct labour cost variances for January.

 Solution

(a) Direct labour total variance:

	£
530 units should cost (× £388)	205,640
But did cost	200,382
Total direct labour cost variance	5,258 Favourable

Handwritten notes:
Std : 530 × 388 = 205640
Actual = 200382
5258 fav

(Act rate – std rate) × Act lab hrs
(3.90 – 4) × 51380 = 5138

Note that this is a favourable variance because actual cost is less than standard.

This variance can now be analysed into its 'price' and 'quantity' elements. The 'price' part is called the labour rate variance and the 'quantity' part is called the labour efficiency variance.

(b) Direct labour rate variance:

The direct labour rate variance reveals how much of the direct labour total variance was caused by paying a different rate for the labour hours worked.

	£
51,380 hours should have cost (× £4)	205,520
But did cost	200,382
Direct labour rate variance	5,138 Favourable

The favourable rate variance indicates that expenditure was £5,138 less than standard because a lower than standard rate was paid for each hour of labour.

π *Labour rate variance:*   (Actual hours paid × standard labour rate per hour) − (actual hours paid × actual direct labour rate per hour).

(c) Direct labour efficiency variance:

The direct labour efficiency variance reveals how much of the direct labour total variance was caused by using a different number of hours of labour, compared with the standard allowance for the production achieved.

	Hours
530 units produced should take (× 97 hours)	51,410
But did take	51,380
Variance	30 Favourable
× standard labour rate per hour (£4)	
Direct labour efficiency variance	£120 Favourable

Handwritten notes:
Act hrs = 97 × 530 = 51410
51380
30
× std rate × 4
120

The favourable efficiency variance of £120 is the saving in labour cost (at standard rates) resulting from using fewer labour hours than the standard expected for this level of output.

 Labour efficiency variance: (Actual production in standard hours × standard direct labour rate per hour) − (actual direct labour hours worked × standard direct labour rate per hour).

Check: £5,138 favourable + £120 favourable = £5,258 favourable (the correct total variance).

3.9.4 Variable overhead cost variances

✋ Exercise

Using the data as before, calculate the variable overhead cost variances for January.

✅ Solution

(a) Variable overhead total variance:

	£
530 units should cost (× £291)	154,230
But did cost	156,709
Total variable overhead cost variance	2,479 Adverse

This variance can now be analysed into its 'price' and 'quantity' elements. The 'price' part is called the variable overhead expenditure variance and the 'quantity' part is called the variable overhead efficiency variance.

(b) Variable overhead expenditure variance:
The variable overhead expenditure variance reveals how much of the variable overhead total variance was caused by paying a different hourly rate of overhead for the hours worked.

	£	
51,380 hours of variable overhead should cost (× £3)	154,140 ✓	*Act hrs × Std OH Rate*
But did cost	156,709	*less Act hrs × Act OH Rate*
Variable overhead expenditure variance	2,569 Adverse	

The adverse expenditure variance indicates that expenditure was £2,569 more than standard because a higher than standard hourly rate was paid for variable overhead.

π *Variable overhead expenditure variance:* Actual overhead cost incurred − (actual hours worked × standard variable production overhead absorption rate per hour).

(c) Variable overhead efficiency variance:
The variable overhead efficiency variance reveals how much of the variable overhead total variance was caused by using a different number of hours of labour, compared with the standard allowance for the production achieved. Its calculation is very similar to the calculation of the labour efficiency variance.

Variance in hours (from labour efficiency variance)	30	Favourable
× standard variable overhead rate per hour (£3)		
Variable overhead efficiency variance	£90	Favourable

The favourable efficiency variance of £90 is the saving in variable overhead cost (at standard rates) resulting from using fewer labour hours than the standard expected for this level of output.

π *Variable overhead efficiency variance:*   (Actual hours worked × standard variable production overhead absorption rate per hour) − (actual production in standard hours × standard variable overhead absorption rate per hour).

Check: £2,569 adverse + £90 favourable = £2,479 adverse (the correct total variance).

3.10 Fixed production overhead variances

In this section you will learn about the fixed production overhead variances in an absorption costing system. The variances in a marginal costing system will be covered in a later section.

The most important point to grasp about fixed production overhead variances is in an absorption costing system:

π *Total fixed production overhead variance:*   This is equal to the under- or over-absorbed fixed production overhead for the period.

When you are analysing the total fixed production overhead variance you are therefore trying to explain the reasons for the over- or under-absorption. Factors which could lead to under-absorption will cause adverse fixed overhead variances. Factors which could lead to over-absorption will cause favourable fixed overhead variances.

3.10.1 The reasons for under- or over-absorption of overhead

There are basically two reasons why fixed overheads are under- or over-absorbed, and they are both linked to the calculation of the overhead absorption rate:

$$\text{Overhead absorption rate} = \frac{\text{Budget fixed overhead}}{\text{Budgeted output}}$$

The overhead will be under- or over-absorbed for either or both of the following reasons:

(a) The actual overhead expenditure was different from budget (this difference is expressed by the overhead expenditure variance).
(b) The actual output was different from budget (this difference is expressed by the overhead volume variance).

It is easiest to look at an example to see how the variances are calculated.

Example

A company manufactures a single product. Budget and actual data for the latest period are as follows:

- *Budget.* Fixed production overhead expenditure £103,000. Production output 10,300 units, in 25,750 hours.
- *Actual.* Fixed production overhead expenditure £108,540. Production output 10,605 units, in 26,700 hours.

3.10.2 The fixed production overhead total variance

This is equal to the over- or under-absorption of overhead.

$$\text{Predetermined overhead absorption rate} = \frac{£103,000}{\text{Budgeted output}} = £10 \text{ per unit}$$

	£
Overhead absorbed during period £10 × 10,605 Units	106,050
Actual overhead incurred	108,540
Fixed production overhead total variance	2,490 Adverse

This variance represents an under-absorption of fixed overheads.

3.10.3 The fixed production overhead expenditure variance

This is the amount of the total variance which is caused by the expenditure on overheads being different from the budgeted amount.

	£
Budgeted fixed production overhead expenditure	103,000
Actual fixed production overhead expenditure	108,540
Fixed production overhead expenditure variance	5,540 Adverse

π   *Fixed overhead expenditure variance*:   Budgeted fixed overheads – actual fixed overheads.

Stop for a moment and look at the difference between the expenditure variances for fixed overhead and for variable overhead. With the variable overhead expenditure variance an allowance is made for the actual number of hours worked (i.e. the budget is flexed to the actual activity level). With the fixed overhead expenditure variance the allowance is not flexed because fixed overhead expenditure should not change if activity levels alter.

3.10.4 The fixed production overhead volume variance

This is the amount of the total variance which is caused by the volume of output being different from the budget.

	Units
Actual output	10,605
Budgeted output	10,300
Difference	305
× fixed production overhead absorption rate (£10)	
Fixed production overhead volume variance	£3,050 Favourable

π   *Fixed overhead volume variance*:   (Actual production in standard hours × fixed overhead absorption rate) − budgeted fixed overhead.

In this case the volume variance is favourable because a higher output than budget was achieved, which would potentially lead to over-absorption.

Check: £5,540 adverse + £3,050 favourable = £2,490 adverse (the correct total variance).

3.10.5 Analysing the fixed production overhead volume variance

We have seen that the fixed production overhead volume variance is the amount of over-or under-absorption caused by the volume of output being different from the budget.

There are two possible reasons why the volume of output might be different form the budget:

1. the number of hours worked might be more than or fewer than budgeted;
2. operations might be carried out more efficiently or less efficiently than standard, resulting in a higher or lower output than expected for the hours worked.

The volume variance can be analysed into two component parts, which explain the potential under- or over-absorption arising due to these two causes.

1. The *fixed production overhead capacity variance* measures the under- or over-absorption that arose due to working fewer or more hours than budgeted.
2. The *fixed production overhead efficiency variance* measures the under- or over-absorption that arose due to working more or fewer hours than would be expected for the actual output produced.

We can now return to our example and analyse the overhead volume variance into its constituent parts. However, this analysis is provided as background knowledge only. The MAPE Syllabus states that the actual analysis of a fixed overhead volume variance into efficiency and capacity components will not be examined.

3.10.6 Fixed production overhead capacity variance

	Hours	
Actual hours worked	26,700	
Budget hours of work	25,750	
Capacity variance in hours	950	Favourable
×fixed production overhead per hour (£4*)		
Fixed production overhead capacity variance	£3,800	Favourable

$$* \text{ Standard fixed production overhead per hour} = \frac{£103,000}{25,750} = £4$$

π *Fixed overhead capacity variance*:   (Actual hours worked – budget hours worked) × standard fixed overhead absorption rate.

In this case the capacity variance is favourable because more hours were worked than budgeted, which led to a potential over-absorption.

3.10.7 Fixed production overhead efficiency variance

	Hours	
10,605 units produced should take (× 25,750/10,300)	26,512.5	
But did take	26,700.0	
Variance in hours	187.5	Adverse
× fixed production overhead per hour (£4)		
Fixed production overhead efficiency variance	£750	Adverse

π *Fixed overhead efficiency variance*:   (Actual hours taken – standard hours for output achieved) × standard fixed overhead absorption rate.

	£	
Check total		
Fixed production overhead capacity variance	3,800	Favourable
Fixed production overhead efficiency variance	750	Adverse
Fixed production overhead volume variance	3,050	Favourable

3.11   Sales variances

In this section we shall be continuing with the study of variances from the viewpoint of reconciling budget and actual profits in an absorption costing system. There are two main variances for sales: the selling price variance and the sales volume variance. These variances can be demonstrated using the following data.

Example

A company manufactures a single product. Budget and actual data for the latest period is as follows:

Budget	
Sales and production volume	81,600 units
Standard selling price	£59 per unit
Standard variable cost	£24 per unit
Standard fixed cost	£4 per unit
Actual results	
Sales and production volume	82,400 units
Actual selling price	£57 per unit
Actual variable cost	£23 per unit
Actual fixed cost	£6 per unit

This data will be used to calculate the sales variances below.

3.11.1   The selling price variance

This variance calculates the profit difference which is caused by charging a different selling price from the standard.

	£	
Selling price per unit should have been	59	
But was	57	
Selling price variance per unit sold	2	Adverse
× units sold (82,400)		
Selling price variance	164,800	Adverse

π *Selling price variance*:   (Actual sales volume × standard selling price per unit) – actual sales revenue.

The adverse variance indicates that the actual selling price was lower than the standard price.

3.11.2   The sales volume variance

This variance calculates the profit difference which is caused by selling a different quantity from that budgeted.

	Units	
Budgeted sales volume	81,600	
Actual sales volume	82,400	
Sales volume variance	800	Favourable
× standard profit per unit (£59 – £24 – £4 = £31)		
Sales volume variance	£24,800	Favourable

 Sales volume (profit) variance: (Budgeted sales units × standard profit per unit) − (actual sales units × standard profit per unit).

The favourable variance indicates that the increased sales volume could have increased profit by £24,800 (if the selling price and the cost per unit had been equal to the standards).

An important point to note from this example is that the sales variances did not make use of the data on actual costs. All of the cost differences are analysed in the cost variances which you have already learned about in this chapter. The sales volume variance is expressed in terms of the *standard* profit lost or gained as a result of the change in sales volume.

3.11.3   The sales volume profit variance

The sales volume variance in an absorption costing system is sometimes called the sales volume profit variance. This helps to emphasise that it measures the change in standard profit caused by the change in sales volume.

3.12   Reconciling the actual and budget profit

Now that you have seen how to calculate all the main operating variances, you should be in a position to produce a statement which reconciles the actual and budget profit for the period.

First, to get some important practice, you should calculate all of the operating variances using the data given in the following exercise. Then you can learn to put all the variances together in a reconciliation statement like the one shown at the end of the solution.

Exercise

A company produces and sells one product only, the standard cost for which is as follows:

	£per unit
Direct material: 11 litres at £2	22
Direct wages: 5 hours at £6	30
Variable overhead	10
Fixed production overhead	20
Total standard production cost	82
Standard gross profit	38
Standard selling price	120

The variable overhead is incurred in direct proportion to the direct labour hours worked.

The unit rate for fixed production overhead is based on an expected annual output of 24,000 units produced at an even rate throughout the year. Assume that each calendar month is equal and that the budgeted sales volume for May was 2,000 units.

The following were the actual results recorded during May.

Number of units produced and sold: 1,750 units

	£	£
Sales revenue		218,750
Directs materials: 19,540 litres purchased and used	41,034	
Direct labour: 8,722 hours	47,971	
Variable overhead	26,166	
Fixed production overhead	37,410	
		152,581
Gross profit		66,169

Calculate the operating variances and present them in a statement which reconciles the budget and actual gross profit for May.

 Solution

Direct material price variance:

	£	
19,540 litres purchased should have costs (× £2)	39,080	
But did cost	41,034	
Direct material price variance	1,954	Adverse

Direct material usage variance:

	Litres	
1,750 units produced should have used (× 11 litres)	19,250	
But did use	19,540	
Variance	290	Adverse
× standard price per litre (£2)		
Direct material usage variance	£580	Adverse

Direct labour rate variance:

	£	
8,722 hours should have cost (× £6)	52,332	
But did cost	47,971	
Direct labour rate variance	4,361	Favourable

Direct labour efficiency variance:

	Hours	
1,750 units produced should take (× 5 hours)	8,750	
But did take	8,722	
Variance	28	Favourable
× standard labour rate per hour (£6)		
Direct labour efficiency variance	£168	Favourable

Variable overhead expenditure variance:

	£	
8,722 hours of variable overhead should cost (× £2)	17,444	
But did cost	26,166	
Variable overhead expenditure variance	8,722	Adverse

Variable overhead efficiency variance:

Variance in hours (from labour efficiency variance)	28	Favourable
× standard variable overhead rate per hour (£2)		
Variable overhead efficiency variance	£56	Favourable

Fixed overhead expenditure variance:

	£	
Budgeted fixed overhead (2,000 units × £20)	40,000	
Actual fixed overhead	37,410	
Fixed overhead expenditure variance	2,590	Favourable

Fixed overhead volume variance:

	Units	
Actual activity level	1,750	
Budgeted activity level	2,000	
Difference	250	
× fixed production overhead absorption rate (£20)		
Fixed overhead volume variance	£5,000	Adverse

Fixed overhead capacity variance:

	Hours	
Actual hours worked	8,722	
Budgeted hours of work (2,000 units × 5 hr)	10,000	
Capacity variance in hours	1,278	Adverse
× Fixed production overhead per hour (£20/5 hr) × £4		
Fixed overhead capacity variance	£5,112	Adverse

Fixed overhead efficiency variance w/f:

Variance in hours (from labour efficiency variance)	28	Favourable
× fixed production overhead per hour (£4)		
Fixed overhead efficiency variance	£112	Favourable

Selling price variance:

	£	
Selling price per unit should have been	120	
But was (£218,750/1,750)	125	
Selling price variance per unit sold	5	Favourable
× units sold (1,750)		
Selling price variance	£8,750	Favourable

Sales volume variance:

	Units	
Budgeted sales volume	2,000	
Actual sales volume	1,750	
Sales volume variance in units	250	Adverse
× standard profit per unit (£38)		
Sales volume variance	£9,500	Adverse

A reconciliation statement begins with the original budgeted profit. It then adds favourable or subtracts adverse variances to arrive at the actual profit for the month.

Profit reconciliation statement for May

		£	£	£
Original budgeted profit:				
2,000 units × £38				76,000
Sales volume variance				(9,500)
Standard gross profit from actual sales				66,500
Selling price variance				8,750
				75,250
Cost variances				
Direct material:	price		(1,954)	
	usage		(580)	
				(2,534)
Direct labour:	rate		4,361	
	efficiency		168	
				4,529
Variable overhead:	expenditure		(8,722)	
	efficiency		56	
				(8,666)
Fixed overhead:	expenditure		2,590	
	capacity	(5,112)		
	efficiency	112		
	volume		(5,000)	
				(2,410)
Actual gross profit				66,169

Note: variances in brackets are adverse.

3.13   Standard marginal costing

You should not be surprised to learn that the only variances in a marginal costing system which are different from those in an absorption costing system are those which involve fixed overheads. You are reminded that when a marginal costing system is in use, all fixed overheads are charged direct to profit without any attempt to attribute to units produced.

3.13.1   The fixed overhead volume variance

This variance does not arise in a marginal costing system. In an absorption costing system it represents the value of the under- or over-absorbed fixed overhead due to a change in production volume. When marginal costing is in use there is no overhead volume variance, because marginal costing does not absorb fixed overhead.

3.13.2   The fixed overhead expenditure variance

This is the only variance for fixed overhead in a marginal costing system. It is calculated in exactly the same way as in an absorption costing system.

3.13.3   The sales volume contribution variance

The sales volume variance in a marginal costing system is sometimes called by this longer name to distinguish it from the sales volume variance in an absorption costing system.

It calculates the standard contribution gained or lost as a result of an increase or decrease in sales volume.

In the previous example the standard contribution per unit is £58.

	£ per unit
Standard selling price	120
Standard variable cost	62
Standard contribution	58

The sales volume variance in a marginal costing system is calculated as follows:

	Units	
Budgeted sales volume	2,000	
Actual sales volume	1,750	
Sales volume variance	250	Adverse
× standard contribution per unit (£58)		
Sales volume variance	£14,500	Adverse

3.13.4 Reconciling the actual and budget profit

The marginal costing variances can now be put together in a reconciliation statement. You should spend some time studying the statement which follows, noting the difference between this statement and the one prepared using absorption costing. Think carefully about the reasons for the differences and ensure that you understand each figure in the statement. The format of the statement is not prescriptive but it is a useful layout because it focuses the reader's attention on the contribution for the period.

Profit reconciliation statement for May: standard marginal costing

		£	£
Original budgeted contribution: 2,000 units × £58			116,000
Sales volume variance			(14,500)
Standard contribution from actual sales			101,500
Selling price variance			8,750
			110,250
Variable cost variances			
Direct material:	Price	(1,954)	
	Usage	(580)	
			(2,534)
Direct labour:	Rate	4,361	
	Efficiency	168	
			4,529
Variable overhead:	Expenditure	(8,772)	
	Efficiency	56	
			(8,666)
			103,579
Actual contribution			
Fixed production overhead			
Budget		(40,000)	
Expenditure variance		2,590	
			(37,410)
Actual gross profit			66,169

Note: variances in brakets are adverse.

3.14   Idle time variances

You may come across a situation where idle time has occurred. Idle time is defined by CIMA as follows.

 Idle time: The period for which a workstation is available for production but is not used due to, e.g., shortage of tooling, material or operators (BS 5191).

During idle time, direct labour wages are being paid but no output is being produced. The cost of this can be highlighted separately in an idle time variance, so that it is not 'hidden' in an adverse labour efficiency variance. In this way, management attention can be directed towards the cost of idle time.

Variable overhead variances can also be affected by idle time. It is usually assumed that variable overhead expenditure is incurred in active hours only – for example, only when the machines are actually running, incurring power costs and so on – therefore variable overhead expenditure is not being incurred during idle hours. The variable overhead efficiency variance is affected in the same way as the labour efficiency variance.

Example

To demonstrate this, suppose that in the previous exercise you were given the following additional information about the actual results recorded during May.

Of the 8,722 hours of direct labour paid for, 500 hours were idle because of a shortage of material supplies.

An idle time variance could be calculated as follows:

Idle hours × standard labour rate per hour
= 500 = £6
= £3,000 adverse

This is the standard cost of wages incurred during the idle time.

These idle hours must be eliminated from the calculation of the labour efficiency variance, so that the efficiency of labour is being measured only during the hours when they were actually working. This gives a much more meaningful measure of labour efficiency.

Direct labour efficiency variance

	Hours	
1,750 units produced should have taken (× 5 hours)	8,750	
But did take (active hours)	8,222	
Variance	528	Favourable
× standard labour rate per hour (£6)		
Direct labour efficiency variance	£3,168	Favourable

The total of these two variances is the same as the original labour efficiency variance (£168 favourable). The effect on the variable overhead variances would be as follows:

Variable overhead expenditure variance:

	£	
8,222 active hours of variable overhead should cost (× £2)	16,444	
But did cost	26,166	
Variable overhead expenditure variance	9,722	Adverse

Variable overhead efficiency variance

	Hours	
1,750 units produced should have taken (× 5 hours)	8,750	
But did take (active hours)	8,222	
Variance	528	Favourable
× standard variable overhead rate per hour (£2)		
Variable overhead efficiency variance	£1,056	Favourable

The total of £8,666 adverse for the two variable overhead variances is not affected by the idle time (you should check this for yourself). However, we have now measured efficiency during active hours only, and we have allowed variable expenditure only for active hours.

3.14.1 Expected idle time

Some organisations may experience idle time on a regular basis. For example, if demand is seasonal or irregular, but the organisation wishes to maintain and pay a constant number of workers, they will experience a certain level of 'expected' or 'normal' idle time during less busy periods.

In this situation the standard labour rate may include an allowance for the cost of the expected idle time. Only the impact of any unexpected or abnormal idle time would be included in the idle time variance.

Example

IT plc experiences seasonal demand for its product. During the next period the company expects that there will be an average level of idle time equivalent to 20% of hours paid. This is incorporated into the company's standard labour rate, which is £9 per hour before the adjustment for idle time payments.

The standard time to produce one unit of output is 3 active (productive) hours.

Actual results for the period were as follows:

Number of units produced	3,263
Actual hours paid for	14,000
Actual active (productive hours)	10,304

Requirement

Calculate the following variances for the period:

(i) the idle time variance;
(ii) the labour efficiency variance.

Solution

The basic standard rate per hour must be increased to allow for the impact of the idle time:

$$\text{Standard rate per hour worked} = \frac{£9.00}{0.8} = £11.25$$

The variances can now be evaluated at this increased hourly rate.

Idle time variance

	Hours	
Expected idle time = 20% × 14,000 hours paid	= 2,800	
Actual idle time = 14,000 − 10,304 hours	= 3,696	
	896	
× standard rate per hour worked (£11.25)		
Idle time variance	£10,080	Adverse

Efficiency variance

	Hours	
3,263 units should have taken (×3)	9,789	
But did take (productive hours)	10,304	
Variance	515	Adverse
× standard rate per hour worked (£11.25)		
Efficiency variance (to the nearest £)	£5,794	Adverse

3.15 Calculating actual data from standard cost details and variances

An excellent way of testing whether you really understand the reasons for and the calculation of operating variances is to 'work backwards' from standard cost data to arrive at the actual results.

Try the following example for yourself before looking at the solution. If you have great difficulty in solving it, then you should go back and reread this chapter to obtain a better understanding of variance analysis.

 Exercise

Q Limited operates a system of standard costing and in respect of one of its products, which is manufactured within a single cost centre, the following information is given.

For one unit of product the standard material input is 16 litres at a standard price of £2.50 per litre. The standard wage rate is £5 per hour and 6 hours are allowed to produce one unit. Fixed production overhead is absorbed at the rate of 120% of direct wages cost. During the last 4 weeks accounting period the following occurred.

• The material price variance was extracted on purchase and the actual price paid was £2.45 per litre.
• Total direct wages cost was £121,500.
• Fixed production overhead incurred was £150,000.
• Variances were as follows:

	Favourable £	Adverse £
Direct material price	8,000	
Direct material usage		6,000
Direct labour rate		4,500
Direct labour efficiency	3,600	
Fixed production overhead expenditure		6,000

Calculate the following for the 4-week period:

(a) budgeted output in units;
(b) number of litres purchased;
(c) number of litres used above standard allowed;
(d) actual units produced;
(e) actual hours worked;
(f) average actual wage rate per hour.

☑ Solution

The best thing to do as a first step is to pull together all of the standard cost information to calculate a standard cost per unit.

A point of departure is to calculate the standard cost per unit, as follows:

	£
Direct material: 16 litres × £2.50 per litre	40
Direct labour: 6 hours × £5 per hour	30
Fixed production overhead: £30 × 120%	36
Total	106

Calculating the required figures is now just a series of exercises in logic. These exercises can seem difficult to the novice – but the logic becomes simple and obvious with familiarity.

(a) If actual fixed overhead was £150,000 and the fixed overhead expenditure variance was £6,000 adverse, then it follows that the budget fixed overhead was £144,000. From this it follows that the budget must have been 4,000 units (that is, £144,000 budgeted overhead/£36 standard overhead per unit).

(b) If the standard material purchase price was £2.50 per litre and the actual purchase price was £2.45, then it follows that the selling price variance per litre is £0.05 per litre favourable. We are told that the material price variance was £8,000 favourable, so it follows that 160,000 litres must have been purchased (that is, £8,000 price variance/£0.05 price variance per litre).

(c) If the direct material usage variance was £6,000 adverse and the standard price of materials is £2.50 per litre, then it follows that the number of litres used above the standard allowance is 2,400 (£6000/£2.50/litre).

(d) If the actual direct wages paid was £121,500 and labour cost variances totalling £900 adverse (£4,500 adverse rate plus £3,600 favourable efficiency) were experienced, then the standard wages for the output achieved was £120,600. It follows that the units produced were 4,020 (that is, £120,600 standard labour cost/£30 standard labour cost per unit).

(e) The total hours actually worked is 24,120 standard hours worked (that is, 4,020 units produced × 6 standard hours per unit) minus the 720-hour favourable labour efficiency variance (that is, £3,600 efficiency variance/£5 standard rate per hour). This gives a total of 23,400 actual hours worked.

(f) If the actual wages paid was £121,500 and the actual hours worked was 23,400, then it follows that the actual wage rate per hour was £5.1923.

3.16 Example: Preparing a reconciliation statement

By way of illustration and revision, a report reconciling budgeted and actual profit via variance analysis will be prepared from the data below.

Kenden Limited is a small company producing a single product, the 'fiixten'. Flixtens have the following production specifications:

Component	Standard quantity	Standard unit price £
FLIX	15	75
TEN	10	75

The standard direct labour hours to produce a flixten are 75; the standard wage rate is £10.50 per hour.

The fixed overhead budget for the year is divided into calendar months, on the basis of equal production per month. The budgeted annual fixed overheads are £645,750 for the budgeted output of 2,460 flixtens per annum. The budgeted annual variable overhead, absorbed on the basis of labour hours, is £184,500.

The above data has been used to arrive at a standard cost for a flixten of £3,000, as shown below:

Flixten standard product cost

	£
Direct materials:	
FLIX (15 × £75)	1,125.0
TEN (10 × £75)	750.0
	1,875.0
Direct labour: (75 hours at £10.50 per hour)	787.5
Variable production overheads:	
(£184,500/2,460 units = £75 per unit or £1 per	
direct labour hour)	75.0
Fixed production overheads: (£645,750/2,460 units)	262.5
Standard product cost	3,000.0

The budgeted sales of flixtens for March were 205 units at a standard selling price of £3,500 each, giving a £500 gross profit per unit and a budgeted profit for the month as follows:

	£	£
Sales		717,500
Cost of sales		
Direct materials	384,375.0	
Direct labour	161,437.5	
	545,812.5	
Variable production overheads	15,375.0	
Fixed production overheads	53,812.5	
		(615,000)
Gross profit (205 units × £500)		102,500
Administration expenses		(13,000)
Selling and distribution expenses		(21,000)
Net profit		68,500

Information relating to Kenden's actual costs and revenues for the month of March is shown below:

	£	£
Sales		612,000
Cost of sales		
Direct materials	342,864	
Direct labour	140,400	
	483,264	
Variable production overheads	14,000	
Fixed production overheads	53,250	
		(550,514)
Gross profit		61,486
Administration expenses		(13,938)
Selling and distribution expenses		(21,613)
Net profit		25,935

Despite the budgeted sales figure of 205 units, actual sales of flixtens in March were only 180 units, at a selling price of £3,400 each.

The company operates a JIT system (explored later in this text), so that there are no components or finished goods stocks. Works in progress is negligible.

The actual direct material cost represents the use of 2,850 FLIXs, which had been acquired at a cost of £199,500, and 1,838 TENs, which had been acquired at a cost of £143,364.

The actual number of direct labour hours worked in March was 14,625, considerably lower than that the production manager had budgeted.

3.16.1 Reconciliation of budgeted and actual profit

From the standard cost information given above, you should have noted that the company employs absorption costing, and the variances appropriate to that particular system are used in the analysis. Adverse variances are shown in brackets, where appropriate.

	£	£
Budgeted gross profit		
205 units × £500 gross profit per unit		102,500
Sales variances		
Sales price variance 181 × (£3,400 − £3,500)	(18,100)	
Sales volume variance		
(205 − 180) × (£3,500 − £3,000)	(12,500)	
		(30,600)
Standard gross profit on actual sales		72,900

	Favourable £	Adverse £	
Cost variances			
Materials usage			
FLIX		11,250.0	
TEN		2,850.0	
Material price			
FLIX	14,250.0		
TEN		5,514.0	
Direct wage rate	13,162.5		
Labour efficiency		11,812.5	
Variable overhead efficiency		1,125.0	
Variable overhead expenditure	625.0		
Fixed overhead expenditure	562.5		
Fixed overhead efficiency		3,937.5	
Fixed overhead capacity		2,625.0	
	28,600.0	39,114.0	(10,514)
Actual gross profit			61,486
Budgeted administration and selling costs (total cost)			(34,000)
Administrative cost variance			(938)
Selling and distribution cost variance (marketing)			(613)
Actual net profit			25,935

As you are aware, cost variances involve a comparison of the standard cost of production with the actual cost of production. In this example, as the company does not hold stocks of finished goods or work in progress, the actual units *produced* are equal to the actual units *sold*. The total cost variance of £10,514(A) in the above reconciliation can be reconciled in turn as follows:

	£
Standard cost of production: 180 × £3,00	540,000
Actual cost of production	550,514
Total cost variance	(10,514)

It is assumed that users of this text will be familiar with the calculation of all the summary variances listed in the reconciliation above. However, for purposes of revision, details of these calculations are provided below. Confident readers may omit this section!

3.16.2 Calculation of cost variances shown in reconciliation above

Hitherto, we have explained the individual variances using a narrative logic. You may have noticed that the definitions of the variances taken from Chapter 6 of CIMA's *Official Terminology* use a rather more sparse algebraic logic. You may find it best to use either of these approaches or a mix of the two for your own working purposes – it all depends on how your mind works. The notes below tend to follow an algebraic reasoning but in appropriate cases a narrative explanation is also given.

Material variances:
Direct material usage variances: (standard quantity − actual quantity) × standard price

FLIX: ((180 × 15) − 2,850) × £75	£11,250(A)
TEN: ((180 × 10) − 1,838) × £75	£2,850(A)

Direct material price variances: (standard price – actual price) × actual quantity

FLIX: (£75 × 2,850) − £199,500	£14,250(F)
TEN: (£75 × 1,838) − £143,364	£5,514(A)

FLIXs used cost £199,500 (given). At standard price, FLIXs used should have cost £213,750 (that is, 2,850 FLIXs × £75). The FLIX material price variance is £14,250 favourable (i.e. £213,750 minus £199,500). Exacdy the same reasoning can be applied to usage of TENs.

Labour variances:
Labour efficiency variance (standard hours – actual hours) × standard rate
(180 × 75 hours – 14,625 hours) × £10.50 £11,812.5(A)

Output of 180 units involves a standard labour requirement of 13,500 hours (180 units × 75 hours per unit), whereas 14,625 hours were used. The labour efficiency variance is therefore 1,125 hours, which has a cost of £11,812.50 adverse (that is 1,125 hours × £10.50).

Wage rate variance: (standard rate − actual rate) × actual hours
(£10.50 × 14,625) − £140,400 £13,162.5(F)

Overhead variances:

From standard cost sheet, variable overhead absorption rate is £1 per direct labour hour

Variable overhead efficiency variance: (standard – actual labour hours) × variable overhead absorption rate

1,125 (see labour efficiency variance above) × £1   £1,125(A)

Variable overhead expenditure variance: budgeted variable overhead for actual hours worked – actual variable overhead incurred

14,625 × £1 − £14,000   £625(F)

Fixed production overhead expenditure: budgeted fixed overhead – actual fixed overhead
£53,812.5 − £53,250   £562.5(F)

Fixed production overhead efficiency: 1,125 hours (see labour efficiency variance above) × £3.50* per hour   £3,937.5(A)

Fixed production overhead capacity: (actual hours worked – budgeted hours worked) × standard fixed overhead per hour
(14,625 – 15,375) × £3.50* per hour   £2,625(A)

*£645,750 budgeted fixed overheads/184,500 budgeted direct labour hours.

3.17 Some miscellaneous ideas

As with any technique, certain refinements and special considerations often have to be considered in the application of standard costing. To illustrate this point, let us consider two examples.

When an operation is producing a wide range of products, it may be inconvenient to base a variance analysis report on a detailed set of calculations relating to each product. The exercise may be simplified by expressing each product in terms of the standard hours required to produce it. Thus one may produce various volumes of 100 different products in a period and express output in terms of the standard hours required to produce the total output concerned. In effect, the standard hour becomes the unit of output and the accountant can base his or her cost variance analysis on the difference between the standard costs for the standard hours work produced and the actual costs of those standard hours.

A full variance analysis requires calculation and use of an average material usage per standard hour and an average selling price per standard hour. The use of such an approach requires a little imagination but involves nothing fundamentally different to the ideas we have explored in this chapter. The general idea is incorporated in Revision Questions 1.3 and 1.4.

Circumstances may arise where a variance is known and you have to work back to one or more of the figures that gave rise to it. Again, this requires a little imagination but involves no new ideas.

Example

Labour efficiency variance = £3,000 favourable
Standard hours required for output achieved = 2,400
Actual hours worked = 2,200

Requirement
What is the standard hourly rate?

Solution

The efficiency variance in hours is 200 favourable (2,400 standard hours minus 2,200 actual hours). Therefore the standard hourly rate must be £15 (that is, £3,000/200 hours).

The general idea is incorporated in Revision Question 7.

3.18   Summary

In this chapter we have explored the means by which performance can be measured by comparison of actual results with the standards used to compile the budget. The technique known as variance analysis involves systematic reconciliation of the budget and actual profit for a given period through calculation of specific cost and sales variances. The concept is that a study of variances allows the manager to identify problems or opportunities on the 'principle of exception' basis.

At the core of this concept is the idea that where there is no exception, there is no problem or opportunity. Some observers consider that this idea may lack substance in the modern economic environment – a proposition that we will consider further as we progress through this text.

Self-test quiz

(1) Distinguish between an 'ideal standard', an 'attainable standard' and a 'basic standard' (Section 3.4).
(2) Explain the term 'cost variance' (Section 3.8).
(3) Explain the manner in which a labour cost variance is split into rate and efficiency component variances (Section 3.9.3).
(4) Explain the term 'variable overhead efficiency variance' (Section 3.9.4).
(5) Explain the manner in which a fixed overhead cost variance is split into expenditure and volume component variances (Section 3.10).
(6) Explain the term 'sales volume variance' (Section 3.11.2).
(7) What are the main differences between variance analyses carried out using (a) absorption costing and (b) marginal costing principles (Section 3.13).
(8) Explain the terms 'idle time' and 'idle time variance' (Section 3.14).
(9) What are the main criticisms of standard costing (Section 3.7).
(10) What factors help to make a standard cost 'meaningful' (Sections 3.6 and, 3.10).

Revision Questions

? Question 1

The following data is to be used to answer questions 1.1 and 1.2 below.   **(2 marks)**

SD plc is a new company. The following information relates to its first period:

	Budget	Actual
Production (units)	8,000	9,400
Sales (units)	8,000	7,100
Break-even point (units)	2,000	
Selling price per unit	£125	£125
Fixed costs	£100,000	£105,000

The actual unit variable cost was £12 less than budgeted because of efficient purchasing.

1.1 If SD plc had used standard absorption costing, the fixed overhead volume variance would have been

(A) £15,638(F)
(B) £17,500(F)
(C) £25,691(F)
(D) £28,750(F)

1.2 If SD plc had used marginal costing, valuing finished goods stock at actual cost, the profit for the period would have been nearest to

(A) £335,200
(B) £337,600
(C) £340,200
(D) £450,400

(3 marks)

The following data is to be used to answer questions 1.3 and 1.4 below.

W plc uses a standard absorption costing system. The absorption rate is based on labour hours. The following data relates to April 2003:

	Budget	Actual
Labour hours worked	10,000	11,135
Standard hours produced	10,000	10,960
Fixed overhead cost	£45,000	£46,200

1.3 The fixed overhead capacity variance to be reported for April 2003 is nearest to

(A) £5,110 (A)
(B) £4,710 (A)
(C) £4,710 (F)
(D) £5,110 (F)

1.4 The fixed overhead efficiency variance to be reported for April 2003 is nearest to

(A) £710 (A)
(B) £730 (A)
(C) £740 (A)
(D) £790 (A)

1.5 A passenger transport company has developed the following formula to forecast the fuel cost to be included in its monthly budget:

$$Y = 10M - 0.4P + 5,000$$

where Y is the total fuel cost ($) per month,
    M is the number of miles travelled per month,
    P is the number of passengers carried per month.

The budgeted and actual miles travelled and passengers carried for April were as follows:

	Budget	Actual
Miles traveled	10,000	9,450
Passengers	6,000	6,050

The actual total cost of the fuel for April was $99,035.
The total fuel cost variance to be reported for April is

(A) $3,565 (F)
(B) $1,955 (F)
(C) $1,955 (A)
(D) $3,565 (A)

? Question 2

You are the management accountant of T plc. The following computer printout shows details relating to April 20X8.

	Actual	Budget
Sales volume	4,900 units	5,000 units
Selling price per unit	£11.00	£10.00
Production volume	5,400 units	5,000 units
Direct materials		
Quantity	10,600 kg	10,000 kg
Price per kg	£0.60	£0.50
Direct labour		
Hours per unit	0.55	0.50
Rate per hour	£3.80	£4.00
Fixed overhead		
Production	£10,300	£10,000
Administration	£3,100	£3,000

T plc uses a standard absorption costing system.
There was no opening or closing work in progress.

Requirements

(a) Prepare a statement that reconciles the budgeted profit with the actual profit for April 20 × 8, showing individual variances in as much detail as the above data permits. **(20 marks)**

(b) Explain briefly the possible causes of

   (i) the material usage variance;
  (ii) the labour rate variance;
 (iii) the sales volume profit variance. **(6 marks)**

(c) Explain the meaning and relevance of interdependence of variances when reporting to managers. **(4 marks)**

(Total marks = 30)

Question 3

A local restaurant has been examining the profitability of its set menu. At the beginning of the year the selling price was based on the following predicted costs:

		£
Starter	*Soup of the day*	
	100 g of mushrooms @ £3.00 per kg	0.30
	Cream and other ingredients	0.20
Main course	*Roast beef*	
	Beef 0.10 kg @ £15.00 per kg	1.50
	Potatoes 0.2 kg @ £0.25 per kg	0.05
	Vegetables 0.3 kg @ £0.90 per kg	0.27
	Other ingredients and accompaniments	0.23
Dessert	*Fresh tropical fruit salad*	
	Fresh fruit 0.15 kg @ £3.00 per kg	0.45

The selling price was set at £7.50, which produced an overall gross profit of 60%.

During October 20X8 the number of set menus sold was 860 instead of the 750 budgeted: this increase was achieved by reducing the selling price to £7.00. During the same period an analysis of the direct costs incurred showed:

	£
90 kg of mushrooms	300
Cream and other ingredients	160
70 kg of beef	1,148
180 kg of potatoes	40
270 kg of vegetables	250
other ingredients and accompaniments	200
140 kg of fresh fruit	450

There was no stock of ingredients at the beginning or end of the month.

Requirements

(a) Calculate the budgeted profit for the month of October 20X8. **(2 marks)**
(b) Calculate the actual profit for the month of October 20X8. **(3 marks)**

(c) Prepare a statement that reconciles your answers to (a) and (b) above, showing the variances in as much detail as possible. **(14 marks)**

(d) Prepare a report, addressed to the restaurant manager, that identifies the two most significant variances and comments on their possible causes. **(6 marks)**

(Total marks = 25)

? Question 4

The following profit reconciliation statement summarises the performance of one of SEW's products for March 20X7.

			£	
Budgeted profit			4,250	
Sales volume variance			850	(A)
Standard profit on actual sales			3,400	
Selling price variance			4,000	(A)
			(600)	
Cost variances	*Adverse*	*Favourable*		
	£	£		
Direct material price		1,000		
Direct material usage	150			
Direct labour rate	200			
Direct labour efficiency	150			
Variable overhead expenditure	600			
Variable overhead efficiency	75			
Fixed overhead expenditure		2,500		
Fixed overhead volume		150		
	1,175	3,650	2,475	(F)
Actual profit			1,875	

The budget for the same period contained the following data:

Sales volume	1,500 units
Sales revenue	£20,000
Production volume	1,500 units
Direct materials purchased	750 kg
Direct material used	750 kg
Direct material cost	£4,500
Direct labour hours	1,125
Direct labour cost	£4,500
Variable overhead cost	£2,250
Fixed overhead cost	£4,500

Additional information

- Stocks of raw materials and finished goods are valued at standard cost.
- During the month the actual number of units produced was 1,550.
- The actual sales revenue was £12,000.
- The direct materials purchased were 1,000 kg.

Requirements

(a) Calculate
- (i)   the actual sales volume;
- (ii) the actual quantity of materials used;
- (iii) the actual direct material cost;
- (iv) the actual direct labour hours;
- (v)   the actual direct labour cost;
- (vi) the actual variable overhead cost;
- (vii) the actual fixed overhead cost.   **(19 marks)**

(b) Explain the possible causes of the direct materials usage variance, direct labour rate variance and sales volume variance.   **(6 marks)**

(Total marks = 25)

 ## Question 5

The following details have been extracted from the standard cost card for product X:

	£/unit
Variable overhead	
4 machine hours @ £8.00/hour	32.00
2 labour hours @ £4.00/hour	8.00
Fixed overhead	20.00

During October 20X7, 5,450 units of the product were made compared with a budgeted production target of 5,500 units. The actual overhead costs incurred were:

	£
Machine-related variable overhead	176,000
Labour-related variable overhead	42,000
Fixed overhead	109,000

The actual number of machine hours was 22,000 and the actual number of labour hours was 10,800.

Requirements

(a) Calculate the overhead cost variances in as much detail as possible from the data provided.   **(12 marks)**

(b) Explain the meaning of, and give possible causes for, the variable overhead variances that you have calculated.   **(8 marks)**

(c) Explain the benefits of using multiple activity bases for variable overhead absorption.   **(5 marks)**

(Total marks = 25)

Question 6

QBD plc produces souvenirs for international airline operators. The company uses a standard absorption costing system. The standard cost card for one of QBD plc's souvenirs is as follows:

		$
Materials	1.5 kg	6.00
Labour	1.6 hours	8.00
Overheads		
Variable	1.6 hours	4.00
Fixed	1.6 hours	12.00
Total cost		30.00
Selling price		40.00

Production and sales information for April:

	Budget	Actual
Production	5,000 units	6,000 units
Sales	5,000 units	4,300 units
Sales revenue	$200,000	$164,800

The resources used and actual costs for April were as follows:

		$
Materials	10,300 kg	38,720
Labour	11,420 hours	71,200
Overhead		
Variable		29,650
Fixed		83,300

The 11,420 labour hours include 2,270 hours of idle time. This was caused by an unexpected machine breakdown.

All of the materials purchased were used during the month.

Requirements

(a) Calculate the budgeted profit/loss for April. **(2 marks)**

(b) Calculate the actual profit/loss for April. **(6 marks)**

(c) Prepare a statement that reconciles the budgeted and actual profits/losses for April 2004 in as much detail as is possible. **(15 marks)**

(d) Calculate the actual profit/loss that would be reported by QBD plc if it used marginal costing. **(2 marks)**

(e) Explain with relevant calculations how the reconciliation statement that you prepared would have been different if QBD plc used standard marginal costing instead of standard absorption costing. **(5 marks)**

(Total = 30 marks)

Question 7

The following uncompleted accounts appear in the ledger of MDX plc for March 20 × 0. The company operates a standard costing system, values stock at standard cost, and uses a single plant-wide standard labour rate of £6 per hour for all employees.

Raw materials

	£		£
Balance b/f	240	price variance	460
Creditors	?	Work in progress	6,000
		Balance c/f	180

Wages control

	£		£
Gross wages	?	Wage rate variance	618
		Work in progress	?

Work in progress

	£		£
Raw materials	6,000	Labour efficiency variance	900
Wages control	?	Finishing goods	34,720
Material usage variance	1,440		
Production overhead control	?		

Production overhead control

	£		£
Expenses – creditors	?	Balance b/f	345
Provision for depreciation	800	Work in progress	?
Volume variance	2,400	Expenditure variance	980
Balance c/f	260		

Data extracted from the standard cost card for MDX plc's only product is as follows:

	£/unit
Direct materials: 5 kg @ £2.40/kg	12.00
Direct labour: 4 hours @ £6/hour	24.00
Fixed overhead	20.00

Budgeted fixed overhead costs are £10,000 per month.

Note: All relevant transactions affecting the above accounts have been identified.

Requirements

Calculate

(i) the actual price paid per kilogram of materials;
(ii) the actual output;
(iii) the production overhead absorbed;
(iv) the actual direct labour hours;
(v) the cost incurred in respect of expense creditors;
(vi) the actual labour rate paid per hour.   **(18 marks)**

Solutions to Revision Questions

 Solution 1

1.1

Budgeted fixed cost	£100,000
Budgeted production	8,000 units
Absorption rate	$\dfrac{£100,000}{8,000 \text{ units}} = £12.50/\text{unit}$
Volume variance	$1,400 \times £12.50 = £17,500 \text{ (F)}$

Therefore the answer is (B).

1.2

Budgeted fixed costs = budgeted contribution to breakeven = £100,000

Budgeted breakeven sales volume =		2,000 units
Budgeted contribution/unit $= \dfrac{£100,000}{2,000} =$		£50
Budgeted selling price	=	£125/unit
So budgeted variable cost	=	£75/unit
So actual variable cost	$= £75 - £12 \;\; =$	£63/unit
So actual contribution/unit	$= £125 - £63 \;\; =$	£62
So actual contribution	$= 7,100 \times £62 =$	£440,200
Less: Actual fixed costs		£105,000
Profit		£335,200

Therefore the answer is (A).

1.3

The absorption rate per standard hour is $\dfrac{£45,000}{10,000} = £4.50$

Budgeted hours worked	10,000
Actual hours worked	11,135
Difference	1,135

Capacity variance = $1,135 \times £4.50 = £5,107.5 \text{ (F)}$

Therefore the answer is (D).

1.4

Standard hours produced	10,960
Actual hours worked	11,135
Difference	175

Efficiency variance = $175 \times £4.50 = £787.5 \text{ (A)}$

Therefore the answer is (D).

THE THEORY PRACTICE OF STANDARD COSTING

1.5

Standard cost	$	$
9,450 miles × 10	94,500	
6,050 passengers × 0.4	2,420	92,080
Fixed cost		5,000
Total		97,080
Actual cost		99,035
Total variance		1,955 (A)

Therefore the answer is (C).

☑ Solution 2

- Work methodically through the exercise, calculating each variance item in turn.
- Note that most of the cost variances are calculated by reconciling standard cost with actual cost – not budget cost to actual cost.
- Note that administration overheads are not absorbed into product costs and hence there is no associated volume variance.

(a) Standard product specification

	£	£
Sales price		10.00
Input costs:		
Materials 2 kg @ 50p	1.00	
Labour 0.5 hours @ £4	2.00	
Fixed production overhead	2.00	
		5.00
Profit		5.00

Note: The actual hours worked were 5,400 × 0.55 = 2,970.

T plc: budget/actual reconciliation statement – April 20X8

	£(F)	£(A)	£
Budgeted profit (5,000 × £5 − £3,000)			22,000
Sales volume profit variance (100 × £5)			500 (A)
Standard profit on actual sales			21,500
Variances:	£(F)	£(A)	
Direct material			
Price (£6,360 − £5,300)		1,060	
Usage (£5,300 − £5,400)	100		
Direct labour			
Rate (£11,286 − £11,880)	594		
Efficiency (£11,880 − £10,800)		1,080	
Fixed production overhead			
Expenditure (£10,300 − £10,000)		300	
Volume (£10,000 − £10,800)	800		
Sales price (4,900 × £1)	4,900		
Administrative cost expenditure	100		
Actual profit	6,394	2,540	3,854 (F)
			25,354

Calculation of actual profit

	£	£
Actual sales revenue		53,900
Actual costs		
Material	6,360	
Labour	11,286	
Production overhead	10,300	
	27,946	
Stock increase (500 units × £5)	2,500	
Cost of sales		25,446
		28,454
Fixed administration		3,100
Actual profit		25,354

The variance calculations shown above are in summary form. In an examination this is perfectly adequate, since the examiner does not need you to explain your calculations in expanded, narrative form. As we progress onwards through the text, we shall increasingly move to this abbreviated form of working. However, on this occasion a fuller explanation of the variance calculations is given below.

Explanation of cost variances

	£	
Direct materials		
Price		
Actual usage at standard cost	5,300	(10,600 kg × £0.50)
Actual usage at actual cost	6,360	(10,600 kg × £0.60)
Material price variance	1,060	Adverse
Usage		
Standard usage for output at standard cost	5,400	(10,800 kg × £0.50)
Actual usage at standard cost	5,300	(10,600 kg × £0.50)
Material usage variance	100	Favourable
Direct labour		
Rate		
Actual hours at standard rate	11,880	(5,400 units × 0.55 hrs × £4)
Actual hours at actual rate	11,286	(5,400 units × 0.55 hrs × £3.80)
Labour rate variance	594	Favourable
Efficiency		
Standard hours at standard rate	10,800	(5,400 units × 0.50 hrs × £4)
Actual hours at standard rate	11,880	(5,400 units × 0.55 hrs × £4)
Labour efficiency variance	1,080	Adverse
Fixed production overhead		
Expenditure		
Budgeted fixed overheads	10,000	
Actual fixed overheads	10,300	
Fixed overhead expenditure variance	300	Adverse
Volume		
Budgeted fixed overheads	10,000	(5,400 units × £2)
Standard fixed overheads	10,800	
	800	Favourable

(b) (i) The material usage variance may be caused by
- improved training of operating personnel;
- the sourcing of a better quality of material than was assumed in the standard cost.

(ii) The labour rate variance may be caused by
- an unanticipated drop in bonus payments;
- the retirement of staff who have reached their maximum points on the salary scale and their replacement by low salary staff.

(iii) The sales volume profit variance may be caused by
- the increase in sales price discouraging customers;
- the adverse effect of a successful advertising campaign run by a competitor.

(c) The term 'interdependence of variances' describes a relationship in which an action taken by management or operating personnel causes more than one (related) variance to be reported. For example, the sourcing of better quality material, as mentioned in part (b), may result in lower usage (favourable material usage variance) but a higher price (adverse material price variance).

An understanding of interdependence is essential if responsibility for outcomes is to be correctly identified. It is therefore crucial to the success of a control system such as standard costing.

☑ Solution 3

- Work methodically through the exercise, calculating each variance item in turn.
- Note that most of the cost variances are calculated by reconciling standard cost with actual cost – not budget cost to actual cost.
- Note that the question invites you to identify which the most significant variances are – using whatever criteria you consider most appropriate.

(a) Budgeted unit cost is £3.00. Therefore the budgeted profit for October 20X8 is

$(750 \times (7.50 - 3.00)) = £3,375$.

(b) The actual profit for October 20X8 is

$(860 \times £7) - £2,548$ actual costs = £3,472.

(c)

	£	
Budgeted profit	3,375	
Sales volume variance (W1)	495	(F)
Budgeted profit on actual sales	3,870	
Sales price variance (W2)	430	(A)
	3,440	

	Price		Usage		
Ingredients	£		£		
Mushrooms	30	(A)	12	(A)	(42)
Cream etc	n/a	–	n/a	–	12
Beef	98	(A)	240	(F)	142
Potatoes	5	(F)	2	(A)	3
Vegetables	7	(A)	11	(A)	(18)
Other	n/a	–	n/a	–	(2)
Fresh fruit	30	(A)	33	(A)	(63)
Actual profit					3,472

Workings

1. Sales volume variance = 110 extra menus sold $\times$ £4.50 unit contribution = £495(F).
2. Sales price variance = £(7.00 − 7.50) $\times$ 860 menus = £430(A).
3. Mushroom price = £(3.00 − 3.33) $\times$ 90 kg = £30(A).
4. Mushroom usage = ((860 $\times$ 0.1 kg) − 90 kg) $\times$ £3 = £12(A).
5. Beef price = £(15.00 − 16.40) $\times$ 70 kg = £98(A).
6. Beef usage = ((860 $\times$ 0.1 kg) − 70 kg) $\times$ £15 = £240(F).
7. Potatoes price = £(0.25 − 0.22) $\times$ 180 kg) = £5(F).
8. Potatoes usage = ((860 $\times$ 0.2 kg) − 180 kg) $\times$ 0.25 = £2(A).
9. Vegetables price = £(0.90 − 0.925) $\times$ 270 kg = £7(A).
10. Vegetables usage = ((860 $\times$ 0.3 kg) − 270 kg) $\times$ £0.90 = £11(A).
11. Fresh fruit price = £(3.00 − 3.21) $\times$ 140 kg = £30(A).
12. Fresh fruit usage = ((860 $\times$ 0.15 kg) − 140 kg) $\times$ £3 = £33(A).

> **!** These workings are in short summary form. As you progress through your studies you should become comfortable with this form.

(d) Report

To:	Restaurant manager
Date:	25 November 20X8
From:	Management accountant
Ref:	RM99/25

Food variance report – October 20X8

- Sales volume variance (£495 favourable). There was an increase of 110 set menus, possibly caused by the reduction in price, but perhaps also caused by an overall increase in the demand for meals within this restaurant because of favourable press comment.
- Sales price variance (£430 adverse). Management has reduced prices in order to combat competition and to attract more business.

Signed: Management accountant

Solution 4

- The question invites you to work backwards from the variance items to the source figures used to calculate them. The student whose study of variance analysis has consisted of merely memorising formulae will find this exercise difficult. The student who understands the logic of variance analysis will find it much easier.
- Note that requirement (b) does not follow on from requirement (a). An imperfect answer to requirement (a) need not prevent an examinee from obtaining full marks for requirement (b).

(a) The first step is to present the given budgeted information in a more usable form.

Budgeted information

	£	£
Sales		20,000
Material: 750 kg @ £6/kg	4,500	
Labour: 1,125 hours @ £4/hour	4,500	
Variable overhead	2,250	
Fixed overhead	4,500	
		15,750
Profit		4,250

Standard cost per units

	£
Materials − 0.5 kg × £6/kg	3.00
Labour − 0.75 hour £4/hour	3.00
Variable overhead − 0.75 hour × £2/hour	1.50
Fixed overhead − £3/unit	3.00
Total	10.50

(i) The budget profit is £4,250 (that is, £20,000 sales less £15,750 costs) giving a standard profit per unit of £2.8333 (that is, £4,250/1,500 units). If the sales volume variance is £850 adverse, then it follows that unit sales must have been 300 less than budget (that is, £850/£2.8333). Hence, the actual sales volume was 1,200 units.

(ii) The material usage variance is £150 adverse and this corresponds to 25 kg usage above standard. Standard usage was 775 kg (that is, 1,550 units produced × 0.5 kg per unit) and it follows that actual usage was 800 kg.

(iii) The material price variance is £1 per kg favourable (that is £1,000 material price variance/1,000 kg purchased). It follows that the actual purchase price must have been £5 per kg (that is, £6 standard price per kg less £1 per kg variance) giving a total material cost of £5,000.

(iv) The labour efficiency variance corresponds to 37.5 hours adverse (that is, £150 variance/£4 per hour standard rate). Standard labour usage was 1,162.5 hours (that is, 1,550 units output × 0.75 hours per unit). Hence, actual labour usage was 1,200 hours.

(v) The rate variance was £0.1666 per hour adverse (that is, £200 rate variance/1,200 hours) giving an actual rate of £4.1666 per hour. It follows that the actual labour cost was £5,000 (that is, 1,200 hours × £4.1666).

(vi) The standard variable overhead cost was £2,325 (that is, 1,550 units output × £1.50 per unit). The variable overhead variances total £675 adverse, hence the actual variable overhead must be £3,000.

(vii) The actual fixed overhead cost is £2,000 (that is, £4,500 budget less £2,500 favourable expenditure variance).

(b) • The adverse direct materials usage variance may have been caused by the purchase of materials of an inappropriate specification, or by the use of machinery that is overdue for maintenance.

• The adverse direct labour rate variance may have been caused by unanticipated additional payments to some employees for overtime working, or the movement of some trainees to a higher wage scale at the end of their training period.

- The adverse sales volume variance may have been caused by a downturn in consumer spending in general, or by the marketing activities of a competitor.

 Solution 5

- Note that there are two sets of variable overheads each using a different overhead absorption basis. It follows that there will be two separate sets of variable overhead variances.
- Note that requirement (c) invites discussion of the principles of overhead absorption – a topic introduced in Foundation level studies.

Overhead cost variances

(a)

	£	
Variable overheads		
Machine-hour related		
Standard overhead for 22,000 machine hours	176,000	(22,000 machine hours × £8)
Actual overhead	176,000	
Variable overhead expenditure variance	–	
Standard overhead for standard machine hours	174,400	(5,450 units × 4 machine hours × £8)
Standard overhead for 22,000 machine hours	176,000	(22,000 machine hours × £8)
Variable overhead efficiency variance	1,600	Adverse
Labour-hour related		
Standard overhead for 10,800 labour hours	43,200	(10,800 labour hours × £4)
Actual overhead	42,000	
Variable overhead expenditure variance	1,200	Favourable
Standard overhead for standard labour hours	43,600	(5,450 units × 2 labour hours × £4)
Standard overhead for 10,800 labour hours	43,200	(10,800 labour hours × £4)
Variable overhead efficiency variance	400	Favourable
Fixed overheads		
Budgeted fixed overhead	110,000	(5,500 units × £20 per cent)
Actual fixed overhead	109,000	
Fixed overhead expenditure variance	1,000	Favourable
Budgeted fixed overhead	110,000	(5,500 units × £20 per unit)
Standard fixed overhead	109,000	(5,450 units × £20 per unit)
Fixed overhead volume variance	1,000	Adverse

(b)

Variance	Meaning	Cause
Machine-related		
Expenditure	The variable overhead costs incurred are exactly in line with those which would have been budgeted for the machine hours worked.	Nil.
Efficiency	The output from the machines is lower than would have been budgeted based on the machine hours worked, therefore less variable overhead has been absorbed.	Necessary maintenance has been deferred, causing operational difficulties and reduced efficiency.
Labour-related		
Expenditure	The actual variable overhead cost incurred is lower than the standard cost allowance for the hours worked by the employees.	Some substitution of lower-paid employees has taken place.
Efficiency	The output produced was higher than would have been expected from the number of labour hours worked and therefore more variable overhead has been absorbed.	The employees were anxious to finish a large order on time to maximise the organisation's chances of receiving significant follow-up work. They therefore worked faster.

(c) The use of multiple activity bases for variable overhead absorption can have the following benefits:

- more realistic product costs may be produced, resulting in improved pricing and decision-making in general;
- management will be more aware of the link between activity and cost behaviour, and will have more incentive to focus on the relationships between these two variables;
- cost reduction activities within this area are more likely to be successful;
- it may become apparent that costs are not driven solely by output volumes, and therefore the focus of managerial attention may be significantly broadened. This may encourage managers to adopt a 'holistic' view of the organisation.

 Solution 6

(a)

Budgeted profit per unit	$10.00
Budgeted production and sales	5,000 units
Budgeted profit	$50,000

(b)

	$	$
Sales		164,800
Total costs incurred	223,370	
Closing stock:		
1,700 × $30	51,000	
Cost of sales		172,370
Actual loss		7,570

(c)

Cost variances	*Adverse*	*Favourable*	
	$	$	$
Material price		2,480	
($38,720 − (10,300 × $4))			
Material usage	5,200		
(10,300 − (6,000 × 1.5)) × $4			
Labour rate	14,100		
($71,200 − (11,420 × $5))			
Labour efficiency		2,250	
((11,420 − 2,270) − (6,000 × 1.6)) × $5			
Labour idle time	11,350		
2,270 × $5			
Variable overhead expenditure	6,775		
($29,650 − ((11,420 − 2,270) × $2.5)			
Variable overhead efficiency		1,125	
((11,420 − 2,270) − (6,000 × 1.6)) × $2.5			
Fixed overhead expenditure	23,800		
($83,800 − (5,000 × $12))			
Fixed overhead capacity		8,625	
((11,420 − 2,270) − (5,000 × 1.6)) × $7.5			
Fixed overhead efficiency		3,375	
((11,420 − 2,270) − (6,000 × 1.6)) × $7.5			
Totals	61,225	17,855	43,370 (A)
Actual loss			7,570

(d)

The actual loss would be greater under marginal costing due to the non absorption of fixed overhead costs into the unsold stock items.

The loss would increase by 1,700 units $\times$ \$12 = \$20,400 so that under marginal costing the loss would be \$27,970.

(e)

There would be no change to the budgeted profit as there was no budgeted change in the level of stocks.

The sales volume variance would be valued on a contribution basis so that it increases to \$15,400 Adverse (700 units $\times$ \$22), an increase of \$8,400 adverse.

The fixed overhead capacity and efficiency variances would not exist, thus removing favourable cost variances totalling \$12,000.

There would be no other changes and so, by totalling the above, it can be seen that they equate to \$20,400 adverse, which equals the increase in the size of the loss as per part (d) above.

✅ Solution 7

(i) (£6,640 − £240)/2,475 kg purchased* = £2.59 per kg
   *(£6,400 − £460)/£2.40

(ii) Budgeted volume: £10,000/£20   500 units per month

Volume variance	120 units (F)
Actual output	620 units

(iii) Overhead absorbed = 620 $\times$ £20 = £12,400

(iv)
Standard hours: 620 $\times$ 4	2,480
Add:efficiency variance	150 (A)
Actual direct labour hours	2,630

(v) £12,400 production overhead is transferred to WIP (620 $\times$ £20)
   To balance: production overhead control account expense creditors = £10,265

(vi) Gross wages = £16,398 (rate £618 + efficiency £900 + standard £14,880)
   Actual total labour hours = 2,630 (from (iv))
   Actual labour rate per hour = £16,398/2,630 = £6.235

4

Standard Costing and Performance Evaluation

Standard Costing and Performance Evaluation

4

LEARNING OUTCOMES

After completing this chapter, you will be able to

▶ calculate and explain planning and operational variances;

▶ discuss the behavioural implications of setting standard costs;

▶ apply standard costing methods within costing systems and demonstrate the reconciliation of budgeted and actual profit margins;

▶ prepare reports using a range of internal and external benchmarks and interpret the results.

4.1 Introduction

In this chapter we will explore further aspects of the practice of standard costing. In particular, we will consider more detailed analysis of particular variances, the separation of variances into operational and planning components and the preparation of performance reports for management based on standard costing.

We will also conduct a general exploration of the role of standard costing in performance evaluation and consider how that role may be changing in the modern economic environment. You should become aware that the relevance of a number of traditional management accounting practices is being questioned in the era of flexible manufacturing and a service-based economy.

4.2 Material mix and yield variances

The direct material usage variance measures the change in total direct material cost brought about by using a non-standard amount of material in production. Sometimes it is possible to subdivide the usage variance into a direct material mix variance and a direct material yield variance. This subdivision is most likely to be found in process industries, where a standard input mix is the norm, and recognisable individual components of input are combined during the production process to produce an output in which the individual items are no longer separately identifiable. Paint manufacture provides a typical example: if a blue paint is required, the basic paint base will be introduced to the mixing process, along with the blue dye; at the input stage, both raw process materials are separately identifiable, but at the end of the process, blue paint emerges, with the individual components no longer separately identifiable.

In many process industries, it may be necessary from time to time to vary the input *mix* – perhaps because of shortages of raw material, or in order to take advantage of attractive input prices. Whether the input mix is a standard or a non-standard one, there is a possibility that the *outcome* from the process will differ from that which was expected. In addition to *unexpected* differences in yield, it is perfectly *normal* in some processes for the physical volume of output from the process to be less than the total volume of input, that is, there may be *unavoidable* losses inherent in the operation of an efficiently working process. In the blended whisky industry, for example, such losses arise from evaporation, and the volume of output from the process is *expected* to be less than the volume of the input. The direct material *mix* variance measures the change in cost brought about by an alteration to the *constituents* of the input mix, while the direct material *yield* variance measures the change in cost brought about by any deviation in output from the *standard* process output.

The data below will be used to calculate mix and yield variances in the subsequent examples.

Example

A company has the following standards for a mix to produce 500 kg of product C:

Input	kg	Cost/kg	Total cost of mix	
A	200	£1.00	£200	
B	400	£1.60	£640	
	600		£840	600 kg of input should produce 500 kg of C at a standard cost of £1.68/kg

In a particular period, the actual results of the process were as follows:

Actual input	kg	Actual cost/kg	Total actual cost
A	300	£1.00	£300
B	300	£1.60	£480
	600		£780

Actual output: 400 kg of C

Note that, in the above data, there is no direct material *price* variance, as the actual cost per kilogram of inputs A and B was the standard cost in each case. The *whole* of the direct material variance is thus due to changes in the *usage* thereof. The total variance is the difference between the standard cost of the *output* of 400 kg of C (400 × £1.68 = £672) and the actual cost of £780. This gives an adverse direct material usage variance of £108. This material usage variance may be split into mix and yield components.

(a) Direct material mix variance

For an input of 600 kg:

Material	Actual input kg	Standard mix of input kg	Mix variance kg	Standard price per kg £	Mix variance £
A	300	200	100 (A)	1.00	100 (A)
B	300	400	100 (F)	1.60	160 (F)
	600	600			60 (F)

The material mix variance demonstrates the cost impact of using an ingredient mix different from that which is standard. That standard mix of 600 kg input is 200 kg of A and 400 kg of B. The actual mix of the 600 kg input is 300 kg of A and 300 kg of B. In this case, ingredient A has been substituted for ingredient B in the mix – and the net cost impact of this is £60 favourable.

Material mix variance: (Actual material input × standard cost per unit) – (actual total material input in standard proportions × standard cost per unit).

The CIMA *Terminology* offers an alternative methodology for working the material mix variance.

This other methodology works the components of the mix variance on the basis of the difference between budget usage for output achieved and the difference between the standard average and the standard cost of the materials input. In this case the standard average price of the material used is £1.40 per kg (that is £840/600 kg). This may be illustrated by reworking the mix variance calculated above using the alternative methodology:

Material	(a) kg	(b) kg	(c) kg	(d) £	(e) £	(f) £	(g) £
A	300	160	140	1.40	1.00	0.40	56 (F)
B	300	320	−20	1.40	1.60	−0.20	4 (F)
						Total	60 (F)

Key:
(a) actual usage
(b) budget input for output achieved A = 200 kg/500 kg × 400 kg, B = 400 kg/500 kg × 400 kg
(c) mix variance (kg), (a) − (b)
(d) standard average price per kg
(e) standard price per kg
(f) (e) − (d)
(g) mix variance (£), (c) × (f).

The logic here is more complex but it may be argued that it gives a more rigorous analysis of the situation. We are using more of the cheap ingredient and less of the expensive ingredient. So, it might be argued, both components of the mixture variance should be favourable.

Material mix variance (alternative methodology): ((Actual input quantity − budget material input quantity for the output produced) × (standard weighted average cost per unit input − standard cost per input unit)).

When answering an examination question simply requiring the calculation of a mix variance, the student is advised to always use the simple method illustrated at the start of this section. However, students should be aware that alternatives do exist and that the examiner may invite the student to demonstrate familiarity with these.

(b) Direct material yield variance

Standard cost per kg of output = £840/500 = £1.68

	kg	
600 kg input should have yielded	500	of C
But did yield	400	of C
Yield variance	100	(A)
x standard cost per kg of output (£1.68)		
Yield variance	£168	(A)

The material yield variance demonstrates the cost impact of generating above or below standard output from a given quantity of input. In this case, the input of 600 kg is associated with a standard output of 500 kg, but the actual output was only 400 kg.

The yield variance is 100 kg adverse (that is, 500 kg standard output − 400 kg actual output).

The cost impact of this is £168 adverse.

Material yield variance: (Standard output for actual input − actual output) × standard cost per unit of output.

The current edition of the *Terminology* permits use of both methods and earlier editions specified use of a third method. All possible methods give the same end result. Students are often confused when they see a mix variance in a text or model answer calculated using a method they are unfamiliar with.

The sum of the direct material mix variance and the direct material yield variance can be seen to be £108 adverse, which, in the absence of a direct material price variance, is equal to the total direct material variance.

The direct material mix and yield variances must be interpreted with care, as there is a very strong interrelationship between them. If we consider the concept of a *standard* mix, it is clear that such a mix will represent the combination of inputs that provides an acceptable quality of output at the least possible cost. If some *other* combination of inputs could produce a *lower* cost output without detriment to quality, then *this* alternative would have been selected as the standard. Any change in the input mix must therefore be expected to have an impact on the *yield* from the process, as well as on the price of the input mix. It is highly unlikely that any meaningful control can be exercised over the output from a process independent of the input to it, and thus the two variances should be considered together.

4.3 Labour mix and yield variances

The same logic applied in the calculation of materials mix and yield variances can equally well be applied to labour costs. When several different classes of labour are engaged then the labour efficiency variance can be split into mix and yield components.

This is best demonstrated through study of a simple example.

Example

The standard labour input associated with the production of one unit is as follows:

- 4 hours of skilled labour at £15 per hour;
- 6 hours of unskilled labour at £10 per hour.

The standard labour cost of one unit is £120. The standard total labour input associated with production of one unit is 10 hours at an average hourly rate of £12 (that is, £120/10 hours). It can also be seen that the standard labour mix is 40% skilled and 60% unskilled.

During Period 6,

- 25 units are produced;
- 95 hours of skilled labour are used;
- 175 hours of unskilled labour are used;
- £3,267.50 wages are paid.

We are required to calculate the labour cost variance and analyse this into labour rate and labour efficiency component variances. We are then required to analyse the labour efficiency variance into labour mix and labour yield components.

Step 1 – calculation of labour cost variance
This is the difference between the standard labour cost of producing 25 units and the actual labour cost incurred.

	£
Actual labour cost incurred (given)	3,267.50
Standard labour cost of 25 units (25 × £120)	3,000.00
Labour cost variance	267.50 (A)

Step 2 – calculation of labour rate and labour efficiency variances

The labour rate variance is the difference between (actual hours worked × standard rate) and the actual wages paid. The labour efficiency variance is (standard hours required for output achieved − actual hours worked) multiplied by the standard hourly rate.

	£
Labour rate variance	
(95 skilled hrs × £15) + (175 unskilled hrs × £10) − £3,267.50	92.50 (A)
Labour efficiency variance	
((100 standard − 95 actual skilled hrs) × £15) +	
((150 standard − 175 actual unskilled hrs) × £10)	175.00 (A)
Sum total (labour cost variance)	267.50 (A)

Step 3 – calculation of labour mix and labour yield variances

Labour mix variance

For 270 hours worked:

Grade	Actual hours	Standard mix of hours	Mix variance hours	Standard rate per hr £	Mix variance £
Skilled	95	(40%) 108	13 (F)	15	195 (F)
Unskilled	175	(60%) 162	13 (A)	10	130 (A)
	270	270			65 (F)

Labour yield variance

270 hours of work should yield (270 hr/ 10 hrs/units)	27 units
But did yield	25 units
Yield variance	2 units (A)
x std cost £120 per unit	
Yield variance	£240 (A)

Check: mix variance £65(F) + yield variance £240(A) = total efficiency variance £175(A).

The variance analysis carried out in Step 3 indicates that a cost advantage has been achieved by substituting unskilled for skilled labour in the production process. However, that advantage has been more than offset by a cost disadvantage arising from the diminished efficiency of the whole workforce.

Again, in dealing with the labour mixture variance, the *Terminology* offers an alternative methodology:

π *Labour mix variance (alternative methodology)*: ((Actual hours worked − budget hours worked for the output produced) × (standard weighted average cost per hour worked − standard cost per hour worked))

Reworking the earlier example using this alternative methodology gives the following result:

Labour	(a) hours	(b) hours	(c) hours	(d) £	(e) £	(f) £	(g) £
Skilled	95	100	−5	12.00	15.00	−3.00	15(F)
Unskilled	175	150	25	12.00	10.00	2.00	50(F)
						Total	65(F)

Key:

(a) actual hours

(b) budget hours for output achieved skilled = 25 units × 4 hours, unskilled = 25 units × 6 hours

(c) mix variance (hours), (a) − (b)

(d) std avg rate per hour, £120/10 hour
(e) standard rate
(f) (e) − (d)
(g) mix variance (£), (c) × (f).

The logic in this case is more complicated, but the result is the same as that given in the simple method above. Again, you are always recommended to use the simple method if the requirement is merely to calculate the labour mix variance.

It should be appreciated that the example given is set in a manufacturing environment, but the technique may be most applicable in a service or professional environment. For example, an audit operation typically makes use of several well-defined grades of staff ranging from Partner to Junior. The calculation of a labour mix variance in regard to an audit may give some powerful insights into the effectiveness with which particular jobs were run. One of the key factors that can determine the performance of a professional practice is the manner in which the work of senior/qualified staff is integrated with that of their juniors.

4.4 Sales variances

In Chapter 2, we considered the calculation of the sales volume variance. In its simplest form, this variance is

(budget − actual sales units) × standard profit per unit

However, it is capable of being expressed in several different ways and is capable of more detailed analysis. The principal alternative ways in which the sales volume variance can be expressed are as follows:

(a)

π *Sales volume profit variance*: ((Budgeted sales units × standard profit per unit) − (actual sales units × standard profit per unit))

This is commonly used to reconcile budget and standard profit as part of a control report when an absorption costing system is in use.

(b)

π *Sales volume contribution variance:* ((budgeted sales units × standard contribution per unit) − (actual sales units × standard contribution per unit))

This is commonly used to reconcile budget and standard contribution as part of a control report when a marginal costing system is in use.

(c)

π *Sales volume revenue variance*: ((budgeted sales units × standard selling price per unit) − (actual sales units × standard selling price per unit))

This is commonly used as a stand-alone element in a sales control report.

Example

The above three alternatives may be illustrated by the following simple example:
ABC Ltd sells the Unit. Details of Unit sales in September were as follows:

Budget – 1,200 units
Actual – 1,100 units

Standard profit per unit – £100
Standard contribution per unit – £150
Standard selling price per unit – £200.

The three alternative sales volume variances listed above are

(1) Profit – £10,000
(2) Contribution – £15,000
(3) Revenue – £20,000.

The sales volume variance (whichever version of it you are using) can be analysed into mix and quantity components using the same logic encountered in regard to materials usage and labour efficiency variances.

Example

XY Ltd sells two products, X and Y, details for the current period as follows:

	Standard mix (units)	Standard profit (£ pu)	Average profit (£ pu)
X	2	5	
Y	3	6	
Total	5	28	5.60

Budget sales – 200 units X and 300 units Y
Actual sales – 180 units X and 310 units Y

It is apparent that the sales volume profit variance for the period is £40 adverse (that is (20 units X adverse × £5) plus (10 units Y favourable × £6)
We can split this into a sales quantity profit variance and a sales mix profit variance as follows:

Sales quantity profit variance   £56 (A)
(500 units Budget – 490 units Actual) × £5.60 per unit

Sales mix profit variance

	Standard mix (units)	Actual mix (units)	Variance (units)	Variance (£)
X	196	180	16 (A)	80 (A)
Y	294	310	16 (F)	96 (F)
Total	490	490		£16 (F)

The standard mix is the total unit sales (490) multiplied by 2/5 to give X and 3/5 to give Y The mix variances in units are multiplied by the individual standard profits per unit to give the mix variance in £.

As with the other mix variances, there are several alternative means of calculating the sales mix profit variance. That used above is the simplest and they all produce the same result.

The example used relates to the sales volume profit variance, but exactly the same procedure can be used for its contribution and revenue variance alternatives.

4.5 Planning and operational variances

Some variances will arise through factors that are entirely, or almost entirely, within the control of management. These may be referred to as *operational* variances. Other variances can arise from changes in factors external to the business, and may be referred to as *planning* variances.

The *Official Terminology* defines operational and planning variances as follows:

 Operational variance: A classification of variances in which non-standard performance is defined as being that which differs from an *ex post* standard. Operational variances can relate to any element of the standard product specification.

 Planning variance: A classification of variances caused by *ex ante* budget allowances being changed to an *ex post* basis. Also known as a revision variance.

Management will wish to draw a distinction between these two variances in order to gain a realistic measure of operational efficiency. As planning variances are self-evidently *not* under the control of operational management, it cannot be held responsible for them, and there is thus no benefit to be gained in spending time investigating such variances at an operational level. Planning variances may arise from faulty standard-setting, but the responsibility for this lies with *senior,* rather than *operational,* management.

It should be noted that *all* deviations of cost between actual and budgeted can be subdivided and attributed to either planning or operational causes. The example below illustrates this more general application of the techniques.

Big plc set up a factory to manufacture and sell 'Advance', a new consumer product. The first year's budgeted production and sales were 1,000 units. The budgeted sales price and standard costs for 'Advance' were as follows:

	£	£
Standard sales price (per unit)		200
Standard costs (per unit)		
Raw materials (10 kg at £10)	100	
Labour (6 hours at £8)	48	
		(148)
Standard contribution (per unit)		52

Actual results for the first year were as follows:

	£'000	£'000
Sales (1,000 units)		316
Production costs (1,000 units)		
Raw materials (10,800 kg)	194.4	
Labour (5800 hours)	69.6	
		(264)
Actual contribution (1,000 units)		52

The managing director made the following observations on the actual results:

In total, the performance agreed with budget; nevertheless, in every aspect other than volume, there were large differences.

Sales were made at what was felt to be the highest feasible price, but we now feel that we could have sold for £330 with no adverse effect on volume. Labour costs rose dramatically with increased demand for the specialist skills required to produce the product, and the general market rate was £12.50 per hour – although we always paid below the general market rate whenever possible.

The raw material cost that was expected at the time the budget was prepared was £10 per kilogram. However, the market price relating to efficient purchases of the material during the year was £17.00 per kilogram.

It is not proposed to request a variance analysis for the first year's results. In any event, the final contribution was equal to that originally budgeted, so operations must have been fully efficient.

Despite the managing director's reluctance to calculate it, the traditional variance analysis is as follows:

	£	£
Sales margin volume variance		
(Actual sales volume = budgeted sales volume)		–
Sales margin price variance		
(Actual selling price − standard selling price) × actual sales volume		
(£316 − £200) × 1,000		116,000 (F)
Material price		
(Standard price − actual price) × actual quantity		
(£10 − £194,400/10,800) × 10,800	86,400 (A)	
Material usage		
(Standard quantity − actual quantity) × standard price		
(10,000 − 10,800) × £10	8,000 (A)	
		94,400 (A)
Wage rate		
(Standard rate − actual rate) × actual hours		
(£8 − £69,600/5,800) × 5,800	23,200 (A)	
Labour efficiency		
(Standard hours − actual hours) × standard rate		
((1,000 × 6) − 5,800) × £8	1,600 (F)	
		21,600 (A)
Total variances		–

Reconciliation:

	£
Budgeted contribution (1,000 × £52)	52,000
Add: adverse cost variances	116,000
Less: favourable sales variances	(116,000)
Actual contribution	52,000

As the managing director states, and the above analysis shows, the overall variance for the company was zero: the adverse cost variances exactly offset the favourable sales margin price.

However, this analysis does not clearly indicate the efficiency with which the company operated during the period, as it is impossible to tell whether some of the variances arose from the use of inappropriate standards, or whether they were due to efficient or inefficient implementation of those standards. In order to determine this, a revised *ex post* plan should be constructed, setting out the standards that, with hindsight, *should* have been in operation during the period. These revised *ex post* standards are shown under (B) below.

	(A)		(B)		(C)	
	Original plan	£	*Revised ex post plan*	£	*Actual result*	£
Sales	(1,000 × £200)	200,000	(1,000 × £330)	330,000	(1,000 × £316)	316,000
Materials	(10,000 × £10)	100,000	(10,000 × £17)	170,000	(10,800 × £18)	194,400
Labour	(6,000 × £8)	48,000	(6,000 × £12.50)	75,000	(5,800 × £12)	69,600

	£	£
Planning variances (A − B)		
Sales price	130,000 (F)	
Material price (100,000 − 170,000)	70,000 (A)	
Wage rate	27,000 (A)	
		33,000 (F)
Operational variances		
Sales price (B − C)	14,000 (A)	
Material price (10,800 × £1)	10,800 (A)	
Material usage (800 × £17)	13,600 (A)	
Wage rate (5,800 × £0.50)	2,900 (F)	
Labour efficiency (200 hrs × £12.50)	2,500 (F)	
		33,000 (A)
Total variances		−

A comparison of (B) and (C) produces *operational* variances, which show the difference between the results that were actually achieved and those that might legitimately have been achievable during the period in question. This gives a very different view of the period's operations. For example, on the cost side, the wage rate variance has changed from adverse to favourable, and the material price variance, while remaining adverse, is significantly reduced in comparison to that calculated under the traditional analysis; on the sales side, the sales margin price variance, which was particularly large and favourable in the traditional analysis, is transformed into an *adverse* variance in the revised approach, reflecting the fact that the company failed to sell at prices that were actually available in the market. A comparison of the original plan (A) with the revised plan (B) allows the planning variances to be identified. As noted at the beginning of this section, these variances are uncontrollable by *operating*, staff, and may or may not have been controllable by the *original* standard-setters at the start of the budget period. Where a revision of standards is required due to environmental changes that were not foreseeable at the time the budget was prepared, the planning variances are truly uncontrollable. However, standards that failed to anticipate *known* market trends when they were set will reflect faulty standard-setting: it could be argued that these variances *were* controllable (avoidable) at the planning stage.

Example

It would be useful to give a second example of planning and operational variances. For this example, we shall return to the data from the earlier section on material mix and yield variances.

You will recall that the standard mix was one that gave a cost of good output of £1.68 per kg, being the input cost of £840 divided by the standard output of 500 kg. In determining this optimal mix, the interaction between the input, the output and the cost of the input had to be taken into account and minimised. Where there is substitutability between inputs, a number of possible mixes may be feasible, for example an alternative mix might be the one shown below:

Input	kg	Cost/kg £	Total cost of mix £
A	325	1.00	325
B	275	1.60	440
	600		765

In this case, let us assume that the 600 kg of input has an expected output of 450 kg, so that the cost per kg is

£765/450 = £1.70

Despite resulting in a product of the right quality, this mix would *not* be chosen as the standard, because it has a higher cost per kg than the optimal mix at the expected input prices.

However, suppose that the actual results recorded in a particular period were as follows:

Actual input	kg	Actual cost/kg £	Total cost £
A	200	1.00	200
B	400	2.00	800
	600		1,000

Actual output: 500 kg of C

The cost per kg of output is now

£1,000/500 = £2

In this case, there would be *no* mix or yield variance, as the input to the process was in the standard mix and produced the standard output. The only variance reported would be an adverse *price* variance of £160 (400 × (£1.60 − £2.00)), reflecting the higher cost per kg of material B in the period under consideration. However, it is clear that the increase in the *price* of B renders the current standard mix *suboptimal*. If B has a price of £2, the *alternative* mix of 325 kg of A and 275 kg of B gives a *lower* output price per kg than the current standard mix, as shown below:

Input	kg	Cost/kg £	Total cost of mix £
A	325	1.00	325
B	275	2.00	550
	600		875

With output of 450 kg, the cost per kg of this mix is

£875/450 = £1.9444

This cost is lower than the cost of £2 per kg that is obtained when the original 'optimal' standard mix is retained in the face of changed prices. A more sophisticated variance analysis system would compare the actions of the operational management with the standards that *would* have been set had the conditions that *actually* prevailed been known at the time the standard was set. In this example, had the price of B been known to be £2 per kg, the alternative mix would have become the standard, and would have been the basis for comparison with the actual result.

The revised standard cost of the actual output is

500/£1.9444 = £972.22

The actual cost incurred was £1,000, giving a material cost variance of £27.78 adverse.

The material mixture variance may be calculated as follows:

Input	Standard mix kg	Actual mix kg	Variance kg	Standard cost £	Variance £
A	325	200	125 (F)	1	125 (F)
B	275	400	125 (A)	2	250 (A)
					125 (A)

The material yield variance is simply the difference between standard (450 kg) and actual (500 kg) yield for the 600 kg input multiplied by the standard cost per kg output.

This gives a result of £97.22 favourable (that is 50 kg × £1,9444).

	£
Material mix variance	125.00 (A)
Material yield variance	97.22 (F)
Material usage variance	27.78 (A)

Suppose that, in the same circumstances, the following results had been recorded.

Actual input	kg	Actual cost/kg £	Actual cost £
A	325	1.00	325
B	275	2.00	550
	600		875

Actual output: 450 kg of C

The actual results are identical to that *would* be expected if the comparison is made with the *revised* standard, and thus there can be no *operational* variance. However, a *planning* variance has occurred. The expected cost of 450 kg of C, based on the original standard mix and input prices, was 450 × £1.68 = £756. The *revised* standard cost of 450 kg of C was £875. The difference of £119 between the two figures results from the change in the price of B, which represents a *planning* variance beyond the control of the operating management.

The formal calculation of the variance is

450 × (£1.68 − £1.94) = £119 adverse (remember the £1.94 is rounded)

It is interesting to note that a failure to revise the standard in these circumstances might encourage management to continue to operate with the *original* standard mix, which would, in fact, be against the company's best interests.

On the face of it, the calculation of operational and planning variances is an improvement over the traditional analysis. However, you should not overlook the considerable problem of data collection for the revised analysis: where does this information come from, and how can we say with certainty what should have been known at a particular point in time?

4.6 Capacity ratios

Capacity ratios are measures of performance in the use of capacity. They are different from standard costing variances because they are expressed in terms of percentages. They are included in this chapter because they provide information which is similar to that provided by the fixed overhead variances.

4.6.1 Standard hour

Before you can learn how to calculate and interpret the most common capacity ratios, you must have a thorough understanding of what is meant by a standard hour.

CIMA's *Terminology* defines a standard hour or minute as follows.

> *Standard hour or minute*: The amount of work achievable, at standard efficiency levels, in an hour or minute. A standard hour is a useful way of measuring output when a number of dissimilar products are manufactured.

Example

A company manufactures tables, chairs and shelf units. The standard times allowed to manufacture one unit of each of these are as follows:

	Standard time per unit
Table	3 hours
Chair	1 hour
Shelf unit	5 hours

Production output during the first two periods of this year was as follows:

	Units produced	
	Period 1	Period 2
Table	7	4
Chair	5	2
Shelf unit	3	5

It would be difficult to monitor the trend in total production output based on the number of units produced. We can see that 15 units were produced in total in Period 1 and 11 units in Period 2. However, it is not particularly meaningful to add together tables, chairs and shelf units because they are such dissimilar items. You can see that the mix of the three products changed over the two periods and the effect of this is not revealed by simply monitoring the number of units produced.

Standard hours present a useful output measure which is not affected by the mix of products. The standard hours of output for the two periods can be calculated as follows:

	Standard hours per unit	Period 1		Period 2	
		Units produced	Standard hours	Units produced	Standard hours
Table	3	7	21	4	12
Chair	1	5	5	2	2
Shelf unit	5	3	15	5	25
Total standard hours produced			41		39

Expressing the output in terms of standard hours shows that in fact the output level for Period 2 was very similar to that for Period 1.

It is important for you to realise that the actual hours worked during each of these periods was probably different from the standard hours produced. The standard hours figure is simply an expression of how long the output should have taken to produce, to provide a common basis for measuring output.

4.6.2 Calculating the capacity ratios

CIMA's *Terminology* describes the following three most commonly used capacity levels, together with a worked example of the calculation of the capacity ratios.

> *Full capacity*: Output achievable if sales, orders, supplies, workforce, for example, were all available.
> *Practical capacity*: Full capacity less an allowance for known unavoidable volume losses.
> *Budgeted capacity*: The standard hours planned for a period, taking into account budgeted sales, supplies, workforce availability and efficiency expected.

On the following given data, the related ratios are set out below:

Full capacity standard hours	100
Practical capacity standard hours	95
Budgeted capacity standard hours (budgeted input hours 90, at 90% efficiency)	81
Actual input hours	85
Standard hours produced	68

$$\text{Idle capacity ratio} = \frac{(\text{Practical capacity} - \text{budget capacity})}{\text{Practical capacity}} \times 100$$

$$= \frac{95 - 81}{95} \times 100 = 15\%$$

This means that the budgeted activity level would not utilise 15 per cent of the practical capacity.

$$\text{Production volume ratio} = \frac{\text{Standard hours produced}}{\text{Budgeted capacity}} \times 100$$

$$= \frac{68}{81} \times 100 = 84\%$$

This means that the actual output achieved amounted to only 84 per cent of the budgeted output.

$$\text{Efficiency ratio} = \frac{\text{Standard hours produced}}{\text{Actual hours}} \times 100 = \frac{68}{85} \times 100 = 80\%$$

This means that an 80 per cent efficiency level was achieved, compared with a budget of 90 per cent efficiency. This ratio may be measured in either direct labour or machine hours, as appropriate.

4.7 Investigation and interpretation of variances

The calculation of variances is not sufficient of itself to ensure better management control. Variances only become useful when *action* is taken as a result of their calculation. The aim of variance analysis is to facilitate management by exception, allowing management to concentrate on those areas where action is necessary, without wasting time on matters which are performing in line with expectations.

Once the variances have been calculated, management has the task of deciding which variances should be investigated. It would probably not be worthwhile or cost-effective to investigate every single variance. Some criteria must be established to guide the decision as to whether or not to investigate a particular variance. Some general factors which may be taken into account include the following and we will return to consider some of them in more detail later in this section:

(a) *The size of the variance.* Costs tend to fluctuate around a norm and therefore 'normal' variances may be expected on most costs. The problem is to decide how large a variance must be before it is considered 'abnormal' and worthy of investigation.

A rule of thumb may be established that any variance which exceeds, say, 5 per cent of its standard cost may be worthy of investigation. Alternatively control limits may be set statistically and if a cost fluctuates outside these limits it should be investigated.

(b) *The likelihood of the variance being controllable.* Managers may know from experience that certain variances may not be controllable even if a lengthy investigation is undertaken to determine their causes. For example, it may be argued that a material price variance is less easily controlled than a material usage variance because it is heavily influenced by external factors.

(c) *The likely cost of an investigation.* This cost would have to be weighed against the cost which would be incurred if the variance were allowed to continue in future periods.

(d) *The interrelationship of variances.* Adverse variances in one area of the organisation may be interrelated with favourable variances elsewhere. For example, if cheaper material is purchased this may produce a favourable material price variance. However, if the cheaper material is of lower quality and difficult to process, this could result in adverse variances for material usage and labour efficiency.

(e) *The type of standard that was set.* You have already seen that an ideal standard will almost always result in some adverse variances, because of unavoidable waste and so on. Managers must decide on the 'normal' level of adverse variance which they would expect to see.

Another example is where a standard price is set at an average rate for the year. Assuming that inflation exists, favourable price variances might be expected at the beginning of the year, to be offset by adverse price variances towards the end of the year as actual prices begin to rise.

4.7.1 Percentage variance charts

We have seen that the size of a variance may be used as a guide to managers to indicate whether the variance is worthy of investigation. However, it may be difficult for managers to appreciate the significance or the trend of variances when they are presented in absolute terms.

A percentage variance chart can provide a useful graphical presentation of variances that is easier for managers to understand and interpret than a series of figures presented in a tabular format. By presenting the variances over time any trend can be identified, and this can be used to decide whether any control action is required.

Example

Product L has a standard material cost of £7 per unit. Details of output and the recorded material cost variances for the last four periods are as follows:

Period	Output Units	Usage variance £	Price variance £
1	5,800	8,120 (A)	6,090 (F)
2	2,470	2,940 (A)	2,075 (F)
3	4,600	4,185 (A)	3,220 (F)
4	3,100	2,170 (A)	1,520 (F)

The fluctuating output and the corresponding fluctuations in variances make it difficult for managers to see whether there is any trend in the recorded variances.

STANDARD COSTING AND PERFORMANCE EVALUATION

In order to prepare a percentage variance chart it is necessary to express each variance as a percentage of the total standard cost of material for the output achieved.

Period	Standard material cost of output @ £7 per unit £	Usage variance £	%	Price variance £	%
1	40,600	8,120 (A)	20 (A)	6,090 (F)	15 (F)
2	17,290	2,940 (A)	17 (A)	2,075 (F)	12 (F)
3	32,200	4,185 (A)	13 (A)	3,220 (F)	10 (F)
4	21,700	2,170 (A)	10 (A)	1,520 (F)	7 (F)

The percentage variances can now be plotted on a percentage variance chart (Figure 4.1).

The chart shows a clear trend in each variance. This trend was not clearly visible from the absolute figures. It appears that the variances may be interrelated; in Period 1 the material purchased was 15% cheaper than standard, which may have caused the 20% adverse usage variance, perhaps because the material was of inferior quality. However, the trend in variances shows that, as the price of material has increased (reducing percentage favourable price variance), the usage has tended to move closer to standard levels (reducing percentage material usage variance).

Since both variances are trending towards a zero percentage, it may not be necessary to undertake a detailed investigation at this stage. If you look back at the table of absolute variances, you will see that it would have been difficult to reach this conclusion from the information presented there.

4.7.2 The reasons for variances

Before we look in detail at variance investigation models, it will be useful to think about *why* actual performance might differ from standard performance. Four principal sources of variances can be identified, and we shall briefly examine each in turn:

(i) *Inefficient operations.* Currently attainable standards should be achievable by expending a reasonable amount of effort, and incorporate normal levels of machine efficiency, non-productive time, spoilage and waste. Variances from such standards may result from faulty machinery, departures from laid-down procedures or human error. The underlying cause of the inefficiency should be sought and eliminated.

(ii) *Inappropriate standards.* Setting standards can be time-consuming and expensive, particularly when there are large numbers of different products or services which consume large numbers of different inputs, and inaccurate standards may simply be the result of an unwillingness to invest sufficient resources to ensure their accuracy. It can be difficult not only to develop accurate standards in high-technology firms, but also to keep them up to date, as the rapid pace of change can overtake standards after

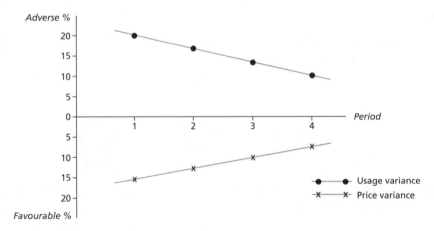

Figure 4.1 Percentage variance chart

only a short time in operation. If frequent changes occur in the *prices* of input factors, standards may quickly become out of date, and variances become less a measure of the purchasing department's efficiency or inefficiency than a reflection of general market conditions. When variances arise as a result of inappropriate standards, the standards need to be revised or updated – and kept under frequent review.

(iii) *Errors in recording actual results.* Humans being error prone, the amounts recorded for actual costs may be inaccurate. There can be few people who have never made an arithmetic slip, transposed numbers or misclassified a particular type of cost. It is improbable that any benefit would accrue to an investigation when the cause of the variance turns out to be a measurement error of this sort.

(iv) *Random or uncontrollable factors.* When setting a standard, it is usual to select a representative value; this well frequently be the mean, or other measure of central tendency. However, although this *single* value has been taken as a standard, the *reality* of the situation is that a *range* of outcomes is possible, even when the process is under control. This is an important point to bear in mind when considering the concept of a standard, because there is an implicit assumption that it represents a *single-point* acceptable measure. It should be understood to represent a band or *range* of possible acceptable measures. Although the band itself may be predictable, it is not possible to predict the *exact* value of an individual unit within it. As long as the process is under control (i.e. the value falls within the range of acceptable outcomes), an observation that *differs* from the standard would be regarded merely as a *random* or *uncontrollable* variance. By definition, a random deviation calls for no corrective action.

4.7.3 Investigation models

In an ideal world, variances would only be investigated when the benefits of an investigation exceed its cost. The difficulty arises in determining whether this is likely to be the case. Management can adopt one of two approaches to the problem: the application of a simple rule of thumb; or the use of a statistical model (with or without a built-in cost/benefit measurement).

Rules of thumb

By definition, these will be based on arbitrary criteria, but need not be quite as crude as the name suggests. For example, for key cost items, a small percentage deviation might prompt an investigation; for less significant cost items, either a higher percentage cut-off or a cutoff point expressed in absolute cost terms might be applied ('investigate all variances over £2,000 or 30 per cent of standard cost, whichever is the lower').

The obvious advantages of such a method are its inherent simplicity and ease of application. However, the choice of cut-off values is subjective: it relies on judgement and intuition rather than statistical probabilities, and thus fails to capture the statistical significance of variances, or to weigh the costs of an investigation against its potential benefits.

Statistical models

A formal statistical model enables management to determine the probability that a particular variance comes from a process that is in control, and an investigation will only be carried out when the probability of that falls below a particular predetermined level (typically expressed in terms of a number of standard deviations from the mean). The model assumes that two mutually exclusive states exist for a process – it is either 'in control' or 'out of control'. In the former case, variances will be due to random fluctuations around the standard, and merit no further action. In the latter case, variances indicate that investigation is called for, and that action will be able to bring the process back into line. A prerequisite of the model is that the 'in control' state is capable (or assumed to be capable) of being expressed in the form of a probability distribution.

Let us take as an example of the standard material content of a product. We shall assume that this figure, say 20 g of a particular chemical, represents the mean value of a large number of observations of the production process operating under conditions of normal efficiency, and that the observations display a normal distribution with a standard deviation of 2 g. On the particular day under review, 20,000 units were produced, with a total usage of 480 kg – an average of 24 g per product. This represents two standard deviations from the mean of 20 g You should recall that, in a normal distribution, 95.45 per cent of all observations can be expected to fall within ± two standard deviations of the mean. Thus, in our example, if the process is under control, the probability of the average usage being two standard deviations from the mean is a mere 2.275 per cent (100 − 95.45%/2). In other words, it is highly *unlikely* that an observation of 24 g would come from a distribution with a mean of 20 g and a standard deviation of 2 g, the distribution representing a process under control. Such an observation is much more likely to derive from a totally *different* distribution, and, given the two mutually exclusive states mentioned above, this would imply to management that the process was out of control for the day under review, and investigation would be called for.

Statistical control charts

The formal means of distinguishing between random variations in an 'in control' process and variances indicating an 'out of control' situation is known as statistical quality control. A convenient means of recording and visually appraising variances is a *control chart*, on which successive cost observations are plotted in the form of a graph. The chart shows certain fixed points, representing the expected distribution of the particular item, and only actual observations which fall *outside* predetermined limits would be regarded as non-random and worth investigating. Visual analysis or statistical procedures can be employed to identify trends that indicate that a process is *heading* out of control, even though current observations are insufficient by themselves to prompt an investigation.

Figure 4.2 is a control chart of a normally distributed item, which takes as its 'in control' parameters – its *control limits* – two standard deviations from the mean (i.e. as there can only be a 4.55 per cent chance (100 − 95.45%) that an observation falling *outside* these parameters could result from a process in control, management considers that there is a high probability that such an observation would come from a process *out of control*).

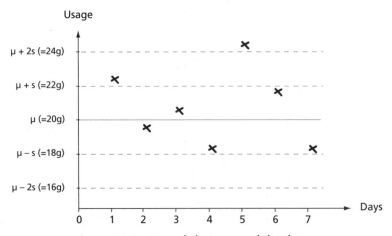

Figure 4.2 Control chart: normal distribution

The data employed are those from our previous example, extended to include actual observations from prior and subsequent days to that previously examined. It can be seen that all observations, other than the one of 24 g, fall within the control limits, and would be considered random fluctuations of a process under control.

Not surprisingly, statistical quality control charts tend to be used to plot data measured in *physical quantity* terms, such as number of rejects or (as in our example) material usage. It should be noted, however, that they cannot distinguish between variances due to inappropriate standards or measurement errors, and those due to inefficient operations.

As indicated at the beginning of this section on investigation models, statistical decision models can be extended to incorporate the costs and benefits of an investigation. A discussion of such models lies outside the scope of this book, but interested readers are referred to Drury (see reading list) for an example. To the caveat mentioned above, however, should be added the severe difficulty of determining, or at least quantifying to an acceptable degree of accuracy, both the cost of an investigation and the benefits expected to accrue from it. This is, of course, a problem common to most mathematical decision-making models, and goes some way towards explaining the relatively infrequent use of many of them, including the techniques just mentioned.

4.7.4 Interrelationship of variances

We shall now consider the question of the interrelationship of variances in a little more detail. A simple example will illustrate the dangers of looking at variances in isolation.

Example

Let us assume that a purchasing manager takes a conscious decision to buy a quantity of slightly substandard direct material for a particularly low price. In order to meet the company's quality criteria, heavy spoilage and labour overruns are incurred when the material is put into production. The aim of the manager is to reduce the *total* costs of manufacturing for the company as a whole, by trading off a favourable price variance against expected adverse efficiency variances. If the manager's strategy works, the *overall* variance will be *favourable*, despite the substantial adverse labels attaching to the individual efficiency variances. Conversely, if the strategy *fails*, the overall variance will be *adverse*, despite the large favourable price variance. (An equally valid strategy might be to acquire more *expensive* material, which causes an *adverse* material price variance, in the expectation that product quality will be improved and give rise to reductions in warranty and servicing costs that exceed the increased material cost.) It is important to keep in mind that there are many interdependencies among a company's activities – the 'favourable' or 'adverse' label pinned on an individual variance should not lead management to make unwarranted value judgements and draw unjustified conclusions concerning a period's operations.

Managers should not regard a standard costing system as a straitjacket that constrains or stifles individual initiative, and prevents them from taking an overall view of the company and its objectives. For this reason, it would be wrong to give too much emphasis to any one performance measure. Such a narrow focus encourages managers to make decisions that maximise their own reported performance in terms of the measure, at the expense of profit maximisation for the company as a whole.

A further problem resulting from the interrelationship of variances results from the traditional focus of responsibilities within organisations. Responsibility for material price variances generally rests with the purchasing manager, and responsibility for material efficiency variances with the production manager. The problem revolves around the responsibility for the joint price/efficiency variance, which is invariably buried within the purchasing manager's variance, as the following example demonstrates.

Example

The product cost of X includes 2 Kg of direct material Y, at a standard cost of £2 per Kg. In a particular period, in order to produce a budgeted requirement of 1,000 units of X, 2,300 kg of Y are used, at an actual cost of £2.20 per Kg.

Conventional variance analysis on the above data would be as follows:

	£
Material price variance (£2.20 − £2.00) × 2,300	460 Adverse
Material usage variance (2,300 − 2,000) × £2.00	600 Adverse
Total material variance	1,060 Adverse

However, the buyer, while accepting responsibility for the price variance on the 2,000 kg in the *standard allowance* for actual production − £0.20 × 2,000 = £400 − might legitimately claim that the additional £60 (300 kg @ £0.20) included in the adverse variance ascribed to *his* activities is more properly attributable to the *production manager*. From the purchasing manager's point of view, if the production manager had operated efficiently, and produced in accordance with the standard quantities, only 2,000 kg would have been required for the actual production of 1,000 units. The extra 300 kg would not have been needed, and − certainly in a JIT system − not even purchased. However, in practice, this distinction between the *pure* price variance − £400 − and the *mutual* price/efficiency variance − £60 − is not often drawn (unless management bonuses depend upon individual variances − an undesirable situation for the reasons outlined above). The efficiency variance, other things being equal, is considered to be of greater significance than the price variance, in view of the more direct influence that the respective manager can exert over it. As a consequence, the management report may be prepared in a manner which seeks to minimise criticism on the part of the production manager of the measurement methods. A joint price/efficiency variance is less likely to cause disagreement − with its concomitant potential for organisational discord − if it is lost within the total *price* variance rather than the *efficiency* variance, particularly as price variances are often regarded more as reflections on forecasting ability than an ability to buy at a particular price.

Normal practice in assigning the joint price/efficiency variance may be rationalised by pointing out that, in reality, it is usual to calculate the material price variance at the point of *receipt* of material, rather than the point of use. Receipt and use will be separated by time in anything other than a JIT system. At the point of receipt, it is not known whether there will be a usage variance or not, and therefore it can be argued that the price variance is properly regarded as the sole responsibility of the buyer. However, this ignores the fact that purchases are ultimately a function of *usage,* and inefficiencies in the production department must inevitably be reflected in adverse price variances for the buyer, irrespective of the point at which the variance is calculated. It could also be argued in this situation that the buyer could generate favourable variances for himself by purchasing substandard material, which then causes inefficiencies in the production department and leads to greater quantities being bought, with concomitant increases in the buyer's favourable variance (this strategy should not be possible, however, in a situation in which a company pursues a policy of minimum standards in the quality of its purchases).

4.8 Behavioural considerations

4.8.1 Organisational goals

This section offers no more than a brief summary of the behavioural aspects of accounting control systems.

It is clear that standard costing and budgetary control systems should be designed in such a way that individuals are encouraged to behave in a manner which is consistent with the overall aims of the organisation. The seminal study of the human problems associated with budgets was published more than 45 years ago *(Argyris,* 1953), but its findings are still pertinent today: budget pressure can lead to tension and a 'them and us' philosophy;

this pressure is exacerbated by accountants measuring their success in terms of the number of errors and weaknesses identified in production (and the reporting system making these faults public); and the budget, which in itself is neutral, is often the scapegoat for assertive patterns of leadership. Obviously, the management accountant has an important role to play in ensuring that the accounting control systems take account of behavioural considerations, in order that these problems are minimised.

4.8.2 Target levels for standards and budgets

There is substantial research evidence to suggest that specific quantitative goals can have a strong motivational appeal, but careful consideration must be given to the degree of difficulty represented by the target figures. A major problem faced by the standard/budget setter is that cultural, organisational and personality factors, together with the degree of task uncertainty associated with specific jobs, conspire to affect individual managers' responses to standards in different ways, making an optimal degree of difficulty impossible to specify for all cases. The most that can be said by way of generalisation is the following: if higher levels of performance are to be achieved, the budget set must be *accepted* by management; up to the point where it is no longer accepted, the more demanding the target, the better the response; and demanding targets are seen as more relevant than less difficult goals, although targets that are perceived as too difficult will result in negative attitudes.

Against this background, *Becker and Green* (1962) made the following suggestions regarding revisions to budget levels in the light of actual performance:

(i) Levels of aspiration will rise, and budgets can and should be revised, if performances meet or slightly *exceed* expectations. If no revision takes place, employees will perform at the *budget* level, when they could be performing at *higher* than budget level.

(ii) Performances just slightly *below* budget expectations require feedback rather than budget changes, in order that budgetees will strive for targets in the future.

(iii) Performances *well below* the budget should probably lead to a downward revision of the budget. If such a revision is *not* made, the employees' level of aspiration will fall, with the concomitant danger that levels of aspiration and output will fall much more than is necessary. The budget should only be revised downwards to the level where it is once more perceived as being *attainable*.

The implication of the research on targets is that the optimum level of motivation is often unlikely to be achieved in practice. At this optimum level, therefore, adverse variances are to be expected *and accepted*; it would be counterproductive to use such variances as a punitive device in an overall reward system, as such a policy would encourage managers to seek looser standards, to the detriment of overall company performance (see Section 3.8.5).

Interestingly, there is a conflict between the use of budgets as *motivating devices* and their use in *planning*. Tight budgets that are not expected to be achieved most of the time are unlikely to be of much help for planning purposes, and consideration should be given to the use of separate budgets for each requirement.

4.8.3 Performance measures and evaluation

Performance measures should encourage *goal congruence*. This state is said to exist when the perceived best interests of managers coincide with those of the organisation, and prompt the former to voluntarily take decisions that achieve the objectives of the latter. Needless to say, only if the measure is a *suitable* indicator will it improve organisational performance, and performance measures are far from infallible. If an *unsuitable* measure is adopted, dysfunctional consequences may follow – managers may be motivated to act in a way which is organisationally undesirable, either because they concentrate only on maximising the *measure,* regardless of organisational realities, or because they modify their behaviour in order to *appear* to be obtaining the desired result. We will consider other examples of such dysfunctional behaviour later in this text. Similarly, we will see the dangers of concentrating on a single measure of performance. It has been suggested that these problems can be overcome by adopting *multiple* measures. In order to avoid subjective judgements regarding the relative impact of the different measures on overall organisational performance, weights are attached to each, giving rise to the possibility of a *composite* measure of a manager's efficiency and effectiveness.

The way in which accounting measures are *used* by top management can also provoke undesirable behaviour. Too much emphasis on adverse performance is likely to lead to a feeling of injustice, but too little emphasis can also be demotivating, by implying that the standards or budget have little relevance. In a classic study, *Hopwood* (1976, *Accounting and Human Behaviour)* identified three distinct styles of performance evaluation: budget-constrained (rigid adherence to budget); profit-conscious (more flexible use of the budget, and emphasis on long-term considerations); and non-accounting (budgets little used in performance evaluation). The reward system will usually mirror the style – with a budget-constrained style, achieving targets results in rewards, and failing to achieve targets in punishment; with the profit-conscious style, good reasons for an overspend can result in rewards, and achievement of budget in undesirable ways to punishment; in the non-accounting style, rewards and punishment are not directly related to the attainment of budgeted figures, and thus the budget is of little importance in this context. *Hopwood* listed a number of problems associated with the budget-constrained style, including high job-related tension, manipulation of accounting information, and poor relations with supervisors and colleagues. The profit-conscious style appears to avoid these problems, while concomitantly ensuring an active involvement with the financial aspect of the operations.

More recent research emphasises the importance of the level of task uncertainty, and it has been suggested that higher levels of stress or poorer management performance do not stem from budget style as such, but rather from a *mismatch* of budget style and task context.

4.8.4 Participation in setting standards and budgets

If budget holders are genuinely able to influence standard setting and the make-up of their budgets – as opposed to simply being pressurised into accepting the figures presented to them – three benefits are said to follow for the organisation:

(i) The attitude of managers towards the accounting system itself will improve, reducing the potential for dysfunctional behaviour.
(ii) The standards and budgets are likely to be seen by managers as more relevant, which increases the likelihood of their acceptance as target figures.
(iii) Communication within the organisation will be improved, with a concomitant potential for increased control.

Unfortunately, the empirical research presents conflicting evidence on the usefulness of participation. One possible explanation for the conflicting results in the influence of personality variables on the effectiveness of participation. A high degree of participation has been found to be effective only for individuals with a *low* level of authoritarianism and a consequent *high* need for independence; highly authoritarian individuals with *low* independence needs remain relatively unaffected by the approach, and may well perform better within a framework of externally set standards. The appropriateness of participation should be assessed against this background, and, rather than adopting a blanket approach to it, an attempt should be made by top management to identify those organisational and personal situations where the evidence would point to the effectiveness of participative approaches.

4.8.5 Budget bias

If the performance of managers is to be measured against budgets, and the relevant individuals participate in setting them, it is plainly in the managers' interest, other things being equal, to influence the performance criteria built into the budgets. However, participation in the setting of standards can lead to bias in their formulation.

There is an assumption that this bias is in one direction only, and will invariably lead to the creation of *slack* budgets, containing targets that can be achieved easily. There is certainly considerable empirical evidence to support a common response of understating revenues and overstating costs, but the bias can work in *both* directions: after all, conservative forecasts might disappoint top management at the time they are made, and lead to an undesirable examination of the basis of the projections; whereas an optimistic forecast can please them – albeit increasing the risk of later disapproval if the optimism appears subsequently to be misplaced.

The potential for bias can be regarded as a function of the particular style of performance evaluation adopted by the organisation: a budget-constrained style is likely to give rise to a *high* degree of bias; if standards and budgets are used in a more flexible profit-conscious style, the level of budget bias is likely to be considerably *lower*.

4.9 Standard costing in the modern business environment

4.9.1 Criticisms of standard costing

There has recently been some criticism of the appropriateness of standard costing in the modern business environment. The main criticisms include the following:

- Standard costing was developed when the business environment was more stable and operating conditions were less prone to change. In the present dynamic environment, such stable conditions cannot be assumed. If conditions are not stable, then it is difficult to set a standard cost which can be used to control costs over a period of time.
- Performance to standard used to be judged as satisfactory, but in today's climate constant improvement must be aimed for in order to remain competitive. The focus in a traditional standard costing environment is on minimising costs rather than on improving quality and customer care.

- Standard costing variances tend to be prepared on an aggregate basis. In today's manufacturing environment there is a need for variances specific to production lines and even individual batches.
- Product life cycles tend to be shorter with the result that standard costs become quickly out of date.
- The emphasis on labour variances is no longer appropriate with the increasing use of automated production methods.
- Standard costing variances are usually reported at the end of each month. In order to be flexible and responsive to changes in the external environment, managers need information more frequently.

4.9.2 Addressing the criticisms

An organisation's decision to use standard costing depends on its effectiveness in helping managers to make the correct planning and control decisions. Many of the above criticisms can be addressed by adaptations to traditional standard costing systems.

- Standard costs must be updated regularly if they are to remain useful for control purposes.
- The use of demanding performance standards can help to encourage continuous improvement.
- The standard costing system can be adapted to produce a broader analysis of variances that are less aggregated.
- It is possible to place less emphasis on labour cost variances and focus more on variances for quality costs, variable overhead costs, and so on.
- Real time information systems have been developed which allow for corrective action to be taken sooner in response to reported variances.
- Standard costing may still be useful even where the final product or service is not standardised. It may be possible to identify a number of standard components and activities for which standards may be set and used effectively for planning and control purposes.

4.9.3 Standards and variances: a cautionary note

An important theme running through this book is the search for continuous improvement, and its importance in the modern, globally competitive market. Thus, despite the heavy emphasis placed by the syllabus on variance accounting, and the calculation, investigation and interpretation of variances, it is appropriate that this discussion of standard costing concludes with the (slightly edited) words of Drury (2000):

It is claimed that the concept of setting standards is not consistent with a . . . philosophy of continuous improvement. When standards are set, a climate is created whereby they represent a target to be achieved and maintained, rather than a philosophy of constant improvement. The . . . philosophy requires that actual performance measures be reported over time, rather than comparisons against a standard, so that the trend in performance can be monitored. Presenting performance measures over time communicates useful feedback information in the amount of rate of change in performance.

However, there is nothing in the process of variance analysis which makes it *inherently* incompatible with continuous improvement; rather, it may be argued that it is the way in which standards have *traditionally* been formulated and maintained which leads to the view quoted above. The standard against which actual performance is measured in variance analysis represents a type of *benchmark*. This benchmark is expressed in financial terms, and has traditionally been *internally* determined, by reference to a company's own costs and procedures.

4.10 Benchmarking

There is now an increasing interest in the use of benchmarking as a means of establishing 'best practice', or standards, by the examination of the practices of *other* organisation relative to a company's own procedures. Benchmarking at its best establishes attainable standards by the examination of both *external* and internal information. If the standards which a firm employs are regularly reviewed in the light of information gained in external as well as internal benchmarking exercises, these standards will embrace continuous improvement by becoming increasingly demanding. The reporting of variances against these updated attainable standards will indicate progress towards them.

External benchmarking is the practice of comparing the critical performance indicators of different organisations. This is frequently carried out by groups of firms that agree to pool information. These firms may not operate in the same geographic areas or may not even be in the same sectors – it is unlikely that direct competitors will agree to voluntarily share information. One can benchmark against an unwilling partner, but the exercise then has to depend only on information that is in the public domain or that can be obtained by covert means.

Benchmarked performance indicators may include 'labour cost per unit of output' in a manufacturing concern or 'fee income per dental surgeon' in a dental practice. A benchmarking exercise will usually consider a range of appropriate performance indicators. If a firm finds that it is performing less well than others in respect of any one Indicator, then the relevant area of the operation will be a focus for attempted improvements.

Benchmarking can be used as a tool in the establishment of standard manufacturing costs. However, benchmarking is a general performance management tool and is considered further in Chapter 7.

The use of internal benchmarking as an element in standard costing systems and the setting of standards has many advocates.

Extract from 'Looking in the mirror' (internal benchmarking)

John P. Puckett III and Philip S. Siegel, *Journal of Business Strategy,* **May–June 1997**
Republished with permission, Emerald Group Publishing Limited.

Most senior executives view external benchmarking as an indispensable management tool. Finding out how their companies stack up against industry leaders provides a yardstick by which to measure performance and, equally important, role models to emulate. For some it has become an obsession to which they devote enormous resources.

But external benchmarking, despite its benefits, is overrated. Many companies are spending countless dollars and man-years seeking something that's right under their noses. By looking in the mirror and appreciating the divergence of performance within their own organisations, they can benchmark to make these internal differences apparent and to help uncover opportunities for capitalising on their unique strengths. The simple truth is a company's own best practices are usually superior to the best company's average practices.

Internal benchmarking will yield solutions that leverage existing knowledge and create more tangible value than external benchmarking. Six factors make this possible:

- It is easier to gather the data. External benchmarking relies on competitive data that is not readily available. When the data is available, it may be neither accurate nor timely. Moreover, it allows a comparison at only one point in time and does not provide a way to continually improve performance. With internal benchmarking, the data is always right at your fingertips.

- The comparisons are more relevant. They are more relevant because they relate to your business. You are not comparing yourself to a business that, in truth, is not the same as yours.

- It is easier to take action on the results. External benchmarking will identify differences between your company and competitors, but it will not tell you why you are different. Internal benchmarking lets you take that next step and, through a series of interviews and best practice sharing, really understand what behaviors are driving those differences.

- It allows you to set sound targets. Performance targets are no longer viewed as arbitrary and unrealistic. A process is in place. Individuals across the organisation are involved. The goals seem achievable because someone in the company is already achieving them. Buy-in increases; whining decreases.

- Internal champions exist. Internal benchmarking makes heroes out of the people who already have best practices in place. Pointing to Jane Doe in the phoenix branch, rather than company X or Y, personalises the effort. Everyone knows them and can identify with them. They may even be motivated by them. And, again, since someone in the company is currently doing it, there are no excuses.

- It allows continuous improvement. There is always going to be variance in performance across an organisation. Sharing best practices lets management keep raising the bar. One region achieves a record productivity level; a few months later, another region breaks that record. Now, all of the company's regions have an even higher target to shoot for.

Realising the maximum value

The factors most ripe for internal benchmarking are productivity ratios, efficiency response time, cost ratios and pricing performance. Many of the numerators for such ratios come from a company's finance department, while the denominators often come from information kept by the business units. For example, in many organisations, finance keeps overhead cost data and sales keeps account data, so if you want to benchmark overhead per account, you must combine data sources. You may have to do some digging. Usually, however, there are just one to four high-level metrics that make the most sense for a company to track, with a larger set of measures underlying them.

Internal benchmarking is most valuable when a company has multiple comparable units. These may be business units, branches, plants, sales offices, countries, even products. For example, how does widget plant A's reject rate compare with widget plant B's? Or what is the Asia/Pacific region's unit cost per account vis-à-vis that of Europe?

4.11 Developments and current thinking in the application of standard costing

4.11.1 McDonaldisation – Another angle on things

Much contemporary discussion concerning the relevance of standard costing in the modern economic environment turns around the manner in which shortened product life cycles and increased customisation of products marginalise the whole concept of the standard cost. Furthermore, the associated 'static optimisation' approach to performance evaluation (through comparison of actual and standard) tends to avoid the whole thrust of modern thinking in areas such as total quality management, continuous improvement and business process re-engineering.

However, one should approach this discussion with a certain caution. In 1993 the American sociologist George Ritzer published his seminal work 'The McDonaldization of Society' (Pine Forge Press), a text which has been reprinted in revised editions on several subsequent occasions. The thrust of this text is that the delivery to market of large-volume, homogenous products (along the lines of McDonald's fast food) offers several advantages which may be grouped under the following headings:

- *Efficiency.* Such products are usually cheap to produce, quick to deliver and efficient in their use of resources. This follows the traditional 'scientific management' approach whereby standardisation of products and production methods leads to cost minimisation.
- *Calculability.* Such products place an emphasis on quantitative considerations such as weight, size, waiting time and price. For example, one measure of the real economic exchange rates of currencies is based on the price of a 'Big-Mac' in the different countries concerned.
- *Predictability.* Buyers can confidently purchase a product anywhere they are without having to give too much thought to the matter. A Big-Mac purchased in Chicago is the same as one purchased in Manchester.
- *Control.* The delivery of such products involves the use of a known set of materials and a simple, pre-determined set of tasks. It is therefore easy and meaningful to evaluate performance through comparison of actual inputs with standard inputs.

Ritzer claims that McDonaldisation is a social and organisational phenomenon. We need not explore this too deeply, but it is apparent that it is a phenomenon which is entirely consistent with 'Taylorism', scientific management and standard costing (see 'What is a Fair Day's Work?' in Section 2.5.4). The conceptual underpinning of McDonaldisation is pure 'scientific management'. It might be argued that the thrust of this is deeply traditional and runs counter to the 'new economy' concepts referred to in the first paragraph of this section.

4.11.2 Diagnostic reference groups

One specific area where standard costing currently appears to be flourishing is in healthcare management. For the purposes of remunerating healthcare providers and evaluating the performance of those providers, it is often deemed necessary to determine the standard cost of providing healthcare to persons suffering from specific medical conditions.

One response to this is the use of the diagnostic reference group (DRG) otherwise known as the healthcare resource group or case mix group. The medical conditions from which patients admitted to hospital are suffering can be classified into DRGs. Most practical applications of this approach involve the adoption of between 600 and 800 DRGs.

Patients within a given DRG all suffer from broadly the same medical condition and will receive broadly the same treatment.

Healthcare funders (insurance companies or the NHS) may undertake to pay a given amount per day to a hospital for the treatment of patients within a particular DRG. That per day rate will be determined with reference to the standard cost of treating a patient within the DRG – having regard to the resources required and the amount that the hospital has to pay for those resources. At the same time, the performance of a hospital may be evaluated by comparing its actual per day costs for given DRGs with the relevant standards. If a hospital incurs a cost of £5,000 per day for treating a patient requiring a liver transplant and the standard cost (or benchmark cost) is £4,000 per day, then this comparison offers a comment on the efficiency of the hospital concerned. Similarly, if a hospital takes 23 days to treat a particular DRG and the standard is 19 days, then this also is a comment on its efficiency.

However, the DRG approach is not without its critics. The clinical treatments available for any illness are varied. In the case of heart disease they range from a heart transplant at one extreme to merely counselling on lifestyle and diet at the other extreme. Each patient is different having regard to the detailed nature of the disease, its degree of progression and their own strength and state of general health. The clinician should evaluate each patient individually and decide on the programme of surgery, drugs and lifestyle counselling that is appropriate in each case. However, if a hospital is paid a fixed daily rate for treating a patient in a given DRG, then the clinician will be most reluctant to provide treatment above or below the standard package for that DRG. If treatment is provided above standard, then the hospital will not be paid any additional fee, and treatment below standard may result in unpleasant accusations of malpractice being levelled by both patients and funding providers.

The logic of the DRG approach is that each patient who presents with a given set of symptoms is offered a standard package of treatments – which may not always be entirely appropriate. A clinician may be tempted simply to offer the standard package to each patient in a DRG even though he or she may suspect that package to be inadequate in some cases and excessive in others. In effect, the approach may induce a degree of McDonaldisation with all patients served the medical equivalent of a Big-Mac. Unless great sensitivity is exercised in its application, the use of DRGs may result in clinical practice being distorted by what is essentially a financial control system.

4.12 Summary

In this chapter we have continued our exploration of the manner in which standard costing can be used as an element in performance evaluation. We have seen that many observers have suggested that standard costing may be in the process of becoming last year's model' in terms of its usefulness in the modern economic environment. The modern trend in performance evaluation is towards the use of internal and external benchmarking. Nevertheless, standard costing is a simple approach that is both well understood and widely used.

We will make further reference to various aspects of standard costing and benchmarking as we proceed through this text.

Self-test quiz

(1) Explain the manner in which a materials usage variance is split into mix and yield component variances (Section 4.2).

(2) In the context of a company audit exercise, what is the likely cause of an adverse labour mix variance (Section 4.3)?

(3) Explain the term 'planning variance' (Section 4.5).

(4) Explain the term 'operational variance' (Section 4.5).

(5) What is an 'ex-post standard' (Section 4.5)?

(6) State at least two drawbacks concerning the split of variances into planning and operational components (Section 4.6).

(7) List the factors that might influence the decision on whether or not to investigate a particular variance (Section 4.7).

(8) Explain the link between the standard cost concept and 'internal benchmarking' (Section 4.10).

(9) Explain the link between the standard cost concept and the 'Diagnostic Reference Groups' used in healthcare management (Section 4.11.2).

(10) How do 'Taylorism' and 'scientific management' contribute to the standard costing concept (Section 4.11.1)?

Revision Questions

? Question 1

The following data relates to both questions 1.1 and 1.2 below.

P Ltd operates a standard costing system. The following information has been extracted from the standard cost card for one of its products:

Budgeted production		1,250 units
Direct material cost	7 kg @ £4.10 per kg	£28.70 per unit
Actual results for the period were as follows:		
Production		1,000 units
Direct material (purchased and used)	7,700 kg	£33,880

It has subsequently been noted that the market price of the material was £4.50 per kg during the period.

1.1 The value of the planning variance is

(A) £1,225 (A)
(B) £2,800 (A)
(C) £3,500 (A)
(D) £4,375 (A)
(E) £5,950 (A)   **(2 marks)**

1.2 The value of the material usage variance is

(A) £2,870 (A)
(B) £3,080 (A)
(C) £3,150 (A)
(D) £3,587.50 (A)
(E) £3,937.50 (A)   **(2 marks)**

The following data is to be used to answer questions 1.3 and 1.4 below.

SW plc manufactures a product known as the TRD100 by mixing two materials.
The standard material cost per unit of the TRD100 is as follows:

		£
Material X	12 litres @ £2.50	30
Material Y	18 litres @ £3.00	54

In October 2002, the actual mix used was 984 litres of X and 1,230 litres of Y. The actual output was 72 units of TRD 100.

1.3 The total material mix variance reported was nearest to

(A) £102 (F)
(B) £49 (F)
(C) £49 (A)
(D) £151 (A)

(3 marks)

1.4 The total material yield variance reported was nearest to

(A) £102 (F)
(B) £49 (F)
(C) £49 (A)
(D) £151 (A)

(2 marks)

The following data is to be used to answer questions 1.5, 1.6 and 1.7 below.
Q plc sells a single product. The standard cost and selling price details are as follows:

	£
Selling price per unit	200
Unit variable costs	124
Unit fixed costs	35

During October 2002, a total of 4,500 units of the product were sold, compared to a sales and production budget of 4,400 units. The actual cost and selling price details were as follows:

	£
Selling price unit	215
Unit variable costs	119
Unit fixed costs	40

1.5 The budgeted margin of safety is closest to

(A) 100 sales units
(B) £154,000 sales value
(C) £334,000 sales value
(D) £475,000 sales value

(2 marks)

1.6 The sales volume contribution variance for October was

(A) £4,100 (F)
(B) £5,600 (F)
(C) £7,600 (F)
(D) £9,600 (F)

(2 marks)

1.7 The sales price variance for October was

(A) £20,000 (F)
(B) £21,500 (F)

(C) £66,000 (F)

(D) £67,500 (F)

(2 marks)

(Total = 20 marks)

1.8 The standard ingredients of 1 kg AB are 0.7 kg A (cost £5 per kg) and 0.3 kg B (cost £8 per kg). In the current period, 100 kg AB has been produced using 68 kg A and 32 kg B. The material mixture variance is

(A) nil.

(B) £10 (A)

(C) £6 (F)

(D) £12 (F)

(E) £6 (A)

1.9 Based on original standards, the standard requirement for the work achieved in the current period is 100 labour hours at a rate of £12 per hour. However, labour efficiency has increased by 20% (that is, 20% more output can be achieved from the same hours) and the standard has been revised to allow for this. The labour efficiency planning variance is

(A) £100 (F)

(B) £150 (F)

(C) £60 (F)

(D) nil.

(E) £200 (F)

The following data are to be used to answer questions 1.10 and 1.11 below.

The following extract from a standard cost card shows the materials to be used in producing 100 litres of an agricultural fertiliser.

Material H	30 litres	@ $4.00 per litre
Material J	50 litres	@ $3.50 per litre
Material K	40 litres	@ $6.50 per litre
	120	

During April 5,400 litres of the agricultural fertiliser were produced using the following materials:

Material H	1,860 litres
Material J	2,450 litres
Material K	2,740 litres
	7,050

1.10 The total material mix variance to be reported for April is nearest to

(A) $2,636 (A)

(B) $1,219 (A)

(C) $1,219 (F)

(D) $2,636 (F)

1.11 The total material yield variance to be reported for April is nearest to

(A) $2,636 (A)

(B) $1,219 (A)

(C) $1,219 (F)

(D) $2,636 (F)

Question 2

Super Clean products Ltd manufactures 'Whizzoh'. Whizzoh comprises three basic ingredients, the standard mix and price of which are as follows:

To produce 1 kg of Whizzoh:

HCB (hydrocarbon base)	0.9 kg at 5 p per kg
SHC (sodium hypochlorite)	0.1 kg at 21 p per kg
WM7 (a secret formula)	0.05 kg at 29 p per kg
	1.05 kg

SHC and WM7 are the active ingredients and are interchangeable. Super Clean Products Ltd's production facilities are highly automated and there is no direct labour. Fixed overheads are budgeted at £10,000 per month and production is budgeted to run at 20,000 kg of Whizzoh per month. Fixed overheads are absorbed through HCB usage. During the course of January, 21,500 kg of Whizzoh are produced with the following figures for material consumption:

HCB	19,100 kg at 5.1 p per kg
SHC	2,800 kg at 20 p per kg
WM7	980 kg at 33 p per kg
	22,880 kg

Fixed overheads during the period were £10,000.

Requirement

Reconcile standard and actual costs in January using a full variance analysis. **(25 marks)**

 Question 3

PH plc operates a modern factory that converts chemicals into fertiliser. Because the demand for its product is seasonal, the company expects that there will be an average level of idle time equivalent to 20% of hours paid. This is incorporated into the company's standard costs, and the standard labour rate of £6.00 per hour paid is then adjusted accordingly. Any difference between the expected and the actual amount of idle time is reported as the 'idle time variance' and is valued at the adjusted wage rate.

Data for each of the 4 months from January to April 2002 is as follows:

	January	February	March	April
Actual hours paid	10,000	14,000	17,000	30,000
Actual productive hours	7,200	10,304	12,784	23,040
Standard hours produced	6,984	9,789	11,889	20,966
Idle time variance	£6,000 (A)	£6,720 (A)	£6,120 (A)	?
Efficiency variance	£1,620 (A)	£3,863 (A)	£6,713 (A)	?

Requirements

(a) Calculated the idle time variance and the efficiency variance for April.   **(4 marks)**

(b) (i) Using the data provided and your answer to (a) above as appropriate, prepare a percentage variance chart that shows the trend of these variances. (Use graph paper and show both variances on the same chart.)

  (ii) Comment on the usefulness of presenting the information in this format.

(10 marks)

(c) Comment briefly on the possible inter-relationships between the idle time variance and the efficiency variance.   **(4 marks)**

(d) Explain briefly the factors that should be considered before deciding to investigate a variance.   **(7 marks)**

(Total = 25 marks)

 ## Question 4

Variance analysis involves the separation of individual cost variances into component parts. The benefit that may be derived from variance analysis depends on the interpretation and investigation of the component variances. A company has recently been carrying out a study on its use of variance analysis.

Requirements

Explain, with the aid of simple numeric examples, for each of the following variance analysis exercises:

- their logic, purpose and limitation; and
- how the management accountant should go about investigating the component variances disclosed.
    (a) The separation of the fixed overhead volume variance into capacity utilisation and efficiency components.
    (b) The separation of the materials usage variance into materials mixture and materials yield components.
    (c) The separation of the labour rate variance into planning and operational components.

Solutions to
Revision Questions

1.1

 Solution 1

Planning variance		£
Ex-ante Standard	7 kg × £4.10 × 1,000	28,700
Ex-post Standard	7 kg × £4.50 × 1,000	31,500
Variance		2,800 (A)

Therefore the answer is (B).

1.2

Material usage variance		kg
Ex-post standard	7 kg × 1,000	7,000
Actual		7,700
Variance		700 × £4.50/kg = £3,150 (A)

Therefore the answer is (C).

1.3

	Actual mix litres	Standard mix litres	Difference litres	Price £	Variamce £
X	984	885.6	98.4 (A)	2.50	246.0 (A)
Y	1,230	1,328.4	98.4 (F)	3.00	295.2 (F)
Totals	2,214	2,214.0	nil		49.2 (F)

Therefore the answer is (B).

1.4

$$\text{Expected output} = \frac{2,214}{30} \quad = 73.8 \text{ units}$$

Actual output	= 72.0 units
Shortfall	= 1.8 units
1.8 units × £84/unit	= 151.2 (A)

Therefore the answer is (D).

1.5

Budgeted fixed costs = 4,400 units × £35/unit	= £154,000	
Budgeted contribution/unit = £200 − £124	= £76	
	= 2,026 units	
Budgeted breakeven point (units) = $\dfrac{£154,000}{£76}$		
Budgeted sales units	= 4,400.00 units	
Budgeted margin of safety (units) = 4,400 − 2,026	= 2,374	
Budget margin of safety (sales value) = 2,374 × £200	= £474,800	

Therefore the answer is (D).

1.6

$$100 \text{ units } \times (£200 - £124) = £7,600(F)$$

Therefore the answer is (C).

1.7

$$4,500 \text{ units } \times (£200 - £215) = £67,500(F)$$

Therefore the answer is (D).

1.8 Answer: (E)

£6 adverse – standard mix is 70 kg A plus 30 kg B, from which it follows that the mixture variance is 2 kg A @ £5 (favourable) plus 2 kg B @ £8 (adverse).

1.9 Answer: (E)

£200 favourable. Since output that required 100 hours under original standards now requires 83.333 hours (100 hours/1.2), it follows that the planning efficiency variance is 16.666 hours favourable with a cost of £200 (16.666 × £12).

1.10

	Actual mix litres	Standard mix litres	Difference litres	Standard price $/litre	Variance $
H	1,860	1,762.5	97.5	4.00	390.00 (A)
J	2,450	2,937.5	(487.5)	3.50	1,706.25 (F)
K	2,740	2,350.0	390.0	6.50	2,535.00 (A)
Total	7,050	7,050	nil		1,218.75 (A)

Therefore the answer is (B).

1.11

Standard cost per litre of output:

		$
H	30 litres @ $4.00	120.00
J	50 litres @ $3.50	175.00
K	40 litres @ $6.50	260.00
Total		555.00 per 100 litres

Actual input of 7,050 litres should yield 100/120 litres of output =   5,8750 litres
Actual output   5,400 litres
Shortfall   475 litres

475 litres @ $555.00 per 100 litres = $2,636.25 (A)

Therefore the answer is (A).

 # Solution 2

- In answering this, it is critical to appreciate that you are being invited to reconcile standard and actual costs – not budget and actual costs. Failing to grasp this is one of the most common problems that student accountants have when undertaking variance analysis exercises.
- In specifying 'a full variance analysis' the question invites calculation of material mix/ yield variance and fixed overhead capacity usage/efficiency variances.
- Notes that since budget fixed overheads equals actual fixed overheads, there will be no fixed overhead expenditure variance.

Standard material cost of 1 kg of Whizzoh is

	Input kg	Unit cost p/kg	Total cost £
HCB	0.90	5	0.0450
SHC	0.10	21	0.0210
WM7	0.05	29	0.0145
	1.05		0.0805

Standard overhead cost of 1 kg Whizzoh is

0.9 kg of HCB @ £0.55555 = £0.50.

The £0.55555 absorption rate is budgeted overheads (£10,000) divided by budgeted HCB usage (18,000 kg).

Variance calculations	£	£
Standard cost of output		
Materials: (21,500 kg × £0.0805)	1,730.75	
Overheads: (21,500 kg × 0.9hrs × £0.5555)	10,749.89	
Total		12,480.64
Actual cost of output		
Materials	1,857.50	
Overheads	10,000.00	
Total		11,857.50
Cost variance		623.14 (F)
	£	£
Material price variance		
A: 19,100 kg × (5 p − 5.1 p)	(19.10) (A)	
B: 2,800 kg × (21 p − 20 p)	28.00 (F)	
C: 980 kg × (29 p − 33 p)	(39.20) (A)	
Total		(30.30) (A)
Material mixture variance		
A: (19,611 kg standard − 19,100 kg actual) × 5 p	25.57 (F)	
B: (2,179 kg standard − 2,800 kg actual) × 21 p	(130.40) (A)	
C: (1,089 kg standard − 980 kg actual × 29 p	31.76 (F)	
Total		(73.07) (A)

	£
Material yield variance	
$((22,880\,kg/1.05) - 21,500\,kg) \times £0.0805$	(23.38) (A)
Fixed overhead capacity	
$(19,100\,kg\ actual - 18,000\,kg\ budget) \times £0.55555$	611.11 (F)
Fixed overhead efficiency	
$(19,350\,kg\ standard - 19,100\,kg\ actual) \times £0.55555$	<u>138.89</u> (F)
Cost variance total	<u>623.00</u> (F)

Note: In calculating the mixture variance for A, the standard amount of A in the mix is 22,880 kg (actual input)/1.05 × 0.09.

 ## Solution 3

(a) Standard rate per hour worked $= \dfrac{£6.00}{0.8} = £7.50$

Idle time variance:

Expected idle time = 20% × 30,000 hours = 6,000 hours
Actual idle time = 30,000 − 23,040 = <u>6,960</u> hours
 <u>960</u> hours

960 hours × £7.50 per hour = £7,200 (A)

Efficiency variance:

Standard hours produced = 20,966
Actual hours worked = <u>23,040</u>
 <u>2,074</u> hours

2,074 hours × £7.50 per hour = £15,555 (A)

(b) (i) Calculations for graph (expressing variances as % of standard)

Idle time	*Standard cost of expected Idle time*	*Idle time variance*	
	£	£	%
January	15,000	6,000 (A)	40 (A)
February	21,000	6,720 (A)	32 (A)
March	25,500	6,120 (A)	24 (A)
April	45,000	7,200 (A)	16 (A)

Efficiency	*Standard cost of Standard hours Produced*	*Efficiency variance*	
	£	£	%
January	52,380	1,620 (A)	3 (A)
February	73,418	3,863 (A)	5 (A)
March	89,168	6,713 (A)	8 (A)
April	157,245	15,555 (A)	10 (A)

See graph below.

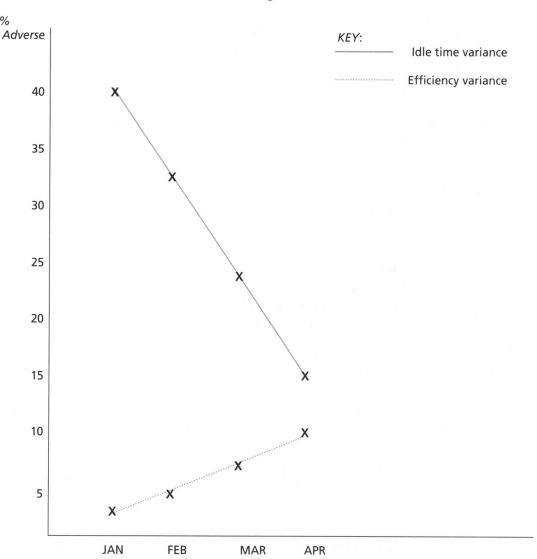

(ii) Many managers find the graphical presentation of variances easier to understand than a series of figures presented in a tabular format. By presenting the variances over time the trend can be identified, and this is used to decide if any control action is required.

In this question, the variances have been expressed as percentages of the standard cost, rather than expressing them in monetary amounts. The use of percentages removes the changes in the monetary size of the variances caused by changing activity levels and this improves the trend information that is provided.

(c) The idle time variance and the efficiency variance are sub-variances of the overall efficiency variance.

As can be seen from the control chart, the idle time variance has reduced over the period, while the efficiency variance has increased. This could be because the employees are deliberately taking longer to complete their tasks to avoid being idle because of a lack of work.

(d) There are a number of factors to be considered before investigating a variance. These include

- the size of the variance;
- the likelihood of identifying the cause of the variance;
- the likelihood that the cause of the variance is controllable;
- the likely cost of correcting the cause;
- the cost of the investigation.

The overall factor that will determine whether or not to investigate a variance is whether or not there will be a positive benefit from the investigation.

 ## Solution 4

- The question invites you to develop examples to illustrate the calculation of certain variances. A student whose study of variance analysis consisted of memorising formulae would have difficulty.
- Note that the question specifies simple examples. In developing an example to illustrate material mixture and yield variances, you should use only two materials.
- Note that the question invites an exploration of the labour rate variance. You should not include a labour efficiency variance in your example.

(a) The materials usage variance shows the standard costs of the variation in quantity of materials used from the standard for a given level of output. The mixture component arises from using different relative proportions of the constituent raw materials from the budget. The yield component reflects any difference between the actual output achieved and that expected based upon the standard operation. For example:

	Standard	*Actual*
Input for 100 kg of product AB	60 kg of A at £1.00/kg	64 kg of A at £1.10/kg
	40 kg of B at £1.30/kg	38 kg of B at £1.25/kg

The materials usage variance is £1.40 adverse, that is, 2 kg B × £1.30 − 4 kg A × £1.00.

The materials mixture component is £0.84 favourable, that is 2.8 kg B × £1.30 − 2.8 kg A × £1.00.

Alternatively, the materials mix variance can be worked on an average ingredient price of £1.12 (i.e., £112/10 kg). In this case the mix variance is (2.8 kg A × £0.12) + (2.8 kg B × £0.18) = £0.84 favourable.

The materials yield component is £2.24 adverse, that is, 2 kg of AB at standard cost of (0.6 × 1 + 0.4 × 1.30).

(b) The purpose is the same as for part (a). The limitation is that this model assumes that there is no change in the quality of the product AB produced from different proportions of A and B. This is not likely to be true in practice where 'side' chemical reactions may become more prevalent, which may render the product unsuitable for its intended purpose. Investigation of the variances would consider the following.

- *Mixture variance*: ingredients used, material control and wastage;
- *Yield variance*: efficiency of equipment and the quality of materials used.

(c) The labour rate variance is the difference between the actual cost incurred for the actual hours worked and the costs for working the actual amount of hours using the budgeted labour rate. The operational component arises from any changes in the rate of pay, which were a consequence of the way labour was operated, for example allowing a discretionary extra payment for poor working conditions. The planning component shows the change in labour rate due to inadequacies to inaccuracies in the preparation of the original budget. For example, the anticipated annual pay increase may have been different from that obtained by the workforce:

Actual hours worked	100
Actual wages paid	£500
Original standard wage rate	£4.00 per hour
Revised standard wage rate for the period	£5.20 per hour

The labour rate variance is £100 adverse, that is $(500 - (4 \times 100))$.

The operational component is £20 favourable, that is $(500 - (5.20 \times 100))$.

The planning component is £120 adverse, that is (100×1.20).

Again, the purpose is the same as for part (a). The limitation of this subdivision is that it is rare for there to be a controllable (operational) reason for the labour rate variance. In general, labour rates are fixed by the marketplace, that is they are uncontrollable (planning) variances.

Thus, this subdivision is an unnecessary complication that will rarely provide an insight that is an improvement on that provided by the labour rate variance. However, any investigation would focus on the establishment of wages rates and labour recruitment, whereas investigation of the operational variance would look at the actual payment of wages and the control of payroll.

The Theory and Practice of Budgeting

The Theory and Practice of Budgeting

5

LEARNING OUTCOMES

When you have completed study of this chapter you will be able to

▸ explain why organisations prepare forecasts and plans;

▸ calculate projected product/service volumes employing appropriate forecasting techniques;

▸ calculate projected revenues and costs based on product/service volumes, pricing, pricing strategies and cost structures;

▸ describe and explain the possible purposes of budgets including planning, communication, co-ordination, motivation, authorisation, control and evaluation;

▸ evaluate and apply alternative approaches to budgeting;

▸ calculate the consequences of 'what if scenarios and evaluate their impact on master profit and loss account and balance sheet.

5.1 Introduction

In this chapter we will consider the manner in which an understanding of cost and revenue structures can be applied in the construction of forecasts, plans and budgets. The preparation of budgets and their use in the control of operations are core management accounting functions. Budgets are widely used in the manufacturing, services, public and voluntary sectors.

The basic concepts and practices involved in budgeting are explored in this chapter.

5.2 The purposes of budgeting

Budgets have two main roles:

(1) They act as authorities to spend, that is, they give authority to budget managers to incur expenditure in their part of the organisation.

(2) They act as comparators for current performance, by providing a yardstick against which current activities can be monitored, and they may be used as targets to motivate managers.

These two roles are combined in a system of budgetary planning and control.

5.2.1 Budgetary planning and control

Planning the activities of an organisation ensures that the organisation sets out in the right direction. Individuals within the organisation will have definite targets that they will aim to achieve. Without a formalised plan the organisation will lack direction, and managers will not be aware of their own targets and responsibilities. Neither will they appreciate how their activities relate to those of other managers within the organisation.

A formalised plan will help to ensure a co-ordinated approach and the planning process itself will force managers to continually think ahead, planning and reviewing their activities in advance.

However, the budgetary process should not stop with the plan. The organisation has started out in the right direction but to ensure that it continues on course it is management's responsibility to exercise control.

Control is best achieved by comparison of the actual results with the original plan. Appropriate action can then be taken to correct any deviations from the plan.

The two activities of planning and control must go hand in hand. Carrying out the budgetary planning exercise without using the plan for control purposes is performing only part of the task.

5.2.2 What is a budget?

A budget could be defined as 'a quantified plan of action relating to a given period of time'.

For a budget to be useful it must be quantified. For example, it would not be particularly useful for the purposes of planning and control if a budget was set as follows: 'We plan to spend as little as possible in running the printing department this year'; or 'We plan to produce as many units as we can possibly sell this quarter'.

These are merely vague indicators of intended direction; they are not quantified plans. They will not provide much assistance in management's task of planning and controlling the organisation.

These 'budget' could perhaps be modified as follows: 'Budgeted revenue expenditure for the printing department this year is £60,000'; and 'Budgeted production for the quarter is 4,700 units'.

The quantification of the budgets has provided:

(a) a definite target for planning purposes; and
(b) a yardstick for control purposes.

The thrust of this approach is that the budget provides an internal benchmark against which performance can be evaluated. If the department or business achieves its budget turnover and/or profit for the period that it is deemed to be performing well. Conversely, if it fails to achieve budget then it is deemed to be performing badly. This approach to performance evaluation has been subject to a variety of criticisms and we will explore these criticisms as we proceed through the text.

A budget can also have a variety of other uses relating to the legitimisation of decisions taken within an organisation. The process of preparing and obtaining approval for a spending budget may provide the channel through which authorisation is granted to commit resources.

In theory, a budget should be a motivating but 'neutral' tool. The practice of budgeting should not distort the processes it is meant to serve. However, at this point it should be noted that the process of establishing a budget and its subsequent use in control and performance evaluation can have a variety of behavioural effects within the organisation. These effects are not always obvious or intended. Sometimes, they can harm the organisation. Behavioural aspects of budgeting are considered fully in Chapter 6.

5.2.3 The budget period

You may have noticed that in each of these 'budgets' the time period was different. The first budget was prepared for a year and the second budget was for a quarter. The time period for which a budget is prepared and used is called the 'budget period'. It can be any length to suit management purposes but it is usually 1 year.

The length of time chosen for the budget period will depend on many factors, including the nature of the organisation and the type of expenditure being considered. Each budget period can be subdivided into control periods, also of varying lengths, depending on the level of control which management wishes to exercise. The usual length of a control period is 1 month.

5.2.4 Strategic planning, budgetary planning and operational planning

It will be useful at this stage to distinguish, in broad terms, between three different types of planning:

1. strategic planning
2. budgetary planning
3. operational planning.

These three forms of planning are interrelated. The main distinction between them relates to their time span which may be short term, medium term or long term.

Strategic planning
Strategic planning is concerned with preparing long-term action plans to attain the organisation's objectives.

Budgetary planning
Budgetary planning is concerned with preparing the short- to medium-term plans of the organisation. It will be carried out within the framework of the strategic plan. An organisation's annual budget could be seen as an interim term step towards achieving the long-term or strategic plan.

Operational planning
Operational planning refers to the short-term or day-to-day planning process. It is concerned with planning the utilisation of resources and will be carried out within the framework set by the budgetary plan. Each stage in the operational planning process can be seen as an interim step towards achieving the budget for the period.

Remember that the full benefit of any planning exercise is not realised unless the plan is also used for control purposes. Each of these types of planning should be accompanied by the appropriate control exercise covering the same time span.

STUDY MATERIAL P1

188

THE THEORY AND PRACTICE OF BUDGETING

5.3 The preparation of budgets

The process of preparing and using budgets will differ from organisation to organisation. However, there are a number of key requirements in the design of a budgetary planning and control process.

5.3.1 Co-ordination: the budget committee

The need for co-ordination in the planning process is paramount. The interrelationship between the functional budgets (e.g., sales, production, purchasing) means that one budget cannot be completed without reference to several others.

For example, the purchasing budget cannot be prepared without reference to the production budget, and it may be necessary to prepare the sales budget before the production budget can be prepared. The best way to achieve this co-ordination is to set up a budget committee. The budget committee should comprise representatives from all parts of the organisation: there should be a representative from sales, a representative from marketing, a representative from personnel and so on.

The budget committee should meet regularly to review the progress of the budgetary planning process and to resolve any problems that have arisen. These meetings will effectively bring together the whole organisation in one room, to ensure that a co-ordinated approach is adopted to budget preparation.

5.3.2 Participative budgeting

CIMA defines participative budgeting as:

 Participative budgeting: A budgeting system in which all budget holders are given the opportunity to participate in setting their own budgets.

This may also be referred to as 'bottom-up budgeting'. It contrasts with imposed or top-down budgets where the ultimate budget holder does not have the opportunity to participate in the budgeting process. The advantages of participative budgeting are as follows:

- *Improved quality of forecasts to use as the basis for the budget:* Managers who are doing a job on a day-to-day basis are likely to have a better idea of what is achievable, what is likely to happen in the forthcoming period, local trading conditions and so on.
- *Improved motivation:* Budget holders are more likely to want to work to achieve a budget that they have been involved in setting themselves, rather than one that has been imposed on them from above.

The main disadvantage of participative budgeting is that it tends to result in a more extended and complex budgetary process. However, the advantages are generally accepted to outweigh this disadvantage.

5.3.3 Information: the budget manual

Effective budgetary planning relies on the provision of adequate information to the individuals involved in the planning process.

Many of these information needs are contained in the budget manual.

A budget manual is a collection of documents that contains key information for those involved in the planning process. Typical contents could include the following.

(a) An introductory explanation of the budgetary planning and control process, including a statement of the budgetary objective and desired results.

Participants should be made aware of the advantages to them and to the organisation of an efficient planning and control process. This introduction should give participants an understanding of the workings of the planning process, and of the sort of information that they can expect to receive as part of the control process.

(b) A form of organisation chart to show who is responsible for the preparation of each functional budget and the way in which the budgets are interrelated.

(c) A timetable for the preparation of each budget. This will prevent the formation of a 'bottleneck' with the late preparation of one budget holding up the preparation of all others.

(d) Copies of all forms to be completed by those responsible for preparing budgets, with explanations concerning their completion.

(e) A list of the organisation's account codes, with full explanations of how to use them.

(f) Information concerning key assumptions to be made by managers in their budgets, for example the rate of inflation, key exchange rates and so on.

(g) The name and location of the person to be contacted concerning any problems encountered in preparing budgetary plans. This will usually be the co-ordinator of the budget committee (the budget officer) and will probably be a senior accountant.

5.3.4 Early identification of the principal budget factor

The principal budget factor is the factor that limits the activities of the organisation. The early identification of this factor is important in the budgetary planning process because it indicates which budget should be prepared first.

For example, if sales volume is the principal budget factor then the sales budget must be prepared first, based on the available sales forecasts. All other budgets should then be linked to this.

Alternatively, machine capacity may be limited for the forthcoming period and therefore machine capacity is the principal budget factor. In this case the production budget must be prepared first and all other budgets must be linked to this.

Failure to identify the principal budget factor at an early stage could lead to delays later on when managers realise that the targets they have been working with are not feasible.

5.3.5 The interrelationship of budgets

The critical importance of the principal budget factor stems from the fact that all budgets are interrelated. For example, if sales is the principal budget factor this is the first budget to be prepared. This will then provide the basis for the preparation of several other budgets, including the selling expenses budget and the production budget.

However, the production budget cannot be prepared directly from the sales budget without a consideration of stockholding policy. For example, management may plan to increase finished goods stock in anticipation of a sales drive. Production quantities would then have to be higher than the budgeted sales level. Similarly, if a decision is taken to reduce the level of material stocks held, it would not be necessary to purchase all of the materials required for production.

5.3.6 Using spreadsheets in budget preparation

It is clear from just this simple example that changes in one budget can have a knock-on effect on several other budgets. For this reason spreadsheets are particularly useful in budget prepaid ration. Budgetary planning is an or iterative, or repetitive, process. Once the first set of budgets has been prepared they will be considered by senior managers. They may require amendments to be made or they may wish to see the effect of changes in key decision variables.

A well-designed spreadsheet model can take account of all of the budget interrelationships. This means that it will not be an onerous task to alter decision variables and produce revised budgets for management's consideration.

In Modern times, the budgetary process has a major IT element.

Spreadsheets and databases as budgeting tools

Bob Scarlett, *CIMA student,* **July 1999**

Most organisations use the spreadsheet as the main tool in budgeting and business planning. However, the spreadsheet was developed and introduced as a personal productivity aid. Its use in budgeting for medium- to large-size organisations may be problematic. A new category of business software has recently emerged, designed for use in budget management. One US software supplier has claimed that sales of this category (including products such as Comshare Commander Budget and Hyperion Pillar) are among the fastest growing in business management software. These products are highly developed database systems.

The limitations of spreadsheets

The process of creating a budget in a large organisation is a complex operation. Each area in the organisation needs to prepare a plan and these plans need to be collated and consolidated. The system must then accommodate adjustments on a top-down and bottom-up basis. A budgeting operation based on spreadsheets has the following problems:

- *It is inflexible and error prone.* A large number of spreadsheets can be linked and consolidated but this process presents many difficulties. Calculations are complex and mistakes are easily made. Random 'what-if' analyses across centres may become very difficult to carry out.
- *It is a single-user tool in a multi-user environment.* A large number of spreadsheet users are involved using similar templates over periods of weeks. This involves massive duplication of effort and gives rise to risks relating to loss of data integrity and consistency of structure.
- *It lacks 'functionality'.* There are many users in the budget management process ranging from cost centre managers to the chief financial officer. All require ready access to the system in order to input data to it and draw information from it. The budget controller must be able to track revisions. Spreadsheet based systems are notorious for complexity – and they can be anything but easy to use.

Spreadsheet-based budgeting systems may be perfectly adequate for the small and simple operation. However, the limitations of such systems may become increasingly apparent as larger and more complex operations are considered.

User requirements

Modern organisations operate in a dynamic environment where the budgeting process involves numerous iterations and changes carried out at very short notice. The type of changes the budget system must accommodate include basic figures, organisation structure and calculation logic. The budget users have to be able to revise the budget to allow for changed assumptions or changed structures in a matter of minutes.

To expand on this:

- Budget holders and cost centre managers need a simple interface with the system which allows them to input data to and draw information from the system without any major learning requirement. It should be possible to view data drawn from the system in simple tabular form.
- Budget managers and divisional mangers receive consolidations of the various departmental budgets. They need to be able to determine who has input their contribution to the consolidated budget and who has not. They need to be able to identify changes to the budget which have been entered at a subordinate level. Above all, they need to be able to carry out top-down changes to the budget to accommodate 'what-if' enquiries and changes in the organisational structure which move items of cost and revenue from one area of the budget to another.
- System administrators design, operate and update the system. They are usually qualified accountants who have a good knowledge of IT. They need a robust system which is easy to understand and where the various interfaces are not excessively technical. The system should allow its administrator to rearrange the system and bolt new modules onto the system without great IT sophistication.

What is needed is a system consisting of a group of linked modules which can be updated in two directions: changed data introduced at cost centre level should automatically feed up through to the various summaries; a new expense line, introduced just once, should feed its way down through to every cost centre. The impact of a departmental reorganisation on the budget should be accommodated by a simple re-coding of relevant data items.

The modern budget management system

The preparation of a large and complex budget is an exercise in data processing. The spreadsheet is, arguably, not well suited to this. The type of system that meets the above requirements is likely to be a database. Such systems have existed for many years but they have been associated mainly with the collation and reporting of large volumes of data. Specifically, they lacked a capability to allow random top-down, what-if analyses.

It is this last feature that distinguishes the modern budget management systems such as Comshare and Hyperion. Such systems contain a capability that allows the budget manager to undertake what-if analyses. For example, the budget manager can postulate the impact of a 12 per cent increase in fuel costs across all cost centers while all other data is held constant. This facility provides what many US budget managers call 'real-life budgeting'. A budget can be revised instantly without having to alter subordinate databases and rework the whole model.

A true multi-user capability allows shared access to a single database (or set of related databases) where users employ common definitions and data without any duplication of work. However, appropriate arrangements should be incorporated for the security and integrity of data. A developed budget management system should incorporate security features – including restricted access to certain account code items (e.g. management salaries).

Budgeting in a large operations is a complex process that requires the support of all the members of the organisation who are engaged in it. To gain the enthusiastic support of managers it is essential that the user interfaces, where data is input and information is extracted, are both familiar and 'user-friendly'.

5.3.7 The master budget

The master budget is a summary of all the functional budgets. It usually comprises the budgeted profit and loss account, budgeted balance sheet and budgeted cash flow statement. It is this master budget that is submitted to senior managers for approval because they should not be burdened with an excessive amount of detail. The master budget is designed to give the summarised information that they need to determine whether the budget is an acceptable plan for the forthcoming period.

5.4   Preparation of operational budgets

In this section, you will be working through an example of the preparation of operational budgets. Try to apply your knowledge from your earlier studies of cost accounting to prepare the budgets before looking at our solution.

  Exercise: preparing operating budgets

A company manufactures two products, Aye and Bee. Standard cost data for the products for next year are as follows:

	Product Aye per unit	*Product Bee per unit*
Direct materials		
X at £2 per kg	24 kg	30 kg
Y at £5 per kg	10 kg	8 kg
Z at £6 per kg	5 kg	10 kg
Direct wages		
Unskilled at £3 per hour	10 hours	5 hours
Skilled at £5 per hour	6 hours	5 hours

Budgeted stocks for next year are as follows:

	Product Aye units	Product Bee units
1 January	400	800
31 December	500	1,100

	Material X kg	Material Y kg	Material Z kg
1 January	30,000	25,000	12,000
31 December	35,000	27,000	12,500

Budgeted sales for next year: Product Aye 2,400 units. Product Bee 3,200 units.
Prepare the following budgets for next year:

(a) production budget, in units;
(b) material purchases budget, in kg and by value;
(c) direct labour budget, in hours and by value.

 Solution

(a) Production budget for next year

	Product Aye units	Product Bee units
Sales units required	2,400	3,200
Closing stock at end of year	500	1,100
	2,900	4,300
Less opening stock	400	800
Production units required	2,500	3,500

(b) Material purchases budget for next year

	Material X kg	Material Y kg	Material Z kg	Total £
Requirements for production				
Product Aye	60,000	25,000	12,500	
Product Bee	105,000	28,000	35,000	
	165,000	53,000	47,500	
Closing stock at end of year	35,000	27,000	12,500	
	200,000	80,000	60,000	
Less opening stock	30,000	25,000	12,000	
Material purchases required	170,000	55,000	48,000	
	£	£	£	
Standard price per kg	2	5	6	
Material purchases value	340,000	275,000	288,000	903,00

(c) Direct labour budget for next year

	Unskilled labour hours	Skilled labour hours	Total £
Requirements for production			
Product Aye	25,000	15,000	
Product Bee	17,500	17,500	
Total hours required	42,500	32,500	
	£	£	
Standard rate per hour	3	5	
Direct labour cost	127,500	162,500	290,000

5.4.1 Using stock control formulae in budget preparation

In this example the required closing stocks for material and for finished goods were detailed in the question data. You should recall from your earlier studies that there exist a number of stock control formulae that could be used to determine the required stock levels, taking into account such factors as supplier lead time.

The procedure used to prepare the budgets would be the same, but they would be based on more detailed calculations of the required stock levels.

5.4.2 Budget interrelationships

This example has demonstrated how the data from one operational budget becomes an input in the preparation of another budget. The last budget in the sequence, the direct labour budget, would now be used as an input to other budgets. The material purchases budget will also provide input data for other budgets. For example, the material purchases budget would probably be used in preparing the creditors budget, taking account of the company's intended policy on the payment of suppliers. The creditors budget would indicate the payments to be made to creditors, which would then become an input for the cash budget and so on.

The cash budget is the subject of the next section of this chapter.

5.5 The cash budget

The cash budget is one of the most vital planning documents in an organisation. It will show the cash effect of all of the decisions taken in the planning process.

Management decisions will have been taken concerning such factors as stockholding policy, credit policy, selling price policy and so on. All of these plans will be designed to meet the objectives of the organisation. However, if there are insufficient cash resources to finance the plans, they may need to be modified or, perhaps, action might be taken to alleviate the cash restraint.

A cash budget can give forewarning of potential problems that could arise so that managers can be prepared for the situation or take action to avoid it.

There are four possible cash positions that could arise:

Cash position	*Possible management action*
Short-term deficit	Arrange a bank overdraft, reduce debtors and stocks, increase creditors.
Long-term deficit	Raise long-term finance, such as loan capital or share capital.
Short-term surplus	Invest short term, increase debtors and stocks to boost sales, pay creditors early to obtain cash discount.
Long-term surplus	Expand or diversify operations, replace or update fixed assets.

A detailed understanding of cash management is outside the scope of the IMPM syllabus. However, you should notice that the type of action taken by management will depend not only on whether a deficit or a surplus is expected, but also on how long the situation is expected to last.

For example, management would not wish to use surplus cash to purchase fixed assets, if the surplus was only short term and the cash would soon be required again for day-to-day operations.

Cash budgets therefore forewarn managers of the following:

(a) Whether there will be cash surpluses or cash deficits.
(b) How long the surpluses or deficits are expected to last.

5.5.1 Preparing cash budgets

You will have studied the basic principles of cash budget preparation at Foundation level. However, in case you have forgotten the basics we shall review them now and work through a basic example.

The examiner has stressed that your studies should emphasise the interpretive aspects of budget preparation. Therefore, we shall also look in outline at how to interpret the cash budget that you have prepared.

(a) The format for cash budgets

There is no definitive format that should be used for a cash budget. However, whichever format you decide to use, it should include the following:

(i) *A clear distinction between the cash receipts and cash payments for each control period.* Your budget should not consist of a jumble of cash flows. It should be logically arranged with a subtotal for receipts and a subtotal for payments.

(ii) *A figure for the net cash flow for each period.* It could be argued that this is not an essential feature of a cash budget. However, you will find it easier to prepare and use a cash budget in an examination if you include the net cash flow. Also, managers find in practice that a figure for the net cash flow helps to draw attention to the cash flow implications of their actions during the period.

(iii) *The closing cash balance for each control period.* The closing balance for each period will be the opening balance for the following period.

(b) Depreciation is not included in cash budgets

Remember that depreciation is not a cash flow. It may be included in your data for overheads and must therefore be excluded before the overheads are inserted into the cash budget.

(c) Allowance must be made for bad and doubtful debts

Bad debts will never be received in cash and doubtful debts may not be received. When you are forecasting the cash receipts from debtors you must remember to adjust for these items.

Exercise: cash budget

Watson Ltd is preparing its budgets for the next quarter. The following information has been drawn from the budgets prepared in the planning exercise so far.

Sales value	June (estimate)	£12,500
	July (budget)	£13,600
	August	£17,000
	September	£16,800
Direct wages	£1,300 per month	
Direct material purchases	June (estimate)	£3,450
	July (budget)	£3,780
	August	£2,890
	September	£3,150

- Watson sells 10% of its goods for cash. The remainder of customers receive 1 month's credit.
- Payments to creditors are made in the month following purchase.
- Wages are paid as they are incurred.
- Watson takes 1 month's credit on all overheads.
- Production overheads are £3,200 per month.
- Selling, distribution and administration overheads amount to £1,890 per month.
- Included in the amounts for overhead given above are depreciation charges of £300 and £190, respectively.
- Watson expects to purchase a delivery vehicle in August for a cash payment of £9,870.
- The cash balance at the end of June is forecast to be £1,235.

Prepare a cash budget for each of the months from July to September.

 ## Solution

Watson Ltd cash budget for July to September

	July £	August £	September £
Sales receipts			
10% in cash	1,360	1,700	1,680
90% in 1 month	11,250	12,240	15,300
Total receipts	12,610	13,940	16,980
Payments			
Material purchases (1-month credit)	3,450	3,780	2,890
Direct wages	1,300	1,300	1,300
Production overheads	2,900	2,900	2,900
Selling, distribution and administration overhead	1,700	1,700	1,700
Delivery vehicle	–	9,870	–
Total payments	9,350	19,550	8,790
Net cash inflow/(outflow)	3,260	(5,610)	8,190
Opening cash balance	1,235	4,495	(1,115)
Closing cash balance at the end of the month	4,495	(1,115)	7,075

5.5.2 Interpretation of the cash budget

This cash budget forewarns the management of Watson Ltd that their plans will lead to a cash deficit of £1,115 at the end of August. They can also see that it will be a short-term deficit and can take appropriate action.

They may decide to delay the purchase of the delivery vehicle or perhaps negotiate a period of credit before the payment will be due. Alternatively, overdraft facilities may be arranged for the appropriate period.

If it is decided that overdraft facilities are to be arranged, it is important that due account is taken of the timing of the receipts and payments within each month.

For example, all of the payments in August may be made at the beginning of the month but receipts may not be expected until nearer the end of the month. The cash deficit could then be considerably greater than it appears from looking only at the month-end balance.

If the worst possible situation arose, the overdrawn balance during August could become as large as £4,495 − £19,550 = £15,055. If management had used the month-end balances as a guide to the overdraft requirement during the period then they would not have arranged a large enough overdraft facility with the bank. It is important, therefore, that they look in detail at the information revealed by the cash budget, and not simply at the closing cash balances.

5.5.3 Cash budget: second example

In the last example you saw how a cash budget can be used to forewarn managers of the cash effect of their planning decisions. A cash budget can also be used as a cash planning tool, as you will see when you work through the following example where it is used to decide on the payments to be made to suppliers.

 Exercise

A redundant manager who received compensation of £80,000 decides to commence business on 4 January year 8, manufacturing a product for which he knows there is a ready market. He intends to employ some of his former workers who were also made redundant but they will not all commence on 4 January. Suitable premises have been found to rent. Material stocks costing £10,000 and second-hand machinery costing £60,000 have already been bought out of the £80,000. The machinery has an estimated life of 5 years from January year 8 and no residual value.

Other data is as follows:

1. Product will begin on 4 January and 25% of the following month's sales will be manufactured in January. Each month thereafter the production will consist of 75% of the current month's sales and 25% of the following month's sales.
2. Estimated sales are:

	Units	£
January	–	–
February	3,200	80,000
March	3,600	90,000
April	4,000	100,000
May	4,000	100,000

3. Variable production cost per unit:

	£
Direct materials	7
Direct wages	6
Variable overhead	2
	15

4. Raw material requirements for January's production will be met from the stock already purchased. During January, 50% of the materials required for February's production will be purchased. Thereafter it is intended to buy, each month, 50% of the materials required for the following month's production requirements. The other 50% will be purchased in the month of production.
5. Payment for raw material purchases will usually be made 30 days after purchase, but it will be possible to delay payment if necessary for another month. The manager does not intend to use this course of action too frequently because of the danger of adversely affecting the business's credit rating. Ten % of the business's purchases will be eligible for a 5% discount if payment is made immediately on delivery.
6. Direct workers have agreed to have their wages paid into their bank accounts on the 7th working day of each month in respect of the previous month's earnings.

7. Variable production overhead: 60% is to be paid in the month following the month it was incurred and 40% is to be paid 1 month later.

8. Fixed overheads are £4,000 per month. One-quarter of this is paid in the month incurred, one-half in the following month and the remainder represents depreciation on the second-hand machinery.

9. Amounts receivable: a 5% cash discount is allowed for payment in the current month and 20% of each month's sales qualify for this discount. Fifty per cent of each month's sales are received in the following month, 20% in the third month and 8% in the fourth month. The balance of 2% represents anticipated bad debts.

10. The manager's intended cash policy is to maintain a minimum month-end cash balance of £5,000. If cash balances are likely to be lower than this then supplier payment will be delayed as described above.

Prepare a cash budget for each of the first 3 months of year 8, taking account of the requirement to maintain a minimum month-end cash balance of £5,000. All calculations should be made to the nearest pound.

☑ Solution
Initial workings

	January	February	March	April
1. *Monthly production (units)*				
25% of following month's sales	800	900	1,000	1,000
75% of current month's sales	–	2,400	2,700	3,000
	800	3,300	3,700	4,000

2. *Material purchases*	£	£	£	£
Material cost of production	5,600	23,100	25,900	28,000
50% of following month's requirements	11,550	12,950	14,000	
50% of current month's requirements		11,550	12,950	
Purchases	11,550	24,500	26,950	

3. *Wages payments*			
Previous month production volume (units)		800	3,300
× £6 = wages paid in month		£4,800	£19,800

4. *Variable overhead*	January	February	March
	£	£	£
Variable overhead cost of production	1,600	6,600	7,400
60% paid in following month		960	3,960
40% paid 1 month later		–	640
		960	4,600

5. *Fixed overhead*			
	£	£	£
One-quarter paid as incurred	1,000	1,000	1,000
One-half paid in following month	–	2,000	2,000
	1,000	3,000	3,000

6. *Sales receipts*		
	£	£
Monthly sales	80,000	90,000
Received in current month × 95% × 20%	15,200	17,100
Received in following month × 50%		40,000
Total receivable	15,200	57,100

The next step is to begin to build up the cash budget so that it is possible to see how much cash is available to pay for the material purchases. The discount for early payment will be taken, as long as this does not cause the cash balance to fall below the minimum required balance of £5,000.

Cash budget for January to March, year 8

	January £	February £	March £
Sales receipts (W6)	–	15,200	57,100
Cash payments			
Wages (W3)	–	4,800	19,800
Variable overhead (W4)	–	960	4,600
Fixed overhead (W5)	1,000	3,000	3,000
Payments, excluding material purchases	1,000	8,760	27,400
Material payments (W7)	1,097	9,343	28,112
Total cash payments	2,097	18,103	55,512
Net cash flow	(2,097)	(2,903)	1,588
Opening cash balance	10,000	7,903	5,000
Closing cash balance	7,903	5,000	6,588

7. *Payments for material purchases*

	January £	February £	March £
Opening cash balance	10,000	7,903	5,000
Cash inflow (from budget)	–	15,200	57,100
Cash outflow, excluding materials (from budget)	1,000	8,760	27,400
	(1,000)	6,440	29,700
Cash available	9,000	14,343	34,700
Material payments			
January: 10% of January paid			
10% × 11,550 × 95% (Note 1)	(1,097)		
February: pay for January purchases			
(maximum amount possible) (Note 2)		(9,343)	
March			
Pay for January balance			(1,052)
February purchases (W2)			(24,500)
10% of March paid: 10% × 26,950 × 95%			(2,560)
Closing cash balance	7,903	5,000	6,588

Notes:

1. The remaining balance of January purchases (£11,550 × 90% = £10,395) is carried forward for later payment.
2. The remaining balance of January purchases (£10,395 − £9,343 = £1,052) must be paid in March.

5.6 Rolling budgets

Rolling budgets can be particularly useful when future events cannot be forecast reliably. The CIMA *Terminology* defines a rolling budget as:

> *Rolling budget:* A budget continuously updated by adding a further accounting period (month or quarter) when the earliest accounting period has expired. Its use is particularly beneficial where future costs and/or activities cannot be forecast accurately.

For example, a budget may initially be prepared for January to December year 1. At the end of the first quarter, that is, at the end of March year 1, the first quarter's budget is deleted. A further quarter is then added to the end of the remaining budget, for January to March year 2. The remaining portion of the original budget is updated in the light of current conditions. This means that managers have a full year's budget always available and the rolling process forces them to continually plan ahead.

It is not necessary for all of the budgets in a system to be prepared on a rolling basis. For example, many organisations will use a rolling system for the cash budget only.

In practice, most organisations carry out some form of updating process on all their budgets, so that the budgets represent a realistic target for planning and control purposes. The formalised budgetary planning process will still be performed on a regular basis to ensure a co-ordinated approach to budgetary planning.

The use of rolling budgets has motivational effects which may induce improved performance.

Extract from 'Budgets on a roll: recalculating a business's outlook several times a year'

Randy Myers, *Journal of Accountancy,* **December 2001. © 2001. Reprinted with permission of AICPA**

For years, senior managers at REL Consultancy Group handled budgeting and revenue forecasting much the way most other companies do. As year-end approached, they would evaluate performance, set sales targets for the upcoming year and then work to see that everyone met or exceeded the goals.

Unfortunately, the process didn't always produce the intended results.

'Invariably,' recalls Stephan Payne, president of the London-based global management consulting firm, 'one of the account directors would land a couple of good clients early in the year and make his annual budget well before the year closed. More often than not, he'd then take his foot off the gas and coast.'

To make the budgeting process more timely and relevant, the firm embraced a more complex, albeit intuitive, approach to financial forecasting – the rolling budget. Rather than creating an annual financial forecast that remains static for the year, he and his colleagues now produce an 18-month budget and then update projections every month – in effect, recalculating the whole budget. As the firm's actual sales figures come in each month, directors plug them into their forecasting model in place of what they had projected, then roll the budget forward one more month.

No more free rides

The result: an always-current financial forecast that reflects not only the company's most recent monthly results but also any material changes to its business outlook or the economy. In addition, it provides fewer opportunities for account directors to ride the coattails of past performance.

'Now, even the guy who booked a million dollars' worth of business in one month can't sit still because 30 days later, we're going to have an entirely new forecast,' Payne says, adding, 'It's a dynamic process that makes a lot more sense.'

Although traditional 1-year budgets are still the norm at most companies large and small, many accountants argue that rolling budgets can be a far more useful tool. Unlike static budgets, they encourage managers to react more quickly to changing economic developments or business conditions. They discourage what is too often a fruitless focus on the past ('Why didn't we meet our numbers?') in favor of a realistic focus on the future. And they produce forecasts that, over the near term, are never more than a few months old, even when companies are rolling them forward on a quarterly basis – the more common approach – rather than REL's monthly basis.

'A static budget simply doesn't reflect the pace of business today,' says Jill Langerman, CPA, president and CFO of the accounting firm Fair, Anderson & Langerman in Las Vegas. 'If at midyear you add a new product to your lineup, you want to calculate the costs and profit margins associated with that and reflected those calculations in your budget OSC to reflect the impact that it will have on your remaining product lines. That way, you can set an accurate performance target and make informed decisions about whether you're now free to invest more in the remaining product lines or perhaps add a new line. If you're not incorporating these new analyses into your budget, it becomes a rather useless document.'

Implementing rolling budgets doesn't necessarily require any fundamental change in the way a company has been doing its budgets – except, of course, it no longer does the job just once a year. However, companies that decide to step up to rolling budgets may want to take advantage of the decision to make a change and consider what else they can do to improve the process. After all, if a company can get everyone on board to make such a fundamental change, a further nudge to make the process more effective and efficient in other ways may be possible, too.

5.7 Forecasting and planning

In preparing budgets it is usually necessary to develop the budget around a set of forecasts. The budget officer needs to know what sales of different products will be, what labour rates will be, what material costs will be and so on. It is not always possible to state with absolute certainty what these figures will be, so certain forecasting techniques may be deployed.

Time series analysis is one such technique. A time series is a series of values that vary over time. When plotted on a graph, a time series may reveal a trend or a relationship.

Such exercises can be carried out with varying levels of mathematical refinement. The simplest possible exercise in 'linear regression' is as follows:

Example

Month	Units produced	Costs £
1	100	1,200
2	150	1,550

We are required to forecast costs for month 3 when production of 120 units is planned.

On the assumption that the components of costs are either fixed or fully variable, then a model for cost behaviour can be developed using an equation in the form:

$$y = a + bx$$

where y is monthly costs, a is monthly fixed costs, b is variable cost per unit and x is output. As x rises by 50, y rises by 350, Hence b must be 7 and a is 500.

So we have deduced that the variable cost per unit (b) is £7, the fixed costs per month (a) are £500. So, if planned output (x) in month 3 is 120 units then we can forecast that costs in month 3 will be £1,340 (i.e. £500 fixed costs plus (£7 × 120 units) variable costs).

Example

A product called the Unit is on sale. The information below gives the actual monthly and cumulative sales of Units during the period month 1 to month 9.

Month	Total sales	Month sales
1	1,000	1,000
2	1,580	580
3	2,100	520
4	2,400	300
5	2,650	250
6	2,850	200
7	3,190	340
8	3,510	320
9	3,690	180

We are required to produce a forecast for sales of Units in month 10.

Inspection of these figures shows that there is a 'trend'. Monthly Unit sales are declining – but not at an even rate (such as sales each month being 150 Units lower than the previous month). The decline month 1 to month 2 is 420 Units, whereas the decline month 8 to month 9 is only 140 Units.

The figures may be represented graphically as in Figure 5.1.

The trend is apparent but the curve is not smooth. There are probably a number of random elements that are influencing sales – perhaps the amount of rain, what happens to be shown on television or developments in the political situation.

One approach to developing a forecast for month 10 Unit sales is to develop a mathematical model to relate time and Unit sales. Essentially, this involves producing an algebraic equation to link the two. One mathematical technique to do this is known as regression analysis.

The widespread use of PC systems has influenced how this technique is applied.

The relationship between time and cumulative sales is a curve. The simplest algebraic form of a curve is represented by the equation:

$$y = Ax^n$$

In this case we can adopt y as the cumulative sales, x as the months and A as Unit sales in month 1. The figure n is a constant and the analyst has to determine its value.

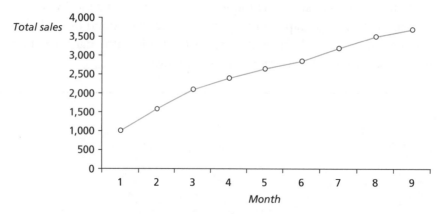

Figure 5.1 Cumulative sales of Units

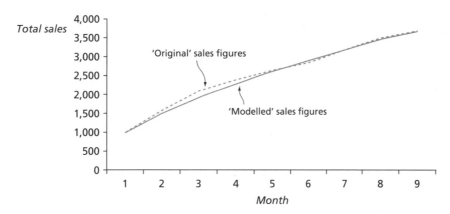

Figure 5.2 Mathematically modelled cumulative sales of Units

The figures can be set up on a computer spreadsheet as shown below. The months are entered in the left-hand column. The equation is entered in all the cells in the center column with x being set as the value of the matching month's figure. The value for n in all the cells is linked to a number entered in a reference cell below the main tabulation.

A series of iterations can then be carried out by changing the value of n. It can be determined very quickly that 0.6 gives 'a line of nearest fit'. The resulting tabulation appears as follows:

Spreadsheet Month	Total sales
1	1,000
2	1,516
3	1,933
4	2,297
5	2,627
6	2,930
7	3,214
8	3,482
9	3,737

These figures are not a perfect match – but they closely fit the actual figures recorded above. They follow the general trend but do not allow for the random events that cause minor fluctuations around that trend.

These 'mathematically modelled' figures may be shown graphically as in Figure 5.2.

If the relationship between cumulative months (x) and cumulative Unit sales is

$$y = 1,000X^{0.6}$$

therefore, which x is 10, then y (cumulative month 1 to month 10 sales) is 3,981 and forecast month 10 sales is 244 Units. This forecast is unlikely to be perfect, but no forecast ever is.

5.8 Time series

5.8.1 The concept

One practical application of regression analysis in business forecasting is time series analysis. This approach was implicitly used in the previous section, at an elementary level, to prepare forecasts of costs and sales. A time series is the name given to a set of observations taken at equal intervals of time, for example daily, weekly, monthly and so on. The observations can be plotted on a graph against time to given an overall picture of what is happening. Time intervals are usually plotted on the horizontal axis.

Time series can be constructed for total annual exports, monthly unemployment figures, daily average temperatures and so on.

Example

The following data relates to the sale of Units by ABC ltd. These are the quarterly totals taken over 4 years from 2002 to 2005.

Year	Q1	Q2	Q3	Q4
2002	25	20	22	36
2003	30	28	31	48
2004	41	40	47	61
2005	54	50	60	82

These sales figures may be presented graphically in the form of a time series as follows:

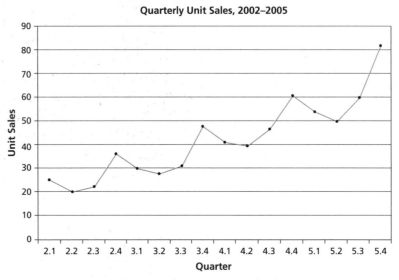

Quarterly Unit Sales, 2002–2005

The graph gives a clear impression of how sales have moved over the 4-year period. It can be seen that sales have increased throughout the period but with seasonal variations. Sales seem to surge towards the end of the year then fall back during the middle of the year. Perhaps the Unit is a product with a seasonal sales pattern (e.g. wellington boots being sold mainly in winter or electric razors being sold mainly around Christmas)?

The purpose of time series analysis is to examine the above graph in order to develop a model that will represent how Unit sales move over time. Typically, that model is represented in the form of an algebraic equation or a line drawn on a graph.

In the case shown, we may wish to use time series analysis to develop a model to predict what the Unit sales will be in 2006. One complication we have in doing this is that sales do not move over time in a neat, uniform manner. There are a number of factors that may influence how sales move over time.

5.8.2 Factors that cause variations

Various factors may cause a time series to move in the manner shown above. These factors include:

(a) *Long-term trend.* This is the key factor that causes the time series to move when the impact of short-term fluctuations has been ironed out. In the case illustrated above, the long-term trend is for Unit sales to rise. Long-term trends may relate to things such as change in the size or age structure of population, change in average income levels and technological progress.

(b) *Cyclical variations.* This is the way in which long-term cycles in trade cause demand to rise and fall. The UK economy has long been prone to 5-year trade cycles whereby the general level of demand in the economy tends to fluctuate around a long-term growth trend. Some observers have claimed that this cycle is associated with the frequency of general elections and the tendency of governments to stimulate the economy in the period before an election. The period considered in the illustrative example is too short to allow the impact of such cyclical variations to be visible.

(c) *Seasonal variations.* This is the way in which sales within a year follow a seasonal pattern. Such a pattern is clearly visible in the example, with sales peaking in winter and bottoming in summer.

(d) *Random (or stochastic) variations.* This is the tendency for sales figures to be influenced by utterly random and unpredictable factors. Examples of these are strikes, terrorist attacks, hurricanes and so on.

5.8.3   Time series modelling

As indicated above, the purpose of time series modelling is to develop a model based on past observations of some variable (e.g. unit sales) in order to forecast what unit sales will be in some future period. Typically, a time series model will incorporate the trend and the seasonal variations. Random variations are, by definition, impossible to forecast and are not incorporated in the model. Long-term cyclical variations normally lie outside the period for which the model is to be used and are not incorporated in the model.

The normal point of departure in designing a model is to take a number of observations of some variable over time and identify a trend. One can do this with varying degrees of mathematical refinement. The simplest approach is to plot the observations on a graph and draw a line of nearest fit through them. That line is the trend and it may be expressed as an equation in the form $y = a + bx$ (assuming it is a straight line). But, using a curve equation in the form $y = a + bx^n$ is possible and may be appropriate.

Another approach to identify a trend is to use moving averages. For example, go back to the figures used in the example in Section 5.8.1. If we take the observations for all quarters in 2002, add them up (giving 103) and then divide by 4, we arrive at 25.75. This figure may be taken as being on the trend line as at the end of quarter 2, 2002, since the averaging gives a 'de-seasonalised' figure. That exercise can be repeated for subsequent quarters (averaging the observations for the two previous and two subsequent quarters) and this gives a series of de-seasonalised trend figures as follows:

Quarter	
2.2	25.75
2.3	27.00 (i.e. (20 + 22 + 36 + 30)/4)
2.4	29.00
3.1	31.25
3.2	and so on

One can identify a trend using a variety of different methods and alternative levels of mathematical refinement. Be aware that the whole modelling exercise is one in preparing a simplified representation of a complex reality. Using a very basic approach will usually give results of a quality very near to those obtained using a sophisticated approach.

Once a trend has been identified, variations from that trend can be averaged in order to determine the standard seasonal variations – and the time series model is then complete. The model can be used to forecast what sales will be in future time periods.

A time series model can be based on the assumption that the seasonal variations are either (a) fixed lump amounts (the additive model) or (b) constant proportions of the trend (the multiplicative model). One has to exercise judgement in determining which is most appropriate. Clearly, if the trend is rising and the seasonal variations appear to be increasing in absolute terms, then a multiplicative model will probably be most appropriate.

Example

C Ltd sells units, and quarterly unit sales in year 1 were as follows – 65 (q1), 80 (q2), 70 (q3) and 85 (q4). Inspection of these figures indicates a trend in unit sales (see Solution) which may be represented by the equation

$$y = 50 + 10x,$$

where y = unit sales and x is the quarter number (with year 1 – quarter 1 being '1').

Solution

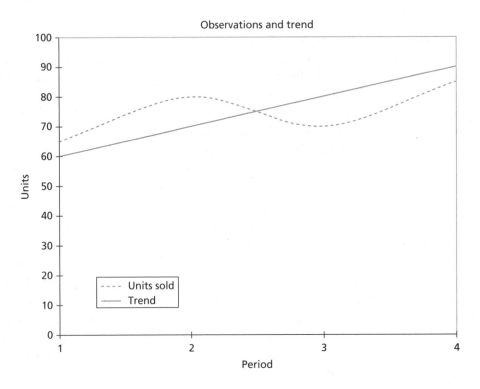

Observations and trend

How might these figures be used to develop a time series model in order to forecast unit sales in each quarter of year 2, using (a) an additive modelling approach and (b) a multiplicative modelling approach?

The point of departure is to take the actual unit sales and compare the trend figures with the actual figures for year 1 in order to determine the seasonal variation for each quarter. This variation can be expressed as (a) a lump sum for each quarter (the additive model) or (b) a percentage of trend (the multiplicative, or proportional, model).

C Ltd – unit sales time series analysis

	Period	Units sold	Trend	(a) Variation	(b) var %
Year 1 q1	1	65	60	5	8.333
Year 1 q2	2	80	70	10	14.286
Year 1 q3	3	70	80	−10	−12.500
Year 1 q4	4	85	90	−5	−5.556

Note that the multiplicative model season variations may be expressed in several different ways. For example, the quarter 3 factor may be expressed as an indexation 87.5% or 0.875.

One may then apply these variation figures to trend projections in order to produce a quarterly forecast for unit sales in Year 2. The two modelling approaches produce two alternative forecasts under headings (a) and (b).

Unit sales, budget for year 2

	Period	Trend	Year 2 forecast Add. (a)	Mult. (b)
Year 2 q1	5	100	105	108
Year 2 q2	6	110	120	126
Year 2 q3	7	120	110	105
Year 2 q4	8	130	125	123

Note that this is the simplest possible example. In particular, we are basing our analysis on only one set of observations (those for year 1). In practice, one would prefer to calculate the seasonal variations on the basis of the average of two or three sets of observations. Thus, if one observed quarter 1 variations from trend (additive model) of 6 (year A), 5 (year B) and 7 (year C) then one would adopt the average of the three (6) as the quarter 1 seasonal variation. The averaging process has the effect of 'ironing out' the impact of random variations over the past period you are considering.

5.9 Sensitivity analysis

There is always a significant degree of uncertainty concerning many of the elements incorporated within a business plan or budget. The budget officer is often required to report on such uncertainty in some way. There are various approaches to this issue and one of the most widely used is 'sensitivity analysis'.

A sensitivity analysis exercise involves revising the budget on the basis of a series of varied assumptions.

Example

The budget for quarter 1 is as follows:

	£
Sales: 100 Units @ £40 per unit	4,000
Variable costs: 100 Units @ £20 per unit	(2,000)
Fixed costs	(1,500)
Profit	500

There is some uncertainty over the variable cost per unit and that cost could be anywhere between £10 and £30, with £20 as the 'expected' outcome. We are required to carry out a sensitivity analysis on this.

One approach to this would be to present the budget shown above as an 'expected' case but with two other cases as 'worst' and 'best' possible outcomes.

Worst-case budget (£30 Unit variable cost)

	£
Sales: 100 Units @ £40 per unit	4,000
Variable costs: 100 Units @ £30 per unit	(3000)
Fixed costs	(1,500)
Profit/(loss)	(500)

Best case budget (£10 Unit variable cost)

	£
Sales: 100 Units @ £40 per unit	4,000
Variable costs: 100 Units @ £10 per unit	(1,000)
Fixed costs	(1,500)
Profit	1,500

The position may be represented graphically as in Figure 5.3.

Figure 5.3 indicates that the operation remains profitable over 75% of possible outcomes. The budget user thus obtains an impression of the possible impact of the uncertainty.

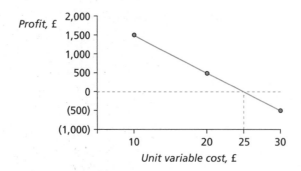

Figure 5.3   Sensitivity to unit variable cost

One can project the sensitivity cases through to the balance sheet as well as the profit and loss account. Let us say that the actual balance sheet at the start of quarter 1 is:

Balance sheet at the start of quarter 1

Fixed assets	5000
Debtors	1500
Cash/(Overdraft)	500
Net Assets	**7000**
Equity	5000
Profit & Loss	2000
Capital	**7000**

We determine that sales are all on 6 weeks' credit and all expenses are paid for immediately they are incurred. Then we can produce three alternative case budget end quarter 1 balance sheets as follows:

Budget balance sheets at the end of quarter 1

	Expected	*Worst*	*Best*
Fixed assets	5000	5000	5000
Debtors	2000	2000	2000
Cash/(Overdraft)	500	(500)	1500
Net Assets	**7500**	**6500**	**8500**
Equity	5000	5000	5000
Profit & Loss	2500	1500	3500
Capital	**7000**	**6500**	**8500**

Calculation of the individual balance sheet figures should be fairly obvious. But, let us consider the worst case cash balance as an example:

Cash inflow from Sales	£	2,000 (being 50% of Sales)
Cash outflow for expenses		−4,500
Cash inflow from opening debtors		1,500
Opening cash balance		500
End cash balance		−500

In practical budgeting, there may be uncertainty concerning a large number of factors within the budget, and sensitivity analysis may consist of a series of complex 'what if?' enquires – reworking the budget, on the basis of a range of different scenarios. In large organisations with complicated budgets, such exercises may be very demanding. In the pre-computer era, the relevant calculations were all carried out manually. This could be a time-consuming and error-prone exercise.

Computer spreadsheets have made the task much easier. However, the spreadsheet has to be designed carefully in order to facilitate sensitivity analysis exercises. A well-designed spreadsheet allows a single correction (on a unit price or an hourly wage rate) to update the whole budget. Spreadsheet modelling is one of the most critical of the practical skills required by management accountants.

5.10   Zero-based budgeting

Certain approaches to the construction of budgets have been developed in recent years. In this and the following sections, we will consider three of these: zero based budgeting (ZBB), programme-planning budgeting systems (PPBS) and activity-based budgeting (ABB). These three methods have one thing in common – they place an emphasis on the outputs of the process being budgeted for. They all tend to start from the results that the budget is intended to achieve and work backwards to the resources needed to achieve those results, the reverse of more traditional budgeting practices. In the modern context, the process of establishing a budget is an intelligent exercise in business planning wherein alternative means of achieving given objectives are identified and evaluated.

ZBB, PPBS and ABB are probably most applicable to costs which contain a substantial discretionary element, and as such they are most commonly encountered in service departments of commercial operations, the public sector and the not-for-profit sector.

 Discretionary cost: A cost whose amount within a time period is determined by a decision taken by the appropriate budget holder. Marketing, research and training are generally regarded as discretionary costs. Control of discretionary costs is through the budgeting process.

Like all budgeting techniques, ZBB is designed to be used in setting levels of *future* expenditures. As all cost-reduction techniques must, by definition, relate to the reduction of future costs (past costs being sunk), it follows that cost-reduction programmes and budgeting procedures are inextricably entwined. The CIMA *Official Terminology* defines zero-based/priority-based budgeting as:

Zero-based/priority-based budgeting: Method of budgeting that requires all costs to be specifically justified by the benefits to be expected.

This approach is particularly pertinent in public sector organisations, where funds are determined by tax revenues and government grants and allocations, that is, the income of the organisation is exogenously set. The aim of the fundholder is to achieve the best service levels possible within the given budget.

In traditional budgeting, *existing* expenditure levels form the baseline for discussions about future expenditure. Implicit in the traditional approach is an assumption and acceptance that current expenditure is adding value to the customer, and the focus of its attention is simply the justification of any proposed *increases* in that expenditure – it therefore adopts an incremental philosophy to budgeting. The rejection of this baseline as a starting point is what gives ZBB its name. An incremental approach is most likely to be applied to discretionary costs, as it is these costs that have no demonstrable relationship with volume or activity measures. The ZBB approach requires *all* activities to be justified and prioritised before the decision to devote resources to particular ones is taken.

All activities are subjected to the most basic scrutiny, and answers sought to such fundamental question as:

(a) Should the activity be undertaken at all?
(b) If the company undertakes the activity, how *much* should be done and how *well* should it be done (e.g. should an economy or a deluxe service level be provided)?
(c) How should the activity be performed – in-house or subcontract?
(d) How much would the various alternative levels of service and provision cost?

In order to answer these questions, all existing and potential organisational activities must be described and evaluated in a series of 'decision packages', giving the following four-step process to a ZBB exercise:

1. Determine the activities that are to be used as the object of decision packages – the provision of home support for the elderly or provision of catering facilities for the workforce, for example – and identify the manager responsible for each activity.
2. Request the managers identified in (1) above to prepare a number of alternative decision packages for those individual activities for which they are responsible. (At least three packages are normally requested: one that sets out what could be delivered with funding maintained at the *current* level; one for a *reduced* level of funding, e.g. 80 per cent of the current level; and one for an enhanced level of funding, e.g. 120 per cent of the current level.)
3. Rank the decision packages in order of their contribution towards the organisation's objectives.
4. Fund the decision packages according to the ranking established under (3) above until the available funds are exhausted.

5.10.1 Advantages of ZBB

The following advantages are claimed for ZBB:

(i) It avoids the complacency inherent in the traditional incremental approach, where it is simply assumed that future activities will be very similar to current ones.
(ii) ZBB encourages a questioning approach, by focusing attention not only on the cost of an activity, but also on the benefits it provides, as the relative benefits of different types and levels of expenditure. Forcing managers to articulate benefits encourages them to think clearly about their activities.
(iii) Preparation of the decision packages will normally require the involvement of many employees, and thus provides an opportunity for their view to be considered. This involvement may produce useful ideas, and promote job satisfaction among the wider staff.

5.10.2 Disadvantages of ZBB

The following disadvantages of ZBB need to be pointed out:

(i) The work involved in the creation of decision packages, and their subsequent ranking by top management, is very considerable, and has given rise to the cynical description of the process as 'Xerox-based budgeting'.

(ii) The ranking process is inherently difficult, as value judgements are inevitable. This is a particular problem in public sector bodies, where choices between very disparate programmes must often be made: for example, it would be extremely difficult to formulate criteria that would allow an unambiguous ranking when decision packages related to public health must be measured against those relating to law and order. Nevertheless, such rankings are made, explicitly or implicitly, whatever funds allocation system is used; bringing the allocation problems into the open could be viewed as an advantage rather than a disadvantage of ZBB. However, without clear and explicit ranking criteria, the human brain finds ranking difficult. If 'a' is preferred to 'b', and 'b' is preferred to 'c', it should follow that 'a' is preferred to 'c'. Unfortunately, experiments have shown that humans are often unable to produce such logical progressions when faced with a large number of choices.

(iii) In applying ZBB, 'activities' may continue to be identified with traditional functional departments, rather than cross-functional activities, and thus distract the attention of management from the real cost-reduction issues. For example, in discussing value-added and non-value-added activities above, it was argued that the costs incurred in a warranty department are largely a function of the reliability of products, which itself is a function of actions and decisions taken elsewhere. If the warranty department is treated as an activity under ZBB, the focus of the decision packages is likely to be on providing the same level of customer service at reduced cost, or enhancing the level of customer service for the same cost. The main driver behind the department's cost – product reliability – may remain unaddressed in ZBB, as it is with the blanket cut approach.

5.10.3   ZBB in practice

ZBB has been adopted more widely in the public sector than the private, although examples of organisations regularly adopting a full ZBB approach are rare. Full-scale ZBB is so resource-intensive that critics claim that its advantages are outweighed by its implementation costs. However, it is not necessary to apply ZBB to the whole of an organisation; benefits can be gained from its application to specific areas. For example, in the public sector, a decision could be made regarding the overall size of the childcare budget, and ZBB could be applied to allocate resources within that particular field; similarly, in a business organisation, ZBB could be applied to individual divisions on a rotational basis. This selective application ensures that a thorough reappraisal of activities is undertaken regularly, but not so regularly that the process itself is a major drain on organisational resources.

Notwithstanding the criticisms, the main plank of the ZBB approach – the rejection of past budgets as a planning baseline – is being increasingly accepted. Two surveys of UK local authorities – the first undertaken in 1983 and the second in 1988 – showed the use of the approach increasing from 48 to 54 per cent over the period.

5.11   Programme-planning budgeting systems

Programme-planning budgeting systems (PPBS) – a well-understood short title, in the absence of the acronym, is *programme budgeting* – is used quite widely in the public sector and not-for-profit organisation to avoid excessive costs and to ensure that expenditure is focused on programmes and activities that generate the most beneficial results.

As we have seen, traditional budgeting systems, whether in the public or the private sector, are heavily *input*-oriented, with the main emphasis on detailed financial controls. They also lean towards existing organisational units such as departments or divisions. In contrast, PPBS is expressed in terms of *programmes* (functional groups of activities with a common objective), rather than along traditional subdivisional lines, and is *output*- and *objective*-oriented, focusing on *end* items – the ultimate output of services of the organisation – rather than specific inputs. This form of budget structure has one obvious advantage, namely the ease with which it identifies the budget appropriations with the organisations's objectives, thus facilitating a more rational allocation of resources.

The steps involved in PPBS can be simply (if rather simplistically) stated:

1. specify the objectives of the various programmes;
2. measure the output in terms of the objectives;
3. determine the total costs of the programmes for several future periods;
4. analyse alternatives, and go for those with the greatest cost–benefit in terms of the objectives;
5. systematically implement the selected alternatives.

Some explanation of these steps is necessary. Effectiveness can be judged only against pre-determined benchmarks set by the organisation. Yet the activities performed by public sector and not-for-profit organisations are often difficult to measure in a tangible way, and can take several years to be measurable, while requiring the annual funding of the related programmes; multiple measures will often be required to overcome these difficulties. Many programmes will also have multiple results, and a choice must usually be made regarding the relative weights attached to them. Further, there will often be questions regarding the legitimacy of causal relationships when measuring these results: particular outcomes could be brought about by the actions of more than one programme, given the nature of public sector and not-for-profit organisations and their objectives.

On a more positive note, one feature of PPBS that should be particularly beneficial is that managers making budget requests are expected to be able to state clearly what would happen if their requests were cut by, say, 10 per cent. Thus the director of leisure services in a local authority should be in a position to say that such a cut would reduce the hours that a swimming pool could open, for example, or require that the grass in public parks be cut every 10 days instead of once a week. This feature of PPBS is, in its result, somewhat similar to ZBB, since different levels of service are associated with each level of requested funding. The interest in PPBS probably owes much to an increasing public demand for accountability by public and other not-for-profit organisations: taxpayers appear to have become dissatisfied with the performance of central and local government agencies; and donors to charitable causes have expressed concern about the proportion of contributed funds devoted to administrative expenses. PPBS specifies goals clearly, and allows people to see where their money is going and, eventually, to see whether or not it is spent *effectively*.

Exercise

The Alpha Sufferers Group is a national charity offering support to sufferers and funding medical research. You have been invited to attend a trustees' meeting at which the following report on this year's performance and next year's annual budget will be discussed. No further supporting information is provided for the trustees. The trustees have used an incremental approach to determine the budget.

The treasurer has heard of 'PPBS' and wonders if it would be useful in the their not-for-profit organisation.

Criticise the current method of budgeting and explain the application (give specific examples) and possible advantages of PPBS to such an organisation.

| | 20X3 | | 20X4 | |
	Budget £	Actual £	Budget £	Actual £
Income				
Subscriptions	20,000	18,000	20,000	
Donations received	160,000	200,000	220,000	
Fund-raising	500,000	440,000	484,000	
	680,000	658,000	724,000	
Expenditure				
Employees	60,000	60,000	60,000	
Premises	8,000	8,000	8,000	
Office expenses	28,000	33,000	30,000	
Administration	30,000	42,000	40,000	
Research	300,000	320,000	350,000	
Printing	25,000	30,000	25,000	
Room rental	15,000	12,000	15,000	
Donations made	200,000	230,000	260,000	
	666,000	735,000	788,000	
Excess of income over expenditure	14,000	77,000	(64,000)	

 Solution

The approach used to construct the budget is the 'traditional' approach to budgeting: looking at items line by line' and for a period of 1 year only. Presumably, the budget for the coming year was set by taking last year's actual figures and 'adding or subtracting' a bit to reflect expectations or intentions, and to use up the last year's 'unexpected' surplus of income over expenses.

The major criticisms of this approach in such a not-for-profit organisation are:

1. The emphasis is on annual figures, yet the activities of the charity (support and research) extend over a much longer time period.
2. There is no information in the budget about planned or actual achievements, such as the number of sufferer contacted and helped, the level of awareness of the condition, or increased knowledge of cause or treatment. All that is shown is whether the levels of expenditure were as authorised, and if income targets were achieved.
3. There has been no attempt to identify the costs of the different activities. For example, if one objective and activity is to put sufferers in touch with each other, then that would incur costs from several categories – employees, premises, office, administration, printing and so on. But it is impossible to tell from the figures presented how much was spent, or authorised, in achieving that individual objective.
4. There is no evidence that resources (cash, employee time, etc.) are being used in the most productive way. Indeed, there is no information at all as to how efficiently or effectively resources are being used.

A PPBS would overcome these problems with the traditional approach, because the emphasis would be on programmes and activities and how best to use resources to achieve the overall effectiveness of the charity in the medium and long term.

Application of PPBS

The trustees must undertake the following steps:

1. Review the charity's long-term objectives – for example, establish likely causes of the condition, put sufferers in touch with each other and so on.
2. Specify the activities and programmes necessary to achieve the overall objectives; for example, offer research grants to universities, fund a laboratory, maintain a database of sufferers, organise regional meetings and social events, distribute a regular newsletter or magazine and so on.
3. Evaluate the alternative activities and programmes in terms of both costs and likely benefits, that is, specify costs of putting sufferers in contact with each other via a newsletter and so on.
4. Select the most appropriate programmes.
5. Analyse the programmes selected, asking such questions as 'if we reduce the resources allocated to this programme by x per cent, what will happen to the level of achievement of objectives?'

Advantages of PPBS

By changing to a PPBS approach to budgeting, and thus taking a longer view than just 1 year, the trustees should be in a much better position to make informed decisions about the optimal use of their resources to achieve their clearly defined and understood objectives.

5.12 Activity-based budgeting

In recent years, a body of 'activity-based techniques' (ABTs) has been developed. These include activity-based costing, activity-based management (explored in Chapter 8) and activity-based budgeting (ABB). The logical thrust behind all ABTs is that cost control and management should focus on the outputs of a process rather than on the inputs to that process.

ABT's are, arguably, most applicable to service-sector operations, the public sector, the not-for-profit sector and indirect costs in a manufacturing environment.

The traditional approach to budgeting presents costs under functional headings, that is, costs are presented in a manner that emphasises their nature. Thus, the traditionally arranged budget for a local authority public cleansing department over a given period might appear as follows:

Item of cost	£
Wages	140,000
Materials	28,000
Vehicle hire	35,000
Equipment hire	18,000
Total	221,000

The weakness of this approach is that it gives little indication of the link between the level of activity of the department and the cost incurred. The budget might be restated as an activity-based budget as follows:

Activity	£	Number of activities
Street sweeping	84,000	4,000
School cleaning	68,000	800
Park cleaning	39,000	130
Graffiti removal	30,000	150
	221,000	

This approach provides a clear framework for understanding the link between costs and the level of activity. Using the traditional approach, many of the costs listed under traditional functional headings might simply be considered 'fixed'. However, research often shows that, in the long run, few costs really are fixed. If one can identify appropriate 'cost drivers', then a very high proportion of costs reveal themselves to be variable.

For example, if the department is instructed to increase the frequency of street sweeping by 25 per cent then this will increase the budgeted number of street sweepings (the 'cost driver') from 4,000 to 5,000. A single street-sweeping activity appears to cost £21 (i.e. £84,000 costs divided by 4,000 street sweepings); therefore, if the number of street sweepings rises from 4,000 to 5,000, then one might expect costs to increase by £21,000.

Another example is in the review of capacity utilisation. If it is known that the resources devoted to street sweeping have a capacity of 4,800 sweepings and only 4,000 sweepings are being budgeted for, then one might consider the possibility of reducing the capacity in some way.

Of course, ABBs and traditional budgets are not mutually exclusive. The two can be prepared in parallel or they can be integrated.

5.13 Efficiency and effectiveness in the not-for-profit sector

The not-for-profit (NFP) sector incorporates a wide range of operations including central government, local authorities, charitable trusts and executive agencies. The central thing about such operations is that they are not primarily motivated by a desire to make profit.

The ultimate objective of a commercial business is to generate a profit for its owners. Such a business may take a short or long-term view of the manner in which it wishes to do this. There are often alternative routes available which are capable of achieving this objective and management has to choose between them. However, there is a clear primary objective from which subsidiary objectives may be derived.

The objectives of NFP organisations may be partly legislated for, partly constitutional and partly political. For example, the Driver and Vehicle Licensing Agency (based at Swansea, UK) is charged with keeping records of vehicle registration and issuing driving licenses and road tax disks to motorists. This is a legal obligation. Mencap (a British Charity) has an obligation to act in order to provide assistance for the mentally handicapped written into its constitution.

Sunderland City Council has an obligation to run local schools – but has a wide measure of discretion over how it does this. It can spend money on salaries for teachers or it can switch some of that money into acquiring IT systems and making greater use of Computer Assisted Learning. It can provide teaching of classical Greek or it can reinforce its sports provision. The relevant choices the Council makes are determined by a political process. Parties contesting local elections will include their spending proposals in party manifestos and the voters will elect the Party with the most popular proposals.

However, practical problems with management in the NFP sector include the following:

- objectives may be vague or poorly understood;
- objectives may change regularly over time;
- radically different means may be available to achieve given objectives.

A further consideration is that the relationship between 'objectives' and 'means' is often poorly understood. For example, one public objective is 'to contain street crime within limits considered to be acceptable'. One means of achieving that objective is through the use of traditional police foot patrols. In fact, police foot patrols may be a poor method of containing many forms of street crime. The use of police response units using fast cars is much more cost effective. As soon as a crime is detected by video surveillance or a report from the public, the police can be on the scene quickly. A police officer in a fast car can cover much more ground than an officer on foot. That said, regular police foot patrols may make the public feel more relaxed as they go about their daily business.

However, many local politicians will advocate the need to 'have more bobbies on the beat' in their manifestos. This reflects some lack of clarity over objectives. Is the objective of policing to contain crime or to make the public feel more comfortable? The two are not the same at all. Are police foot patrols a means to achieve an objective, or are they an objective in themselves?

In recent years, much of the discussion concerning NFP sector management has concerned the promotion of the twin concepts of 'efficiency' and 'effectiveness'.

5.13.1 Efficiency

Efficiency concerns making the maximum possible use of a given set of resources; that is, it involves a straight comparison of output and input, for example the total cost per kilometre of road resurfaced.

Many UK local authorities in the 1970s were judged to be making an inefficient use of the resources available to them. They undertook most of their activities (such as road resurfacing or refuse disposal) using large numbers of directly employed council staff. It was often found that these in-house operations cost far more to achieve given outputs than comparable private sector operations.

Financial management initiatives in the 1980s required local authorities to put many of their works programmes 'out to tender'. Private contractors may submit bids in order to undertake specific works for the local authorities. The current private finance initiatives involve continuing private sector participation in the maintenance and operation of facilities such as schools and prisons. For example, in the past a contractor may have built a school for a local authority and simply handed it over to the authority. The more modern approach might involve the contractor building the school and then leasing it to the authority. The contractor thus remains responsible for aspects of its maintenance and management after completion. The contractor will now have an incentive to carefully consider the trade-off between construction costs and operating costs. Possible economies in the construction phase may be associated with higher operating costs later on and the contractor now has in interest in both.

Experience over the last 20 years suggests that this process has generally improved efficiency and achieved greater 'value for money' in local authorities – although the concept is not without its critics.

5.13.2 Effectiveness

Effectiveness concerns finding the cheapest combination of means to achieve a given objective.

This concept is a little more difficult to handle than efficiency. An NFP organisation will normally have a number of stated objectives. For example, a public authority may have 'containing youth crime within acceptable levels' as one of its objectives. It has several means by which it may achieve this objective, including:

- providing 'school attendance officers' to ensure that children are not truanting from school (Education Department);
- providing leisure facilities in the form of sports grounds and youth clubs (Recreation Department);
- providing assistance for disadvantaged or problem families (Social Services Department);
- providing police patrols to arrest or deter young criminals (Police Department);
- providing Young Offenders Institutions at which young criminals may be detained (Prisons Department).

All of these departmental activities contribute to achievement of the objective. The problem is to find the optimum combination of spending for all of the departments together. Practical solutions to this problem lie at the core of budgeting and planning techniques such as ZBB and PPBS.

An aggressive policy of arresting and detaining young criminals may achieve the required objective – but at high cost. Imprisoning a criminal is a very expensive 'last resort' and may turn a marginal criminal into a habitual one. Experience suggests that much crime can be deterred by less aggressive methods. A high proportion of crime is committed by young men in the 13–18 age group. Ensuring that children all attend school regularly and that adequate youth recreational facilities are available may address 'the causes of crime'.

An insensitive financial cut back in one area (e.g. making a school attendance officer redundant) can have a high cost impact in other areas when truanting schoolchildren commit petty crime. The key to effectiveness is in finding an optimum pattern of spending to achieve a given objective.

Finding that optimum pattern will usually involve determining a programme of activities which cuts right across traditional departmental boundaries. The emphasis in modern public sector planning tends to be on outputs rather than inputs. It should be appreciated that the departments within an organisation may be efficient – but the organisation as a whole may be ineffective if the overall pattern of departmental activity has not been carefully planned. Conversely, an organisation may have detailed inefficiencies in its operation, but be effective nevertheless.

Effectiveness is, by its very nature, rather more difficult to measure than efficiency. However, it should be appreciated that performance in an NFP organisation is a function of both efficiency and effectiveness. Performance management and measurement have to take account of this.

5.14 Summary

In this chapter, we have explored the budgeting concept. It has been seen that the process of establishing a budget is an exercise in business planning wherein alternative courses of action are identified and evaluated. Once it has been adopted, the budget may be used as a tool of control and a benchmark against which performance may be evaluated.

Modern approaches to budgeting place an emphasis on finding cost effective means of achieving given objectives. The point of departure is to identify the objectives of the organisation and then determine the cheapest combination of resources that can achieve those objectives. Hence, the emphasis is on the outputs of the operation rather than on the inputs.

Self-test quiz

(1) Define the term 'budget' (Section 5.2.2).

(2) Distinguish between 'budgetary planning' and 'budgetary control' (Section 5.2.1).

(3) Distinguish between 'strategic planning' and 'operational planning' (Section 5.2.4).

(4) What is the difference between 'bottom-up' and 'top-down' budgeting (Section 5.3.2)?

(5) What is the 'principal budget factor' (Section 5.3.4)?

(6) List problems that may be encountered in using a spreadsheet system to prepare and operate the budget of a large organisation (Section 5.3.6).

(7) State the main differences likely to be encountered between budget profit and budget cash flow (Section 5.5).

(8) What advantages are claimed for the use of rolling budgets (Section 5.6)?

(9) Distinguish between an additive model and a multiplicative model in time series analysis (Section 5.8.3).

(10) What are the main factors that distinguish ZBB and PPBS from more traditional budgeting practices (Sections 5.10 and 5.11).

(11) Distinguish between efficiency and effectiveness in the not-for-profit sector (Section 5.13).

Revision Questions

5

? Question 1

1.1 AW plc is preparing its maintenance budget. The number of machine hours and maintenance costs for the past 6 months have been as follows:

Month	Machine hours	£
1	10,364	35,319
2	12,212	39,477
3	8,631	31,420
4	9,460	33,285
5	8,480	31,080
6	10,126	34,784

The budget cost allowance for an activity level of 9,340 machine hours, before any adjustment for price changes, is nearest to

(A) £21,000
(B) £30,200
(C) £33,000
(D) £34,300

1.2 M plc uses time series analysis and regression techniques to estimate future sales demand. Using these techniques, it has derived the following trend equation:

$$y = 10,000 + 4,200x$$

where y is the total sales units and x is the time period.

It has also derived the following seasonal variation index values for each of the quarters using the multiplicative (proportional) seasonal variation model:

Quarter	Index value
1	120
2	80
3	95
4	105

The total sales units that will be forecast for time period 33, which is the first quarter of years 9, are

(A) 138,720
(B) 148,720
(C) 176,320
(D) 178,320

1.3 Q limited used an incremental budgeting approach to setting its budgets for the year ending 30 June 2003.

The budget for the company's power costs was determined by analysing the past relationship between costs and activity levels and then adjusting for inflation of 6%.

The relationship between monthly cost and activity levels, before adjusting for the 6% inflation, was found to be:

$$y = £(14,000 + 0.0025x^2)$$

where y = total cost and x = machine hours.

In April 2003, the number of machine hours was 1,525 and the actual cost incurred was £16,423. The total power cost variance to be reported is nearest to

(A) £3,391 (A)
(B) £3,391 (F)
(C) £3,740 (F)
(D) £4,580 (F)

1.4 H Limited uses a combination of regression analysis and time series analysis to predict its future sales volumes. An analysis of past data has shown that the underlying trend of the company's sales is well represented by the formula:

$$y = 100x + 2,400$$

where y is the total sales units for a period and x is the quarterly period number.

The seasonal variation index values based on the same past data is:

Quarter 1	105%
Quarter 2	96%
Quarter 3	90%
Quarter 4	109%

The increase in budgeted sales volumes between quarter 3 and quarter 4 next year, which are periods 17 and 18, will be

(A) 100 units
(B) 119 units
(C) 432 units
(D) 888 units   **(Total marks = 20)**

Question 2

You are given the following information about a company's costs in the past two quarters.

	Q_1	Q_2
Production (units)	10,000	15,000
Sales (units)	9,000	15,000
Costs	£'000	£'000
Direct material		
A	50	75
B	40	60
Production labour	180	230
Factory overheads	80	95
Depreciation	14	14
Administration	30	30
Selling expenses	29	35

For accounting purpose, the company values inventory of units at a constant standard cost. In quarter 3:

- Sales and production will be 18,000 units.
- Material A will rise in price by 20% relative to earlier quarters.
- Production wages will rise by 12.5% relative to earlier quarters.
- The selling price per unit will remain constant at £40.
- Expenses are all paid in the month in which they are incurred.
- Sales are all on 2 month's credit terms. Seventy per cent sales are paid for on the due date while the remaining 30% are paid for 1 month after the due date.

Requirements
(a) Prepare a budget profit statement for quarter 3. **(12 marks)**
(b) Prepare a budget cash-flow statement for quarter 3. **(13 marks)**
(Total marks = 25)

Question 3

R plc is an engineering company that repairs machinery and manufactures replacement parts for machinery used in the building industry. There are a number of different departments in the company including a foundry, a grinding department, a milling department and a general machining department. R plc prepared its budget for the year ending 31 December 2003 using an incremental budgeting system.

The budget is set centrally and is then communicated to each of the managers who have responsibility for achieving their respective targets. The following report has been produced for the general machining department for October 2003:

	Budget	Actual	Variance
Number of machine hours	9,000	11,320	2,320 (F)
	$	$	$
Cleaning materials	1,350	1,740	390 (A)
Steel	45,000	56,000	11,000 (A)
Other direct materials	450	700	250 (A)
Direct labour	29,000	32,400	3,400 (A)
Production overheads	30,000	42,600	12,600 (A)
Total	105,800	133,440	27,640 (A)

The Manager of the general machining department has received a memo from the Financial Controller requiring him to explain the serious overspending within his department.

The Manager has sought your help and, after some discussion, you have ascertained the following:

- The cleaning materials, steel and other direct materials vary in proportion to the number of machine hours.
- The budgeted direct labour costs include fixed salary costs of $4,250; the balance is variable in proportion to the number of machine hours.
- The production overhead costs include a variable cost that is constant per machine hour at all activity levels, and a stepped fixed cost which changes when the activity level exceeds 10,000 machine hours. A further analysis of this cost is shown below:

Activity (machine hours)	3,000	7,000	14,000
Costs ($)	13,500	24,500	45,800

Requirements

(a) Prepare a revised budgetary control statement using the additional information that you have obtained from the Manager of the general machining department. **(10 marks)**

(b) (i) Explain the differences between an incremental budgeting system and a zero-based budgeting system. **(4 marks)**

   (ii) Explain why R plc and similar organisations would find it difficult to introduce a system of zero-based budgeting. **(4 marks)**

(c) Explain the benefits of involving the managers of R plc in the budget setting process, rather than setting the budget centrally as is R plc's current policy. **(7 marks)**

(Total = 25 marks)

Question 4

Y plc is currently preparing its budgets for the year ending 30 September 20X1.

The sales and production budgets have been completed and an extract from them is shown below.

	Production units	Sales units	Sales value
	£'000	£'000	£'000
January	900	1,000	50,000
February	850	800	40,000
March	1,000	900	45,000
April	1,200	1,100	55,000
May	1,250	1,300	65,000
June	1,175	1,200	60,000
July	1,100	1,150	57,500
August	*	1,050	52,500

* To be determined

Budgeted production costs are:

	£/unit
Direct materials	14
Direct labour	12
Variable overhead	6
Fixed overhead*	8
Production cost	40

*Fixed overheads are absorbed on a unit basis assuming a normal production level of 14 m units per year.

Direct materials are purchased in the month of usage and, where settlement discounts are available, Y plc's policy is to pay suppliers so as to receive these discounts. It is expected that 60% of Y plc's material costs will be received from suppliers who offer a 2% discount for payment in the month of purchase. Other material suppliers are to be paid in the month following purchase.

Direct labour costs are paid 75% in the month in which they are incurred, and 25% in the following month.

Variable overhead costs are paid in the month in which they are incurred.

Fixed overhead costs include £16m depreciation. Fixed overhead expenditure accrues at a constant rate throughout the year and is paid 40% in the month in which it is incurred and 60% in the following month.

In addition to production costs, Y plc expects to incur administration overhead costs of £500,000 per month and selling overhead costs of 2% of sales value. These costs are to be paid in the month in which they are incurred.

Y plc's customers are expected to pay for items as follows:

- in the month of sale   20%
- in the month after sale   55%
- in the month 2 months after sale   15%
- in the month 3 months after sale   5%

Customers paying in the month of sale are given 1% discount. Five per cent of sales are expected to be bad debts.

In addition to the above, Y plc expects that

- new machinery is to be acquired on 1 February 20X1, costing £15m, this is to be paid for in May 20X1;
- corporation tax of £10m will be payable in June 20X1;
- a dividend of £7.5 m will be paid to shareholders in July 20X1;
- the bank balance at 1 April 20X1 will be £14.5 m.

Requirements

(a) Prepare Y plc's cash budget for the period April–July 20X1, showing clearly the receipts, payments and resulting balances for each month separately. **(20 marks)**

(b) Use your answer to part (a) to explain clearly:
  (i)   feed-forward control
  (ii) feedback control. **(5 marks)**

(Total marks = 25)

Question 5

PMF plc is a long-established public transport operator that provides a commuter transit link between an airport and the centre of a large city.

The following data has been taken from the sales records of PMF plc for the last 2 years:

Quarter	Number of passengers carried	
	Year 1	*Year 2*
1	15,620	34,100
2	15,640	29,920
3	16,950	29,550
4	34,840	56,680

The trend equation for the number of passengers carried has been found to be

$$x = 10,000 + 4,200q$$

where x = number of passengers carried per quarter and
  q = time period (year 1 quarter 1: $q = 1$)
   (year 1 quarter 2: $q = 2$)
   (year 2 quarter 1: $q = 5$)

Based on data collected over the last 2 years, PMF plc has found that its quarterly costs have the following relationships with the number of passengers carried:

Cost item	Relationship
Premises costs	$y = 260,000$
Premises staff	$y = 65,000 + 0.5x$
Power	$y = 13,000 + 4x$
Transit staff	$y = 32,000 + 3x$
Other	$y = 9,100 + x$

where y = the cost per quarter (£), and x = number of passengers per quarter.

Requirements

(a) Using the trend equation for the number of passengers carried and the multiplicative (proportional) time series model, determine the expected number of passengers to be carried in the third quarter of year 3. **(7 marks)**

(b) Explain why you think that the equation for the Transit staff cost is in the form $y = 32,000 + 3x$. **(3 marks)**

(c) Using your answer to part (a) and the cost relationship equations, calculate for each cost item and in total, the costs expected to be incurred in the third quarter of year 3. **(3 marks)**

(d) Explain briefly why there may be differences between the actual data for the third quarter of year 3 and the values you have predicted. **(5 marks)**

(e) Prepare a report, addressed to the Board of Directors of PMF plc, that briefly explains the following in the context of measuring the *effectiveness* of the transport services:
  • why the company should consider the use of non-financial performance measures;
  • three non-financial performance measures that could be used. **(7 marks)**

(Total marks = 25)

Question 6

Nossex County Council (NCC) is responsible for the normal range of services associated with a major local authority. NCC is organised into departments each responsible for a particular activity, for example education, social services, parks and gardens and so on. Each department has an annual budget that is used in both the planning and control of activities.

After its budgets for 20X4/X5 had been approved by NCC's finance committee, it is found that due to government restrictions on the level of NCC's council tax, total expenditure will have to be reduced to a level 8% below that originally planned for.

Shortly after receiving news of this, NCC's Finance Committee Chairman (councillor Ron Scroggs) makes the following statement during the course of an interview on Radio Nossex:

> We do not like what has happened but we shall have to make the best of things. It seems to me that the fairest thing to do is to cut back the present 20X4/X5 budget for each department by 8%. In this manner the misery will be spread evenly and everyone will suffer the same. The details of how this cut back will affect particular services can be left to the individual departmental heads to decide.

Requirements

In your capacity as chief executive of NCC write a report for NCC's Finance Committee on the situation explaining why you agree or disagree with the approach that Scroggs advocated in the radio interview.   **(25 marks)**

 Question 7

MNO Ltd manufactures a product known as the Unit. A large number of other companies also manufacture the Unit and the market price of the Unit is forecast to be £210 during 20X1. Market demand for the Unit is highest towards the end of the year. Customers prefer to place orders with manufacturers who are able to deliver Units immediately from their inventory.

A summarised version of MNO's balance sheet at 31 December 20X0 is shown below.

Summarised balance sheet of MNO Ltd as at 31 December 20X0

	£
Plant and equipment (net)	780,000
Inventory	80,000
Debtors	125,000
Cash at bank	30,000
Creditors	(20,000)
Net assets	995,000
Share capital	100,000
16% loan from shareholders	500,000
Retained earnings	395,000
Capital	995,000

During 20X1, MNO is committed to

- repaying £125,000 of the 16% loan from shareholders in June and paying £40,000 interest on the loan in June and £30,000 interest in December;
- paying interest on its bank overdraft at a rate of 5% per quarter on the balance outstanding on the last day of each quarter;
- incurring fixed overhead costs (excluding depreciation) at a rate of £200,000 per quarter (all such costs are paid in the month in which they are incurred);

- incurring variable production costs at a rate of £100 per Unit (75% of these costs are paid for in the month they are incurred and 25% in the month after they are incurred).

  MNO's accounting policies include

- providing for depreciation at a rate of 5% per quarter on the net book value (i.e. cost less depreciation) of plant and equipment outstanding at the end of each quarter;
- valuing inventory (or 'stock') at a standard production cost of £160 per unit.

In early January 20X1, MNO's executives meet in order to discuss commercial strategy for the coming year. The sales director advocates an aggressive strategy (Strategy 1), involving new investment, high inventories and an expansion of sales. The finance director advocates a conservative strategy (Strategy 2) involving no new investment, minimising inventories and the adoption of a 'tight' credit policy on sales.

Relevant details concerning the two strategies are described in the following section.

Strategy 1

- In January, acquire new production equipment at a cost of £360,000.
- Offer 60% (by sales value) of customers, 2 months' credit and require the rest to pay immediately.
- Make sales at a rate of 900 units per month (quarters 1 and 2) and 1,300 units per month (quarters 3 and 4).
- Produce at the rate of 1,200 units per month (quarters 1 and 2) and 1,100 units per month (quarters 3 and 4).
- A review of outstanding debts at the end of 20X1 is forecast to result in a bad debt writeoff totalling £64,000 (all relating to quarter 4 sales).

Strategy 2

- Continue the existing credit policy of offering 50% (by sales value) of customers 1 month's credit and require the rest to pay immediately.
- Make sales at a rate of 800 units per month (quarters 1 and 2), 1,000 units per month (quarter 3) and 1,100 units per month (quarter 4).
- Produce at a rate of 850 units per month (quarters 1 and 2) and 1,000 units per month (quarters 3 and 4).
- A review of outstanding debts at the end of 20X1 is forecast to result in a bad debt writeoff totalling £10,000 (all relating to quarter 4 sales).

Requirements

(a) Prepare a cash-flow budget and a profit budget for MNO on the basis of Strategy 1. The budgets should be split into quarterly intervals showing cash-flow and profit forecasts for each individual quarter. **(20 marks)**

(b) Prepare a cash-flow budget and a profit budget for MNO on the basis of Strategy 2. The budgets should be split into quarterly intervals showing cash flow and profit forecast for each individual quarter. **(20 marks)**

(c) Compare and contrast the two sets of budgets you have prepared in answer to requirements (a) and (b). Advise MNO's management on the relative merits of the two alternative strategies. Advise which strategy should be adopted. **(10 marks)**

(Total marks = 50)

Note: In preparing your answer you may assume that cash is held on current account where it earns no interest and any cash deficit requirement is satisfied by drawing down on the overdraft facility.

Question 8

'Traditional budgeting systems are incremental in nature and tend of focus on cost centers. Activity-based budgeting links business planning to the budgeting process with a view to finding the most cost-effective means of achieving objectives.'

Requirements

(a) Explain the weaknesses of an incremental budgeting system.   **(5 marks)**

(b) Describe the main features of an activity-based budgeting system and comment on the advantages claimed for its use.   **(10 marks)**

(Total marks = 15)

Solutions to Revision Questions

Solution 1

1.1

Use high and low points to determine the cost behaviour pattern based on past data:

	Machine hours	£
High	12,212	39,477
Low	8,480	31,080
Difference	3,732	8,397

$$\text{Variable cost per machine hour} = \frac{£8,397}{3,732} = £2.25$$

By substitution, the fixed cost is

£39,477 − (12,212 × £2.25) = £12,000

For an activity level of 9,340 machine hours, the budget cost allowance would be

£12,000 + (9,340 × £2.25) = £33,015

Therefore the answer is (C)

1.2

$x = 33$, so trend value is = 10,000 + (4,200 × 33) = 148,600
Seasonal variation index value = 120
Forecast sales units = 148,600 × 120% = 178,320

Therefore the answer is (D)

1.3

The budget cost allowance for 1,525 machine hours is

$$= £14,000 + 0.0025 \ (1,525^2)$$
$$= £14,000 + (0.0025 × 2,325,625)$$
$$= £14,000 + £5,814$$
$$= £19,814$$

Add 6% for inflation = £21,003
Thus the total variance is £16,423 − £21,003 = £4,580 (F)

Therefore the answer is (D)

1.4

Quarter 3 units $= [(100 \times 17) + 2,400] \times 90\% = 3,690$
Quarter 4 units $= [(100 \times 18) + 2,400] \times 109\% = 4,578$
Difference $= 888$

Therefore the answer is (D)

✓ Solution 2

- The question gives two sets of figures linked to alternative levels of output and sales. A simple linear regression approach can be used to determine the cost structure of the business and thus forecast costs for quarter 3.
- Note that some costs vary with production and some costs vary with sales.

Applying a linear regression approach to the figures supplied, the cost structure forecast for quarter 3 is as follows:

	Unit VC	Quarter FC
	£	£
Material A	6.00	
Material B	4.00	
Production labour	11.25	90,000
Factory overheads	3.00	50,000
Depreciation		14,000
Administration		30,000
Selling expenses	1.00	20,000
Total	25.25	204,000

(a) The budget profit statement for quarter 3 is:

	£	£
Sales revenue		720,000
Costs		
Materials	180,000	
Wages	292,500	
Factory overheads	104,000	
Depreciation	14,000	
Administration	30,000	
Selling expenses	38,000	
		658,500
Profit		61,500

(b) The budget cash-flow statement for quarter 3 is:

	£	£
Cash inflow:		
Q2 month 1		60,000
Q2 month 2		200,000
Q2 month 3		200,000
Q3 month 1		168,000
		628,000
Cash outflow		
Materials	180,000	
Wages	292,500	
Factory overheads	104,000	
Administration	30,000	
Selling expenses	38,000	
		644,500
Net cash flow		(16,500)

Seventy per cent of month 1 sales from Q_2 will be paid during Q_2. The other 30% of those sales will be paid in Q_3. Q_2 month 1 sales therefore give rise to a £60,000 cash inflow (i.e. 5,000 units $\times$ £40 $\times$ 30%) in Q_3. The same logic is applied to sales in later months.

 Solution 3

(a) Analyse budget cost of direct labour:

	$
9,000 hours total cost	29,000
Fixed cost	(4,250)
Therefore variable cost of 9,000 hours	24,750

$$\text{Variable cost per houre} = \frac{\$24,750}{9,000} = \$2.75$$

Therefore

Budget cost of 11,320 hours	$
Variable (11,320 $\times$ $2.75)	31,130
Fixed	4,250
	35,380

Use high/low technique to analyses production overheads (ignore 14,000-hour activity level to eliminate the effect of the step fixed cost):

	Hours	$
High	7,000	24,500
Low	3,000	13,500
Difference	4,000	11,000

$$\text{Variable cost} = \frac{\$11,000}{4,000}\text{hours} = \$2.75 \text{ per hour}$$

Variable cost of 14,000 hours = 14,000 $\times$ $2.75 = $38,500
Total cost of 14,000 hours = $45,800
Fixed cost (for activity levels above 10,000 hours) = $7,300

	Original budget	Flexed budget	Actual	Variance
Number of machine hours	9,000	11,320	11,320	
	$	$	$	$
Cleaning materials	1,350	1,698	1,740	42 (A)
Steel	45,000	56,600	56,000	600 (F)
Other direct materials	450	566	700	134 (A)
Direct labour	29,000	35,380	32,400	2,980 (F)
Production overheads	30,000	38,430	42,600	4,170 (A)
Totals	105,800	132,674	133,440	766 (A)

(b) (i) An incremental budgeting system is a system whereby budgets are prepared by adjusting the previous period's budget/actual values for expected changes in the level of activity and for expected price changes.

A zero-based budgeting system is a system whereby all proposed activities have to be justified. Once the activity itself has been justified, then the method of carrying out the activity needs to be considered and the chosen method justified on a cost benefit basis.

(ii) R plc is an engineering company that operates in the repairs and maintenance sector of engineering.

This type of business has difficulty in predicting the exact nature of its customer's requirements as this depends on their needs in response to machinery failures.

For R plc and similar organisations to introduce zero-based budgeting, assumptions would have to be made as to the exact nature of the customer requirements. If these assumptions were to differ significantly from the actual customer requirements, the budget would be invalid.

(c) The main benefits of involving managers in the budget-setting process include:

Goal congruence – the manager will see their organisational target as a personal target because, by their setting it, they believe it to be achievable;

Motivation – the manager will be motivated to achieve the target, because not to do so would be a personal failure;

Accuracy/detail – the manager will have the detailed knowledge to prepare a budget that accurately identifies the resource requirements needed to achieve the target set.

 Solution 4

(a) Cash budget

	April £'000	May £'000	June £'000	July £000
Receipts				
Sales	44,140	51,870	58,130	56,885
Payment				
Material	15,478	17,010	16,673	15,635
Labour	13,800	14,850	14,325	13,425
Variable overhead	7,200	7,500	7,050	6,600
Fixed overhead	8,000	8,000	8,000	8,000
Administrative overhead	500	500	500	500
Selling overhead	1,100	1,300	1,200	1,150
Machinery	–	15,000	–	–
Corporation tax	–	–	10,000	–
Dividend	–	–	–	7,500
	46,078	64,160	57,748	52,810
Balance b/f	14,500	12,562	272	654
Net cash movement	(1,938)	(12,290)	382	4,075
Balance c/f	12,562	272	654	4,729

Workings

	April £'000	May £'000	June £'000	July £'000
Direct material				
Purchases	16,800	17,500	16,450	15,400
Payment in month	9,878	10,290	9,673	9,055
1-month credit	5,600	6,720	7,000	6,580
	15,478	17,010	16,673	15,635
Direct labour				
Monthly cost	14,400	15,000	14,100	13,200
Payment in month	10,800	11,250	10,575	9,900
1 month in arrears	3,000	3,600	3,750	3,525
	13,800	14,850	14,325	13,425
Sales receipts				
20% in month (×99%)	10,890	12,870	11,880	11,385
55% in month after sale	24,750	30,250	35,750	33,000
15% 2 months after sale	6,000	6,750	8,250	9,750
5% 3 months after sale	2,500	2,000	2,250	2,750
	44,140	51,870	58,130	56,885

Each year	£'000
Fixed overhead	112,000
Less depreciation	16,000
Cash expense	96,000 = £8,000,000 per month

(b) (i) Feed-forward control occurs when, in compiling the budget, the cash flows predicted differ from those desired, resulting in the amendments to budgets or activities. Feed-forward is a proactive form of control, exercised before the event. For example, the capital expenditure on machinery might be deferred or financed differently to avoid the anticipated cash deficit in May.

(ii) Feedback control, on the other hand, is exercised after the activity has taken place, and involves comparing actual outcomes with those predicted in the budget. It is reactive control, and would result in an explanation being required should the cash expenditure on material in a given month differ by more than (say) 5% of budgeted value.

✓ Solution 5

(a) The trend values for quarter 3 of each year based upon the equation

$$X = 4,200q + 10,000$$

can be calculated as

Year 1 $(4,200 \times 3) + 10,000 = 22,600$ passengers
Year 2 $(4,200 \times 7) + 10,000 = 39,400$ passengers

This can be compared with the past data provided to establish the seasonal variation:

	Trend	Past data	%
Year 1	22,600	16,950	75
Year 2	39,400	29,550	75

Thus it seems that the quarter 3 values are 75% of their equivalent trend values.

The trend value for the third quarter of year 3, adjusted for the seasonal variation, will thus be

$$[(4,200 \times 11) + 10,000] \times 75\% = 42,150 \text{ passengers}$$

(b) The reason for the cost equation for the Transit staff being in the format shown is that it is a mixed cost, that is, it comprises a fixed element of £32,000 and a variable element of £3 for each passenger. This could be because the remuneration package provides for a fixed salary plus a bonus.

(c)

Cost item	Relationship	Cost
		£
Premises costs	$y = 260,000 + 0x$	260,000
Premises staff	$y = 65,000 + 0.5x$	86,075
Power	$y = 13,000 + 4x$	181,600
Transit staff	$y = 32,000 + 3x$	158,450
Other	$y = 9,100 + x$	51,250
		737,375

(d) There are a number of reasons why the actual data may differ from that predicted:

- The prediction of the number of passengers carried assumes that the underlying growth shown by the trend equation will continue into year 3.
- The prediction of the number of passengers carried assumes that the seasonal variation in the third quarter of year 3 will be the same as it was in the same quarter in previous years.
- The predicted costs are based on simple linear cost relationships that have probably been derived from past data using of linear regression analysis techniques on past data. In reality, costs rarely behave in a linear fashion, though this may be a reasonable approximation.
- Actual costs may be affected by a number of cost drivers other than, or in addition to, the number of passengers carried.
- The calculation does not consider the effects of price changes on the costs.

(e) | | **Report** |
| --- | --- |

To:	Board of Directors of PMF plc	*From:*	Management Accountant
Subject:	Non-financial performance measures	*Date:*	21 November 2001

Introduction

Further to our recent meeting, I have considered some of the non-financial performance measures that we may use in addition to our existing budgetary control procedures.

Findings

As a public transport operator, we operate in a service sector where the quality of the service we provide is paramount to our continued success. We should, therefore, focus on the needs of our customers and our employees to ensure that we continue to deliver the service required.

Among the measures that we can use to measure our effectiveness are

- the percentage of trains that arrive within 2 minutes of schedule;
- the percentage of trains that depart within 2 minutes of schedule;

- the percentage of trains cancelled in a period;
- the failure rate of our ticket machines;
- the failure rate of our ticketing gates;
- the failure rate of the escalators in our stations;
- the failure rate of our signaling system; and
- the number of injuries per thousand passengers carried.

> **Examiner's Note:**
> Candidates were required to identify any *three* suitable measures and briefly describe them.

Conclusion

These non-financial measures are as important as those that we currently use to control our costs and revenues. If we can improve our customers' perceptions of our performance, then we will continue to remain profitable and can improve still further in the future.

Signed: Management Accountant.

 Solution 6

- The critical thing to note here is that the approach advocated by Councillor Scroggs places an emphasis on 'inputs' to the process. It shows little awareness of outputs and objectives.
- The question invites you to discuss modern budgeting practices such as ZBB and PPBS.

From: Chief executive
To: Finance committee
Re: Budget savings

What the chairman is proposing is a course of action based on the incremental approach to budgeting. This approach seeks to determine budgets by taking past patterns of spending and using them as the basis for determining future patterns. For example, in establishing the budget for this year, one might take last year's budget and add or subtract an equal percentage to/from the spending of each department.

This approach is simple and avoids having to think too hard about what one is doing. It also avoids difficult political disputes by seeking to maintain an established *status quo* between spending departments.

However, the incremental approach to budgeting is essentially passive. It is generally considered to have various adverse features including the following:

- An 8% cut in the budget for parks and gardens may cause far less misery than a 5% cut in the budget for social services; blanket spending cuts can have very uneven effects in terms of the misery they cause.
- A given public objective (e.g. the welfare of old people) is best achieved by a carefully integrated pattern of spending within several departments (e.g. residential homes, meals on wheels, home helps and mobile libraries); unselective spending cuts in one area

TEH THEORY AND PRACTICE OF BUDGETING

(e.g. home helps) might cause substantial new requirements to be created in others (e.g. residential homes) if obligations are to be fulfilled.

- A selective rearrangement of spending may have far less impact on the standard of services than blanket cuts; for example, a reduction in police officer numbers might be partly offset by small increases in spending on 'traffic calming' measures and video surveillance in public areas.

The incremental approach to budgeting is not considered to be the most satisfactory available. A variety of proactive approaches to budget determination exists including PPBS and ZBB. It is suggested that these might be used to good effect on this occasion.

 ## Solution 7

- This question addresses many of the issues explored in this and the preceding two chapters. It can be worked through without the use of a computer spreadsheet, but it provides a good spreadsheet modelling exercise. If you are adept in the use of a spreadsheet, then you may be able to construct the required four budgets very quickly indeed.
- Note that the profit budget tends to follow on from the cash flow budget because of the calculation of overdraft interest. This suggest the sequence in which the budgets should be arranged.
- The two sets of budgets should be constructed in a manner that allows them to be readily compared.
- When comparing the two strategies, be aware that profitability is not the sole relevant measure of performance.

(a) MNO Ltd: cash-flow budget for 20X1, Strategy 1

	Q1 £	Q2 £	Q3 £	Q4 £	20X1 £
Opening cash balance	30,000	(435,540)	(623,217)	(459,393)	30,000
Customer receipts	465,200	567,000	718,200	819,000	2,569,400
Capital expenditure	(360,000)				(360,000)
Variable costs	(350,000)	(360,000)	(332,500)	(330,000)	(1,372,500)
Fixed overheads	(200,000)	(200,000)	(200,000)	(200,000)	(800,000)
Loan interest		(40,000)		(30,000)	(70,000)
Loan repayment		(125,000)			(125,000)
Cash flow	(444,800)	(158,000)	185,700	259,000	(158,100)
'Initial' closing balance	(414,800)	(593,540)	(437,517)	(200,393)	
Overdraft interest	(20,740)	(29,677)	(21,876)	(10,020)	(82,312)
'Final' closing balance	(435,540)	(623,217)	(459,393)	(210,413)	(210,412)

MNO Ltd: profit budget for 20X1, Strategy 1

	Q1 £	Q1 £	Q3 £	Q4 £	20X1 £
Sales	567,000	567,000	819,000	819,000	2,772,000
Opening stock	(80,000)	(224,000)	(368,000)	(272,000)	(80,000)
Variable costs	(360,000)	(360,000)	(330,000)	(330,000)	(1,380,000)
Fixed overheads	(200,000)	(200,000)	(200,000)	(200,000)	(800,000)
Depreciation	(57,000)	(54,150)	(51,443)	(48,870)	(211,463)
Closing stock	224,000	368,000	272,000	176,000	176,000
Loan interest	(20,000)	(20,000)	(15,000)	(15,000)	(70,000)
Overdraft interest	(20,740)	(29,677)	(21,876)	(10,020)	(82,312)
Bad debt write-off				(64,000)	(64,000)
Net profit	53,260	47,173	104,681	55,110	260,225

(b) Cash-flow budget of MNO Ltd for 20X1, Strategy 2

	Q1 £	Q2 £	Q3 £	Q4 £	20X1 £
Opening cash balance	30,000	121,250	5,250	118,000	30,000
Customer receipts	545,000	504,000	609,000	682,500	2,340,500
Capital expenditure					–
Variable costs	(253,750)	(255,000)	(296,250)	(300,000)	(1,105,000)
Fixed overheads	(200,000)	(200,000)	(200,000)	(200,000)	(800,000)
Loan interest		(40,000)		(30,000)	(70,000)
Loan repayment		(125,000)			(125,000)
Cash flow	91,250	(116,000)	112,750	152,500	(240,500)
'Initial' closing balance	121,250	5,250	118,000	270,500	
Overdraft interest	–	–	–	–	–
'Final' closing balance	121,250	5,250	118,000	270,500	270,500

Profit budget of MNO Ltd for 20X1, Strategy 2

	Q1 £	Q2 £	Q3 £	Q4 £	20X1 £
Sales	504,000	504,000	630,000	693,000	2,331,000
Opening stock	(80,000)	(104,000)	(128,000)	(128,000)	(80,000)
Variable costs	(255,000)	(255,000)	(300,000)	(300,000)	(1,110,000)
Fixed overheads	(200,000)	(200,000)	(200,000)	(200,000)	(800,000)
Depreciation	(39,000)	(37,050)	(35,198)	(33,438)	(144,685)
Closing stock	104,000	128,000	128,000	80,000	80,000
Loan interest	(20,000)	(20,000)	(15,000)	(15,000)	(70,000)
Overdraft interest	–	–	–	–	–
Bad debt write-off				(10,000)	(10,000)
Net profit	14,000	15,950	79,802	86,562	196,315

(c) The most conspicuous feature in comparing the two alternative strategies is that Strategy 1 yields about £60,000 more profit than Strategy 2. So, is Strategy 1 automatically preferable? The following observations are relevant in answering this question:

- Strategy 2 follows existing sales policies and the associated sales forecasts are, therefore, probably reliable; Strategy 1 follows new sales policies and the associated sales forecasts must incorporate estimates/assumptions about what will happen; the reliability of these estimates/assumptions may be uncertain and this makes Strategy 1 riskier than Strategy 2.
- Strategy 1 involves accumulating a £200,000 overdraft balance; this is a cause for some concern even though such a balance need not be a problem for a profitable company with an annual turnover approaching £3 m.
- Strategy 2 results in a cash surplus of £270,000 to be accumulated by the end of 20X1; this can be paid out to MNO's shareholders as dividends – thus reducing the capital employed in the business and without any adverse impact on its profitability.

Taking into account the above factors, it seems that Strategy 2 might be preferred under certain circumstances. Those circumstances might apply if the owners of MNO are anxious to follow a low-risk strategy and extract funds from the business.

Solution 8

(a) Incremental budgeting uses year 1 budget as the starting point for the preparation of year 2 budget. It is assumed that the basic structure of the old budget is acceptable and that adjustments will be made to allow for changes in volume, efficiency and price levels. The focus, therefore, tends to be on the existing use of resources rather than on identifying objectives and alternative strategies for the future budget period. It is argued that incremental budgeting does not question sufficiently the costs and benefits of operating a particular resource allocation structure.

Incremental budgeting may, therefore, be argued to have weaknesses in that:

- the resource allocation is not clearly linked to a business plan and the consideration of alternative means of achieving objectives;
- there is a tendency to constrain new high-priority activities;
- there is insufficient focus on efficiency and effectiveness and the alternative methods by which they may be achieved;
- it often leads to arbitrary cuts being made in order to meet overall financial targets;
- it tends not to lead to management commitment to the budget process.

(b) The main features and potential advantages of activity-based budgeting are:

 (i) The major focus is on the planning of resource allocation that aims at efficiency, effectiveness and continuous improvement. Features may include:
  - the impact of change from the present activity levels are made more apparent;
  - key processes and constraints are identified and resource requirements related thereto are quantified;
  - efforts are made to identify critical success factors and the performance indicators that are most relevant for such factors.
 (ii) Activities are seen as the key to effective planning and control.
 (iii) It is argued that activities consume resources and that efforts should be focused on the control of the cause of costs not the point of incidence.
 (iv) Costs are traced to activities with the creation of 'cost pools' that relate to an activity.
 (v) It is easier to eliminate non-value-adding activities.
 (vi) Focus may be on total quality management with emphasis on process control through identification of cost drivers.

Budgetary Control

Budgetary Control

6

6.1 Introduction

In the previous chapter we explored the basic concepts, approaches and techniques that are used in the establishment of budgets. In this chapter, we consider the manner in which budgets are used to control the operations of an organisation. Budgetary control is the practice of systematically comparing actual results achieved with those budgeted for. The results of this comparison are used to direct the attention of management to problems and opportunities through the 'principle of exception'. Broadly, those areas that perform to budget are considered satisfactory while those that depart from budget are identified and investigated. Where components of a budget relate to the responsibilities of individual executives, then budgetary control may act as a means of securing adherence of those executives to corporate objectives.

The practice of standard costing and variance analysis (considered in Chapters 2 and 3) provides the means by which a budgetary control report might be prepared.

The point of departure is to consider basic business control system theory and explore the use of that theory in the practice of budgetary control. We will then go on to consider practical aspects of budgetary control with particular emphasis on responsibility accounting and behavioural/motivational issues.

6.2   The Theory of Systems

A system is a set of related parts co-ordinated to accomplish a set of goals. In accountants' daily activities they will encounter constant references to a variety of systems such as a transportation system, a communication system, a reward system, a budgeting system or a stock control system. Any situation which involves the handling or manipulation of resources, be they human, financial or information, may be structured by way of a system to produce an output or goal.

6.3   System design

6.3.1   The characteristics and components of a system

There are a number of key characteristics and components of a system:

(a) inputs
(b) process
(c) outputs
(d) environment
(e) boundary.

We shall now consider each of these in turn.

(a) *Inputs.* Inputs may take the form of people, energy, materials, equipment, money or data. These inputs may be received individually or in combination and can originate from a number of diverse sources.

(b) *Process.* Some form of activity is carried out as a result of receiving input, with the aim of adding value to that input to produce an output. These processing activities may include assembling, machining, recording and so on.

(c) *Outputs.* Once processing is complete, the finished, processed product or service is passed out to the environment. This may involve the delivery of goods to a customer or the transmission of goods or information to a new system or subsystem.

(d) *Environment.* A system's environment is often defined as those external elements that have direct or indirect influence on the process and the elements of a system. Every system operates within the context of an environment and it interacts with the environment by receiving inputs from it and delivering outputs to it. For example, a manufacturing company will receive its raw materials from specific component suppliers, but when these components are processed they will be delivered to the customer. Business environment can be viewed as internal environment and external environment. Factors that fall within the boundaries of the organisation constitute internal environment, factors beyond the organisational boundaries form the external environment.

(e) *Boundary.* The systems boundary separates the system and its components from its environment. Systems boundaries may or may not be physical. However, sometimes boundaries are not easily identifiable. Whether physical or not, the system boundary defines and separates the components of a system from the environment and from any other systems within that environment.

6.3.2   Control systems

A control system is designed to facilitate the operation of a process through the reporting of information generated by the process and prompting appropriate changes to the inputs in response to appraisal of that information. The different ways in which information may be used to prompt changes in inputs to the process are the following.

Feedback control systems

Most budgetary control systems work on the feedback principle. Information on actual results experienced is obtained from the process and compared with control data (a plan, budget or standard). Deviations from the control data will usually prompt feedback in order to bring actual results back in line with plan. This is negative feedback – where action is prompted to return the process to its original planned course. For example, if costs are rising above budget then negative feedback will prompt managers to cut costs.

But a control system can work with positive feedback. In this case, feedback prompts actions to reinforce a deviation from plan, for example, if unit sales are rising above budget in some areas, then this may imply an opportunity and positive feedback will prompt attempts to increase unit sales still further.

Feedforward control systems

In some situations, feedback control is inappropriate. It involves acting 'after the event' to bring the process back to its planned course. This may be costly if things have gone badly wrong. By contrast, feedforward control works on the basis of forecast results.

For example, if *forecast* costs start to rise above budget then action may be prompted on the feedforward principle to prevent such a deviation from ever actually occurring. 'Target costing' (discussed in Chapter 8) is sometimes described as a system in feedforward control. A target rate of return is set for a product or project, and if it is forecast that this target is not going to be achieved, then action is prompted (by way of product re-engineering or other similar management initiative) in order to ensure that the target is achieved.

6.4 Feedback control loops and system operation

Control within budgetary control systems is conventionally exercised by feedback loops that gather information on past performance from the output side of a system, department or process, which is then used to govern future performance by adjusting the input side of the system.

The manner in which a feedback control loop might work in the context of a budgetary control system may be illustrated by the following diagram.

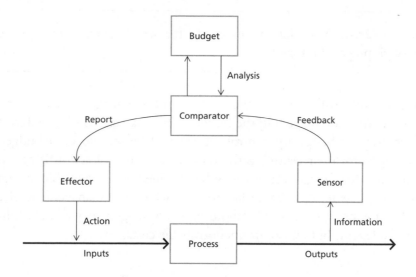

BUDGETARY CONTROL

The components of the control system illustrated are the following.

Sensor. Sensors are the measuring and recording devices of the system. In the context of budgetary control, the basic management accounting system acts as the sensor by collecting and reporting information on costs and revenues.

Comparator. This is the mechanism by which actual results are compared with plan. In the context of a budgetary control system, the exercise of preparing a monthly control report (commonly called operating statistics or something similar) is the comparator. The report seeks to reconcile budget with actual results through the calculation of variances. Reporting of those variances prompts actions intended to eliminate adverse variances or exploit favourable variances.

Effector. The usual effector is a manager or supervisor acting on the report containing the results of the comparison between actual and budget, and taking the actions required for adjustment to be made. An effector could also be an automatic process, such as an automated stock reordering system that checks stock levels and automatically reorders when the preset reorder quantity is reached.

The general subject of systems design is explored more fully in CIMA's Paper P4 – *Organisational Management and Information Systems.*

6.5 Budgetary control information

Budgetary control is achieved by comparing the actual results with the budget. The differences are calculated as variances and management action may be taken to investigate and correct the variances if necessary or appropriate.

- If costs are higher or revenues are lower than the budget, then the difference is an *adverse* variance.
- If costs are lower or revenues are higher than the budget, then the difference is a *favourable* variance.

6.5.1 Budget centres

The CIMA *Official Terminology* defines a budget centre as follows.

 Budget centre: A section of an entity for which control may be exercised through prepared budgets.

Each budget center will have its own budget and a manager will be responsible for managing the centre and controlling the budget. This manager is often referred to as the budget-holder. Regular budgetary control reports will be sent to each budget-holder so that they may monitor their centre's activities and take control action if necessary. Costs attributed to individual budget centres may be classified as 'controllable' or 'uncontrollable'. Controllable costs relate to those factors over which the management of the budget centre have direct control, for example labour hours. Managers may be held fully responsible for controllable costs but less so for uncontrollable costs.

The structure of budget centres that an organisation adopts will normally correspond to its own organisational structure. Thus each division, department or section will have its own budget. For example, an equipment manufacturer may be organised in the form of three operating divisions, each working from its own factory site:

(1) heavy equipment manufacture division;
(2) medium equipment manufacture division;
(3) light equipment manufacture division.

Each division will have its own budget for both costs and sales revenues. Not only is each division a budget centre, but it is also a 'responsibility centre' for the purposes of management accounting. The costs and revenues associated with the operations of each division will be collated and reported periodically for the purposes of comparison with budget. Responsibility centres are discussed more fully in Chapter 9.

It should be appreciated that an organisation might be organised on regional rather than functional lines – and there might be North, South and East regional divisions. In such a case both the budget and the responsibility centres would match the organisational structure; the general point being that budgetary control would follow the responsibility accounting principal. Each divisional budget would relate to a clearly defined organisational unit with its own manager. That manager would be held responsible for achieving the budget.

The individual divisional budgets could be split into subsidiary departmental budget. For example, the costs contained in the budget for (1) heavy equipment manufacture division could be split into budgets for

(1.1) Assembly line A
(1.2) Assembly line B
(1.3) Paint Shop.

Again, each of these is a budget centre and a responsibility centre – with actual costs incurred being periodically reported for each and compared with a budget. The departmental managers would be responsible for keeping departmental costs within budget.

Key issues to consider in the design and operation of budget centres include

- The budget centres should strictly match organisational units. Any departure from this breaches the responsibility accounting principal since no one manager is responsible for achieving a particular budget.
- The responsibility centres should strictly match the budget centres. Any departure from this means that the nature of the costs reported does not strictly match those being budgeted for. If some actual costs are being charged to one department but are in the budget of another, then the whole budgetary control exercise is debased.
- The extent to which 'uncontrollable' costs are attributed to individual departments should be minimised. But consider our earlier discussion (see Chapter 4) concerning activity-based costs. Few costs really are 'uncontrollable' – it is just a matter of determining which activities such costs relate to and who controls the level of those activities.

6.5.2 Budgetary control reports

If managers are to use the budgets to control effectively, they must receive regular control information.

The budgetary control reports should be

(a) *Timely*. The information should be made available as soon as possible after the end of the control period. Corrective action will be much more effective if it is taken soon after the event, and adverse trends could continue unchecked if budgetary reporting systems are slow.

(b) *Accurate*. Inaccurate control information could lead to inappropriate management action. There is often a conflict between the need for timeliness and the need for accuracy. The design of budgetary reporting systems should allow for sufficient accuracy for the purpose to be fulfilled.

(c) *Relevant to the recipient*. Busy managers should not be swamped with information that is not relevant to them. They should not need to search through a lot of irrelevant information to reach the part that relates to their area of responsibility. The natural reaction of an individual faced with this situation could be to ignore the information altogether.

   The budgetary reporting system should ideally be based on the exception principle, which means that management attention is focused on those areas where performance is significantly different from budget. Subsidiary information could be provided on those items that are in line with the budget.

   Many control reports also segregate controllable and non-controllable costs and revenues, that is the costs and revenues over which managers can exercise control are highlighted separately in the reports.

(d) *Communicated to the correct manager*. Control information should be directed to the manager who has the responsibility and authority to act upon it. If the information is communicated to the wrong manager its value will be immediately lost and any adverse trends may continue uncorrected. Individual budget-holders' responsibilities must be clearly defined and kept up to date in respect of any changes.

Budgetary control reports can be prepared with varying degrees of frequency, timeliness, accuracy and detail. For example, you can report at weekly, monthly or quarterly intervals. You can report figures accurate to the nearest £0.1 m or to the nearest penny.

Obviously, the greater the volume and sophistication of control reporting, the greater is its cost. In determining the style of reporting appropriate to an organisation one should have regard to the costs and benefits of reporting. The marginal benefits of additional reporting start to decline as the volume of reporting and the associated cost of reporting rise. An optimum position should be sought having regard to the needs of the organisation.

The design of a budgetary control report depends very much on the inclination of users. We have already seen examples of budgetary control reports in our earlier study of standard costing. In those cases, the reports took the form of reconciliations of budget and actual profit through the calculation of cost and sales variances.

But, alternative styles are possible. A simple example to illustrate a common format is as follows.

ABC Manufacturing Ltd

Operating Statement
September 2004

£ millions	Quarter (01/06–30/09			Year to Date (01/01–30/09)		
	Actual	*Budget*	*Variance*	*Actual*	*Budget*	*Variance*
Sales	24.1	22.9	+5.2%	84.0	92.4	−9.1%
Costs	18.6	18.8	−1.1%	69.6	70.1	−0.7%
Profit	5.5	4.1	+34.1%	14.4	22.3	−35.4%

In this case, the 'variances' are (actual–budget)/budget. These variances are not the same as the cost and sales variances we considered in Chapters 2 and 3. A plus percentage means that Actual exceeded Budget-it does not mean that it had an adverse impact on Profit.

A common feature in modern control reports is a forecast to year end position. Adding such a feature to the above report would involve inserting a third set of columns under the heading 'Forecast to Year End (01/01–31/12)'. This adds an element of feedforward to the report.

6.6 Fixed and flexible budgets

When managers are comparing the actual results with the budget for a period, it is important to ensure that they are making a valid comparison. The use of flexible budgets can help to ensure that actual results are monitored against realistic targets.

Example

A company manufactures a single product and the following data shows the actual results for the month of April compared with the budgeted figures.

Operating statement for April

	Actual	Budget	Variance
Units produced and sold	1,000	1,200	(200)
	£	£	£
Sales revenue	110,000	120,000	(10,000)
Direct material	16,490	19,200	2,710
Direct labour	12,380	13,200	820
Production overhead	24,120	24,000	(120)
Administration overhead	21,600	21,000	(600)
Selling and distribution o/head	16,200	16,400	200
Total cost	90,790	93,800	3,010
Profit	19,210	26,200	(6,990)

Note: variances in brackets are adverse. Also, the figures described as variances (budget–actual) are not variances for standard costing and variance analysis purposes.

Looking at the costs incurred in April, a cost saving of £3,010 has been made compared with the budget. However, the number of units produced and sold was 200 less than budget, so some savings in expenditure might be expected. It is not possible to tell from this comparison how much of the saving is due to efficient cost control, and how much is the result of the reduction in activity.

Similarly, it is not possible to tell how much of the fall in sales revenue was due to the fall in activity. Some of the sales revenue variance may be the result of a difference in the sales prices but this budget comparison does not show the effect of this.

The type of budget in use here is a fixed budget. A fixed budget is one that remains unchanged regardless of the actual level of activity. In situations where activity levels are likely to change, and there is a significant proportion of variables costs, it is difficult to control expenditure satisfactorily with a fixed budget.

A flexible budget can help managers to make more valid comparisons. It is designed to show the expected revenue and the allowed expenditure for the actual number of units produced and sold. Comparing this flexible budget with the actual expenditure and revenue it is possible to distinguish genuine efficiencies.

6.6.1 Preparing a flexible budget

Before a flexible budget can be prepared managers must identify which costs are fixed and which are variable. The allowed expenditure on variable costs can then be increased or decreased as the level of activity changes. You will recall that fixed costs are those costs that will not increase or decrease over a given range of activity. The allowance for these items will therefore remain constant.

We can now continue with the example.

Management have identified that the following budgeted costs are fixed.

	£
Direct labour	8,400
Production overhead	18,000
Administration overhead	21,000
Selling and distribution overhead	14,000

It is now possible to identify the expected variable cost per unit produced and sold.

	Original budget (a)	Fixed cost (b)	Variable cost (c) = (a) − (b)	VC per unit (c)/1,200
Units produced and sold	1,200			
	£	£	£	£
Direct material	19,200	–	19,200	16
Direct labour	13,200	8,400	4,800	4
Production overhead	24,000	18,000	6,000	5
Administration overhead	21,000	21,000	–	–
Selling and distribution o/head	16,400	14,000	2,400	2
	93,800	61,400	32,400	27

Now that managers are aware of the fixed costs and the variable costs per unit, it is possible to 'flex' the original budget to produce a budget cost allowance for 1,000 units produced and sold.

The budget cost allowance for each item is calculated as follows:

Cost allowance = budgeted fixed cost +
(number of units produced and sold × variable cost per unit)

For the costs that are wholly fixed or wholly variable the calculation of the budget cost allowance is fairly straightforward. The remaining costs are semi-variable, which you will recall means that they are partly fixed and partly variable. For example, the budget cost allowance for direct labour is calculated as follows:

Cost allowance for direct labour = £8,400 + (1,000 × £4) = £12,400

The budgeted sales price per unit is £120,000/1,200 = £100 per unit. If we assume that sales revenues follow a linear variable pattern (i.e. the sales price remains constant) the full flexible budget can now be produced.

Flexible budget comparison for April

	Cost/revenue allowances			Actual	
	Fixed	Variable	Total	cost/revenue	Variance
	£	£	£	£	£
Sales revenue			100,000	110,000	10,000
Direct material	–	16,000	16,000	16,490	(490)
Direct labour	8,400	4,000	12,400	12,380	20
Production overhead	18,000	5,000	23,000	24,120	(1,120)
Administration overhead	21,000	–	21,000	21,600	(600)
Selling and distn. o/h	14,000	2,000	16,000	16,200	(200)
	61,400	27,000	88,400	90,790	(2,390)
Profit			11,600	19,210	7,610

Note: variances in brackets are adverse.

This revised analysis shows that in fact the profit was £7,610 higher than would have been expected from a sales volume of 1,000 units.

The largest variance is a £10,000 favourable variance on sales revenue. This has arisen because a higher price was charged than budgeted. We know this because flexing the budget has eliminated the effect of changes in the volume sold, which is the only other factor that could have increased sales revenue.

Could the higher sales price have been the cause of the shortfall in sales volume? We do not know the answer to this, but without a flexible budget comparison it was not possible to tell that a different selling price had been charged. The cost variances in the flexible budget comparison are almost all adverse. These overspendings were not revealed when a fixed budget was used and managers may have been under the false impression that costs were being adequately controlled. In Chapter 1, you learnt how each total cost variance can be analysed to reveal how much of the variance is due to higher resource prices and how much is due to higher resource usage.

6.6.2   Using flexible budgets for planning

You should appreciate that whereas flexible budgets can be useful for control purposes they are not particularly useful for planning. The original budget must contain a single target level of activity so that managers can plan such factors as the resource requirements and the product pricing policy. This would not be possible if they were faced were faced with a range of possible activity levels. The budget can be designed so that the fixed costs are distinguished from the variable costs. This will facilitate the preparation of a budget cost allowance for control purposes at the end of each period, when the actual activity is known.

6.6.3   Flexible budgets

Now that you have got the idea of how a flexible budget can be prepared, work through the following exercise to consolidate your understanding.

In this exercise, as in practice, you will need to investigate the cost behaviour patterns to determine which costs are fixed, which are variable and which are semi-variable.

The first step in investigating cost behaviour patterns is to look at the cost data. You should be able to easily spot any fixed costs because they remain constant when activity levels change.

The easiest way to identify the behaviour patterns of non-fixed costs is to divide each cost figure by the related activity level. If the cost is a linear variable cost, then the cost per unit will remain constant. For a semi-variable cost the unit rate will reduce as the activity level increases.

You will then need to recall how to use the high–low method to determine the fixed and variable elements of any semi-variable costs.

Exercise

Lawrence Ltd operates a system of flexible budgets, and the flexed budgets for expenditure for the first two quarters of Year 3 were as follows:

Flexed budgets – Quarters 1 and 2

	Quarter 1	Quarter 2
	Units	Units
Sales	9,000	14,000
Production	10,000	13,000
	£	£
Budget cost allowances		
Direct materials	130,000	169,000
Production labour	74,000	81,500
Production overhead	88,000	109,000
Administration overhead	26,000	26,000
Selling and distribution overhead	29,700	36,200
Total budget cost allowance	347,700	421,700

Despite a projected increase in activity, the cost structures in Quarters 1 and 2 are expected to continue during Quarter 3 as follows:

(a) The variable cost elements behave in a linear fashion in direct proportion to volume. However, for production output in excess of 14,000 units the unit variable cost for production labour increases by 50%. This is due to a requirement for overtime working and the extra amount is payable only on the production above 14,000 units.
(b) The fixed cost elements are not affected by changes in activity levels.
(c) The variable elements of production costs are directly related to production volume.
(d) The variable element of selling and distribution overhead is directly related to sales volume.

Prepare a statement of the budget cost allowances for Quarter 3. The activity levels during Quarter 3 were as follows.

	Units
Sales	14,500
Production	15,000

 Solution

If you divide each cost figure by the relevant activity figure, you will find that the only wholly variable cost is direct material, at £13 per unit.

You can also see that the only wholly fixed cost is administration overhead since this is a constant amount for both activity levels, £26,000.

For the remaining costs you will need to use the high–low method to determine the fixed and variable elements.

Production labour

	Production units	£
Quarter 2	13,000	81,500
Quarter 1	10,000	74,000
Change	3,000	7,500

$$\text{Variable cost} = \frac{£7,500}{3,000} = £2.50 \text{ per unit}$$

$$\text{Fixed cost} = £81,500 - (£2.50 \times 13,000) = £49,000$$

Production overhead

	Production units	£
Quarter 2	13,000	109,000
Quarter 1	10,000	88,000
Change	3,000	21,000

$$\text{Variable cost per unit} = \frac{£21,000}{3,000} = £7 \text{ per unit}$$

Fixed cost = £109,000 − (£7 × 13,000) = £18,000

Selling and distribution overhead

	Sales units	£
Quarter 2	14,000	36,200
Quarter 1	9,000	29,700
Change	5,000	6,500

$$\text{Variable cost per unit sold} = \frac{£6,500}{5,000} = £1.30 \text{ per unit}$$

Fixed cost = £36,200 − (£1.30 × 14,000) = £18,000

We can now prepare a statement of the budget cost allowances for quarter 3.

	£	Quarter 3 Budget cost allowance £
Direct material (15,000 units × £13)		195,000
Production labour:		
Fixed	49,000	
Variable up to 14,000 units (14,000 × £2.50)	35,000	
Variable above 14,000 units (1,000 × £3.75)	3,750	
		87,750
Production overhead:		
Fixed	18,000	
Variable (15,000 × £7)	105,000	
		123,000
Administration overhead: fixed		26,000
Selling and distribution overhead:		
Fixed	18,000	
Variable (14,500 × £1.30)	18,850	
		36,850
Total budget cost allowance		468,600

6.6.4 Extrapolating outside the relevant range

In the preceding example you were told that the cost structures would remain unaltered despite the increase in activity. In examinations, and in practice, if you need to do a similar extrapolation outside the range for which you have available data, you should always state the assumption that the observed behaviour patterns will still be applicable.

6.7 Behavioural aspects of budgetary control

Throughout the previous discussion on the budgetary control concept, the emphasis has been on economic considerations. There is, however, another very important aspect of budgetary control systems and this is its impact on the human beings who will operate and be judged by those systems.

It is only comparatively recently that the results of years of study of personal relationships in the workplace have percolated into the field of management accounting. It is now recognised that failure to consider the effect of control systems on the people affected could result in a lowering of morale and a reduction of motivation. Further, those people may be induced to do things that are not in the best interests of the organisation.

Specific behavioural issues encountered in budgeting include the following.

6.7.1 Motivation and co-operation

To be fully effective, any system of financial control must provide for motivation and incentive. If this requirement is not satisfied, managers will approach their responsibilities in a very cautious and conservative manner. It is often found that adverse variances attract investigation and censure but there is no incentive to achieve favourable variances. Failure to distinguish controllable from uncontrollable costs in budgetary control can alienate managers from the whole process.

Personal goals and ambitions are, in theory, strongly linked to organisational goals. These personal goals may include a desire for higher income and higher social standing. To simultaneously satisfy the goals of the organisation and the goals of the individual there must be 'goal congruence'. That is, the individual manager perceives that his or her own goals are achieved by his or her acting in a manner that allows the organisation to achieve its goals. The problem is that reliance on budgetary control systems does not always result in goal congruence.

The success of a budgetary control system depends on the people who operate and are affected by it. They must work within the system in an understanding and co-operative manner. This can only be achieved by individuals who have a total involvement at all stages in the budget process. However, it is often found that

- A budget is used simply as a pressure device. If the budget is perceived as 'a stick with which to beat people', then it will be sabotaged in all sorts of subtle ways.
- The budgeting process and subsequent budgetary control exercises induce competition between individual departments and executives. Managers may be induced to do things in order to 'meet budget' that are not in the best interests of the business as a whole.

6.7.2 Failure of goal congruence

It has been seen that an essential element in budgetary control is performance evaluation. Actual results are compared with budget or standard in order to determine whether performance is good or bad. What is being evaluated is not just the business operation but the managers responsible for it. The purpose of budgetary control is to induce managers to behave in a manner that is to the best advantage of the organisation. Compliance with budget is enforced by a variety of negative and positive sanctions.

When adverse variances are reported for operations then this implies poor performance by the managers of the operations. If they are unable to correct or explain away the adverse variances, then they may suffer negative sanctions. They may have forgo salary increases, or they may be demoted to a less prestigious post. Other more subtle negative sanctions are possible that anyone who has ever worked for a large organisation will be aware of.

Positive inducements may be offered to encourage managers to avoid adverse variances. A manager who meets budget may be granted a performance-related salary bonus, promotion, a new company car or use of the executive dining room.

Consequently, the manager has a considerable incentive to ensure that the department or operation he is responsible for achieves its budgeted level of performance. However, there are a variety of ways of doing this that might not be to the advantage of the organisation as a whole.

For example, the manager of a production line can cut costs and hence improve its reported performances by reducing quality controls. This may result in long-term problems concerning failure of products in service, loss of customer goodwill and rectification costs – but these are not the concern of the production line manager. This is a clear failure of goal congruence.

The control system is capable of distorting the process it is meant to serve – or 'the tail wags the dog'. The enforcement of a budgetary control system requires sensitivity if this is not to happen.

6.7.3 The budget as a pot of cash

In some environments managers may come to consider the budget as a sum of money that has to be spent. This arises particularly in service departments or public sector organisations, the performance of which is gauged mainly through comparison of actual and budget spending.

The manager of a local authority 'street cleaning' department may be given an annual budget of £120,000 to clean the streets. The manager knows that she will be punished if she spends more than £120,000 in the year. She also knows that if she spends less than £120,000 in the year then her budget will probably be reduced next year. Such a reduction will involve a personal loss of status in the organisation and will make her job more difficult in the next year.

In order to ensure that she does not overspend her annual budget in the current year the manager may spend at a rate of £9,000 per month for the first 11 months of the year. This can be achieved by reducing the frequency of street cleaning and using poor-quality materials. It allows a contingency fund to be accumulated in case of emergencies.

However, in the final month of the year the manager has to spend £21,000 if she wishes to ensure that her whole budget is fully used. She might achieve this by using extra labour and high-quality materials.

Does this behaviour make sense? Of course it does not. The whole pattern of behaviour is distorted by the control system. It means that local residents have a substandard service for 11 months of the year and money is wasted in the 12th month.

It is, however, a fact that suppliers to government departments and local councils often experience a surge in orders towards the end of the financial year. This surge is caused by managers placing orders at the last moment in order to ensure that their full budget for the year is committed.

6.7.4 Budget negotiation

Budgets are normally arrived at by a process of negotiation with the managers concerned. A budget may actually be initiated by departmental managers and then corrected as a result of negotiation with the budget officer.

Clearly, a manager has an incentive to negotiate a budget that is not difficult to achieve. This produces a phenomenon known as 'padding the budget' or 'budgetary slack'. A manager will exaggerate the costs required to achieve objectives. This has the following results:

- If the manager succeeds in padding his budget, then the whole control exercise is damaged. Comparison of actual with budget gives no meaningful measure of performance and the manager is able to include inefficiencies in his operation if he wishes.
- A successful manager becomes one who is a hard negotiator. The problem with this is that the negotiations in question are between colleagues and not with customers. 'Infighting' may become entrenched in the management process.

- A great deal of time and energy that could be directed to the actual management of the business is distracted by what are essentially administrative procedures.

These are all examples of a control system distorting the processes they are meant to serve.

6.7.5 Influence on accounting policies

Any management accountant who has been engaged in the preparation of financial control reports will be familiar with attempts by managers to influence the accounting policies that are used. For example, the apportionment of indirect costs between departments often contains subjective elements. Should security costs be apportioned on the basis of floor space or staff numbers?

The manner in which the indirect costs are apportioned can have a considerable impact on how the performance of individual departments is perceived. This position creates the scope and incentive for managers to argue over accounting policies.

If a manager perceives that her department's performance is falling below budget, then she may sift through the costs charged to her department and demand that some be reclassified and charged elsewhere. The time and energy that goes into this kind of exercise has to be diverted from that available for the regular management of the business.

6.7.6 Budget constrained management styles

When the performance of a manger is assessed by his ability to meet budget, then he is likely to adopt a conservative approach to new business opportunities that appear. The immediate impact of new business ventures is likely to be a rise in capital and operating costs – with an adverse impact on current period profit. The benefits of such ventures may only be felt in the long term. Hence, when a new opportunity appears, the manager evaluating it may only perceive that its acceptance will result in below-budget performance in the current period – and turn it down on this ground alone. Another consideration is that reliance on budgetary control is an approach to management that involves sitting in an office and reading financial reports. Such an approach (in conjunction with features such as executive dining rooms) may result in an unsatisfactory corporate culture based on hierarchies and social divisions. Large organisations that rely heavily on budgetary control systems often take on an 'ossified' character.

Yet another consideration is that a reliance on budgetary planning may induce managers to favour projects and developments that are most amenable to the construction of budgets. Projects that involve little uncertainty and few unknowns are easy to incorporate in budgets and hence managers may be more inclined to adopt such projects than the alternatives. Projects that involve significant uncertainties may be attractive if they incorporate some combination of high expected returns and low cost interim exit routes – but a budget constrained manager may be disinclined to adopt such projects simply because they are difficult to incorporate in budgets. Some writers (see Section 6.8.3, 'contingency theory') suggest that the budgetary approach may be particularly inappropriate in a dynamic and turbulent business environment.

The general conclusion concerning this and previous points is that good budgetary control can offer certain benefits. However, when budgetary control is enforced in a rigid or insensitive manner it may end up doing more harm than good.

6.7.7 Budgets and motivation

Much of the early academic work on budgets concerned the extent to which the 'tightness' or looseness' of a budget acted as an incentive or disincentive to management effort. This was the issue of 'budget stretch'. Seminal works in this general area included studies by A.C. Stedry (see his 1960 text 'Budget Control and Cost Behaviour') and G.H. Hofstede (see his 1968 text 'The Game of Budget Control').

The main thrust of the findings that emerged from these studies was

- loose budgets (i.e. ones easily attainable) are poor motivators
- as budgets are tightened, up to a point they become more motivational
- beyond that point, a very tight budget ceases to be motivational.

The role of budget participation and the manner in which aspirations and objectives are stated was also explored in certain studies. It was suggested that the participation of managers in budget setting was a motivational factor – but see earlier discussion concerning budget padding and negotiation.

6.8 Modern developments in control systems

6.8.1 The problem of discretionary costs

'Discretionary costs' are so called because of their lack of a clear relationship between the input to the process and the output of that process. Such costs are encountered in all operations but are particularly significant in services. For example, the output of a firm's legal department is hard to measure, making it very difficult to determine the amount of resource that the organisation should devote to this type of activity. This can be contrasted with direct material input requirements for a production process – here, the process is well understood, and it is relatively straightforward to budget for the input required to arrive at any particular desired output.

The techniques discussed in this text with reference to engineered (or 'variable') costs can also be applied to discretionary costs. One obvious way to make the budgeting of discretionary costs easier is to convert such costs from the discretionary category to the engineered category. This necessarily demands the development of suitable output measures for discretionary costs, and requires that there is at least some understanding of how the input to a process impacts on these required outputs. For example, some decades ago, in an insurance company, the processing of insurance claims may have been considered to be a discretionary cost. However, in most insurance organisations, this has now been converted to an engineered cost, as analysis of the work undertaken has enabled an understanding to be gained of the amount of time that is typically required to process a claim, and thus the relationship between the number of claims to be processed and the resources required to facilitate this. Obviously, this relationship will not be a direct one, and would not be expected to hold for any individual claim; there will inevitably be a great variability in the time taken between the shortest and the longest claims processed. Nevertheless, over a reasonable time period, an average can be established that will enable a budget to be set on a more rational basis than the traditional incremental approach. Similarly, the analysis required for activity-based costing (see Chapter 8) will also facilitate an understanding of the relationship between inputs and outputs of a process, and offers the possibility for more rational budgeting of discretionary costs. Where discretionary costs *cannot* be converted to approximate engineered costs, ZBB (see Chapter 5) offers an approach to determining the level of resource to be given to this type of activity.

Engineered costs can be controlled on a short-term basis using traditional standards. Discretionary costs, by definition, cannot be controlled on the basis of *output,* because of the difficulty in measuring or specifying outputs in financial terms. Nevertheless, *some* output measures for discretionary costs should be developed, where possible, in order to set minimum standards of performance. For example, a company's legal department may have a service requirement to respond to legal queries within 2 hours of receipt of the query, or the training department may be required to run a minimum number of programmes within the financial year.

Inputs to discretionary categories can also be controlled. For example, discretionary departments may have 'staff numbers' budgets in addition to financial budgets.

6.8.2 Developments from financial modelling and budgeting packages

The use of 'budgeting packages' has been encountered earlier in this text (see 'Spreadsheets and databases as budgeting tools' in Chapter 5).

When such packages were first introduced in the 1960s and 1970s their impact was to free accountants and managers from many of the time and resource constraints of manual systems:

- Computer accounting provided basic data faster and in more detail.
- Consolidation of monthly management accounts could be faster and more complete.
- Processing problems and limitations no longer precluded the preparation and review of alternative budgets and forecasts, assuming the formulation of detailed alternative hypotheses.

The advent of PCs in the 1980s made computer systems available to small- and medium-sized enterprises for the first time. In some cases, this made the operation of full management accounting systems become economic. In the pre-PC era many smaller businesses did not prepare monthly management accounting reports or used crude approximations in place of proper accounting practices.

For example, backflush accounting is introduced in Chapter 8 as a 'modern' accounting system. In fact, variations on backflush accounting were widely used in the pre-PC era as a 'cheap and cheerful' means of preparing monthly management accounts. The standard cost of goods completed was deducted from costs incurred to give both monthly cost of sales and end month stock figures.

6.8.3 Rethinking the purpose of the monthly report and decision support systems

Various organisations will emphasise different priorities, but possible system aims include

- monitoring progress towards a range of predetermined performance measures, including budgets and standards, financial requirements and cost improvement or service improvement targets;
- direction attention to significant variations and to events that could produce significant deviations in the future;
- acting as an agenda, a way of structuring regular discussion of results and progress and plans;

- providing an overall view of all the activities, not necessarily to answer specific questions, but possibly aimed at a non-executive director broad view.

There is considerable scope for discussion of the list of potential objectives for and determinants of management accounting systems. Such discussion goes beyond the scope of this book, but be aware that within the academic community there are two main schools of thought over the design of management reporting systems:

1. Contingency theory – particularly associated with the academic David Otley The idea here is that reporting systems develop in response to the individual needs of particular businesses and sectors. For example, a business operating in a 'certain, static and calm' environment may well find that a reporting system based on traditional standard costing and budgetary control is entirely satisfactory. But this becomes progressively less likely to be the case as one moves further into an uncertain, dynamic and turbulent business environment.

2. Institutional theory – associated with the academics Paul Di Maggio and Walter Powell. The idea here is that reporting systems develop in response to the internal dynamics of organisations. Rather than responding to individual environmental needs, reporting systems tend to follow industry norms regardless of specific advantage.

The term 'isomorphism' (or, 'change making things equal') is commonly encountered in the discussion of institutional theory. Organisations adopt reporting systems that they perceive to be normal or best practice in their sector (mimetic process). The practice of benchmarking is an example of mimetic process. In order to adopt what they perceive to be best practice, organisations adopt the systems and processes of sector leaders without thinking too hard about whether or not those systems and practices are well suited to their own particular needs.

6.8.4 Beyond budgeting

The whole concept of budgeting turns around the idea that the operation of an organisation can be meaningfully planned for in some detail over an extended period into the future. Further, that this plan can be used to guide, control and co-ordinate the activities of numerous departments and individuals within the organisation.

The traditional budgeting concept has its critics:

In one division with 300 employees and $100 m in annual costs, their operating budget was more than four inches thick and involved over 100 business units. They completed the budget six months into the current fiscal year with managers and directors under great pressure to revise the budget to meet corporate goals. But each revision was just an editorial exercise in changing the numbers, not in revising operating activities. These were only changes in a lengthy and cumbersome document that few understood. Budget complexity drives out meaning and relevance.

Bruce Neumann, Streamlining Budgeting in the New Millenium (*Strategic Finance* 12/2001)

The modern economic environment is associated with a rapidly changing environment, flexible manufacturing, short product life-cycles and products/services which are highly customised. The 'lean business' and the 'virtual business' are responses to this. Such businesses own limited assets of the traditional kind but assemble resources as and when needed to meet customer demand. The keys to their operation are flexibility and speed of response. They are able to move quickly to exploit opportunities as they arise and do not operate according to elaborate business plans.

In an age of discontinuous change, unpredictable competition, and fickle customers, few companies can plan ahead with any confidence – yet most organisations remain locked into a 'plan-make-and-sell' business

BUDGETARY CONTROL

model that involves a protracted annual budgeting process based on negotiated targets and that assumes that customers will buy what the company decides to make. Such assumptions are no longer valid in an age when customers can switch loyalties at the click of a mouse.

J Hope and R Fraser. Beyond Budgeting (*Strategic Finance* 10/2000)

'Beyond Budgeting' (BB) is the generic name given to a body of practices intended to replace budgeting as a management model. The core concept is the need to move from a business model based on centralised organisational hierarchies to one based on devolved networks.

BB is identified with the 'Beyond Budgeting Round Table' (BBRT). The latter is:

'. . . at the heart of a new movement that is searching for ways to build lean, adaptive and ethical enterprises that can sustain superior competitive performance. Its aim is to spread the idea through a vibrant community'.

BBRT website

BBRT is a research consortium which was set up in 1998 to promote research into and the adoption of BB. At its centre is the eight strong 'BBRT team', the best known of whom are Robin Fraser and Jeremy Hope. The full round table community consists of the team, business and academic associates and the member businesses.

Budgeting is a pervasive exercise that provides the administrative basis for organisational planning and control in many traditionally run organisations. The vision of the Chief Executive is translated into a plan which is expressed in the form of a budget. Once that budget is adopted, then the management function becomes one of securing compliance. Budgeting is a core management process which provides stability and reduces risk. This becomes a cultural phenomenon reflecting a hierarchical approach to management whereby subordinate managers are judged on how far they succeed in complying with orders. It is an approach which has been linked to some high-profile business failures. For example, managers at WorldCom claimed that working life was all about satisfying the demands of CEO Bernie Ebbers and a small group of his associates:

'You would have a budget and he would mandate that you had to be 2 percent under budget. Nothing else was acceptable'

BBRT advances the idea that budgeting should be abolished and an alternative business model should be substituted in its place. BB is a 'responsibility model' whereby managers are given goals which are based on benchmarks linked variously to world class performance, peers, competitors and/or earlier periods. This requires an adaptive approach whereby authority is devolved to managers. An organisation run in this manner will be more a network than a hierarchy. The whole spectrum of modern management techniques and aids should be incorporated in an implementation of the BB model. IT networks provide easy communication between different component parts of an organisation together with its customers, associates and suppliers. Quality programmes (TQM), process engineering (BPR), supply chain management (SCM), balanced scorecards and activity accounting all have a role. Advocates of BB claim that it does not provide a softer environment for management than budget compliance. Both individual and team performance should have a high visibility in a devolved management environment.

For example, a performance control report based on the scorecard principle might appear as follows:

XYZ Ltd, Performance Control Report for Quarter 4
Scorecard

	Actual	Target	Var (%)
Financials:			
Revenue (£)	18,360,000	17,500,000	**4.91**
Income/Expenditure	1.055	1.040	**1.44**
Earnings (£)	181,900	170,000	**7.00**
Market capitalisation (£)	190,800,000	200,000,000	**(4.60)**
Customers:			
Customer satisfaction (points)	8.731	9.000	**(2.99)**
Returns (%)	2.89(%)	2.00(%)	**(44.50)**
Processes:			
Delivery error (%)	0.86(%)	0.90(%)	**4.44**
Design error (points)	1.976	2.000	**1.20**
Design-delivery time (days)	94	90	**(4.44)**
Staff:			
Staff satisfaction (points)	7.310	8.000	**(8.63)**
Training hours per FTE staff member	4.217	3.500	**20.49**

That gives a fuller impression of performance than a straight actual-budget comparison and the approach can be refined much further. Results can be reported using graphics and trends. It is possible to adopt industry averages or trend analysis based projections as the relevant benchmarks instead of fixed targets.

A BB implementation should incorporate the following six main principles :

(1) An organisation structure with clear principles and boundaries; a manager should have no doubts over what he/she is responsible for and what he/she has authority over; the concept of the internal market for business units may be relevant here.

(2) Managers should be given goals and targets which are based on relative success and linked to shareholder value; such targets may be based on key performance indicators and benchmarks following the balanced scorecard principle.

(3) Managers should be given a high degree of freedom to make decisions; this freedom is consistent with the total quality management and business process reengineering concepts; a BB organisation chart should be 'flat'.

(4) Responsibility for decisions that generate value should be placed with 'front line teams'; again, this is consistent with TQM and BPR concepts.

(5) Front line teams should be made responsible for relationships with customers, associate businesses and suppliers; direct communication between all the parties involved should be facilitated; this is consistent with the SCM concept.

(6) Information support systems should be transparent and ethical; an activity based accounting system which reports on the activities for which managers and teams are responsible is likely to be of use in this regard.

BB is essentially an approach that places modern management practices within a cultural framework.

'The process of management is not about administering fixed budgets, it is about the dynamic allocation of resources'

Lord Browne, former CEO of BP

Researchers have explored the history of BB implementations to determine whether or not these have delivered improved results. BBRT has reported several case studies, the best known of which is that of Svenska Handelsbanken. This Swedish bank abandoned budgeting in 1972 and switched to delegation model (involving 600 autonomous work units) that avoids formal planning and target setting. Branch managers run their own businesses and are able to decide how many staff they need, where they obtain support services from and what products they market to which customers. Branch performance is assessed using measures such as customer profitability, customer retention and work productivity.

The Svenska Handelsbanken model might indicate a higher level of corporate risk with all that would imply for cost of money and market capitalisation. However, it is claimed that the model favours flexibility. In the absence of a fixed plan, products and projects are designed to allow easy modification and exit routes. This view suggests that the model invites a different approach to risk management rather than the acceptance of higher risk.

All the cases studied are different, but the following general benefits for BB are claimed:

- Faster response time – operating within a flexible organisational network and with strategy as an 'adaptive process' allows managers to respond quickly to customer requests.
- Better innovation – managers working within an environment wherein performance is judged on the basis of team and business unit results encourages the adoption of new innovations. Relations with customers and suppliers through SCM may facilitate the adoption of new working methods and technologies.
- Lower costs – in the context of BB managers are more likely to perceive costs as scarce resources which have to be used effectively than as a budget 'entitlement' that has to be used. BB is also likely to promote an awareness of the purposes for which costs are being incurred and thereby the potential for reductions.
- Improved customer and supplier loyalty – the leading role of front line teams in dealing with customers and suppliers is likely to deepen the relevant relationships.

As with many innovations in management practice, BB was a creature of its time. It appeared in the mid-1990s at a time when globalisation and advances in IT were tending to speed up the business environment. In particular, customers had greater choice and expected faster service. The key competitive constraint in most business situations is no longer land, labour or capital. For example, if labour is locally scarce then work can be outsourced to India or manufacturing can be relocated to China. In many practical business situations the key competitive factor is likely to be intellectual and knowledge based in character.

The BB model appeared as a set of information-age best practices which was attuned to the new situation. BB is intended to be an exercise in mobilising competent managers, skilled workers and loyal customers.

However, traditional budgeting still has its defenders. Such defenders claim that while budgeting may be associated with a 'command and control' management style, it is the management style that is the problem and not budgeting.

Budgeting (extract)

Penelope S. Greenberg and Ralph H. Greenberg, *Strategic Finance,* **August 2006 ©
Institute of Management Accountants.**

Who needs budgets? You do. Your budgeting process can target information that needs to flow within your organisation and to your B2B partners. (Extract) (Budgeting) *Penelope Sue Greenberg Ralph H. Greenberg.*

Budgets aren't just about the numbers. They're about communicating vital information within the organisation. And in the very near future, the budgeting function in your organisation may be called on to serve as a role model for communicating information in business-to-business (B2B) collaborative planning processes.

[Author's note : see discussion of Supply Chain Management in Chapter 8 below]

Budget bashing has become a popular topic and has even led to the suggestion that budgets are outdated and no longer needed, but don't be too hasty in advocating that your organisation dump its budgeting process. Although such a position might make you popular with some colleagues, it isn't in your organisation's best interests. The reason? The most important aspect of your budgeting process soon may be as a communication model for reducing information asymmetries and uncertainties between your organisation and its B2B partners. The communication procedures that your organisation has developed for its strategic and operational budgeting process may provide the best blueprint for effective, efficient interorganisational communication.

Keep Your Budgets

Talk regarding the budgeting process frequently revolves around target revenues and costs and how these targets are set, used and misused. But rather than suggest dumping the budget, a much better approach is to determine why problems exist and fix them. If your process promotes a command-and-control environment, then incorporate more participation. If your incentive system is too restrictive or if it invites managers to create slack, then revise it. If the financial targets are no longer appropriate for your evolving organisation, then expand or change the targets. Many companies have successfully implemented and used balanced scorecards and other methods to identify targets, and, even before balanced scorecards, they used performance evaluation based on world-class benchmarks.

Any revisions to your budgeting procedures should recognise that the biggest benefit of the current process is probably in enhancing interdepartmental communication throughout your organisation in order to coordinate efforts and attain strategic and operational goals. The budgeting process allows upper-level operating and financial managers to communicate information about the strategic and operational goals of the organisation. These executives have access to business intelligence efforts and to the tools to assess the competitive environment. They need to communicate many aspects of the big picture (the organisation and the environment) and how these aspects impact each part of the organisation.

The budgeting process also allows lower-level operating and financial managers and frontline employees to have their fingers on the pulse of the organisation. They understand the business processes and procedures. Because they often have valuable information that can impact both short- and long-term goals and priorities, they need to have a process for communicating both internal and external perspectives on their assigned tasks.

This communication is critical because information asymmetries exist among departments and levels within the organisation. Also, a company needs to recognise and deal with uncertainties in its environment, such as the changing nature of competition.

B2B Collaboration

As business-to-business partnerships flourish, many organisations are developing closer ties than ever before. These relationships involve inter-organisational coordination, communication and information sharing at an unprecedented level. If your budgeting process has been done correctly, it has already identified the information that needs to flow from one unit to another within your organisation, so it should provide a good baseline for communicating with your B2B partners. In both intra- and inter-organisational planning, the type and amount of information, as well as the level of communication, depend on the situation, the interdependence and interactions between units, and whether those interactions are product or process focused.

6.9   Summary

Budgetary control is one of the classic management accounting techniques. It allows performance to be monitored by systematically comparing actual results achieved with budget. A variety of practices have been developed to make this comparison meaningful – but the management accountant should be aware that budgetary control can easily distort the processes it is meant to serve.

An article extract taken from Strategic Finance (the publication of CIMAs sister body in the US, The Institute of Management Accountants) now follows. This extract contains a wide extract-ranging discussion of modern budgeting practices and their link with IT and techniques such as ERP, ABC and ABM.

Self-test quiz

(1) Distinguish between 'feedback' and 'feedforward' in the context of a budgetary control system (Section 6.4).
(2) Explain the term 'budget centre' (Section 6.5.1).
(3) Distinguish between a 'controllable' cost and an 'uncontrollable' cost in the context of budgetary control (Section 6.5.1).
(4) What is a 'budget period' and what is a 'budget interval' (Section 6.5.2)?
(5) How does one identify the optimum budget interval for control reporting purposes (Section 6.5.2)?
(6) What advantages are claimed for the use of flexible budgets (Section 6.6)?
(7) Explain the term 'failure of goal congruence' in the context of budgetary control (Section 6.7.2).
(8) What is a 'budget constrained management style' (Section 6.7.6)?
(9) Distinguish between a 'discretionary cost' and an 'engineered cost' (Section 6.8.1).
(10) 'Beyond budgeting' is commonly defined in terms of what it is not (non-reliance on budgets), but what is it (Section 6.8.4)?

Reading

Streamlining budgeting in the new millennium (extract)

Bruce Neumann, *Strategic Finance,* December 2001
Published by the Institute of Management Accountants, Monteuale, NJ. For more information about reprints from Strategic Finance Contact PARS International.

Is your budget causing dysfunctional behavior within your organisation? If employees pad, stuff, under- and over-forecast revenue during the budgetary process, then the budget isn't serving as a useful tool like it could. So how do you create a budget that motivates employees to achieve targets and doesn't get filed it in the bottom of a drawer? Two formats – the activity budget and the global budget – promptly provide more useful information to department managers, unlike traditional resource-oriented budgets that are bogged down with needless details. You might consider this leading-edge approach 'hotrod budgeting.'

Companies obviously need budget. After all, the budget addresses the major area of concern to the business: allocating resources to produce the most cost-effective and, therefore, best profits and return on investment. It links together all of the activities that the firm undertakes into one clear set of targets, but, to be successful, the operational budgeting process will involve all of the following steps:

- Planning;
- Controlling;
- Coordination;
- Motivation; and
- Evaluation.

Let the operational management and staff own the budget

There are approaches to the budgetary process that motivate employees to achieve targets and others that do the opposite. I've observed two common attitudes towards budgets in large, centrally run organisations. First, the central planners think that they are in charge and often act as police over the rest of business, which creates resentment and results in an 'us-and-them' attitude. If senior managers dictate the budget, operational personnel are alienated from ownership of the budget, and if a budget is implemented as a stick to use on managers, it will waste time, effort and money.

Second, the budget may be tossed into the bottom drawer and forgotten until next year: 'We have satisfied the accountants this year, so let's get on with the real job.' The result: Employees

BUDGETARY CONTROL

in operations then use their own guidelines to run the business, and the whole budget process has been an almost complete waste of time.

So why not let operational managers implement the budget? Where operational managers put the budgets in place, they are then responsible for those targets and are more likely to try to achieve them. When circumstances change due to unforeseen happenings, then operational managers shouldn't be held responsible for such events.

The role of ERP systems

In order to manage their organisations more effectively, many large- and mid-sized firms are turning to enterprise resource planning (ERP) software.

[Author's note: ERP systems are explored in Chapter 8, they are planning systems which allow the resource requirements of given output levels to be projected.]

The goal of many technology-driven budgeting and planning processes is to link the general accounting system with all other finance systems and also with marketing management (sales orders), procurement, human resources management, inventory management and so on. In brief, ERP is designed to provide seamless interfaces among all operating and managerial systems in the in the organisation.

All of the linkages in the ERP model must be included in the budget document. Consequently, meaningful relationships may be obscured. Here's an example. I'm currently conducting activity-based costing (ABC) studies on large organisation where the ERP model is so complex and no one understands it.

In one division with 300 employees and $100 m in annual costs, their operating budget was more than four inches thick and involved over 100 business units. They completed the budget 6 months into the current fiscal year with managers and directors under great pressure to revise the budget to meet corporate goals. But each revision was just an editorial exercise in changing the numbers, not in revising budgetary relationships or operating activities. Very few managers understood the linkages in the budgeting model. In other words, no real events were likely to change as a result of preparing the budget. There were only changes in a lengthy and cumbersome document that few understood.

Budgeting in the new millennium will continue to use ever-more-complex ERP systems. In the event that ERP models continue to expand, it's likely that budgets will again be relegated to the bottom drawer. Budget complexity, unfortunately, drives out meaning and relevance at a time when budget reality and relevance should be paramount. Since obscuring meaningful relationships in complex budget models will most likely accelerate, budget directors and line managers should attempt to reverse this trend. I'll show you how.

How to streamline the budget

As finance professionals, you can use activity budgeting and global budgeting or 'morph' the two to simplify and streamline budgetary documents. These budgets can be motivational to those who use them because they're easy to understand and department managers can see the changes flow through them. They're user-oriented. Because they aren't bogged down in details and complex financial terms, simplified budgets will get used by department managers for strategic management and cost management activities rather than being filed and forgotten.

Activity Budgeting. In this new millennium, activity-based costing (ABC) will expand into strategic cost management or activity-based management (ABM) and activity budgeting.

Modeled on ABC or ABM, activity budgeting is a new budget format whereby budget costs are arrayed according to the expected costs of activities rather than products, services or resources. When a budget reflects activities in the business units, it's easy to understand and use. Functional categories – such as materials and labor – collapse, and new process-oriented categories – such as acquiring customers, retaining customers and providing IT services – replace them. Most ABC experts recommend the magic seven activities, where most organisational units can represent their key activities with seven descriptors.

The results

You'll end up with highly summarised budget formats that are much more understandable than budget formats reflecting the general ledger. Leave the general ledger to finance and accounting professionals because operating managers don't need that level of detail anyway. They can better understand and use activity budgets than documents that are four inches thick.

I forecast the activity budgets will supercede resource budgets because of their inherent linkages that present a cause-and-effect relationship between activities and products or services (cost objects). Process modifications, quality improvements and systems design changes aren't easily linked to traditional resource budgets, but such changes are easily entered into activity budgets.

Get in the fast lane

It's perplexing why companies continue to produce budgets that just don't get used and are the cause of dysfunctional behavior such as padding the budget. If you find the traditional budget doesn't get used by operational managers, then stop creating it. Instead, provide the managers with an activity or global budget from which they can easily glean the information they need. You'll be glad you did because the budgetary process will no longer be a waste of time, effort and money, and everybody will have a more realistic picture of the company's finances and operations.

Revision Questions

? Question 1

1. Within the context of a budgetary control system:

1.1. Explain the distinction between information feedback and feedforward.
1.2. Explain the distinction between a controllable cost and an uncontrollable cost.
1.3. Explain the distinction between a fixed and a flexible budget.
1.4. Explain the term 'failure of goal congruence'.
1.5. Explain the term 'budget slack'.

? Question 2

(a) Explain briefly the differences between fixed and flexible budgets.   **(5 marks)**
(b) Prepare a report, addressed to the board of directors, clearly explaining the advantages/
   disadvantages of using fixed/flexible budgets as part of a budgetary control system.
                                                                                      (10 marks)
(c) Spreadsheets are often used by accountants to assist in the preparation of budgets.
      Describe how a spreadsheet may be used to prepare a sales budget and explain the
   advantages of using spreadsheets to assist in this task. (Your answer should refer to
   input, use of formulae, and output reports.)   **(10 marks)**
                                                                                 (Total marks = 25)

? Question 3

(a) The following report has been prepared, relating to one product for March 20X7. This
   has been sent to the appropriate product manager as part of PDC Ltd's monitoring
   procedures.

Monthly variance report – March 20X7

	Actual	*Budget*	*Variance*	*%*
Production volume (units)	9,905	10,000	95 A	0.95 A
Sales volume (units)	9,500	10,000	500 A	5.00 A
Sales revenue (£)	27,700	30,000	2,300 A	7.67 A
Direct material (Kg)	9,800	10,000	200 F	2.00 F
Direct material (£)	9,600	10,000	400 F	4.00 F
Direct labour (hours)	2,500	2,400	100 A	4.17 A
Direct labour (£)	8,500	8,400	100 A	1.19 A
Contribution (£)	9,600	11,600	2,000 A	17.24 A

The product manager has complained that the report ignores the principle of flexible budgeting and is unfair.

Requirements

Prepare a report addressed to the management team that comments critically on the monthly variance report.

Include as an appendix to your report the layout of a revised monthly variance report that will be more useful to the product manager.

Include row and column headings, but do not calculate the contents of the report.

(15 marks)

(b) Explain the differences between budgetary control and standard costing/variance analysis. In what circumstances would an organisation find it beneficial to operate both of these cost control systems?   **(5 marks)**

(c) Explain briefly how a database may be used to collect the information required to prepare a report such as that illustrated in part (a) above.   **(5 marks)**

(Total marks = 25)

? Question 4

The following monthly budgeted cost values have been taken from the budget working papers of MZ Ltd for the year ended 30 September 20X0.

	Activity level		
	60%	70%	80%
	£	£	£
Direct materials	30,000	35,000	40,000
Direct labour	40,500	47,250	54,000
Production overhead	46,000	52,000	58,000
Selling overhead	15,000	17,000	19,000
Administration overhead	28,000	28,000	28,000
	159,500	179,250	199,000

During September 20X0, actual activity was 1,292 units (which was equal to 68% activity)

	£
Direct materials	33,500
Direct labour	44,000
Production overhead	46,250
Selling overhead	16,150
Administration overhead	27,800
	167,700

Requirements

(a) Prepare a budgetary control statement for MZ Ltd on a flexible budget basis for the month of September 20X0.   **(7 marks)**

(b) Explain the difference between fixed and flexible budgets, and state when each should be used to control costs.   **(8 marks)**

(c) The preparation of budgets is an important task that relies on the identification of the principal budget factor.

Explain the term 'principal budget factor' and state its importance in the budget preparation process.   **(5 marks)**

(d) Explain the role of the budget committee in the budget preparation process. **(5 marks)**

(Total marks = 25)

? Question 5

The chief executive of your organisation has expressed concern about the expenditure on staff training. Individual costs are often mentioned in discussing departmental budgets but he is not aware of the overall activities or the control mechanism. He has requested that a training programme be prepared and submitted for his approval.

Requirements

(a) Explain the nature of training costs from a control view point. **(5 marks)**
(b) List the costs you would include in a training programme. **(5 marks)**
(c) State how a training programme report could be prepared and the advantages such a report would offer. **(5 marks)**
(d) Explain briefly how the performance of the training function could be controlled and evaluated. **(5 marks)**

(Total marks = 20)

? Question 6

The following statement was made by a business consultant:

The problem with any control system is that it can distort the process it is meant to serve. Budgeting and budgetary control can distort the operations of the organisation they are being applied to. This distortion often takes a subtle form that people are unaware of, but it can increase costs and reduce the quality of the service that is being provided.

Requirements

(a) Explain the various ways in which budgeting and budgetary control can distort the processes they are meant to serve. **(5 marks)**
(b) Explain the manner in which such distortions can increase costs and reduce the quality of the service being provided. **(5 marks)**
(c) Suggest approaches to budgeting and budgetary control that might help to avoid the problems referred to in (a) and (b). **(5 marks)**

(Total marks = 15)

? Question 7

MPL Ltd is a company specialising in providing consultancy services to the catering industry. MPL Ltd prepared its operating statement for period 5 of the year ending

31 August 2000. This was as follows:

	Budget	Actual	Variance
Chargeable consultancy hours	2,400	2,500	100
	£	£	£
Administration staff salaries – fixed	15,000	15,750	750
Consultants' salaries – fixed	80,000	84,000	4,000
Casual wages – variable	960	600	360
Motor and travel costs – fixed	4,400	4,400	–
Motor and travel costs – variable	1,600	2,610	1,010
Telephone – fixed	600	800	200
Telephone – variable	2,000	2,150	150
Printing, postage & stationary – variable	2,640	2,590	50
Premises and equipment costs – fixed	3,200	3,580	380
Total costs	110,400	116,480	6,080
Fees charged	180,000	200,000	20,000
Profit	69,600	83,520	13,920

While the directors are pleased that the actual profit exceeded their budget expectations they are interested to know how this has been achieved. After the budgets had been issued to them, the consultants expressed concern at the apparent simplicity of assuming that costs could be classified as being either fixed or varying in direct proportion to chargeable consultancy hours.

Requirements

(a) As the newly appointed management accountant, prepare a report addressed to the board of directors of MPL Ltd that
  (i) explains the present approach to budgeting adopted in MPL Ltd and discuss the advantages and disadvantages of involving consultants in the preparation of future budgets; **(10 marks)**
  (ii) critically discusses the format of the operating statement for period 5. **(5 marks)**
(b) explains how a spreadsheet could be set up so that a flexed budget and variance calculations could be rapidly produced by inserting only the actual data, assuming that variable costs are thought to vary in line with chargeable consultancy hours. **(10 marks)**

(Total marks = 25)

? Question 8

AHW plc is a food processing company that produces high-quality, part-cooked meals for the retail market. The five different types of meal that the company produces (Products A to E) are made by subjecting ingredients to a series of processing activities. The meals are different, and therefore need differing amounts of processing activities.

Budget and actual information for October 2002 is shown below:

Budgeted data

	Product A	Product B	Product C	Product D	Product E
Number of batches	20	30	15	40	25
Processing activities per batch					
Processing activity W	4	5	2	3	1
Processing activity X	3	2	5	1	4
Processing activity Y	3	3	2	4	2
Processing activity Z	4	6	8	2	3

Budgeted costs of processing activities:

	£'2000
Processing activity W	160
Processing activity X	130
Processing activity Y	80
Processing activity X	200

All costs are expected to be variable in relation to the number of processing activities.

Actual data

Actual output during October 2002 was as follows:

	Product A	Product B	Product C	Product D	Product E
Number of batches	18	33	16	35	28

Actual processing costs incurred during October 2002 were as follows:

	£'2000
Processing activity W	158
Processing activity X	139
Processing activity Y	73
Processing activity Z	206

Requirements

(a) Prepare a budgetary control statement (to the nearest £'2000) that shows the original budget costs, flexible budget costs, the actual costs and the total variances of each processing activity for October 2002. **(15 marks)**

Your control statement has been issued to the Managers responsible for each processing activity and the Finance Director has asked each of them to explain the reasons for the variances shown in your statement. The Managers are not happy about this as they were not involved in setting the budgets and think that they should not be held responsible for achieving targets that were imposed upon them.

(b) Explain briefly the reasons why it might be preferable for Managers **not** to be involved in setting their own budgets. **(5 marks)**

(c) (i) Explain the difference between fixed and flexible budgets and how each may be used to control production costs and non-production costs (such as marketing costs) within AHW plc. **(4 marks)**

   (ii) Give two examples of costs that are more appropriately controlled using a fixed budget, and explain why a flexible budget is less appropriate for the control of these costs. **(3 marks)**

   Many organisations use linear regression analysis to predict costs at different activity levels. By analyzing past data, a formula such as

   $$y = ax + b$$

   is derived and used to predict future cost levels.

(d) Explain the meaning of the terms y, a, x and b in the above equation. **(3 marks)**

(Total = 30 marks)

Solutions to Revision Questions

6

✔ **Solution 1**

1.1 Feedback involves obtaining information from the past operation of a process and using that information as a guide for the control of that process. Feedforward involves forecasting information in regard to the future operations of a process and using that as a guide for control. Both approaches may feature in a budgetary control report (feedback being year-to-date figures, with feedforward being forecast-to-year-end figures).

1.2 A controllable cost is one which is influenced by decision of the budget holder. An uncontrollable cost is one which is not so influenced. It is often argued that uncontrollable costs should not be brought within the remit of the budgetary control process. However, the contrary argument is that few costs really are uncontrollable if they are studied to determine the activities they relate to and who determines the level of such activities.

1.3 A fixed budget is one which is based on given levels of output and/or activity. A flexible budget is one which is based on the actual level of output/activity that takes place but at given price levels, wages rates and efficiency levels. The comparison of actual with flexed budget therefore eliminates 'volume variances' and allows a more immediate comparison of the two sets of figures.

1.4 A failure of goal congruence occurs when a manager is induced by a business control system to do something that is not in the best interests of the organisation as a whole. For example, a departmental manager may be induced to reduce quality control costs in his department in order to stay within his overall operating cost budget. Such a measure may keep the manager within his budget but it may give rise to a reduction in product quality that impacts adversely on the performance of the organisation as a whole.

1.5 Budget slack is considered to arise when a budget holder negotiates a budget that involves a lower level of performance than that which is realistically possible. For example, a departmental manager may negotiate a cost budget in excess of that which is really required to enable the department to perform its function. Such a budget will make the manager's task easier in the current period. The gap between required costs and budget costs is the budget slack.

Solution 2

- This is fairly straightforward question that invites comment on the material we have explored in the chapter. In answering it you may care to consider the distinction between a flexed budget and the standard cost for the output achieved. Why are the two likely to differ?
- The requirement concerning spreadsheets may now seem rather dated to the average reader. In fact this question is now some years old.

(a) A fixed budget is one which is set before the beginning of an accounting period, and that shows, in financial terms, the results of the budgeted, or planned, activities for the forthcoming period. The budget therefore is based on single-point estimates with respect to the variables such as sales quantity, production volume, production mix and so on. The fixed budget is used for planning purposes.

Whereas a fixed budget is useful for planning, it is deficient when used as a control device. This is because actual activity will almost always differ from that envisaged in the budget, and therefore the budget, if it is to be used as a comparator, must be flexed to the actual level of activity. Thus, the actual outcome is compared with a flexed budget, set after the event, which portrays the budgeted costs and revenues of the activity that actually took place.

(b) **Report**

To:	Board of directors
From:	Management accountant
Date:	20 November 20X6
Subject:	Fixed and flexible budgets

A fixed budget is a budget such as the master budget, which is set before the start of the financial year, and which formalises our expectations of the likely activities undertaken in the year.

The advantages of such a budget are

- in compiling the budget the various elements of the organisation are co-ordinated;
- it is useful as a comparator for the actual outcomes;
- without a formalised budget it would be difficult to achieve focus around the desired strategy;
- it may be useful in external negotiations with banks and other lenders.

The disadvantages are

- like any financial statement, it may give a false impression of accuracy;
- it grows increasingly out of date, and therefore loses its validity as time passes;
- inappropriate use, as for example in budgetary control, may be harmful.

Flexible budgets are those that recognise cost behaviour and that are changed, after the event, to reflect the actual level that took place. Their advantages are

- they are primarily intended for use in budgetary control, and are appropriate as comparators;
- the variances that are produced give valid indications of relative performance.

The disadvantages of flexible budgets are

- fairly obviously, a flexible budget cannot be used for planning purposes because of the multiple levels of activity involved;

- focus on control of costs/revenues against a flexible budget may distract attention from strategic issues, such as the fact that market share is dropping;
- there is always a problem in separating costs by behaviour. If this cannot be undertaken with some accuracy, the quality of the flexible budget and its usefulness as a control tool suffer.

(c) A spreadsheet that would produce a sales budget would normally contain three areas:

1. An input area, into which is input raw data, for example on sales volumes, sales prices, discounts allowable, mix of sales growth rates predicted.
2. A working area, containing relationships between the inputs. This is where the calculations take place. Cells within this area will draw upon information into the required output. Cells in this area may be protected, to maintain the integrity of the model.
3. An output area, where the sales budget and supporting schedules are presented in a form suitable for use. This may allow a multi-dimensional analysis of sales revenue, showing it by product, currency unit, geographical area, customer type and so on.

Such a spreadsheet can be used to perform repetitive or predetermined calculations, for example in situations such as in sales budgeting, where prices, volumes, can be fed into the spreadsheet that contains the required model. This will, thereafter, almost instantly produce the required output, whether this is a budget for total sales, for sales by region, by sales outlet or by product.

The creation of a spreadsheet model can be seen as being similar to devoting resources to capital expenditure. It takes time and resources to build the initial model, but having done this, the task of producing budgets becomes much more efficient, and budget variations can be accomplished with ease ('what if?' questions). Without a spreadsheet, in a complex organisation, such variations may be impossible due to their time requirement.

The sales budget created on a spreadsheet will therefore have the advantage of being less time-consuming, and therefore cheaper to produce than a manual equivalent. Of greater significance, however, is its ability to be easily amended and interrogated, so that its value in use is incomparably greater than that of the manually created budget.

Signed: Management Accountant

 ## Solution 3

- This question can be answered at varying levels of refinement. However, the preparation of a full answer requires you to draw on all you have learned about accounting.
- In particular, you should introduce what you have studied in previous chapters concerning standard costing and variance analysis.

(a) **Memorandum**

To:	Management team
From:	Management accountant
Date:	21 May 20X7
Re:	Format of monthly variance reports

I have recently undertaken a review of the formats used for the monthly variance reports on product performance that are utilised throughout this organisation, and have concluded that as they stand they could well mislead users. The problem is caused largely by the way in which product information is presented, rather than in the information itself, and therefore I have a number of recommendations to make.

1. Volumes and values should be separated, and reported separately to avoid confusion.
2. The report computes variances by comparing financial figures that result from dissimilar volume levels. Volume levels should be the same, to ensure comparability.
3. The percentage variance figures may draw attention away from the absolute impact of each variance, which is illustrated by the monetary value of the variance.
4. No indication is given of the out-turn that would have been expected from the actual level of activity (flexed budget).
5. No controllable fixed costs are included. If such exist, they should be separately identified.
6. Year-to-date information should be shown as well as information for the reporting period.

A more appropriate layout is shown in Appendix A attached.

Appendix A

	Per unit	Original budget units	Flexed budget units	Actual units	Quantity variance	Price variance	Total variance
Sales volume		x	x	x			
Production volume		x	x	x			
	£	£	£	£	£	£	£
Sales	x	x	x	x	x	x	x
Direct material	x	x	x	x	x	x	x
Direct labour	x	x	x	x	x	x	x
Stock adjustment			x	x			
Contribution	x	x	x	x			x
Fixed costs		x	x	x		x	x
Profit		x	x	x			x

An identical layout might also be used for the presentation of year-to-date information.

(b) A standard cost is the cost of an individual product component or operation, whereas a budget is the cost or value associated with a larger organisational unit such as a department. Budgetary control focuses on various techniques in order to control what may be largely negotiated or discretionary cost, whereas standard costing uses work and method study and design engineering to reduce operation times, material requirements and unit costs.

A single organisation may use standard costing to control manufacturing costs, and budgetary control to control the costs of support services and departments such as personnel or marketing.

(c) A database could be used to hold the inputs of information, which may come at different times, and from different sources, and which are held centrally before being input to the variance report. Staff may either input information manually to the database or it may be picked up automatically from accounting records or production reports, thus saving on time and reducing the risk of error or omission. From the information in the database, the required output can be produced in any format, perhaps by using macros.

✓ Solution 4

(a) • MateWrials cost is variable at £500 per 1% of activity.
   • Labour cost is variable at £675 per 1% of activity.

- Production overhead costs are £10,000 fixed and vary at £600 per 1% of activity.
- Selling overhead costs are £3,000 fixed and vary at £200 per 1% of activity.
- Administration overhead costs are fixed.

Budget at 68% activity

	Flexed budget £	Actual £	Variance £
Direct material	34,000	33,500	500 (F)
Direct labour	45,900	44,000	1,900 (F)
Production overhead	50,800	46,250	4,550 (F)
Selling overhead	16,600	16,150	450 (F)
Administration overhead	28,000	27,800	200 (F)
	175,300	167,700	7,600 (F)

(b) Budgets show the planned costs and revenues which an organisation expects in a future period. They can be divided into two categories.

Fixed budgets are set before the start of an accounting period, are not susceptible to change, and are used as a plan for the future. Their use is most appropriate where resources have to be tightly controlled, as in cash control.

Fixed budgets may be set before or after the actual performance is known. If they are set after the event, they are set on the basis of the level of activity which was actually undertaken. This allows valid comparison to be made against the costs and revenues which were actually recorded, facilitating operational control. Budget flexing can also be undertaken before activity commences, to show predicted costs/revenues at a number of activity levels (as per the budget working papers). This gives management a prior understanding of the financial consequences of a number of possible activity levels.

The use of flexible budgets is most appropriate where activity levels are likely to change, and a substantial proportion of the costs is variable.

(c) The principal budget factor is a constraint, around which the budget is constructed. In any organisation there will be one area of operations which constrains the ability of the organisation to improve its financial performance. This is frequently sales volume, but it equally may be availability of skilled staff, of processing equipments, of material and so on. The starting point of the budget should be a consideration of the principal budget factor. This acts as a co-ordination device, allowing the budget to be produced in a way which allows the budget of each functional department, or budget centre, to be co-ordinated and linked.

(d) The preparation of a budget requires inputs from a number of different departments, each of which, while working towards the overall objective(s) of the organisation, may have its own particular priorities and interests. The role of the budget committee is to prevent the focus of the organisation from being lost through factors such as inertia, or the pursuit of self-interest on the part of individual managers. The budget committee, therefore, ensures that all proposals which are accepted for inclusion in the budget are co-ordinated and realistic, and further the goals of the organisation, so that the final budget which is approved represents an integrated series of departmental and functional targets achievable by all parties. The members of the budget committee should have sufficient experience and seniority to be able to ensure that the budget targets set are realistic, and should meet regularly to review the budgetary planning process and to resolve problems.

BUDGETARY CONTROL

 Solution 5

- The critical thing to appreciate is that training costs are normally 'discretionary' in character. That is, they do not relate directly to the volume of output or productive activity in the business.
- In answering the question you should draw on your full knowledge of business training. What is the full range of activities and practices that might be classified as 'staff training'?
- Staff training involves both inputs and outputs. The control and evaluation of training costs should relate to both of these. One problem with discretionary costs is that it is sometimes difficult to identify the outputs that flow from them.

(a) *The nature of training costs from a control viewpoint*

From a control viewpoint, training costs are discretionary costs. In other words, management decides what levels of training they wish to achieve and then budget for the expenditures that will be required to achieve those training levels. The decision as to the training levels required is a technical one – the result of training technology and experience – rather than an accounting one. The expenditure budgeted for training reflects that required objective. It is not normally susceptible to changes in volume of output, though it might be to the number of personnel or to the skills or length of service of personnel. Thus, from a control viewpoint, training costs will tend to be substantially fixed.

(b) *Training costs included in a training programme*

These costs would be for the following:

(i) External courses – Fees, travel, subsistence, expenses and so on; and

(ii) Internal courses – Space charges for buildings used, for example rentals, depreciation on buildings, maintenance and cleaning of buildings, light and heat.

– Depreciation on training equipment used, for example overhead projectors, desks.
– Consumables, for example paper, flip charts.
– Labour on training staff (direct costs on courses, e.g. internal and external lectures), support administrative staff and managerial training/personnel staff.
– Catering expenses and so on, for students and staff.
– Extra costs or loss of production by employees on courses and away from their normal work.

(c) *Preparation of a training programme report*

The training programme report would consists of

1. a statement of what the training programme aims to achieve, analysed by different types of training and/or courses;
2. the costs of each type of training activity/course, analysed by types of expenditure as listed in part (b) above. If possible, these would be separated into direct costs per activity/course and other fixed costs incurred for the whole activity;
3. the expected benefits from each type of course/activity.

The advantages of such a report would be that it would

1. show the net benefits per class of training course/activity;
2. show the assumptions on which benefits from training are calculated;
3. provide an opportunity to compare internal costs with charges by outside organisations that offer training facilities/courses;

4. highlight the relative incremental benefits of each type of course;

5. give an analysis of how the total budget is spent.

(d) *Controlling the performance of the training function*

Control of the training function would arise as indicated in (a) above, that is, by comparing expected benefits with the discretionary costs budgeted and by comparing actual costs with those budgeted.

In evaluating the training function, it would be advisable to try to check on the benefits actually obtained. This might require sample surveys; or 'before and after' surveys on, for example, production levels or reject costs; or post-course surveys, to learn of benefits that students had achieved. There is, nevertheless, a big element of 'faith' in the concept of benefit from training in industry.

☑ Solution 6

- This is a discursive question that invites discussion of various behavioural issues associated with financial control systems.

(a) Both the process of establishing a budget, and the use of that budget in the control process, can distort a business operation. To the extent that a budget provides a target and a performance yardstick, failure to achieve budget may be perceived by managers as an indication of poor performance that carries personal sanctions. A manager who fails to achieve budget may forgo promotions or salary increases.

A manager has, from the outset, an interest in securing an 'easy' budget. The process of establishing a budget may therefore become an exercise in bargaining and negotiation. The manager is thus distracted from running his department, and the budget that emerges from the process may be more a reflection of the manager's negotiating skills than any sort of objective statement.

Once a budget is established, a manager may be induced to do things that are not in the best interest of the business to ensure that he achieves it. Such things might include declining new business that offers only long-term advantages, or reducing costs in areas (such as quality control) that may have no immediate impact on the manager's own department. It can work the other way, too: a manager may incur unnecessary expenditure in order to ensure that all his budget is used, in order to prevent the next year's budget from being cut back.

(b) The process of budget negotiation may result in a pattern of spending that reflects the internal politics of an organisation and the bargaining position of individual managers. Such a pattern is unlikely to enable the organisation to achieve its objectives in the most cost-effective manner. This is particularly critical in a public sector or service organisation where the nature of output is not always tangible.

Where one departmental manager acts in a manner intended primarily to ensure that his own department achieves current period budget, unnecessary costs can arise in the long run. A cutback in quality control costs may result in more in-service failures of finished goods and lower customer satisfaction. However, the costs associated with these factors may not be attributable to the individual departmental manager.

It is frequently found that control systems linked to periodic reporting can induce cyclical behaviour in a manufacturing organisation. A manager who has a production budget for the quarter may be tempted to organise production in a manner calculated

BUDGETARY CONTROL

to maximise completions in the current quarter. This may involve splitting one 600-unit production batch into two batches of 300 units, since it is only possible to complete a 300-unit batch in one quarter. This allows current-period budget to be achieved, but it may not be the most economic pattern of production.

(c) As with many things in life, it is not the idea behind budgeting that is the problem, but the way in which it is used.

If a budget is perceived to be a form of sanction, and failure to achieve budget is thought to result in punishment, then the likelihood of the sort of problems described above is high.

The personal performance of individual managers should be assessed using a range of indicators, and achievement of budget should be only one of these. In any event, it is particularly critical that performance should be considered over a long period, not merely over the current budget control period.

☑ Solution 7

- The question invites comment on a variety of behavioural, quantitative, presentational and IT issues relevant to budgeting and budgetary control.
- Note that the question does not actually invite preparation of a flexed budget.

Report
To: Board of directors
From: Management accountant
Date: 5 February 2000
Subject: Budgets and performance measurement

Introduction
Further to our brief discussion I have considered the matters that you have raised and I set out detailed responses below.

(a) (i) *Present approach to budgeting*
As the budgets were 'issued to' the consultants it seems that they were set centrally and imposed on them. As one of the purposes of a budget is to motivate people to improve their performance, care is needed to ensure that the efficiency level of the budget is in line with the consultants' expectations of reasonableness. This is referred to as the consultants' aspiration level.

An alternative approach is to encourage the consultants to participate in the budget-setting process. This should lead to the creation of a target that is accepted by the consultants as being their own target. The consultants are motivated to achieve their own target, or feel that they have failed personally.

The danger of allowing consultants to participate in the budget-setting process is that they may try to set an 'easy' target, particularly if their performance is being measured against it. The inclusion of budgetary slack by the consultants can be difficult to remove once it has been included in a draft budget.

(ii) *Format of the operating statement*
The operating statement identifies those costs that are fixed and variable in relation to chargeable consultancy hours. However, no attempt is made in the statement to

determine the costs that would be expected in respect of the actual chargeable consultancy hours.

The variable costs should be flexed to the actual activity level and the variances recalculated, with indications as to whether the variances are adverse or favourable.

Further, the report should identify the controllable costs so that the consultants' attention is focused towards these variances so that, if they are significant, action is taken.

(b) A spreadsheet could be set up as follows to automate the variance calculation process.
  • Column headings: original budget, flexed budget, actual, variance.
  • Row headings: chargeable consultancy hours, costs (by item of cost).

A possible layout is shown below.

	Original budget	Flexed budget	Actual	Variance
Chargeable consultancy hours				
Administration staff salaries				
Consultants' salaries				
Casual wages				
Motor and travel costs				
Telephone				
Printing, postage and stationery				
Premises and equipment costs				
Total costs				
Fees charged				
Profit/(loss)				

A separate input area within the spreadsheet can be used to hold budget cost data expressed as a rate per consultancy hour, budget hours and actual hours. This can be used to produce the budget column above and also to provide the basis for the flexible budget. An alternative is to input the budget data and then to insert formulae to flex the original budget variable cost values by multiplying them by

$$\frac{\text{Actual chargeable consulatancy hours}}{\text{Original budget chargeable consultancy hours}}$$

to determine the total expected variable cost of the actual activity. This is added to the budgeted fixed cost (which is not expected to change in relation to activity-level changes). This gives the flexible budget.

Actual costs are then inserted into the spreadsheet, and other formulae are input in order to compare actual costs with the flexible budget, thus determining the variances.

Solution 8

(a) Cost driver rates:

$$W \quad \frac{£160,000}{(20 \times 4) + (30 \times 5) + (15 \times 2) + (40 \times 3) + (25 \times 1)} = £395$$

$$X \quad \frac{£130,000}{(20 \times 3) + (30 \times 2) + (15 \times 5) + (40 \times 1) + (25 \times 4)} = £388$$

$$Y \quad \frac{£80,000}{(20 \times 3) + (30 \times 3) + (15 \times 2) + (40 \times 4) + (25 \times 2)} = £205$$

$$Z \quad \frac{£200,000}{(20 \times 4) + (30 \times 6) + (15 \times 8) + (40 \times 2) + (25 \times 3)} = £374$$

Actual activities during October 2002:

W $(18 \times 4) + (33 \times 5) + (16 \times 2) + (35 \times 3) + (28 \times 1) = 402$
X $(18 \times 3) + (33 \times 2) + (16 \times 5) + (35 \times 1) + (28 \times 4) = 347$
Y $(18 \times 3) + (33 \times 3) + (16 \times 2) + (35 \times 4) + (28 \times 2) = 381$
Z $(18 \times 4) + (33 \times 6) + (16 \times 8) + (35 \times 2) + (28 \times 3) = 552$

Budgetary control statement

Processing activity	Original budget £'000	Flexible budget £'000	Actual costs £'000	Variance £'000
W	160	159	158	1 (F)
X	130	135	139	4 (A)
Y	80	78	73	5 (F)
Z	200	206	206	0
Totals	570	578	576	2 (F)

(b) It might be preferable for Managers not to be involved in setting their own budgets because

- budgetary slack is avoided, and more appropriate targets produced;
- they cannot use budgets to play games which disadvantage other budget holders;
- they may not have sufficient time available to devote to the budgeting process because of other pressures and thus the budgets that they prepare are rushed and inappropriate;
- they may have little knowledge of budgeting and be unprepared for such a task.

(c) (i) A fixed budget is a budget based upon a single level of activity, whereas a flexible budget recognises the relationships between costs and activity and allows target costs to be determined for the actual level of activity achieved.

Where costs are caused by activity, a flexible budget provides a fairer basis of comparison with actual results than a fixed budget. Fixed budgets should be used to control discretionary costs within AHW plc.

(ii) *Research and Advertising.* Since these costs are not directly related to activity, they both should be controlled against a pre-set expenditure limit, which is a form of fixed budget.

(d) The terms in the equation mean:

y = total cost of the period;
a = variable cost/unit of activity;
x = activity level of the period;
b = period fixed cost.

Budgeting and
Performance Evaluation

Budgeting and Performance Evaluation

7

LEARNING OUTCOMES

When you have completed study of this chapter you will be able to

▶ evaluate projected performance by calculating key metrics including profitability, liquidity and asset turnover ratios;

▶ discuss the role of non-financial performance indicators and compare and contrast traditional approaches to budgeting with recommendations based on the 'balanced scorecard';

▶ evaluate the criticisms of budgeting particularly from the advocates of techniques that are 'beyond budgeting'.

7.1 Introduction

In the previous two chapters, we have explored the budgeting concept and the manner in which budgets can be used to plan and control the operations of an organisation. We have also encountered the criticisms that have been levelled at the use of budgets, having particular regard to changes in the economic and business environment that may have limited the usefulness of more traditional budget practices.

The gravitational force of the budgeting system makes it extremely difficult for most firms to escape the world of compliance and control. Only by overcoming the constraints of the traditional budgeting approach can managers build a business model that operates at high speed; is self-questioning, self-renewing and self-controlling.

> J. Hope & R. Fraser, Beyond Budgeting (Strategic Finance, October 2000)
> (*Note*: Most of the article is included as a Reading item in Chapter 6)

In this chapter, we will consider the manner in which the performance of a business, organisation or function may be evaluated. In doing this we will have regard to both budget figures, actual results and innovative approaches which fall under the heading of 'beyond budgeting'.

7.2 Performance evaluation

The manner in which analysis of published financial reports can be used to evaluate performance is explored fully in CIMA's Paper P8 – *Financial Analysis*. Many of the techniques encountered therein can also be deployed in the review of budgets and internal financial control reports. However, the analyst should be aware that the preparation of budgets and internal reports may be less constrained by accounting standards and statutory requirements than is the case with published reports.

With that caveat, let us consider the key metrics used in performance evaluation. These can be applied to both budgets to give a measure of projected performance and actual reported results. Bear in mind that we may be considering the performance of individual organisational segments as well as a whole business or organisation.

7.2.1 The profit and loss account

(a) Turnover

An understanding of the profitability of the business could start with a review of turnover. Turnover is important in both absolute and relative terms. Increases or decreases in sales may be attributable to changes in selling prices or sales volume, or a combination of both.

Turnover of a business may be varied in nature. There may be seasonal differences, many products or segments, and different product mixes.

Understanding the reasons for movements in the level and structure of turnover may explain why performance has improved or worsened in the past and give us insights as to what might happen in the future.

(b) Profitability

There are a number of profit figures appearing in the profit and loss account. Each may be used to evaluate the profitability of the business.

Gross profit margin: Gross profit/Turnover

Factors relevant to an appreciation of the gross profit margin may include

- breakdown by product, geographical area or other segment;
- purchase details such as bulk discounts, purchasing errors, wastage or theft;
- selling prices of products over the period.

Operating profit margin: Operating profit/Turnover

Factors relevant to an appreciation of the operating profit margin may include

- the manner in which overheads are distributed between products and organisational segments;
- the technology used by an organisation which determines the relative proportion of its costs chargeable to gross and operating profit.

Net profit is rather less useful than gross or operating profit for the purposes of performance evaluation. Net profit is profit after deduction of finance costs and these are influenced by decisions which do not relate to the economic performance of the business.

(c) Elements of cost

Individual elements of cost may be reported, for example:

telephone cost ratio = telephone costs/sales;
Advertising cost ratio = advertising costs/sales.

7.2.2 Return on capital employed

The overall performance of a business operation depends on the operating profit that it is generating relative to the value of the capital engaged in achieving that profit. The simplest measure of this is return on capital employed (ROCE), as shown below.

Operating profit/capital employed.

Capital employed is the book value of the Net Assets employed by the business or business segment that is under review. The term 'return on investment' (RoI) is often used almost interchangeably with ROCE. However, the term 'RoI' is more commonly applied to the performance of a project rather than a business.

We will encounter ROCE and its variants when we consider detailed aspects of responsibility centre accounting in Chapter 9.

7.2.3 Asset turnover

The asset turnover shows the amount of turnover the business generates relative to the capital it employs.

Asset turnover = Turnover/capital employed

This metric gives an impression of the efficiency with which capital is being used. Obviously, it contributes to overall performance as measured by ROCE, since

Operating profit margin × Asset turnover = ROCE

If asset turnover can be raised, then ROCE will also rise.

One may consider the efficiency with which individual components of assets are being used. For example:

Stock days = (Stock held/purchases) × 365
Debtor days = (Debtor balance/sales) × 365

These figures give the average number of days trade held in the form of stock and debtors – the working capital of the business. The lower these figures are, the higher is ROCE. One wishes to operate a business with the lowest possible levels of stock and debtors. That said, these working capital items are assets which do contribute to the operating profit of the business.

Factors that one might consider in obtaining an appreciation of the various aspects of asset turnover include

- stock holding policy having regard to the calculation of optimum stock holding levels, just-in-time production strategies or commercial initiatives that have stock holding implications;
- credit sales policy, having regard to the fact that sales on credit terms might be made at enhanced prices;
- the technology that is being used having regard to the fact that one may operate a labour intensive production operation as the alternative to holding high capital assets.

The mirror image of asset turnover is liability turnover. The main example of this is

Creditor days = Creditor balance/purchase × 365

This figure reports the average time the business takes to pay its suppliers. In theory, keeping this figure high will increase ROCE – but at the possible cost of damage to supplier relationships.

7.2.4 Liquidity

While not central to the aspects of performance evaluation we are considering, liquidity is another aspect of management that might be considered. Liquidity, as a broad concept, refers to the manner in which cash is circulated through the business – and it should not be confused with 'solvency' which is a legal consideration. Measures of liquidity involve comparison of current assets (debtors, stock and cash) with current liabilities (trade creditors and bank overdraft)

There are several metrics which may be used to measure liquidity and these include

Current (or 'liquidity') ratio = Current assets/current liabilities
Acid test (or 'quick') ratio = (Cash + debtors)/current liabilities
Cash conversion period = Stock days + debtor days − creditor days

In considering these metrics it will be appreciated that the lower they are, the higher will be the ROCE. On the other hand, very low values for these metrics may imply some difficulty in meeting financial obligations as they become due.

Management of working capital is one area of administration that contributes to the performance of a business operation. If the business can be run in a manner that allows its CCP to be kept low, then this will keep the Capital Employed low and minimise operating costs relating to the holding of stock and debtors.

7.3 Exercise

Let us explore the use of the metrics specified above through use of a simple exercise.

Exercise

In early 2004 your client has been requested to sell a large volume of goods on extended credit terms to a potential new customer called GHI Ltd, which has been trading for three years. GHI is a wholesaler and most of its business costs are purchases. Your client has expressed some doubts about the financial stability of GHI and has asked for your advice.

You have obtained copies of the two most recent sets of GHI's audited accounts which are summarised as follows:

All figures in £'000	2002	2003
Equipment net of depreciation	1,200	1,100
Premises	800	450
Stock	280	540
Debtors	160	490
Cash/(Overdraft)	80	(90)
Creditors	(140)	(390)
Net Assets	2,380	2,100
Share Capital	800	800
Loan from Directors	1,100	700
Cumulative Retained Profits	480	600
Capital	2,380	2,100
Turnover (Sales)	2,400	2,900
Operating Profit	160	210
Dividends Paid	40	90

The Managing Director of GHI has made the followings statement to your client:

GHI has a consistent history of profitability. We are investing in the future of the company and this has strained our cash flow position. However, GHI is poised for growth and our acceptance of you as a supplier will be an opportunity for you to participate in our inevitable success

Requirements

(a) Calculate the following business metrics for GHI in 2002 and 2003 – ROCE, profit margin on sales, liquidity (or current) ratio, debtor days, stock days, creditor days and cash conversion period.

(b) Critically appraise the Managing Director's comment quoted above and advise your client on whether or not he or she should extend significant amounts of credit to GHI.

 Solution

(a) GHI Ltd – key business metrics

	2002	2003
ROCE	6.7%	10.0%
Profit margin	6.7%	7.2%
Liquidity	3.7	2.1
Debtor days	24	62
Stock days	46	73
Creditor days	23	53
CCP	47	82

Most of the figures given above are fairly obvious. But some imagination is required in certain cases. For example, in calculating stock days and creditor days one needs to know 'purchases' – a figure which is not given. What we can do in this case is adopt operating costs as a proxy for purchases. Operating costs is sales minus operating profit. We are told that most business costs are purchases so the resultant stock and creditor days figures are meaningful and allow a clear inter-period comparison.

For example, Stock days for 2002 is

$$(280/(2,400-160)) \times 365 = 46 \text{ days}$$

that is, end 2002 Stock balance divided by 2002 operating costs. Note that our stock and creditor days positions for 2003 are both based on end 2003 balances. One could argue that it would be more appropriate to base these figures on an average of end 2002 and end 2003 balances. The argument against such an averaging is that the end 2002 balance is old history, and what was happening at end 2003 is far more current.

(b) The performance of this business appears to have been both respectable and improving having regard to both ROCE and profit margin. Those are the key performance metrics, but they do not tell the whole story. The asset turnover and liquidity position of the business has changed in a manner that should prompt some serious questions:

- Stock days has risen dramatically. Why has this happened? Does the extra stock really exist and how has it been valued?
- Debtor days has risen dramatically. Why has this happened? Do the extra debtors actually exist and what is the chance of bad debts arising?
- Creditor days has risen dramatically. Why has this happened? Are suppliers continuing to make deliveries as normal?

That apart, there is clear evidence of assets being stripped out of the business by its owners. Property has been sold, a director loan partly repaid and dividends have been increased. These may not impact immediately on the key performance metrics – which are essentially 'backward looking' measures reporting only what has happened over a short period in the immediate past. But what is happening suggests a clear lack of commitment on the part of its directors that might impact on performance in the longer term.

To form a fuller evaluation of performance one would need to obtain a range of forward looking indicators – linked to things like market share, quality of service, response time to customer orders, proportion of customer repeat business being achieved, staff turnover and relationships with suppliers. These are considered in the discussion of non-financial performance indicators below.

7.4 Understanding the business

It is sometimes considered that financial analysis involves the direct application of a routine set of numerical calculations to a set of financial reports. This is only one part of the task. In order to interpret those calculations it is important to understand the relationships between the data and the underlying reasons for the current situation.

Financial analysis requires an understanding of the products, services and operating characteristics of the business. The business operates within an industry consisting of businesses with similar operating characteristics. If the analysis invites comparison of the business with the industry norms, it is important to identify the key characteristics of the industry and so establish benchmarks such as gross profit ratios, debtor collection days and so on.

However, one should exercise care in evaluating performance on the basis of comparison with industry 'benchmarks' (a concept introduced in Chapter 2). No two businesses are the same and one can never be sure that one is comparing likes. For one thing, ROCE and related metrics tend to move with the plant replacement cycle. A business with old, heavily depreciated equipment is likely to report a higher ROCE than one with new equipment. But this does not imply that the former is performing better than the latter in a strictly economic sense.

7.5 Reporting a performance evaluation

Broadly, the following approaches to reporting an evaluation are possible.

(a) Horizontal analysis
Horizontal analysis involves a line-by-line comparison of one set of data with another (e.g. the current year's accounts with those of the previous year or with budgets). Identifying the percentage movements in this way can reveal indicators of the performance of the business, but more importantly, it can prompt further lines of enquiry. We have seen examples of this at several points earlier in this text.

(b) Trend analysis
Trend analysis is horizontal analysis extended over several years. The GHI example considered above involves use of a form of trend analysis. The most significant observations were drawn from consideration of the movement in metrics between 2002 and 2003.

(c) Vertical analysis
Vertical analysis involves expressing the data as a percentage of a critical component of the financial statements. Components of the balance sheet are usually expressed as a percentage

of total assets. The profit and loss account items are usually expressed as a percentage of total sales. This type of analysis can give important clues as to the financial condition and operations of the business. For example, a company may maintain a high percentage of assets in cash, stocks or debtors in order to increase its liquidity.

The reporting of a performance evaluation can be carried out for a whole business or for individual segments of a business. In this context your attention is drawn to the discussion of budget centres and responsibility centres elsewhere in this text. Budgets should be assembled and results reported in a manner that is consistent with the organisational structure. This allows the performance of individual responsibility areas to be budgeted for and then evaluated.

Let us consider the following simple financial control report:

Light manufacturing division:

Operating statement for September 2004

	£'000	'000 units	£ per unit	% Sales
Sales	450	1,200	0.375	100
Costs:				
Materials	120		0.100	27
Labour	240		0.200	53
Overheads	40		0.033	9
Total	400		0.333	89
Profit	50		0.042	11

Is a material cost of £120,000 good or bad? In itself, the figure tells you very little. But if you express it relative to something else then it takes on more meaning. When expressed as £0.10 per unit or as 27 per cent of sales value then one gets a clearer idea of what is involved.

If you are told that the corresponding figures for materials £ per unit were £0.08 per unit in 9/03 and £0.07 per unit in 9/02, then you get a much clearer view of how performance is moving. If you are told that the light manufacturing industry average materials £ per unit is £0.09, then you get still more insights into what is happening.

One key thing to be aware of is that consideration of a given figure or performance metric may tell you little when considered in isolation. It becomes most meaningful only when set in some context – compared with previous years results to reveal a trend, compared with budget to reveal a divergence from plan or compared with an industry benchmark to reveal a departure from the norm. Even then, caution should be exercised in drawing conclusions too easily.

7.6 Non-financial performance indicators

The use of traditional financial performance metrics is widespread, but the practice has its problems. For example:

- They only tell you what has happened over a limited period in the immediate past.
- They give you no indication of what is going to happen in the future.
- They are vulnerable to manipulation and to the choice of accounting policy on matters such as depreciation and stock valuation.
- They do not relate to the strategic management of the business and may induce 'short-termism' – an issue explored further in Chapter 9.

So, if we wish to obtain a fuller evaluation of performance, then we have to turn to a range of Non-financial performance indicators (NFPIs).

Certain academic writers have developed models of performance evaluation for strategic advantage and these are considered more fully in CIMA's Paper P6 – *Business Strategy*. The general thrust behind these is that performance indicators should be developed that relate to the long-term strategic development of the organisation.

This follows the principle advocated by management guru/writer Tom Peters:

What gets measured gets done.

The performance indicators adopted for a given business or business segment should relate to its key success factors – those things that are most likely to determine its success or failure. NFPIs can be expressed in either quantitative and qualitative terms. For example, it might be reported that we have a 5 per cent market share (a quantitative measure) and we are first supplier of preference to almost all our established customers (a qualitative measure).

Let us consider a number of NFPIs, how they might be expressed and relevant information relating to them might be gathered.

(a) *Competitiveness*:
   - sales growth by product or service;
   - size of customer base;
   - market share by product, service or customer group.
   Regular market surveys drawing on both internal and external sources of information can be used to compile reports.

(b) *Activity level*:
   - number of Units sold;
   - labour and machine hours worked;
   - number of passengers carried;
   - number of overdue debts collected.
   Relevant information could be drawn mainly from internal sources, with appropriate checks to ensure accuracy.

(c) *Productivity*:
   - manufacturing cost per unit produced;
   - capacity utilisation of facilities and personnel;
   - average number of units produced per day or per man-day;
   - average setting up time for new production run.
   Again, most of this information could be drawn from internal sources.

(d) *Quality of service*:
   - number of units rejected in manufacturing;
   - number of units failing in service;
   - number of visits by representatives to customer premises;
   - number of new accounts gained or lost;
   - number of repeat customer orders received.
   Again, most relevant information would be available from internal sources but this could be reinforced by periodic customer surveys.

(e) *Customer satisfaction*:
   - average time taken to respond to customer enquiry or order;
   - expressed customer satisfaction with sales staff;
   - expressed customer satisfaction with technical representatives;
   - number of customer complaints received.

Relevant information would have to come mainly from customer surveys although some internal sources could be selectively used. Customer surveys can be carried out on a regular structured basis or on an occasional informal basis. If a sample of customers is being used to compile information, then care has to be taken that the sample is significant in size and representative in structure.

(f) *Quality of staff experience*:
- days absence per week;
- staff turnover rate;
- number of new qualifications/courses completed by staff;
- number of new staff skills certified;
- expressed job satisfaction;
- qualification levels of newly recruited staff.

Some information could be taken from internal sources but much would have to come from colleges and external trainers. Exit interviews and confidential staff opinion surveys could also be used.

(g) *Innovation*:
- number of new products or services brought to market;
- proportion of Sales relating to new products;
- technical lead relative to competitors;
- lead time to bring new products to market.

This kind of information would have to be taken from a variety of internal and external sources. The slightly subjective nature of what constitutes a 'new product' is such that this may be an area where an external assessor or consultant might be used to prepare the report.

These sort of performance indicators have the advantage of being 'forward looking'. That is, they are likely to address factors that relate to how well or badly the business will perform in the future.

For example, a service business with a high staff turnover rate is at a disadvantage. If experienced and qualified staff are constantly leaving and being replaced, then this may not contribute to the quality of service being offered to customers. We have all experienced visits to a shop, travel agent or garage where we have been served by an inexperienced and obviously new member of staff – who is unfamiliar with our account history and appears to have limited knowledge of the products that he or she is trying to sell. We find it much more satisfactory to be served by an experienced member of staff who knows his or her customers and products.

Yet, a deterioration in the standard of staff being employed (as evidenced by the indicators listed above under quality of staff experience) would not impact greatly on current period ROCE. A focus on current ROCE might actually induce a business to make greater use of poorly paid, junior staff in order to minimise operating costs. The impact of this on the business might be felt only in the long term.

As with any performance indicator, an NFPI has to be viewed in some context in order to be most meaningful. A good control report will express indicators in terms of a deviation from plan, relative to an industry benchmark or as part of a trend analysis covering comparable earlier periods.

Further, it is best to consider performance indicators as part of a package giving a multidimensional impression of how the organisation is performing.

Example

One example of the use of NFPIs frequently reported in management literature is that of BAA plc (formerly the British Airports Authority). This is the case of a service company that attempts to evaluate its own performance in terms of the quality it is able to offer to customers.

It has identified about 12 key success factors which include access, aesthetics, cleanliness, comfort, staff competence, staff courtesy, reliability, responsiveness and security. These take on board the factors that customers appreciate when using an airport–short distances to walk from point of arrival to point of departure, safety from attack or robbery, easy availability of luggage trolleys and wheel chairs and so on.

BAA carries out regular surveys involving interviews with customers, consultant reports, analysis of operational data, and monitoring customer feedback. Appropriate indicators for each factor are reported and studied through comparison between different airports and trend analysis over time. For example, if airport A persistently reports a higher level of theft from customers than other airports–then this might prompt the introduction of additional security measures at airport A. If complaints about staff courtesy at airport D have been on a persistent upward trend over time, then this might prompt enquiries into staff supervision at that site and/or additional staff training.

A customer survey might include a question as follows:

'Your impression of the service available in the cafeterias at Airport B is best described as

(A) Most satisfactory
(B) Satisfactory
(C) Acceptable
(D) Less than acceptable
(E) Unsatisfactory.

Answering this involves a qualitative judgement on the part of the customer, but the survey results can be reported and evaluated in quantitative terms. For example, if 80% of customers offered A or B answers to this question, then the impression given is that the standard of service at Airport B cafeterias is not a problem–and it may even serve as a model of best practice for other airports.

This line of discussion leads us into the more modern models of performance evaluation which fall broadly under the 'Beyond Budgeting' heading encountered in Chapter 6.

7.7 Benchmarking

It is often found that performance is difficult to compare by a simple comparison of actual and budget profit. A variety of refinements have therefore been developed to assist in the establishment of business plans and in monitoring the achievement of those plans.

The term 'benchmarking' has become associated with a growing desire by companies to seek out the best available performance, internal or external, as a comparator ('benchmark') against which to measure their own performance. We have already encountered the term in Chapter 1 in the context of standard costing. The standard cost of a product or activity is a form of benchmark. However, it is conventionally arrived at through a work study exercise which is internal to the process being managed. Some argue that the standard cost concept offers a very limited form of benchmark and a wider view should be taken. The *Official Terminology* defines it as follows.

> *Benchmarking.* The establishment, through data gathering, of targets and comparators, through whose use relative levels of performance (and particularly areas of underperformance) can be identified. By the adoption of identified best practices it is hoped that performance will improve.

The data-gathering exercise referred to in the definition is not necessarily an easy one: obtaining the information required in order to benchmark against competitors in non-financial areas can be problematic. Financial information is much more readily available than non-financial information. Obviously, non-financial information about competitors' products can be obtained by 'reverse engineering' them (i.e. buying a competitor's products and dismantling them, in order to understand their content and configuration), and from product literature, trade associations and press comment. However, the product is the end result of the *processes* that a business follows, and thus effective benchmarking required an understanding of the processes of other businesses. Getting information about their processes is much more difficult than getting information about their products. For example, how do competitors process customer orders, deal with customer enquiries, conduct their relationships with suppliers? The need to gain an understanding of business processes in other companies has given rise to two types of 'benchmarking': intra-group and inter-industry.

With intra-group benchmarking, groups of companies in the same industry agree that similar units within the co-operating companies will pool data on their processes. The processes are benchmarked against each other, and, at an operational level, 'improvement task forces' are established to identify and transfer 'best practice' to all members of the group. In interindustry benchmarking, a non-competing business with similar processes is identified and asked to participate in a benchmarking exercise. For example, a distributor of personal computers may approach a distributor of hi-fi equipment to establish a benchmarking relationship. The two companies are not in direct competition, but there are obviously many similarities in the characteristics of their sources of supply, distribution channels and customers. There are benefits to both participants in such a scheme, as they are each able to benefit from the experience of the other, and establish 'best practice' in their common business processes.

Almost any aspect of a manufacturing or service operation can be benchmarked. For example, benchmarking is now quite widely used in the public sector. Local authorities may exchange data on matters such as cost per km of roadway maintained, cost per primary school pupil in education, cost per tonne of refuse collected and so on. Benchmarking against non-local authorities may also be useful. An insurance company may provide a useful benchmark (cost per sq. metre of office space maintained, cost per customer enquiry processed) which a local authority may use to measure the performance of its office functions.

Benchmarking exercises may be undertaken as one-off projects in particular areas or on a continuing basis. Where an adverse discrepancy is identified between an own performance indicator and that of the benchmark reference, this may indicate an area for improvement. That said, it may simply indicate a difference of circumstances. For example 'cost per primary school pupil in education' will be higher than average for a local authority which has a high proportion of special needs pupils on its books. Similarly, lower than average 'cost per tonne of sewage disposed of' does not reflect a more efficient operation if it is achieved simply by pumping raw sewage into the sea off a local beach. As with all forms of business control system, a degree of sensitivity is required in the manner in which benchmarks are selected and the manner in which the resultant comparisons are interpreted.

The motivation for collaborating with other companies in a benchmarking exercise is clear: it enables a company to improve its performance by learning from the experience of others. Obviously, there is a danger in intra-group benchmarking that competitors may gain more from the process than one's own firm, and this is an issue that will be of concern to management. However, this concern may be tempered by the knowledge that yet other competitors are outside the system. Nevertheless, the attraction of inter-industry benchmarking in providing less of a direct commercial threat is obvious.

Benchmarking is a 'hot' management topic that has attracted the interest of practitioners, academics, writers and consultants.

Benchmarking

Bob Scarlett – *CIMA Insider*, October 2003

Benchmarking is the process of improving performance by continuously identifying, understanding (studying and analysing), and adapting outstanding practices and process found inside and outside the organisation and implementing the results

(American Productivity and Quality Centre, 1997)

Benchmarking is an approach to performance management that starts with the premise that whatever the process (supply, production, sales or services), performance can best be measured and managed by comparing that process with an appropriate outside entity that is already achieving world-class performance. The outside entity used to provide the benchmark need not operate within the same sector as our process. Further the benchmark can be from either another organisation (an 'external' benchmark) or a different segment within the same organisation (an 'internal' benchmark).

A benchmark provides a standard of excellence against which to measure and compare. Benchmarks are performance measures – How many? (e.g. 'customers served per staff member per hour') How quickly? (e.g. 'delivery time to customer') How high? (e.g. 'proportion of sales giving rise to repeat business') How low? (e.g. 'proportion of output being defective'). To be meaningful, a benchmark should relate to a 'key performance indicator', that is something within the business process that has a major influence on results. Establishing benchmarks is a necessary part of benchmarking but of itself does not provide an understanding of best practices nor does knowledge of the benchmarks lead necessarily to improvement. Benchmarking is the learning of lessons about how best performance is achieved. Rather than merely measuring performance, benchmarking focuses on how to improve any given business process by exploiting 'best practices' by discovering the specific practices responsible for high performance, understanding how these practices work and adapting and applying them to the organisation. A benchmarking exercise may take the form of a process comparison which does not involve the use of metrics.

Some writers identify three distinct approaches to benchmarking:

(1) *Metric benchmarking*. The practice of comparing appropriate metrics to identify possible areas for improvement;

(2) *Process benchmarking*. The practice of comparing processes with a partner as part of an improvement process;

(3) *Diagnostic benchmarking*. The practice of reviewing the processes of a business to identify those which indicate a problem and offer a potential for improvement.

The Xerox corporation is often cited as the pioneer in benchmarking practice. When it wanted to improve performance in its warehousing and distribution operation it did not go down the then conventional road of process redesign. Rather, it identified the business which was acknowledged as being the very best at warehousing and distribution – the L.L. Bean catalogue merchant. L.L. Bean agreed to undertake a co-operative benchmarking project. Over a period the two exchanged data on various aspects of their inventory handling and processing of orders. As a result of this, Xerox identified those areas in its own operation which were performing at below Bean's standards and acted to implement improvements. One critical point to note is that Xerox did not adopt another office equipment business as its model – it adopted a business operating in a different sector altogether.

Benchmarking in all its varied forms is becoming increasingly widespread in industry, services and the public sector. In particular, it is perceived to offer a more sophisticated tool in performance management than more traditional approaches such as standard costing. The general thrust behind this idea is that standard costing belongs in the era when goods were produced in long continuous production runs and a high proportion of costs were 'product specific'. In the new economy, goods tend to be highly customised, contain a significant service element and are produced in short discontinuous production runs on a JIT basis. A large proportion of product costs are determined at the design stage or are 'customer specific', that is they relate to the manner in which the goods are provided to the customer. Efficiency is therefore very much a function of product engineering, the flexibility of the production operation and customer relationship management. It is argued that the traditional budgetary control report based on standard costing simply does not address these issues.

A comprehensive system of benchmarking can provide a much fuller impression of how well or badly an operation is performing. And, it is more likely to give an indication of those areas in the operation that are amenable to improvement. That said, benchmarking has its critics. For example:

Benchmarking relies on competitive data that isn't readily available. When the data is available, it may be neither accurate nor timely. Moreover, it allows a comparison at only one point in time and does not provide a way to continually improve performance.

John Pucket, Boston Consulting Group (quoted from 1997)

That is fair comment, but the discussion above indicates some of the ways in which such criticism might be answered. For one thing, benchmarking need not rely on competitive data. As with most business techniques, benchmarking has to be carried out well if it is to yield results.

7.8   The balanced scorecard

Actions that are taken to improve the economic performance of a business do not always lead to an improvement in short-term financial performance, and may actually lead to a deterioration in this performance. For example, increased spending on product development may lead to enhanced product innovation, but there will invariably be a time lag between the expenditure and the financial rewards expected to follow from it. Similarly, reducing the lead time from receipt of a customer order to the delivery of the product will have positive outcomes in terms of increased customer satisfaction and a likely reduction in the level of stocks held in the company. However, financial accounting requires stocks to be valued at full absorption cost; under this convention, a decline in stockholding is associated with a reduction in reported profit, which, in isolation, would be seen as a negative outcome. Such examples illustrate the importance of ensuring that information that is passed up the organisation from operating units contains sufficient non-financial information for management to assess the financial results of the subunits in the correct context. It is similarly important that the measures are such that employees are encouraged to take actions that are consistent with long-run profitability: the old maxim 'what gets measured gets attention' remains true.

The inclusion of non-financial information alongside financial information has become known as the 'balanced scorecard approach' associated with writings by Kaplan and Norton. The *Official Terminology* defines it as follows.

> *Balanced scorecard approach*. An approach to the provision of information to management to assist strategic policy formulation and achievement. It emphasises the need to provide the user with a set of information which addresses all relevant areas of performance in an objective and unbiased fashion. . . .

The contents of a balanced scorecard will vary from business to business, but most include the following measures; *profitability* – the 'financial perspective'; *customer satisfaction* – the 'customer perspective'; *innovation* – the 'innovation and learning perspective'; and *internal efficiency* – the 'internal business perspective'. An example of the types of measures used to assess performance under the four 'perspectives' just listed is provided by *Kaplan and Norton*. The firm to which their measures relate is a semiconductor company, and they are reproduced in the form of Figure 7.1.

By providing all this information in a single report, management is able to assess the impact of particular actions on all perspectives of the company's activities.

Determining the specific items to include in a balanced scorecard requires a business to examine its operation carefully, in order to address the following three questions:

1. What are the critical success factors?
2. What performance measures can be used to monitor attainment against the critical success factors?
3. What changes must be made to organisational processes in order to facilitate the improvement of performance against the critical success factors?

As changes take place in its market, so the critical success factors of a business may change. The questions listed above must thus be regularly revisited, illustrating yet again the dynamism of the modern business environment, and the importance of ensuring that information is provided that gives a clear indication of the actions that are required to deal with environmental turbulence.

7.9 Performance evaluation in the not-for-profit sector

The special characteristics of performance in the Not-for-profit (NFP) sector were discussed in Chapter 5. The central issue is that an NFP organisation exists to achieve certain objectives and an evaluation of its performance in achieving those objectives must have regard to a combination of efficiency and effectiveness factors. The organisation should achieve the maximum output from the resources at its disposal (efficiency) and at the same time it should organise those resources in a manner that achieves a given result by the cheapest route (effectiveness).

Many of the performance indicators considered above can be applied to NFPs. For example, in evaluating the performance of a local authority one might consider

- cost per km of road maintained;
- cost per child in school;
- cost per square metre of grass verge mown;
- cost per tonne of sewage disposed of.

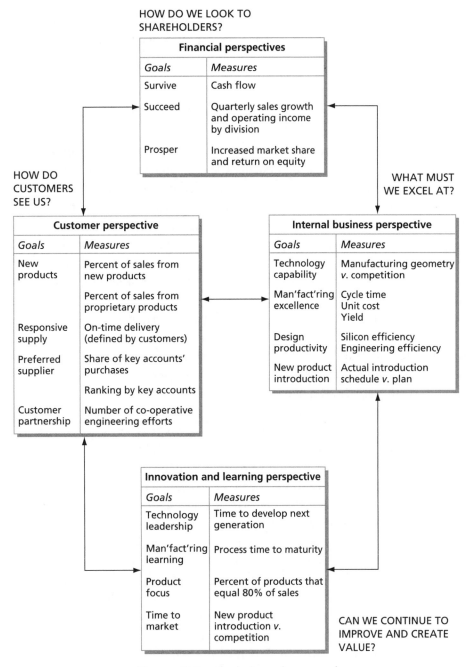

Figure 7.1   The balanced scorecard

These are all quantitative measures and care should be taken in their interpretation. For example, town A' s sewage disposal cost might be half that of town B. Does that mean that A is more efficient than B? Not necessarily, because A might be pumping raw sewage direct into the sea whereas B treats sewage and transports it for disposal. If A is a resort town then its 'efficiency' in disposing of sewage might have a variety of adverse knock-on effects. In considering performance one has to consider qualitative factors. A variety of qualitative indicators might also be considered in tandem with the quantitative ones listed above:

- number of claims made by motorists arising from pot holed roads;
- number of local children obtaining 2 A level GCEs or equivalent;
- rating of local road system by the Automobile Association;
- number of complaints from visitors concerning smell/taste of sea water.

Benchmarking is probably the most important recent innovation in performance evaluation in the NFP sector. The standard benchmarking practice can be used:

- study processes in the organisation and select which are to be benchmarked;
- secure suitable benchmark partners;
- compare appropriate figures and indicators with partners;
- adopt and implement 'best practices'.

A benchmark partner for one local authority need not necessarily be another local authority. For example, if the activity being benchmarked is 'office costs', then one could benchmark against an insurance company or a mail order company. However, while such benchmark partners might give a local authority an idea about its efficiency in certain areas, they would offer little guidance on effectiveness. If the authority is seeking guidance on the appropriate combination of spend on police, social services, housing and so on in order to provide a certain level of welfare for elderly residents (a quest for effectiveness), then the appropriate benchmark partners would have to be other authorities providing a similar service.

In the United Kingdom, benchmarking and its associated concept of 'best practice' are now widely used in public sector performance evaluation. The Department of the Environment rates all local authorities on the basis of periodic reviews. The use of appropriate performance indicators are a central element in these reviews. Such indicators have regard to both quantitative and qualitative factors.

As with all performance evaluation exercises, it must be appreciated that the calculation of a particular indicator will probably mean little unless it is set in some sort of context. Calculating the value of a particular indicator at 7.2 means little, until it is compared with a budget, set in a trend or set against a best practice benchmark.

One final comment in this area should be made. You are reminded of the Peter principle – 'What gets measured gets done'. If a performance evaluation is based on an incorrect or incomplete range of metrics, then the system can induce the wrong things to get done. For example, in the late 1990s the performance of hospitals was judged on the length of their waiting lists. Specifically, the average time taken for a referred patient to have a first consultation was adopted as a key performance indicator. It is claimed that this induced hospitals to concentrate on patients with minor illnesses since they could be treated quickly and cleared off the list. The small number of patients requiring major treatments often had to wait longer than was the case before the performance indicator was adopted.

Hospital waiting lists were reduced, but not in a wholly neutral manner. Some people gained and some lost as a result of the system. That was never the intention.

7.10 Summary

In this chapter we have considered various aspects of performance evaluation and have seen the limitations of the more traditional methods linked to simple financial metrics and budget compliance. Much of material covered in the previous chapter is also relevant in this regard.

We have then proceeded to consider the more modern models of performance evaluation associated with Benchmarking and the Balance Scorecard. These techniques coupled with NFPIs are associated with the Beyond Budgeting concept. It is suggested that these ideas are better attuned to the modern economic environment than the more traditional approaches.

In this and the preceding two chapters we have explored the nature of budgeting and its role in business planning, business control and performance evaluation. We have seen how the general idea works and what its limitations are.

A promotional article issued over the Internet by a firm of consultants now follows in a somewhat abridged form. This article contains a wide-ranging discussion of modern thinking and practices in the area of organisational performance evaluation.

Self-test quiz

(1) Explain the term 'ROCE' (Section 7.2.2).
(2) Is an increase in the cash conversion period most likely to cause ROCE to fall or to rise (Section 7.2.4)?
(3) Distinguish between 'horizontal analysis' and 'vertical analysis' in the context of budgetary control reporting (Section 7.5).
(4) What is a non-financial performance indicator (Section 7.6)?
(5) State four NFPIs that might be used to measure service quality (Section 7.6).
(6) State four NFPIs that might be used to measure quality of staff experience (Section 7.6).
(7) Explain the term 'benchmarking' (Section 7.7).
(8) Distinguish between 'metric benchmarking' and 'process benchmarking' (Section 7.7).
(9) What are the four performance perspectives that feature in the balanced scorecard (Section 7.8)?
(10) How might the Peter principle influence management behaviour in the context of a performance evaluation system (Section 7.9).

Reading

7

There is a substantial body of writing on general budgeting and performance management topics. The following item gives a flavour of this.

A guide to performance measurement and non-financial indicators

Andrew Mosely, Metapraxis Ltd

The need for a range of performance measures:

Organisational control is the process whereby an organisation ensures that it is pursuing strategies and actions which will enable it to achieve its goals. The measurement and evaluation of performance are central to control and mean posing four basic questions:

1. What has happened?
2. Why has it happened?
3. Is it going to continue?
4. What are we going to do about it?

The first question can be answered by performance measurement. Management will then have to hand far more useful information than it would otherwise have in order to answer the other three questions. By finding out what has actually been happening, senior management can determine with considerable certainty which direction the company is going in and, if all is going well, continue with the good work. Or, if the performance measurements indicate that there are difficulties on the horizon, management can then lightly effect a touch on the tiller or even alter course altogether with plenty of time to spare.

As to the selection of a range of performance measures which are appropriate to a particular company, this selection ought to be made in the light of the company's strategic intentions which will have been formed to suit the competitive environment in which it operates and the kind of business that it is.

For example, if technical leadership and product innovation are to be the key source of a manufacturing company's competitive advantage, then it should be measuring its performance in this area relative to its competitors. But if a service company decides to differentiate itself in the marketplace on the basis of quality of service, then, amongst other things, it should be monitoring and controlling the desired level of quality.

305

BUDGETING AND PERFORMANCE EVALUATION

Whether the company is in the manufacturing or the service sector, in choosing an appropriate range of performance measures it will be necessary, however, to balance them, to make sure that one dimension or set of dimensions of performance is not stressed to the detriment of others. The mix chosen will in almost every instance be different. While most companies will tend to organise their accounting systems using common accounting principles, they will differ widely in the choice, or potential choice, of performance indicators.

Authors from differing management disciplines tend to categorise the various performance indicators that are available as follows:

(1) competitive advantage   (4) flexibility
(2) financial performance   (5) resource utilization
(3) quality of service   (6) innovation.

These six generic performance dimensions fall into two conceptually different categories. Measures of the first two reflect the success of the chosen strategy, that is ends or results. The other four are factors that determine competitive success, that is means or determinants.

Another way of categorising these sets of indicators is to refer to them either as upstream or as downstream indicators, where, for example, improved quality of service upstream leads to better financial performance downstream.

Upstream Determinants and Downstream Results

Performance Dimensions	Types of Measures
Competitiveness	Relative market share and position sales growth, Measures re customer base
Financial Performance	Profitability, Liquidity, Capital Structure, Market Rations, etc.
Quality of Service	Reliability, Responsiveness, Appearance, Cleanliness, Comfort, Friendliness, Communication, Courtesy, Competence, Access, Availability, Security etc.
Flexibility	Volume Flexibility, Specification and Speed of Delivery Flexibility
Resource Utilisation	Productivity, Efficiency, etc.
Innovation	Performance of the innovation process, Performance of individual innovations, etc.

Source: 'Performance Measurement in Service Businesses'
by Lin Fitzgerald, Robert Johnston, Stan Brignall, Rhian Silvestro and Christopher Voss, p. 8.

Who does the analysis?

Whether the indicators are of the financial variety or of the non-financial sort, usually it is the functional managers themselves who prepare their own indicators from data generated from within their own departments.

Financial vs. non-financial

In many companies in the United Kingdom, as in the United States of America, the familiar cry 'everything here is viewed in terms of the bottom line!' can be heard. In this sort of corporate environment, financial indicators remain the fundamental management tool and could be said to reflect the capital market's obsession with profitability as almost the sole indicator of corporate performance. Opponents of this approach suggest that it encourages management to take a number of actions which focus on the short term at the expense of investing for the long term. It results in such action as cutting back on R & D revenue expenditure in an effort to minimise the impact on the costs side of the current year's P & L, or calling for information on profits at too frequent intervals so as to be sure that targets are being met, both of which actions might actually jeopardise the company's overall performance rather than improve it.

In general terms, the opponents of 'the bottom line school' state that because of the preeminence of money measurement in the commercial world, the information derived from the many stages preceding the preparation of the annual accounts, such as budgets, standard costs, actual costs and variances, are actually just a one-dimensional view of corporate activity. Increasingly, over the past decade, they have been emphasising that executives should come to realise the importance of the non-financial type of performance measurement.

Research in support of this approach has come up with new dictums for the workplace: 'the less you understand the business, the more you rely on accounting numbers' and 'the nearer you get to operations, the more non-financial performance indicators you realise could be valuable aids to better management'; or 'graphs and bars carry much more punch than numbers for the non-financial manager'.

But there is still a lot of resistance. Executives tend to avoid using multiple indicators because they are difficult to design and sometimes difficult to relate, one to another. They have a strong preference for single indicators of performance which are well tried and which produce ostensibly unambiguous signals. But the new school lays great emphasis on the fact that multiple indicators are made necessary by the sheer complexity of corporate activity.

The case for non-financial performance indicators

Professor R.S. Kaplan of Harvard Business School in The Evolution of Management Accounting states, '. . . if senior managers place too much emphasis on managing by the financial numbers, the organisation's long term viability becomes threatened.' That is, to provide corporate decision makers with solely financial indicators is to give them an incomplete set of management tools.

The essential case is twofold; first that not every aspect of corporate activity can be expressed in terms of money and secondly that if managers aim for excellence in their own aspects of the business, then the company's bottom line will take care of itself.

So what do non-financial indicators relate to? They relate to the following functions:

- manufacturing and production
- sales and marketing
- people
- research and development
- the environment.

Whether the company is a manufacturer or a service provider, to be successful its management should be concerned to ensure that

- products move smoothly and swiftly through the production cycle
- warranty repairs are kept to a minimum and turned round quickly
- suppliers' delivery performance is constantly monitored
- quality standards are continually raised
- sales orders, shipments and backlog are kept to a minimum
- there is overall customer satisfaction
- labour turnover statistics are produced in such a way as to identify managerial weaknesses
- R & D costs do not escalate
- the accounting and finance departments really understand the business.

Looking at each of these areas in turn,

(*Author's note: for reasons of brevity, only the Manufacturing and Production function is considered in this extract. Anyone interested in performance measures relevant to the other four functions should refer to the original article at*: www.fpm.com/journal/mattison.htm)

The following non-exhaustive list of performance measures is relevant. No one indicator should be over emphasised and no one indicator should reign supreme for long in the corporate consciousness of executives or management gurus.

Manufacturing and production indicators
The sheer volume, variety and complexity of managerial issues surrounding the production process makes this area of corporate activity a particularly rich one for non-financial indicators. Performance indicators can be devised for all operational areas.

non-financial indicators, depending on the exact nature of the production process, might include the following:

- indicators deriving from time and motion studies
- production line efficiency
- ability to change the manufacturing schedule when the marketing plan changes
- reliability of component parts of the production line
- production line repair record
- keeping failures of finished goods to a minimum
- ability to produce against the marketing plan
- product life cycle.

indicators concerned with controlling production quality – right first time

- measurement of scrap
- tests for components, sub-assemblies and finished products
- fault analysis
- 'most likely reasons' for product failures
- actual failure rates against target failure rates
- complaints received against the quality assurance testing programme
- annualised failures as a percentage of sales value
- failures as a percentage of units shipped
- various indicators of product/service quality
- various indicators of product/service reliability.

indicators concerned with the purchasing department's external relationships with its suppliers

- inventory levels and timing of deliveries
- 'just in time' inventory control measurements
- stock turnover ratio
- weeks stocks held
- suppliers delivery performance
- analysis of stock-outs
- parts delivery service record
- percentage of total requests supplied in time
- percentage supplied with faults.

indicators of sales delivery and service

- shipments vs. first request date
- average no. of days shipments late
- response time between enquiry and first visit.

Final Note

Many executives will talk freely in terms of quality and standards, 'just in time' inventory control and of other performance measurement yardsticks and may be quite knowledgeable about them, but when questioned as to the exact nature of the non-financial measurements that they actually have in place in the company will be hard-pressed to tell the researcher what the company is in fact measuring on an on-going basis. There is a lot of lip-service paid to these measures, as opposed to those of a purely financial nature, which are of course to a great extent the product of regulation and company law. So, much remains to be done to broadcast the merits of non-financial performance measurement indicators.

Revision Questions

7

? Question 1

1.1 State three reasons why ROCE might be considered to be 'limited' as a performance indicator.

1.2 State why compliance with budget might not be an appropriate indicator for performance evaluation in 'the new economy'.

1.3 State why it might not be to the long-term advantage of a business to operate with the lowest possible stock days.

1.4 Distinguish between financial and non-financial performance indicators.

1.5 Distinguish between quantitative and qualitative performance indicators.

1.6 Suggest three performance indicators that might be used to measure 'responsiveness to customers'.

1.7 Distinguish between efficiency and effectiveness in an NFP organisation.

1.8 Explain why benchmarking is particularly appropriate for performance evaluation in local authorities.

1.9 Suggest five performance indicators that might be appropriate for benchmarking at a University, having particular regard to the value of the qualifications that the University awards.

1.10 Suggest three possible areas of criticism for benchmarking.

? Question 2

CM Limited was formed 10 years ago to provide business equipment solutions to local businesses. It has separate divisions for research, marketing, product design, technology and communication services, and now manufactures and supplies wide range of business equipment (copiers, scanners, printers, fax machines and similar items).

To date it has evaluated its performance using monthly financial reports that analyse profitability by type of equipment.

The Managing Director of CM Limited has recently returned from a course on which it had been suggested that the 'Balanced Scorecard' could be a useful way of measuring performance.

Requirements

(a) Explain the 'Balanced Scorecard' and how it could be used by CM Limited to measure its performance. **(13 Marks)**

While on the course, the Managing Director of CM Limited overhead someone mention how the performance of their company had improved after they introduced 'Benchmarking'.

(b) Explain 'Benchmarking' and how it could be used to improve the performance of CM Limited. **(12 Marks)**

(Total Marks = 25)

? Question 3

HJL provides consultancy services to companies considering improving their telephone and communication systems, including those operated using computer technology. HJL employs a number of consultants and measures its performance based on profitability and the number of chargeable hours. Performance measures make comparisons between actual and budget performance using budgets that are developed on an incremental approach which adds 5% to the budget of the previous year.

The Managing Director has returned from a management training conference which provided her with a basic understanding of the use of alternative performance measures. Two of these were The Balanced Scorecard and Benchmarking. She has asked you, as a management accountant, to prepare a report to be discussed at the next meeting of the Board of Directors. The report should explain these terms and how the performance of the company may improve if HJL were to introduce these new performance measures.

Requirements

Prepare a report, to be discussed at the next meeting of the Board of Directors, that

(a) reviews the suitability of the existing performance measures used by HJL;

(b) explains 'The Balanced Scorecard' and recommends, with reasons, performance measures that could be used if it were introduced in HJL;

(c) explains 'Benchmarking' and the potential impact on operations within HJL if it were to be introduced.

Solutions to Revision Questions

✓ Solution 1

1.1
- It only reports what has happened in the previous short period.
- It is based on subjective book values for assets and profit.
- Concentration on current ROCE may induce 'short-termism' in managers.

1.2 Compliance with budget is the classic 'command and control' approach to management and performance evaluation. It may have been appropriate in an era when the business environment was very stable and predictable. It may then have been possible to produce meaningful plans that were capable of execution. However, the modern environment is much more fluid – where the market constantly changes and success is dependant on the ability to respond quickly to new developments and customer demand.

1.3 Stock is an asset which engages capital in the business. That capital has a cost so there is a temptation to minimise stock holding. But stock is also a valuable business asset which is needed to provide the maximum chance of satisfying customers and even out any irregularities in the flow of deliveries and production. It may be technically possible to operate with minimal stock but this is not always commercially advantageous.

1.4 A financial performance indicator is a number drawn from money values, for example, profit margin, ROCE, debtor days and so on. Typically those money values are taken from the financial reports of an organisation which are prepared on the basis of relevant accounting standards. A non-financial performance indicator is one which is not drawn primarily from accounting data. For example, the delivery lead time in days measures the time it takes from order to delivery for a customer purchase.

1.5 A quantitative indicator relates to some aspect of the operation that is amenable to being expressed as a number. For example, a 10-day delivery lead time is a quantitative indicator. 'A reputation for being a reliable supplier' is a qualitative indicator – although it may be possible to express it in quantitative terms (e.g. '75% of customers place us in the upper quartile of supplier reliability').

1.6
- Delivery lead time (days)
- Customer rating on willingness to customise products/services

- Number of customer orders/enquiries leading to completed sales
- Customer rating on standard of answers to technical enquiries.

1.7 Efficiency relates to securing the maximum output from a given set of inputs. For example, if we say that 95 standard hours work were performed during 100 available hours labour, then we might say we were operating at 95 per cent efficiency. Effectiveness relates to finding the optimum combination of inputs to achieve a given objective. For example, we might say that the most effective means of containing youth crime is to spend £1 m on police, £1.5 m on school support services and £0.5 on sports clubs.

1.8 Local authorities are engaged in a complex operation intended to secure a variety of different public objectives. One often finds that it is difficult to measure efficiency by conventional means since outputs cannot be expressed in clear and unambiguous terms. Also, effectiveness is difficult to achieve since there are often various means available to achieve given objectives and one has to 'juggle' them. Benchmarking is therefore very suitable to local authorities since it allows them to compare like aspects of their activities and outputs. If 'best practice' can be identified, then this acts as a guideline for all.

1.9
- Employer rating of degrees and qualifications.
- Government (UK and overseas) rating of degrees and qualifications.
- Student/alumni rating of degrees and qualifications.
- Number of alumni in employment within 12 months of graduating.
- Average salary of alumni 5 years after graduation.
- Number of alumni in management/professional employment 5 years after graduating.
- Number of alumni judged to have achieved 'national fame' status inside 10 years after graduating.

1.10
- Organisations and businesses differ in so many detailed respects that it may be difficult to find a benchmark partner that provides a genuine like-for-like comparison.
- Potential benchmark partners may be reluctant to exchange commercially sensitive information.
- Different approaches to the provision of activities may be possible, for example, using different combinations of labour and equipment to produce the same product. There may be no such thing as 'best practice'.
- The whole culture of benchmarking is 'mimetic' – whereby organisations copy each other's practices in order to achieve some form of legitimacy. It may be better for all to adopt distinct practices in order to suit detailed differences in history and circumstances.

✅ Solution 2

(a) The balanced scorecard was developed and refined during the 1980s and 1990s. It has the aim of breaking the reliance of traditional performance measurement systems on financial performance measures, and widening the scope of performance measurement and therefore of managerial attention, to include both financial and non-financial information. By developing a wider focus of attention, the balanced scorecard encourages managers to look at the relationships between different aspects of performance, and highlights the links between improving operational performance and achieving improvements in financial performance.

The balanced scorecard contains three basic elements:

1. A customer perspective, where the focus is on measuring and improving customer satisfaction. CM Limited might measure the incidence of customer complaints, or of repeat purchases, as proxies for customer satisfaction.

2. The learning and growth perspective assesses the organisation's ability to satisfy, develop and motivate its employees. Key measures here assess employee retention, productivity and satisfaction. CM Limited would use questionnaires, surveys and/ or interviews to gain information on these areas. It would seek to determine, for example, whether employees felt that they were supported in their work, and how satisfied they were with their working conditions.

3. The internal business process perspective assesses the efficiency of the value creating process, and gathers information on areas such as innovation, operations and after-sales service. CM Limited could gather information on the percentage of sales from new products, sales growth compared with competitors and speed of response to customer service requests.

The effect of making improvements in these three areas is that profitability, cashflow and other measures in the financial perspective should improve. The balanced score-card, however, explicitly links the operational perspectives to the financial perspective, so that a change in any of the former can be seen to have an influence on the latter. If a balanced scorecard approach were to be introduced, the focus of CM Limited's managerial attention would move from being on products to a more holistic model, in which the key performance measures, linked to the achievement of objectives, are identified and monitored. Thus, objectives are more likely to be achieved, since the key performance indicators have been identified.

(b) Benchmarking is used by many organisations as a way of achieving process improve-ments and cost reduction. The objective of benchmarking is to become 'best in class' in the chosen areas and to constantly compare your own performance with that of an appropriate comparator. Many business processes are not unique to businesses located in a single industry (which will be CM Limited's competitors), and therefore best in class performance might be found in a company which undertakes the same process, but in a quite different industry. By exchanging information concerning costs/times/ resource requirements of the process, firms may learn from one another, and become aware of any areas of inefficiency which they may have, and thus gain an insight into where their cost reduction efforts should be targeted.

CM Limited sells business equipment, so it could investigate the possibility of bench-marking its order taking, delivery, stockholding and similar procedures against those of a similar firm located in a different geographical area. Or, it could perhaps benchmark against a local firm selling and repairing air-conditioning units or electrical white goods.

Benchmarking improvements could impact upon the 'internal business process' of the bal-anced scorecard, causing efficiency improvements. Should employee training requirements be required, then 'learning and growth' changes would need to be made. In the short term, there might be a deterioration in the cash flow of CM Limited, but as the improvements begin to have an effect, the financial perspective will improve.

Solution 3

Report

To: Board of Directors
From: Management Accountant
Subject: Performance Measures
Date: 24 November 2004

Introduction

Further to your request, I consider in this report our existing performance measures and then set out explanations of the balanced scorecard and benchmarking approaches and how our performance could improve if we introduced these alternative performance measures.

(a) Existing performance measures

Our present performance measures focus attention on our profitability and our level of chargeable hours, the latter of course being a key factor in achieving our profitability targets.

These targets are set in the form of a budget which is based upon increasing our performance by 5% over that previously budgeted. This arbitrary increase does not necessarily reflect the change in the circumstances in which HJL operates. As a result, the budget may become dysfunctional. It also suggests that the organisation's sole performance indicator is one that focuses on financial aspects. There are many other aspects that contribute towards the company's performance which need to be monitored.

(b) The Balanced Scorecard

The balanced scorecard is an approach to the provision of information to management to assist strategic policy formulation and achievement. It emphasises the need to provide the user with a set of information which addresses all relevant areas of performance in an objective and unbiased fashion.

The balanced scorecard comprises four perspectives: financial perspective, customer perspective, internal business perspective and innovation and learning perspective.

The financial perspective considers how we look to our shareholders and thus focuses on measures of short- and long-term profitability and growth. Our present performance measures of profitablility and number of chargeable hours is very much focused on these financial measures, but they should not be the only measures that are used.

The customer perspective considers how our customers see us. This is important because if our customers are pleased with the service they receive, then we will continue to be their preferred supplier and hopefully they will recommend us to their business contact group so that we obtain more work. Measures that could be used include the number of customer referrals received, the proportion of quotations accepted by the customer, the extent to which our projects and recommendations are delivered on time to our customers.

The internal business perspective monitors what we must excel at if we are to succeed. This perspective looks at our ability to remain up to date and design new communications systems in an efficient manner. We need to compare our systems with those recommended by our competitors and measure the time taken to introduce new systems that take advantage of technological developments.

The innovation and learning perspective considers whether we can continue to improve and create value by the advice that we give to our customers. Measures that could be used in this area include our position in the industry in relation to introducing new systems compared to our competitors, and the amount of expenditure on training per employee.

The overall concept of the balanced scorecard is that all four types of performance measure are equally important to ensure the continuing success of a company.

(c) Benchmarking

There are two types of benchmarking: intra group and inter-industry.

Intra group benchmarking involves groups of companies in the same industry agreeing to pool data on their processes. Best practices are identified from this pooled data and as a result the performance of all of the group companies can improve.

Inter-industry benchmarking is used by non-competing businesses that have similar processes. HJL could consider using this type of benchmarking by working with other consultancy businesses who provide services other than those connected with communications, such as marketing consultants.

Benchmarking enables a company to improve its performance by learning best practice from other organisations. Benchmarking establishes targets and comparators and through their use relative levels of performance (particularly areas of underperformance) can be identified. By the adoption of identified best practices it is hoped that performance will improve.

Conclusion

I should be pleased to discuss these matters with you at our next meeting.

8

Developments in
Management Accounting

Developments in Management Accounting

8

8.1 Introduction

In this chapter we will consider developments in the business environment over the last 25 years and the impact that these developments have had on the practice of management accounting. In particular, we will consider activity-based techniques (ABTs), throughput accounting and backflush accounting.

8.2 The modern economic environment

8.2.1 Traditional Production processes

In manufacturing industry (and one can identify parallels in the service sector), there have traditionally been three main methods of organising production, each one representing the least-cost method of satisfying customer needs:

(i) *Jobbing production.* Where customers require goods to be produced to their own particular specifications. In such an environment, each order is a one-off, manufactured

321

to customer order. Typically, only low stocks are held and production is organised in a manner calculated to achieve flexibility. That is, machines and personnel are arranged in a manner that allows production to be shifted quickly from one job to another.

(ii) *Batch production*. Where production takes place in the form of discrete production runs. Typically, production is not to specific customer order and some stock holding of both finished goods and components may be essential. Given that production facilities have to switch quickly from output of one product to another, a degree of flexibility has to be incorporated in the operation. Such flexibility in plant arrangement and machine design may be at the expense of unit cost.

(iii) *Mass production*. Where a standard product is in continuous or near continuous production. This approach prioritises low unit cost at the expense of flexibility. If customer dispatches and supplier deliveries can be phased evenly (through use of JIT and SCM technique – discussed below), then it may be possible to operate with very low stock holdings.

The mass production model is typical of traditional industry. This approach is vulnerable to fluctuations in the market. A temporary down turn in customer demand may result in a build-up in stocks of finished goods and it may be difficult or expensive to suspend production when this happens. It may be very difficult to accommodate product features customised to the needs of individual customers. The weakness of the mass production model is that it lacks flexibility. It involves sacrificing a lot in exchange for low unit production cost.

8.2.2 The background to change

Cost is an important competitive weapon. Low-cost producers will have an advantage in the marketplace over those whose cost base is higher. However, cost is only one competitive weapon and it is one that has become of declining importance in recent years. Other dimensions of competition have become increasingly important: product reliability, product innovation, shortened time to market, and flexibility of response to customer demands – these last three being features of time-based competition.

It is obvious that a manufacturer would gain competitive advantage if he were able to produce the diversity of output seen in a jobbing system at a cost associated with mass production. In recent years, some manufacturers, most notably the Japanese, have been successful in moving towards this. Furthermore, the products of these manufacturers have an enviable reputation for reliability. These suppliers have clearly gained competitive advantage in the marketplace, forcing competitors to follow or exit the market. Consumers, given the opportunity to enjoy diversity and reliability at a mass-produced cost, have reacted not unexpectedly by requiring all manufacturers to offer these features. Further, a corollary of the requirement for greater diversity has been a shortening of product life cycles.

This fundamental shift in demand patterns dictates a need for companies to constantly review and redesign existing products, and to shorten the time to market of each new line in order to ensure satisfactory returns from it. Against this new background, companies will find it increasingly difficult to gain economic returns from an expensive, dedicated mass-production line operated in traditional way. Means must be found whereby manufacturing facilities cannot only accommodate the production of existing lines and their inevitable redesigned successors, but also facilitate the rapid introduction of new products at minimum cost. The challenge of the modern, globally competitive market is to offer an increased and increasing choice of high-quality products at a cost traditionally associated with mass production; to enjoy economies of scale, along with the economies of scope that result from the increased manufacturing flexibility. This challenge can be met by investment in new technology, and the adoption of alternative production management strategies. Those who successfully meet this challenge are the 'world-class manufacturers' that provide the benchmark against which other manufacturers are measured.

'World class' organisations make products using the latest manufacturing technologies and techniques. Those products are typically sold around the world and are generally viewed as being first rate in terms of quality, design, performance and reliability. Companies such as Toyota, BMW and Boeing have been described at various times as being world-class manufacturers. The world-class manufacturer will probably invest heavily in research, product design, CAD/CAM technology. It will also make extensive use of modern management concepts such as Total quality management (TQM), flexible manufacturing systems and customer relationship management. These concepts variously known as advanced manufacturing technologies (AMTs) or the new manufacturing are discussed in detail below.

8.3 The new manufacturing

8.3.1 Computer-aided design

At the initial design stage of a product, the considerable space occupied by the drawing tables of a typical design office has been replaced by computer terminals, and the time taken to work through an initial engineering drawing – and, more importantly, rework the drawing – has shortened dramatically as a result of the softwares currently available. Computer-aided design (CAD) allows huge numbers of alternative configurations to be analysed both for cost and utility. CAD allows quality and cost reduction to be built in at the design stage of a product. The advanced graphics facilities of the typical CAD program enable the draughtsman not only to move parts around the design, and instantly appreciate the effect of these changes on the finished product, but also to manipulate the drawing, and view the design from any desired angle (and even, in the case of the latest generation of software, 'walk through' it). The use of a database to match, where possible, the requirements of the new design with existing product parts will enable the company to minimise stockholdings by reducing the total number of product parts required.

8.3.2 Computer-aided manufacturing

The manufacturing process is carried out by a range of machinery that, together with its concomitant software, comes under the collective heading of computer-aided manufacturing (CAM). Significant elements of CAM are computer numerical control (CNC) and robotics. CNC machines are programmable machine tools that are capable of performing a number of machining tasks, such as cutting and grinding. A computer program stores all the existing manufacturing configurations and set-up instructions for a particular machine or bank of machines, facilitating a change in configuration in a matter of seconds via the keyboard; changes to existing configurations and new configurations are easily accommodated. CNC therefore offers great flexibility and dramatically reduced set-up times. Furthermore, unlike human operators, who tire and are error-prone, CNC machines are able to repeat the same operation continuously in an absolutely identical manner, to a completely consistent level of accuracy and machine tolerance. CNC also promotes flexibility through allowing machines to switch from output of one product to another very quickly.

Two brief examples will serve to illustrate the dramatic impact of CAM on manufacturing flexibility, and the time taken to develop a product and bring it to the market. Nissan, the car producer, found that the time taken to completely retool car body panel jigs in their intelligent body assembly system (IBAS) fell from 12 months to less than 3 months by reprogramming the process machinery by computer and using computerised jig robots. Similar advances have been made in the resetting of machines and in the exchange of dies. These changes have reduced the changeover time in moving from one process to another. Again it is a Japanese company, Toyota, that provides one of the best examples of the advances made in this area. As the speed of production changeover increases under CAM, the possibility of producing smaller and smaller batch sizes at an economic cost also increases, so that the production schedule can be driven more and more by customer requirements rather than the constraints of the traditional manufacturing process.

8.3.3 Computer-integrated manufacturing

The ultimate extension – and logical long-term direction – of AMT in the production environment is computer-integrated manufacturing (CIM), which brings together all the elements of automated manufacturing and quality control into one coherent system. The 'ideal' technological world of CIM – the fully automated production facility, controlled entirely by means of a computer network with no human interference – is not yet with us (and, indeed, with its overtones of 'ghost factories', would not necessarily be universally welcomed).

A somewhat watered-down version of CIM is already with us, however, in the form of a flexible manufacturing system (FMS) discussed below. The FMS cell is often referred to as an 'island of automation' in the context of a more traditionally organised facility.

8.3.4 Flexible manufacturing systems

The FMS is 'an integrated production system which is computer controlled to produce a family of parts in a flexible manner . . . a bundle of machines that can be reprogrammed to switch from one production run to another'. It consists of a cluster of machine tools and a system of conveyor belts that shuttle the work piece from tool to tool in a similar fashion to the traditional transfer line used in mass (large-batch) production. Thus the benefits lie in being able to switch quickly from making one product to another.

The major strength of an FMS system is its ability to manufacture not just a family of parts, but a family of products. By using this system, General Electric has been able to produce a range of diesel engines that are of considerably different sizes on the same automated production line, without substantially retooling and time-consuming start-ups.

The FMS normally incorporates CAD and CAM features. It is an approach to manufacturing that is well attuned to modern market economics, where products have short life-cycles, are produced in short discontinuous runs (see discussion of JIT below) and are often highly customised to the needs of individual customers.

One notable aspect of an FMS (or any AMT environment) is that efficiency is a product of product design and plant flexibility rather than a direct result of low unit production costs. A traditional standard costing and variance analysis system may not be very effective in this environment. For one thing, once one moves away from a traditional mass production

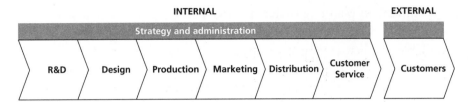

Figure 8.1 The value chain

operation, a high proportion of production costs are either designed into a product or are facility costs not directly specific to any one product. Running a cost system that places a focus on things like the 'direct material usage variance' may tell one almost nothing about how well or badly a production operation is performing.

8.4 The value chain

The driving force behind the adoption of AMTs is a thorough appreciation of the relationship between *all* the factors within the value chain – the sequence of business factors by which *value* is added to the organisation's products and services. The value chain is illustrated in Figure 8.1.

- *Research and development.* The generation of, and experimentation with, ideas for new products, services or process.
- *Design.* The detailed planning and engineering of products, services or process.
- *Production.* The co-ordination and assembly of resources to produce a product or deliver a service.
- *Marketing.* The process by which potential customers learn about and value the attributes of the organisation's products or services, and are persuaded to buy them.
- *Distribution.* The mechanism by which the organisation's products or services are delivered to the customer.
- *Customer service.* The support activities provided to customers.

Functions within the value chain are not necessarily sequential; the organisation can gain important competitive advantages by activating individual parts of the chain concurrently. The major consideration is their smooth *co-ordination* within the framework of the organisation as a whole.

8.5 Production operations systems and management strategies

8.5.1 Material requirements planning

The traditional way to determine material requirements is to monitor stocks constantly; whenever they fall to a predetermined level, a preset order is placed to replenish them. This approach involves the replenishment of any one stock item independently of all others. In reality, the demand for a particular stock item is a function of the assemblies and sub-assemblies of which it forms a part. This traditional approach (involving re-order level and economic order quantity calculations) originates in the pre-computer era.

Material requirements planning (MRP or MRP1) is a technique that aims to ensure that material resources – raw materials, bought-in components and in-house subassemblies – are made available just before they are needed by the next stage of production or despatch. It also seeks to ensure that these resources are delivered only when required, so that stocks are kept to an absolute minimum. The technique enables managers to track orders through the entire manufacturing process, and helps the purchasing and production control departments to move the precise amount of material at the right time to the correct production/distribution stage. MRP1 is only practical with the availability of a full computer model of the production and associated materials procurement requirement for the coming period. MRP1 appeared in the 1960s with the arrival of computers in management.

The MRP is a computerised production planning system that begins with the setting of a master production schedule, and, working backwards, uses the information from this top-level schedule to determine the raw material, component and sub-assembly requirements at each of the earlier stages in the production process. Obviously, the ability of the system to deliver what is required in the correct place at the correct time will be dependant on the quality of the information that is put into the computer model.

The data in the system is analysed to produce a *material requirements* plan for purchasing and manufacturing. As the system is computerised, schedules can easily be reworked to accommodate changes to customer requirements. For example, if a customer requests that product X be delivered in the current month rather than product Y, which had previously been ordered, and that delivery of product Y be deferred until the following month, the MRP system can quickly reschedule all the activities that go to producing these requirements, in order to meet the new needs of the customer.

Prerequisites for the successful operation of an MRP system are as follows:

(i) *Strict schedule adherence.* The operation of informal expediting systems, or the informal alteration of production priorities, will quickly destroy the potential benefits of the system. Workers must be educated to understand the importance of schedule adherence, and controls should be in place to ensure this adherence. A further possible problem is that the system assumes unlimited capacity in all work centres, whereas in reality some work centres always behave as bottlenecks. This contradiction destroys the accuracy of MRP scheduling logic, and makes it ineffective for capacity planning and control.

(ii) *Accurate base data.* Data accuracy is vital to the system; if a plan is based on inaccurate data, it may be impossible to adhere to the schedule. For example, if the information in the inventory file is incorrect, perhaps stating that certain sub-assemblies are available when in fact they are not, the whole production schedule will be incapable of being completed in the manner envisaged. The difficulties encountered in keeping inventory records and 'bill of materials' (listing of materials and components required for products) up to date have been a major cause of failure in the implementation of MRP systems. Similarly, it is vital that the bill of materials file is accurate, and regularly updated to reflect any changes in product composition. An enormous effort is required in a typical company to bring the data inputs to a high enough level of accuracy to support an MRP system. However, without such accuracy, the MRP system will not bring about the expected benefits.

8.5.2 Manufacturing resources planning

When MRP is extended beyond the planning of raw materials, components and sub-assemblies to encompass other input resources, such as machine capacity and labour, so that the system provides a fully integrated planning approach to the management of all the company's manufacturing resources, it is known as manufacturing resources planning (MRP2). It is clear that the *caveats* mentioned above will only increase in importance when the system's database becomes larger and more complex.

Even if the data in an MRP system – either MRP1 or MRP2 – is accurate, and there is 100 per cent schedule adherence, this does not, of itself, mean that the company operating the system will be a world-class manufacturer. It has been argued that many western companies adopt an operations research focus in management, and this approach has been adopted in applying both MRP systems. An operations research approach takes input parameters as given. For example, production times, delivery times and design features are regarded as constants, and within this static framework the optimal production and purchasing plan is sought. This is the 'static optimisation' philosophy of performance management that is entirely consistent with the standard costing and budgeting models considered above.

This is not to argue that MRP systems are incompatible with world-class manufacturing or continuous improvement – indeed, Japanese companies such as Nissan use MRP2 – but simply to point out that applying MRP to an *existing* set of circumstances may improve the *efficiency* with which existing operations are carried out, but this efficiency may still lead to a level of cost that is *higher* than could be achieved if the parameters themselves were challenged. MRP2 appeared in the 1970s, very much as a straight line development from MRP1.

8.5.3   Optimised production technology

Like MRP systems, Optimised production technology (OPT) requires detailed information about inventory levels, product structures, routings and set-up and operation timing for each and every procedure of each product. However, unlike MRP, the technique actively seeks to identify and remove – or optimise the use of – bottleneck resources within a manufacturing process, in order to avoid unnecessary build-ups of stock. A bottleneck resource is the thing in the production process that limits overall output. We have already encountered this idea in the context of critical path analysis, limiting factor analysis and the principal budget factor.

Drury (2000) gives an excellent and concise description of the OPT approach, which is worth reproducing in full:

The OPT philosophy contends that the primary goal of manufacturing is to make money. Three important criteria are identified to evaluate progress towards achieving this goal. These are throughput, inventory and operating expenses. The goal is to maximise throughput while simultaneously maintaining or decreasing inventory and operating expenses.

The OPT approach determines what prevents throughput from being higher by distinguishing between bottlenecks and removing them or, if this is not possible, ensures that they are fully utilised at all times. Non-bottleneck resources should be scheduled and operated based on constraints within the system, and should not be used to produce more than the bottlenecks can absorb. The OPT philosophy therefore advocates that non-bottleneck resources should not be utilised to 100 per cent of their capacity, since this would merely result in an increase in inventory. Thus idle time in non-bottleneck areas is not considered detrimental to the efficiency of the organisation. If it were utilised, it would result in increased inventory without a corresponding increase in throughput for the plant.

With the OPT approach, it is vitally important to schedule all non-bottleneck resources within the manufacturing system based on the constraints of the system (i.e. the bottlenecks). For example, if only 70 per cent of the output of a non-bottleneck resource can be absorbed by the following bottleneck resources, then 30 per cent of the utilisation of the non-bottleneck is simply concerned with increasing inventory. It can therefore be argued that by operating at the 70 per cent level, the non-bottleneck resource is achieving 100 per cent efficiency.

The above description makes it clear that the objective of OPT is to maximise throughput of products, which necessitates the maximisation of output from bottlenecks. Everything else is subservient to this end, so, for example, buffer stocks might be held ahead of bottlenecks, and quality checked *before* product enters the bottleneck. Non-bottlenecks should be paced by the bottlenecks, and should not produce merely for stock.

It has been suggested that overheads should be changed to products on the basis of throughput time, defined as the time taken from initial input to the production line to removal from the line as a finished good. In using this as the allocation base, top management is flagging up to operating management that product costs can be reduced by cutting down throughput time.

8.5.4 ERP, CRM and SCM

MRP1, MRP2 and OPT are essentially business planning techniques, whereby the full resource requirements of a given plan of action can be identified and those requirements satisfied in the most cost-effective manner. The approach is entirely consistent with the budgeting model that we explored in earlier chapters.

However, things have not stopped there and the 1990s saw further developments along this line. During the 1990s, enterprise resource planning (ERP) systems tended to displace the old MRP systems. ERP involves the use of elaborate computer systems to provide plans for every aspect of the business – not just confining attention to material supplies and manufacturing. ERP system design and installation became one of the major products sold by firms of business consultants. ERP systems are frequently associated and integrated with budgeting systems.

Another parallel development was customer relationship management (CRM) systems. These contained all the information about customers and customer requirements. They are often integrated with ERP systems and involve websites and e-commerce facilities. A CRM system may allow receipt of a customer order to automatically prompt the scheduling of necessary production facilities and the ordering of components.

The ultimate development of this kind was supply chain management (SCM), which became very much the 'hot topic' in business management circles in the late 1990s. SCM systems go beyond individual companies and seek to integrate the flow of information between different companies on a supply chain. Thus, if company A schedules production of a certain number of units, then information concerning this would feed through to A's component supplier B, via an SCM system. B's production control would automatically schedule production and delivery at the appropriate time of the components required by A.

To be effective, SCM system have to be associated with a high degree if mutual confidence among the participating businesses. This may involve placing personnel from one business in the premises of another to ensure that appropriate manufacturing standards and specifications are met. It may also involve sharing information about product design and cost structures.

The MRP, ERP and SCM represent a line of development associated with the use of computers and IT to undertake very detailed planning and resource scheduling exercises. However, many observers feel that this approach may be nearing the end of its life cycle. The elaborate, integrated ERP systems of the 1990s may be passing out of use. It is claimed that they involve unnecessary data collection, over-elaborate bills of materials and inefficient workflows. The current move is towards the alternative 'lean enterprise' and its associated information system requirements. The thrust of the lean enterprise concept is that production scheduling and resource acquisition should respond quickly and flexibly to customer demand rather than being the subject of an elaborate planning exercise. Once again, we encounter the idea that modern thinking in management places an emphasis flexibility and short response time rather than elaborate forward planning.

8.5.5 Just-in-time concept

There can be few students of business-related topics who have not heard of just-in-time (JIT) production methods. The CIMA *Official Terminology* defines JIT as follows.

> *JIT:* A system whose objective is to produce or procure products or components as they are required by a customer or for use, rather than for stock. A JIT system is a 'pull' system, which responds to demand, in contrast to a 'push' system, in which stocks act as buffers between the different elements of the systems, such as purchasing, production and sales.

JIT production is defined as follows.

> *JIT production:* A production system which is driven by demand for finished products whereby each component on a production line is produced only when needed for the next stage.

And JIT purchasing is defined as follows.

> *JIT purchasing:* A purchasing system in which material purchases are contracted so that the receipt and usage of material, to the maximum extent possible, coincide.

The JIT is best described as a 'philosophy', or approach to management, as it encompasses a commitment to continuous improvement and the pursuit of excellence in the design and operation of the production management system. The logical thrust behind JIT is that production and resource acquisition should be 'pulled' by customer demand rather than being 'pushed' by a planning process. A JIT-based production operation responds quickly to customer demand and resources are required and utilised only when needed. In order to be able to operate in this manner, an organisation must achieve excellence in all areas of management.

An attempt to gains from the adoption of JIT usually exposes problems that were previously hidden. An analogy with a boat sailing along a river is often used to explain this result, as seen in Figure 8.2.

The production process in a multi-product plant represents the boat, and the levels of stocks that a company holds are the determinants of the water level of the river. A high level of raw material and component stocks, work in progress and finished goods would indicate that the river is extremely deep. As these stock are reduced, the water level reduces. The bed of the river may contain rocks, the height and quantity being determined by the number of problems that a company faces in its production. The 'rocks' may be caused by poor production scheduling, machine breakdown, absenteeism, inefficient plant layout, excessive rework, schedule interruption through order expediting and so on. However,

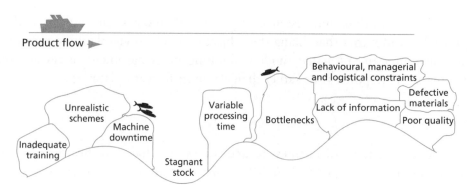

Figure 8.2 The just-in-time concept

these rocks do not cause a problem to the boat on the surface, provided that the water depth – the level of inventory – is sufficient to cover them. As the water level, the inventory goes down, the rocks – the problems within the company – will be exposed. The inevitable consequence of this is that the boat will crash into the rocks and will be damaged.

This damage can be avoided in one of the two ways. The first, the traditional western way, is to keep the water level deep – maintain high levels of stocks. An alternative way, and the way consistent with the JIT philosophy, is to remove the rocks, so that the boat can sail quite safely in a much lower level of water. Operating on a JIT basis with low inventories requires a first class operation in all the areas of

- production scheduling
- supplier relations
- plant maintenance
- information systems
- quality controls
- customer relations.

In a JIT environment, 'family groups' of products – products with similar production requirements – are manufactured in separate cells along production-line principles. That is, all the machines needed to carry out the manufacture of a particular product family are arranged in the form of a discrete 'mini' assembly line. The machines are grouped closely together in the sequential order required by processing, and products move from machine to machine in a constant flow, without 'queuing' by machines or returning to stores, thus minimising lead times and work in progress. The reader will recognise similar features and aims to those described earlier with an FMS.

The traditional manufacturing environment operates on a 'push-through' basis, in which one process supplies parts to the next process without regard to the latter's immediate ability to continue work on those parts. Work in progress in an unavoidable features of such a system. In contrast, the JIT system works on a 'pull' principle, whereby one workstation 'pulls' the part from the previous station; work will not begin in any workstation until the signal to part has been received from the next station in the process. The bin, or container, that is passed to the previous workstation to give the 'pull' signal, is known in Japanese as the 'kanban', hence the use of this word to describe JIT systems. As production only commences once the 'pull' signal has been received, this has the obvious consequence of keeping work in progress at a low level. One consequence of the 'pull' system, however, is that problems in any part of the system will immediately halt the production line, as earlier workstations will not receive the 'pull' signal and later stations will not have their own 'pull' signals answered. As noted above, this would have the powerful effect of concentrating all minds on finding a long-term solution to the problem.

The analogy of the boat and the river emphasised the role of buffer stocks in protecting the traditional manufacturing system against shortages caused by innate problems such as poor-quality production or machine breakdowns. JIT operates with minimal stock levels; its approach is to 'get it right first time', and the aim is 'zero defects'. In the absence of the attainment of this 'ideal' situation, JIT is still able to cut scrap and rework. If transfer batches are small, product is quickly manufactured and quality checked – any problems are quickly found and only a small amount of work in progress will need to be reworked.

The JIT manufacturer plays an active and constructive part in ensuring that cost savings are made by suppliers. Cost teams from the manufacturer regularly visit suppliers' plants, perform audits on the information supplied to them, and suggest ways in which the suppliers' operations might be carried out more efficiently and achieve greater synchronisation and harmony with the manufacturer's own specifications. This co-operation with a limited number of suppliers provides the manufacturer with a high degree of control of the upstream activities in the value chain, even though the supplier has legal ownership of these parts of the chain. There is an element of commonality with SCM (discussed above) in this.

8.6 Total quality management

Total quality management (TQM) may be defined as the continuous improvement in quality, productivity and effectiveness obtained by establishing responsibility for process as well as output. In this, every process has an identified process owner within the organisation and every person in an organisation operates within a process and contributes to its improvement. The idea is that quality is the key strategic variable in achieving strategic advantage. When a customer considers buying a product he is influenced in his choice of supplier by factors other than the technical specification of the product – such as speed of delivery, customisation, reliability, ease of placing an order and attractiveness of design. All these are quality-related factors. The TQM movement argues that ability to deliver these quality-related factors is a function of process, that is it is a function of how the organisation works.

The role that quality plays in ensuring an efficient and effective operation has already been encountered within the context of JIT. Operating on a demand-pull basis with minimal stocks requires a high level of quality at all levels in the manufacturing operation.

There are two recurring themes that run through much of the literature on TQM. These are 'terms' and 'empowerment'. Employee empowerment is considered to liberate talents and facilitate the deployment of skills. Teams are considered to improve the co-ordination of functions and skills within the organisation. The co-operative ethic lies at the heart of what TQM is all about.

The TQM is a philosophy and a movement rather than a body of techniques. There are many alternative definitions and models of TQM. However, the central idea is that quality is the key strategic variable in business and it is a variable that is amenable to organisational culture. The idea is that quality should be a feature that is rooted in the structure of the organisation. Quality should impact on the way that the organisation is run and on the way that staff are recruited, assessed, promoted and rewarded. The view that quality is something imposed on staff by inspectors is anathema to the TQM movement. W Edwards

DEVELOPMENTS IN MANAGEMENT ACCOUNTING

Deming, widely accepted as the founder of the TQM movement, argued that mass inspection of goods ties up resources and does not improve quality. Quality has to come from within the process rather than being imposed on it from without.

The main features of a TQM-oriented organisation include

- Top priority is given to satisfying customers and the organisation is structured in a way that ensures interest convergence of owners, employees, suppliers and management in achieving this. Managers should act as facilitators rather than controllers.
- People are considered to be the key internal guarantors of success. Decision-making processes are participative. Management is both visible and accessible.
- Constant change is considered a way of life and the organisation is structured in a manner that readily embraces change. The organisation structure is flat, requiring employees to use initiative and communicate directly with customers and suppliers.
- The organisation pursues continuous improvement and not static optimisation. The concept of 'an optimum defects level' rooted in traditional cost accounting is entirely alien to TQM. Performance is measured against an external benchmark and not against an internal standard, in order to emphasise the possibility of improvement.
- The emphasis is on prevention of problems and faults rather than detection. Employees have a wide span of activity but a short span of control.

Achieving and improving quality is the central theme that runs through all of these features. This is particularly relevant in the era of flexible manufacturing when products are highly customised and product life cycles are short. Customer service and product innovation have become major elements in the quality of products that are being offered.

One feature of traditional management accounting is that it may not report the cost of quality failure and quality assurance. Poor-quality work results in costs, but those costs may be 'buried' at several points in the management accounting system and thus not be specifically reported. For example, the costs of quality failure may include

- internally rejected and test-failed units;
- compensation/replacement for units rejected and returned by customers;
- rectification costs;
- compensation for units failed in service with customers;
- loss of customer goodwill and market reputation.

It is notable that some of these things are opportunity costs that have no immediate impact on accounting costs and are not reported through a conventional management accounting system.

The adoption of a TQM approach is likely to require the provision of comprehensive cost of quality reports that are supplied on a frequent basis to all levels in the organisation. This involves identifying the costs of quality control, quality failure and quality assurance – and collecting them together for management information and reporting purposes. It is only when the costs of quality are known that the measures needed to achieve and maintain high quality can be justified.

The role of design in determining product costs has already been encountered. Quality is engineered into products at the design stage. In the modern era, 90 per cent of product costs may be determined at the design stage – and a traditional costing system reporting costs and variances in discrete 1-month periods may be of limited relevance in evaluating performance. Reporting product costs on a life-cycle basis ('life cycle costing') therefore allows a much fuller understanding of the costs and benefits of quality.

TQM is a cultural thing and over the years it has attracted critics as well as followers. The debate between the two groups is explored in the article titled 'Quality streak' in the Readings section of this chapter.

TQM is a popular management topic but it has its critics.

Quality Streak

Bob Scarlett, *CIMA Insider*, 9 September 2001, (pp. 22–23)

The problems with TQM

There are two recurring themes that run through much of the literature on TQM. These are 'teams' and 'empowerment'. Employee empowerment is considered to liberate talents and facilitate the deployment of skills. Teams are considered to improve the co-ordination of functions and skills within the organisation. The co-operative ethic lies at the heart of what TQM is all about.

However, 20 years' experience of TQM has raised awkward questions.

Do employees and management really find 'empowerment' to be liberating? Empirical studies suggest that 'empowerment' often amounts to the delegation of additional duties to employees. Limits have to be placed on what employees can do, so empowerment is often associated with rules, bureaucracy and form-filing That apart, many employees find most satisfaction from outside work activities and are quite happy to confine themselves to doing what they are told while at work. The proponents of TQM are often very work-centred people themselves and tend to judge others by their own standards.

Do teams contribute to organisational effectiveness? Just calling a group of people who work in the same office 'a team' does not make it a team. A team requires a high level of co-operation and consensus. Many competitive and motivated people find working in a team environment to be uncongenial. It means that every time you want to do anything you have to communicate with and seek approval from fellow team members. In practice, this is likely to involve bureaucracy and form filling.

Is quality really a function of system? TQM tends to proceed from the assumption that variations in quality can be explained by features in the organisational system. The idea is that by changing the system you can improve quality. However, it can be argued that TQM merely moves empowerment from management to employees. It has been argued that the latter cannot be expected to succeed where the former have failed.

Experience with TQM

Management literature offers many examples of the success of TQM and the benefits that some organisations have obtained from it.

However, experience is not all good. Many organisations that have attempted TQM have found that it involves a great deal of additional bureaucracy. When the attempt is anything less than fully committed, then the results can be unfortunate. Some organisations have found themselves with two parallel structures. A new TQM structure is set up complete with committees and teams – but the old hierarchical structure remains in existence which actually amounts to 'the real organisation'.

One UK study (A.T. Kearney) reported found that only 20 per cent of organisations who had tried TQM reported positive results from it. A US study (Arthur D. Little) put the figure somewhat higher at 30 per cent. Celebrated failures include

- Florida Power and Light Company discontinued its TQ programme after extensive employee complains concerning excessive paperwork. This decision was taken in spite of the company having won Japan's 'Deming Prise' for quality management in 1989.
- British Telecom launched a TQ programme in the late 1980s but was reported (*The Economist*, 18 April 1992) to have abandoned most of it after 3 years. It was claimed that BT became bogged down in TQ-related bureaucracy and took some time to recover from it.

Conclusion

In appraising TQM one has to appreciate that it is not a well-defined technique that can offer a 'quick fix' solution to specific perceived problems. Rather, it is an organisational philosophy that embraces a wide variety of different techniques and ideas. For example, JIT and benchmarking are closely associated with TQM.

The general theme of TQM is the need to move away from a traditional hierarchic organisation structure in order to respond to the demands of an increasingly customer service–oriented business environment where quality is the key strategic variable. Those organisations which have made a success of TQM are ones which understand its limitations and are prepared to take the long view.

8.7 Synchronous manufacturing

The title 'synchronous manufacturing' was coined in 1984, when leading exponents of OPT felt that the focus of the latter, as evidenced by its nomenclature, had become too narrow. The change in name allowed the newly emerging procedures and concepts of JIT and TQM to be integrated with the basic principles of OPT. It is interesting to note, however, that the guiding force behind both OPT and synchronous manufacturing is the identification and management of 'bottleneck resources' – Eli Goldratt prefers to use the term 'theory of constraints'.

Synchronous manufacturing has been defined as follows.

> *Synchronous manufacturing:* . . . an all-encompassing manufacturing management philosophy that includes a consistent set of principles, procedures and techniques where every action is evaluated in terms of the common global goal of the organisation.

Note the use of the word 'philosophy' in the definition: this is the key to distinguishing it from its narrower, technique-based predecessor, OPT. The word 'optimised' in the latter implied that an 'optimum' position was possible, which runs counter to a belief in continuous improvement; and the words 'production' and 'technology' failed to capture the richness of the range of constraints and challenges faced by the firm in achieving its objectives – market constraints, and logistical, managerial and behavioural constraints need to be added to the physical constraints of production capacity.

A set of seven 'principles' are associated with synchronous manufacturing:

1. Do not focus on balancing capacities, focus on synchronising the flow.
2. The marginal value of time at a bottleneck resource is equal to the throughput rate of the products processed by the bottleneck.
3. The marginal value of time at a non-bottleneck resource is negligible.
4. The level of utilisation of a non-bottleneck resource is controlled by other constraints within the system.
5. Resources must be utilised, not simply activated.
6. A transfer batch may not, and many times should not, be equal to the process batch.
7. A process batch should be variable both along its route and over time.

Principle 5 requires a brief explanation: as we saw with OPT, it is possible to *activate* resource, particularly a non-bottleneck resource, beyond what is useful or productive for the system; however, that resource will only be *utilised* if the activation contributes positively to company performance. In other words, activating a resource without utilising it is both wasteful and costly.

An alleged weakness of the conventional JIT philosophy is its approach of improving the process everywhere in the system. According to synchronous manufacturing principles 2 and 3, the return on improvements at a *bottleneck* resource is enormous. But the return on improvement made at *non-bottlenecks* is marginal at best, and often of no consequence at all. In other words, whether *across-the-board* improvement activities have any impact on the organisational goal of making money is not known. The synchronous manufacturing philosophy, on the other hand, required managers to focus on those areas of operations that offer the greatest potential for *global* improvements. This process of *focused* improvement becomes a vital part of its own particular approach to continuous improvement throughout the entire organisation.

Another criticism of the basic JIT model is that it is unable to pre-plan the production schedule for any resource in the process except final assembly, and thus the schedule does not consider the resulting loads at the bottleneck work stations. Consequently, it may not effectively utilise the bottleneck resources and, since bottlenecks determine the throughput for the entire system, the resulting throughput may be less than optimum.

8.8 The emphasis on continuous improvement

What emerges from all the previous discussion is that a world-class business achieves its objectives by pursuing a policy of continuous improvement in those factors that have been shown to be important to customers in today's market place. These are

(i) Innovation in design;
(ii) Flexibility in process;
(iii) Short product lead times;
(iv) High quality at all levels in the operation;
(v) Low cost engineered into product and process.

It has been seen that the benefits from these features will not be realised through the slavish application of technologies and techniques. Similarly, a management accounting system which emphasises a compliance with standard costs over given short periods is not likely to be helpful. Long-term benefits will only be achieved by a commitment on the part of all employees to the philosophy of continuous improvement. The search for continuous improvement must become a personal as well as a corporate goal, or the full benefits of technologies and techniques – either individually or in combination – will not accrue to the firm, to the detriment of its competitive position.

Management accounting must assist a search for continuous improvement by supplying relevant information, that is information that helps management to choose the actions necessary to achieve the desired organisational goals, and information that measures the movement of the firm towards those goals. The onus is very much on the management accountant to develop new costing systems and performance measures that will support world-class manufacturing and world-class management.

8.9 Activity-based costing

8.9.1 Traditional versus activity-based cost

We have seen earlier in this text that the modern business environment is one which is much more dynamic than that in which traditional management accounting practices were developed. This applies also to the manner in which we determine the costs of individual products and services.

Traditional cost accounting involves attributing indirect costs to individual products on the basis of an overhead absorption base related to some proxy such as direct labour hours or machine hours ('volume-related measures'). One can apply this approach with varying degrees of sophistication but it is unlikely to give an unambiguous result in modern circumstances.

In the 'new manufacturing' environment a high proportion of costs are indirect and the only meaningful way to attribute such costs to individual products is through a study of the activities that give rise to them. One is seeking an approach to product costing that reflects the manner in which costs are actually incurred and the question is whether or not traditional absorption costing offers such an approach for both decision-making and performance evaluation purposes. This last question can be split into three strands:

1. Are production overheads significant relative to total full absorption cost?
2. Is there any causal link between the incurrence of these production overhead costs and the production volume, and hence products?
3. Are there causal links between the incurrence of production overhead and the particular product that are not volume-related?

Part (1) is important in the context of materiality. If production overhead costs represent only 1 per cent of total production costs, the argument as to how that 1 per cent should be spread among products would not have the same significance as one relating to the spreading of an amount representing, say 50 per cent of total production costs. In fact, overhead costs have become an increasing proportion of production costs during this century, and in many industries now represent the single largest element of product costs. This change in the make-up of production costs has two main causes: the nature of the production process itself, and the nature of competition faced by firms.

In terms of production processes, it would be hard to think of a single industry in which there has not been a significant shift from the use of human labour to the use of machinery.

The effect has been a reduction in the cost of direct labour and an increase in long-term variable production overhead (fixed costs) through increased depreciation charges. Furthermore, modern manufacturing machinery tends to be much more accurate than manual labour, so wastage of material has also declined over time, leading to a further fall in the proportion of direct costs in the total mix.

In the early part of this century, much competition was on the basis or price. While price remains an important competitive weapon in many industries, there are also other factors that determine a firm's success. As we saw in an earlier chapter, businesses now compete on time, quality, innovation and so on. This had led many producers to offer a great variety of products, and necessitated very complex production schedules. This complexity and diversity has also been responsible for some of the increase in production overheads in recent decades.

It will readily be appreciated that, as overheads have become an increasing proportion of total production cost, any arbitrariness in the method in which they are charged to products assumes increasing significance in a decision-making context.

Part (2) asked whether there was any causal link between the incurrence of production overhead costs and the production volume, and hence products. As noted above, some short-term variable overheads are observed to change in response to a volume-related measure, such as direct labour or machine hours worked – that is, there is a causal link between the production volume and the level of production overhead cost incurred. We gave the example of the volume-related activity of running a machine, which results in the variable overhead cost of power being incurred. However, other production overhead expenditure, such as the cost of material procurement, clearly has no direct relationship with the number of direct labour hours worked or the number of hours machines are operating. Nevertheless, the production volume-related basis that appears to drive some short-term variable overheads is usually used to absorb all overheads. It can be argued that this is the only sensible way to operate: by definition, the long-term variable production overheads are fixed in the short term; in the short term, therefore, there can be no causal link between any particular volume-related activity and the particular overheads incurred. Any absorption of cost must be arbitrary, but an absorption must be made nevertheless in order to meet financial accounting requirements. However, it follows that the information is unlikely to be useful for decision-making purposes.

Part (3) asked whether there were causal links between the incurrence of production overhead and the particular product that were not volume-related. In many companies, overhead continues to be absorbed by products on the same basis year after year, with little thought being given to the appropriateness for decision-making of this basis in a situation in which overhead is increasing relative to direct cost. However, the activity-based costing (ABC) approach is based on the premise that there may be a causal link between these overheads and individual activities, particularly when a perspective of more than one year is taken.

We must conclude that traditionally calculated product costs are not useful for decision-making, as they are unable to provide satisfactory explanations for the behaviour of costs. This does not mean, however, that ABC costs, without modification, are decision-relevant.

ABC and ABM have been very much at the leading edge of management accounting practices since the late 1980s.

Activity-Based Techniques

Bob Scarlett, *CIMA Insider,* **May 2002**

For the last 15 years, activity-based techniques (ABTs) have been at the forefront of developments in management accounting. The advent of ABTs has been associated with changes in production technology and organisational practices.

The origins of ABC

In the early 1980s, many organisations became aware that their traditional cost accounting systems were generating information that was either misleading or irrelevant. Organisations and manufacturing processes were becoming increasingly complex, products were becoming more highly customised and product life cycles were shortening. It was found that calculating product costs using traditional volume-based absorption methods (such as direct labour hours or machine hours) no longer produced meaningful results.

For example, let us say that a business manufactures many products including the X and the Y. Production of the two takes place at a rate of 10 units per hour and total production is 500 units of each in the period. Overheads in the period are £100,000 and a total of 20,000 direct labour hours are worked on all products. If the business uses a traditional overhead absorption rate of £5 per labour hour, then the overhead cost of both the X and the Y will be £0.50 per unit.

Enquiry reveals that X manufacture is organised in the form of 2 production runs per period and Y manufacture is organised in the form of 10 production runs per period. Enquiry also reveals that overhead costs mainly related to 'batch level activities' associated with machine set-ups and materials handling for production runs. If there are a total of 1,000 production runs in the period, then overheads may be attributed to products at a rate of £100 per run. On that basis the overheads cost of X will be £0.40 (2 runs X £100/500 units) and the overhead cost of the Y will be £2.00 (10 runs X £100/500 units).

The reported unit costs of £0.40 (X) and £2.00 (Y) are activity based, recognising that overhead costs are incurred through batch level activities. It is likely that this statements offers a more meaningful version of product costs than the traditional unit-volume-based version of £0.50 for both the X and the Y. ABC gives more meaningful results because it attributes costs to products in a more sensitive manner that recognises the way in which overhead costs are actually incurred.

In the case described, production of the Y is a more complex operation than production of the X. The need to organise Y production in frequent small batches (perhaps because it is perishable) means that it requires greater resource usage than production of the X – something that ABC recognises but traditional product costing does not.

This is particularly critical in the modern manufacturing environment. Continuous mass production of simple, homogenous products is becoming increasingly rare. Production now typically takes place in short, discontinuous runs and a high proportion of product costs are determined at the design phase. Hence, an increasing proportion of overhead costs are incurred at batch level or product level.

ABC is capable of providing a statement of product costs which may be used with confidence for both performance management and decision-making in the modern world.

Activity-based management (ABM)

The terms ABC and ABM are sometimes used interchangeably. This is inappropriate since ABC refers only to the actual technique used to determine the cost of activities and the cost of the outputs that those activities achieve. The aim of ABC is to provide improved cost data for use in managing the activities of a business.

ABM is a broader concept. It refers to the fundamental management philosophy that focuses on the planning, execution and measurement of activities as the key to competitive advantage. ABC and ABB are likely to be elements in the practice of ABM. A business that uses ABC and ABB is likely to have a good appreciation of its own cost structures and is therefore able to apply that appreciation for a variety of management purposes ranging from product design to departmental efficiency measurement.

It is often found that the adoption of ABC and ABB yields only disappointing results in terms of profitability and performance. A recent American study by the Institute of Management Accountants disclosed that 80 per cent of ABC users reported that ABC had not yet resulted in any profit increase. Why should this be so?

One problem identified by researchers is that the information generated by ABC and ABB systems has to be used effectively in order to achieve the expected results:

An ABC implementation failure could be defined as the inability of a company to move from simply generating ABC information towards actually using the information.

Roberts & Silvester, 'Why ABC failed and why it may yet succeed', JCM 1996

The writers quoted above suggest that organisations sometimes contain structural barriers to change that make it difficult to progress from ABC to ABM. The design and installation of sophisticated accounting systems is pointless if the information from those systems is not used.

8.10   Transaction analysis and cost drivers

As noted above, overhead in traditional systems is absorbed by products using volume-related measures. The activity-based approach, where appropriate, seeks explanations other than volume for the level of overhead. In this context, it is recognised that overhead costs are incurred in carrying out a number of different types of transactions. These have been summarised as follows:

(i) logistical transactions, that is those activities that relate to the organisation of the flow of materials and other resources throughout the production process;

(ii) balancing transactions, that is those that relate to ensuring that the supply of resources is matched with the demand for them;

(iii) quality transactions, that is those concerned with ensuring output conforms to requirements;

(iv) change transactions, that is those concerned with meeting customers' requirements for altered specifications, product designs, delivery dates and so on.

The important point about the transactions identified by Miller and Vollman is that the primary driver behind them is usually not production volume. For example, logistical and balancing transactions are likely to be driven by the number of batches produced, rather than the total number of individual units. Similarly, change transactions might be related to the number of customers and number of different product types, rather than the volume of production. By identifying non-volume-related drivers, a better understanding of the behaviour of costs in the long term is provided. Such an analysis also facilitates the aggregation of cost-by-cost object, such as distribution channel, which again provides a better understanding for the management of the business than traditional approaches are able to produce.

The resources necessary to carry out the above transactions will tend to be variable in the short term only in an upward sense. As the number of customers increases, the potential for change transactions, for example, also increases. If the number or mix of customers were to change in the short term, in such a way that the overall workload is reduced, it is unlikely that any of the personnel employed to carry out the change transactions would be dismissed. Similarly, a short-term increase in the workload might be absorbed by existing staff, and overtime may be worked, which may or may not increase costs, depending on individual contracts. However, if the increased workload persists, more staff will eventually be hired. As the volume of these change transactions increases, the total overhead cost of the business will increase. In a traditional costing system (Figure 8.3), the increased cost of these transactions is automatically transferred to particular products by the use of a volume-related absorption rate. However, as noted above, such costs are not primarily volume-driven. It is conceivable that, for example, small batches of highly customised products could give rise to costs in terms of all four types of transactions listed above. Through the operation of a traditional costing system, the increased costs associated with carrying out these small-batch transactions will be spread among all the products on an inappropriate volume-related basis, such as direct labour hours or machine hours. It is this sort of anomaly that has led to the criticism of traditional costing as being arbitrary in its cost absorption, and thus providing information that is not useful for decision-making.

The ABC identifies the activities that cause cost to be incurred, and searches for the fundamental cost drivers of these activities. Once the activities and their drivers have been identified, this information can be used to attach overhead to those cost objects (e.g. products) that have actually caused the cost to be incurred. In comparing the ABC approach with the traditional approach, the obvious starting point is a comparison of the costs of individual products as determined under a traditional costing system with those same costs under an ABC system (Figure 8.4). However, this would be a pointless exercise if it simply stopped there: for a given sales revenue and a given level of total costs, the overall company profit will be precisely the same whatever method of allocation is used to allocate the total cost between individual product lines.

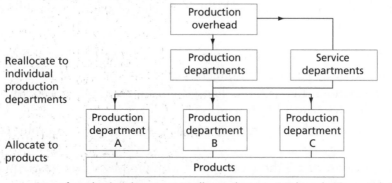

Sum of production departments' allocated costs = total production overhead

Figure 8.3 Traditional product costing system

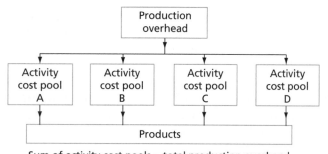

Sum of activity cost pools = total production overhead

Figure 8.4 Activity-based costing system

8.11 Favourable conditions for ABC

The purpose of moving from a traditional costing system to an ABC system must therefore be based on the premise that the new information provided will lead to action that will increase the overall profitability of the business. This is most likely to occur when the analysis provided under the ABC system differs significantly from that which was provided under the traditional system, which is most likely to occur under the following conditions:

  (i) When production overheads are high relative to direct costs, particularly direct labour.
 (ii) Where there is great diversity in the product range.
(iii) Where there is considerable diversity of overhead resource input to products.
(iv) When consumption of overhead resources is not driven primarily by volume.

Information from an ABC analysis may indicate opportunities to increase profitability in a variety of ways, many of which are long term. For example, an activity-based analysis often reveals that small-batch items are relatively expensive to produce, and are therefore unprofitable at current prices. A number of responses to this information could be adopted. The first response might be to consider stopping production of such items, and concentrate on the apparently more profitable high-volume lines. Another approach would be to investigate how the production process could be organised in such a way as to bring the cost of producing small-batch items closer to that of producing high-volume goods. By identifying the cost of carrying out particular activities, the new approach provides opportunities for directing attention to matters of cost control. It can therefore be viewed as a much longer-term technique than the word 'costing' in the title suggests. The establishment of an ABC product cost may thus be considered to be merely the beginning of a process, rather than an end in itself. The recent use of the term activity-based management suggests this forward-looking orientation, which is assuming increasing importance. Activity-based management is discussed briefly in a later section.

8.12 Establishing an activity-based product cost

8.12.1 Comparison with traditional costing

Figures 8.4 and 8.5 illustrate the differences between a traditional product costing system and an ABC system.

A simplified description of the various steps associated with the operation of the basic ABC approach, and a comparison with the traditional coasting costing approach, is given below. An example is set out in Section 8.12.4.

- *Step 1 – Identify the main production-related activities of the organisation.* In a traditional cost system, these will often be related to the department, for example machining, assembly, ordering, receiving, packing and despatching. Note that, for ABC, 'activities' can apply to services as well as to products.
- *Step 2 – Identify the cost (cost pool) of each of the activities identified in Step 1.* This analysis would include the direct costs of the activities, and might include some apportioned costs, such as recent and rates, but it would exclude costs that would have been allocated to departments under a traditional system. For example, under the latter, a production department would be charged an allocation to cover the cost of the receiving department, but in an activity-based system, the receiving department either becomes an activity cost pool in itself, or is part of a greater activity cost pool and is not reallocated to production departments.
- *Step 3 – Determine the cost driver for each activity identified in Step 1.* The cost driver is the thing that best explains why resources are consumed by a particular activity, and therefore why the activity incurs cost, that is, it provides an explanation of the size of the cost pool. For example, although the resources consumed by the order processing activity can be explained by the number of orders processed, a more precise explanation might be the number of items processed therein, that is an order for one item will usually take less processing than an order for ten items, but ten single-item orders will require more processing than an order for ten items. A decision must be made as to what constitutes the most appropriate driver.
- *Step 3a – Select the activity cost pools and cost drivers that will be used within the system.* This step reflects the need for some compromise within an ABC system. As we have just seen, in order processing, the driver could be the number of orders processed, or the number of items per order. The outcome of the process will clearly be dependent on the particular decision made. The diagram above does not show Step 3a separately, but makes the implicit assumption that a driver can be identified.
- *Step 4 –* Calculate a cost driver rate for each activity cost pool in the same way as an overhead rate is calculated in a traditional system.

$$\text{Cost driver rate} = \frac{\text{Activity cost pool}}{\text{Activity driver}}$$

- *Step 5 –* Apply the activity cost driver rates to products (cost units) to arrive at an activity-based product cost.

8.12.2 Analysis of activities

The original impetus for the adoption of ABC is often the desire to provide a more accurate unit product cost. Indeed, the first reference to ABC, which appeared in the *Official Terminology* as late as 1991, is consistent with this objective: ABC was defined as: 'Cost attribution to cost units on the basis of benefit received from indirect activities, e.g. ordering, setting up, and assuring quality.' However, any unit cost, no matter how it is derived, can be misinterpreted. There is temptation to adopt a simplistic approach, which would say, for example, that if it cost £1,000 to produce ten units, it will cost £10,000 to produce

100 units. As we know, this in incorrect in the short term, owing to the existence of short-term fixed costs. The ABC approach does not eliminate this problem any more than the traditional approach. The alternative to presenting full absorption costing information in a traditional costing system has been to provide the user with a statement which distinguishes clearly between the variable cost of production and the fixed cost of production. This carries an implication for the decision-maker that if the variable cost of production is £50 for 10 units, the additional cost of producing a further 40 units will be 40 × £5 = £200. Activity-based costing, on the other hand, can provide the user with a more sophisticated breakdown of cost. This breakdown relates cost to the level of activities undertaken. The structure of reporting will vary from company to company, but Cooper (1992) has suggested that four levels of activity, which he terms a hierarchy of cost, will commonly be found in practice. These are shown below:

(i) *Unit-level activities.* These are activities where the consumption of resources is very strongly correlated with the number of units produced. Costs traditionally defined as direct costs would fall into this category, for example direct material and direct labour.

(ii) *Batch-level activities.* Some activities – for example, machine set-up, materials handling and batch inspection – consume resources in proportion to the number of batches produced, rather than in proportion to the number of units produced. By identifying the consumption of resources at a batch rather than a unit level, it is easier than in a traditional costing system for a user to visualise the changing cost that will come about in the long term by changing a product mix or production schedule.

(iii) *Product-level activities.* Consumption of resources by, for example, administration, product specification or purchasing may be related to the existence of particular products. If the activity is performed to sustain the existence of a particular product line, it is a product-level activity.

(iv) *Facility-level activities.* Even within an ABC system, it is accepted that there are some costs that relate simply to being in business and that therefore cannot be related in any way to the production of any particular product line. Grounds maintenance, plant security and property taxes would be examples of this type of cost.

Consideration of (i)–(iv) shows that the difference between traditional costing and ABC costing will be dependent on the proportion of overhead cost that falls into each of the four categories. If this overhead is made up primarily of (i) and (iv), it is obvious that the traditional approach and the ABC approach will lead to very similar product costs. However, if the bulk of overhead cost falls into category (ii) and/or category (iii), there will be a very significant difference between the two.

 Exercise

A company produced three products, the standard costs of which are shown below:

	P	R	S
	£	£	£
Direct material	50	40	30
Direct labour (@ £10/hour)	30	40	50
Production overhead*	30	40	50
	110	120	130
*Absorbed on basis of direct labour hours			
Quantity produced/sold (units)	10,000	20,000	30,000

The company wishes to introduce ABC, and has identified two major cost pools for production overhead and their associated cost drivers.

Information on these activity cost pools and their drivers is given below:

Activity cost pool	Cost driver	Cost associated with activity cost pool
Receiving/inspecting quality assurance	Purchase requisitions	£1,400,000
Production scheduling/machine set-ups	Number of batches	£1,200,000

Further relevant information on the three products is also given below:

	P	R	S
Number of purchase requisitions	1,200	1,800	2,000
Number of set-ups	240	260	300

From the information given, calculate the activity-based production cost of products, P, R and S. Also, comment on the differences between the original standard costs and the activity-based costs you calculate.

 ## Solution

We are in a position to move straight to Step 4, that is the calculation of the cost-driver rates.

$$\text{Cost-driver rate for receiving/inspecting quality assurance} = \frac{£1,400,000}{5,000} = £280$$
per purchase requisition

$$\text{Cost-driver rate for production scheduling/machine set-ups} = \frac{£1,200,000}{800} = £1,500$$
per set-up

Therefore ABC production costs of these products are as follows.

	P	R	S
	£	£	£
Direct material	50.00	40.00	30.00
Direct labour	30.00	40.00	50.00
Production overhead:			
Receiving/inspecting/quality assurance			
£280 × 1,200/10,000	33.60		
£280 × 1,800/20,000		25.20	
£280 × 2,000/30,000			18.66
Production scheduling/machine set-ups			
£1,500 × 240/10,000	36.00		
£1,500 × 260/20,000		19.50	
£1,500 × 300/10,000			15.00
	149.60	124.70	113.66

Comparison of the ABC cost with the original traditionally calculated cost reveals that product S was significantly overcosted by the traditional system relative to the ABC system, while product P was seriously undercosted. Product S is high-volume product with a high direct labour content, while product P is a low-volume product with a low direct labour content; this result is therefore to be expected. Both the activities in this simple example are batch-related, not unit-related. ABC reflects this reality in its allocation of production overhead costs to the product. The traditional approach allocated all production overhead costs to products as if the overheads were driven by unit-level activities, that is the number of direct labour hours worked – with the inevitable costing consequence seen above.

You should note that this example, with only two activity cost pools, will almost certainly have necessitated some arbitrary cost allocations. All that is being claimed is that the resulting ABC costings give a better insight into the cost of producing the products than traditional costs.

The debate as to whether ABC is actually a new technique, or whether it simply encourages a more accurate tracing of costs to products in a manner that is perfectly consistent with the traditional approach, is interesting but sterile – and misses the point of ABC, as is demonstrated in the rest of this chapter. Nevertheless, it is worth pointing out that ABC product costs are full absorption costs and, as such, suffer from the same type of deficiencies in a decision-making context as do traditional full absorption costs – they are historical, based on current methods of organisation and operation and, at the level of the product, contain allocations of joint/common costs, a point which is illustrated in the comprehensive example of ABC appearing later in this chapter. However, it can be strongly argued that ABC has an important 'attention-directing' role to play in both cost management and decision-making Indeed, the cost management, or monitoring, role of ABC is explicitly acknowledged in the definition which appears in the latest CIMA *Official Terminology:*

> *ABC:* An approach to the costing and monitoring of activities which involves tracing resource consumption and costing final outputs. Resources are assigned to activities and activities to cost objects based on consumption estimates. The latter utilise cost drivers to attach activity costs to outputs.

This particular role is discussed below.

In decision-making, it is arguable that activity-based costs are much more helpful than traditional costs in determining the costs relevant for decision-making and, more particularly, in drawing attention to the likely impact on long-run variable costs of short-term decisions. This point is discussed further later in the chapter.

Exercise – activity-based costing

(a) Distinguish between,
   (i) short-run variable costs and long-run variable costs, and give an example of each;
   (ii) the marginal cost and the average cost of production, and describe the conditions likely to cause such costs to vary.
(b) Explain how long-run variable production costs are allocated to cost units in traditional costing methods. In what ways are modern manufacturing methods making this approach less relevant?

8.12.3 Cost management and ABC

The ABTs have a wide range of applications in the areas of business planning and decision-making The application of an awareness of operational activities in the management of a business is known as Activity-Based Management'. You will encounter the approaches which fall under the ABM heading as part of your studies for CIMA's Paper P2, *Management Accounting – Decision-Making.*

8.12.4 A comprehensive example of ABC

Exercise section I: traditional analysis

A company manufactures three products – X, Y and Z, whose direct costs are given below:

	X	Y	Z
	£	£	£
Direct material	67.92	63.27	56.79
Direct labour (@ £3/hour):			
Machining	13.08	14.73	17.01
Assembly	24.00	27.00	31.20
	105.00	105.00	105.00

The data below was used in calculating the direct labour costs above, and will be used to determine the production overhead charged to each product under the 'traditional' costing method.

	X	Y	Z	Total
Machine time (hours)	11.00	9.00	8.00	
Direct labour (hours)				
Machining	4.36	4.91	5.67	
Assembly	8.00	9.00	10.40	
Production (units)	50,000	30,000	16,250	
Total machine hours	500,000	270,000	130,000	900,000
Total labour hours				
Machining	218,000	147,300	92,137	457,437
Assembly	400,000	270,000	169,000	839,000
				1,296,437

Information on the company's overheads is as follows:

Production overhead	£'000	£'000
Indirect labour		
Machinery	900	
Assembly	600	
Purchasing/order processing	600	
Factory management	100	
		2,200
Power		
Machining	400	
Assembly	100	
		500
Indirect materials		
Machining	200	
Assembly	200	
Purchasing	100	
Factory management	100	
		600
Depreciation		
Machining	600	
Assembly	300	
Purchasing	200	
Building	400	
		1,500
Security		100
Grounds maintenance		100
Total production overhead		5,000

Prepare a traditional overhead analysis and calculate product costs for the three products. Assume that the machining department uses a machine hour absorption rate and the assembly department a labour hour rate.

 Solution

Step 1 – Assign production overhead to cost centres

	£'000	£'000
Machining		
Indirect labour	900	
Power	400	
Indirect materials	200	
Depreciation	600	
		2,100
Assembly		
Indirect labour	600	
Power	100	
Indirect materials	200	
Depreciation	300	
		1,200
Purchasing/order processing		
Indirect labour	600	
Indirect materials	100	
Depreciation	200	
		900
Factory management		
Indirect labour	100	
Indirect materials	100	
Depreciation	400	
Security	100	
Ground maintenance	100	
		800
Total production overhead		5,000

Step 2 – Reallocate services department costs to production departments on a suitable basis

	£'000	£'000
Machining		
Indirect costs (from step 1)	2,100	
Reallocation of service centre costs	600	
		2,700
Assembly		
Indirect costs (from step 1)	1,200	
Reallocation of service centre costs	1,100	
		2,300
Purchasing/order processing		
Indirect costs (from step 1)	900	
Reallocate on basis of direct labour cost	(900)	
		–
Factory management		
Indirect costs (from step 1)	800	
Reallocate on basis of direct labour cost	(800)	
		–
Total production overhead		5,000

Step 3 – Calculate absorption rate
Machining: based on total machine hours

$$\frac{\text{Total overhead costs}}{\text{Total machine hours}} = \frac{£2,700,000}{900,000} = £3 \text{ per machine hour}$$

Assembly: based on total assembly labour hours

$$\frac{\text{Total overhead costs}}{\text{Total labour hours}} = \frac{£2,300,000}{839,000} = £2.74 \text{ per machine hour}$$

Step 4 – Calculate full product cost

	X £	Y £	Z £
Direct cost (as before)	105.00	105.00	105.00
Production overhead:			
Machining	30.00	27.00	24.00
Assembly	21.92	24.66	28.50
	156.92	156.66	157.50

Exercise section II: ABC analysis – allocating all costs to products

The information and data in the following tables will be used to determine cost drivers and calculate overheads.

Product X	*Product Y*	*Product Z*
High volume	Medium volume	Low volume
Large batches	Medium batches	Small batches
Few purchase orders placed	Medium purchase orders placed	Many purchase orders placed
	Medium components	Many components
Few customer orders placed	Medium customer orders placed	Many customer orders placed

	Product X	Product Y	Product Z	Total
Typical batch size	2,000	600	325	
No. of production runs	25	50	50	125
No. of inspections	25	50	50	125
Purchase orders placed	25	100	200	325
Customer orders received	10	100	200	310

Prepare an ABC analysis and calculate product costs.

Solution

- Step 1 – Identify production-related activities

	£'000	£'000
Analysis of indirect labour		
Machining		
Supervision	100	
Set-up	400	
Quality control	400	
		900
Assembly		
Supervision	200	
Quality control	400	
		600
Purchasing/order processing		
Resource procurement	300	
Customer liaison/expediting	300	
		600
Factory management		
General administration		100
		2,200

Activities
1. Machining
2. Machine set-up
3. Machining quality control
4. Assembly
5. Assembly quality control
6. Resource procurement
7. Customer liaison/expediting
8. Factory management.

The table below shows the specific details of

- Step 2 – identify the cost of activities;
- Step 3 – identify cost driver;
- Step 4 – reallocate factory management costs pro rata to other costs.

STEP 2	£'000	Total £'000	STEP 3	STEP 4 £'000	Total £'000
1. Machining					
Supervision	100				
Power	400				
Indirect materials	100				
Depreciation	600				
		1,200	Machine running time	230	1,430
2. Machine set-up					
Indirect labour	400				
Indirect materials	50				
		450	No. of set-ups (batch size)	85	535
3. Machining quality control					
Indirect labour	400				
Indirect materials	50				
		450	No. of inspections (batch size)	85	535
4. Assembly					
Supervision	200				
Power	100				
Indirect materials	100				
Depreciation	300				
		700	Direct labour hours worked	135	835
5. Assembly quality control					
Indirect labour	400				
Indirect materials	100				
		500	No. of inspections (batch size)	95	595
6. Resource procurement					
Indirect labour	300				
Indirect materials	50				
Depreciation	100				
		450	No. of orders placed (product batch size)	85	535
7. Customer liaison/expediting					
Indirect labour	300				
Indirect materials	50				
Depreciation	100				
		450	No. of orders rec'd (product)	85	535
8. Factory management (see note)					
Indirect labour	100				
Indirect materials	100				
Depreciation	400				
Security	100				
Grounds maintenance	100				
		800	No obvious (size of business?)	(800)	0
		5,000		0	5,000

There is no obvious driver for the common costs collected under the heading 'factory management', so they have been reallocated to other activity cost pools on the basis of their total costs.

- Step 5 – Calculate overhead from cost drivers.

  Rate per machine hour

  $$\frac{\text{Total overhead costs}}{\text{Total machine hours}} = \frac{£1,430,000}{900,000} = £1.59 \text{ per machine hour}$$

  Rate per set-up

  $$\frac{\text{Total overhead costs}}{\text{Total set-ups}} = \frac{£535,000}{125} = £4,280 \text{ per batch}$$

Rate per machining inspection

$$\frac{\text{Total overhead costs}}{\text{Total inspections}} = \frac{£535,000}{125} = £4,280 \text{ per batch}$$

Assembly rate per direct labour hour

$$\frac{\text{Total overhead costs}}{\text{Total assembly hours}} = \frac{£835,000}{839,000} = £1.00 \text{ per labour hour}$$

Rate per assembly inspection

$$\frac{\text{Total overhead costs}}{\text{Total inspections}} = \frac{£595,000}{125} = £4,760 \text{ per batch}$$

Rate per order placed

$$\frac{\text{Total overhead costs}}{\text{Total orders placed}} = \frac{£535,000}{325} = £1,646 \text{ per order}$$

Rate per order received

$$\frac{\text{Total overhead costs}}{\text{Total orders received}} = \frac{£535,000}{310} = £1,726 \text{ per order}$$

- Step 6 – Calculate full product cost.

	X	Y	Z
	£	£	£
Direct costs (as before)	105.00	105.00	105.00
Overhead			
Per machine hour	15.90	14.31	12.72
Per set-up			
£4,280/2,000	2.14		
£4,280/600		7.13	
£4,280/325			13.17
Per machine inspection			
£4,280/2,000	2.14		
£4,280/600		7.13	
£4,280/325			13.17
Assembly rate @ £1 per DLH	8.00	9.00	10.40
Per assembly inspection			
£4,760/2,000	2.38		
£4,760/600		7.93	
£4,760/325			14.65
Per order placed			
£1,646 × 25/50,000	0.82		
£1,646 × 100/30,000		5.49	
£1,646 × 200/16,250			20.26
Per order received			
£1,726 × 10/50,000	0.35		
£1,726 × 100/30,000		5.75	
£1,726 × 200/16,250			21.24
Overhead subtotal	31.73	56.74	105.61
Direct costs + overheads	136.73	161.74	210.61

Rationalisation of overhead charged

Product	Overhead (£)	Production	Total (rounded)
	£		£'000
X	31.73	50,000	1,580
Y	56.74	30,000	1,700
Z	105.61	16,250	1,720
			5,000

Comparison of product costs under each method

	X	Y	Z
'Traditional'	156.92	156.66	157.50
Activity-based costing	136.73	161.74	210.61

Product Z – with a low total production volume, many purchase and customer orders, and frequent small production runs – has a significantly higher cost under ABC than under the 'traditional' method. The opposite is the case with product X, which has a high total production volume, relatively few orders and large production runs.

✋ Exercise section III: ABC analysis – excluding facility-level costs

In the calculation in section II the ABC costs, like traditional costs, contain an allocation of the factory management costs within each cost driver – or absorption – rate. Factory management costs were allocated to other activities simply because of the lack of an identifiable driver with which to associate them with products. Factory management is a 'facility-level' activity and, as such, cannot be identified directly with another activity, and certainly not with a particular product.

Despite the lack of an identifiable driver, it can be argued that this cost should not be identified arbitrarily with the other activities, but should be left within its own cost pool.

If this is done, Step 4 in the ABC analysis above would be omitted, and the calculation would proceed as follows

ABC analysis when factory management costs are not reallocated to other activities
This shows the detail for

- Step 2 – Identify the cost of activities
- Step 3 – Identify cost drivers

STEP 2	£'000	STEP3
1. Machining	1,200	Machine running time
2. Machine set-up	450	No. of set-ups (batch size)
3. Machining quality control	450	No. of inspections (batch size)
4. Assembly	700	Direct labour hours worked
5. Assembly quality control	500	No. of inspections (batch size)
6. Resource procurement	450	No. of orders placed (product/batch size)
7. Customer liaison/expediting	450	No. of orders received (product)
8. Factory management	800	No obvious driver (size of business)
	5,000	

- Step 4 – Omitted
- Step 5 – Calculate overhead from cost drivers.

Rate per machine hour

$$\frac{\text{Total overhead costs}}{\text{Total machine hours}} = \frac{£1,200,000}{900,000} = £1.33 \text{ per machine hour}$$

Rate per set-up

$$\frac{\text{Total overhead costs}}{\text{Total set-ups}} = \frac{£450,000}{125} = £3,600 \text{ per batch}$$

Rate per machining inspection

$$\frac{\text{Total overhead costs}}{\text{Total inspections}} = \frac{£450,000}{125} = £3,600 \text{ per batch}$$

Assembly rate per direct labour hour

$$\frac{\text{Total overhead costs}}{\text{Total assembly hours}} = \frac{£700,000}{839,000} = £0.83 \text{ per labour hour}$$

Rate per assembly inspection

$$\frac{\text{Total overhead costs}}{\text{Total inspections}} = \frac{£500,000}{125} = £4,000 \text{ per batch}$$

Rate per order Placed

$$\frac{\text{Total overhead costs}}{\text{Total orders placed}} = \frac{£450,000}{325} = £1,385 \text{ per order}$$

Rate per order received

$$\frac{\text{Total overhead costs}}{\text{Total orders received}} = \frac{£450,000}{310} = £1,452 \text{ per order}$$

Factory management costs of £800,000 have no obvious driver, and are not included in the costs above.

- Step 6 – Calculate full product cost

	X £	Y £	Z £
Direct costs (as before)	105.00	105.00	105.00
Overhead			
Per machine hour	13.33	12.00	10.67
Per set-up			
£3,600/2,000	1.80		
£3,600/600		6.00	
£3,600/325			11.08
Per machine inspection			
£3,600/2,000	1.80		
£3,600/600		6.00	
£3,600/325			11.08
Assembly rate @ £0.83 per DLH	6.67	7.51	8.67
Per assembly inspection			
£4,000/2,000	2.00		
£4,000/600		6.67	
£4,000/325			12.31
Per order placed			
£1,385 × 25/50,000	0.69		
£1,385 × 100/30,000		4.62	
£1,385 × 200/16,250			17.05
Per order received			
£1,452 × 10/50,000	0.29		
£1,452 × 100/30,000		4.84	
£1,452 × 200/16,250			17.87
Overhead subtotal	26.58	47.64	88.73
Direct costs + overheads	131.58	152.64	193.73

Rationalisation of overhead charged

Product	Overhead	Production	Total Tail
	£		£'000
X	26.58	50,000	1,329
Y	47.64	30,000	1,429
Z	88.73	16,250	1,442
			4,200

In this second approach, the £800,000 factory management costs have been left unallocated. Obviously, for stock valuation purposes, it would be necessary to allocate them to products, albeit on an arbitrary basis. They could be allocated to products in proportion to the allocation of other overhead costs, as shown below:

Product	Total Overhead (1)	Factory management cost (2)	Total production overhead allocated (1) + (2)
	£'000	£'000	£'000
X	1,329	253	1,582
Y	1,429	272	1,701
Z	1,442	275	1,717
	4,200	800	5,000

Apart from minor rounding differences, the total allocation as shown in the final column above is identical to that in the same column in section II, and thus the total overhead charged to the three products is identical under both approaches. However, the second approach may be much more helpful to management by directing attention to the resource implications of manufacturing particular products. For example, the table below shows product Y's comparative costs.

ABC COST OF PRODUCT Y	Factory management costs allocated to other activities £	Factory management treated as a separate activity £	
Direct costs (as before)	105.00	105.00	
Overhead			
Unit-level activity cost			
Per machine hour	14.31	12.00	
Assembly rate	9.00	7.51	
Batch-level activity cost			
Per set-up	7.13	6.00	
Per machine inspection	7.13	6.00	
Per assembly inspection	7.93	6.67	
Per order placed	5.49	4.62	
Product-level activity cost			
Per order received	5.75	4.84	
Overhead subtotal	56.74	47.64	
Facility-level activity cost			
Factory management costs:		9.10	(£272,000/30,000)
Total production overhead	56.74	56.74	
Direct costs + overheads	161.74	161.74	

In the first analysis, the cost-driver rates do not give an accurate reflection of the resource consumption implications of performing particular activities, as they contain an arbitrary allocation of factory management costs. The second analysis provides cost-driver rates that do reflect truly the long-run costs of performing particular activities. This information may be useful to management in identifying cost-reduction opportunities, as well as for product costing purposes.

In addition to identifying 'factory management' as a separate cost pool, the table above has also grouped costs in accordance with the hierarchy outlined above. This provides management with a clear view of the resource consumption that will result in the long run, if production of Y is maintained at 30,000 units and the organisation of production remains the same. If the volume of production of Y were to change, both ABC analyses draw management's attention to the fact that the change in overhead resource consumption brought about by the change in volume would not be proportionate to the change in the number of units produced. In the first analysis, even the resource consumption of unit-level activities would not change proportionately to the change in production volume, as there is no reason to expect the facility-level costs of factory management, included therein via the allocation process, to change proportionately with change in volume. In the second analysis, where there are no arbitrary cost allocations, the resource consumption of unit-level activities would change proportionately with the change in volume. However, the change in consumption of the other overhead resources would depend on precisely how the change in volume was achieved – for example, were there more batcher? For example, volume could be expanded by increasing the size of each batch of Y, in which case the consumption of batch-level resources would remain constant, despite the rise in volume. ABC analyses thus provide a clearer insight into the way in which resource consumption, and ultimately cost, will change as a result of the specific changes in activities that accompany a particular change in volume.

It pays to know your abc

Sarah Perrin, *Management Today,* **December 1997 Full Text: © Haymarket Publishing Ltd. 1997**

It's difficult to calculate the true cost of a product when the same resources are used to generate different goods, says Sarah Perrin. Activity-based costing may be the answer.

Businessmen may think they already know how profitable their widgets are. They know the materials and labour costs which, hopefully, are covered by the price. But what about those extra indirect costs? For example, does the marketing department spend a major percentage of its time on one product line, devising promotions to shift stock? Does the finance department have to keep chasing one customer for payment? All these activities incur a cost whenever the same resources are being harder to calculate the true cost of a product.

Activity-based costing (ABC) is one answer. It takes every cost generated by the business and allocates it proportionately to the products or services that it has helped create. Customers too can be analysed to see whether some are more costly to serve than others. Only once all costs have been allocated do you have a complete picture of how profitable each of the different products or services really are.

That's the simple explanation, but the process is easier talked about than done. 'It's difficult to get a simple explanation of activity-based costing', says Colin Drury, professor of accounting at the University of Huddersfield. 'It's about trying to break an organisation down into many different activities rather than departments. It's about finding the causes of costs.'

The process itself does appear complex to the uninitiated. It requires the identification of all the activities performed within the company. 'For small or medium-sized companies, I would expect to divide the business into 300–400 activities', says John McKenzie, director of consulting for ABC software developer Armstrong Laing. Most departments could be broken down into 30–50 activities. Within accounts receivable, for example, one key activity would be chasing late payers. Having identified that activity, the next step is to customers. This can be done by getting staff to fill out time sheets or answer questionnaires. You can then estimate the cost of debt-chasing activity and allocate it proportionately over those late-paying accounts. Suddenly you have a better idea of how much each customer costs to service. By applying the technique to all the other departments, and all the activities within departments, the complete cost picture for each product or client appears.

So far so good. But it is what you do with the information that counts. Hence the term 'activity-based management' (ABM). One example of ABM would involve looking at all the activities in the company and breaking them down into four types: those that add value to a customer, those that add value to the business; non-value-added activities (such as correcting mistakes in invoices); and sustaining activities (such as the annual audit, which is required by law). Those non-value-added costs can then be compared with their value-added counterparts. If they make up a high proportion of the total, then there is scope for cost-cutting 'Sustaining and non-value-added costs often come out at around 50% of the total', says McKenzie. 'That's when you find you can eliminate some of them. That's when people get excited.'

Further analysis shows which products or customers are profitable. You can find yourself in the uncomfortable position of learning that, say, 10% of your company's products account for 100% of profits. In other words, 90% are loss-making or just breaking even.

8.12.5 Variance analysis and ABC

An ABC approach to the analysis of overhead costs is possible. This follows the ABC logic that all overheads are variable if one understands what they vary with. Let us illustrate the approach with a simple example.

Example

ABC Ltd produces the Unit and all overheads are associated with the delivery of Units to its customers. Budget details for the period include £8,000 overheads, 4,000 Units output and 40 customer deliveries. Actual results for the period are £7,800 overheads, 4,200 units output and 38 customer deliveries.

The overhead cost variance for the period is

Actual cost	£	7,800
Standard cost		8,400 (4,200 Units at £2 per Unit standard cost)
Cost variance		600 Fav

Applying the traditional fixed overhead cost variance analysis gives the following result:

Volume variance	£	400 Fav (£8,400 standard cost− £8,000 budget cost)
Expenditure variance		200 Fav (£8,000 budget cost− £7,800 actual)
Cost variance		600 Fav

Adopting an ABC approach gives the following result:

Activity variance	£	800 Fav ((42 standard − 38 actual deliveries) × £200)
Expenditure variance		200 Adv ((38 deliveries × £200) − £7,800)
Cost variance		600 Fav

The ABC approach is based on an assumption that the overheads are essentially variable (but variable with the delivery numbers and not the Units output). The ABC cost variances are based on a standard delivery size of 100 Units and a standard cost per delivery of £200. Both of these figures are derived from the budget. The activity variance reports the cost impact of undertaking more or less activities than standard, and the expenditure variance reports the cost impact of paying more or less than standard for the actual activities undertaken.

8.13   Throughput accounting

In this chapter we are discussing the development of synchronous manufacturing, and the identification of bottleneck resources. In this context we will now go on to learn about throughput accounting, a new type of management accounting system that has been developed to provide management information that is more suited to the new manufacturing philosophy.

8.13.1   The theory of constraints

The concept behind the throughput accounting system was first formulated and developed by Goldratt and Cox (1986) in the United States of America in a book called *The Goal.* Godlratt (1990) developed the concept and eventually gave it the name the theory of constraints (TOC) by which name it is known today in the United States of America. The theory was picked up and turned into an accounting system in the United Kingdom, where it has become known as throughput accounting (TA). Goldratt and Cox developed the technique to help managers improve the overall profitability of the firm. The theory focuses attention on constraints or bottlenecks within the organisation which hinder speedy production. This main concept is to maximise the rate of manufacturing output, that is the throughput of the organisation. The idea being TOC is that raw materials should be turned into products that are immediately shipped to customers at the greatest possible speed, in a similar way to JIT system.

The important concept behind TOC is that the production rate of the entire factory is set at the pace of the bottleneck – the constraining resource. Hence, in order to achieve the best results TOC emphasises the importance of removing bottlenecks or, as they are called in the United States of America, binding constraints from the production process. If they cannot be removed they must be coped with in the best possible way so that they do not hinder production unduly. In order to do this, network diagrams need to be drawn to identify the bottlenecks or binding constraints. Figure 8.5 illustrates a simple network chart where the assembly and test process is the bottleneck.

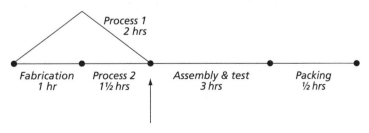

Figure 8.5   Network chart of a manufacturing process

In Figure 8.5 it can be seen that the assembly and test process is the bottleneck and that in order to maximise throughput, a buffer stock is needed prior to the assembly and test process so that its employees never have to wait for components from prior processes.

TOC identifies three types of cost.

1. Throughput contribution = sales revenue − completely variable costs this is usually = sales revenue − direct material cost.

   (Labour costs tend to be partially fixed and are excluded normally. Direct material cost includes purchased components and material handling costs.)

2. *Conversion costs.* These are all operating costs, excluding completely variable costs, which are incurred in order to produce the product, that is labour and overhead, including rent, utilities and relevant depreciation.

3. *Investments.* These include all stock, raw material, work in progress, finished goods, research and development costs, costs of equipment and buildings and so on.

The aim is to increase throughput contribution while decreasing conversion costs and investment costs. TOC is a short-term profit maximising technique that is very similar in approach to marginal costing. The only real difference is that the contribution may be more realistic in that all conversion costs are assumed to be fixed costs. Bottleneck decisions are in reality linear programming decisions as TOC attempts to do the following:

> Maximise throughput contribution (sales revenue − direct materials)
> Subject to:
> > Production capacity (supply constraints)
> > Production demand (demand constraints)

The TOC is quite widely used in the United States of America by companies such as Ford Electronics, General Motors and Avery Dennison, some of which claim that it has revolutionised their business. It is also used by a number of UK companies, sometimes in the form of throughput accounting, discussed next.

8.13.2 Throughput accounting

In the United Kingdom Galloway and Waldron (1988/89) developed TA from the theory of constraints. It is very similar in concept to TOC but it is an accounting-based technique whereas TOC is not. Eli Goldratt has always stressed the differences between the two systems. This may have been because he is not over-fond of cost accountants or their methods and at one time one of his sayings was that 'cost accounting is the number 1 enemy of productivity'. TA is an extreme version of variable costing as, like TOC, it treats only direct material as variable and all labour and overhead costs as fixed. It operates through a series of ratios and differs from all other management accounting systems because it emphasises throughput first, stock minimisation second and cost control third.

Throughput accounting's primary concern is the rate at which a business can generate profits. In order to monitor this it focuses on the return on the throughput through the bottleneck resource.

Its key measure is

$$\text{Return per time period} = \frac{\text{sales revenue} - \text{material costs}}{\text{time period}}$$

[Assuming materials are the only totally variable costs, Balderstone & Keef (1999)]

This ratio measure the value added by the organisation during a specific period of time, normally 1 hour. As time plays a crucial part in the ratio, managers' attention is automatically drawn to removing bottlenecks that might cause delay in the production process.

If one machine holds up production, because it is inefficient or has inadequate capacity, it is of little use to work the other machines at 100 per cent efficiency as the parts produced will be destined for stock until such time as the bottleneck machine can process them. Eventually when parts are spilling from the storeroom or piled all over the factory floor, the efficient machines will have to stop altogether for a time, in order to allow the bottleneck machine to catch up. Therefore, there is nothing to be gained by measuring and encouraging the efficiency of machines that do not govern the overall flow of work. The same applies to the efficiency of production staff working in the non-bottleneck processes. In fact bonuses that are paid to encourage fast working are at best simply wasted and at worst result in increased storage costs. Furthermore, if workers are encouraged to work too quickly, they are likely to produce more faulty goods and to waste materials. If the goods are destined for the storeroom, this increase in waste serves no purpose except to increase the average cost per unit.

A minor use of the return per time period ratio is to optimise production in the short term. Product return per time period ratio can be used in the same way as limiting factor ratios are used in order to plan how many units of each product should be made in order to maximise profit. The limiting factor is the first factor that prevents a manufacturing company expanding production towards infinity, and the ratio is contribution/limiting factor. The products are ranked according to this ratio; that is according to their use of the limiting factor, the one with the highest contribution per key or limiting factor being the best financially. In TA the key or limiting factor is the bottleneck. The return per time period ratio can be modified and used in a similar way to the P/V ratio. The amended ratio for ranking products is

$$\text{Product return per minute} = \frac{\text{sales price} - \text{material costs}}{\text{Minutes on key/bottleneck resource}}$$

This is illustrated in detail in the following example.

Exercise – contrasting TA with the limiting factor approach

A company produces two products, A and B, the production costs of which are shown below:

	A	B
	£	£
Direct material cost	10	10
Direct labour cost	5	9
Variable overhead	5	9
Fixed overhead	5	9
Total product cost	25	37

Fixed overhead is absorbed on the basis direct labour cost.

The products pass through two processes, Y and Z, with associated labour cost of £10 per direct labour hour in each. The direct labour associated with the two products for these processes is shown below:

	Time taken	
Process	Product A	Product B
Y	10 min	39 min
Z	20 min	15 min

Selling prices are set by the market. The current market price for A is £65 and that for B, £52. At these prices, the market will absorb as many units of A and B as the company can produce. The ability of the company to produce A and B is limited by the capacity to process the products through Y and Z. The company operates a two-shift system, giving 16 working hours per day. Process Z is a single-process line and 2 hours in each shift will be downtime. Process Y can process two units simultaneously, although this doubles the requirement for direct labour. Process Y can operate for the full 16 working hours each day.

Requirement

What production plan should the company follow in order to maximise profits?

 Solution

In order to find the profit maximising solution in any problem, the constraints which prevent the profit from being infinite must be identified; the greater the number of constraints, the more difficult the problem is to solve. In the simplest case, where there is only one binding constraint, the profit maximising solution is found by maximising the contribution per unit of the scarce resource, that is binding constraint. Linear programming may be used to solve the problem where more than one constraint is binding for some, but not all, feasible solutions. Where the number of products is limited to two, and such constraints are relatively few in number, the problem can easily be expressed graphically to reveal the profit maximising solution, and/or the problem can be expressed in the form of a set of simultaneous equations. As the number of potentially binding constraints increases, the use of a computer becomes the only feasible way to solve the necessary number of simultaneous equations.

In this question, the only constraint is the company's ability to process the product. The total daily processing time for processes Y and Z are

$$\text{Maximum process time Y} = 2 \times 6 \text{ hours} \times 60 \text{ mins} = 1,920 \text{ minutes}$$
$$\text{Maximum process time Z} = 12 \text{ hours} \times 60 \text{ mins} = 720 \text{ minutes}$$

So the maximum number that could be produced of each of the two products is

	Product A Maximum units	Product B Maximum units
Y	$\frac{1,920}{10} = 192$	$\frac{1,920}{39} = 49.23$
Z	$\frac{720}{20} = 36$	$\frac{720}{15} = 48$

In the case of both products, the maximum number of units which can be produced in Process Y exceeds the number that can be produced in Process Z, and thus the capacity of Process Y is not a binding constraint. The problem therefore becomes one of deciding how to allocate the scarce production capacity of Process Z in such a way as to maximise profit.

Traditional approach – maximising the contribution per minute in Process Z

Contribution of A = £65 (selling price) − £20 (variable cost) = £45
Contribution of B = £52 (selling price) − £28 (variable cost) = £24
Contribution of A per minute in process Z = £45 − 20 = £2.25
Contribution of B per minute in process Z = £24 − 15 = £1.60

The profit maximising solution is therefore to produce the maximum possible number of units of A, 36, giving a contribution of £45 × 36 = £1,620.

Throughput approach – maximising throughput per minute in bottleneck resource Z

Throughput of A = £65 (selling price)/£10 (material cost) = £55
Throughput of B = £52 (selling price)/£10 (selling price) = £42

Contribution of A per minute in process Z = £55/20 = £2.75
Contribution of B per minute in process Z = £42/15 = £2.80

The profit maximising solution is therefore to produce the maximum number of units of B, 48, giving a throughput of £42 × 48 = £2,016.

It is clear that, given the different solutions, the two approaches cannot both lead to profit maximisation. Which technique is correct depends on the variability or otherwise of labour and variable overheads, which in turn depends on the time horizon of the decision. This type of profit maximisation technique is a short-term one and in today's world labour is likely to be fixed in the short term and so it can be argued that TA provides the more correct solution. Variable overheads would need to be analysed to assess their variability.

Marginal costing rose to popularity in the 1930s when labour costs were usually variable as the workforce was usually paid on a piece-rate basis. Since then textbooks, at least, have always assumed that labour is a variable cost in the short term. All that has happened with TA is that it tends to recognise the present reality, which is that most cost excluding materials are now fixed in the short term.

The marginal costing approach should of course be modified to accommodate this, as it requires only variable costs to be used to calculate contribution. If only material costs are variable, then only those costs should be used in the calculation of contribution. Thus there should be no difference between the two systems in this respect.

8.13.3 Throughput cost control and effectiveness measures

Although the measure of return per period is a valuable measure for speeding up the flow of work and eliminating bottlenecks it ignores the costs involved in running the factory. There is little to be gained if throughput and, therefore, revenue are increased marginally but in order to achieve this labour and overhead costs increase considerably. The throughput accounting ratio measures this:

$$\text{TA ratio} = \frac{\text{Value added per time period}}{\text{Conversion cost per time period}} \quad \text{i.e.} \quad \frac{\text{sales} - \text{Materials}}{\text{labour} + \text{overhead}}$$

This ratio will obviously be greater than one for a profitable company and the aim will be to increase it to an acceptably high level. If a product has a ratio of less than one, the organisation loses money every time it is produced.

Traditional efficiency measures such as standard costing variances and labour ratios can no longer be used with TA because traditional efficiency cannot be encouraged. (The labour force must not be encouraged to work to produce for stock.) A process efficiency ratio of throughput/cost can still be used.

Effectiveness is, however, the more important measure:

$$\text{Current effectiveness ratio} = \frac{\text{Standard minutes of throughout achieved}}{\text{Minutes available}}$$

This measures effectiveness and compares it to a current standard.

Traditional variances can also be misleading in a throughput environment. For example, if overtime was worked at the bottleneck to increase throughput an adverse labour rate variance would arise. Generally adverse variances are considered bad. However, in throughput environment this would be good and would increase profits as long as the extra labour cost was less than the increase in value added.

TA's aim, like JIT, must always be to minimise production time taken and so all non-value-added elements in the production lead time need to be eliminated or minimised so that process time approaches the lead time.

$$\text{Lead time} = \text{set-up time} + \text{waiting time} + \text{process time} + \text{inspection time} + \text{move time}$$

8.13.4 Summary of throughput accounting

Table 8.1 highlights the difference between TA and traditional product costing.

So far TA has only been considered in relation to manufacturing organisations but it has been used very successfully in service industries as well. For example, it has been used to speed up and reduce costs in checking customers' creditworthiness. In one company this process took a long time, often longer than a week, and held up further activities. Before TA was used, over-qualified people were used to make basic credit decisions and this caused the delays in deciding on creditworthiness. Afterwards ordinary members of staff were allowed to make decisions in the majority of cases and only difficult ones were referred to experts. This meant that decisions were made much faster, normally within 24 hours, and the cost of the function was reduced.

Table 8.1 Difference between throughput accounting and traditional product cost systems

Throughput accounting	Traditional product costing
Value is added when an item is sold	Value is added when an item is produced
Schedule adherence and meeting delivery dates are the key to work effectively	Full utilisation of labour and machine time is the key to working efficiently
Variance analysis only investigates why the scheduled mix was not produced	Variance analysis investigates whether standards were achieved
Labour and traditionally defined variable overheads are not normally treated as variable costs	Labour and traditionally defined variable overheads are treated as variable costs
Stock is valued in the P&L and balance sheet at material cost only (i.e. variable cost)	Stock is valued in the P&L and balance sheet at total production cost

The TA has been criticised for being unduly short term because all costs apart from material costs tend to be treated as fixed. It could be argued that the use of traditional marginal costing is not always correct because those that use it tend to treat direct labour as a variable cost, which is not realistic. It could be argued, and has been by some that labour is more fixed than an item of machinery and its associated costs, as that can be removed and sold within a few weeks. Staff cannot be made redundant as quickly and the cost may be greater. Having said that, in the long term all costs are variable and all options possible but TA only considers the current situation and way of improving it.

Marginal costing and throughput accounting rely on the calculation of contribution (sales–variable cost) and as such there is no difference between them. Because direct labour was paid on a piece-rate, it was largely a truly variable cost when marginal costing was developed early this century. Today, textbooks tend to use the same definition of variable costs for marginal costing purpose even though it is usually no longer relevant. Once this problem has been overcome the two systems are seen to be the same in principle, marginal costing dealing with short-term one-off decisions and throughput accounting providing a planning and control system.

Make or buy decisions should nearly always be made from a strategic viewpoint and not from a short-term marginal cost point of view. But assume for a moment that a short-term decision is needed and marginal costing is used, and that it suggests that the product under consideration should be made rather than bought in. If this product uses valuable capacity on the machine before the bottleneck machine, then the holding of buffer stock could be jeopardised under certain circumstances. This was a real scenario at Allied Signal Ltd. Because throughput accounting was used, management declined the opportunity to make the product under consideration (Darlington 1995). Again conflict occurred between the two systems, but the consequence of using spare capacity should have been considered in any system; throughput accounting simply drew attention to it.

It is also argued that by concentration on the relationship between sales and materials, TA neglects other costs. This is not a valid criticism as the TA ratio incorporates conversion costs per time period. However, the purpose of throughput accounting, and especially TOC, is not so much to control costs as to demonstrate ways of improving profit by increasing production flow. It is an attention-directing system. The criticisms can be countered but nevertheless throughput accounting is not a technique that will suit all organisations.

8.14   Backflush accounting

Traditional cost accounting systems track the sequence of raw materials and components moving through the production systems, and as a consequence are called 'sequential tracking systems'. As JIT is an entirely different system it requires its own cost accounting system. The absence of stocks makes choices about stock valuation systems unnecessary and the rapid conversion of direct material into cost of goods sold simplifies the cost accounting system. The approach is known as backflush accounting.

Backflush accounting delays the recording of costs until after the events have taken place, then standard costs are used to work backwards to 'flush' out the manufacturing costs. There are two events that trigger the records kept in most backflush accounting systems:

- The first is the purchase of raw materials, In a true JIT system where absolutely no raw material stock is held, even this trigger is not relevant and raw materials are 'flushed' when the second trigger is activated.

- The second trigger is either the transfer of goods to finished goods stock or, in a true JIT system, the sale of goods. Two examples of possible backflush accounting systems are given in Tables 8.2 and 8.3.

This is the system used by Toyota in its UK factory. In true Japanese style it manipulates employees to behave in a certain way. First employees must concentrate on achieving sales

Table 8.2 System 1. A small stock of raw material is held but no finished goods stock

	Dr £	Cr £
1. Raw materials are purchased – £3,200		
Stock control	3,200	
Creditors control		3,200
2. Conversion costs are incurred – £3,000		
Conversion cost control	3,000	
Individual a/cs		3,000
3. Goods sold – £6,000 worth at standard cost		
Cost of goods sold	6,000	
Stock control		2,900
Conversion costs allocated		3,100
4. Under- or over-allocation of conversion costs		
Conversion costs allocated	3,100	
Cost of goods sold		100
Conversion costs control		3,000

Table 8.3 System 2. No raw material stock is held but same finished goods stock is held

	Dr £	Cr £
1. Raw materials are purchased – no entry		
2. Conversion costs are incurred – £3,000		
Conversion cost control	3,000	
Individual a/cs		3,000
3. Finished goods units produced £6,000		
Finished goods control	6,000	
Creditors control		2,900
Conversion costs allocated		3,100
4. Finished goods sold – £5,900		
Cost of goods sold	5,900	
Finished goods control		5,900
5. Under- or over-allocation of conversion costs		
Conversion costs allocated	3,100	
Cost of goods sold		100
Conversion costs control		3,000

The figures are the same as for System 1, but the transfer to finished goods is assumed to be £6,000 and the cost of goods sold is £5,900 leaving a finished goods stock of £100.

because cost of sales is the trigger – nothing gets recorded until the sale is made. Second there is no benefit in producing goods for stock. In traditional systems which have a finished goods, stock managers can increase profit by producing more goods than are sold in a period because an increase in finished goods stock reduces the cost of sales in traditional financial account (Figure 8.6).

The model just described may be altered to cope with work in progress in the system by using a raw and in progress account (RIP) in place of the stock control account. All other entries remain the same (Figure 8.7).

The backflush accounting model cannot be used by all organisations. It can only be used where a JIT-type system is in operation. Where it is used it does have advantages. The traditional system is time consuming and expensive to operate, as it requires a considerable amount of documentation, such as material requisitions and time sheets to support it in order to maintain the WIP records and job cards. If a company operates with low stock levels, the benefits of operating the traditional costing system are few. By introducing a black-flush system a considerable amount of clerical time is saved.

From the backflush accounting examples it can be seen that JIT eliminates direct labour as a cost category. Instead labour is treated as an indirect cost and is included in conversion

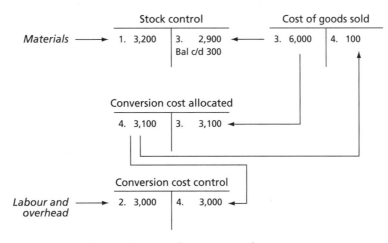

Figure 8.6   Ledger accounts for system 1

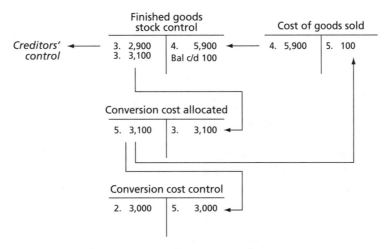

Figure 8.7   Ledger accounts for system 2

cost with the overheads. This is because production is only required when demand requires it and so production labour will be paid regardless of activity. All indirect costs are treated as a fixed period expense. With JIT, failed or rework must be almost eliminated if the system is to work and so no accounts for this will exist in blakflush accounting whereas they are required in traditional systems.

The backflush accounting model does not conform to the accepted financial accounting proceducers for external reporting in the United Kingdom. This is because work in progress is treated as an asset in the financial accounts and in backflush accounting it is not shown to exist although in practice a small amount does. This can be countered by claiming, quite rightly, immateriality. If only one-tenth of one day's production is held in work in progress, then it is immaterial. It can also be claimed that it is immaterial if the work in progress does not change from one period to the next as opening and closing stock will cancel each other out.

Backflush accounting can be criticised because of the lack of information that it provides. Some argue, quite rightly, that in reality it is impossible to eliminate all stock as a truck arriving with raw material creates stock until it is moved to and used in production. If backflush accounting is used in a system where a substantial amount of stock is held, a physical stock-take will be needed, because the system does not record the quantity of stock. Instead it is derived on paper by the difference between the standard cost of material in the goods sold and the amount of materials purchased. This must be checked by a physical stock-take from time to time.

8.15 Summary

In this chapter, we have considered modern developments in the manufacturing, business and economic environment. We have explored the manner in which these developments have resulted in the adoption of new management philosophies such as TQM, JIT and TOC. Further, we have reviewed the new management accounting techniques such as ABC, throughput accounting and backflush accounting that have appeared in response to the modern environment.

This section concludes with an article on the manner in which modern management practices such as JIT, TQM and OPT interface with the more traditional management accounting practice of standard costing. The extract shown poses the possible incompatibilities between modern priorities and traditional practice.

Some writers have indicated that modern management philosophies may be incompatible with traditional financial control technique. In the article below, Lucas poses a number of issues for consideration in this regard.

Standard costing and its role in today's manufacturing environment

Mike Lucas, *Management Accounting*, April 1997. Reproduced by permission of the Institute of Management Accountants, Monteuale, NJ. www.imanet.org

In recent years, writers such as Kaplan and Johnson, Ferrara and Modern and Lee have argued that standard costing variance analysis should not be used for cost-control and performance-evaluation purposes in today's manufacturing world. Its use, they argue, is likely to induce behaviour which is inconsistent with the strategic manufacturing objectives that companies need to achieve in order to survive and prosper in today's intensely competitive international economic environment.

The case against standard costing

Drury, for example, has described how the scientific management principles of F.W. Taylor provided the impetus for the development of standard costing systems. The scientific management engineers divided the production system into a number of simple repetitive tasks in order to obtain the advantages of specialisation and to eliminate the time wasted by workers changing from one task to another.

Once individual tasks and methods have been clearly defined it is a relatively simple matter to set standards of performance using work study and time and motion study. These standards of performance then serve as the basis for financial control: monetary values are assigned to both standards and deviations from standard, that is variances. These variances are then attributed to particular operations/responsibility centers.

Companies operating in today's manufacturing environment, however, are likely to have strategies based on objectives such as improving quality, increasing flexibility to meet customer's individual requirements, reducing manufacturing lead times and delivery times, reducing inventories and unit costs. To help achieve these objectives, manufacturing strategies such as just-in-time (JIT), advanced manufacturing technology (AMT) and continuous improvement are often applied. Kaplan et al. argue that standard costing is counter-productive in such an environment. The major criticisms levelled at standard costing variance analysis are as follows:

1. *In a JIT environment, measuring standard costing variances for performance evaluation may encourage dysfunctional behaviour.*
   The primary purpose of the JIT production system is to increase profits by decreasing costs. It does this by eliminating excessive inventory and/or workforce. Items will be produced only at the time they are needed and in the precise amounts in which they are needed – thus removing the necessity for inventories. Running the business without inventories requires the ability to produce small batch sizes economically. In order to do so, set-up times must be reduced. Performance measures should therefore be such as to motivate managers and workforce to work towards reducing set-up times in order to achieve the sub-goal of economic small batch size as a prerequisite for achieving the lower inventories. Performance measures that benefit from large batch sizes or from producing for inventory should therefore be avoided; standard costing variances are just such measures!
2. *In an AMT environment, the major costs are those related to the production facility rather than production volume-related costs such as materials and labour which standard costing is essentially designed to plan and control.*
   Standard costing is concerned with comparing actual cost per unit with standard cost per unit. Fixed costs imputed to the product unit level are only notionally 'unit' costs. Any difference between the actual and the standard fixed cost per unit is not therefore meaningful for controlling operations, as it does not necessarily reflect under- or overspending – it may simply reflect differences in production volume.

What matters is the total fixed overhead expenditure rather than the fixed overhead cost per unit.

Therefore, in an AMT environment, standard costing variances have at best a minor role to play and at worst they may be counter-productive in so far as they force managers to focus on the wrong issues. An activity-based cost management (ABCM) system may be more appropriate, focusing on activities that drive the cost in service and support departments which form the bulk of controllable costs.

3. *In a JIT/AMT/continuous-improvement environment, the workforce is usually organised into empowered, multi-skilled teams controlling operations autonomously.*
   The feedback they require is real time and in physical terms. Periodic financial variance reports are neither meaningful nor timely enough to facilitate appropriate control action.

4. *In a total quality management (TQM) environment, standard costing variance measurement places an emphasis on cost control to the likely detriment of quality.*
   TQM requires a total managerial and worker ethos of improving and maintaining quality, and of resolving problems relating to this. The emphasis of standard costing is on cost control; variance analysis is likely to pull managerial and worker interest away from perhaps critical quality issues. Thus cost control may be achieved at the expense of quality and competitive advantage.

5. *A continuous improvement environment requires a continual effort to do things better, not achieve an arbitrary standard based on prescribed or assumed conditions.*
   Ferrara has suggested that standard costing based on engineering standards – which in turn are predicted on the notion of a 'one best way' – is only appropriate in the static, bygone world of cost-plus pricing (the world in which the Scientific Management School lived?). In such a world, a standard cost is established specifying what a product should cost and to this is added the required profit mark-up to arrive at the selling price. Cost management then consists of ensuring that standards are adhered to.

   In today's intensely competitive environment (the argument goes), we no longer look to the total unit cost in order to determine selling price; instead, we use the selling price to help determine the cost the market will allow. This allowable or target cost per unit is a market-driven cost that has to be achieved if desired profits are to be achieved. In a highly competitive, dynamic world there is likely to be considerable downward pressure on this allowable cost. Cost management must therefore consist of both cost maintenance and continuous cost improvement.

   In such a competitive improvement-seeking environment, of what value is standard costing based on predetermined engineering standards which create a mind-set of achieving the standard rather than of continuous cost reduction?

6. *In a largely automated production system, it argued, the processes are so stable that variances simply disappear.*
   Gagne and Discenza, for example, contend that 'with the use of statistical quality control and automation, the production processes are very consistent and reliable.

Variances often cease to exist.' If this is true, emphasis should be switched to the product design stage as most costs are effectively committed during this phase. A target cost that is achievable through the designer's efforts can be established and the designer then controls the design activities of a new product using the target cost as an economic guideline.

Self-test quiz

(1) Explain the terms MRP1 and MRP2 (Sections 8.5.1 and 8.5.2).
(2) How does the 'static optimisation' philosophy link MRP and standard costing concepts (Section 8.5.2)?
(3) How does IT contribute to the practices of ERP and SCM (Section 8.5.4)?
(4) What are the main features of JIT (Section 8.5.5)?
(5) How do the terms 'team' and 'empowerment' feature in TQM (Section 8.6)?
(6) List possible problems with the practice of TQM (Section 8.6).
(7) Explain the relationship between ABC and ABM (Section 8.9.1).
(8) List at least four management practices known as ABTs (Sections 8.9–8.12).
(9) Explain the central feature of backflush accounting (Section 8.14).
(10) State why JIT, TQM and AMTs may not always be entirely compatible with the practice of standard costing (Section 8.15).

Revision Questions

8

Question 1

1.1 What is a flexible manufacturing system and how does it relate to changes in the economy?

1.2 Explain materials requirements planning and contrast it with more traditional approaches to stock management.

1.3 Explain the Just-in-Time concept.

1.4 Explain the characteristics of a backflush accounting system.

1.5 Explain the features that make ABC more relevant to the modern manufacturing environment than traditional product costing technique.

1.6 Explain 'throughput accounting'.

1.7 Explain the 'total quality management' philosophy and its relevance to the modern economic environment.

1.8 Explain the meaning of the term 'the New Economy' and its relevance to the practice of management accounting.

Question 2

'Japanese companies that have used just-in-time (JIT) for five or more years are reporting close to a 30 per cent increase in labour productivity, a 60 per cent reduction in inventories, a 90 per cent reduction in quality rejection rates, and a 15 per cent reduction in necessary plant space. However, implementing a JIT system does not occur overnight. It took Toyota over twenty years to develop its system and realise significant benefits from it.'

Source: Sumer C. Aggrawal, *Harvard Business Review*

Requirements

(a) Explain how the benefits claimed for JIT in the above quotation are achieved and why it takes so long to achieve those benefits. **(15 marks)**

(b) Explain how management information systems in general (and management accounting systems in particular) should be developed in order to facilitate and make best use of JIT. **(10 marks)**

(Total marks = 25)

> ❗ The following two questions draw both on the issues explored in this chapter and on a wider range of management accounting and business management topics. In preparing answers to these questions you should consider your earlier studies of management accounting and general knowledge of business.

Question 3

ST plc produces three types of processed foods for a leading food retailer. The company has three processing departments (Preparation, Cooking and Packaging). After recognising that the overheads incurred in these departments varied in relation to the activities performed, the company switched from a traditional absorption costing system to a budgetary control system that is based on activity-based costing.

The foods are processed in batches. The budgeted output for April was as follows:

	Output
Food A	100 batches
Food B	30 batches
Food C	200 batches

The number of activities and processing hours budgeted to process a batch of foods in each of the departments are as follows:

	Food A Activities per batch	Food B Activities per batch	Food C Activities per batch
Preparation	5	9	12
Cooking	2	1	4
Packaging	15	2	6
Processing time	10 hours	375 hours	80 hours

The budgeted departmental overhead costs for April were:

	Overheads $
Preparation	100,000
Cooking	350,000
Packaging	50,000

Requirements

(a) For food A ONLY, calculate the budgeted overhead cost per batch:
   (i) using traditional absorption costing, based on a factory-wide absorption rate per processing hour;
   (ii) using activity-based costing.

(b) Comment briefly on the advantages of using an activity-based costing approach to determining the cost of each type of processed food compared to traditional absorption costing approaches. You should make reference to your answers to requirement (a) where appropriate.

(c) The actual output for April was

	Output
Food A	120 batches
Food B	45 batches
Food C	167 batches

Prepare a flexed budget for April using an activity-based costing approach. Your statement must show the total budgeted overhead for each department and the total budgeted overhead absorbed by each food.

(d) Discuss the advantages that ST plc should see from the activity-based control system compared to the traditional absorption costing that it used previously.

Question 4

As part of a total quality management (TQM) programme in a large manufacturing company, quality costing has been introduced and is regarded as useful by senior managers. They are now planning to extend the TQM programme, and quality costing, from manufacturing to the whole of the company. You have been asked to devise a TQM programme, including appropriate quality measures and calculations of quality cost in the management accounting section of the finance department.

Requirements

(a) Briefly explain each of the four categories of quality cost (prevention cost, appraisal cost, internal failure cost and external failure cost). Give examples of each category appropriate to a manufacturing environment, and examples relevant to management accounting. **(8 marks)**

(b) Explain how this cost categorisation mentioned in (a) above can be used to help to develop performance measures within management accounting. Explain and justify a set of performance measures that can be used by the finance director in assessing the management accounting service. **(12 marks)**

(Total marks = 20)

Question 5

(a) 'It may be argued that in a total quality environment, variance analysis from a standard costing system is redundant.'

Discuss the validity of this statement. **(8 marks)**

(b) Using labour cost as the focus, discuss the differences in the measurement of labour efficiency/effectiveness where (i) total quality management techniques and (ii) standard cost variance analysis are in use. **(7 marks)**

(Total marks = 15)

Question 6

ABC Ltd produces a large number of products including the A and the B. The A is a complex product of which 1,000 are made and sold in each period. The B is a simple product of which 25,000 are made and sold in each period. The A requires one direct labour hour to produce and the B requires 0.6 direct labour hours to produce.

ABC Ltd employs 12 salaried support staff and a direct labour force that works 400,000 direct labour hours per period. Overhead costs are £500,000 per period.

The support staff are engaged in three activities – six staff engaged in receiving 25,000 consignments of components per period, three staff engaged in receiving 10,000 consignments of raw materials per period and three staff engaged in disbursing kits of components and materials for 5,000 production runs per period.

Product A requires 200 component consignments, 50 raw material consignments and 10 production runs per period. Product B requires 100 component consignments, 8 raw material consignments and five production runs per period.

Requirements
(a) Calculate the overhead cost of the A and the B using a traditional system of overhead absorption based on direct labour hours. **(10 marks)**
(b) Identity appropriate cost drivers and calculate the overhead cost of the A and the B using an activity-based costing system. **(10 marks)**
(c) Compare your answers to (a) and (b) and explain which gives the most meaningful impression of product costs. **(5 marks)**
(Total marks = 25)

 ## Question 7

It has been suggested that much of the training of management accountants is concerned with *cost control* whereas the major emphasis should be on *cost reduction*.

Requirements
(a) Distinguish between cost control and cost reduction. **(10 marks)**
(b) Give three examples each of the techniques and principles used for
  (i) cost control and
  (ii) cost reduction. **(10 marks)**
(c) Discuss the proposition contained in the statement. **(5 marks)**
(Total marks = 25)

Scenario for questions 8–10
During the last 20 years, KL's manufacturing operation has become increasingly automated, with computer-controlled robots replacing operatives. KL currently manufactures over 100 products of varying levels of design complexity. A single, plant-wide overhead absorption rate (OAR), based on direct labour hours, is used to absorb overhead costs.

In the quarter ended March 20 × 9, KL's manufacturing overhead costs were

	£'000
Equipment operation expenses	125
Equipment maintenance expenses	25
Wages paid to technicians	85
Wages paid to storemen	35
Wages paid to dispatch staff	40
	310

During the quarter, Rapier Management Consultants were engaged to conduct a review of KL's cost accounting systems. Rapier's report includes the following statement:

In KL's circumstances, absorbing overhead costs in individual products on a labour-hour absorption basis is meaningless. Overhead costs should be attributed to products using an activity-based costing (ABC) system.

We have identified the followings as being the most significant activities:

1. receiving component consignments from suppliers;
2. setting up equipment for production runs;
3. quality inspections;
4. dispatching goods orders to customers.

Our research has indicated that, in the short term, KL's overheads are 40 per cent fixed and 60 per cent variable. Approximately half the variable overheads vary in relation to direct labour hours worked and half vary in relation to the number of quality inspections. This model applies only to relatively small changes in the level of output during a period of 2 years or less.

Equipment operation and maintenance expenses are apportionable as follows: component stores (15 per cent), manufacturing (70 per cent) and goods dispatch (15 per cent).

Technician wages are apportionable as follows: equipment maintenance (30 per cent), setting up equipment for production runs (40 per cent) and quality inspections (30 per cent).

During the quarter:

- a total of 2,000 direct labour hours were worked (paid at £12 per hour);
- 980 component consignments were received from suppliers;
- 1,020 production runs were set up; 640 quality inspections were carried out; and
- 640 quality inspections were carried out; and
- 420 goods orders were dispatched to customers.

? Question 8 (see scenario)

KL's production during the quarter included components *r*, *s* and *t*. The following information is available:

	Component r	Component s	Component t
Direct labour hours worked	25	480	50
Direct material costs	£1,200	£2,900	£1,800
Component consignments received	42	24	28
Production runs	16	18	12
Quality inspections	10	8	18
Goods orders dispatched	22	85	46
Quantity produced	560	12,800	2,400

In April 20x9 a potential customer asked KL to quote for the supply of a new component *(z)* to a given specification. 1,000 units of *z* are to be supplied each quarter for a 2-year period. They will be paid for in equal instalments on the last day of each quarter. The job will involve an initial design cost of £40,000 and production will involve 80 direct labour hours £2,000 materials, 20 component consignments, 15 production runs, 30 quality inspections and 4 goods dispatches per quarter.

KL's sales director comments:

Now we have a modern ABC system, we can quote selling prices with confidence. The quarterly charge we quote should be the forecast ABC production cost of the units plus the design cost of the z depreciated on a straight-line basis over the 2 years of the job – to which we should add a 25 per cent mark-up for profit. We can base our forecast on costs experienced in the quarter ended March 20x9.

Requirements

(a) Calculate the unit cost of components *r*, *s* and *t*, using KL's existing cost accounting system (single-factory, labour-hour OAR). **(5 marks)**

(b) Explain how an ABC system would be developed using the information given. Calculate the unit cost of components *r*, *s* and *t*, using this ABC system. **(11 marks)**

(c) Calculate the charge per quarter that should be quoted for supply of component *z* in a manner consistent with the sales director's comments. Advise KL's management on the merits of this selling price, having regard to factors you consider relevant.

Note: KL's cost of capital is 3 per cent per quarter. **(9 marks)**

(Total marks = 25)

Question 9 (see scenario)

It is often claimed that ABC provides better information concerning product costs than traditional management accounting techniques. It is also sometimes claimed that ABC provides better information as a guide to decision-marking. However, one should treat these claims with caution. ABC may give a different impression of product costs but it is not necessarily a better impression. It may be wiser to try to improve the use of traditional techniques before moving to ABC.

Comment by KL's management accountant on the Rapier report

Requirements

(a) Explain the ideas concerning cost behaviour that underpin ABC. Explain why ABC may be better attuned to the modern manufacturing environment than traditional techniques. Explain why KL might or might not obtain a more meaningful impression of product costs through the use of ABC. **(10 marks)**

(b) Explain how the traditional cost accounting system being used by KL might be improved to provide more meaningful product costs. **(6 marks)**

(c) Critically appraise the reported claim that ABC gives better information as a guide to decision-making than do traditional product costing techniques. **(9 marks)**

(Total marks = 25)

Question 10 (see scenario)

The lean enterprise [characterised by 'just in time' (JIT) total quality management (TQM) and supportive supplier relations] is widely considered a better approach to manufacturing. Some have suggested, however, that ABC hinders the spread of the lean enterprise by making apparent the cost of small batch sizes.

Comment by an academic accountant

Requirements

(a) Explain the roles that JIT, TQM and supportive supplier relations play in modern manufacturing management. How might the adoption of such practices improve KL's performance? **(10 marks)**

(b) Explain what the writer of the above statement means by 'the cost of small batch sizes'. Critically appraise the manner in which this cost is treated by KL's existing (single OAR-based) cost accounting system. Explain the benefits that KL might obtain through a full knowledge and understanding of this cost. **(10 marks)**

(c) Explain and discuss the extent to which academic research in the area of management accounting is likely to influence the practice of management accounting. **(5 marks)**

(Total marks = 25)

Solutions to Revision Questions

8

☑ Solution 1

1.1 An FMS is a manufacturing facility designed, organised and operated in a manner to facilitate swift changes in production. It is likely to be very different from a traditional production line which is organised for continuous production of a single product. FMS facilities typically consist of clusters of equipment which can be reprogrammed quickly as required. Such flexibility has a cost and makes demands on personnel. However, FMS facilities are adapted to the needs of a swiftly changing market and JIT production systems.

1.2 Traditional materials planning in the pre-computer era involved constantly monitoring stock levels and re-ordering whenever they fell below certain specified levels. This was an inherently passive approach. MRP involves preparing detailed procurement plans based on projected output and placing orders in order to ensure that materials are delivered as and when they are needed. The ability of a large, complex operation to operate with MRP (and its later variants – MRP2 and ERP) depends very much on the availability of reliable computer systems.

1.3 JIT is an approach to production that involves obtaining materials, components and use of facilities as and when they are needed. It also involves arranging to supply customers with goods only as and when they are required. It is therefore characterised by small but frequent deliveries, low stock levels and short, discontinuous batch production. Operating in this manner makes considerable demands on staff, facilities and the production planning operation.

1.4 Backflush accounting is an approach that avoids the cost-tracking approach that is characteristic of traditional accounting. The latter usually involves maintaining detailed records of costs incurred in order to determine the cost of products on a cumulative basis. Backflush costing and its variants work the other way. When production costs are incurred they are charged to a conversion cost account. When production is completed, the standard cost of the units concerned is credited to the conversion cost account. The balance outstanding on the latter at any time will therefore be the stock of raw materials and work in progress – sometimes described as the 'RIP' account. It is an approach considered well adapted to a JIT environment (where stocks are low and cost variances are few), but it is not new. It is similar in character to low-cost practice commonly used in the pre-computer era to prepare monthly management accounts.

1.5 ABC is an approach to cost determination which involves careful study of the activities that give rise to costs and the manner in which those activities vary with the level and structure of output. It seeks to attribute costs to products through the identification and use of appropriate 'cost drivers'. This contrasts with more traditional practice which involved the use of volume related, and often arbitrary, overhead absorption bases. ABC is more demanding than traditional practice but it is better attuned to the modern environment. A modern manufacturing operation typically involves a far more complex range of activities than was the case 30 years ago and a higher proportion of costs are likely to be indirect. A more sensitive approach to cost determination is therefore appropriate.

1.6 Throughput accounting is the term used to describe an approach to accounting which places an emphasis on production volumes, production times and contribution. In the practice of TA, the assumption is frequently made that the only truly variable cost in an operation is that of the materials used. The key TA performance indicator for any period is:

(Sales Revenue – Material Cost)/Production Time (hours).

By considering this indicator for 'the bottleneck facility' management may be guided in optimising the use of production facilities. Throughput accounting is therefore closely associated with the 'theory of constraints'.

1.7 TQM is a management philosophy which involves use of a range of advanced management techniques. Its central concept is that 'quality' is the key strategic variable in a business and that it is a variable that is amenable to organisational culture. The key concepts associated with the provision of quality in an organisation are 'empowerment' and 'teams'. TQM is very much the antithesis of the traditional 'command and control' concept associated with budgeting that we encountered earlier in this text. TQM involves the devolution of authority to multi-skilled, empowered teams in the organisation. It is claimed the TQM provides the organisational flexibility needed to cope with an environment where product life cycles are short, products are highly customised and products have a high service element. The empowerment and motivation of individual staff to deal directly with customers is therefore critical to success.

1.8 The 'New Economy' is a buzz word which became popular in management literature in the late 1990s. Essentially, it referred to a business environment in which it was expected that 'lean' and 'virtual' businesses would emerge as the dominant species. Traditional businesses with factories and offices would be replaced by loosely organised alliances which would obtain the use of facilities and resources only as and when needed. The goods being produced were expected to have an increasingly high service content (e.g. the software and associated system support in a PC costing more than the equipment). The key to success in this environment would be 'flexibility'. It was also claimed that new metrics (other than profit or return on investment) would be needed in order to evaluate the performance of such businesses. The spectacular collapse of many high profile New Economy businesses (Enron and World.com being examples) during the recession of the early 2000s has brought the term into some disfavour lately.

✅ Solution 2

In answering this question it is important to appreciate that JIT is not merely a stock management technique. Rather, it is a management philosophy.

(a) The benefits of JIT, as described by Aggrawal, are gained by a revolutionary change in work practices, company culture and external relationships. JIT is not just about running a production facility with less inventory, it is a way of working that reduces traditional practices which do not add value to the product. Such 'non-value adding' practices include warehousing and stock movement within the factory, testing for quality control, running machinery merely to accumulate large stocks of WIP at a bottleneck down the line and setting-up machinery to run a batch of different specification or product.

The new company culture gives workers the power to manage the production process by moving to where they are needed on the production line or by solving their own problems (quality circles). This requires co-operation between workers and a new approach to management. Furthermore, the workers self-test their work to provide quality assurance and must feel free to halt production if there is a problem. Workers need to be multi-skilled, that is there can be no demarcation across traditional skill boundaries, so that set-up times and maintenance down-time may be minimised. These new working practices coupled with new technology reduce inefficiencies in the production process and result in new working patterns.

New external relationships must be developed, especially with suppliers of materials and components. The supplies must be defect-free, on-time and delivered more frequently in smaller lots. There should be no inspection of goods received. Therefore, new standards need to be established with tighter tolerances, warranties and changed packing requirements. In return, the supplier will become the sole supplier, but will take on board the responsibility for R&D for the items supplied.

All of the above changes are quite radical and involve everyone concerned with the production process. The JIT philosophy will work only when workers are empowered, that is free to make decisions and own up to mistakes; this cultural change for both workers and management requires much training and much practice. Thus, the benefits of JIT do not appear overnight.

(b) The introduction of a JIT production process will result in smaller batch sizes, that is smaller production runs and more changeovers, lower inventory levels and more frequent deliveries, fewer direct labour and machine hours, but more indirect labour for quality assurance, software development, R & D and so on.

Thus, we see a need for faster gathering, grouping and analysis of performance for control purposes. Fortunately, computer-controlled processes capture much of the information required, such as what was done, when it was done, how long it took and what was produced. This enables traceable costs to be collected and monitored for each cost centre. This process must start at the component level, and for every stage in the production process the number of set-ups, orders, inspections, labour and machine time, and so on must be built into the product cost-control exercise.

Electronic data interchange will enable the system to match the pace of frequent deliveries on to the shop floor, and as a Kanban system will be used the day-to-day variation in inventory will be small. A complete production scheduling system will be required such as MRP2. This will allow for management accounting exercises such as capacity utilisation to be carried out.

The empowered workers will not require variance analysis, but motivational control will be more important and will use physical performance indicators, such as average set-up time or number of defects. Standard costing will still be required, but mainly as a foundation in preparing the financial accounting reports. To control the rising indirect costs, budget control will become more important. Cost planning will need to cater for blueprints for new products or production methods and for cost reduction as an ongoing process.

Thus, the development in management information systems is more of evolution and change in emphasis, as opposed to the revolution on the shop floor when JIT is introduced.

Solution 3

(a)

$$\text{Budgeted processing hours} = (10 \times 100) + (375 \times 30) + (800 \times 200)$$
$$= 1,000 + 11,250 + 16,000$$
$$= 28,250$$

Budgeted cost $= \$500,000$

$$\text{Budgeted absorption rate per processing hour} = \frac{\$500,000}{28,250} = \$17.70$$

Budgeted overhead cost per unit of A $= 0.1 \times \$17.70 = \$1.77$

Activity	Budgeted cost $000	Number of activities	Cost driver rate
Preparation	100	3,170	31.546
Cooking	350	1,030	339.806
Packaging	50	2,760	18.116

Budgeted overhead cost per unit of A $= [(31.546 \times 5) + (339.806 \times 2) + (18.116 \times 15)]/100 = \$11.09$.

(b)

The use of an activity-based approach to attributing overhead costs to product units, rather than the traditional absorption costing basis, is that by using an activity-based approach a fairer recognition of the costs of producing an item is obtained.

In part (a), it can be seen that the unit overhead cost of product A is significantly higher under an ABC approach. This is caused, at least in part, by the smaller batch size compared to most of the other products and the fact that the incidence of the overhead costs occurs in respect of batches of production rather than individual units.

(c)

Flexible budget

Activity	A $	B $	C $	Total $
Preparation	18,928	12,776	63,218	94,922
Cooking	81,553	15,291	226,990	323,834
Packaging	32,609	1,630	18,152	52,391

Workings			
Preparation	$31.546 \times [(120 \times 5) + (45 \times 9) + (167 \times 12)]$		95,827
Cooking	$339.806 \times [(120 \times 2) + (45 \times 1) + (167 \times 4)]$		323,834
Packaging	$18.116 \times [(120 \times 15) + (45 \times 2) + (167 \times 6)]$		52,391

(d)

A budgetary control system based on activity-based costing provides more meaningful variances than traditional absorption costing, because the amount that should be expended is measured in relation to the cause of each of the costs, rather than simply one single assumed cause such as number of machine hours.

As a consequence, the manager responsible can more clearly identify how the cost may be controlled and thereby seek to control the cost and reduce variances.

Furthermore, the use of an ABC system requires a manager to investigate the cause of costs prior to setting their budget. As a consequence, they have a better understanding of the cause of the costs and thus how they may be controlled.

☑ Solution 4

This question requires candidates to demonstrate their understanding of quality cost by providing examples, and to apply the approach to developing an appropriate set of performance measures for the management accounting function.

(a) *Prevention costs:*

These are investments made in machinery, technology and educational programmes with the intention of reducing the number of defective items. Examples are

- *Manufacturing*: Automated production processes such as robotics: the use of quality circles for process improvements.
- *Management accounting*: Replacing manual operations with computers; the use of regular staff training programmes.

Appraisal costs:

These are the costs of monitoring and inspection compared with predetermined standards of performance, before release to customers. Examples are

- *Manufacturing*: Product and process testing for quality by quality control staff; the costs of test equipment.
- *Management accounting*: The use of computer audits to check the reliability of computer software; the use of batch input controls to confirm the validity of data processing.

Internal failure costs:

These refer to failure costs discovered before delivery to customers. Examples are as follows.

- *Manufacturing*: The cost of scrapped production; the costs of rework and corrections.
- *Management accounting*: The costs of reprocessing input errors; the costs of producing replacement reports.

External failure costs:

These refer to failure costs discovered after delivery to customers. Examples are as follows.

- *Manufacturing*: The cost of meeting warranty claims from customers; the loss of repeat orders from customers.
- *Management accounting*: The costs associated with poor decision-making arising from inaccurate or untimely information to management; the costs associated with resolving external audit queries.

(b) How cost categorisation can help develop performance measures.

The breaking down of costs into the four categories identified in (a) provides a useful structure of data collection. Also, defining these cost categories helps to clarify an understanding of the issues involved in developing the objectives of management accounting within the organisation.

Rather than looking at the totality of quality costs within management accounting, a VFM approach can usefully be attempted in each quality cost area. For example, some of these quality cost areas are likely to be more critical than others, such as the provision of cost information for pricing purposes.

In this way, quality cost categorisation focuses attention on areas of both high expenditure and high importance, and may provide a basis for benchmarking the management accounting function against that of comparable organisations.

Appropriate quality and performance measures:
It needs to be recognised that management accounting has internal customers, that is other departments in the organisation and senior management. Their opinions on the service they receive are critical. Indeed many organisations are currently considering outsourcing their accounting functions.

Appropriate performance objectives should address issues such as

- the usefulness of management accounting information – in other words, relevance to user needs;
- the timeliness of reports and cost exercises;
- the flexibility in response to user requests;
- the availability of accounting personnel to resolve queries;
- value for money.

Specific performance measures could then be, for example:

- the number of computer downtime hours in a period;
- the number of reports issued on time;
- ratings from internal customer satisfaction surveys;
- benchmarking management accounting costs and activities against those of comparable organisations.

 ## Solution 5

(a) Standard costing involves the setting of standards at agreed levels of price and performance and the measurement of actual events against such standards in order to monitor performance. The variance analysis will measure changes in performance and price for sales, material, labour and overhead. A basic assumption is that the standards will apply over a time period during which they provide a suitable base against which to measure actual events.

A total quality environment adopts a different philosophy:
- it aims towards an environment of zero defects at minimum cost. This conflicts with the idea of standard costs, which, for example, accept that a planned level of yield loss has been built into material standards.
- it aims towards the elimination of waste, where waste is defined as anything other than the minimum essential amount of equipment, materials, space and worker time. Standard costs may be set at currently attainable levels of performance that built in an accepted allowance for 'waste'.
- it aims at continuous improvement. The focus is on performance measures that illustrate a continuous trend of improvement rather than 'steady-state' standard performance that is accepted for a specific period.

- it is an overall philosophy requiring awareness by all personnel of the quality requirements in providing the customer with products of agreed design specification. Standard costing tends to place control of each variance type with specific members of management and work-force. This view may cause conflicting decisions as to the best strategy for improvement.

(b) Standard costing will measure labour efficiency in terms of the ratio of output achieved: standard input. This measure focuses on quantity and does not address other issues of effectiveness. Effectiveness is a broader concept that incorporates the idea of trying to find the cheapest method of achieving a given result. Effectiveness in a total quality context implies high quality with a focus on value-added activities and essential support activities. Efficiency (in terms of output) may be achieved at a cost. In a total quality context, such costs may be measured as internal or external failure costs that will not be identified in the standard cost variance measure.

In a standard cost system, individual labour task situations are used as a basis for efficiency measurement. In a total quality environment it is more likely that labour will be viewed in multitask teams who are responsible for the completion of a part of the production cycle. The team effectiveness is viewed in terms of measures other than output, including incidence of rework, defect levels at a subsequent stage in production, and defects reported by the customer.

☑ Solution 6

This is a basic product costing question that invites students to demonstrate their understanding of the principles of ABC.

(a) Overhead costs of £500,000 and direct labour hours of 400,000 give an overhead absorption rate of £1.25 per hour.

Applied to the two products this OAR gives overhead costs as follows:

	Per unit £
A	1.25
B	0.75

(b) Three appropriate cost drivers are

(i) receiving components;
(ii) receiving raw materials;
(iii) disbursing kits of components and raw materials.

Relating overhead costs to these drivers using the number of indirect staff engaged in each activity as the basis gives the following results:

- receiving components – £250,000; £10 per receipt;
- receiving raw materials – £125,000; £12.50 per receipt;
- disbursing kits – £125,000; £25 per issue

The products therefore attract overheads as follows:

	Total £	Per unit £
A	2,875	2.87
B	1,225	0.05

(c) Advocates of ABC would argue that the product costs shown in (b) are more meaningful than those shown in (a) because the former are based on a more sensitive analysis of the activities giving rise to overhead costs.

It is clear that the relative cost impact of the activities involved in producing the two products appears much more clearly when ABC is used.

☑ Solution 7

In some types of popular management literature the terms 'cost control' and 'cost reduction' are used as if they are interchangeable. Actually, they mean very different things. The question invites students to explore relevant differences.

(a) Cost control is the process of containing costs to some predetermined norm. This is usually carried on by the formal comparison of actual results with those planned – the routine of budgets and standard costs and operating statements and the investigation of variances. Cost reduction is the wider-ranging attempt to reduce costs below the previously accepted norm or standard, preferably without reducing quality or effectiveness. This is a dynamic rather than routine process, quite possibly only carried out at infrequent intervals, for example at time of financial crisis.

(b) A wide range of examples can be given.
   (i) *Cost control:*
      Budgetary control
      Standard costing
      Setting of spending limits by level of management
      Procedures for formal authorisation of recruitment
      Control of capital expenditure.
  (ii) *Cost reduction:*
      Value analysis, value engineering
      Systems analysis, O&M
      Work study
      Operations research (OR)
      Standardisation of components and processes
      Product range standardisation/simplification
      Investment appraisal, terotechnology
      Value-for-money analysis
      Arbitrary cutting of overhead budgets
      Zero-based budgeting.

      Any three of the above are sufficient to answer the question.

(c) The cost-control techniques of standard costing and budgetary control would tend to support the proposal. However, a study of OR techniques (essentially cost-reduction techniques) and of recent developments, reported in *Management Accounting*, would lead to the conclusion that current practice is not purely control, but active cost reduction.

There has been considerable interest in a range of topics relating to new manufacturing techniques, and to Japanese methods – quality management, quality costs, JIT stock and production control, flexible manufacturing systems and computer-integrated manufacturing.

There has also been interest in a range of other innovations, in IT making management accounting faster and more effective especially with developments in data capture and transmission, in strategic management accounting and the links between management accounting and long-range planning, and in the extension of management accounting in areas where it has been relatively underdeveloped in service industries and the public sector, often with the development of new techniques such as data envelopment analysis.

Solution 8

The question covers much the same ground as Question 2 in this chapter. It invites students to demonstrate a grasp of the basic principles of ABC and how they compare to traditional product costing.

(a) Labour hour overhead absorption rate:

$$\frac{£310,000}{2,000} = £155 \text{ per labour hour}$$

Traditional unit costs:

	r	s	t
	£	£	£
Direct labour costs	300	5,760	600
Direct material costs	1,200	2,900	1,800
Overheads	3,875	74,400	7,750
Total costs	5,375	83,060	10,150
Cost per unit	£9.60	£6.49	£4.23

Workings for r

Direct labour costs	25 × £12	£300
Direct material costs	as stated	£1,200
Overheads	25 × £155	£3,875
Cost per unit	£5,375/560	£9.60

(b) An ABC system would be developed by analysing the cause of overhead costs as a function of the support activities carried out within the organisation. The 'cost drivers' are then used to apportion costs in a meaningful way to the different products produced in a multi-product company.

Rapier Consultants have already identified the cost drivers for KL, that is

- receiving components from suppliers;
- setting up production runs;
- quality inspections;
- dispatching goods to customers.

The apportionment of costs to r, s and t is carried out as follows:

Step 1 – Determine the total costs for each activity (£'000).

Activities	Operations £	Maintenance £	Costs Technicians £	Stores £	Dispach £	Total £
Receiving supplies	18.75	3.75	3.83	35.00		61.33
			34.00			
Set-ups	87.50	17.50	17.85			156.85
Quality inspections			25.50			25.50
Dispatching goods	18.75	3.75	3.83		40.00	66.33
Total	125.00	25.00	85.00	35.00	40.00	310.00

Operations (equipment), maintenance and the portion of technicians' wages for maintenance are all apportioned on the book value of equipment.

Workings for set-up cost activities:
Operations and maintenance have 70% of their costs apportionable to manufacturing (i.e. set-ups):

$$125 \times 0.70 = 87.50$$

and

$$25 \times 0.70 = 17.50$$

Technicians have 40% of their cost apportionable to set-ups, that is

$$85 \times 0.40 = 34$$

They also have 30% of their costs apportionable to maintenance, which in turn has 70% of its costs apportionable to set-ups, that is

$$85 \times 0.30 \times 0.70 = 17.85.$$

Step 2 – Calculate the cost for each activity.

		£
Receiving suppliers	£61,330/980	62.58
Set-ups	£156,850/1,020	153.77
Quality inspections	£25,500/640	39.84
Dispatching goods	£66,330/420	157.93

Step 3 – Apply these rates to calculate the unit costs.

	r £	s £	t £
Direct labour costs	300.00	5,760.00	600.00
Direct material costs	1,200.00	2,900.00	1,800.00
Receiving supplies	2,628.36	1,501.92	1,752.24
Set-ups	2,460.32	2,767.86	1,845.24
Quality inspections	398.40	318.72	717.12
Dispatching goods	3,474.46	13,424.05	7,264.78
Total	10,461.54	26,672.55	13,979.38
Cost per unit	£18.68	£2.08	£5.82

Example working for overhead costs: receiving supplies for r

$$£62.58 \times 42 = £2,628.36$$

(c) Quarterly charge (for 1,000 units):

		£
Design costs	£40,000/8	5,000
Direct labour	80 × £12	960
Direct materials		2,000
Overheads		
Receiving supplies	£62.58 × 20	1,252
Set-ups	£153.77 × 15	2,307
Quality inspections	£39.84 × 30	1,195
Dispatching goods	£157.93 × 4	632
Total		13,346
25% mark-up		3,337
Charge per quarter		16,683

The actual quarterly marginal cost is as follows:

	£
Design costs: £40,000/7.02	5,698
Direct labour	960
Direct materials	2,000
Variable overheads:	
Labour-related:	
80 × ((310,000 × 0.6 × 0.5)/2,000)	3,720
Inspection-related:	
30 × ((310,000 × 0.6 × 0.5)/640)	4,359
	16,737

The method suggested by the sales director does not cover the actual marginal costs.

In the short term, the use of Rapier's analysis of fixed and variable overheads allows the traditional method to give a more accurate costing. Work needs to be undertaken to discover the reasons for the discrepancies between the two methods, that is a more fundamental understanding of cost drivers and their unit costs is still required.

Workings for the actual quarterly marginal cost 7.02 represents the cumulative discount factor for the eight quarters at 3 per cent per quarter.

The labour-related overhead is found from the fact that 60 per cent of the overheads are variable of which 50 per cent vary with labour hours, that is

$$\frac{310,000 \times 0.6 \times 0.5}{2,000} = \text{per labour hour.}$$

 Solution 9

- The question invites an evaluation of ABC practice relative to traditional product costing.
- It also invites discussion of how the traditional product costing system used by KL might be improved. This invites students to draw on knowledge gained in their Foundation level studies or equivalent.

(a) Activity-based costing (ABC) is based on the principle that all overhead costs can vary over the medium to long term and that each category varies with the level of support activity that is being provided. This is a more sophisticated argument than the simplistic division into fixed or variable costs with respect to one measure of activity, that is production output.

This more complicated approach was developed in response to a significant change in many modern manufacturing environments. Specifically, these change include

- constant and low levels of materials and products owing to the implementation of just-in-time (JIT) principles;
- constant and how direct labour costs owing to the high level of automation and a multi-skilling and teamworking approach;
- high capital investment cost, driving up overheads;
- many production set-ups to provide a wide range of customer-specific products while keeping low product inventory – this will influence the production overhead costs;
- more paperwork and progress expediting is required to ensure supply of materials and delivery of product – this also drives production overheads.

The ABC approach is to identify the relevant activities that drive up overhead costs, and to use the need for these activities for each product, as the basis for apportionment of these costs. Advocates claim that this is more attuned to the situation of high overhead and low direct costs than the traditional method, which catered for the opposite situation.

The company KL manufactures several products:

r complex, low-volume product;

s a simple, high-volume product;

t an intermediate product in terms of composition and volume.

The traditional system will tend to over-apportion costs to large volumes of production and under-apportion costs to complicated products.

Thus *r* will be undercharged and *s* overcharged by both inadequacies in the traditional system. This may make the product costs grossly inaccurate in some situations.

(b) The existing system uses a single overhead absorption rate (OAR), which produces the gross inaccuracies highlighted in part (a). This could be replaced with several OARs, one for each cost centre, and, rather than using direct labour hours, direct material costs, machine hours or power usage might be chosen as the basis for apportionment.

This might reflect more accurately the extra costs attributable to more complex products but would not reflect the extra costs attributable to small production batches.

Thus the system needs to be fully augmented with a complete analysis of overhead cost drivers to give meaningful results.

(c) The proponents of ABC claim that it gives more meaningful results in both AMT industries and service industries. Specifically, they state that it gives not only accurate and meaningful product costs, but that it also gives management a handle on controlling and reducing overhead costs.

This is based on the fuller understanding gained of how the overhead costs vary with the operating strategy and indirect support activities undertaken within the organisation.

Management decision-making for pricing, project appraisal, buy-or-make options, and so on depend on an accurate and meaningful cost analysis. The ABC system is the most sophisticated system developed for this purpose.

ABC produces an average cost per unit. However, when this changes with the level of activity (e.g. a stepped fixed cost, a discount on bulk purchases, etc.) this average cost per unit may not be the marginal cost per unit that should be taken into consideration.

Although the theory of ABC is simple, the process of analysis required to implement it is complex and costly. If the analysis is flawed, then the results obtained will also be flawed and may be less accurate and less meaningful than the 'arbitrary' traditional approach.

Solution 10

This is another question that invites students to draw on their general knowledge of modern development in management.

(a) The just-in-time (JIT) philosophy aims to enable scheduled production targets to be met while reducing to a minimum non-added-value activities of maintaining more than minimal stock levels of raw materials, subassemblies, work in progress and finished goods.

To achieve this aim, customer relations must be close to enable accurate demand forecasts and relevant product offerings. The factory layout and product design may need to be simplified and a multitask and teamwork culture needs to be established among the workforce. Supplier relationships are crucial and long-term contracts, including component research and development, will follow from a focus on reliable delivery of many on-specification and on-time batches of small quantities of materials.

These are all attributes of a world-class manufacturing standard in an advanced manufacturing technology environment. The old ways of mass production of a single product, in a dedicated production facility with large buffer stockholding, have been replaced with a flexible production facility producing small batches of different product variations, which have shorter life cycles.

Total quality management (TQM) aims to ensure that quality is the primary concern of every employee at every stage of producing a good or service. This implies empowerment of the workforce, that is each individual has responsibility and authority, for example, to stop the production line if necessary to maintain quality.

Both JIT and TQM radically alter the management function from directing to supporting, from organising to coaching, from deciding to facilitating, from problem-solving to providing resources. KL makes a wide variety to complex product and to be economic and to maintain customer satisfaction it will be forced to adopt such practices.

(b) It is not always economic to manufacture every product on a continuous basis. Therefore, a great deal of manufacturing is organised in the form of batches. Production lines periodically switch from one product to another. Operating in this manner will usually involve holding stocks of each product and producing fresh batches of each product as stocks are depleted by sales.

Manufacturing in large, infrequent batches incurs high inventory-holding costs. Manufacturing in small, frequent batches minimises holding costs but may give rise to certain additional costs. For example:

- set-up costs – that is, the opportunity cost of lost production capacity as machinery and the workforce reorganise for a different product;
- extra materials-handling costs as the materials and subassemblies and so on, used for the previous batch are replaced with those required for the next batch;
- quality costs – every time a new batch is commenced more emphasis (workers' and inspectors' time) must be put into assuring that quality is maintained;
- increased paperwork (or software data entry) and expediting corresponding to increased movements of smaller amounts of raw materials, subassemblies and finished products.

All the above factors give rise to costs and it is these costs that the writer is referring to. These costs will be relatively higher in small-batch production than in large-batch production.

The purpose of any cost accounting system is to attribute production costs to individual products in a meaningful way. One weakness with KL's existing cost accounting system is that it may not adequately identify the full costs of small-batch production. Some of those costs (high labour and material usage in early production) are direct and will be correctly allocated to the products they relate to.

The factory overheads are distributed over all batches at a single overhead rate, for example labour hour rate, which takes no account of batch sizes. So, overheads are absorbed in a manner that discriminates in favour of small batches at the expenses of large batches.

Adopting a cost accounting system that allows a more meaningful treatment of small-batch costs (and ABC is not the only option) offers advantages including the following:

- by providing an accurate figure for batch-size costs, it allows the calculation of accurate optimum batch sizes for each production;
- by correctly treating and reporting small-batch costs, the need to control and manage those costs may become more apparent to managers;
- better short-term decision-making regarding whether to make a product or to buy it in, and better-informed pricing and portfolio decisions;
- better medium- to long-term decision-making, especially relating to reducing these overhead costs by use of IT, better systems and procedures, a better-trained and more flexible workforce, etc.

(c) Academic accountants are expected to carry out research and publish scholarly papers as well as teach undergraduates. Thus, such writers are likely to communicate new practices to the profession as a whole.

There are also numerous consultancy firms that generate business for themselves on the basis of new practices that produce superior results. They too are likely to communicate the general outline of their proprietary practices.

As to the development of new practices, this usually occurs as an empirical solution to a practical problem. This problem may be encountered by practising accountants, by academic accountants via their research, or by consultant accountants working for a client. The last two categories of accountant may have more resources and time to develop a radically new practice, but all three situations could lead to a new practice.

ABC is an example of a new practice based on old principles but applied in a new way to give new insights into production costing. The academic Kaplan is credited with publicising the idea via academic journals, a book, and in conjunction with a major group of consultants. All the ideas in ABC may have been developed and used individually by different practising accountants, but Kaplan took the time to develop them into a coherent theory for modern manufacturing and service sectors.

Some new practices have been developed by academics and all are communicated, tested, debated and explained to the accounting body as a whole by their activities. Thus academic research plays an important role in the development of new practices within the management accounting profession.

9

Responsibility Centres and
Transfer Pricing

Responsibility Centres and Transfer Pricing

LEARNING OUTCOMES

After completing study of this chapter, you should be able to

▸ discuss the use of cost, revenue, profit and investment centres in devising organisation structure and in management control;

▸ prepare cost information in appropriate formats for cost centre managers, taking due account of controllable/uncontrollable costs and the importance of budget flexing;

▸ prepare revenue and cost information in appropriate formats for profit and investment centre managers, taking due account of cost variability, attributable costs, controllable costs and identification of appropriate measures of profit centre 'contribution';

▸ calculate and apply measures of performance for investment centres (often 'strategic business units' or divisions of larger groups);

▸ discuss the likely behavioural consequences of the use of performance metrics in managing cost, profit and investment centres;

▸ explain the typical consequences of a divisional structure for performance measurement as divisions compete or trade with each other;

▸ identify the likely consequences of different approaches to transfer pricing for divisional decision-making, divisional and group profitability, the motivation of divisional management and the autonomy of individual divisions.

9.1 Introduction

In this chapter, we will explore the manner in which an organisation can be split into 'responsibility centres' for accounting and financial control purposes. The concept of responsibility accounting was encountered earlier in this text within the context of budgeting and budgetary control. The thrust of this approach is that an organisation can be split into parts for each of which an individual manager or management team is responsible.

A budget is prepared for each of the constituent parts ('responsibility centres') and results reported on a strictly consistent basis. Hence, the central method of performance evaluation is the comparison of budget and actual results for each responsibility centre. This comparison can be between particular cost/revenue figures or between particular performance indicators judged appropriate.

We will proceed to consider detailed aspects of the operation of responsibility centres (including 'transfer pricing'), and the manner in which performance indicators are selected and applied. We will also consider the manner in which the selection of performance indicators can influence and/or distort the manner in which responsibility centre managers behave.

9.2 Cost, revenue, profit and investment centres

9.2.1 Cost centres

You should already have encountered cost centres as part of your Foundation level studies. The role that cost centres play in the determination of product costs and, in general, management accounting practice is not therefore explored fully here. The CIMA *Official Terminology* defines a cost centre as:

 Cost centre. A production or service location, function, activity or item of equipment for which costs are accumulated.

A cost centre is used as a 'collecting place' for costs. The cost of operating the cost centre is determined for the period, and then this total cost is related to the cost units that have passed through the cost centre.

For instance, an example of a production cost centre could be the machine shop in a factory. The production overhead cost for the machine shop might be £100,000 for the period. If 1,000 cost units have passed through this cost centre we might say that the production overhead cost relating to the machine shop was £100 for each unit.

The CIMA definition of a cost centre also mentions a service location, a function, an activity or an item of equipment being used as a cost centre. Examples of these might be as follows but you should try to think of some others:

Type of cost centre	Examples
Service location	Stores, canteen
Function	Sales representative
Activity	Quality control
Item of equipment	Packing machine

If you are finding it difficult to see how a sales representative could be used as a cost centre, then work carefully through the following points:

1. What are the costs that might be incurred in 'operating' a sales representative for one period?

   Examples might be the representative's salary cost, the cost of running a company car, the cost of any samples given away by the representative and so on. Say, these amount to £20,000.
2. Once we have determined this cost, the next thing that we need to know is the number of cost units that can be related to the sales representative.

   The cost unit selected might be £100 of sales achieved. If the representative has achieved £200,000 of sales, then we could say that the representative's costs amounted to £10 per £100 of sales. The representative has thus been used as a cost centre or collecting place for the costs, which have then been related to the cost units.

9.2.2 Profit centres

In an organisation, the degree of authority delegated by top management to lower level operating management can be viewed as a continuum. At one end, where complete executive control over activities is maintained by head office, and all decisions are made at the top level, the organisation is totally *centralised*. At the other end, where the degree of autonomy exercised by lower level managers gives them full control over activities and decisions, it would be described as totally *decentralised*. Neither end of this continuum is seen as desirable. In the case of total centralisation, routine decisions best handled (from the point of view of timeliness and detailed knowledge) by the manager at local level will divert valuable top management time and attention from the broader policy and strategic issues that face the firm as a whole. In the case of total decentralisation, it is extremely difficult to obtain a sufficient number of competent subordinate managers to operate the system successfully; not all will have equally good decision-making skills, and top management must therefore be willing to let them make some costly mistakes. Furthermore, head office is faced with the problem of selecting an appropriate performance measurement system that will ensure that the managers of the operating units (often called 'divisions') act in a way that is consistent with the goals of the organisation as a whole (goal congruence). In reality, of course, few organisations operate at these extremes; but as any movement away from complete centralisation necessarily involves a degree of decentralised activity, the problems associated with it must be recognised and solved.

In the weakest form of decentralisation, a simple system of *cost* or *revenue* centres is often used, where managers are responsible for cost containment or revenue generation, respectively. In such cases, a single financial measure may be deemed appropriate, and performance is likely to be evaluated primarily by reference to the materiality of the variances between budgeted and actual costs and revenues. As decentralisation becomes stronger, managers will be responsible for both costs and revenues in their divisions (*profit centres*), and in its strongest form for costs, revenues and the acquisition and disposal of the assets used to support the divisions' activities (*investment centres*). In these situations, other measures of performance are appropriate to reflect the greater degree of independence enjoyed by the managers of the centres, and these measures must be designed to minimise the dysfunctional tendencies that inevitably accompany greater autonomy.

9.2.3 Revenue centres and investment centres

A revenue centre is a responsibility centre that is devoted to raising revenue (or generating sales), without any link to the associated costs. Revenue centres might be encountered in the not-for-profit sector or in the marketing operation of a commercial organisation. The fund raising function of an NFP organisation might be split into revenue centres (with each centre responsible for a geographic area) and a marketing operation might be split into revenue centres (with each responsible for a particular product range).

An investment centre is responsible for justifying, making and then operating particular investments. Hence, an investment centre is responsible for the selection and performance of particular investments. The core technique associated with this is 'investment appraisal', which is not a topic within this particular course. It is explored fully in CIMA's Paper P2 *Management Accounting Decision-Making*. However, the Investment Centre is central to our discussion of strategic business units (SBUs) below.

9.2.4 Reporting responsibility centre results

The reporting of responsibility centre results has already been explored within our study of budgetary control and financial reporting (see Chapters 6 and 7).

The key points to note are:

- The results reported for a given centre should genuinely reflect only those costs and revenues which lie within the control of that centre. Costs that are 'uncontrollable' (e.g. an apportionment of head office overheads) might be either excluded from the report or clearly segregated. The end result is that the results (in terms of profit, contribution and capital employed) reported for a given centre are only those for which the centre's management is strictly responsible.
- The results reported for a centre should be compared only with a meaningful benchmark in order to evaluate performance. With the context of a traditional budgetary control system, this means that the budget may be 'flexed' to allow for the actual level of output/activity achieved. Hence, the financial control report involves a comparison of likes. This issue has been explored earlier in this text.
- Any reported result becomes most meaningful when it is expressed in some context, that is, in the form of a performance indicator. The context may be a comparison of a financial actual with budget, a comparison of a financial actual with some non-financial measure (e.g. to give a cost per unit output), a current actual compared with a previous period actual or an actual compared with some industry-wide benchmark.
- A performance indicator can be either financial or non-financial (see relevant discussion in Chapter 7). For a given business unit, the most meaningful and full form of performance evaluation might involve a mix of performance indicators along the lines of the balanced scorecard. The choice of indicators should be related to the key success factors of the unit.

In the performance evaluation exercise, the management accountant should be aware that there is ultimately no such thing as an uncontrollable cost or a fixed cost – if one takes a long enough view over time and span of activity level. All costs may be considered to vary if you take enough time to research what activities they vary with. It is then just a matter of determining who controls the relevant levels of activity in order to determine which responsibility centre the costs concerned should be attributed to.

The various component parts of the management accounting function relate to one another. Meaningful performance evaluation requires a rigorous cost accounting system. Our discussion of costing systems in Chapter 1 is relevant to subsequent discussion of performance evaluation in Chapter 7 and our discussion of responsibility centres in this chapter.

Responsibility centres and internal markets (extract)

Bob Scarlett, *Financial Management,* **April 2007**

An objective must be set for an autonomous responsibility centre. Determining how far that objective has been achieved provides a performance measure for the centre. The system must be adapted to priorities and circumstances in each case. Accordingly, responsibility centres may be grouped under three main headings:

(1) Cost centre (CC)

This is a responsibility centre to which costs are attributed, but not earnings or capital.

CCs can be designed in two alternative ways: either (a) the CC is given a fixed quantity of inputs and be required to maximise outputs, or (b) a required level of outputs is specified for the CC which must be achieved with minimum inputs. An example of (a) is a public relations department, which is given a fixed budget to spend and has to use this to achieve the best possible result. An example of (b) is a cleaning department, which is given certain areas to clean and has to do this at minimum cost. In both cases, the CC manager is allowed a degree of autonomy in making decisions on how the operation is run. But the system guides the manager to act in a manner which is consistent with the interest of the organisation.

However, the CC offers one particular weakness insofar as it relies on the measurement of financial spend to assess performance. There is no direct incentive for the manager to enhance the quality of output. Costs can always be contained by reducing quality. In the case of a CC, quality reduction is not identified by the use of financial performance metrics.

Many organisations treat their IT departments as cost centres. This often has unfortunate consequences.

The idea that IT is a cost centre and carries no profit or loss is dangerous and should be opposed wherever it is encountered, according to Simon Linsley, head of consultancy, IT and development at Philips. Will Hadfield, *Computer Weekly*, 30 May 2006

This CW article describes how IT system installation projects were usually completed on time and within budget at the electronics firm Philips. However, the manner in which system projects were implemented often gave rise to serious disruption at the operational level, causing stress to the staff of client departments and degraded customer service.

(2) Profit centres (PC)

This is a responsibility centre to which costs and revenues are attributed, but not capital.

In the case of a CC, the manager has autonomy as regards either (a) outputs or (b) inputs – but not both together. In the case of the PC, the manager has autonomy over both inputs and outputs. The objective of a PC is to maximise profit or achieve a profit target. The manager of the PC is allowed to make decisions concerning both the resources used and output (in terms of both quantity and price) achieved.

In the case of a PC, reliance on financial performance measures does not provide any incentive to lower quality. Lowering quality will impact on sales quantity and/or selling price, which will impact on profit. The PC may also induce other behaviour which is in the interests of an organisation. For example, unit costs within a CC may be minimised by use of long continuous production runs and this pattern of production may be favoured accordingly. But, it is a pattern of production which will result in high stock holding and/or lowered response levels to individual customer requirements. These last features will adversely impact on profit and, therefore, a suboptimum pattern of production is less likely to be induced within a PC.

An IT department within an organisation may be organised as a profit centre. Typically, this will involve invoicing client departments for its services and inviting competition from outside consultants for system installation projects.

IT directors should push for the IT function in their organisation to be treated as a profit centre rather than a cost to the business. This was the key message from Glenn Martin, managing director and chief technology officer at financial services firm Cazenove, speaking to the City IT financial services technology forum last week. Christian Annesley, *Computer Weekly*, 15 November 2005

Rather than forcing through system installations in a manner which minimises costs, IT managers are now incentivised to allow for the full operational requirements of client departments when organising projects.

The logic behind responsibility centres suggests that an organisation should be split into decoupled internal components with decision rights in each given to its own management, within certain parameters. Each component trades its services with the others on an arms length basis, giving rise to an 'internal market'.

This concept was applied widely in the British public sector in the 1990s. The BBC under Director General John Birt introduced an internal market amongst its different components – Technology, Production, News and so on. The development of an internal market has also been a feature of NHS reform, whereby different units within the NHS have the character of buyers and providers of services.

So much for the theory. Practical experience has introduced organisations to a concept known as 'failure of the internal market'. For example, the BBC Gramophone Library was rated as the greatest sound archive in the world and it was traditionally run as a cost centre. During the reforms of the 1990s, it became a profit centre and was required to charge user departments in the BBC for the issue of recordings.

Music that was previously provided free by the Library now came with a charge and it wasn't cheap. Which is why all the music shops in Oxford Street were busy with BBC researchers buying far cheaper commercial CDs. At the prestigious Radio 4 daytime current affairs programmes The World at One and PM, staff were barred from using any material from the BBCs gramophone library because the cost was too high. Netribution, '*BBC axes Producer Choice*', March 2006

The BBC's internal market was deeply unpopular and produced unintended effects in the way that managers behaved. It has been largely abandoned in recent years. The reality was that the BBC's Gramophone Library was a vital resource that had to be seen as a cost centre and nothing other than that.

Responsibility centres and internal markets have much to offer. But insensitivity in their use or their use in inappropriate circumstances can result in them doing more harm than good.

9.3 Transfer pricing

In a divisionalised organisation, the managers of the different investment centres are encouraged to operate them as separate economic entities. This separation will only rarely complete, however, as goods and services are often provided by one division to another, particularly in a focused manufacturing environment. A value must obviously be placed on these intra-company transfers, and is known as the *transfer price*. In the absence of divisionalisation, the value that would be placed on goods or services that would otherwise be transferred would be *cost* (however calculated), and this can still be used as a transfer price. An alternative, however, that reflects the autonomous nature of divisions, would be for the selling division to transfer at a price *above* cost, and thus record a profit. It is the character and allocation of such profit, and the concomitant potential for suboptimality for the organisation as a whole, that forms the nub of the transfer-pricing problem.

9.3.1   Aims and features

Any transfer-pricing system should aim to

- ensure that resources are allocated in an optimal manner;
- promote goal congruence;
- motivate divisional managers;
- facilitate the assessment of management performance;
- retain divisional autonomy.

  Its two overriding features should be

- simplicity in calculation and implementation;
- robustness (i.e. not requiring frequent adjustment).

Needless to say, a number of these aims and features can conflict with each other, and prove difficult to achieve in practice. It is highly unlikely that any one method would meet all the requirements of the firm in all circumstances; the best that can be hoped for is a reasonable compromise.

9.3.2   General rules

Although different approaches will result in different figures, limits within which the transfer price should fall can be summarised as follows:

- *Minimum:* The sum of the selling division's marginal cost and the opportunity cost of the resources used. Note that in many practical circumstances, the opportunity cost of the resources used in making a transfer is 'nil'. Hence, it is often stated in management literature that the minimum limit for a transfer price is marginal cost.
- *Maximum:* The lowest market price at which the buying division could acquire the goods or services externally, less any internal cost savings in packaging and delivery.

This is so because (a) the transferor division will not agree to transfer units if the transfer price is set at less than marginal cost plus opportunity cost, and (b) the transferee division will not accept internally transferred units if it can buy them for less cost from an outside supplier. If the marginal cost of unit is £5 and £3 contribution from an outside sale is lost through using that unit for an internal transfer, then the transferor division will not agree to transfer for less than £8. If such a unit can be bought from an outside supplier for £9, then the transferee division will not accept an internally transferred unit at any price greater than £9. So, in this case the lower and upper limits of the transfer price are £8 and £9, respectively.

The difference between the two limits represents the savings made by producing internally as opposed to buying in from outside.

We will now look at a number of different transfer pricing methods, using the example data which follows.

Example

XY has two divisions – A and B. Division A manufactures advanced computer microchips, and most of its production is taken up by division B, which assembles computers. Data for division A are:

Standard unit production cost

	£	£
Direct materials		35
Direct labour		10
Variable manufacturing overhead		5
		50
Fixed overhead*	20	
Fixed selling and administration*	5	
		25
Total cost		75
Normal mark-up: 40%		30
List price to outside buyers		105

*Fixed costs are allocated on the basis of estimated volume.

Estimated production

	Units
Internal transfers	300,000
External sales	200,000
Total production	500,000

9.3.3 Cost-based prices

Four versions of 'cost' are commonly used: marginal cost, absorption cost, standard cost, and marginal cost plus a fixed fee ('two-part tariff'). Actual costs will vary with volume, seasonal and other factors; furthermore, if actual costs are used as a basis for transfer prices, any inefficiency in the producing department will be passed on in the form of increased cost to the receiving department. The use of standard costs is therefore recommended, so that all of the supplying division's efficiencies and inefficiencies are reflected in its own accounts.

(i) **Marginal cost**

If we assume that variable cost can be used as marginal cost, then the transfer price based thereon would be £50. If costs, revenues and volume are as expected, the use of this price will result in a 'loss' for the selling division of £1.5 m:

	£m
Internal transfers: 300,000 @ £50	15.0
External sales: 200,000 @ £105	21.0
	36.0
Total costs: 500,000 @ £75	(37.5)
Loss	(1.5)

This loss must be contrasted with the profit of £15 m that would accrue if all of A's production could be sold externally:

	£m
Sales: 500,000 @ £105	52.5
Total costs – as above	(37.5)
	15.0

However, if no more than the current 200,000 could be sold externally, and the capacity represented by the production of units for internal transfer would otherwise remain idle, there is no opportunity cost associated with a transfer at marginal cost, other things being equal, and division A would be indifferent to the production and transfer.

Obviously, if more than the current 200,000 could be sold externally, A's indifference may change, depending on whether a price in excess of marginal cost is offered. If no excess is offered, A would have a strong *disincentive* to supply B.

(ii) **Absorption cost**

Using this variant of cost gives a transfer price of £70 (variable costs £50 + fixed manufacturing cost £20) and a rather happier income statement:

	£m
Internal transfers: 300,000 @ £70	21.0
External sales: 200,000 @ £105	21.0
	42.0
Total costs – as above	(37.5)
Profit	4.5

Although the new transfer price does not generate the same level of profit as a sale of that quantity to an outside party, nevertheless a contribution towards fixed costs is provided thereby, thus modifying the disincentive noted above. However, as the level of the transfer cost is increased, its effect on the buying division, B, could lead to problems of suboptimalisation for the firm as a whole. For example, suppose B could buy the same components from an *outside supplier* at a cost of £65. An internal transfer price of £70 would force B to buy in a product at £65 that could be manufactured in-house for a variable cost of £50. Although the buying division would 'save' £5 per chip (£70 − £65), the firm would *lose* £4.5 m thereby:

	£
Marginal cost to produce	50
External purchase cost	(65)
Loss if buy in	(15)
300,000 × £15 = £4.5 m	

This loss assumes that the opportunity cost of the released capacity is *less* than £15 per unit. If alternative goods generating *more* than this could be produced with the spare capacity – if, for example, the marginal 300,000 units *could* be sold externally at the list price – then XY would be optimising its resources by buying in the components:

	£
List price	105
Marginal cost	(50)
Contribution	55
Loss if buy in	(15)
Incremental profit	40
300k × £40 = £12 m	

We can see here a clear application of the minimum/maximum rule noted above: the sum of the selling division's marginal cost and the opportunity cost of the resources used (at list price) is £105, the minimum transfer price that the selling division could change without making a loss for the firm, which exceeds the £65 maximum transfer price dictated by the prevailing market price. XY should not transfer the components internally as long as the market price is less than £105.

(iii) **Standard cost**

One of the problems of cost-based systems is that they allow a transferor division to pass on cost inefficiencies to a transferee division. Such inefficiencies can result from anything as simple as high fixed overheads per unit arising from low output levels in the current period, or high unit material costs resulting from machine defects in the current period.

One variant on the absorption cost method is standard cost. Such standards are used irrespective of what actual costs were, with the result that the impact of adverse or favourable cost variances rests with the transferor division. Many business managers would consider that this gives the most equitable distribution of profit.

(iv) **Two-part tariff**

Under this variant, the selling division transfers at marginal cost (including any opportunity cost), but raises a fixed annual fee on the buying division for the privilege of receiving transfers at that price. The theory underlying this approach is that the buying division will have a correct understanding of the selling division's cost behaviour patterns. The buying division will be able to correctly identify the appropriate marginal cost when calculating the optimum output level. The fixed fee is designed to cover a share of the selling division's fixed costs and provide a return on the capital employed in it, and thus both selling and buying divisions should be able to record a profit on intra-company transfers.

Drawbacks of this system include:

- The supplying division has no incentive to supply units swiftly, because individual units do not generate a profit.
- A profit is made when the fixed fee is transferred.

9.3.4 Market-based prices

The price of a comparable product or service in the market can be seen as an objective basis for the transfer price between divisions. It is the price that reflects the autonomous nature of divisionalisation, inasmuch as it simulates the price that would be offered and paid by fully independent entities. If the selling division is operating efficiently relative to its competitors, it would be expected to show a profit at such a price, and, similarly, a market-based price should not cause problems for an efficiently managed buying division, as the only alternative to an internal transfer would be to buy the goods of services in the open market at that price.

However, it is not always easy to determine the appropriate market price to use

- A comparable product might not be available on the market;
- Different suppliers will quote different initial prices;
- Different buyers command different discounts and credit terms, depending on the order size and their status.

- Current market prices may reflect temporary aberrations in trading conditions, and thus might not prevail in the longer term.
- An internal transfer of goods may involve savings in advertising, packaging and delivery costs, and thus an external market price would not be entirely appropriate.

 Exercise

The XY group comprises two divisions – X and Y Each divisional manager is paid a salary bonus linked to divisional profit. X produces the Exe and Y produces the Why. There is a 'perfect' outside market for the Exe with a going market price of £20 over which X has no influence. One unit of the Exe is incorporated in each unit of the Why.

The marginal cost of an Exe is £10 and the marginal cost of a Why (excluding the cost of the component Exe) is £10.

At unit selling price £50 no Whys are sold but demand for Whys rises by 100 units per period with each £5 reduction in the unit selling price.

Requirements

(a) Assuming that there is no production constraint in division X, tabulate the contribution generated by XY from sales of Whys ranging from nil to 500 units per period in 100-unit increments. Use this tabulation to identify the optimum unit selling price (usp) and output of the Why.

(b) Tabulate the contribution generated by division Y from sales of Whys ranging from nil to 500 units per period at 100-unit increments with the Exe being transferred from X to Y at market price. Use this tabulation to identify the unit selling price (usp) and output of the Why that is likely to be induced if Exes are transferred from X to Y at market price.

(c) Assuming that there is a production constraint in division X (with each unit of Why produced resulting in an outside sale of a unit of Exe being forgone), tabulate the contribution generated by XY from sales of Whys ranging from nil to 500 units per period in 100-unit increments. Use this tabulation to identify the optimum unit selling price (usp) and output of the Why.

(d) Comment on the results you have produced in answer to requirements (a) to (c) and outline any 'general rule' for transfer pricing that they might suggest.

 Solution

(a) Optimum usp and output with no capacity constraint in X

Units Why	USP £	Sales £	MC £	XY Cont. £
0	50	0	0	0
100	45	4,500	2,000*	2,500
200	40	8,000	4,000	4,000
300	35	10,500	6,000	4,500
400	30	12,000	8,000	4,000
500	25	12,500	10,000	2,500

* The marginal cost is £20 per unit of Why (£10 + £10)

It can be seen that the optimum usp is £35 and output is 300 units. The critical point is that transferring Exe to Y involves no opportunity cost to X or XY as a whole.

(b) Induced usp and output

The marginal cost per unit charged to division Y will be:

	£
Transfer price of Exe (market price)	20
Marginal cost of Why	10
	30*

Units Why	USP £	Sales £	MC £	Division Y Cont. £
0	50	0	0	0
100	45	4,500	3,000*	1,500
200	40	8,000	6,000	2,000
300	35	10,500	9,000	1,500
400	30	12,000	12,000	0
500	25	12,500	15,000	(2,500)

The transfer price system is likely to induce division Y to charge a usp of £40 and an output of 200 units. This maximises Y's contribution but is suboptimal from the point of view of XY as a whole, since we have proved in part (a) that the optimum usp is £35, with no capacity constraint.

(c) Optimum usp and output with capacity constraint in X

Units Why	USP £	Sales £	MC £	Op. cost £	XY cont. £
0	50	0	0	0	0
100	45	4,500	2,000	1,000	1,500
200	40	8,000	4,000	2,000	2,000
300	35	10,500	6,000	3,000	1,500
400	30	12,000	8,000	4,000	0
500	25	12,500	10,000	5,000	(2,500)

The critical thing here is that each unit of Why sold results in the sale of a unit of Exe (with £10 contribution) being forgone. Hence, an opportunity cost of £10 results from each unit of Why sold.

It can be seen that the optimum usp is £40 and output is 200 units. In this case, the transfer price of £20 (being marginal cost plus opportunity cost, or market price) induces optimum behaviour from the point of view of XY as a whole.

(d) What the above analysis suggests is that the general rule for transfer pricing is that units should be transferred at marginal cost plus opportunity cost. Where there is no production constraint in X then this rule gives a transfer price of £10, which will induce the optimum usp and output in Y.

Where there is a production constraint in X then the rule gives a transfer price of £20 (£10 marginal cost plus £10 opportunity cost) and this now induces the optimum usp and output in Y. In these circumstances, the rule specifies a transfer price that will usually approximate to market price.

As with all mathematical models, this rule provides a theoretical case that may be very difficult to apply in practice. For one thing, what constitutes 'opportunity cost' may vary from day to day.

The general point concerning transfer pricing is that a system based on marginal cost plus opportunity cost of resources used (commonly known as 'opportunity cost') is commonly considered to provide the mathematically correct method of transfer pricing, but it has practical limitations. This issue is explored in the Readings item 'Opportunity Cost: the Mathematically correct transfer price . . .' appended.

9.3.5 Marginal cost

We have already seen that the use of marginal cost as a transfer price penalises the selling division by forcing it to transfer goods below total cost. In this case, the selling division will be providing a concealed subsidy to the buying division.

In this section, we will look in a little more detail at the potential behavioural impact of a transfer pricing system based on marginal cost.

Economic theory suggests that, where the market is imperfect, marginal cost is the correct price to use if the group's profit is to be optimised. Marginal cost is assumed to equate with variable cost in this discussion. Table 9.1 contains data that illustrates this. Up to five units are demanded, according to the selling price asked. The transfer price between the divisions is marginal cost plus 100 per cent mark-up to cover fixed costs and profit. The receiving division will wish to continue selling units until the 'perceived marginal cost' (i.e. the transfer price of the component plus the receiving division's own marginal cost) is equal to marginal revenue. This occurs after the second unit, and so the receiving division will sell only two units – assuming its management acts selfishly and wishes to maximise the division's contribution rather than that of the group. The maximum contribution under these circumstances will be £14. (At this point, the supplying division will make a contribution of £20 and so the group's total contribution will be £34.) However, from the group's perspective the receiving division should continue to sell until the group's marginal cost is equal to the marginal revenue – this occurs at the fourth unit, where a contribution of £42 is made. (This is the point where neither a profit nor a loss is made and so sales would stop after three units.)

Using marginal cost as a basis for transfer pricing does little for the morale and motivation of the supplying division as that division will always make a loss to the extent of its fixed costs. Using marginal cost plus a mark-up helps to overcome this, but the receiving division may not then be aware of the marginal cost itself. Even if the receiving division is aware of the marginal cost, the managers will be tempted to act in the interests of the division rather than that of the group.

We have seen that a two-part tariff system can help in this situation, but it does have its limitations.

Table 9.1

	Supplying division			Receiving division			
Units	Marginal cost per unit £	Units	Transfer price £	Marginal cost per unit £	Perceived total marginal cost £	True total marginal cost £	Selling price £
1	10	1	20	5	25	15	35
2	10	2	20	6	26	16	30
3	10	3	20	7	27	17	25
4	12	4	24	8	32	20	20
5	12	5	24	9	33	21	15

9.3.6 Dual pricing

The dual price method of transfer pricing was introduced in order to overcome the problems caused by using marginal cost, namely poor morale in the selling division, and lack of motivation by the receiving division to maximise the group's profit. The dual pricing method uses two prices:

1. The supplying division is credited with a price based on total cost plus a mark-up.
2. The receiving division is debited with marginal cost.

This means that the selling division is allowed to earn a profit and the receiving division has the correct information in order to make the correct selling decision to maximise the group's profit. The difference between the two prices will be debited to a group account – a transfer price adjustment account. At the end of the year, the profits of the two divisions, and hence of the group, will be overstated to the extent of the price difference. In order to correct this, the total amount in the transfer price adjustment account must be subtracted from the two profits to arrive at the correct profit for the group as a whole.

Dual pricing can also be used with market price in place of marginal cost for the receiving division. This can aid the supplying division in a particular circumstance. For example, where market prices are very volatile and the market price of the component suddenly collapses, it may be unrealistic to expect the supplying division to cope with the decrease. Under these circumstances, the receiving division would wish to buy elsewhere if the transfer price set was higher than the market price. So, the supplying division could be credited with total cost-plus and the receiving division debited with the much reduced market price. The receiving division would then be happy to continue to buy internally.

However, despite its advantages, dual pricing is not used widely in practice for the following reasons:

- It is a complicated system to operate when many goods are being transferred between a number of different divisions.
- It involves head office in the accounting side and so notification of transactions must be sent to the head office. Head office involvement goes against the principle of decentralisation and as a result the managers of the divisions may feel they are not being given the freedom they might expect as managers of an autonomous division.
- If total cost plus and market price is used because prices have collapsed, it may cocoon the divisional managers of the supplying division from the rigours of the market place.
- Total cost plus and marginal cost may not prove helpful either. Very few organisations require the economic theory approach of using marginal costs to optimise profit, and taxation issues and repatriation of funds are often of more importance when setting transfer prices.

9.3.7 Profit-maximising transfer prices

One can consider more complex situations where both marginal cost and marginal revenue move with output level.

It is possible to determine a range of transfer prices within which divisional managers will be motivated to operate at the level of output which maximises profit for the organisation as a whole. The following exercise will demonstrate this.

Exercise

CD Ltd has two divisions, C and D. C transfers all its output to D, where the units are finished before being sold on the external market. Recent costs and revenues are as follows:

Monthly output units	Cost incurred in division C £'000	Cost incurred in division D £'000	Division D revenue £'000	Company profit £'000
14	150	60	350	140
15	163	64	371	144
16	177	69	392	146
17	194	77	412	141
18	211	85	431	135

The profit-maximising output for the company as a whole is 16 units per month. In order to determine the range of transfer prices that will encourage both divisions to operate at this level, we need to consider each division's marginal cost and marginal revenue.

Each divisional manager will be willing to increase supply until the point is reached where marginal cost = marginal revenue. Therefore, we need to look at the marginal costs and revenues for each division.

Monthly output units	Marginal cost Division C £'000 per unit	Net revenue Division D £'000 per unit	Net marginal revenue Division D £'000 per unit
14	–	(350–60) 290	–
15	(163–150) 13	307	(307–290) 17
16	14	323	16
17	17	335	12
18	17	346	11

Division C will be willing to increase output until the marginal cost exceeds the marginal revenue, or the transfer price. In order to be encouraged to produce and transfer 16 units, the profit-maximising output, the transfer price must exceed £14,000 per unit, which is the marginal cost of the 16th unit. However, the transfer price must be lower than £17,000 per unit, otherwise Division C will wish to expand output to 17 units.

Division D will be willing to purchase 16 units from Division C as long as the transfer price is lower than £16,000 per unit. However, if the price is as low as £12,000 per unit, Division D will wish to purchase 17 units.

A transfer price must therefore be selected that is higher than £14,000 per unit but lower than £16,000 per unit.

To check this for yourself, select a transfer price within this range of, say, £15,000 per unit.

- Division C would be willing to supply 16 units at this price, but not 17 units, since the 17th unit would have a marginal cost of £17,000.
- Division D would be willing to purchase 16 units at this price, but not 17 units, since the net marginal revenue for the 17th unit is only £12,000.

9.3.8 Negotiated transfer prices

We have seen that transfer prices may be determined by various means, including the use of mathematical formulae based on opportunity cost and by determining the correct transfer price to encourage all divisions to operate at the profit-maximising output level.

Alternatively, transfer prices could be set through a process of negotiation between the buying and selling divisions. It could be argued that this is the correct procedure in a truly autonomous system, with no interference whatsoever from central management or head office. The resulting transfer price should be acceptable to both the buying and selling division since the relevant managers have been directly responsible for the negotiations.

However, there are disadvantages to the use of negotiated transfer prices.

- The negotiations may be protracted and time-consuming
- The managers may find it impossible to reach agreement. In this case, central management may need to intervene. If a transfer price is imposed as a consequence, then this may cause behavioural problems and would negate the objective of giving autonomy to divisions. On the other hand, central managers might act simply as arbitrators in any dispute during negotiations, providing a mediation service to assist the negotiations to reach a conclusion that is acceptable to all concerned.
- The managers may not be negotiating from an equal basis. For example, one of the managers may be more experienced than the other with the result that the outcome of negotiations may be unfair. This could lead to poor motivation and consequent behavioural problems.

9.3.9 Other behavioural considerations

Transfer prices tend to vary over the product life cycle according to Cats-Baril et al. (1988). During the introductory phase, they suggest a cost plus fixed fee or cost plus a profit share. During the growth phase, they suggest a price related to the closest substitute and during maturity a price based on identical products. This is common sense to a large extent. It is probably only during the maturity stage that identical substitutes exist and during the introductory phase there may be no basis other than cost on which to base the price.

Using any actual cost or cost plus as a transfer price does not motivate the supplying division to act in the interest of the group. Standard or predetermined costs should always be used in place of actual cost. If actual cost is used, the supplying division is not encouraged to be efficient, and control costs as inefficiencies are passed on to the receiving division by way of a higher transfer price. It is even worse if a mark-up is used because the selling division is encouraged to *push up the actual cost* as this will increase the mark-up, and increase the division's profit. Standard costs are at least subject to scrutiny when they are set once a year and the receiving division has a chance to challenge them. If standard cost is used, the selling division has an incentive to control actual costs below that level and so increase its own profits.

It is usual to imagine transfer pricing taking place in vertically integrated manufacturing organisations. This is not the norm today. Transfer pricing takes place in many different types of organisation and it can have a profound effect on behaviour. For example, a garage carries out a number of different activities that are linked to the activities of another section. The activities include selling new cars, selling old cars, servicing cars sold, general repairs, repairing and servicing used cars accepted in part payment, providing financing and so on. A transfer price is used to transfer a used car accepted in part-payment for a new car between the new car sales and used car sales divisions. A transfer price will also have to be established for transferring the cost of servicing and repairing these cars for sale between the servicing division and the used car sales division. These prices will have considerable implications for the profitability of the different sections and on the actions of the employees when making sales deals. If performance measurement and assessment is to be fair, transfer prices need to be set carefully.

Transfer prices can also be used to deter competitors. If a vertically integrated company concentrates profits at the stage of production where there is least competition, competitors may be attracted to enter. On the other hand, competitors operating at the other stages may be disadvantaged by the low profits the vertically integrated company is taking and they may not be able to achieve a satisfactory return if they are only operating in a limited area of the value chain. Neghandhi (1987) cites cases of US oil companies and Japanese trading and manufacturing companies doing this.

9.3.10 Opportunity Cost – the 'mathematically correct' transfer price

In designing a transfer pricing system, the management accountant should have regard to the following main requirements:

- The system should provide an *equitable* distribution of profit between divisions.
- The system should be *neutral* in that it does not induce sub-optimal behaviour.
- The system should be *simple* and transparent in order to be cost-effective.

The benchmarks against which any transfer pricing system can be judged are therefore (1) equity, (2) neutrality and (3) simplicity.

All sorts of different transfer pricing systems are possible. But, there are two extreme positions:

- Outside market selling price – above which no strategic business unit (SBU) would accept transfers in.
- Marginal cost – below which no SBU would agree to make transfers out.

For obvious reasons, the receiving SBU will never accept transfers at above market price and the supplier SBU will never agree to make transfers at below its marginal cost of production. One other possible transfer pricing system is 'opportunity cost' – the costs incurred and contribution foregone by the transferor division as the direct result of making a transfer.

Let us use a simple worked example to explore the merits of three alternative transfer pricing systems in two different sets of circumstances.

Example

AB Ltd has two divisions – A and B. Division A produces Units at a marginal cost of £5 each. Division B produces Products (each incorporating 1 Unit), at a marginal cost of £3 each (excluding the cost of the Unit). The outside selling price of the Unit is £10 and that of the Product is £12.

Question

Should AB adopt a transfer price system based on (i) marginal cost, (ii) market selling price or (iii) opportunity cost? In answering this question, one should consider two alternative Scenarios – (1) where there is no capacity constraint in A and (2) where A is operating at full capacity and Unit transfers to B mean that outside sales must be foregone.

Solution

Scenario 1 (no capacity constraint in A)

The manufacture of Products is to the advantage of AB as a whole. The total cost of manufacture is £8 per Product (£5 in A and £3 in B), the selling price is £12 – giving a contribution of £4 per Product. But the manager of B is the person who will decide whether or not Products are manufactured. He/she will be guided in this only by the impact such manufacture has on the profit of Division B.

Let us consider the likely outcome, given each of the three alternative transfer pricing systems. Consider the impact on the profit of B from the manufacture of one Product, given each possible transfer pricing system:

Impact on B profit from manufacture of one Product

Transfer price system	(i) Marginal cost	(ii) Market price	(iii) Opportunity cost
Transfer price	−5	−10	−5
B marginal cost	−3	−3	−3
Selling price	12	12	12
Contribution	4	−1	4

In this case, the opportunity cost to A of transferring one Unit is the same as marginal cost. A simply manufactures 1 extra Unit and its opportunity cost is the marginal cost thereof. Transfer pricing systems based on marginal and opportunity cost both achieve the 'correct' result, in that the manager of B would manufacture and sell the Product. However, a transfer pricing system based on market price experiences the 'wrong' result. The manager of B would decline to manufacture the Product – sub-optimal or dysfunctional behaviour that is not in the interests of AB as a whole.

Scenario 2 (capacity constraint in A)

The manufacture of Products is to the disadvantage of AB as a whole. The total cost of manufacture is £8 per Product and £5 contribution has to be foregone as a result of reducing outside sales from A by one Unit. Hence the manufacture and sale of a product at £12 gives rise to a negative contribution to AB as a whole of £1.

Impact on B profit from manufacture of one Product

Transfer price system	(i) Marginal cost	(ii) Market price	(iii) Opportunity cost
Transfer price	−5	−10	−10
B marginal cost	−3	−3	−3
Selling price	12	12	12
Contribution	4	−1	−1

In this case, the opportunity cost to A of transferring one Unit is its marginal cost of production (£5) plus the contribution foregone (£5) by being forced to reduce sales to outside customers by one Unit. Hence, the transfer price at opportunity cost is £10. Transfer pricing systems based on market price and opportunity cost both achieve the correct result – the manager of B would decline to manufacture the Product. However, a transfer pricing system based on marginal cost might induce the wrong result. If the manager of B could force the transfer of a Unit at a transfer price of £5, then division B might benefit but AB as a whole would lose.

Note that only the transfer pricing system based on opportunity cost produces the correct outcome in both scenarios.

General Conclusion

Having regard to the workings and discussion above, what are we to conclude?. Let us appraise each of the three transfer pricing systems considered against the relevant benchmarks.

Equity

A transfer price system based on marginal cost cannot be relied on to produce a fair distribution of profit between divisions. It leaves no element of profit with the transferor division and this is entirely inappropriate if the transferor has to forego profitable outside business in order to manufacture the Unit being transferred. Similarly, a transfer price based on market price cannot be relied on to produce a fair distribution of profit given that it allows the transferor to earn a full market profit on a transaction which involves no risk or management cost. Neither of these systems are satisfactory if rigidly applied in all possible circumstances.

A system based on opportunity cost is more sensitive in this regard since it takes account of circumstances. If the transferor does not have to forego outside business in order to make a transfer, then there is no reason why the transferor should make a profit from a risk free internal transfer – and opportunity cost achieves that result. Conversely, if the transferor has to forego a market profit to make the transfer, then the transfer should carry a market profit margin – and opportunity cost achieves that result. A case can be made that opportunity cost gives the most equitable result.

Neutrality

Both marginal cost– and market price–based transfer systems can induce dysfunctional behaviour in certain circumstances. However, opportunity cost avoids this possibility under all circumstances. Transfer at opportunity cost means that the manager of the transferee division will always be charged the amount the company as a whole incurs and foregoes in order to make the transfer. In theory, an opportunity cost–based transfer pricing system offers perfect neutrality.

Simplicity

Marginal cost and market price–based systems are usually fairly simple to operate. Marginal cost is easy to calculate and market price (so long as there is one) is easy to identify.

However, opportunity cost can be ambiguous since it depends on the precise circumstances of the business at any given moment in time. In the worked example above, whether or not Division A is operating at full capacity may vary from day to day. Hence, determining an appropriate transfer price for a particular Unit will require detailed investigation and negotiations every time a transfer is made. An opportunity cost–based transfer price system may be theoretically correct but it may be too complicated for practical use.

In designing management accounting systems, the accountant must have regard to various priorities. This often involves judicious compromise between theoretical correctness and practicality.

9.4 Taxation and other financial aspects of transfer pricing

International and intra-group trading is a very important part of business today. One-third of the UK's exports to Europe are intra-group transactions. Foreign-owned assets in Europe and the USA increased considerably during the 1980s and 1990s. During the 1980s, foreign-owned assets in the USA tripled, but the tax paid changed very little, as more than half the companies involved reported no taxable income (Pear, 1990).

International intra-group transfer pricing has its own special considerations, and so a multinational organisation will have matters other than behavioural ones to consider when it sets its transfer prices. There is a natural inclination to set transfer prices in order to minimise tax payments, or to repatriate profits from one country to another or minimise payments to minority shareholders. These three aspects will now be considered.

RESPONSIBILITY CENTRES AND TRANSFER PRICING

9.4.1 Taxation

If a group has subsidiaries that operate in different countries with different tax rates, the overall group corporation tax bill could be reduced by manipulating the transfer prices between the subsidiaries.

For example, if the taxation rate on profits in Country X is 25 per cent and in Country Y it is 60 per cent, the group could adjust the transfer price to increase the profit of the subsidiary in Country X and reduce the profit of the subsidiary in Country Y.

Thus, if the subsidiary in Country X provides goods or services to the subsidiary in Country Y, the use of a very high transfer price would maximise the profits in the lower-tax country, and minimise the profits in the higher-tax country.

There is also a temptation to set up marketing subsidiaries in countries with low corporation tax rates and transfer products to them at a relatively low transfer price. When the products are sold to the final customer, a low rate of tax will be paid on the difference between the two prices.

According to a survey by Ernst and Young (1995), more than 80 per cent of multinational companies viewed transfer pricing as a major international tax issue, and more than half of those companies saw it as the major issue. The taxation authorities in most countries monitor transfer prices in an attempt to control the situation and in order to collect the full amount of taxation due. Double taxation agreements between countries mean that companies pay tax on specific transactions in one country only. However, if the company sets an unrealistic transfer price in order to minimise tax, and the tax authority spots this, the company will pay taxation in both countries, that is, double taxation. This additional payment can amount to millions of pounds and, as a result, is quite an effective deterrent. On the other hand, the gains of avoiding taxation may be even greater.

There have been many cases of transfer price fixing for one reason or another over the years. One of the most notorious of UK transfer pricing cases was that of Hoffman La Roche, as it was then called. Hoffman La Roche had developed the drugs of Librium and Valium. The products were imported into the UK at prices of £437 and £979 per kilo, respectively. The UK tax authority accepted the prices; however, the Monopolies Commission sprang into life and questioned the prices on the grounds that the same chemical ingredients, which were unbranded, could be obtained from an Italian company for £9 and £28 per kilo. Hoffman La Roche argued on two grounds: (1) that the price was not set on cost but on what the market would bear, and (2) they had incurred the research and development costs and so had to recover those in the price. However, this was not accepted and they were fined £1.85 m in 1960.

More recently in the UK in 1992, Nissan was caught for unpaid tax of £237 m for falsely inflated invoices that were used to reduce profits. The freight charges were inflated by 40–60 per cent by a Norwegian company. The next year Nissan was required to pay £106 m in unpaid tax in the USA because the authorities felt that part of their USA marketing profits were being transferred to Japan as transfer prices on imports of cars and trucks were too high. Interestingly, the Japanese tax authorities took a different view and returned the double tax, which is a very rare occurrence.

Most countries now accept the Organisation for Economic Co-operation and Development's (OECD) 1995 guidelines. These guidelines were produced with the aim of standardising national approaches to transfer pricing as part of the OECD's charter to encourage the freedom of world trade. They provide guidance on the application of 'arm's length' principles. They state that where necessary transfer prices should be adjusted using an 'arm's length' price, that is, a price that would have been arrived at by two unrelated companies acting independently. There are three methods the tax authorities can use to determine an arm's length price.

The first is the comparable price method. This is the most widely used and involves setting the arm's length price by using the prices of similar products, that is, the market price or an approximation to one. The method is known as using comparable uncontrolled prices (CUPS) and is the preferred method wherever possible. This may seem a straightforward basis but as most international trade is carried out between related companies meaningful comparisons are hard to find. For example, in the UK in the 1980s, it was possible to use independent car distributorships to find a CUP but now that car manufacturers have developed their own dependent distributor networks, finding arm's length comparability is much more difficult.

Where a CUP cannot be found, or is inappropriate, one of two gross margin methods should be used. These involve a review of gross margins in comparable transactions between uncontrolled organisations. The resale price method is used for the transfer of goods to distributors and marketing operations where goods are sold on with little further processing. The price paid for a final product by an independent party is used and from this a suitable mark-up (to allow for the seller's expenses and profit) is deducted. The second gross margin method is the cost-plus method. Here an arm's length gross margin is established and applied to the seller's manufacturing cost.

These methods are of little help when attempting to establish an arm's length price for intangible property such as a patent right or trade name. Also, much of the data needed may not be in the public domain and so setting fair transfer prices is not easy. In the past, this did not matter so much but today it is often up to the taxpayer to 'prove' the price.

For example, the US section 482 regulations on transfer pricing cover 300 pages and the onus is on the taxpayer to support the transfer price with 'timely' documentation. If this is not done, a non-deductible penalty of up to 40 per cent of the arm's length price may be levied. In the past in the UK, it was up to the tax authorities to detect cases of inappropriate transfer pricing. This left the UK vulnerable to a certain amount of tax leakage. But now under the self-assessment regulations, the onus has switched to the taxpayer to provide correct information. Failure to demonstrate a reasonable attempt at an arm's length price in the tax return will give rise to a penalty of 100 per cent of any tax adjustment. Other European countries are also tightening their regulations in response to the USA and OECD's moves.

To safeguard the position, the taxpayer may enter into an Advanced Pricing Agreement (APA) with the relevant two tax authorities involved. This is a new approach and is done in advance to avoid any dispute and the costly penalty of double taxation and penalty fees. According to the Ernst and Young (1995) survey referred to earlier, more than 60 per cent of companies intend to do or are doing this.

Exercise

Assume that Division A, which is part of the ABC group, manufactures a single product M. Division A's maximum capacity is 450,000 Ms a year. It sells 420,000 Ms to external customers at a price of £75.95 a unit. This gives Division A a contribution of £30.50 a unit.

Division B is also part of the ABC group but is situated in a different country to Division A. Division B purchases 120,000 units of product M each year from a local company X (which is not part of the group) at a local currency price which is equivalent to £65.33 a unit.

It has been suggested that, in the interests of maximising the group's profit, Division B should purchase Ms from Division A. As there are no marketing costs involved when transferring goods to Division B, Division A would set the transfer price for an M at £69.60. This would give Division A the same contribution as an external sale, i.e. £30.50 per unit. Division A would give Division B's orders priority and so some external customer orders could no longer be met.

Requirements

Should Division B continue to purchase from company X or switch to Division A in order to maximise the group's profit if:

(a) the tax rate in the country in which Division A operates is 40% and the tax rate in Division B's country is 50%;

(b) the tax rate in the country in which Division A operates is 55% and the tax rate in Division B's country is 10%?

(Assume that changes in the contribution can be used as a basis for calculating changes in tax charges and that Division B generates sufficient profit from other activities to absorb any tax benefits.)

 Solution

The problem can be solved by using relevant costs, that is, by considering the change in contribution and tax paid only (Tables 9.2 and 9.3):

Table 9.2

	£'000	Answer (a) Tax £'000	Answer (b) Tax £'000
Current position-B buys from X:			
B buys 120,000 Ms @ £65.33	7,839.6		
This is set against profits taxed @			
50%/10% – this reduces B's tax liability by		(3,919.8)	(783.96)
A sells 420,000 Ms externally			
@ contribution £30.50	12,810		
A's tax @ 40%/55%		5,124	7,045.5
If B buys from A:			
B buys 120,000 Ms @ £69.60	8,352		
This is set against profits taxed @			
50%/10% – this reduced B's tax liability by		(4,176)	(835.2)
A sells 450,000 Ms			
@ contribution £30.50	13,725		
A's tax @ 40%/55%		5,490	7,548.75

Summary:

Table 9.3

If B switches to A:	Answer (a) Workings £'000	Answer (a) Net gain/(loss) £'000	Answer (b) Net gain/(loss) £'000
Decrease in B's contribution	7,839.6–8,352	(512.4)	(512.40)
Tax saving on B's decreased contribution	(3,919.8)–(4,176)	256.2	51.24
Increase in A's contribution	12,810–13,725	915.0	915.00
Tax increase for A @ 40% or 55%	5,124–5,490	(366.0)	(503.25)
Net gain to group		292.8	(49.41)

So, Division B should buy from Division A in order to maximise group profit in scenario (a) and from Company X in scenario (b).

9.4.2 Repatriation of funds

During the 1970s, in particular, repatriation of funds from a subsidiary to the group's HQ was not always easy. For example, the Andean Common Market Pact (1970) limited the amount of profit that could be repatriated to 14 per cent of registered capital. Repatriation of funds was particularly important to the company if inflation was very high, as it was in South America in the 1970s. Funds remaining unused in the host country would rapidly lose value but if they could be repatriated immediately their value was saved. If dividends could not be repatriated, prices to subsidiaries could be increased so that the subsidiary's profits were smaller and funds were repatriated by the higher price paid for the goods. Research into foreign companies in South America at that time showed that pharmaceutical companies inflated transfer prices between 30 and 300 per cent.

Where import duty exists on goods imported into a country, it is obviously advantageous to keep the transfer price as low as possible in order to avoid high duty payments.

9.4.3 Minority shareholders

Transfer prices can also be used to reduce the amount of profit paid to minority shareholders by artificially depressing a subsidiary's profit. Eiteman and Stonehill (1989) cite the case of the Ford Motor Co. buying out minority share interests in its British subsidiary in 1961 to avoid transfer price problems. Tate and Lyle was another company to have problems in this area. In a similar way different profit sharing schemes in different parts of the group can influence the way in which transfer prices are set.

9.5 Investment centres and performance measures

9.5.1 Investment centres/strategic business units

At the beginning of this chapter, we mentioned a third type of responsibility centre, in addition to cost centres and profit centres. The third type of responsibility centre is an investment centre.

The manager of an investment centre will be responsible for the costs and revenues of the centre in the same way as the manager of a profit centre. The revenues may be earned from external sales or through transfers made to other responsibility centres. The difference is that, in addition, the manager of an investment centre will be responsible for the capital investment in the centre, for example, in terms of fixed assets and working capital.

This means that the investment centre's performance can be monitored according to the profit earned relative to the capital invested in the centre.

> 🔑 An *investment centre* is defined in the CIMA Terminology as being: *A profit centre with additional responsibilities for capital investment and possibly for financing, and whose performance is measured by its return on investment.*

> 🔑 The term investment centre is to some extent interchangeable with the term strategic business unit (SBU). The CIMA Terminology provides the following definition for an SBU: *A section, within a larger organisation, responsible for planning, developing, producing and marketing its own products or services.*

SBUs may be treated as profit centres but they are more usually treated as investment centres, as an organisation's SBUs cannot be compared and assessed by the profit they generate alone, since they will inevitably differ in terms of size and operating characteristics at the very least. As a consequence, a means of comparing the benefit of investing in each SBU is needed. This section will use the terms investment centres and SBUs as interchangeable.

Each investment centre or SBU will have a manager and management team in charge of activities and performance. The aim of head office management must be to

- motivate the manager of the investment centre, and the team, to achieve the goals of the group;
- provide the right incentive for the manager, and his or her team, to make decisions that are consistent with the goals of the group's management.

One of the traditional methods of doing this is by using a return on investment (ROI) as a target performance measure, and tying in the management's bonus payments to its achievement. Investments will only be undertaken if they increase the investment centre's ROI.

9.5.2 Return on investment

ROI is almost a universal measure. It was introduced early this century and is still widely used today as a key performance measure for SBUs by many organisations throughout the world. Japan is the main exception to this, where return on sales (ROS) plays a more important role. (This is largely due to the differences in financing.) One of the problems of using ROI is that it has a variety of slightly different definitions and meanings according to how it is to be used. For example, return on net assets (RONA) and return on capital employed (ROCE) are also names given to very similar measures of profit over assets.

When used for internal performance measurement the formula for the return on investment is

$$\text{ROI} = \frac{\text{Operating profit before tax}}{\text{Net operating assets}}$$

Table 9.4 Investment centres

	A £'000	B £'000	C £'000
Sales	400	400	800
Profit	40	40	40
Assets	200	400	400
Profit/sales ratio (ROS)	10%	10%	5%
	×	×	×
Asset turnover ratio	2	1	2
	=	=	=
ROI	20%	10%	10%

The manager of an SBU (or investment centre) is not usually responsible for, or in control of, the tax paid and so, if the measure is to be fair, taxation should be excluded. Also, only those assets that are actually being used in the business unit should be used in the calculation, as these are the only assets the investment centre's management is responsible for. In the UK, the term 'operating assets' is taken to mean net assets (as stated above), that is, both fixed and current assets minus current liabilities. In the USA, only fixed and current assets are used in the ROI calculation. This treats the current liabilities as part of the financing – a method which has considerable advantages.

$$\text{ROI} = \frac{\text{Pre-tax profit}}{\text{Net assets}} = \frac{\text{Pre-tax profit}}{\text{Sales}} \times \frac{\text{Sales}}{\text{Net assets}}$$

These two ratios can be used to assess the performance of investment centres. Table 9.4 illustrates this; it shows the ratios for three investment centres, A, B and C.

If, and this is a big if, the three SBUs are identical in terms of business area and assets, it is possible to say that A is the best investment centre in terms of performance. If the management of investment centre C wishes to emulate A, they need to improve ROS, the profit/sales ratio. Perhaps, their operating costs are too high in comparison to A, or they might be discounting the product(s) in order to increase sales turnover.

The management of B should look at the other ratio and try to improve the unit's asset turnover. Their factory or business may not be operating close to 100 per cent capacity and, as a consequence, the equipment or resources are not being fully utilised.

When interpreting the ratio, care must be taken with the valuation of the assets. If the assets are new, they will not have been depreciated by a great deal, but as they age, depreciation will reduce the asset value and the asset turnover ratio will appear to improve – but all that has happened is that the asset base has decreased.

9.5.3 The problems with ROI

ROI is not an ideal internal performance measure. It has a number of problems that are listed below:

- *Percentage return versus the size of investment.* Is it better to have a return of 15 per cent on £100,000, or to have a 12 per cent return on £200,000? Shareholders would probably prefer the higher return on the smaller amount because this gives them the freedom to invest the remainder of their funds at the highest alternative rate on the stock market. A manager would probably prefer the lower return on the larger amount – as long as it was an adequate return. This is because business growth safeguards his job and as the business grows, the manager's role also expands and becomes more interesting. As a consequence, the aims of management and shareholders may differ.

Using ROI as a measure tends to limit growth – is it the intention of the directors of the group to do this? If the directors require a 15 per cent ROI for the group, and an SBU currently earns an 18 per cent return, the SBU management are unlikely to undertake investments which will reduce their ROI towards the required level. It is partly a psychological issue – the management will feel that they are doing well and that if they let the ROI fall to, say, 14.5 per cent they would have failed. The directors on the other hand might prefer growth and a return of 14.5 per cent rather than the existing size and a ROI of 18 per cent.

- *Short- versus long-term returns.* Generally speaking, a business has to invest now in order to obtain positive cash flows and profits in the future. Thus, a successful business is always reducing the profit it could earn this year in order to create a situation which will generate a greater profit in the future. But what are the rules for this? What is an acceptable current ROI, and what is the required ROI in the long term? The ROI measure does not help solve this problem.

If a manager's performance is judged on the ROI of his SBU this year, there is always the possibility that he will endeavour to make this as large as possible and, as a consequence, not invest for the future. His success in achieving a high ROI may bring him promotion to the board of directors; if this is so, another manager will have to sort out the mess he has left behind. By the time the new manager is appointed, the lack of investment in the SBU is probably beginning to show in a reducing ROI, and it will be a hard battle for the new manager to turn the SBU round.

One way to overcome this problem is to exclude items that benefit the future such as R&D, staff development and advertising from the initial calculation of profit.

	£'000	£'000
Sales		600
Less cost of sales		300
Gross profit		300
Less operating costs		170
Profit generated by operations		130
Less cost benefiting the future		
R&D	40	
Advertising	20	
Staff development	20	80
Net profit		50

The ROI can be calculated on both the profit generated by operations and the final net profit if required.

- *Different businesses and industries have different ROIs.* Traditional manufacturing organisations tend to have a large number of physical assets – tangible fixed assets. An advertising company, by comparison, does not have a great deal in the way of tangible fixed assets – its employees and their skills are the main assets of the organisation. This means that the ROI of an advertising company will normally appear to be much greater than that of, say, a steel company.
- *Massaging the ROI.* Wherever a single performance measure is used to assess a manager's performance there is the likelihood that the manager will attempt to make the measure

look as good as possible. If a large bonus depends on the measure being met the chances of the manager massaging the measure grows considerably. Is this what the head office directors intend? The asset base of the ratio can be altered by increasing or decreasing the creditors and debtors, that is, by speeding up or delaying payments to and from the business unit. A 5 per cent discount will tend to reduce the debtors, but if they would have paid in the next month anyway it is likely to be a costly exercise. Companies regularly work a considerable amount of overtime at the end of the financial year, so as to complete orders and invoice customers within the financial year, thereby increasing the annual sales revenue. A fortnight later, at the beginning of the next year, the production employees wait for work because all the orders in the pipeline have been completed ahead of schedule. The overtime cost reduces the overall profit unnecessarily.

- *Intra-group transfers.* Where goods or services are transferred between different investment centres within the group, managers must feel that the transfer price is fair, as it affects profit and, therefore, the ROI of the investment centre. If one SBU is required to transfer at a low price for taxation or other purposes, and ROI is used as a performance measure, the SBU's management may find the use of the measure demotivating.
- *Asset value.* It is quite usual for ROI to compare the profit earned during the year with the assets in place at the end of the year. If the business is growing, this will always understate the return, as the latest assets purchased will not have had a chance to start to earn a profit. This could conceivably deter management from purchasing new assets altogether, but they will certainly think carefully before purchasing them towards the end of the financial year.

The central problem with ROI (otherwise known as ROCE) is that reliance on it as a performance indicator can induce divisional managers to destroy the business they are being paid to run.

Michael Black, the vice-president of management consultancy CSC index, tells of a bank that bought a growing life insurance firm and imposed a strict return-on-capital regime. It was the wrong test to use: any growing insurance company will eat capital because costs come early, whereas returns take longer. But management remuneration was tied to capital, so it fired the sales force and the firm stopped growing. After four years return on capital (and managers' pay) had soared – but the insurance business was worth half its original price. Says Black: 'The bank had in effect paid the managers to destroy the company'.
Simon Caulkin, 'Stampede to Replace the Principle of Profit', *The Observer*, 1/97

ROI is a relative performance measure that contains no element of scale. The linking of management remuneration to ROI can result in a manager slimming down their business to a small high-yield core. This can result in the loss of a large volume of perfectly profitable trade. It is often argued that what is required is an 'absolute' measure of performance expressed in pounds or dollars. That brings us to Residual Income.

9.5.4 Residual income (RI)

The concept of residual income may have been around for a century or so, but it was certainly used in the 1950s by General Electric to overcome some of the problems encountered with ROI. For example, the information in Table 9.5 relates to the current performance of the three SBUs within the group ABC. If the directors of the group ask the SBU managers to improve their performance and aim for a group ROI of 20 per cent, what is likely to happen? The management of C will probably expand the business and reduce its ROI somewhat. The management of B will contract the business by selling assets that are not giving an adequate return. The managers of A will probably feel rather smug as they may feel that they are operating as the directors require. They are unlikely to expand slightly and reduce A's ROI to 20 per cent, but this is precisely what the group's directors require.

A residual income requires that each division's profit must bear a charge for capital – in this instance, 20 per cent. The residual figure is known as 'residual income', as shown in Table 9.6. The management of each SBU is required to maximise the unit's residual income. This is achieved if any project providing a return in excess of 20 per cent is accepted.

Table 9.5

	A £'000	B £'000	C £'000	Total £'000
Profit	110	100	35	245
Assets	500	1,000	100	1,600
ROI	22%	10%	35%	15.3%

Table 9.6

	A £'000	B £'000	C £'000
Profit	110	100	35
Less			
Capital charge (500 × 20%)	100	(1,000 × 20%) 200	(100 × 20%) 20
Residual income	10	(100)	15

Example

The managers of A have a project under consideration which involves purchasing £20,000 of assets in order to earn an annual profit of £4,100.

The effect on the residual income (RI) and ROI are shown in Table 9.7.

Table 9.7

	A £'000	
Profit (110 + 4.1)	114.1	ROI = 114.1/520 = 21.9%
less		
Captial charge (520 × 20%)	104.0	
Residual income	10.1	

The project would be accepted if the investment centre's performance is monitored using the RI approach, because the project offers a marginal increase in RI.

The ROI shows a slight decrease on the previous figure; therefore, the managers may be unwilling to accept the project if monitored on this basis.

The RI will always increase if a proposed project offers an ROI which exceeds the percentage capital charge.

Residual income has never been a particularly widely used technique in practice. Drury (1996) reported a survey that showed that 20 per cent of companies used RI whereas 55 per cent used a target ROI to assess the performance of the divisions. But ROI was not relied on, as measures such as profit before tax and the ability to stay within budget were generally regarded as being more important than ROI.

9.5.5 Current thinking about performance metrics

The problems associated with reliance on traditional financial performance metrics have been explored earlier in this text. A range of financial metrics judged to be more appropriate to the New Economy has been developed. These include economic value added (EVA) and cash flow return on investment (CFROI).

According to a recent survey by the US Institute of Cost and Management Accountants, nearly two-thirds of companies are losing faith in accounting based performance measures and are seeking new 'value criteria' to get a better handle on their businesses.

Driving the stampede to the new measures (or 'metrics' as they are fashionably known) is the obsession with shareholder value, itself booted merrily along by the tidal swell of management share options. What performance measurements best correlate with movements in a company's share price?

Simon Caulkin, 'Stampede to Replace the Principle of Profit', *The Observer*, 1/97

EVA is a variant on RI which is more attuned to the economics of a business than to the traditional accounting model. Both EVA and RI are 'profit less finance cost of capital'. But, whereas RI is based on the traditional accounting model, EVA adopts an economic valuation of the capital employed in the business. Hence, for EVA calculation purposes, the capital figure is based on assets at replacement cost – or, even possibly the whole business unit at estimated sales value.

Similarly, calculation of EVA will adopt an economic version of profit – distinguished from the traditional accounting profit by its treatment of certain items. For example, the EVA calculation may involve capitalising certain R&D costs that would be charged direct to profit on the basis of current accounting standards.

CFROI is the yield for a business unit taking the economic value of its assets as the capital base and using projected future cash flows as the return. This involves the use of discounted cash flow technique which is explored fully in CIMA's Management Accounting Decision Management (P2) course. However, be aware that CFROI is a forward-looking measure linked to what is forecast to happen in the future rather than what has happened in the past. Obviously, one has to have reservations about a performance measure based on forecasts, but the logic is significant.

The selection of appropriate metrics to measure business unit performance is essentially a behavioural and business economics issue. As indicated in the quotation above, the current thinking is that metrics should be adopted that are linked to the drivers of shareholder value. Performance should be evaluated and managers rewarded on the basis of achieving objectives that cause share price to rise.

The executive 'share option' is a classic example of issues that link management motivation and business performance. A manager is given an option to buy company shares at a future date at a specified price (say $5). If the current share price is $4, then the manager is motivated to do whatever is needed to get the share price over $5 by the date on which the executive options can be exercised. By going down the executive share option route, company owners do not even have to think too hard about value drivers and performance metrics.

However, experience has shown that this can be a dangerous strategy. Managers can be induced to do things that get the share price above a certain price on a certain date – without regard to what might happen later. This is just a variation on the problems that can arise from the use of budget compliance or ROCE/ROI/RI as the key performance indicators.

In practice, a more sophisticated approach may involve the adoption of packages of financial and non-financial performance indicators along the lines of the balanced scorecard.

Example

SM Ltd manufactures and sells mugs. These mugs carry logos to the order of customers. It has a capacity to produce up to 3,000,000 mugs per year. Its cost structure is £1,950,000 fixed production costs per year plus £0.50 variable production costs per mug. The market unit price for mugs is £2.00.

SM's profit statement for 2004 may be summarised as follows:

	£
Sales (1.5 m mugs)	3,000,000
Production Cost of Sales	2,700,000
Gross Profit	300,000
Marketing & Admin. Costs	400,000
Net Profit	(100,000)

There were no significant stocks of unsold mugs throughout 2004.

Concerned by the loss, SM's directors engage a new Chief Executive at the start of 2005. The new CE is to be paid a salary package comprised:

(1) a fixed salary of £50,000 per year,
(2) a performance bonus being 15% of Net Profit before deduction of the bonus.

SM's accounting policies include absorption costing, with stock valued at full production cost.

During 2005, the new CE did the following:

- Raised production to 2,500,000 mugs,
- Raised sales to 1,800,000 mugs,
- Raised Marketing & Admin costs (including CE salary) to £650,000

At the end of 2005 the CE met SM's directors and made the following statement:

'Gentlemen, thankyou for giving me the opportunity to exercise and develop my management skills in your business. I am delighted that I have been able to put your business successfully on track. I have now accepted a new appointment which will involve turning around another struggling company'.

Requirements

(a) Prepare a summary Profit Statement for SM in 2005. Calculate the CE's bonus.
(b) Evaluate the performance of SM and the CE having regard to any criteria you consider relevant. State whether or not the CE deserves his bonus.
(c) Having regard to the foregoing, explain the advantages of non-financial relative to financial performance measures.

Solution

(a)

SM Profit Statement, 2005

		£
Sales (1.8 m mugs)		3,600,000
Production costs	3,200,000	
Closing stock	896,000	
Production cost of sales		2,304,000
Gross profit		1,296,000
Marketing & admin. Costs		650,000
Net profit		646,000

CE bonus = £646,000 × 15% = £96,900

(b) The Net profit achieved looks remarkable, but it may be just a pure mathematical manipulation. A sharp rise in stock allows a significant element of fixed costs to be carried forward into 2006. One wonders about the worth of that stock given that the mugs carry customised logos.

If the stock has to be written off, then that will more than wipe out the profit achieved in 2005.

If production had been set at the same level as sales in 2005, then the profit achieved would have only been £100,000.

The CE certainly does not deserve his performance bonus. He appears to have carried out a cynical manipulation linked to an inappropriate choice of performance measure. Quite apart from the matter of a flawed performance measurement system, what the CE has done raises questions about his integrity.

(c) The use of simple financial performance measures may very easily induce dysfunctional behaviour. In this case, the choice of 'profit' as the performance measure seems obvious - but it invites manipulation. For one thing, the objective given to the CE is far too 'short term'.

A more sensitive approach to performance measurement in this case might involve the adoption of a number of non-financial performance indicators linked to the development of new customers, sales volume and minimising the cash conversion period of the business.

9.6 Summary

In this chapter, we have considered the manner in which a business can be split into 'strategic business units' (or 'divisions') for organisational and control purposes. The thrust behind this approach is that each unit functions as an independent business with its management taking its share of the associated risks and rewards. In this manner, the managers are motivated to adopt courses of action which are consistent with the overall objective of maximising shareholder value.

The approach involves various difficulties. One difficulty is the design and operations of a transfer pricing system for transactions between divisions in the same business. Another difficulty is selecting appropriate performance metrics to be used as determinants of management remuneration.

Handling these difficulties is a central part of the design and operation of management accounting systems.

Self-test quiz

(1) Explain the following terms and distinguish between them: cost centre, profit centre and investment centre (Section 9.2).
(2) Is there any such thing as an 'uncontrollable' cost in the context of divisional performance evaluation (Section 9.2.4)?
(3) What is the main problem with running a business unit as a cost centre (Section 9.2.4)?
(4) What is a transfer price (Section 9.3)?
(5) What are the likely minimum and maximum limits for a transfer price (Section 9.3.2)?
(6) Why does 'opportunity cost' offer a theoretically correct transfer price (Section 9.3.10)?
(7) How might transfer prices be used as a tax avoidance device (Section 9.4)?
(8) List at least four problems that may be encountered with use of ROI (or ROCE) as the main divisional performance indicator (Section 9.5.3).
(9) Explain and distinguish between RI and EVA (Section 9.5.5).
(10) Explain how the executive 'share option' is intended to influence management behaviour (Section 9.5.5).

Revision Questions

? Question 1

1.1 Division A transfers 100,000 units of a component to Division B each year.

The market price of the component is £25.
Division A's variable cost is £15 per unit.
Division A's fixed costs are £500,000 each year.

What price would be credited to Division A for each component that it transfers to Division B under

(i) dual pricing (based on marginal cost and market price)?
(ii) two-part tariff pricing (where the Divisions have agreed that the fixed fee will be £200,000)?

	Dual pricing	*Two-part tariff pricing*
(A)	£15	£15
(B)	£25	£15
(C)	£15	£17
(D)	£25	£17
(E)	£15	£20

1.2 TM plc makes components which it sells internally to its subsidiary RM Limited, as well as to its own external market. The external market price is £24.00 each unit, which yields a contribution of 40% of sales. For external sales, variable costs include £1.50 each unit for distribution costs, which are not incurred on internal sales.

TM plc has sufficient capacity to meet all of the internal and external sales. In order to maximise group profit, the component should be transferred to RM Limited at a price for each unit of:

(A) £9.60
(B) £12.90
(C) £14.40
(D) £22.50
(E) £24.00

1.3 Divisions A and B are part of the same group. Division A makes a component, two of which are used in each unit of a product made by Division B. There is no established market for the component. The transfer price for the component is Division A's variable cost plus 60%. Division A's variable cost is £10 per unit of component;

Division B's variable costs for the product, excluding components from Division A, are £6 per unit.

Division B

Units produced	1	2	3	4	5	6	7	8	9	10	11	12
Marginal revenue, £	46	44	42	40	38	36	34	32	30	28	26	24

How many units of the product will the management of Division B sell if they act so as to maximise the division's profit?

(A) 4
(B) 5
(C) 6
(D) 7
(E) 8

Data for Questions 1.4 and 1.5

CF Multinational transferred 10,000 units of product Z from its manufacturing division in the USA to its selling division in the UK during the year just ended.

The manufacturing cost of each unit of product Z was $150 (60% of which was variable cost). The market price for each unit of product Z in the USA was $270. The USA division's profit after tax for its sales to the UK division for the year just ended was $900,000.

The UK division incurred marketing and distribution costs of £30 for each unit of product Z and sold the product for £200 a unit. The UK tax rate was 30%. (Exchange rate: £1 = $1.5)

1.4 If product Z had been transferred at the USA market price, the tax rate in the USA must have been

(A) 15%
(B) 20%
(C) 25%
(D) 30%
(E) 33%

1.5 If the transfers had been made at variable cost, the UK division's profit after tax would have been

(A) £490,000
(B) £770,000
(C) £840,000
(D) £960,000
(E) £1,100,000

1.6 Division Q makes a single product. Information for the division for the year just ended is:

Sales	30,000 units
Fixed costs	£487,000
Depreciation	£247,500
Residual income	£47,200
Net assets	£1,250,000

Head Office assesses divisional performance by the residual income achieved. It uses a cost of capital of 12% a year.

Division Q's average contribution per unit was

(A) £14.82
(B) £22.81
(C) £28.06
(D) £31.06
(E) £32.81

1.7 EF plc has 3 divisions – P, Q and R – whose performance is assessed on return on investment (ROI). The ROI for the divisions for the coming year is expected to be 24%, 28% and 23%, respectively. EF plc operates a policy that all surplus cash balances are transferred to Head Office.

Three new proposals are now being considered:
P is considering investing £75,000 in order to increase profit by £21,600 each year.

Q is considering selling a machine, forecast to earn a profit of £2,500 in the coming year, for its net book value of £7,000.

R is considering giving a $2\frac{1}{2}$% discount for prompt payment. This should reduce debtors by £20,000. R's sales revenue is £500,000 each year and a 50% take up of the offer is expected.

The following division(s) will REJECT the proposal under consideration because of its effect on ROI:

(A) P
(B) Q
(C) P and Q
(D) P and R
(E) Q and R

? Question 2

CD plc is organised on a divisional basis. Two of the divisions are the Components division and the Products division. The Components division produces components d, e and f. The components are sold to a wide variety of customers including Products division at the same price. The Products division uses one unit of component d, e and f, respectively, in products X, Y and Z.

Recently, Products division has been forced to work below capacity because of limits in the supply of components from Components division. CD's chief executive has therefore directed Components division to sell all its output to Products division.

Price, cost and output data for Components division are as follows:

Component	d	e	f
	£	£	£
Unit selling price	20	20	30
Unit selling cost	7	12	10
Period fixed cost	50,000	100,000	75,000

Components division has a maximum output capacity of 50,000 of which each component must number at least 10,000.

Price, cost and output data for Products division are as follows:

Products	X £	Y £	Z £
Unit selling price	56	60	60
Unit variable cost	10	10	16
Period fixed cost	100,000	100,000	200,000

Products division has been forced to operate at 20,000 units below capacity because of the lack of components coming from Components division. Products division is able to sell all the output it can produce at the current selling price.

Requirements

(a) Assuming all components are supplied to Products division, calculate the different component and product output mixes that would maximise the profit of:
  (i) the Components division;
  (ii) the Products division;
  (iii) CD plc as a whole.
(b) Comment on the effectiveness of the transfer pricing system used by CD plc and on the merits of preventing Components division from selling outside the company.

? Question 3

(a) Outline and discuss the main objectives of a transfer pricing system.
(b) Transfer prices based on 'total cost-plus' are inappropriate. Discuss.
(c) Discuss the major factors to be considered when setting transfer prices for an international group.

? Question 4

B Limited, producing a range of minerals, is organised into two trading groups: one handles wholesale business and the other sales to retailers.

One of its products is a moulding clay. The wholesale group extracts the clay and sells it to external wholesale customers as well as to the retail group. The production capacity is 2,000 tonnes per month but at present sales are limited to 1,000 tonnes wholesale and 600 tonnes retail.

The transfer price was agreed at £200 per tonne in line with the external wholesale trade price at the 1st July which was the beginning of the budget year. As from 1st December, however, competitive pressure has forced the wholesale trade price down to £180 per tonne. The members of the retail group contend that the transfer price to them should be the same as for outside customers. The wholesale group refute the argument on the basis that the original budget established the price for the whole budget year.

The retail group produces 100 bags of refined clay from each tonne of moulding clay which it sells at £4.00 a bag. It would sell a further 40,000 bags if the retail trade price were reduced to £3.20 a bag.

Other data relevant to the operation are:

	Wholesale group £	Retail group £
Variable cost per tonne	70	60
Fixed cost per month	100,000	40,000

You are required to

(a) calculate the estimated profit for the month of December for each group and for B Limited as a whole based on transfer prices of £200 per tonne and of £180 per tonne when producing at:
   (i) 80% capacity;
   (ii) 100% capacity utilising the extra sales to supply the retail trade;

(b) comment on the results achieved under (a) and the effect of the change in the transfer price; and

(c) propose an alternative transfer price for the retail sales which would provide greater incentive for increasing sales, detailing any problems that might be encountered.

? **Question 5**

PQR is a company that develops bespoke educational computer software. The company is based in Germany. It has recently acquired two companies: W and Z.

W is a well-established company that is also based in Germany. It develops educational computer software and was a direct competitor of PQR.

Z, which is based in Malaysia, is a new but rapidly growing company that develops off the shelf educational software and also produces CD ROMs. Z was acquired so that it could produce CD ROMs for PQR and W.

The Managing Director of PQR has now realised that the acquisition of these two companies will cause problems for him in terms of planning, control and decision-making He is thinking of implementing a decentralised structure but is unsure of the advantages and disadvantages of such a structure, of how much autonomy to grant the new companies, and also which performance measure to use to appraise their performance. Consequently he has contacted you, the Finance Director of PQR, for help.

Requirements

Write a report to the Managing Director which:

 (i) explains the advantages and disadvantages that would be experienced by PQR in operating a decentralised structure;
 (ii) explains which types of responsibility centres you would recommend as being most appropriate for W and Z in a decentralised structure;
(iii) critically evaluates the possible use of the financial performance measures 'return on capital employed' and 'residual income' for the decentralised structure of PQR;
(iv) discusses the issues that need to be considered in relation to setting transfer prices for transfers made from Z to PQR and W.

? **Question 6**

Division A and Division B are both parts of C plc. A makes product i and B makes product j. Every unit of product j requires one unit of product i as a component. B purchases most of its i requirement from A although sometimes it makes purchases from outside suppliers.

Relevant details of products i and j are tabulated as follows:

	Product i	Product j
Established selling price £	30	50
Variable costs per unit		
Material	8	5
Transfers from A	–	30
Labour	5	3
Overhead	2	2
Total	15	40
Fixed costs	500,000	225,000
Annual outside demand units	100,000	25,000
Plant capacity	130,000	30,000

Investment in Divisions:

(A) £ 6,625,000
(B) £ 1,250,000

Division B is currently achieving an ROI below target. Its manager blames this on the high transfer price of product i. The manager of Division A claims that the current transfer price (£30) is appropriate since 'it is determined by the market'. The manager of Division B argues that the transfer price for the i should be set 'at production cost plus a reasonable mark up'.

The manager of Division B has made two specific proposals aimed at improving his ROI:

1. Pay £50,000 per year for new premises which should allow an additional 5,000 units of j to be sold each year at the existing price
2. The Board of C plc should intervene to reduce the transfer price of i

Requirements

(a) Write a report explaining the merits to C plc of the proposed new investment by Division B. **(5 marks)**
(b) Write a report explaining the impact of the proposed investment on the annual profit of C plc and the divisional profits of A and B, respectively. Explain the likely attitude of the Divisional managers to the investment on the basis of your findings. **(6 marks)**
(c) Advise C plc's Board on the proposal of the Division B manager concerning transfer price. Explain the general considerations that are involved in the determination of transfer prices. In answering this, consider how the position would be affected if the capacity of Division A were only 125,000 units of i. **(9 marks)**
(Total marks = 20)

Solutions to Revision Questions

☑ Solution 1

1.1 Answer: (B)

Dual price transfer price from division A's point of view is market price £25. This ensures that the supplying division can earn a profit.

The two-part tariff transfer price per unit is marginal cost £15.

1.2 Answer: (B)

Using the general profit-maximising rule, the transfer price should be (marginal cost plus opportunity cost). There is sufficient capacity to meet all demands, therefore the opportunity cost is zero and the internal variable cost should be used: $(£24 \times 60\%) - £1.50 = £12.90$.

1.3 Answer: (B)

Variable cost of components for B's product = $£10 \times 2 = £20$
Transfer price = variable cost plus 60% = £32
Division B's variable cost per product = £6
Total variable/marginal cost to B = £38

B will sell till its marginal cost equals marginal revenue, that is, when marginal revenue = £38.

1.4 Answer: (C)

	$
Market price	270
Less Total cost	150
Pre-tax profit	120
Post-tax profit per unit	
$900,000/10,000 units	90
Therefore tax is	30

Tax as a percentage of pre-tax profit = $30 + $120 \times 100 = 25\%$

1.5 Answer: (B)

	£	£
Market price in UK		200
Less: Transfer price $150 \times 0.6 \times 1/1.5	60	
UK costs	30	90
		110
Less: Tax 30%		33
		77 $\times$ 10,000 units = £770,000

431

1.6 Answer: (D)

	£
Capital charge £1.25 m × 12%	150,000
Residual income	47,200
Profit	197,200
Depreciation	247,500
Fixed costs	487,000
Total contribution	931,700
Contribution per unit	£31.06

1.7 Answer: (E)

P's return: $\dfrac{21,600}{75,000}$ = 29% accept, because higher than expected 24%.

Q's return: $\dfrac{\text{Decrease in profit}}{\text{Decrease in capital}} = \dfrac{(£2,500)}{(£7,000)}$

$= 36\%$ reject, because average ROI will reduce

R's return: $\dfrac{\text{Cost of discount}}{\text{Reduction in debtors}} = \dfrac{(£500,000 \times 50\% \times 2\frac{1}{2}\%)}{(£20,000)} = \dfrac{(£6,250)}{(£20,000)}$

$= 31\%$ reject, because average ROI will reduce

 ## Solution 2

Tips

- This is a simple question that illustrates the central problem behind transfer pricing. It turns around the concept of marginality. You must understand issues connected with marginal cost and marginal revenue.
- The critical issue is that the pattern of output that maximises the reported profit of the Products division is based on a distorted perception of marginal cost. The Products division manager will perceive the marginal cost of components as being their market selling price – not the true marginal cost to CD plc as a whole.
- Another issue is that the manager of the Components division is indifferent between whether he sells to outside customers or to the Products division. Requirement (b) invites you to comment on the implications of this for CD plc.

(a) The rankings of the products can be determined in each case by simply calculating the contributions of the products from the three alternative points of view.
  (i) *Components division*

	d £ per unit	e £ per unit	f £ per unit
Selling price	20	20	30
Variable cost	7	12	10
Contribution	13	8	20
Ranking	2nd	3rd	1st

The division profit will be maximised by a mix of:
10,000 d/X
10,000 e/Y
30,000 f/Z

(ii) *Products division*

	X	Y	Z
	£ per unit	£ per unit	£per unit
Selling price	56	60	60
Variable cost	10	10	16
Transfer cost of d,e,f	20	20	30
Contribution	26	30	14
Ranking	2nd	1st	3rd

The division profit will be maximised by a mix of:
10,000 d/X
30,000 e/Y
10,000 f/Z

(iii) *CD plc as a whole*

	X	Y	Z
	£ per unit	£ per unit	£per unit
Selling price	56	60	60
Variable cost	10	10	16
Component variable cost	7	12	10
Contribution	39	38	34
Ranking	1st	2nd	3rd

The whole company's profit will be maximised by a mix of:
30,000 d/X
10,000 e/Y
10,000 f/Z

(b) A perfect transfer pricing system has to satisfy three criteria. First, it has to give a 'fair' impression of divisional profit. Second, it has to avoid distorting the decision-making processes in the business. Third, it has to be cheap and simple to operate. In practice, almost no system of transfer pricing is capable of meeting all three of these criteria.

The transfer pricing system used by CD plc involves transfers at 'market selling price' accompanied by an obligation to supply all components internally. This system possibly meets the first and third criteria, but it certainly does not meet the second. For one thing, who decides which components are to be prioritised? If the decision is left to the Components division, then it is likely that a pattern of output will emerge (see (i) above) that gives an aggregate profit to the two divisions of £1,165,000 − £100,000 less than the maximum possible (see (iii) above).

One possibility, if 'outside' sales are allowed, is that production of Z could be discontinued and all the output of component f be sold to outside customers. This would increase aggregate profit by £60,000 over the maximum otherwise possible – by foregoing £300,000 net revenue but avoiding £160,000 of variable costs and £200,000 of fixed costs.

 Solution 3

Tip

A straightforward essay-type question. Remember to read the question carefully and plan your answer.

(a) The objectives of a transfer pricing system are:
(i) to record intra-company transfers;
(ii) to enable a fair evaluation of divisional performance;

      (iii) to motivate divisional managers to make sound decisions and achieve goal congruence;

      (iv) to reduce the overall tax burden in international transfers;

      (v) to encourage a healthy inter-divisional competitive spirit;

      (vi) to preserve the autonomy of divisional managers.

(b) Transfer prices based on 'total cost-plus' are often used when there is no competitive market for the product. However, these prices include fixed costs, which can be mis-read as variable costs leading to incorrect pricing and output decisions. The receiving division could make a suboptimal decision to restrict output to below that of the optimal level of the group.

    The inefficiencies of the supplying division are passed on to the receiving division when actual full costs are used as a basis for setting transfer prices. This would not provide a fair representation of divisional performance evaluation and will undermine divisional autonomy.

    Furthermore, when actual cost-plus is used, there is actually an incentive for the supplying division to overspend. This is because all of the costs incurred will be passed on, and the supplying division will also earn a profit on all costs incurred.

(c) When setting transfer prices for an international group, the following points need to be considered:

    Taxation – transfer prices must be set so that the tax burden for the group as a whole is minimised.

    Repatriation of funds – this is an important factor to consider when dealing with countries with a high inflation rate or stringent foreign exchange regulations. Transfer prices have to be set depending on where and in which currency cash balances should be held.

    Currency risk management – decisions concerning in which currency to invoice and in which currency to settle invoice and so on.

    Import duties – transfer prices kept as low as possible when goods are imported into countries with high import duties.

    Minority shareholders – transfer prices can be used to reduce the amount of profit paid to minority shareholders.

    Profit sharing – profit sharing in different parts of the group can influence the transfer price set.

 ## Solution 4

Tips

- You will need to calculate profit figures for four different situations. Do not waste time by starting from scratch each time. It is much quicker to use your first profit calculation as a base, and then adjust this profit figure for the effects of changes in capacity and transfer price.
- There is no single correct answer to part (c). Your answer may be quite different from ours but as long as it is accompanied by logical reasoning you should earn all the marks available.

(a) (i) *80% capacity; transfer price £200 per tonne*

		Wholesale group £'000		Retail group £'000	B Ltd total £'000
Internal transfers	600t × £200	120		–	
External sales	1,000t × £180	180	60,000 bags × £4	240	
		300		240	
Variable costs	1,600t × £70	112	600t × £60	36	
Transfer charge				120	
Fixed cost		100		40	
Monthly profit		88		44	132

80% capacity; transfer price £180 per tonne

	Wholesale group £'000	Retail group £'000	B Ltd total £'000
Monthly profit as above	88	44	132
Change in transfer charge 600t × £20	(12)	12	
Monthly profit	76	56	132

(ii) *100% capacity; transfer price £200 per tonne*

	Wholesale group £'000		Retail group £'000	B Ltd Total £'000
Monthly profit from (a) (i)	88		44	132
Extra internal transfer charge 400t × £200	80		(80)	
Extra variable costs 400t × £70	(28)	400t × £60	(24)	(52)
Extra external sales	–	40,000 bags × £3.20	128	128
Redn. in revenue from existing sales	–	60,000 bags × £0.80	(48)	(48)
Monthly profit	140		20	160

100% capacity, transfer price £180 per tonne

	Wholesale group £'000	Retail group £'000	B Ltd Total £'000
Monthly profit from (a) (ii)	140	20	160
Change in transfer charge 1,000 × £20	(20)	20	
Monthly profit	120	40	160

(b) Profit for B Limited as a whole would not be affected by the change in transfer price but operating at 100% capacity produces a £28,000 increase in profit.

However, the profit earned by the Retail group would be lower at 100% capacity for both transfer prices. Therefore, there is a lack of goal congruence because the manager of the Retail group will prefer to operate at 80% capacity, to the detriment of the company as a whole.

(c) At the moment, the Retail group is bearing all of the effect of the revenue reduction as a result of the lower external selling price.

The transfer price needs to be set so as to encourage the Retail group to be willing to increase output.

Perhaps, the best approach would be to have a separate transfer price for the extra output, which provides each group with a fair share of the incremental contribution earned.

	£'000
Incremental contribution from 20% increase in capacity (160 − 132)	28
Equal share credited to wholesale group	14
Plus incremental variable costs (from (a) (ii))	28
Transfer charge for extra 20% capacity	42

The resulting monthly profit will be, at 100% capacity:

	Wholesale group £'000	Retail group £'000	B Ltd total £'000
Monthly profit from (a) (ii)	120	40	160
Change in transfer charge			
Existing charge 400t × £180	(72)	72	
Revised charge as above	42	(42)	
Revised monthly profit	90	70	160

Both groups will experience an increase in profit on the extra output and both will therefore be willing to increase activity to 100p10.5 capacity.

The recommended transfer price structure is, therefore,

- £180 per tonne for the first 600 tonnes transferred
- £105 (£42,000/400t) per tonne for the next 400 tonnes transferred

Possible problems that might be encountered include:

- If the potential external market for wholesale increases there will be an opportunity cost involved in supplying the Retail group
- Confusion may arise with a two-tier transfer pricing structure

 Solution 5

Report

To: Managing Director
Re: Acquisition of W and Z and decentralisation issues

From: Finance Director
Date: 26 May 2004

Further to our recent acquisition of W and Z, I have prepared a report which I hope addresses the concerns which you have raised.

Advantages and disadvantages that we would experience by operating a decentralised structure

Advantages
- Improved decision-making process – quality and speed.
- Motivational – delegation of decision-making.
- Autonomy for divisional managers.
- Allow top management to focus on strategic rather than operational matters.
- Reduce head office bureaucracy.
- Good training ground for junior and middle management.

Disadvantages

- Dysfunctional decision-making, where divisions make decisions in their own best interests which may not be good from the company's viewpoint.
- Costs of activities that are common to all divisions may be greater for a decentralised organisation rather than a centralised one.
- Loss of control by top management as decision-making is delegated to the divisional managers.

The above advantages and disadvantages of decentralisation would apply to our company. However, some of those in favour and against are linked. For example, the ability of decentralised operations managers to make speedy decisions will increase the lack of control in circumstances in which the head office cannot be informed of these decisions in a timely manner. This was more important in the past. Whereas Z is based overseas, modern communications like email will enable us to keep in close contact.

Responsibility centres and decentralised structures

Types of responsibility centres include

- cost centres,
- profit centres,
- investment centres.

Conditions

- Divisional structure is best suited to those companies engaged in several dissimilar activities.
- Activities should be as independent as possible for decentralisation to be successful.

Recommendation

- W and Z could become cost centres, profit centres or investment centres.
- W and Z have already operated independently so maintaining this structure would seem feasible. Therefore, a profit or investment centre structure may work.
- W and Z would need to be integrated with our systems, policies and procedures.
- Integration of the two companies with our company must be done in such a way as to promote goal congruence and to discourage sub-optimal behaviour.

There are, however, potential problems which may make decentralisation difficult:

- PQR and W were direct competitors. This situation must cease and the companies should work through their client lists and decide who will manage particular clients so that crossover between clients is avoided, thus eliminating internal competition.
- They should also seek to find a way to strengthen their position in the market by working together in order to secure new clients and business going forward.
- Obvious decisions should be taken such as agreeing target markets and not competing against each other when bidding for work (bespoke offerings). Once the lines have been drawn, the two companies would be free to operate within their own sectors.
- There may be some synergies between the work and offerings of Z and both PQR and W. This may be particularly true in the area of identifying new business opportunities – buyers of bespoke software may have some generic needs and vice versa. Salespeople/bidding

teams (W) need to be trained to identify these opportunities. If divisions are autonomous, some reward structure may be payable. Alternatively, a separate sales/marketing division covering all the companies may be considered.

Financial performance measures – ROCE and RI

The objective of performance measurement is to

- promote goal congruence;
- encourage initiative and motivation;
- provide feedback to management;
- encourage long-term rather than short-term views.

The method of performance measurement we will choose depends on the form of decentralisation chosen for W and Z.

Autonomous units (which is being recommended) should have:

(1) Financial targets – revenue generation, cashflow, profit, ROCE, RI.
(2) Non-financial targets – market share, sales growth, product development and so on.

We will need to set the targets centrally and implement them locally. By doing so, we should be able to avoid some of the pit falls associated with decentralisation. Once the plans have been agreed, local managers will have the autonomy to implement the plans working within the parameters we set.

Return on capital employed

This is also known as ROI and is calculated as follows

$$\text{ROCE} = \frac{\text{Earnings before interest and tax}}{\text{Capital employed}} \times 100\%$$

This method has the following advantages and disadvantages.

Advantages
- Widely used and accepted.
- As a relative measure, it enables comparisons to be made between divisions or companies of different sizes.
- It can be broken down into secondary ratios for more detailed analysis.

Disadvantages
- May lead to dysfunctional decision-making. For example, a division with a current ROCE of 30% would not wish to accept a project offering a ROCE of 25%, as this would reduce its current figure.
- Different accounting policies can confuse comparisons.
- ROCE increases with the age of assets if NBVs are used, thus giving managers an incentive to hang on to possibly inefficient, obsolete machines.

Residual income

Residual income is divisional profit less an imputed interest charge for invested capital.

The imputed interest charge is the amount of capital employed in the division multiplied by the cost of capital.

This method has the following advantages and disadvantages.

Advantages
- It reduces ROCE's problem of rejecting projects with an ROCE in excess of the company's target, but lower than the division's current ROCE.
- The cost of financing a division is brought to the attention of divisional managers.

Disadvantages
- Does not facilitate comparisons between divisions.
- Does not relate the size of a division's profit to the assets employed in order to obtain that profit.

Transfer prices for Z

It is likely that Z will be asked to supply off the shelf products and CD-ROMs for the customers of PQR and W. Therefore, transfer pricing will be an issue for PQR. The transfer price should be set at marginal cost plus opportunity cost to ensure profit maximisation for the group. However, if no opportunity cost exists, then the transfer price will be set at marginal cost. If this situation arises, it will be demotivating for Z as no profit is realised and may, therefore, discourage them from transferring to PQR and W. PQR, therefore, needs to monitor inter company activity carefully to ensure that the correct decisions are made. If a situation is envisaged where Z transfers at marginal cost only, then the company would need to consider avoiding dysfunctional behaviour remedying this by introducing a two-part tariff system or a dual pricing system.

Another issue to consider when operating in two countries is that the group can use its transfer pricing policies to move profits around the world and thereby minimise the global tax liability. Where there are differential tax rates, it is beneficial to set a transfer price which results in the highest taxable profit in the country with the lowest tax rates.

 ## Solution 6

(a) So long as the proposed project does not displace other sales (i.e. that there is no opportunity cost associated with the 5,000 extra j units sold) then the impact is as follows:

C plc

Extra annual revenues	£	250,000
Variable costs – i		75,000
Variable costs – j		50,000
Fixed costs		50,000
Profit		75,000

Clearly, the project offers a profit advantage and it should be adopted.

(b) The problem arises out of how the extra profit is distributed between the two divisions. Using the £30 transfer price the impact is as follows:

		Division A	Division B
Capital employed	£	6.525 m	1.125 m
Profit at existing sales levels		1.375 m	0.025 m
ROI at existing sales levels		21%	2%
Impact of proposal			
Sales/Transfers		150,000	250,000
Variable costs		75,000	50,000
Transfer costs		nil	150,000
Fixed costs		nil	50,000
Profit		75,000	nil
Total profit with proposal		1.450 m	0.025 m
ROI with proposal		22%	2%

The transfer pricing system works in a manner that locates all the incremental profit from the project with Division A. Given that the decision-maker is the manager of Division B, this makes adoption of the project problematic. In spite of its merits, the project might not be adopted since B takes all the risk but none of the reward.

(c) Any transfer pricing system has to reconcile two basic criteria: (1) that the system should provide an equitable distribution of profit between divisions and (2) that the system should not distort decision-making behaviour. In practice, it is difficult to find any transfer pricing system or any unique transfer price for an intermediate good that does reconcile these two criteria.

C plc's existing system is based on market price. This does, under some circumstances, provide for a fair distribution of profit between the divisions. However, it may distort decision-making As seen in the example explored, an attractive project may be declined because the benefit it offers is all concentrated with a division that does not decide on the project or operate it. This is clearly inappropriate since B has to take the risk of the project but A gets all the rewards.

This suggests that a transfer price should be set at a level nearer to the marginal cost. If the transfer price for the i were set at marginal cost, then all the reward from the project would reside with Division B, which may be a reasonable result. A small mark up on marginal cost might provide a reward to A without being a significant disincentive to A.

However, the merits of particular systems and prices depend very much on circumstances. If Division A only had a capacity of 125,000 units and it was directed to supply B in order to run the project, then C plc as a whole would incur an opportunity cost of £15 for each unit of i transferred to support extra production of j. This £15 is the contribution from the outside sales of i that would have to be foregone. In this case, the merits of the project would become neutral when a £75,000 opportunity cost (5,000 units × £15) is considered. The transfer price of £30 would correctly reflect C plc's cost for the units transferred (£15 variable cost plus £15 opportunity cost) and there would be no scope for dysfunctional behaviour. The manager of Division B would correctly perceive that the project would offer nil profit.

If there is an efficient outside market for i, then it might be very difficult to have any transfer price other than £30. Any price higher than that would induce Division B to buy outside. Division A would vigorously resist any lower price, particularly, if the Division was operating at full capacity.

So long as Division A is operating comfortably inside capacity, then a case might be made for reducing the transfer price below the outside market price. This is so because an internal transfer does not involve the risk or administrative costs of an outside sale. In the circumstances specified in the question, a transfer price of £25 might well be justified and ultimately acceptable to both divisional managers.

Preparing for the Examination

Revision Questions

Foreword

The revision questions given below are mostly old CIMA examination questions, which have been lightly adapted in some cases. Some of these are taken from old MAPE papers and are unambiguously suitable for use as practice examination questions.

Questions taken from papers under discontinued schemes do not all follow the style or arrangement of the current MAPE paper. Such questions should therefore be considered as teaching or study exercises although you may be sure that their content and standard is appropriate for that purpose. Students should refer carefully to old MAPE papers when preparing to sit the examination in order to ensure that they are familiar with the style and arrangement of questions that they are likely to encounter.

That said, the questions in this chapter have been split into four sections (A multi-choice, A non-multi-choice, B and C) which are intended to correspond approximately to the arrangement of the Performance Evaluation examination paper. A number of the questions in Section C may be considered as general teaching or study exercises which are relevant to any part of the Performance Evaluation paper.

The relevance of the Revision Questions to the Learning Outcomes is tabulated below. Note that the Learning Outcomes are listed in the order in which they appear in this text. That is, an order which provides a logical study sequence. This is not the same as the order in which the Learning Outcomes are listed in the Syllabus.

Learning outcomes	Questions
Chapter 2 – Cost Accounting Systems (A)	
Compare and contrast marginal and absorption costing methods in respect of profit reporting and stock valuation	2.7, 7.9, 22a,
Apply marginal and absorption costing approaches in a job, batch and process environments	1.1, 1.3, 2.4, 4.7, 4.8, 9.2,
Prepare ledger accounts according to context: marginal or absorption based in job, batch or process environments, including WIP and related accounts	3.9, 3.10, 6.6, 8.2, 9.3, 9.7, 10.6, 11.7, 26, 28, 35
Chapter 3 – The Theory and Practice of Standard Costing (B)	
Explain why and how standards are set in a manufacturing and service industries with particular reference to the maximisation of efficiency and minimisation of waste	1.4, 4.9, 18
Calculate and interpret material, labour, variable overhead, fixed overhead and sales variances	1.5, 2.6, 3.1, 3.2, 3.3, 4.5, 4.6, 5.1, 5.2, 6.3, 6.4, 6.5, 7.2, 9.8, 10.9, 10.10, 12.3, 20d,

Learning outcomes	Questions
Prepare and discuss a report which reconciles budget and actual profit using absorption and/or marginal costing principles	22b, 22c, 23, 25,

Chapter 4 – Standard Costing and Performance Evaluation (A and B)

Calculate and explain planning and operational variances	1.6, 1.7, 1.8, 9.5, 11.1, 11.2,
Discuss the behavioural implications of setting standard costs	22d
Apply standard costing methods within costing systems and demonstrate the reconciliation of budgeted and actual profit margins	7.5, 7.6, 10.1, 10.2, 11.3, 14a,
Prepare reports using a range internal and external benchmarks and interpret the results	14b, 14c,

Chapter 5 – The Theory and Practice of Budgeting (C)

Explain why organisations prepare forecasts and plans	3.4, 20f, 34, 38
Calculate projected product/service volumes employing appropriate forecasting techniques	2.8, 2.9, 5.5, 7.1, 8.1, 12.5, 13f,
Calculate projected revenues and costs based on product/service volumes, pricing, pricing strategies and cost structures	2.5, 2.10, 4.4, 4.10, 7.3, 7.4, 8.3, 10.4, 10.7, 10.11, 13a, 13b,
Describe and explain the possible purposes of budgets including planning, communication, co-ordination, motivation, authorisation, control and evaluation	20c, 30,
Evaluate and apply alternative approaches to budgeting	5.3, 5.8, 6.7, 13c, 13d, 13e, 20a,
Calculate the consequences of 'What if' scenarios and evaluate their impact on master profit and loss account and balance sheet	31, 44, 46

Chapter 6 – Budgetary Control (C)

Explain the ideas of feedback and feed-forward control and their applications in the use of budgets for control	2.3, 16, 19,
Explain the concept of responsibility accounting and its importance in the construction of functional budgets that support the overall master budget	20e
Identify controllable and uncontrollable costs in the context of responsibility accounting and explain why 'uncontrollable' costs may or may not be allocated to responsibility centres	22f,
Evaluate performance using fixed and flexible budget reports	4.2, 41
Explain the impact of budgetary control systems on human behaviour	4.3, 17c,

Chapter 7 – Budgeting and Performance Evaluation (C)

Evaluate projected performance by calculating key metrics including profitability, liquidity and asset turnover ratios	11.8, 11.9, 12.2, 27,
Discuss the role of non-financial performance indicators and compare and contrast traditional approaches to budgeting with recommendations based on the 'balanced scorecard'	5.4, 8.9, 8.10, 10.8, 17a,
Evaluate the criticisms of budgeting particularly from the advocates of techniques that are 'beyond budgeting'	15, 17d,

Chapter 8 – Developments in Management Accounting (A)

Explain the role of MRP and ERP systems in supporting standard costing systems, calculating variances and facilitating the posting of ledger entries	2.1, 2.2, 6.8, 6.10, 14e,
Evaluate the impact of JIT manufacturing methods on cost accounting and the use of 'backflush' accounting when WIP stock is minimal	1.9, 3.8, 5.6, 14f, 36, 43,
Compare activity-based costing with traditional marginal and absorption costing methods and evaluate its potential as a system of cost accounting	8.4, 8.5, 8.6, 9.6, 24, 32, 33, 37, 45,

Explain the origins of throughput accounting as 'super variable costing' and its application as a variant of marginal or variable costing	1.2, 7.7, 7.8, 9.1, 11.4, 11.5, 11.6, 12.1, 22e,

Chapter 9 – Responsibility Centres and Transfer Pricing (D)

Discuss the use of cost, revenue, profit and investment centres in devising organisation structure and in management control	4.1, 21,
Prepare cost information in appropriate formats for cost centre managers, taking due account of controllable/uncontrollable cost and the importance of budget flexing	41
Prepare revenue and cost information in appropriate formats for profit and investment centre managers, taking due account of cost variability, attributable costs, controllable costs and identification of appropriate measures of profit centre 'contribution'	3.5, 3.6, 3.7,
Calculate and apply measures of performance for investment centres (often strategic business units or divisions of larger groups)	1.10, 5.9, 5.10, 6.1, 6.2, 10.3, 17b, 40,
Discuss the likely behavioural consequences of the use of performance metrics in managing cost, profit and investment centres	17f, 39
Explain the typical consequences of a divisional structure for performance measurement as divisions compete or trade with each other	14d, 17e, 29, 42,
Identify the likely consequences of different approaches to transfer pricing for divisional decision-making, divisional and group profitability, the motivation of divisional management and the autonomy of individual divisions	5.7, 6.9, 8.7, 8.8, 9.4, 10.5, 12.4,

Reference to Syllabus items:

(A) – Cost Accounting Systems
(B) – Standard Costing
(C) – Budgeting
(D) – Control and Performance Measurement of Responsibility Centres

Note: Some of the Revision Questions draw on more than one of the Learning Outcomes. The indexing above relates questions to the main Learning Outcome that those questions (and sub-questions, where relevant) draw on. Some of the questions and sub-questions are most accessible only to students who have completed study of the whole course.

Section A – Multi-choice questions

 Question 1

The following data are given for sub-questions 1.1 and 1.2 below.

The following data relate to a manufacturing company. At the beginning of August, there was no inventory. During August 2,000 units of product X were produced, but only 1,750 units were sold. The financial data for product X for August were as follow:

	£
Materials	40,000
Labour	12,600
Variable production overheads	9,400
Fixed production overheads	22,500
Variable selling costs	6,000
Fixed selling costs	19,300
Total costs for X for August	109,800

1.1 The value of inventory of X at 31 August using a marginal costing approach is

(A) £6,575
(B) £7,750
(C) £8,500
(D) £10,562   **(2 marks)**

1.2 The value of inventory of X at 31 August using a throughput accounting approach is

(A) £5,000
(B) £6,175
(C) £6,575
(D) £13,725   **(2 marks)**

1.3 A company has a budget to produce 5,000 units of product B in December. The budget for December shows that for Product B the opening inventory will be 400 units and the closing inventory will be 900 units. The monthly budgeted production cost data for product B for December is as follows:

Variable direct costs per unit	£6.00
Variable production overhead costs per unit	£3.50
Total fixed production overhead costs	£29,500

The company absorbs overheads on the basis of the budgeted number of units produced.

The budgeted profit for product B for December, using **absorption costing**, is

(A) £2,950 lower than it would be using **marginal costing**.
(B) £2,950 greater than it would be using **marginal costing**.
(C) £4,700 lower than it would be using **marginal costing**.
(D) £4,700 greater than it would be using **marginal costing**.   **(2 marks)**

1.4 Y has set the current budget for operating costs for its delivery vehicles, using the formula described below. Analysis has shown that the relationship between miles driven and total monthly vehicle operating costs is described in the following formula:

$$y = £800 + £0.0002x^2$$

where

y is the total monthly operating cost of the vehicles, and
x is the number of miles driven each month

The budget for vehicle operating costs needs to be adjusted for expected inflation in vehicle operating costs of 3%, which is not included in the relationship shown above.

The delivery mileage for September was 4,100 miles, and the total actual vehicle operating costs for September were £5,000.

The total vehicle operating cost variance for September was closest to

(A) £713 Adverse
(B) £737 Adverse
(C) £777 Adverse
(D) £838 Adverse   **(2 marks)**

1.5 The CIMA official definition of the 'variable production overhead efficiency variance' is set out below with two blank sections.

'Measures the difference between the variable overhead cost budget flexed on _____ and the variable overhead cost absorbed by _____.'

Which combination of phrases correctly completes the definition?

	Blank 1	Blank 2
(A)	actual labour hours	budgeted output
(B)	standard labour hours	budgeted output
(C)	actual labour hours	output produced
(D)	standard labour hours	output produced

(2 marks)

The following data are given for sub-questions 1.6 to 1.8 below.
The following data relate to Product Z and its raw material content for September.

Budget
Output   11,000 units of Z
Standard materials content   3 kg per unit at $4.00 per kg

Actual
Output   10,000 units of Z
Materials purchased and used   32,000 kg at $4.80 per kg

It has now been agreed that the standard price for the raw material purchased in September should have been $5 per kg.

1.6 The materials planning price variance for September was

(A) $6,000 Adverse
(B) $30,000 Adverse
(C) $32,000 Adverse
(D) $33,000 Adverse   (2 marks)

1.7 The materials operational usage variance for September was

(A) $8,000 Adverse
(B) $9,600 Adverse
(C) $9,600 Favourable
(D) $10,000 Adverse   (2 marks)

1.8 The materials operational price variance for September was

(A) $6,000 Adverse
(B) $6,400 Favourable
(C) $30,000 Adverse
(D) $32,000 Adverse   (2 marks)

1.9 A company operates a just-in-time purchasing and production system and uses a back-flush accounting system with a single trigger point at the point of sale. A summary of the transactions that took place in June (valued at cost) is:

	£
Conversion costs incurred	890,000
Finished goods produced	1,795,000
Finished goods sold	1,700,000
Conversion costs allocated	840,000

The two items debited to the cost of goods sold account in June would be

	£		£
(A)	890,000	and	95,000
(B)	1,700,000	and	50,000
(C)	1,700,000	and	95,000
(D)	1,795,000	and	50,000

(2 marks)

1.10 Division Y has reported annual operating profits of £40.2 m. This was after charging £6 m for the full cost of launching a new product that is expected to last 3 years. Division Y has a risk adjusted cost of capital of 11% and is paying interest on a substantial bank loan at 8%. The historical cost of the assets in Division Y, as shown on its balance sheet, is £100 m, and the replacement cost has been estimated at £172 m.

Ignore the effects of taxation.

The EVA® for Division Y is

(A) £23.28 m

(B) £25.28 m

(C) £29.20 m

(D) £30.44 m

(2 marks)

Question 2

2.1 *Definition 1*: 'A system that converts a production schedule into a listing of materials and components required to meet the schedule so that items are available when needed.'

Definition 2: 'An accounting system that focuses on ways by which the maximum return per unit of bottleneck activity can be achieved.'

Which of the following pairs of terms correctly matches definitions 1 and 2 above?

	Definition 1	*Definition 2*
(A)	Manufacturing resources planning (MRP2)	Backflush accounting
(B)	Material requirements planning (MRP1)	Throughput accounting
(C)	Material requirements planning (MRP1)	Theory of constraints
(D)	Supply chain management	Throughput accounting

(2 marks)

2.2 Which of the following statements is/are true?

(i) Enterprise Resource Planning (ERP) systems use complex computer systems, usually comprehensive databases, to provide plans for every aspect of a business.

(ii) Flexible Manufacturing Systems (FMS) are simple systems with low levels of automation that offer great flexibility through a skilled workforce working in teams.

(iii) Just-in-time (JIT) purchasing requires the purchasing of large quantities of inventory items so that they are available immediately when they are needed in the production process.

(A) (i) only

(B) (i) and (ii) only

(C) (i) and (iii) only

(D) (ii) and (iii) only

(2 marks)

2.3 Which of the following statements apply to feed-forward control?

  (i) It is the measurement of differences between planned outputs and actual outputs.
 (ii) It is the measurement of differences between planned outputs and forecast outputs.
(iii) Target costing is an example.
(iv) Variance analysis is an example.

(A) (i) and (iii)
(B) (i) and (iv)
(C) (ii) and (iii)
(D) (ii) and (iv)   **(2 marks)**

2.4 The final stage of production adds Material Z to units that have been transferred into Process D and converts them to the finished product. There are no losses in Process D. Data for Process D in the latest period are shown below:

	Units
Opening work in progress	225
Material Z: 80% complete	
Conversion costs: 80% complete	
Units transferred in	500
Units transferred out	575
Closing work in progress	150
Material Z: 60% complete	
Conversion costs: 40% complete	

The equivalent units to be used in the calculations of the cost per equivalent unit for Material Z and Conversion Costs, assuming first-in-first-out (FIFO) costing are

	Material Z	Conversion costs
(A)	485	455
(B)	485	500
(C)	575	455
(D)	575	500

(2 marks)

2.5 If the budgeted fixed costs increase, the **gradient** of the line plotted on the budgeted Profit/Volume (P/V) chart will

(A) increase.
(B) decrease.
(C) not change.
(D) become curvi-linear.   **(2 marks)**

2.6   A company operates a standard costing system and prepares monthly financial statements. All materials purchased during February were used during that month. After all transactions for February were posted, the general ledger contained the following balances:

	Debit £	Credit £
Finished goods control	27,450	
Materials price variance	2,400	
Materials usage variance		8,400
Labour rate variance	5,600	
Labour efficiency variance		3,140
Variable production overhead variance	2,680	
Fixed production overhead variance		3,192

The standard cost of the goods produced during February was £128,500.

The actual cost of the goods produced during February was

(A) £96,998
(B) £124,448
(C) £132,552
(D) £160,002   **(2 marks)**

2.7   Overheads will always be over-absorbed when

(A) actual output is higher than budgeted output.
(B) actual overheads incurred are higher than the amount absorbed.
(C) actual overheads incurred are lower than the amount absorbed.
(D) budgeted overheads are lower than the overheads absorbed.   **(2 marks)**

2.8   The following extract is taken from the production cost budget of L plc:

Output	2,000 units	3,500 units
Total cost	£12,000	£16,200

The budget cost allowance for an output of 4,000 units would be

(A) £17,600
(B) £18,514
(C) £20,400
(D) £24,000   **(2 marks)**

2.9   A company uses time series and regression techniques to forecast future sales. It has derived a seasonal variation index to use with the multiplicative (proportional) seasonal variation model. The index values for the first three quarters are as follows:

Quarter	Index value
Q1	80
Q2	80
Q3	110

The index value for the fourth quarter (Q4) is

(A) −270
(B) −269
(C)   110
(D)   130   **(2 marks)**

2.10 The budgeted profit statement for a company, with all figures expressed as percentages of revenue, is as follows:

	%
Revenue	100
Variable costs	30
Fixed costs	22
Profit	48

After the formulation of the above budget, it has now been realised that the sales volume will only be 60% of that originally forecast.

The revised profit, expressed as a percentage of the revised revenue, will be

(A) 20%
(B) 33.3%
(C) 60%
(D) 80%   (**2 marks**)

? **Question 3**

The following data are given for sub-questions 3.1 to 3.3 below.

A company uses standard absorption costing. The following information was recorded by the company for October:

	Budget	Actual
Output and sales (units)	8,700	8,200
Selling price per unit	£26	£31
Variable cost per unit	£10	£10
Total fixed overheads	£34,800	£37,000

3.1 The sales price variance for October was

(A) £38,500 favourable
(B) £41,000 favourable
(C) £41,000 adverse
(D) £65,600 adverse   (**2 marks**)

3.2 The sales volume profit variance for October was

(A) £6,000 adverse
(B) £6,000 favourable
(C) £8,000 adverse
(D) £8,000 favourable   (**2 marks**)

3.3 The fixed overhead volume variance for October was

(A) £2,000 adverse
(B) £2,200 adverse
(C) £2,200 favourable
(D) £4,200 adverse   (**2 marks**)

3.4 A master budget comprises the

(A) budgeted income statement and budgeted cash flow only.
(B) budgeted income statement and budgeted balance sheet only.
(C) budgeted income statement and budgeted capital expenditure only.
(D) budgeted income statement, budgeted balance sheet and budgeted cash flow only. **(2 marks)**

The following data are given for sub-questions 1.5 and 1.6 below.
The annual operating statement for a company is shown below:

	£'000
Sales revenue	800
Less variable costs	390
Contribution	410
Less fixed costs	90
Less depreciation	20
Net income	300
Assets	£6.75 m

The cost of capital is 13% per annum.

3.5 The return on investment (ROI) for the company is closest to

(A) 4.44%
(B) 4.74%
(C) 5.77%
(D) 6.07% **(2 marks)**

3.6 The residual income (RI) for the company is closest to

	£'000
(A)	467
(B)	487
(C)	557
(D)	577

(2 marks)

3.7 A company has reported annual operating profits for the year of £89.2 m after charging £9.6 m for the full development costs of a new product that is expected to last for the current year and two further years. The cost of capital is 13% per annum. The balance sheet for the company shows fixed assets with a historical cost of £120 m. A note to the balance sheet estimates that the replacement cost of these fixed assets at the beginning of the year is £168 m. The assets have been depreciated at 20% per year.

The company has a working capital of £27.2 m.

Ignore the effects of taxation.

The Economic Value Added® (EVA) of the company is closest to

(A) £64.16 m
(B) £70.56 m
(C) £83.36 m
(D) £100.96 m **(2 marks)**

3.8 Which of the following definitions are correct?

   (i) Just-in-time (JIT) systems are designed to produce or procure products or components as they are required for a customer or for use, rather than for inventory;
   (ii) Flexible manufacturing systems (FMS) are integrated, computer-controlled production systems, capable of producing any of a range of parts and of switching quickly and economically between them;
   (iii) Material requirements planning (MRP) systems are computer-based systems that integrate all aspects of a business so that the planning and scheduling of production ensures components are available when needed.

   (A) (i) only
   (B) (i) and (ii) only
   (C) (i) and (iii) only
   (D) (ii) and (iii) only   **(2 marks)**

3.9 RJD Ltd operates a standard absorption costing system. The following fixed production overhead data is available for one month:

Budgeted output	200,000	units
Budgeted fixed production overhead	£1,000,000	
Actual fixed production overhead	£1,300,000	
Total fixed production overhead variance	£100,000	Adverse

The actual level of production was

   (A) 180,000 units.
   (B) 240,000 units.
   (C) 270,000 units.
   (D) 280,000 units.   **(2 marks)**

3.10 WTD Ltd produces a single product. The management currently uses marginal costing but is considering using absorption costing in the future.

The budgeted fixed production overheads for the period are £500,000. The budgeted output for the period is 2,000 units. There were 800 units of opening inventory at the beginning of the period and 500 units of closing inventory at the end of the period.

If absorption costing principles were applied, the profit for the period compared to the marginal costing profit would be

   (A) £75,000 higher.
   (B) £75,000 lower.
   (C) £125,000 higher.
   (D) £125,000 lower.   **(2 marks)**

Question 4

4.1   Which of the following best describes an investment centre?

(A) A centre for which managers are accountable only for costs.
(B) A centre for which managers are accountable only for financial outputs in the form of generating sales revenue.
(C) A centre for which managers are accountable for profit.
(D) A centre for which managers are accountable for profit and current non-current assets.

(2 marks)

4.2   A flexible budget is

(A) a budget which, by recognising different cost behaviour patterns, is designed to change as volume of activity changes.
(B) a budget for a twelve month period which includes planned revenues, expenses, assets and liabilities.
(C) a budget which is prepared for a rolling period which is reviewed monthly, and updated accordingly.
(D) a budget for semi-variable overhead costs only.   **(2 marks)**

4.3   The term "budget slack" refers to the

(A) lead time between the preparation of the master budget and the commencement of the budget period.
(B) difference between the budgeted output and the actual output achieved.
(C) additional capacity available which is budgeted for even though it may not be used.
(D) deliberate overestimation of costs and/or underestimation of revenues in a budget.   **(2 marks)**

4.4   PP Ltd is preparing the production and material purchases budgets for one of their products, the SUPERX, for the forthcoming year.

The following information is available:

SUPERX

Sales demand (units)	30,000
Material usage per unit	7 kgs
Estimated opening inventory	3,500 units
Required closing inventory	35% higher than opening inventory

How many units of the SUPERX will need to be produced?

(A) 28,775
(B) 30,000
(C) 31,225
(D) 38,225   **(2 marks)**

The following data are given for sub-questions 4.5 and 4.6 below

X Ltd operates a standard costing system and absorbs fixed overheads on the basis of machine hours. Details of budgeted and actual figures are as follows:

	Budget	Actual
Fixed overheads	£2,500,000	£2,010,000
Output	500,000 units	440,000 units
Machine hours	1,000,000 hours	900,000 hours

4.5 The fixed overhead expenditure variance is

(A) £190,000 favourable
(B) £250,000 adverse
(C) £300,000 adverse
(D) £490,000 favourable **(2 marks)**

4.6 The fixed overhead volume variance is

(A) £190,000 favourable
(B) £250,000 adverse
(C) £300,000 adverse
(D) £490,000 favourable **(2 marks)**

4.7 A company operates a standard absorption costing system. The budgeted fixed production overheads for the company for the latest year were £330,000 and budgeted output was 220,000 units. At the end of the company's financial year the total of the fixed production overheads debited to the Fixed Production Overhead Control Account was £260,000 and the actual output achieved was 200,000 units.

The under/over absorption of overheads was

(A) £40,000 over absorbed
(B) £40,000 under absorbed
(C) £70,000 over absorbed
(D) £70,000 under absorbed **(2 marks)**

4.8 A company operates a standard absorption costing system. The following fixed production overhead data are available for the latest period:

Budgeted Output	300,000 units
Budgeted Fixed Production Overhead	£1,500,000
Actual Fixed Production Overhead	£1,950,000
Fixed Production Overhead Total Variance	£150,000 adverse

The actual level of production for the period was nearest to

(A) 277,000 units
(B) 324,000 units
(C) 360,000 units
(D) 420,000 units **(2 marks)**

4.9 Which of the following best describes a basic standard?

(A) A standard set at an ideal level, which makes no allowance for normal losses, waste and machine downtime.
(B) A standard which assumes an efficient level of operation, but which includes allowances for factors such as normal loss, waste and machine downtime.
(C) A standard which is kept unchanged over a period of time.
(D) A standard which is based on current price levels. **(2 marks)**

4.10 XYZ Ltd is preparing the production budget for the next period. The total costs of production are a semi-variable cost. The following cost information has been collected in connection with production:

Volume (units)	Cost
4,500	£29,000
6,500	£33,000

The estimated total production costs for a production volume of 5,750 units is nearest to

(A) £29,200
(B) £30,000
(C) £31,500
(D) £32,500   (**2 marks**)

❓ Question 5

The following data are given for sub-questions 5.1 and 5.2 below.

Trafalgar Limited budgets to produce 10,000 units of product D12, each requiring 45 minutes of labour. Labour is charged at £20 per hour, and variable overheads at £15 per labour hour. During September 2003, 11,000 units were produced. 8,000 hours of labour were paid at a total cost of £168,000. Variable overheads in September amounted to £132,000.

5.1 What is the correct labour efficiency variance for September 2003?

(A) £5,000 Adverse
(B) £5,000 Favourable
(C) £5,250 Favourable
(D) £10,000 Adverse

5.2 What is the correct variable overhead expenditure variance for September 2003?

(A) £3,750 Favourable
(B) £4,125 Favourable
(C) £12,000 Adverse
(D) £12,000 Favourable

5.3 Which of the following definitions best describes 'Zero-Based Budgeting'?

(A) A method of budgeting where an attempt is made to make the expenditure under each cost heading as close to zero as possible.
(B) A method of budgeting whereby all activities are re-evaluated each time a budget is formulated.
(C) A method of budgeting that recognises the difference between the behaviour of fixed and variable costs with respect to changes in output, and the budget is designed to change appropriately with such fluctuations.
(D) A method of budgeting where the sum of revenues and expenditures in each budget centre must equal zero.

5.4 Copenhagen plc is an insurance company. Recently, there has been concern that too many quotations have been sent to clients either late or containing errors. The department concerned has responded that it is understaffed, and a high proportion of current staff has recently joined the firm. The performance of this department is to be carefully monitored.

Which ONE of the following non-financial performance indicators would NOT be an appropriate measure to monitor and improve the department's performance?

(A) Percentage of quotations found to contain errors when checked.
(B) Percentage of quotations not issued within company policy of three working days.
(C) Percentage of department's quota of staff actually employed.
(D) Percentage of budgeted number of quotations actually issued.

5.5 Nile Limited is preparing its sales budget for 2004. The sales manager estimates that sales will be 120,000 units if the Summer is rainy, and 80,000 units if the Summer is dry. The probability of a dry Summer is 0.4.

What is the expected value for sales volume for 2004?

(A) 96,000 units
(B) 100,000 units
(C) 104,000 units
(D) 120,000 units

5.6 MN plc uses a Just-in-Time (JIT) system and backflush accounting. It does not use a raw material stock control account. During April, 1,000 units were produced and sold. The standard cost per unit is £100: this includes materials of £45. During April, conversion costs of £60,000 were incurred.

What was the debit balance on the cost of goods sold account for April?

(A) £90,000
(B) £95,000
(C) £105,000
(D) £110,000

5.7 Division A transfers 100,000 units of a component to Division B each year.
The market price of the component is £25 per unit.
Division A's variable cost is £15 per unit.
Division A's fixed costs are £500,000 each year.

What price per unit would be credited to Division A for each component that it transfers to Division B under marginal cost pricing and under two-part tariff pricing (where the Divisions have agreed that the fixed fee will be £200,000)?

	Marginal cost pricing	Two-part tariff pricing
(A)	£15	£15
(B)	£25	£15
(C)	£15	£17
(D)	£25	£17

5.8 Which of the following statements are true?

(i) A flexible budget can be used to control operational efficiency.
(ii) Incremental budgeting can be defined as a system of budgetary planning and control that measures the additional costs that are incurred when there are unplanned extra units of activity.
(iii) Rolling budgets review and, if necessary, revise the budget for the next quarter to ensure that budgets remain relevant for the remainder of the accounting period.

(A) (i) and (ii) only
(B) (ii) and (iii) only
(C) (iii) only
(D) (i) only

5.9 Green division is one of many divisions in Colour plc. At its year-end, the fixed assets invested in Green were £30 m, and the net current assets were £5 m. Included in this total was a new item of plant that was delivered 3 days before the year end. This item cost £4 m and had been paid for by Colour, which had increased the amount of long-term debt owed by Green by this amount.

The profit earned in the year by Green was £6 m before the deduction of £1.4 m of interest payable to Colour.

What is the most appropriate measure of ROI for the Green division?

(A) 13.1%
(B) 14.8%
(C) 17.1%
(D) 19.4%

5.10 Division G has reported annual operating profits of £20.2 m. This was after charging £3 m for the full cost of launching a new product that is expected to last 3 years. Division G has a risk-adjusted cost of capital of 11% and is paying interest on a substantial bank loan at 8%. The historical cost of the assets in Division G, as shown on its balance sheet, is £60 m, and the replacement cost has been estimated at £84 m.

Ignore the effects of taxation.

What would be the EVA for Division G?

(A) £15.40 m
(B) £15.48 m
(C) £16.60 m
(D) £12.96 m   **(Total marks for sub-questions 5.1–5.10 = 20)**

 Question 6

The following data are given for sub-questions 6.1 and 6.2 below.

Summary financial statements are given below for one division of a large divisionalised company.

Summary Divisional Financial Statements for the year ended 31 December

Balance sheet	£'000	Income statement	£'000
Non-current assets	1,500	Revenue	4,000
Current assets	600	Operating costs	3,600
Total assets	2,100	Operating profit	400
		Interest paid	70
Divisional equity	1,000	Profit before tax	330
Long-term borrowings	700		
Current liabilities	400		
Total equity and liabilities	2,100		

The cost of capital for the division is estimated at 12% each year.

Annual rate of interest on the long-term loans is 10%.

All decisions concerning the division's capital structure are taken by central management.

6.1 The divisional Return on Investment (ROI) for the year ended 31 December is

(A) 19.0%
(B) 19.4%
(C) 23.5%
(D) 33.0% **(2 marks)**

6.2 The divisional Residual Income (RI) for the year ended 31 December is

(A) £160,000
(B) £196,000
(C) £230,000
(D) £330,000 **(2 marks)**

The following data are given for sub-questions 6.3 and 6.4 below.

X40 is one of many items produced by the manufacturing division. Its standard cost is based on estimated production of 10,000 units per month. The standard cost schedule for one unit of X40 shows that 2 hours of direct labour are required at £15 per labour hour. The variable overhead rate is £6 per direct labour hour. During April, 11,000 units were produced; 24,000 direct labour hours were worked and charged; £336,000 was spent on direct labour; and £180,000 was spent on variable overheads.

6.3 The direct labour rate variance for April is

(A) £20,000 Favourable
(B) £22,000 Favourable
(C) £24,000 Adverse
(D) £24,000 Favourable **(2 marks)**

6.4 The variable overhead efficiency variance for April is

(A) £12,000 Adverse
(B) £12,000 Favourable
(C) £15,000 Adverse
(D) £15,000 Favourable **(2 marks)**

6.5 The fixed overhead volume variance is defined as

(A) the difference between the budgeted value of the fixed overheads and the standard fixed overheads absorbed by actual production;

(B) the difference between the standard fixed overhead cost specified for the production achieved, and the actual fixed overhead cost incurred;

(C) the difference between budgeted and actual fixed overhead expenditure;

(D) the difference between the standard fixed overhead cost specified in the original budget and the same volume of fixed overheads, but at the actual prices incurred. **(2 marks)**

6.6 Summary results for Y Limited for March are shown below.

	£'000	Units
Sales revenue	820	
Variable production costs	300	
Variable selling costs	105	
Fixed production costs	180	
Fixed selling costs	110	
Production in March		1,000
Opening inventory		0
Closing inventory		150

Using *marginal costing*, the profit for March was

(A) £170,000

(B) £185,750

(C) £197,000

(D) £229,250 **(2 marks)**

6.7 The CIMA definition of zero-based budgeting is set out below, with two blank sections.

'Zero-based budgeting: A method of budgeting which requires each cost element _____, as though the activities to which the budget relates _____.'

Which combination of two phrases correctly completes the definition?

	Blank 1	Blank 2
(A)	to be specifically justified	could be out-sourced to an external supplier
(B)	to be set at zero	could be out-sourced to an external supplier
(C)	to be specifically justified	were being undertaken for the first time
(D)	to be set at zero	were being undertaken for the first time **(2 marks)**

6.8 *Definition A*: 'A technique where the primary goal is to maximise throughput while simultaneously maintaining or decreasing inventory and operating costs.'

Definition B: 'A system whose objective is to produce or procure products or components as they are required by a customer or for use, rather than for inventory.'

Which of the following pairs of terms correctly matches the definitions A and B above?

	Definition A	Definition B
(A)	Manufacturing resource planning	Just-in-time
(B)	Enterprise resource planning	Material requirements planning
(C)	Optimised production technology	Enterprise resource planning
(D)	Optimised production technology	Just-in-time **(2 marks)**

6.9 Division P produces plastic mouldings, all of which are used as components by Division Q. The cost schedule for one type of moulding – item 103 – is shown below.

Direct material cost per unit	£3.00
Direct labour cost per unit	£4.00
Variable overhead cost per unit	£2.00
Fixed production overhead costs each year	£120,000
Annual demand from Division Q is expected to be	20,000 units

Two methods of transfer pricing are being considered:

(i) Full production cost plus 40%
(ii) A two-part tariff with a fixed fee of £200,000 each year

The transfer price per unit of item 103 transferred to Division Q using both of the transfer pricing methods listed above is

	(i) Full production cost plus 40%	*(ii) Two-part tariff*
(A)	£21.00	£9
(B)	£21.00	£15
(C)	£15.00	£19
(D)	£12.60	£9

(2 marks)

6.10 Which of the following statements is/are true?

(i) Computer-integrated manufacturing (CIM) brings together advanced manufacturing technology and modern quality control into a single computerised coherent system.
(ii) Flexible manufacturing systems (FMS) are simple systems with low levels of automation that offer great flexibility through a skilled workforce working in teams.
(iii) Electronic data interchange (EDI) is primarily designed to allow the operating units in an organisation to communicate immediately and automatically with the sales and purchasing functions within the organisation.

(A) (i) only
(B) (i) and (ii) only
(C) (i) and (iii) only
(D) (ii) and (iii) only

(2 marks)

Section A – Non-multi-choice questions

 Question 7

Each of the sub-questions numbered 7.1 to 7.2 below require a brief written response.
  This response should be in note form and should not exceed 50 words.
  Write your answers to these sub-questions in your answer book.

7.1 The overhead costs of RP Limited have been found to be accurately represented by the formula

$$y = £10,000 + £0.25x$$

where y is the monthly cost and x represents the activity level measured as the number of orders.

   Monthly activity levels of orders may be estimated using a combined regression analysis and time series model:

$$a = 100,000 + 30b$$

where a represents the de-seasonalised monthly activity level and b represents the month number.

   In month 240, the seasonal index value is 108.

Requirement

Calculate the overhead cost for RP Limited for month 240 to the nearest £1,000.

(3 marks)

7.2 The following data have been extracted from the budget working papers of WR Limited:

Activity (machine hours)	Overhead cost £
10,000	13,468
12,000	14,162
16,000	15,549
18,000	16,242

In November 2003, the actual activity was 13,780 machine hours and the actual overhead cost incurred was £14,521.

Requirement

Calculate the total overhead expenditure variance for November 2003.

(4 marks)

   The following data are given for sub-questions 7.3 and 7.4 below.
DRP Limited has recently introduced an Activity-based Costing system. It manufactures three products, details of which are set out below:

	Product D	Product R	Product P
Budgeted annual production (units)	100,000	100,000	50,000
Batch size (units)	100	50	25
Machine set-ups per batch	3	4	6
Purchase orders per batch	2	1	1
Processing time per unit (minutes)	2	3	3

Three cost pools have been identified. Their budgeted costs for the year ended 31 December 2004 are as follows:

Machine set-up costs	£150,000
Purchasing of materials	£70,000
Processing	£80,000

7.3   Calculate the annual budgeted number of:

(a) batches
(b) machine set-ups
(c) purchase orders
(d) processing minutes   **(2 marks)**

7.4   Calculate the budgeted overhead unit cost for Product R for inclusion in the budget for 2004.   **(4 marks)**

The following data are given for sub-questions 7.5 and 7.6 below.
SW plc manufactures a product known as the TRD100 by mixing two materials. The standard material cost per unit of the TRD100 is as follows:

			£
Material X	12 litres	@ £2.50	30
Material Y	18 litres	@ £3.00	54

In October 2003, the actual mix used was 984 litres of X and 1,230 litres of Y. The actual output was 72 units of TRD100.

7.5   Calculate the total material mix variance for October 2003.   **(3 marks)**

7.6   Calculate the total material yield variance for October 2003.   **(2 marks)**

The following data are given for questions 7.7 and 7.8 below.
A company produces three products using three different machines. No other products are made on these particular machines. The following data is available for December 2003.

Product	A	B	C
Contribution per unit	£36	£28	£18
Machine hours required per unit			
Machine 1	5	2	1.5
Machine 2	5	5.5	1.5
Machine 3	2.5	1	0.5
Estimated sales demand (units)	50	50	60

Maximum machine capacity for December will be 400 hours per machine.

7.7   (a) Calculate the machine utilisation rates for each machine for December 2003.
                                                                          (2 marks)
          (b) Identify which of the machines is the bottleneck machine.   **(2 marks)**

7.8   (a) State the recommended procedure given by Goldratt in his 'Theory of Constraints' for dealing with a bottleneck activity.   **(2 marks)**
          (b) Calculate the optimum allocation of the bottleneck machine hours to the three products.   **(3 marks)**

7.9 Explain three circumstances where the first-in-first-out (FIFO) valuation method of process costing will give very similar results to the Weighted Average valuation method. **(3 marks)**

? Question 8

8.1 Z plc has found that it can estimate future sales using time-series analysis and regression techniques. The following trend equation has been derived:

$$y = 25,000 + 6,500x$$

where y is the total sales units per quarter and x is the time period reference number.

Z has also derived the following set of seasonal variation index values for each quarter using a multiplicative (proportional) model:

Quarter 1	70
Quarter 2	90
Quarter 3	150
Quarter 4	90

Using the above model, calculate the forecast for sales units for the third quarter of year 7, assuming that the first quarter of year 1 is time period reference number 1.

(3 marks)

8.2 Three products P, Q and R are produced together in a common process. Products P and Q are sold without further processing, but product R requires an additional process before it can be sold. No inventories are held. There is no loss of volume in the additional process for product R.

The following data apply to March.

Output	Product P	3,600 litres
	Product Q	4,100 litres
	Product R	2,800 litres
Selling prices	Product P	£4.60 per litre
	Product Q	£6.75 per litre
	Product R	£10.50 per litre
Costs incurred in the common process		£42,500
Costs incurred in the additional process for R		£19,600

Calculate the value of the common process costs that would be allocated to product R using the sales proxy method (notional sales value method). **(3 marks)**

8.3 A company is preparing its cash budget for February using the following data. One line in the cash budget is for purchases of a raw material, J. The opening inventory of J in January is expected to be 1,075 units. The price of J is expected to be £8 per unit. The company pays for purchases at the end of the month following delivery. One unit of J is required in the production of each unit of product 2, and J is only used in this product. Monthly sales of product 2 are expected to be:

January	4,000 units
February	5,000 units
March	6,000 units

The opening inventory of product 2 in January is expected to be 1,200 units.

The company implements the following inventory policies. At the end of each month, the following amounts are held:

Raw materials: 25% of the requirement for the following month's production

Finished goods: 30% of the following month's sales

Calculate the value for purchases of J to be included in the cash budget for February. **(4 marks)**

The following data are given for sub-questions 8.4 to 8.6 below.

K makes many products, one of which is Product Z. K is considering adopting an activity-based costing approach for setting its budget, in place of the current practice of absorbing overheads using direct labour hours. The main budget categories and cost driver details for the whole company for October are set out below, excluding direct material costs:

Budget category	£	Cost driver details
Direct labour	128,000	8,000 direct labour hours
Set-up costs	22,000	88 set-ups each month
Quality testing costs*	34,000	40 tests each month
Other overhead costs	32,000	absorbed by direct labour hours

* A quality test is performed after every 75 units produced

The following data for Product Z is provided:

Direct materials	budgeted cost of £21.50 per unit
Direct labour	budgeted at 0.3 hours per unit
Batch size	30 units
Set-ups	2 set-ups per batch
Budgeted volume for October	150 units

8.4 Calculate the budgeted unit cost of product Z for October assuming that a direct labour-based absorption method was used for all overheads. **(2 marks)**

8.5 Calculate the budgeted unit cost of product Z for October using an activity-based costing approach. **(3 marks)**

8.6 Explain **in less than 50 words**, why the costs absorbed by a product using an activity-based costing approach could be higher than those absorbed if a traditional labour-based absorption system were used, and identify **two** implications of this for management. **(4 marks)**

The following data are given for sub-questions 8.7 to 8.8 below.

The KL Company provides legal and secretarial services to small businesses. KL has two divisions.

Secretarial Division

This division provides secretarial services to external clients and to the Legal Division. It charges all its clients, including the Legal Division, at a rate of £40 per hour. The marginal cost of 1 hour of secretarial services is £20.

Legal Division

The Legal Division provides legal services. One service, called L&S, involves a combination of legal and secretarial services. Each hour of L&S charged to clients involves 1 hour of legal services and 1 hour of secretarial services. The secretarial element of this service is purchased from the Secretarial Division. The likely demand for L&S at different prices is as follows:

Demand (hours)	Price per hour (£)
0	100
1,000	90
2,000	80
3,000	70
4,000	60
5,000	50

The marginal cost of 1 hour of legal services is £25.

8.7 Calculate the level of sales (hours) and total contribution of L&S that would maximise the profit from this service for the Legal Division. Assume the Legal Division pays the Secretarial Division at a rate of £40 per hour for secretarial services. **(3 marks)**

8.8 Calculate the level of sales (hours) and total contribution that would maximise the profit from L&S for the KL Company as a whole. **(3 marks)**

The following data are given for sub-questions 8.9 and 8.10 below.
T is a large pharmaceutical manufacturing company that is implementing a 'Kaplan and Norton style' Balanced Scorecard for its research and development division. The goals and measures for the 'customer perspective' and the 'financial perspective' have been set.

8.9 For each of the two perspectives given in the question data, state an appropriate performance measure. **(2 marks)**

8.10 List the other two perspectives in the Balanced Scorecard for T's research and development division, and state for each of the perspectives a relevant goal and performance measure. **(3 marks)**

❓ Question 9

9.1 JJ Ltd manufactures three products: W, X and Y The products use a series of different machines but there is a common machine that is a bottleneck.
The standard selling price and standard cost per unit for each product for the forthcoming period are as follows:

	W	X	Y
	£	£	£
Selling price	200	150	150
Cost			
Direct materials	41	20	30
Labour	30	20	36
Overheads	60	40	50
Profit	69	70	34
Bottleneck machine – minutes per unit	9	10	7

40% of the overhead cost is classified as variable

Using a throughput accounting approach, what would be the ranking of the products for best use of the bottleneck? **(3 marks)**

9.2 X Ltd has two production departments, Assembly and Finishing, and two service departments, Stores and Maintenance.

Stores provides the following service to the production departments: 60% to Assembly and 40% to Finishing.

Maintenance provides the following service to the production and service departments: 40% to Assembly, 45% to Finishing and 15% to Stores.

The budgeted information for the year is as follows:

Budgeted fixed production overheads	£
Assembly	100,000
Finishing	150,000
Stores	50,000
Maintenance	40,000
Budgeted output	100,000 units

At the end of the year after apportioning the service department overheads, the total fixed production overheads debited to the Assembly department's fixed production overhead control account were £180,000.

The actual output achieved was 120,000 units.

Calculate the under/over absorption of fixed production overheads for the Assembly department. **(4 marks)**

9.3 A company simultaneously produces three products (X, Y and Z) from a single process. X and Y are processed further before they can be sold; Z is a by-product that is sold immediately for $6 per unit without incurring any further costs. The sales prices of X and Y after further processing are $50 per unit and $60 per unit respectively.

Data for October are as follows:

	$
Joint production costs that produced 2,500 units of X, 3,500 units of Y and 3,000 units of Z	140,000
Further processing costs for 2,500 units of X	24,000
Further processing costs for 3,500 units of Y	46,000

Joint costs are apportioned using the final sales value method.

Calculate the total cost of the production of X for October. **(3 marks)**

9.4 ZP Plc operates two subsidiaries, X and Y X is a component manufacturing subsidiary and Y is an assembly and final product subsidiary. Both subsidiaries produce one type of output only. Subsidiary Y needs one component from Subsidiary X for every unit of Product W produced. Subsidiary X transfers to Subsidiary Y all of the components needed to produce Product W. Subsidiary X also sells components on the external market.

The following budgeted information is available for each subsidiary:

	X	Y
Market price per component	$800	
Market price per unit of W		$1,200
Production costs per component	$600	
Assembly costs per unit of W		$400
Non production fixed costs	$1.5 m	$1.3 m
External demand	10,000 units	12,000 units
Capacity	22,000 units	
Taxation rates	25%	30%

The production cost per component is 60% variable. The fixed production costs are absorbed based on budgeted output.

X sets a transfer price at marginal cost plus 70%.

Calculate the post tax profit generated by each subsidiary. **(4 marks)**

9.5 PP Ltd operates a standard absorption costing system. The following information has been extracted from the standard cost card for one of its products:

Budgeted production	1,500 units
Direct material cost: 7 kg × £4.10	£28.70 per unit

Actual results for the period were as follows:

Production	1,600 units
Direct material (purchased and used): 12,000 kg	£52,200

It has subsequently been noted that due to a change in economic conditions the best price that the material could have been purchased for was £4.50 per kg during the period.

(i) Calculate the material price planning variance.
(ii) Calculate the operational material usage variance. **(4 marks)**

9.6 CJD Ltd manufactures plastic components for the car industry. The following budgeted information is available for three of their key plastic components:

	W	X	Y
	£ per unit	*£ per unit*	*£ per unit*
Selling price	200	183	175
Direct material	50	40	35
Direct labour	30	35	30
Units produced and sold	10,000	15,000	18,000

The total number of activities for each of the three products for the period is as follows:

Number of purchase requisitions	1,200	1,800	2,000
Number of set ups	240	260	300

Overhead costs have been analysed as follows:

Receiving/inspecting quality assurance	£1,400,000
Production scheduling/machine set up	£1,200,000

Calculate the budgeted profit per unit for each of the three products using activity-based budgeting. **(4 marks)**

9.7 CW Ltd makes one product in a single process. The details of the process for Period 2 were as follows:

There were 800 units of opening work in progress valued as follows:

Material	£98,000
Labour	£46,000
Production overheads	£7,600

During the period, 1,800 units were added to the process and the following costs were incurred:

Material	£387,800
Labour	£276,320
Production overheads	£149,280

There were 500 units of closing work in progress, which were 100% complete for material, 90% complete for labour and 40% complete for production overheads.

A normal loss equal to 10% of new material input during the period was expected. The actual loss amounted to 180 units. Each unit of loss was sold for £10 per unit.

CW Ltd uses weighted average costing.

Calculate the cost of the output for the period. **(4 marks)**

9.8 SS Ltd operates a standard marginal costing system. An extract from the standard cost card for the labour costs of one of its products is as follows:

Labour Cost
5 hours × £12   £60

Actual results for the period were as follows:

Production   11,500 units
Labour rate variance   £45,000 adverse
Labour efficiency variance   £30,000 adverse

Calculate the actual rate paid per direct labour hour **(4 marks)**
(Total for Section A = 50 marks)

 Question 10

The following data are given for sub-questions 10.1 and 10.2 below.

A company has a process in which three inputs are mixed together to produce Product S. The standard mix of inputs to produce 90 kg of Product S is shown below:

	$
50 kg of ingredient P at $75 per kg	3,750
30 kg of ingredient Q at $100 per kg	3,000
20 kg of ingredient R at $125 per kg	2,500
	9,250

During March 2,000 kg of ingredients were used to produce 1,910 kg of Product S. Details of the inputs are as follows:

	$
1,030 kg of ingredient P at $70 per kg	72,100
560 kg of ingredient Q at $106 per kg	59,360
410 kg of ingredient R at $135 per kg	55,350
	186,810

10.1 Calculate the materials mix variance for March. **(3 marks)**

10.2 Calculate the materials yield variance for March. **(2 marks)**

10.3 Division L has reported a net profit after tax of £8.6 m for the year ended 30 April 2006. Included in the costs used to calculate this profit are the following items:

- interest payable of £2.3 m;
- development costs of £6.3 m for a new product that was launched in May 2005, and is expected to have a life of 3 years;
- advertising expenses of £1.6 m that relate to the re-launch of a product in June 2006.

The net assets invested in Division L are £3 m.

The cost of capital for Division L is 13% per year.

Calculate the Economic Value Added® for Division L for the year ended 30 April 2006.

(3 marks)

10.4 The following details have been taken from the debtor collection records of W plc:

Invoices paid in the month after sale	60%
Invoices paid in the second month after sale	20%
Invoices paid in the third month after sale	15%
Bad debts	5%

Customers paying in the month after the sale are allowed a 10% discount.

Invoices for sales are issued on the last day of the month in which the sales are made.

The budgeted credit sales for the final 5 months of this year are

Month	August	September	October	November	December
Credit sales	$80,000	$100,000	$120,000	$130,000	$160,000

Calculate the total amount budgeted to be received in December from credit sales.

(2 marks)

10.5 State four aims of a transfer pricing system. **(3 marks)**

10.6 Process 2 takes transfers from Process 1 and converts them to finished goods. Additional materials are added during the process. An abnormal loss occurred part way through the process in April. Output data for April are shown below:

			Equivalent units (kg)	
	kg	From P1	Materials	Conversion
Transferred to finished goods	2,800	2,800	2,800	2,800
Normal loss	200			
Abnormal loss	100	100	100	50
Closing work in progress	700	700	700	150

The losses cannot be sold.

Costs incurred during April were

Transfer from Process 1	£34,200
Materials added	£16,200
Conversion costs	£26,700

There was no opening work in progress at the beginning of the month.

Calculate the value of the abnormal loss that will be debited to the abnormal loss account.

(3 marks)

10.7 D plc operates a retail business. Purchases are sold at cost plus 25%. The management team are preparing the cash budget and have gathered the following data:

1. The budgeted sales are as follows:

Month	£'000
July	100
August	90
September	125
October	140

2. It is management policy to hold inventory at the end of each month which is sufficient to meet sales demand in the next half month. Sales are budgeted to occur evenly during each month.

3. Creditors are paid one month after the purchase has been made.

Calculate the entries for 'purchases' that will be shown in the cash budget for

  (i)   August
  (ii) September
  (iii) October   **(3 marks)**

10.8 ZY is an airline operator. It is implementing a balanced scorecard to measure the success of its strategy to expand its operations. It has identified two perspectives and two associated objectives. They are

Perspective	*Objective*
Growth	Fly to new destinations
Internal capabilities	Reduce time between touch down and take off

  (i) For the 'growth perspective' of ZY, recommend a performance measure and briefly justify your choice of the measure by explaining how it will reflect the success of the strategy.   **(2 marks)**

  (ii) For the 'internal capabilities perspective' of ZY, state data that you would gather and explain how this could be used to ensure the objective is met.   **(2 marks)**

The following data are given for sub-questions 10.9 and 10.10 below.

Q plc uses standard costing. The details for April were as follows:

Budgeted output	15,000 units
Budgeted labour hours	60,000 hours
Budgeted labour cost	£540,000
Actual output	14,650 units
Actual labour hours paid	61,500 hours
Productive labour hours	56,000 hours
Actual labour cost	£522,750

10.9 Calculate the idle time variance for April.   **(2 marks)**

10.10 Calculate the labour efficiency variance for April.   **(2 marks)**

10.11 S plc produces and sells three products–X, Y and Z. It has contracts to supply products X and Y, which will utilise all of the specific materials that are available to make these two products during the next period. The revenue these contracts will generate and the contribution to sales (C/S) ratios of products X and Y are as follows:

	Product X	*Product Y*
Revenue	£10 m	£20 m
C/S ratio	15%	10%

Product Z has a C/S ratio of 25%.

The total fixed costs of S plc are £5.5 m during the next period and management have budgeted to earn a profit of £1 m.

Calculate the revenue that needs to be generated by Product Z for S plc to achieve the budgeted profit.   **(3 marks)**

Question 11

11.1 D Limited manufactures and sells musical instruments, and uses a standard cost system. The budget for production and sale of one particular drum for April was 600 units at a selling price of £72 each. When the sales director reviewed the results for April in the light of the market conditions that had been experienced during the month, she believed that D Limited should have sold 600 units of this drum at a price of £82 each. The actual sales achieved were 600 units at £86 per unit.

Calculate the following variances for this particular drum for April:

(a) Selling price planning variance
(b) Selling price operating variance   **(4 marks)**

11.2 A plastics company operates a process in which all materials are added at the beginning of the process. At the beginning of March, the work-in-process in a plastic moulding machine was 200 units, which were 25% complete with respect to conversion costs. During March, 1,400 units were completed and transferred to the next process. Also during March, 50 units were scrapped due to an operator error at the end of the process, although it is unusual for this to occur. At the end of March, there were 200 units in process, which were 50% complete with respect to conversion costs.

Using the first-in-first-out (FIFO) method, calculate the equivalent units of production for the month of March that would be used in the computation of the cost per equivalent unit for

(a) Material costs
(b) Conversion costs   **(4 marks)**

11.3 A company has a process in which the standard mix for producing 9 litres of output is as follows:

	$
4.0 litres of D at $9 per litre	36.00
3.5 litres of E at $5 per litre	17.50
2.5 litres of F at $2 per litre	5.00
	58.50

A standard loss of 10% of inputs is expected to occur. The actual inputs for the latest period were:

	$
4,300 litres of D at $9.00 per litre	38,700
3,600 litres of E at $5.50 per litre	19,800
2,100 litres of F at $2.20 per litre	4,620
	63,120

Actual output for this period was 9,100 litres.
You are required to calculate

(a) the total materials mix variance
(b) the total materials yield variance   **(4 marks)**

The following data are given for sub-questions 11.4 to 11.9 below.

SM makes two products, Z1 and Z2. Its machines can only work on one product at a time. The two products are worked on in two departments by differing grades of labour. The labour requirements for the two products are as follows:

	Minutes per unit of product	
	Z1	Z2
Department 1	12	16
Department 2	20	15

There is, currently, a shortage of labour and the maximum times available each day in Departments 1 and 2 are 480 minutes and 840 minutes, respectively.

The current selling prices and costs for the two products are shown below:

	Z1	Z2
	£per unit	£per unit
Selling price	50.00	65.00
Direct materials	10.00	15.00
Direct labour	10.40	6.20
Variable overheads	6.40	9.20
Fixed overheads	12.80	18.40
Profit per unit	10.40	16.20

As part of the budget-setting process, SM needs to know the optimum output levels. All output is sold.

11.4 Calculate the maximum number of each product that could be produced each day, and identify the limiting factor/bottleneck. **(3 marks)**

11.5 Using traditional contribution analysis, calculate the 'profit-maximising' output each day, and the contribution at this level of output. **(3 marks)**

11.6 Using a throughput approach, calculate the 'throughput-maximising' output each day, and the 'throughput contribution' at this level of output. **(3 marks)**

11.7 A is a food processing company. The following data have been produced for one of its processes for April. There were no inventories in the process at the beginning or at the end of the month.

	£
Inputs: 2,400 kg at £8 per kg	19,200
Process costs	4,800
Transferred to packing department: 2,060 kg	22,889

There is usually a loss of 10% by weight of inputs during the process. The normal loss does not have a sale value.

During April, there was an abnormal loss that was sold for £400.

Prepare the Process Account and the Abnormal Loss Account to record the events that occurred in this process during April. **(4 marks)**

The following data are given for sub-questions 11.8 and 11.9 below.

The summarised financial statements for P Limited, a potential major supplier, are shown below. Before a contract is signed, the financial performance of P Limited is to be reviewed.

Summary Balance Sheets for P Limited as at year end

	2003	2002
	£'000	£'000
Non-current assets	1,600	1,400
Inventories	300	280
Trade receivables	200	210
Cash	50	10
Trade payables	(280)	(290)
Long-term borrowings	(900)	(800)
Net assets	970	810
Share capital	600	600
Retained earnings	370	210
	970	810

Summary Income Statements for the years

	2003	2002
	£'000	£000
Sales	3,000	2,500
Cost of sales	1,600	1,300
Operating profit	600	450

11.8 Calculate the following financial statistics for P Limited for 2003

    (a) Receivables days
    (b) Payables days
    (c) Inventory days   **(3 marks)**

11.9 Calculate the following financial statistics for P Limited for 2003

    (a) Current ratio
    (b) Acid test (quick ratio)   **(2 marks)**

 **Question 12**

12.1 S Ltd manufactures three products, A, B and C. The products use a series of different machines but there is a common machine, P, that is a bottleneck.

    The selling price and standard cost for each product for the forthcoming year is as follows:

	A	B	C
	$	$	$
Selling price	200	150	150
Direct materials	41	20	30
Conversion costs	55	40	66
Machine P – minutes	12	10	7

Calculate the return per hour for each of the products.   **(4 marks)**

12.2 The following data have been extracted from a company's year-end accounts:

	£
Turnover	7,055,016
Gross profit	4,938,511
Operating profit	3,629,156
Non-current assets	4,582,000
Cash at bank	4,619,582
Short term borrowings	949,339
Trade receivables	442,443
Trade payables	464,692

Calculate the following four performance measures:

(i) Operating profit margin;

(ii) Return on capital employed;

(iii) Trade receivable days (debtors days);

(iv) Current (Liquidity) ratio.   **(4 marks)**

12.3 PQR Ltd operates a standard absorption costing system. Details of budgeted and actual figures are as follows.

	Budget	Actual
Sales volume (units)	100,000	110,000
Selling price per unit	£10	£9·50
Variable cost per unit	£5	£5·25
Total cost per unit	£8	£8·30

(i) Calculate the sales price variance.   **(2 marks)**

(ii) Calculate the sales volume profit variance.   **(2 marks)**

12.4 WX has two divisions, Y and Z. The following budgeted information is available.

Division Y manufactures motors and budgets to transfer 60,000 motors to Division Z and to sell 40,000 motors to external customers.

Division Z assembles food mixers and uses one motor for each food mixer produced.

The standard cost information per motor for Division Y is as follows:

	£
Direct materials	70
Direct labour	20
Variable production overhead	10
Fixed production overhead	40
Fixed selling and administration overhead	10
Total standard cost	150

In order to set the external selling price the company uses a 33·33% mark up on total standard cost.

(i) Calculate the budgeted profit/(loss) for Division Y if the transfer price is set at marginal cost.

(ii) Calculate the budgeted profit/(loss) for Division Y if the transfer price is set at the total production cost.   **(4 marks)**

12.5 RF Ltd is about to launch a new product in June 2007. The company has commissioned some market research to assist in sales forecasting. The resulting research and analysis established the following equation:

$$Y = Ax^{0.6}$$

Where Y is the cumulative sales units, A is the sales units in month 1, x is the month number.
June 2007 is Month 1.
Sales in June 2007 will be 1,500 units.

Calculate the forecast sales volume for each of the months June, July and August 2007 and for that three month period in total. **(4 marks)**

？ Question 13

The following scenario is given for sub-questions (a) to (f).

X Plc manufactures specialist insulating products that are used in both residential and commercial buildings. One of the products, Product W, is made using two different raw materials and two types of labour. The company operates a standard absorption costing system and is now preparing its budgets for the next four quarters. The following information has been identified for Product W:

Sales

Selling price	£220 per unit

Sales demand

Quarter 1	2,250 units
Quarter 2	2,050 units
Quarter 3	1,650 units
Quarter 4	2,050 units
Quarter 5	1,250 units
Quarter 6	2,050 units

Costs

Materials

A	5 kgs per unit @ £4 per kg
B	3 kgs per unit @ £7 per kg

Labour

Skilled	4 hours per unit @ £15 per hour
Semi-skilled	6 hours per unit @ £9 per hour
Annual overheads	£280,000
	40% of these overheads are fixed and the remainder varies with total labour hours. Fixed overheads are absorbed on a unit basis.

Inventory holding policy

Closing inventory of finished goods	30% of the following quarter's sales demand
Closing inventory of materials	45% of the following quarter's materials usage

The management team are concerned that X Plc has recently faced increasing competition in the market place for Product W. As a consequence there have been issues concerning the availability and costs of the specialised materials and employees needed to manufacture Product W, and there is concern that these might cause problems in the current budget setting process.

(a) Prepare the following budgets for each quarter for X Plc:
  (i) Production budget in units;
  (ii) Raw material purchases budget in kgs and value for Material B. **(5 marks)**

(b) X Plc has just been informed that Material A may be in short supply during the year for which it is preparing budgets. Discuss the impact this will have on budget preparation and other areas of X Plc. **(5 marks)**

(c) Assuming that the budgeted production of Product W was 7,700 units and that the following actual results were incurred for labour and overheads in the year:

Actual production	7,250 units
Actual overheads	
Variable	£185,000
Fixed	£105,000
Actual labour costs	
Skilled–£16.25 per hour	£568,750
Semi-skilled–£8 per hour	£332,400

Prepare a flexible budget statement for X Plc showing the total variances that have occurred for the above four costs only. **(5 marks)**

(d) X Plc currently uses incremental budgeting. Explain how Zero Based Budgeting could overcome the problems that might be faced as a result of the continued use of the current system. **(5 marks)**

(e) Explain how rolling budgets are used and why they would be suitable for X Plc. **(5 marks)**

(f) Briefly explain how linear regression analysis can be used to forecast sales and briefly discuss whether it would be a suitable method for X Plc to use. **(5 marks)**

? Question 14

(a) A company uses variance analysis to monitor the performance of the team of workers which assembles Product M. Details of the budgeted and actual performance of the team for last period were as follows:

	Budget	Actual
Output of product M	600 units	680 units
Wage rate	£30 per hour	£32 per hour
Labour hours	900 hours	1,070 hours

It has now been established that the standard wage rate should have been £31·20 per hour.

(i) Calculate the labour rate planning variance and calculate the operational labour efficiency variance.

(ii) Explain the major benefit of analysing variances into planning and operational components. **(5 marks)**

(b) Briefly explain three limitations of standard costing in the modern business environment.
(5 marks)

(c) Briefly explain three factors that should be considered before deciding to investigate a variance. **(5 marks)**

(d) G Group consists of several autonomous divisions. Two of the divisions supply components and services to other divisions within the group as well as to external clients. The management of G Group is considering the introduction of a bonus scheme for managers that will be based on the profit generated by each division.

Briefly explain the factors that should be considered by the management of G Group when designing the bonus scheme for divisional managers. **(5 marks)**

(e) Briefly explain the role of a Manufacturing Resource Planning System in supporting a standard costing system. **(5 marks)**

(f) Briefly explain the main differences between the traditional manufacturing environment and a just-in-time manufacturing environment. **(5 marks)**

? Question 15

The new manufacturing environment is characterised by more flexibility, a readiness to meet customers' requirements, smaller batches, continuous improvements and an emphasis on quality. In such circumstances, traditional management accounting performance measures are, at best, irrelevant and, at worst, misleading.

Requirements
(a) Discuss the above statement, citing specific examples to support or refute the views expressed.
(b) Explain in what ways management accountants can adapt the services they provide to the new environment.

? Question 16

(a) Briefly outline the main features of 'feedback control', and the 'feedback loop' and explain how, in practice, the procedures of feedback control can be transformed into 'feed-forward control'.
(b) Give *four* reasons why the adoption of Total Quality Management (TQM) is particularly important within a Just-in-Time (JIT) production environment.
(c) Briefly outline the advantages and disadvantages of allowing profit centre managers to participate actively in the setting of the budget for their units.
(d) Explain and discuss the similarities and differences between Residual Income and Economic Value Added as methods for assessing the performance of divisions.
(e) Define the 'controllability principle' and give arguments for and against its implementation in determining performance measures.
(f) Discuss the problems that arise specifically when determining transfer prices where divisions are located in different countries. **(Total marks = 30)**

❓ Question 17

(a) A general insurance company is about to implement a Balanced Scorecard. *You are required* to

   (i) State the *four* perspectives of a Balanced Scorecard; and

   (ii) Recommend *one* performance measure that would be appropriate for a general insurance company, for *each* of the four perspectives, and give a reason to support each measure. (You must recommend one measure only for each perspective.) **(5 marks)**

(b) (i) Briefly explain the main features of Economic Value Added (EVA®) as it would be used to assess the performance of divisions. **(2 marks)**

   (ii) Briefly explain how the use of EVA® to assess divisional performance might affect the behaviour of divisional senior executives. **(3 marks)**

(c) Briefly discuss *three* different circumstances where participation in setting budgets is likely to contribute to *poor* performance from managers. **(5 marks)**

(d) W Limited designs and sells computer games. There are many other firms in this industry. For the last 5 years, the senior management has required detailed budgets to be produced for each year with slightly less detailed plans for the following 2 years. The managing director of W Limited has recently attended a seminar on budgeting and heard the 'Beyond Budgeting' arguments that have been advanced by Hope and Fraser, among others.

You are required to

   (i) briefly describe the 'Beyond Budgeting' approach; and **(2 marks)**

   (ii) advise the management of W Limited whether or not it should change its current budgeting system to a 'Beyond Budgeting' approach. **(3 marks)**

The following information is to be used to answer sub-questions (e) and (f)

C plc is a large company that manufactures and sells wooden garden furniture. It has three divisions:

1. The *Wood Division* (WD) purchases logs and produces finished timber as planks or beams. Approximately, two-thirds of its output is sold to the Products Division, with the remainder sold on the open market.

2. The *Products Division* (PD) manufactures wooden garden furniture. The policy of C plc is that the PD must buy all its timber from the WD and sell all its output to the Trading Division.

3. The *Trading Division* (TD) sells wooden garden furniture to garden centres, large supermarkets, and similar outlets. It only sells items purchased from PD.

   The current position is that all three divisions are profit centres and C plc uses Return on Investment (ROI) measures as the primary means to assess divisional performance. Each division adopts a cost-plus pricing policy for external sales and for internal transfers between divisions. The senior management of C plc has stated that the divisions should consider themselves to be independent businesses as far as possible.

(e) For each division, suggest, with reasons, the behavioural consequences that might arise as a result of the current policy for the structure and performance evaluation of the divisions. **(5 marks)**

(f) The senior management of C plc has requested a review of the cost-plus transfer pricing policy that is currently used.

   Suggest, with reasons, an appropriate transfer pricing policy that could be used for transfers *from PD to TD*, indicating any problems that may arise as a consequence of the policy you suggest. **(5 marks)**

Question 18

State the range of behavioural issues that need to be addressed in the establishment of standard costs.

Question 19

Explain the difference between information feedback and feed-forward within the context of a budgetary control system.

Question 20

Requirements

(a) J Limited has recently been taken over by a much larger company. For many years, the budgets in J have been set by adding an inflation adjustment to the previous year's budget. The new owners of J are insisting on a 'zero-base' approach when the next budget is set, as they believe many of the indirect costs in J are much higher than in other companies under their control.

  (i) Explain the main features of 'zero-based budgeting'. **(2 marks)**

  (ii) Discuss the problems that might arise when implementing this approach in J Limited. **(3 marks)**

(b) An analysis of past output has shown that batches have a mean weight of 90 kg and that the weights conform to the normal distribution with a standard deviation of 10 kg. The company has a policy to investigate variances that fall outside the range that includes 95% of outcomes. In September one sample batch weighed 110 kg.

  (i) Calculate whether the material usage variance for this batch should be investigated according to the company policy described above. **(3 marks)**

  (ii) Discuss two other important factors that should be taken into account when deciding whether to investigate this variance. **(2 marks)**

(c) UV Limited is a catering company that provides meals for large events. It has a range of standard meals at fixed prices. It also provides meals to meet the exact requirements of a customer and prices for this service are negotiated individually with each customer.

    Discuss how a 'McDonaldisation' approach to service delivery would impact on budget preparation and control within UV Limited. **(5 marks)**

(d) A management consulting company had budgeted the staff requirements for a particular job as follows:

	£
40 hours of senior consultant at £100 per hour	4,000
60 hours of junior consultant at £60 per hour	3,600
Budgeted staff cost for job	7,600

The actual hours recorded were

	£
50 hours of senior consultant at £100 per hour	5,000
55 hours of junior consultant at £60 per hour	3,300
Actual staff cost for job	8,300

The junior consultant reported that for 10 hours of the 55 hours recorded, there was no work that she could do.

Calculate the following variances:

- Idle time variance
- Labour mix variance
- Labour efficiency variance   **(5 marks)**

(e) ST plc is a medium-sized engineering company using advanced technology. It has just implemented an integrated enterprise resource planning system (ERPS) in place of an old MRP (manufacturing resource planning) system.

Discuss the changes that are likely to be seen after the implementation of the ERPS in

(i) the budget-setting process; and
(ii) the budgetary control process   **(5 marks)**

(f) W Limited has conducted a review of its budget-setting procedures. The review coordinator frequently heard the following comment from staff interviewed:

'It's impossible to make this system work because senior managers want budgets to be a challenging target whereas the finance department require an accurate forecast.'

Discuss the issues raised in this comment, and advise the review coordinator on practical action that could be taken to alleviate the situation described.   **(5 marks)**

? Question 21

State the differences in the financial reporting requirements as between cost, profit, sales and investment centres.

? Question 22

Requirements

(a) A manufacturing company uses a standard costing system. Extracts from the budget for April are shown below:

Sales	1,400 units
Production	2,000 units

	$
Direct costs	15 per unit
Variable overhead	4 per unit

The budgeted fixed production overhead costs for April were $12,800.

The budgeted profit using marginal costing for April was $5,700.

(i) Calculate the budgeted profit for April using absorption costing.   **(3 marks)**
(ii) Briefly explain two situations where marginal costing is more useful to management than absorption costing.   **(2 marks)**

(b) The standard cost schedule for hospital care for a minor surgical procedure is shown below.

Staff: patient ratio is 0.75:1

	£
Nursing costs: 2 days × 0.75 × £320 per day	480
Space and food costs: 2 days × £175 per day	350
Drugs and specific materials	115
Hospital overheads: 2 days × £110 per day	220
Total standard cost	**1,165**

The actual data for the hospital care for one patient having the minor surgical procedure showed that the patient stayed in hospital for 3 days. The cost of the drugs and specific materials for this patient was £320. There were 0.9 nurses per patient on duty during the time that the patient was in hospital. The daily rates for nursing pay, space and food and hospital overheads were as expected.

Prepare a statement that reconciles the standard cost with the actual costs of hospital care for this patient. The statement should contain *five* variances that will give useful information to the manager who is reviewing the cost of hospital care for minor surgical procedures. **(5 marks)**

(c) C plc uses a just-in-time (JIT) purchasing and production process to manufacture Product P. Data for the output of Product P, and the material usage and material price variances for February, March and April are shown below:

Month	Output (units)	Material usage variance		Material price variance	
February	11,000	£15,970	Adverse	£12,300	Favourable
March	5,100	£5,950	Adverse	£4,500	Favourable
April	9,100	£8,400	Adverse	£6,200	Favourable

The standard material cost per unit of Product P is £12.

Prepare a sketch (not on graph paper) of a percentage variance chart for material usage and for material price for Product P for the 3-month period. *(Note:* your workings must show the coordinates of the points that would be plotted if the chart was drawn accurately.) **(5 marks)**

(d) Briefly discuss three reasons why standard costing may *not* be appropriate in a modern business environment. **(5 marks)**

(e) Compare and contrast marginal costing and throughput accounting. **(5 marks)**

(f) T plc is a large insurance company. The Claims Department deals with claims from policy holders who have suffered a loss that is covered by their insurance policy. Policy holders could claim, for example, for damage to property or for household items stolen in a burglary. The Claims Department staff investigate each claim and determine what, if any, payment should be made to the claimant.

The manager of the Claims Department has decided to benchmark the performance of the department and has chosen two areas to benchmark:

- the detection of false claims
- the speed of processing claims.

For each of the above two areas:

(i) state and justify a performance measure
(ii) explain how relevant benchmarking data could be gathered.   **(5 marks)**

Section C

 Question 23

A firm has recently commenced using a standard costing system but the manager is having some difficulty in identifying significant variances, that is, those that require further analysis and investigation.

Requirements

(a) Describe the factors which determine whether or not a variance is significant.

(5 marks)

(b) Suggest ways in which significant variances could be more easily identified.

(10 marks)

 Question 24

Frolin Chemicals Ltd produces FDN. The standard ingredients of 1 kg of FDN are:

0.65 kg of ingredient F	@ £4.00 per kg
0.30 kg of ingredient D	@ £6.00 per kg
0.20 kg of ingredient N	@ £2.50 per kg
1.15 kg	

Production of 4,000 kg of FDN was budgeted for April 20X8. The production of FDN is entirely automated and production costs attributed to FDN production comprise only direct materials and overheads. The FDN production operation works on a JIT basis and no ingredients or FDN inventories are held.

Overheads were budgeted for April 20X8 for the FDN production operation as follows:

Activity	Total amount £
Receipt of deliveries from suppliers	
(standard delivery quantity is 460 kg)	4,000
Despatch of goods to customers	
(standard despatch quantity is 100 kg)	8,000
	12,000

In April 20X8, 4,200 kg of FDN were produced and cost details were as follows:
Materials used:

	kg
F	2,840
D	1,210
N	860

at a total cost of £20,380.

Actual overhead costs: 12 supplier deliveries (cost £4,800) were made and 38 customer despatches (cost £7,800) were processed.

Frolin Chemicals Ltd's budget committee met recently to discuss the preparation of the financial control report for April, and the following discussion occurred:

- *Chief accountant*: 'The overheads do not vary directly with output and are therefore by definition 'fixed'. They should be analysed and reported accordingly.'
- *Management accountant*: 'The overheads do not vary with output, but they are certainly not fixed. They should be analysed and reported on an activity basis.'

Requirements

Having regard to this discussion:

(a) Prepare a variance analysis for FDN production costs in April 20X8: separate the material cost variance into price, mixture and yield components; separate the overhead cost variance into expenditure, capacity and efficiency components using consumption of ingredient F as the overhead absorption base.

(b) Prepare a variance analysis for FDN production overhead costs in April 1998 on an activity basis.

(c) Explain how, in the design of an activity-based management system, you would identify and select the most appropriate activities and cost drivers.

? Question 25

X Ltd uses an automated manufacturing process to produce an industrial chemical, Product P.

X Ltd operates a standard marginal costing system. The standard cost data for Product P is as follows:

Standard cost per unit of Product P

Materials			
A	10 kgs	@ £15 per kilo	£150
B	8 kgs	@ £8 per kilo	£64
C	5 kgs	@ £4 per kilo	£20
	23 kgs		
Total standard marginal cost			£234
Budgeted fixed production overheads			£350,000

In order to arrive at the budgeted selling price for Product P the company adds 80% markup to the standard marginal cost. The company budgeted to produce and sell 5,000 units of Product P in the period. There were no budgeted inventories of Product P.

The actual results for the period were as follows:

Actual production and sales		5,450 units
Actual sales price		£445 per unit
Material usage and cost		
A	43,000 kgs	£688,000
B	37,000 kgs	£277,500
C	23,500 kgs	£99,875
	103,500 kgs	
Fixed production overheads		£385,000

Requirements

(a) Prepare an operating statement which reconciles the budgeted profit to the actual profit for the period. (The statement should include the material mix and material yield variances.) **(12 marks)**

(b) The Production Manager of X Ltd is new to the job and has very little experience of management information. Write a brief report to the Production Manager of X Ltd that

   (i) interprets the material price, mix and yield variances;

   (ii) discusses the merits, or otherwise, of calculating the materials mix and yield variances for X Ltd. **(8 marks)**

? Question 26

(a) M Pty produces 'Biotinct' in a lengthy distillation and cooling process. Base materials are introduced at the start of this process, and further chemicals are added when it is 80% complete. Each kilogram of base materials produces 1 kg of Biotinct.

Data for October are:

Opening work in process	40 kg of base materials, 25% processed	
Cost of opening work in process	Base materials	$1,550
	Processing	$720
Costs incurred in October	Base materials (80 kg)	$3,400
	Conversion costs	$6,864
	Further chemicals	$7,200
Closing work in process	50 kg of base materials, 90% processed	
Finished output	65 kg of Biotinct	

Under normal conditions, there are no losses of base materials in this process. However, in October, 5 kg of partially complete Biotinct were spoiled immediately after the further chemicals had been added. The 5 kg of spoiled Biotinct were not processed to finished goods stage and were sold for a total of $200.

Requirement

Using the FIFO method, prepare the process account for October. **(12 marks)**

(b) One of the company's management accountants overheard the Managing Director arguing as follows: 'These process accounts are complicated to produce, and often conceal the true position. As I see it, the value of partly processed Biotinct is zero. In October, we spent $17,464 and the output was 65 kg. So, the average cost was $268.68 per kg, while the target cost is $170 ($40 for base materials, $70 for processing and $60 for further chemicals). These figures make me concerned about production efficiency.'

Requirement

Explain to the Managing Director any errors in the comment he had made, and discuss whether the data from the process account indicate that there has been production inefficiency. **(8 marks)**

Question 27

Marshall Limited operates a business that sells advanced photocopying machines and offers on-site servicing. There is a separate department that provides servicing. The standard cost for one service is shown below along with the operating statements for the Service Department for the 6 months to 30 September 2003. Each service is very similar and involves the replacement of two sets of materials and parts.

Marshall Limited's budgets for 5,000 services per month.

Standard cost for one service

	£
Materials – 2 sets @ £20 per set	40
Labour – 3 hours @ £11 per hour	33
Variable overheads – 3 hours @ £5 per hour	15
Fixed overheads – 3 hours @ £8 per hour	24
Total standard cost	112

Operating Statements for 6 months ending 30 September 2003

Months	1	2	3	4	5	6	Total
Number of services per month	5,000	5,200	5,400	4,800	4,700	4,500	29,600
	£	£	£	£	£	£	£
Flexible budget costs	560,000	582,400	604,800	537,600	526,400	504,000	3,315,200
Less: Variances:							
Materials							
Price	5,150(F)	3,090(F)	1,100(F)	−2,040(A)	−5,700(A)	−2,700(A)	−1,100(A)
Usage	−6,000(A)	2,000(F)	−4,000(A)	−12,000(A)	−2,000(A)	0	−22,000(A)
Labour							
Rate	26,100(F)	25,725(F)	27,331(F)	18,600(F)	17,400(F)	15,515(F)	130,671(F)
Efficiency	5,500(F)	9,900(F)	12,100(F)	−12,100(A)	−4,400(A)	−11,000(A)	0
Variable overheads							
Spending	−3,500(A)	−3,500(A)	−2,500(A)	−4,500(A)	500(F)	2,500(F)	−11,000(A)
Efficiency	2,500(F)	4,500(F)	5,500(F)	−5,500(A)	−2,000(A)	−5,000(A)	0
Fixed overheads							
Expenditure	−3,000(A)	−5,000(A)	−5,000(A)	−15,000(A)	5,000(F)	5,000(F)	−18,000(A)
Volume	0	4,800(F)	9,600(F)	−4,800(A)	−7,200(A)	−12,000(A)	−9,600(A)
Actual costs	533,250	540,885	560,669	574,940	524,800	511,685	3,246,229

Requirements

(a) Prepare a summary financial statement showing the overall performance of the Service Department for the 6 months to 30 September 2003.   **(4 marks)**

(b) Write a report to the Operations Director of Marshall Limited commenting on the performance of the Service Department for the 6 months to 30 September 2003.

Suggest possible causes for the features you have included in your report and state the further information that would be helpful in assessing the performance of the department.

(16 marks)

Question 28

PQR plc is a chemical processing company. The company produces a range of solvents by passing materials through a series of processes. The company uses the first-in-first out (FIFO) valuation method.

In Process 2, the output from Process 1 (XP1) is blended with two other materials (P2A and P2B) to form XP2. It is expected that 10% of any new input to Process 2 (i.e. transfers from Process 1 plus Process 2 materials added) will be immediately lost and that this loss will have no resale value. It is also expected that in addition to the loss, 5% of any new input will form a by-product, Z, which can be sold without additional processing for £2.00 per litre.

Data from Process 2 for November 2003 was as follows:

Opening work in process

Process 2 had 1,200 litres of opening work-in-process. The value and degree of completion of this was as follows:

	£	% degree of completion
XP1	1,560	100
P2A	1,540	100
P2B	750	100
Conversion costs	3,790	40
	7,640	

Input

During November, the inputs to Process 2 were:

	£
XP1 5,000 litres	15,679
P2A 1,200 litres	6,000
P2B 3,000 litres	4,500
Conversion costs	22,800

Closing work in process

At the end of November, the work in process was 1,450 litres. This was fully complete in respect of all materials, but only 30% complete for conversion costs.

Output

The output from Process 2 during November was:

Z	460 litres
XP2	7,850 litres

Requirement

Prepare the Process 2 account for November 2003. **(17 marks)**
Note: 3 marks will be awarded for presentation. **(Total marks = 20)**

Question 29

The ZZ Group has two divisions, X and Y Each division produces only one type of product: X produces a component (C) and Y produces a finished product (FP). Each FP needs one C. It is the current policy of the group for C to be transferred to Division Y at the marginal cost of £10 per component and that Y must buy all the components it needs from X.

The markets for the component and the finished product are competitive and price sensitive. Component C is produced by many other companies but it is thought that the external demand for the next year could increase to 1,000 units more than the sales volume shown in the current budget for Division X.

Budgeted data, taken from the ZZ Group Internal Information System, for the divisions for the next year is as follows:

Division X

Income statement

Sales	£70,000
Less Cost of sales	
Variable costs	£50,000
Contribution	£20,000
Less Fixed costs (controllable)	£15,000
Profit	£5,000

Production/Sales (units)	5,000 (3,000 of which are transferred to Division Y)
External demand (units)	3,000 (Only 2,000 of which can be currendy satisfied)
Capacity (units)	5,000
External market price per unit	£20

Balance sheet extract

Capital employed	£60,000

Other information

Cost of capital charge	10%

Division Y

Income statement

Sales	£270,000
Less Cost of sales	
Variable costs	£114,000
Contribution	£156,000
Less Fixed costs (controllable)	£100,000
Profit	£56,000

Production/Sales (units)	3,000
Capacity (units)	7,000
Market price per unit	£90

Balance sheet extract

Capital employed	£110,000

Other information

Cost of capital charge	10%

Four measures are used to evaluate the performance of the Divisional Managers. Based on the data above, the budgeted performance measures for the two divisions are as follows:

	Division X	*Division Y*
Residual income	(£1,000)	£45,000
Return on capital employed	8.33%	50.91%
Operating profit margin	7.14%	20.74%
Asset turnover	1.17	2.46

Current policy

It is the current policy of the group for C to be transferred to Division Y at the marginal cost of £10 per component and that Y must buy all the components that it needs from X.

Proposed policy

ZZ Group is thinking of giving the Divisional Managers the freedom to set their own transfer price and to buy the components from external suppliers but there are concerns about problems that could arise by granting such autonomy.

Requirements

(a) If the transfer price of the component is set by the Manager of Division X at the current market price (£20 per component), recalculate the budgeted performance measures for each division. **(8 marks)**

(b) Discuss the changes to the performance measures of the divisions that would arise as a result of altering the transfer price to £20 per component. **(6 marks)**

(c) (i) Explain the problems that could arise for each of the Divisional Managers and for ZZ Group as a whole as a result of giving full autonomy to the Divisional Managers.

(ii) Discuss how the problems you have explained could be resolved without resorting to a policy of imposed transfer prices. **(6 marks)**

Question 30

You have been appointed as the management accountant of the DL Hospital Trust, a newly formed organisation with specific responsibility for providing hospital services to its local community. The hospital trust is divided into a number of specialist units: one of these, unit H, specialises in the provision of a particular surgical operation.

Although the trust does not have profit maximisation as its objective, it is concerned to control its costs and to provide a value-for-money service. To achieve this, it engages teams of specialist staff on a subcontract basis and pays them an hourly rate based upon the direct hours attributable to the surgical operation being carried out.

Surgical team fees (i.e. labour costs) are collected and attributed to each surgical operation, whereas overhead costs are collected and attributed to surgical operations using absorption rates. These absorption rates are based on the surgical team fees. For the year ended 31 December 20X3, these rates were:

Variable overhead	62.5% of surgical team fees
Fixed overhead	87.5% of surgical team fees

Each surgical operation is expected to take 10 hours to complete, and the total fees of the team for each operation are expected to be £2,000.

The budget for the year ended 31 December 20X3 indicated that a total of 20 such surgical operations were expected to be performed each month, and that the overhead costs were expected to accrue evenly throughout the year.

During November 20X2, there were 22 operations of this type completed. These took a total of 235 hours and the total surgical team fees amounted to £44,400.

Overhead costs incurred in unit H in November 20X3 amounted to:

Variable overhead	£28,650
Fixed overhead	£36,950

Requirements

(a) Prepare a statement that reconciles the original budget cost and the actual cost for this type of operation within unit H for the month of November 20X3, showing the analysis of variances in as much detail as possible from the information given.

(15 marks)

(b) The DL Hospital Trust has been preparing its budgets for 20X4, and the finance director has questioned the appropriateness of using surgical team fees as the basis of attributing overhead costs to operations.

You are required to write a brief report to her explaining the arguments for and against the use of this method. **(5 marks)**

? Question 31

The newly appointed group finance director of a medium-sized quoted company has expressed considerable dissatisfaction with the budget prepared before his appointment. He considered that the comparisons of the budget with the results of the first quarter of the current financial year, which he had recently reviewed, were far from helpful in understanding changes in the business environment. He proposes significant changes in the process of budget preparation for next year.

In the past, budgets have been prepared after the third quarter's results were known and the fourth-quarter forecast prepared. This timetable left finance staff very little time to prepare the budgets before the end of the financial year and the start of the new year. The group finance director proposes that the preparation of the budget for the next financial year should be commenced after the half-year results for the current financial year have been completed.

The group finance director wishes to implement the change in the current year, preparing the budget for the next financial year, but there are three problems:

1. Division A has no managing director. He resigned after very poor results for the first quarter followed disappointing results for the last financial year. A search is being made for a new managing director, almost certainly an external appointment, but this could take several months.

   In the meantime, the divisional financial director is acting as managing director as well as carrying out his own duties.
2. Division B has launched in the first quarter of this year a new product range aiming at a new group of customers. This is effectively a new marketing strategy.
3. Division C is installing new plant that will not be fully operational until the third quarter. There are some doubts whether the plant will produce, without modification, products of acceptable quality, as customer requirements have changed since the plant was ordered.

Requirements

Prepare a report, on behalf of the group finance director, to the board, explaining the reasons for the proposed changes in budget preparation and planning for next year.

Discuss the three specific problems and any other anticipated difficulties, and advise how they could be dealt with in the new proposed system. **(20 marks)**

Question 32

F plc supplies pharmaceutical drugs to drug stores. Although the company makes a satisfactory return, the directors are concerned that some orders are profitable and others are not. The management has decided to investigate a new budgeting system using activity-based costing principles to ensure that all orders they accept are making a profit.

Each customer order is charged as follows. Customers are charged the list price of the drugs ordered plus a charge for selling and distribution costs (overheads). A profit margin is also added, but that does not form part of this analysis.

Currently, F plc uses a simple absorption rate to absorb these overheads. The rate is calculated based on the budgeted annual selling and distribution costs, and the budgeted annual total list price of the drugs ordered.

An analysis of customers has revealed that many customers place frequent small orders with each order requesting a variety of drugs. The management of F plc has examined more carefully the nature of its selling and distribution costs, and the following data have been prepared for the budget for next year:

Total list price of drugs supplied	£8 m	
Number of customer orders	8,000	
Selling and distribution costs	*£'000*	*Cost driver*
Invoice processing	280	See Note 2
Packing	220	Size of package – see Note 3
Delivery	180	Number of deliveries – see Note 4
Other overheads	200	Number of orders
Total overheads	880	

Notes:

1. Each order will be shipped in one package and will result in one delivery to the customer and one invoice (an order never results in more than one delivery).
2. Each invoice has a different line for each drug ordered. There are 28,000 invoice lines each year. It is estimated that 25% of invoice processing costs are related to the number of invoices and 75% are related to the number of invoice lines.
3. Packing costs are £32 for a large package and £25 for a small package.
4. The delivery vehicles are always filled to capacity for each journey The delivery vehicles can carry either 6 large packages or 12 small packages (or appropriate combinations of large and small packages). It is estimated that there will be 1,000 delivery journeys each year and the total delivery mileage that is specific to particular customers is estimated at 350,000 miles each year. £40,000 of delivery costs are related to loading the delivery vehicles and the remainder of these costs are related to specific delivery distance to customers.

The management has asked for two typical orders to be costed using next year's budget data, using the current method, and the proposed activity-based costing approach. Details of two typical orders are shown below:

	Order A	Order B
Lines on invoice	2	8
Package size	small	large
Specific delivery distance	8 miles	40 miles
List price of drugs supplied	£1,200	£900

Requirements

(a) Calculate the charge for selling and distribution overheads for Order A and Order B using:

    (i) the current system; and

    (ii) the activity-based costing approach. **(10 marks)**

(b) Write a report to the management of F plc in which you

    (i) assess the strengths and weaknesses of the proposed activity-based costing approach for F plc; and **(5 marks)**

    (ii) recommend actions that the management of F plc might consider in the light of the data produced using the activity-based costing approach. **(5 marks)**

(Total for requirement (b) = 10 marks)

? Question 33

The budget for the Production Planning and Development Department of ABC plc is currently prepared as part of a traditional budgetary planning and control system. The analysis of costs by expense type for the period ended 30 November 20X1 where this system is in use is as follows:

Expense type	Budget %	Actual %
Salaries	60	63
Supplies	6	5
Travel cost	12	12
Technology cost	10	7
Occupancy cost	12	13

The total budget and actual costs for the department for the period ended 30 November 20X1 are £1,000,000 and £1,060,000, respectively.

The company now feels that an activity-based budgeting approach should be used. A number of activities have been identified for the Production Planning and Development Department. An investigation has indicated that total budget and actual costs should be attributed to the activities on the following basis:

Activities	Budget %	Actual %
1. Routeing/scheduling – new products	20	16
2. Routeing/scheduling – existing products	40	34
3. Remedial rerouteing/scheduling	5	12
4. Special studies – specific orders	10	8
5. Training	10	15
6. Management and administration	15	15

Requirements

(a) Prepare *two* budget control statements for the Production Planning and Development Department for the period ended 30 November 20X1 that compare budget with actual cost and show variances using:

- a traditional expense-based analysis;
- an activity-based analysis.

(b) Identify and comment on *four* advantages claimed for the use of activity-based budgeting over traditional budgeting, using the Production Planning and Development example to illustrate your answer.

(c) Comment on the use of the information provided in the activity-based statement that you prepared in (a) in activity-based performance measurement and suggest additional information that would assist in such performance measurement.

? Question 34

A manufacturing company has a materials handling department that provides a service to production departments and to other service departments. The materials handling department has 40 forklift trucks and charges users of the service at a rate per forklift truck hour that is compiled using the following budget information:

- Each forklift truck attracts drivers' salaries of £26,000 per annum plus a bonus of 5 p per cubic metre handled (all paid 4-weekly – based on thirteen 4-week periods per year).
- The forklift trucks are powered by electric batteries. The charge to the materials handling department for keeping the batteries at full power is made at a cost equivalent to £1.50 per forklift truck running hour.
- Forklift trucks cost £26,000 each and are depreciated over 5 years on a straight-line basis with nil residual value.
- Maintenance per forklift truck is implemented by the company maintenance department at an average cost of £120 per truck per 4-week period. This is considered to be a fixed cost.
- Each forklift truck is expected to be used for 80% of company operating time. The budget for company operating time is 115 hours per week.
- The average quantity handled per forklift truck running hour is 10 cubic metres.
- Forklift truck time is charged to users at a rate per running hour based on the above information.

The actual data relating to the 4-week period ended 28 November 20X1 is as follows:

- Forklift truck drivers' salaries: £81,600, bonus £7,400.
- Total power cost £21,800. This is based on the actual time required to keep the batteries at full power where the time is charged at £1.50 per hour.
- Total forklift truck maintenance cost: £6,000.
- Depreciation charge is as per budget.
- The company operated for 120 hours per week with each forklift truck operating on average for 80% of the time. All forklift truck running time was charged to users.

Requirements

(a) Prepare a cost statement for the materials handling department for the 4-week period ended 28 November 20X1 that compares flexed budget with actual costs and shows:
  (i) variances for each expense type;
  (ii) the total cost charged out to user departments;
  (iii) the over-/underabsorption of cost for the period.

(b) Comment on advantages that may be claimed for the use of a charge rate to user departments for the materials handling service that uses budgeted rather than actual costs.

Question 35

Ryman Inc produces three chemical products – X, Y and Z. Raw materials are processed in a single plant to produce two intermediate products – 1 and 2, in fixed proportions. There is no outside market for these intermediate products. 1 is processed further in process A to give X, product 2 is converted into Y by a separate finishing process B. Process B produces both Y and a waste material 'beta' which has no market value. However, beta can be passed through process C in order to convert it into a saleable product Z. Unlimited quantities of Z can be sold at a going market price of £1.50 per kg.

At normal levels of production and sales, 600,000 kg of the common raw material are processed each period, giving an output of 440,000 kg of 1 and 110,000 kg of 2 respectively. After the separate finishing processes described above, the products X, Y and Z emerge as follows:

Product	Quantity kg (£)	Selling price
X	400,000	2.425
Y	100,000	4.500
Z	10,000	1.500

At these normal volumes, material and processing costs are as follows:

£'000	Plant	A	B	C
Materials	320	110	15	1
Labour	150	225	90	5.5
Variable overhead	30	50	25	0.5
Fixed overhead	50	25	5	3
Total	550	410	135	10

Requirements

(a) Draw a diagram to illustrate the flow of materials and products through the various processes. Label the diagram with appropriate titles and quantities to show the normal operation specified in the figures given.

(b) Calculate the cost per unit of products X and Y and the total manufacturing profit for the period attributed to individual products – on both of the following alternative methods of allocating joint costs (i) physical units and (ii) net realisable value. (*Note:* or 'notional sales value at point of separation'.)

(c) Advise Ryman Inc management on a request from a potential customer to buy 10,000 kg of Y for £40,000. Support this advice with a financial analysis and a statement of the critical assumptions contained in this analysis.

 Question 36

PSA Ltd pays its operatives an hourly rate which at the start of 20X2 was forecast to be £10.50 throughout the year. Both hardwood and softwood are used on jobs, the 20X2 costs of which were forecast to be £55 per cubic metre (hardwood) and £9 per cubic metre (softwood). Overheads (absorbed on a labour hour overhead absorption rate [OAR]) for 20X2 were forecast to be £96,000 (fixed) and £72,000 (variable). It was forecast that 24,000 labour hours would be worked on all jobs at an even rate in 20X2. PSA Ltd uses a conventional cost accounting system and reports cost variances at the end of each month, with labour and material variances split into operational and planning components.

At the start of April 20X2 there was no work-in-progress and, during the month, work started on jobs 98, 107 and 109. Jobs 98 and 107 were fully complete by the end of the month. Job 109 was estimated to be 60% complete as regards labour and 80% complete as regards materials. The evaluator had calculated the following requirements for the jobs, based on the original standards specified above:

	Job 98	Job 107	Job 109
Standard labour hours	1,000	600	780
Hardwood (cubic metres)	200	180	120
Softwood (cubic metres)	320	400	300

During April, 2,200 labour hours were worked (wages paid were £24,500), 520 cubic metres of hardwood were used (cost £28,600) and 1,100 cubic metres of softwood were used (cost £9,200). Conditions in the labour market meant that operatives had to be engaged who were less able than those planned for. On average, operatives were able to work only at 4% below the original standard level of efficiency (i.e. expected output per hour is 4% less than standard). Hardwood available during 20X2 is 5% below forecast quality (that is, the output per cubic metre is 5% below standard). During March, the standard price of softwood for 20X2 was revised to £8 per cubic metre. April overheads were £7,800 (fixed) and £6,900 (variable).

Rapier Management Consultants have reported as follows:

Your cost system looks like something from an accounting textbook written 40 years ago. What you need is backflush costing. Rapier will be delighted to design you a backflush costing system for a modest fee.

Requirements

(a) Explain why conventional cost accounting systems use predetermined OARs.
(b) Construct PSA Ltd's April cost control report.
(c) Explain what backflush costing is and (as far as you can on the basis of available information) comment on the suitability of PSA Ltd's operation for backflush costing.

? Question 37

Apollo plc manufactures and sells several products, two of which are Alpha and Beta. Estimated data for the two products for the forthcoming period is as follows:

(i) Product data	Alpha	Beta	Other products
Production/sales units	5,000	10,000	40,000
	£'000	£'000	£'000
Total direct material cost	80	300	2,020
Total direct labour cost	40	100	660

(ii) Variable overhead cost is £1,500,000 of which 40% is related to the acquisition, storage and use of direct materials and the remainder is related to the control and use of direct labour.

(iii) It is current practice for Apollo plc to absorb the two types of variable overhead cost to products using an overall company-wide percentage based on either direct material cost and direct labour cost as appropriate.

(iv) Apollo are considering the use of activity-based costing. The cost drivers for material and labour related overheads have been identified as follows:

	Alpha	Beta	Other products
Direct material related overheads – cost driver is weight of material			
Weight of material/unit	4	1	1.5
Direct labour related overheads – cost driver is number of labour operations			
Labour operations/unit	6	1	2

(v) Market investigation indicates that market prices for Alpha and Beta of £75 and £95 per unit respectively will achieve the estimated sales shown in (i) above.

(vi) Apollo plc require a minimum estimated contribution: sales ratio of 40% before proceeding with the production or sale of any product.

Requirements

(a) Prepare estimated unit product costs for Alpha and Beta where the variable overhead is charged to product units as follows:
   (i) using the existing absorption rates as detailed above,
   (ii) using an activity-based costing approach. **(5 marks)**
(b) Using the information in (a), prepare an analysis that will help Apollo determine whether both A and B should remain in production.
   Your answer should include relevant calculations and discussion and be prepared in a form suitable for presentation to management. **(10 marks)**
(c) Explain how Apollo could make use of target costing in conjunction with activity-based costing with respect to Alpha and Beta. **(5 marks)**

? Question 38

S Limited installs complex satellite navigation systems in cars, at a very large national depot. The standard cost of an installation is shown below. The budgeted volume is 1,000 units installed each month. The operations manager is responsible for three departments, namely purchasing, fitting and quality control. S Limited purchases navigation systems and other equipment from different suppliers, and most items are imported. The fitting of different systems takes differing amounts of time, but the differences are not more than 25% from the average, so a standard labour time is applied.

Standard cost of installation of one navigation system

	£	Quantity	Price (£)
Materials	400	1 unit	400
Labour	320	20 hours	16
Variable overheads	140	20 hours	7
Fixed overheads	300	20 hours	15
Total standard cost	1,160		

The Operations Department has gathered the following information over the last few months. There are significant difficulties in retaining skilled staff. Many have left for similar but better paid jobs and as a result there is a high labour turnover. Exchange rates have moved and commentators have argued this will make exports cheaper, but S Limited has no exports and has not benefited. Some of the fitters have complained that one large batch of systems did not have the correct adapters and would not fit certain cars, but this was not apparent until fitting was attempted. Rent, rates, insurance and computing facilities have risen in price noticeably.

The financial results for September to December are shown below.

Operating Statement for S Limited for September to December

	September £	October £	November £	December £	4 months £
Standard cost of actual output	1,276,000	1,276,000	1,102,000	1,044,000	4,698,000
Variances					
Materials					
Price	5,505 F	3,354 F	9,520 A	10,340 A	11,001 A
Usage	400 A	7,200 A	800 A	16,000 A	24,400 A
Labour					
Rate	4,200 A	5,500 A	23,100 A	24,000 A	56,800 A
Efficiency	16,000 F	0	32,000 A	32,000 A	48,000 A
Variable overheads					
Expenditure	7,000 A	2,000 A	2,000 F	0	7,000 A
Efficiency	7,000 F	0	14,000 A	14,000 A	21,000 A
Fixed overheads					
Expenditure	5,000 A	10,000 A	20,000 A	20,000 A	55,000 A
Volume	30,000 F	30,000 F	15,000 A	30,000 A	15,000 F
Actual costs	1,234,095	1,267,346	1,214,420	1,190,340	4,906,201

'A' = adverse variance 'F' = favourable variance

Requirements

(a) Prepare a report to the operations manager of S Limited commenting on the performance of the company for the 4 months to 31 December. State probable causes for the key issues you have included in your report and state the further information that would be helpful in assessing the performance of the company.   **(15 marks)**

(b) Prepare a short report to the operations manager of S Limited suggesting ways that the budgeting system could be used to increase motivation and improve performance.

(5 marks)

 Question 39

KDS Ltd is an engineering company which is organised for management purposes in the form of several autonomous divisions. The performance of each division is currently measured by calculation of its return on capital employed (ROCE). KDS Ltd's existing accounting policy is to calculate ROCE by dividing the net assets of each division at the end of the year into the operating profit generated by the division during the year. Cash is excluded from net assets since all divisions share a bank account controlled by KDS Ltd's head office.

Depreciation is on a straight-line basis. The divisional management teams are paid a performance-related bonus conditional upon achievement of a 15% ROCE target.

On 20 December 20X1 the divisional managers were provided with performance forecasts for 20X1 which included the following:

Forecast	Net assets at 31 December 20X1 £	20X1 operating profit £	ROCE
Division K	4,400,000	649,000	14.75%
Division D	480,000	120,000	25.00%

Subsequently, the manager of Division K invited members of her management team to offer advice. The responses she received included the following:

- From the divisional administrator: 'We can achieve our 20X1 target by deferring payment of a £90,000 trade debt payable on 20 December until 1 January. I should add that we will thereby immediately incur a £2,000 late payment penalty.'
- From the works manager: 'We should replace a number of our oldest machine tools (which have nil book value) at a cost of £320,000. The new equipment will have a life of 8 years and generate cost savings of £76,000 per year. The new equipment can be on site and operational by 31 December 20X1.'
- From the financial controller: 'The existing method of performance appraisal is unfair. We should ask head office to adopt residual income (RI) as the key performance indicator, using the company's average 12% cost of money for a finance charge.'

Requirements

(a) Compare and appraise the proposals of the divisional administrator and the works manager, having regard to the achievement of the ROCE performance target in 20X1 and to any longer-term factors you think relevant.
(b) Explain the extent to which you agree or disagree with the financial controller's proposal.

? Question 40

Y and Z are two divisions of a large company that operate in similar markets. The divisions are treated as investment centres and every month they each prepare an operating statement to be submitted to the parent company. Operating statements for these two divisions for October are shown below:

Operating Statements for October

	Y £'000	Z £'000
Sales revenue	900	555
Less variable costs	345	312
Contribution	555	243
Less controllable fixed costs (includes depreciation on divisional assets)	95	42
Controllable income	460	201
Less apportioned central costs	338	180
Net income before tax	122	21
Total divisional net assets	£9.76 m	£1.26 m

The company currently has a target return on capital of 12% per annum. However, the company believes its cost of capital is likely to rise and is considering increasing the target return on capital. At present the performance of each division and the divisional management are assessed primarily on the basis of Return on Investment (ROI).

Requirements

(a) Calculate the annualised Return on Investment (ROI) for divisions Y and Z, and discuss the relative performance of the two divisions using the ROI data and other information given above. **(9 marks)**

(b) Calculate the annualised Residual Income (RI) for divisions Y and Z, and explain the implications of this information for the evaluation of the divisions' performance. **(6 marks)**

(c) Briefly discuss the strengths and weaknesses of ROI and RI as methods of assessing the performance of divisions. Explain two further methods of assessment of divisional performance that could be used in addition to ROI or RI. **(5 marks)**

Question 41

M plc designs, manufactures and assembles furniture. The furniture is for home use and therefore varies considerably in size, complexity and value. One of the departments in the company is the Assembly Department. This department is labour intensive; the workers travel to various locations to assemble and fit the furniture using the packs of finished timbers that have been sent to them.

Budgets are set centrally and they are then given to the managers of the various departments who then have the responsibility of achieving their respective targets. Actual costs are compared against the budgets and the managers are then asked to comment on the budgetary control statement. The statement for April for the Assembly Department is shown below.

	Budget	Actual	Variance	
Assembly labour hours	6,400	7,140		
	$	$	$	
Assembly labour	51,970	58,227	6,257	Adverse
Furniture packs	224,000	205,000	19,000	Favourable
Other materials	23,040	24,100	1,060	Adverse
Overheads	62,060	112,340	50,280	Adverse
Total	361,070	399,667	38,597	Adverse

Note: The costs shown are for assembling and fitting the furniture (they do not include time spent travelling to jobs and the related costs). The hours worked by the Manager are not included in the figure given for the assembly labour hours.

The Manager of the Assembly Department is new to the job and has very little previous experience of working with budgets but he does have many years' experience as a supervisor in assembly departments. Based on that experience he was sure that the department had performed well. He has asked for your help in replying to a memo he has just received asking him to 'explain the serious overspending in his department'. He has sent you some additional information about the budget:

1. The budgeted and actual assembly labour costs include the fixed salary of $2,050 for the Manager of the Assembly Department. All of the other labour is paid for the hours they work.
2. The cost of furniture packs and other materials is assumed by the central finance office of M plc to vary in proportion to the number of assembly labour hours worked.

3. The budgeted overhead costs are made up of three elements: a fixed cost of $9,000 for services from central headquarters, a stepped fixed cost which changes when the assembly hours exceed 7,000 hours, and some variable overheads. The variable overheads are assumed to vary in proportion to the number of assembly labour hours. Working papers for the budget showed the impact on the overhead costs of differing amounts of assembly labour hours:

Assembly labour hours	5,000	7,500	10,000
Overhead costs	$54,500	$76,500	$90,000

The actual fixed costs for April were as budgeted.

Requirements

(a) Prepare, using the additional information that the Manager of the Assembly Department has given you, a budgetary control statement that would be more helpful to him.

(7 marks)

(b) (i) Discuss the differences between **the format of the statement** that you have produced and that supplied by M plc. **(4 marks)**

(ii) Discuss the assumption made by the central office of M plc that costs vary in proportion to assembly labour hours. **(3 marks)**

(c) Discuss whether M plc should change to a system of participative budgeting.

(6 marks)

Question 42

CTD Ltd has two divisions – FD and TM. FD is an iron foundry division which produces mouldings that have a limited external market and are also transferred to TM division. TM division uses the mouldings to produce a piece of agricultural equipment called the 'TX' which is sold externally. Each TX requires one moulding. Both divisions produce only one type of product.

The performance of each Divisional Manager is evaluated individually on the basis of the residual income (RI) of his or her division. The company's average annual 12% cost of capital is used to calculate the finance charges. If their own target residual income is achieved, each Divisional Manager is awarded a bonus equal to 5% of his or her residual income. All bonuses are paid out of Head Office profits.

The following budgeted information is available for the forthcoming year:

	TM division TX per unit	FD division Moulding per unit
	£	£
External selling price	500	80
Variable production cost	366*	40
Fixed production overheads	60	20
Gross profit	74	20
Variable selling and distribution cost	25	4**
Fixed administration overhead	25	4
Net profit	24	12
Normal capacity (units)	15,000	20,000
Maximum production capacity (units)	15,000	25,000
Sales to external customers (unit)	15,000	5,000
Capital employed	£1,500,000	£750,000
Target RI	£105,000	£85,000

*The varible production of TX includes the cost of an FD moulding.

**External sales only of the mouldings incur a variable selling and distribution cost of £4 per unit.

FD division currently transfers 15,000 mouldings to TM division at a transfer price equal to the total production cost plus 10%.

Fixed cost are absorbed on the basis of normal capacity.

Requirements

(a) Calculate the bonus each Divisional Manager would receive under the current transfer pricing policy and discuss any implications that the current performance evaluation system may have for each division and for the company as a whole.   **(7 marks)**

(b) Both Divisional Managers want to achieve their respective residual income targets. Based on the budgeted figures, calculate

   (i) the *maximum* transfer price per unit that the Divisional Manager of TM division would pay.

   (ii) the *minimum* transfer price per unit that the Divisional Manager of FD division would accept.   **(6 marks)**

(c) Write a report to the management of CTD Ltd that explains, and recommends, the transfer prices which FD division should set in order to maximise group profits. Your report should also

   • consider the implications of actual external customer demand exceeding 5,000 units; and

   • explain how alternative transfer pricing systems could overcome any possible conflict that may arise as a result of you recommended transfer prices.

   Note: Your answer must be related to CTD Ltd. You will not earn marks by just describing various methods for setting transfer prices.   **(12 marks)**

(Total marks = 25)

Question 43

X Ltd has recently automated its manufacturing plant and has also adopted a Total Quality Management (TQM) philosophy and a Just in Time (JIT) manufacturing system. The company currently uses a standard absorption costing system for the electronic diaries which it manufacturers.

The following information for the last quarter has been extracted from the company records:

	Budget	*Actual*
Fixed production overheads	$100,000	$102,300
Labour hours	10,000	11,000
Output (electronic diaries)	100,000	105,000

Fixed production overheads are absorbed on the basis of direct labour hours.
The following fixed production overhead variances have been reported:

	$	
Expenditure variance	2,300	(A)
Capacity variance	10,000	(F)
Efficiency variance	5,000	(A)
Total	2,700	(F)

If the fixed production overheads had been further analysed and classified under an Activity Based Costing (ABC) system, the above information would then have been presented as follows:

	Budget	Actual
Costs		
Material handling	$30,000	$30,800
Set up	$70,000	$71,500
Output (electronic diaries)	100,000	105,000
Activity		
Material handling (order executed)	5,000	5,500
Set up (production runs)	2,800	2,600

The following variances would have been reported:

		$	
Overhead expenditure variance	Material handling	2,200	(F)
	Set ups	6,500	(A)
Overhead efficiency variance	Material handling	1,500	(A)
	Set ups	8,500	(F)
Total		2,700	(F)

Requirements

(a) Explain why and how X Ltd may have to adapt its standard costing system now that it has adopted TQM and JIT in its recently automated manufacturing plant. **(9 marks)**

(b) Explain the meaning of the fixed overhead variances calculated under the standard absorption costing system and discuss their usefulness to the management of X Ltd for decision-making **(6 marks)**

(c) For the variances calculated under the ABC classification:
  (i) explain how they have been calculated;
  (ii) discuss their usefulness to the management of X Ltd for decision-making

(10 marks)
(Total marks = 25)

? Question 44

FP sells and repairs photocopiers. The company has operated for many years with two departments, the Sales Department and the Service Department, but the departments had no autonomy. The company is now thinking of restructuring so that the two departments will become profit centres.

The Sales Department

This department sells new photocopiers. The department sells 2,000 copiers per year. Included in the selling price is £60 for a 1-year guarantee. All customers pay this fee. This means that during the first year of ownership if the photocopier needs to be repaired, then the repair costs are not charged to the customer. On average, 500 photocopiers per year need to be repaired under the guarantee. The repair work is carried out by the Service Department who, under the proposed changes, would charge the Sales Department for doing the repairs. It is estimated that on average the repairs will take 3 hours each and that the charge by the Service Department will be £136,500 for the 500 repairs.

The Service Department

This department has two sources of work: the work needed to satisfy the guarantees for the Sales Department, and repair work for external customers. Customers are charged at full cost plus 40%. The details of the budget for the next year for the Service Department revealed standard costs of

Parts	*at cost*
Labour	£15 per hour
Variable overheads	£10 per labour hour
Fixed overheads	£22 per labour hour

The calculation of these standards is based on the estimated maximum market demand and includes the expected 500 repairs for the Sales Department. The average cost of the parts needed for a repair is £54. This means that the charge to the Sales Department for the repair work, including the 40% mark-up, will be £136,500.

Proposed Change

It has now been suggested that FP should be structured so that the two departments become profit centres and that the managers of the Departments are given autonomy. The individual salaries of the managers would be linked to the profits of their respective departments.

Budgets have been produced for each department on the assumption that the Service Department will repair 500 photocopiers for the Sales Department and that the transfer price for this work will be calculated in the same way as the price charged to external customers.

However, the manager of the Sales Department has now stated that he intends to have the repairs done by another company, RS, because they have offered to carry out the work for a fixed fee of £180 per repair and this is less than the price that the Sales Department would charge.

Requirements

(a) Calculate the individual profits of the Sales Department and the Service Department, and of FP as a whole *from the guarantee scheme* if:
  (i) The repairs are carried out by the Service Department and are charged at full cost plus 40%;
  (ii) The repairs are carried out by the Service department and are charged at marginal cost;
  (iii) The repairs are carried out by RS. **(8 marks)**

(b)
  (i) Explain, with reasons, why a 'full cost plus' transfer pricing model may not be appropriate for FP. **(3 marks)**
  (ii) Comment on other issues that the managers of FP should consider if they decide to allow RS to carry out the repairs. **(4 marks)**

(c) Briefly explain the advantages and disadvantages of structuring the departments as profit centres. **(5 marks)**

Question 45

RJ produces and sells two high performance motor cars: Car X and Car Y. The company operates a standard absorption costing system. The company's budgeted operating statement for the year ending 30 June 2008 and supporting information is given below:

Operating statement year ending 30 June 2008

	Car X $000	Car Y $000	Total $000
Sales	52,500	105,000	157,500
Production cost of sales	40,000	82,250	122,250
Gross profit	12,500	22,750	35,250
Administration costs			
Variable	6,300	12,600	18,900
Fixed	7,000	9,000	16,000
Profit/(loss)	(800)	1,150	350

The production cost of sales for each car was calculated using the following values:

	Car X Units	Car X $000	Car Y Units	Car Y $000
Opening inventory	200	8,000	250	11,750
Production	1,100	44,000	1,600	75,200
Closing inventory	300	12,000	100	4,700
Cost of sales	1,000	40,000	1,750	82,250

Production costs

The production costs are made up of direct materials, direct labour, and fixed production overhead. The fixed production overhead is general production overhead (it is not product specific). The total budgeted fixed production overhead is $35,000,000 and is absorbed using a machine hour rate. It takes 200 machine hours to produce one Car X and 300 machine hours to produce one Car Y.

Administration costs

The fixed administration costs include the costs of specific marketing campaigns: $2,000,000 for Car X and $4,000,000 for Car Y.

Required:

(a) Produce the budgeted operating statement in a marginal costing format.　**(7 marks)**

(b) Reconcile the total budgeted absorption costing profit with the total budgeted marginal costing profit as shown in the statement you produced in part *(a)*.　**(5 marks)**

　　The company is considering changing to an activity based costing system. The company has analysed the budgeted fixed production overheads and found that the costs for various activities are as follows:

	$000
Machining costs	7,000
Set up costs	12,000
Quality inspections	7,020
Stores receiving	3,480
Stores issues	5,500
	35,000

The analysis also revealed the following information:

	Car X	Car Y
Budgeted production (number of cars)	1,100	1,600
Cars per production run	10	40
Inspections per production run	20	80
Number of component deliveries during the year	492	900
Number of issues from stores	4,000	7,000

Required:

(c) Calculate the budgeted production cost of one Car X and one Car Y using the activity based costing information provided above. **(10 marks)**

(d) Prepare a report to the Production Director of RJ which explains the potential benefits of using activity based budgeting for performance evaluation. **(8 marks)**

? Question 46

RF Ltd is a new company which plans to manufacture a specialist electrical component. The company founders will invest £16,250 on the first day of operations, that is, Month 1. They will also transfer fixed capital assets to the company.

The following information is available:

Sales

The forecast sales for the first four months are as follows:

Month	Number of components
1	1,500
2	1,750
3	2,000
4	2,100

The selling price has been set at £10 per component in the first four months.

Sales receipts

Time of payment	% of customers
Month of sale	20*
One month later	45
Two months later	25
Three months later	5

The balance represents anticipated bad debts.

*A 2% discount is given to customers for payment received in the month of sale.

Production

There will be no opening inventory of finished goods in Month 1 but after that it will be policy for the closing inventory to be equal to 20% of the following month's forecast sales.

Variable production cost

The variable production cost is expected to be £6·40 per component.

	£
Direct materials	1·90
Direct wages	3·30
Variable production overheads	1·20
Total variable cost	6·40

Notes:

Direct materials: 100% of the materials required for production will be purchased in the month of production. No inventory of materials will be held. Direct materials will be paid for in the month following purchase.

Direct wages: will be paid in the month in which production occurs.

Variable production overheads: 60% will be paid in the month in which production occurs and the remainder will be paid one month later.

Fixed overhead costs

Fixed overhead costs are estimated at £75,000 per annum and are expected to be incurred in equal amounts each month. 60% of the fixed overhead costs will be paid in the month in which they are incurred and 30% in the following month. The balance represents depreciation of fixed assets.

Calculations are to be made to the nearest £1.

Ignore VAT and Tax.

Required:

(a) Prepare a cash budget for each of the first three months and in total. **(15 marks)**

(b) There is some uncertainty about the direct material cost. It is thought that the direct material cost per component could range between £1·50 and £2·20. Calculate the budgeted total net cash flow for the three month period if the cost of the direct material is:
  (i) £1.50 per component; or
  (ii) £2.20 per component. **(6 marks)**

(c) Using your answers to part *(a)* and *(b)* above, prepare a report to the management of RF Ltd that discusses the benefits or otherwise of performing 'what if' analysis when preparing cash budgets. **(9 marks)**

Solutions to Revision Questions

Section A – Multi-choice solutions

 ## Solution 1

1.1 Marginal cost of inventory is an approximation of variable production cost of £62,000. l/8th production in inventory = £7,750

Therefore the correct answer is (B).

1.2 Throughput approach values inventory at direct materials cost = 1/8th of £40,000 = £5,000

Therefore the correct answer is (A).

1.3 Absorption costing overhead rate is £29,500/5,000 units = £5.90 per unit

Absorption costing profit greater by £5.90 × 500 units = £2,950

Therefore the correct answer is (B).

1.4 $y = £800 + (0.0002 \times 4,100^2) = £4,162$

Total budgeted vehicle costs are £4,162 × 1.03 = £4,287

Variance is £4,287 − £5,000 = £713 Adverse

Therefore the correct answer is (A).

1.5 The correct answer is (C).

1.6 Planning price variance

30,000 × ($4.00 − $5.00) = $30,000 Adverse

Therefore the correct answer is (B).

1.7 Operational usage variance

(30,000 − 32,000) × $5.00 = $10,000 Adverse

Therefore the correct answer is (D).

1.8 Operational price variance

32,000 × ($5.00 − $4.80) = $6,400 Favourable

Therefore the correct answer is (B).

1.9 Items debited to cost of goods sold account will be:

Finished goods sold £1,700,000

Difference between conversion costs incurred and conversion costs allocated, that is, £890,000 − £840,000 = £50,000

Therefore the correct answer is (B).

1.10 Adjustments needed are:

1. for launch costs − spread over 3 years; and

2. need to use replacement cost of net assets.

So EVA = (£40.2 m + £4 m) − (£172 m × 11%) = £25.28 m.

Therefore the correct answer is (B).

 Solution 2

2.1 The correct answer is (B).

2.2 The correct answer is (A).

2.3 The correct answer is (C).

2.4

Units		Equivalent Units	
		Material Z	Conversion cost
225	To complete opening wip	45	45
350	Started and finished	350	350
150	Closing wip	90	60
	Total E. U.	**485**	**455**

Therefore the correct answer is (A).

2.5 Therefore the correct answer is (C).

2.6

	£	£
Std cost of goods produced		128,500
Plus adverse variances		
Materials price	2,400	
Labour rate	5,600	
Variable overheads	2,680	10,680
Less favourable variances		
Material usage	8,400	
Labour efficiency	3,140	
Fixed overheads	3,192	(14,732)
Actual cost of goods produced		**124,448**

Therefore the correct answer is (B).

2.7   The correct answer is (C).

2.8

		Difference
Output	2,000 units	3,500 units	1,500 units
Total cost	£12,000	£16,200	£4,200

Variable cost per unit = 4,200/1,500 = £2.80.

Fixed cost = 12,000 − (2,000 × 2.80) = £6,400 *(Note:* Alternatively, you could have used the figures for 3,500 units).

Therefore, the budget cost allowance for 4,000 units = £6,400 + (4,000 × 2.80) = £17,600.

Therefore the correct answer is (A).

2.9   The index values for a multiplicative model with four seasons add to 400.

Therefore the correct answer is (D).

2.10 Assuming the revenue was $100 will lead to the following revised figures:

	Original	Revised
Revenue	100	60
Variable costs	30	18
Fixed costs	22	22
Profit	48	20

Therefore the correct answer is (B) (20/60).

 Solution 3

3.1

Standard selling price	£26
Actual selling price	£31
	£5 × 8,200 = £41,000 Favourable

The correct answer is B.

3.2   Sales profit volume variance

	Units
Budgeted sales	8,700
Actual sales	8,200
	500 × (£26 − £10 − £4) = £6,000 Adverse

The correct answer is A.

3.3   Fixed overhead volume variance

	Units
Budgeted output	8,700
Actual output	8,200
	500 × £4 = £2,000 Adverse

The correct answer is A.

3.4 The correct answer is D.

3.5 ROI $300,000/6,750,000 \times 100 = 4.44\%$

The correct answer is A.

3.6 RI £300 K – 877.5 K ($13\% \times £6.75$ m) = $-£577.5$

The correct answer is D.

3.7

	£m
Profit	89.20
Add	
Current depreciation ($120 \times 20\%$)	24.00
Development costs ($£9.60 \times 2/3$)	6.40
Less	
Replacement depreciation ($£168 \times 20\%$)	33.60
Adjusted profit	86.00
Less cost of capital charge (Working 1)	21.84
EVA	64.16

Working 1
Cost of capital charge

Fixed assets ($£168 - 33.6$)	134.4
Working capital	27.2
Development costs	6.4
	$168.0 \times 13\% = 21.84$

The correct answer is A.

3.8 The correct answer is B.

3.9 OAR $1,000/200 = £5$ per unit

Total variance

Actual	£1,300,000
Absorbed	£1,200,000
	£ 100,000 adverse

£1,200,000/£5 = 240,000

The correct answer is B.

3.10

	Units
Opening inventory	800
Closing inventory	500
Decrease	$300 \times (£500,000/2,000) = £75,000$ lower

The correct answer is B.

Solution 4

4.1   The correct answer is D.

4.2   The correct answer is A.

4.3   The correct answer is D.

4.4

	Units
Sales	30,000
Req'd closing inventory	4,725
Less opening inventory	(3,500)
Production	31,225

The correct answer is C.

4.5

Budget	£2,500,000
Actual	£2,010,000
Variance	£490,000 favourable

The correct answer is D.

4.6

Budgeted volume	500,000 units
Actual volume	440,000 units
	60,000 units

OAR	
2 hours × £2·50	×£5 per unit
Volume variance	£300,000 adverse

The correct answer is C.

4.7

	£
Absorbed (200,000 units × £1·50)	300,000
Incurred	260,000
Over absorbed	40,000

The correct answer is A.

4.8   Actual fixed production

overhead cost	£1,950,000
Total variance	£150,000 adverse
Absorbed	£1,800,000
OAR per unit	£5
	360,000 units

The correct anser is C.

4.9   The correct answer is C.

4.10

High Low Method	Activity	Cost	
Highest	6,500	£33,000	
Lowest	4,500	£29,000	
Difference	2,000	£4,000	
Variable cost per unit		£2	
Substitute into highest activity	6,500	£33,000	Total cost
	6,500 × £2	£13,000	Variable cost
	Difference	£20,000	Fixed cost
Therefore	5,750 × £2	£11,500	Variable cost
		£20,000	Fixed cost
		£31,500	Total cost

The correct answer is C.

✅ Solution 5

5.1 $[(11,000 \times 0.75) - 8,000] \times £20 = £5,000$ Favourable

Therefore the correct answer is (B).

5.2 $(8,000 \times £15) - £132,000 = £12,000$ Adverse

Therefore the correct answer is (C).

5.3 The correct answer is (B).

5.4 The correct answer is (D).

5.5 $(80,000 \times 0.4) + (120,000 \times 0.6) = 104,000$ units

Therefore the correct answer is (C).

5.6

	£
Cost of goods sold	100,000
Less material cost £45 × 1,000	45,000
Conversion cost allocated	55,000
Conversion cost incurred	60,000
Excess charged to cost of goods sold account	5,000
Total debit on cost of goods sold account £100,000 + £5,000 =	105,000

Therefore the correct answer is (C).

5.7 Marginal cost will be the same as variable cost, that is, £15

The two-part tariff transfer price per unit is marginal cost £15. This is because the £200,000 will be transferred as a total fixed fee and not, therefore, as part of the *until* transfer price.

Therefore the correct answer is (A).

5.8 The correct answer is (D).

5.9 The most appropriate measure of ROI will include only assets available to earn profit during the year and will not include interest payable.

Thus ROI will be $£6\,m/(£35\,m - £4\,m) = 19.4\%$

Therefore the correct answer is (D)

5.10 Adjustment needed for launch costs – spread over 3 years, and need to use replacement cost of net assets so EVA = $(£20.2\,m + £2\,m) - (£84\,m \times 11\%) = £12.96\,m$. Therefore the correct answer is (D).

✓ Solution 6

6.1 $400/1700 = 23.5\%$

Therefore the correct answer is (C).

6.2 $400 - (1,700 \times 12\%) = £196,000$

Therefore the correct answer is (B).

6.3 Actual rate is $£336,000/24,000 = £14$ per hour
$$24,000 \times [£15 - £14] = £24,000 \text{ Favourable}$$

Therefore the correct answer is (D).

6.4 $[(11,000 \times 2) - 24,000] \times £6 = £12,000$ Adverse

Therefore the correct answer is (A).

6.5 The correct answer is (A).

6.6 Closing inventory would be valued at $£300,000/1,000 = £300$ per unit.

	£
Turnover	820,000
Production costs [£300,000 − (150 × £300)]	255,000
Other costs	395,000
Profit	170,000

Therefore the correct answer is (A).

6.7 The correct answer is (C).

6.8 The correct answer is (D).

6.9 Full cost

	£
Variable cost	9
Fixed cost = 120,000/20,000=	6
Full cost	15
plus 40%	6
Total cost plus	21

Two-part tariff requires only variable cost of £9 for additional transfers

Therefore the correct answer is (A).

6.10 The correct answer is (A).

Section A – Non-multi-choice questions

 ## Solution 7

7.1 Orders = [100,000 + (30 × 240)] × 1.08 = 115,776
Overhead cost = £10,000 + (£0.25 × 115,776) = £38,944
Answer is £39,000

7.2 Use high/low method to separate fixed and variable budgeted overhead cost:

	Hours	£
High	18,000	16,242
Low	10,000	13,468
Difference	8,000	2,774

Variable cost per machine hour

$$= \frac{£2,774}{8,000} = £0.34675$$

By substitution fixed cost

$$= £13,468 - (10,000 \times £0.34675) = £10,000$$

Budget cost allowance   £
$$= £10,000 + (13,780 \times £0.34675) = 14,778$$
Actual cost =   14,521
                             257 (F)

7.3

Budgeted number of batches		
Product D (100,000/100)	=	1,000
Product R (100,000/50)	=	2,000
Product P (50,000/25)	=	2,000
		5,000
Budgeted machine set-ups		
Product D (1,000 × 3)	=	3,000
Product R (2,000 × 4)	=	8,000
Product P (2,000 × 6)	=	12,000
		23,000
Budgeted number of purchase orders		
Product D (1,000 × 2)	=	2,000
Product R (2,000 × 1)	=	2,000
Product P (2,000 × 1)	=	2,000
		6,000
Budgeted processing minutes		
Product D (100,000 × 2)	=	200,000
Product R (100,000 × 3)	=	300,000
Product P (50,000 × 3)	=	150,000
		650,000 minutes

7.4 *Budgeted cost/set-up*

$$= \frac{£150,000}{23,000} = £6.52 \quad \text{Budgeted unit cost of } \mathbf{R} = \frac{£6.52 \times 4}{50} = £0.52$$

Budgeted cost/purchase orders

$$= \frac{£70,000}{6,000} = £11.67 \text{ Budgeted unit cost of } \mathbf{R} = \frac{£11.67 \times 1}{50} = £0.23$$

Budgeted processing cost per minute

$$= \frac{£80,000}{650,000} = £0.12 \text{ Budgeted unit cost of } \mathbf{R} = £0.12 \times 3 = £0.36$$

*Total budgeted unit cost of **R** is*

		£
Set-up costs	=	0.52
Purchasing costs	=	0.23
Processing costs	=	0.36
Total cost	=	1.11 per unit

7.5

	Actual mix litres	Standard mix litres	Difference litres	Price £	Variance £
X	984	885.6	98.4 (A)	2.50	246.0 (A)
Y	1,230	1,328.4	98.4 (F)	3.00	295.2 (F)
Totals	2,214	2,214.0	nil		49.2 (F)

7.6

$$\text{Expected output} = \frac{2,214}{30} = 73.8 \text{ units}$$

Actual output	= 72.0 units
Shortfall	= 1.8 units
1.8 units × £84/unit	= £151.2 (A)

An alternative would be only 73 complete units of output were expected, thus the shortfall would be 1 unit. The variance would be 1.0 × £84 per unit = £84 adverse.

7.7 (a) Machine utilisation rates

Product Required machine hours	A	B	C	Total
Machine 1	250	100	90	440
Machine 2	250	275	90	615
Machine 3	125	50	30	205

Utilisation rates:

Machine 1 (440/400)	=	10%
Machine 2 (615/400)	=	154%
Machine 3 (205/400)	=	51%

(b) Machine 2 is the bottleneck – it has the highest utilisation and this is greater than 100%.

7.8 (a) The Goldratt procedure is:
- identify the system's bottleneck,
- decide how to exploit or relieve the bottleneck,
- sub-ordinate everything else to relieving the bottleneck,
- elevate the system's bottlenecks,
- when one bottleneck is no longer a constraint, start procedure again (there will always be a new bottleneck).

(b) Optimal allocation would be on the basis of contribution from the bottleneck resource.

Ranking of contribution per product from machine 2 is:

Product	A	B	C
Contribution per unit	£36	£28	£18
Machine 2 hours	5	5.5	1.5
Contribution per machine hour	£7.20	£5.09	£12.00
Ranking	2	3	1

Thus allocation on this ranking

Product C	60 units	Using	90 hours	
Product B	50 units	Using	250 hours	
			340 hours	

This use 340 hours, leaving an available balance of 60 hours.
This will make 60/5.5 = 10.9 units of Product B or 10 whole units.

7.9 FIFO and weighted average methods give very similar results under various circumstances including the following:

1. Where the conversion percentage is virtually constant between accounting periods.
2. Where the conversion costs in work-in-process at the end of the month are very small in relation to the total conversion costs during the month. This is likely to occur where the process time is short and the process is repeated many times in the month.
3. In general, where unit cost fluctuations are minimal between the months.

☑ Solution 8

8.1 $x = 27$ so trend value is $25,000 + (6,500 \times 27) = 200,500$ units

Quarter 3 adjustment is 150%, so forecast is 300,750 units

8.2 Post separation costs per unit are £19,600/2,800 = £7 per litre

Notional price at separation point is £10.50 − £7 = £3.50 per litre

		Weighted sales value is		
	P	3,600 × £4.60 =	£16,560
	Q	4,100 × £6.75 =	£27,675
	R	2,800 × £3.50 =	£9,800
			£54,035

8.3 Allocation of common process costs to R is £42,500 × (£9,800/£54,035) = £7,708

	January units	February units	March units
Sales	4,000	5,000	6,000
Closing inventory:			
30% next month	1,500	1,800	
Less opening inventory	(1,200)	(1,500)	
Production in month	4,300	5,300	

Raw material requirement	*January*
	units
Monthly production	4,300
Closing inventory: 25% of	
next month's production	1,325
Less opening inventory	(1,075)
Material purchases	4,550

Payments for purchases for the cash budget in February are the actual purchases delivered in January, that is,

4,550 units at £8 per unit = £36,400

8.4
Total overhead cost	£88,000
Direct labour hours	8,000
Absorption rate	£11 per direct labour hour

Budgeted unit cost for product Z for October is:

	£
Direct materials	21.50
Direct labour 0.3 × £16	4.80
Overhead costs 0.3 × £11	3.30
Total unit cost	29.60

8.5   Cost driver rates are needed

Set-ups £22,000/88	=	£250 per set-up
Quality tests £34,000/40	=	£850 per test
Other overheads £32,000/8,000 =		£4 per direct labour hour
(note this is not a true cost driver)		

Activity-based cost of product Z

	£
Direct materials	21.50
Direct labour	4.80
Set-up costs 2 × £250/30	16.67
Quality tests £850/75	11.33
Other overhead costs 0.3 × £4	1.20
Total activity-based costs for October	55.50

An alternative approach to these calculations would be:
Set-up costs = [(150/30) × 2 × £250]/150 = £16.67
Quality costs = (2 × £850)/l50 = £11.33

8.6   Costs under ABC could be higher where: there is production complexity not represented in direct labour hours; small batch sizes; or high levels of non-manufacturing activity. This may lead management to: increase batch sizes, simplify processes to reduce activities, or review pricing if this is not in line with ABC costs.
(Three implications are given, though only two are required).

Hours sold	Price per hour	LD view (VC = 25 1 40) Contribution per hour	Contribution	KL view (VC = 25 1 20) Contribution per hour	Contribution
	£	£	£	£	£
0	100				
1,000	90	25	25,000	45	45,000
2,000	80	15	*30,000	35	70,000
3,000	70	5	15,000	25	*75,000
4,000	60	−5	−20,000	15	60,000
5,000	50	−15	−75,000	5	25,000

8.7 The level of sales for the Legal Division that will maximise the profit in the Legal Division is 2,000 hours, giving contribution to the division of £30,000.

8.8 The level of sales for the KL company that will maximise the profit in KL company is 3,000 hours giving a contribution of £75,000.

8.9 Customer perspective performance measure could be the percentage of new product developments delivered to the manufacturing division on time.

Financial perspective performance measure could be the number of projects completed within 5% of the budgeted cost.

8.10 Two perspectives required are 'Internal Business' perspective and 'Innovation and Learning' perspective.

Appropriate objectives or goals could be:
The Internal Business perspective captures the processes at which the division must excel, so a goal might be a continuous stream of new products to the market. A suitable measure could be measuring the trend in the average time it takes to bring new drugs to market.
The Innovation and Learning perspective emphasises how the division can continuously improve and create value. Thus the division's goal might be to maintain its reputation for innovating new products and treatments. A suitable measure might be the number of new patents registered.

 Solution 9

9.1

	W	X	Y
	£	£	£
Selling price	200	150	150
Cost			
Direct materials	41	20	30
Throughput contribution	159	130	120
TP/LF	159/9	130/10	120/7
	£17.66	£13.00	£17.14
Ranking	1st	3rd	2nd

9.2

	Assembly (£)	Finishing (£)	Stores (£)	Maintenance (£)
Overheads	100,000	150,000	50,000	40,000
Reapportion				
Maintenance	16,000	18,000	6,000	−40,000
Stores	33,600	22,400	−56,000	
	149,600	190,400	Nil	Nil
OAR	149,600/100,000			
	£1.496 per unit			

Assembly
Absorbed 120,000 × £1.496	£179,520
Incurred	£180,000
Under absorbed	£480

9.3

$140,000 − $18,000(by product)$122,000
Sales revenue
X (2,500 × $50)	$125,000
Y (3,500 × $60)	$210,000
	$335,000

Split between products
X [($125,000/$335,000) × $122,000] + $24,000 =	$69,522
Y [($210,000/$335,000) × $122,000] + $46,000 =	$122,475
	$191,997 rounding

9.4

	X ($)	Y ($)
Sales		
10,000 × $800	8,000,000	
12,000 × $612	7,344,000	
12,000 × $1,200		14,400,000
Costs		
22,000 × $360	−7,920,000	
12,000 × $1,012		−12,144,000
Fixed costs		
Production 22,000 × $240	−5,280,000	
Non production	−1,500,000	−1,300,000
Profit	644,000	956,000
Tax	−161,000	−286,800
Profit after tax	483,000	669,200

9.5

Planning variance	£ per kg
Ex-ante standard	4.10
Ex-post standard	4.50
	0.40 × 11,200 = £4,480 Adverse

Usage variance	kg
Standard 7 × 1,600	11,200
Actual	12,000
	800 × £4.50 = £3,600 Adverse

9.6

	W	X	Y
	£ per unit	*£ per unit*	*£ per unit*
Selling price	200.00	183.00	175.00
Direct material	50.00	40.00	35.00
Direct labour	30.00	35.00	30.00
Overheads			
Receiving/inspecting etc	33.60	33.60	31.11
Production scheduling	36.00	26.00	25.00
Profit per unit	50.40	48.40	53.89

Cost driver rates
Receiving/inspecting quality assurance   £1,400,000/5,000 = £280 per requisition
Production scheduling/machine set up   £1,200,000/800 = £1,500 per set up

9.7   Equivalent units table

Description	Units	Materials		Labour		Overheads	
		%	EU	%	EU	%	EU
Output	1,920	100	1,920	100	1,920	100	1,920
CWIP	500	100	500	90	450	40	200
			2,420		2,370		2,120
Costs			£		£		£
OWIP			98,000		46,000		7,600
Process			387,800		276,320		149,280
			485,800		322,320		156,880
Less normal loss – 180 × £10			1,800				
			484,000				
EU cost			£200		£136		£74

Value of Output − 1,920 units × (£200 + £136 + £74) = £787,200

9.8

Efficiency variance
Standard hours   57,500
Actual hours   60,000
           2,500 × £12 − £30,000 Adverse

Rate variance
Standard rate   £12.00
Actual rate   £12.75
           £0.75 × 60,000 hours = £45,000 Adverse

 Solution 10

10.1   Mix variance = $500 favourable

	Actual mix			Standard mix		
	kg	*$*	*$*	*kg*	*$*	*$*
P	1,030	75	77,250	1,000	75	75,000
Q	560	100	56,000	600	100	60,000
R	410	125	51,250	400	125	50,000
	2,000		184,500	2,000		185,000

10.2 Yield variance = $196,304 − $185,000 = $11,305 favourable Output was 1,910 kg. The stanard input for this should be 1,910/90% = 2,122.22 kg

	Standard mix of input			Standard mix for output		
	kg	*$*	*$*	*kg*	*$*	*$*
P	1,000	75	75,000	1,061.11	75	79,583
Q	600	100	60,000	636.67	100	63,667
R	400	125	50,000	424.44	125	53,055
	2,000		**185,000**	2,122.22		**196,305**

Alternative method

Standard cost of 1 kg of output is $9,250/90 = $102.78

Expected output was 2,000 × 0.9 = 1,800 kg
Actual output was 1,910 kg

There is a favourable yield of 110 kg.
Therefore, the yield variance is 110 × $102.78 = $11,306 favourable

10.3

	£m	£m
Net profit after tax		8.6
Add		
Interest	2.3	
Development costs	6.3	
Advertising	1.6	10.2
		18.8
Less 1/3 development costs		2.1
		16.7
Less capital charge: 30 × 13%		3.9
EVA		**12.8**

10.4

Month of sale	Factor	Receive December $
November	60% × 90%	70,200
October	20%	24,000
September	15%	15,000
Total		**109,200**

10.5 Any four relevant aims. For example:

1. Ensure optimal allocation of resources;
2. Promote goal congruence;
3. Motivate divisional managers;
4. Facilitate performance measurement;
5. Not stifle autonomy.

10.6

	kg	From P1	Materials	Conversion
		Equivalent units (kg)		
Transferred to finished goods	2,800	2,800	2,800	2,800
Normal loss	200			
Abnormal loss	100	100	100	50
Closing work in progress	700	700	700	150
	3,800	3,600	3,600	3,000
Costs (£)		34,200	16,200	26,700
Cost per E.U. (£)		9.50	4.50	8.90

Abnormal loss $= (100 \times £9.50) + (100 \times £4.50) + (50 \times £8.90) = £1,845$

10.7 All figures are £'000

Month	Sales	Cost of sales	Opening inventory	Closing inventory	Purchase	Paid
July	100	80	40	36	76	
August	90	72	36	50	86	76
September	125	100	50	56	106	86
October	140	112	56			106

10.8 Fly to new destinations: percentage occupancy on flights to new destinations. This will show how popular the routes are.

Reduce ground time: measure baggage unloading/loading times, cleaning times, restocking meals and duty free, staff availability and so on. This will identify the key factor.

10.9 Labour standard for 1 unit is 4 hours $\times$ £9 per hour

$$\begin{aligned} \text{Idle time variance} &= (61,500 - 56,000) \times £9 \\ &= 5,500 \times £9 \\ &= £49,500 \text{ adverse} \end{aligned}$$

10.10

$$\begin{aligned} \text{Efficiency variance} &= (\text{std hours for actual output} - \text{actual hours}) \times \text{std rate} \\ &= [(14,650 \times 4) - 56,000] \times £9 \\ &= (58,600 - 56,000) \times £9 \\ &= £23,400 \text{ favourable} \end{aligned}$$

10.11 Budgeted profit $= £1\,m$. Therefore total contribution $= £6.5\,m$ and contribution from Z must be £3 m.

	Product X	Product Y	Product Z	Total
Revenue	£10 m	£20 m	£12 m	
C/S ratio	15%	10%	25%	
Contribution (£m)	1.5	2.0	3.0	6.5
Fixed costs (£m)				5.5
Profit (£m)				1.0

Solution 11

11.1

A – Original plan	600 × £72 = £43,200
B – Revised ex post plan	600 × £82 = £49,200
C – Actual results	600 × £86 = £51,600

Selling price planning variance is B − A = £6,000 Favourable

Selling price operating variance is C − B = £2,400 Favourable

(Total variance is C − A = £8,400 Favourable to check)

11.2

	Units	Material	Conversion
Opening stock	(200)	(200)	(50)
Completed and transferred	1,400	1,400	1,400
Abnormal loss	50	50	50
Closing stock	200	200	100
Equivalent Units	1,450	1,450	1,500

11.3 Mix variance

	Actual usage in standard proportions	$
D =	4,000 litres at $9 per litre	36,000
E =	3,500 litres at $5 per litre	17,500
F =	2,500 litres at $2 per litre	5,000
	10,000	58,500 (1)

	Actual usage in actual proportions	
D =	4,300 litres at $9 per litre	38,700
E =	3,600 litres at $5 per litre	18,000
F =	2,100 litres at $2 per litre	4,200
	10,000	60,900 (2)

Mix variance is (1) − (2) = $2,400 Adverse

Yield variance

Standard cost of 1 litre is $58.50/9	=	$6.50
Expected output is 10,000 × 90%	=	9,000 litres
Actual output	=	9,100 litres
Yield variance is (9,100 − 9,000) × $6.50 =		$650 Favourable

11.4

	Maximum no of units of Z1	*Maximum no of units of Z2*
Dept 1	480/12 = 40	480/16 = 30
Dept 2	840/20 = 42	840/15 = 56

Department 2 has more capacity than Department 1 for both products, therefore Department 1 is the limiting factor or bottleneck.

11.5

	Z1	Z2
Variable cost	£26.80	£30.40
Sales price	£50.00	£65.00
Contribution	£23.20	£34.60

Calculate contribution per limiting factor (Department 1 time)
Z1 = £23.20/12 = £1.933 per minute
Z2 = £34.60/16 = £2.1625 per minute
So, maximum contribution would be to make as many Z2 as possible, that is, 30 units
× £34.60 = £1,038

11.6 Throughput or throughput contribution is sales less direct materials, so
Z1 is £50 − £10 = £40
Z2 is £65 − £15 = £50

Throughput per bottleneck minute is:
Z1 £40/12 = £3.333
Z2 £50/16 = £3.125

Thus, maximum throughput is by production of maximum number of Zl, that is,
40 units of Zl giving throughput contribution of 40 × £40 = £1,600

11.7

Process account

	kg	£		kg	£
Input materials	2,400	19,200	Normal loss	240	–
Process costs		4,800	Abnormal loss	100	1,111
			Transfer to packing	2,060	22,889
	2,400	24,000		2,400	24,000

Abnormal loss account

	£		£
Process account	1,111	Cash sale	400
		To income statement	711
	1,111		1,111

11.8

(a) Receivables days   200/3,000 × 365 = 24 days
(b) Payables days   280/1,600 × 365 = 64 days
(c) Inventory days   300/1,600 × 365 = 68 days

Note: Alternative answers for these calculations using
average figures would be equally allowable.

11.9

(a) Current ratio	550:280	1.96:1
(b) Quick ratio	250:280	0.89:1

 Solution 12

12.1

	A	B	C
	$	$	$
Selling price	200	150	150
Direct materials	41	20	30
Throughput	159	130	120
Machine P – minutes per unit	12	10	7
Return per factory hour			
	159/12	130/10	120/7
	13·25	13	17·14
×60 minutes	**795**	**780**	**1,028**

12.2

Operating profit margin	$(3,629,156/7,055,016) \times 100 = 51\cdot44\%$
Return on capital employed	$[3,629,156/(4,582,000 + 4,619,582 + 442,443 - 949,339 - 464,692)] \times 100 = 44\cdot10\%$
Trade receivable days	$(442,443/7,055,016) \times 365$ days $= 22\cdot89$ days
Current/liquidity ratio	$(4,619,582 + 442,443)/(949,339 + 464,692) = 3\cdot58$ times

12.3

Sales price variance

Budgeted selling price	£10·00	
Actual selling price	£9·50	
	£0·50	adverse
Actual sales volume (units)	110,000	
	£55,000	adverse

Sales volume profit variance

Budgeted sales volume (units)	100,000	
Actual sales volume (units)	110,000	
	10,000	favourable
Standard profit per unit	£2	
	£20,000	favourable

12.4

(i) Budgeted loss – marginal cost transfer price

		£000
Sales		
Internal	60,000 × £100	6,000
External	40,000 × (£150 × 1·3333)	8,000
		14,000
Variable cost	100,000 × £100	10,000
Contribution		4,000
Fixed costs		
Production	100,000 × £40	4,000
Administration	100,000 × £10	1,000
Loss		(1,000)

(ii) Budgeted profit – absorption cost transfer price

		£000
Sales		
Internal	60,000 × £140	8,400
External	40,000 × (£150 × 1·3333)	8,000
		16,400
Variable cost	100,000 × £100	10,000
Contribution		6,400
Fixed costs		
Production	100,000 × £40	4,000
Administration	100,000 × £10	1,000
Profit		1,400

12.5 Forecast sales volume for June, July and August is:

Month	Cumulative sales (units)	Monthly sales (units)
June	1,500	1,500
July	2,274	774
August	2,900	626

Section B

 Solution 13

(a) Production Budget in units

	Quarter 1	Quarter 2	Quarter 3	Quarter 4	Total
Required by sales	2,250	2,050	1,650	2,050	8,000
Plus required closing inventory	615	495	615	375	375
Less opening inventory	−675	−615	−495	−615	−675
Production Budget	2,190	1,930	1,770	1,810	7,700

Raw Materials purchases budget

Material B	Quarter 1	Quarter 2	Quarter 3	Quarter 4	Total
	kg	kg	kg	kg	kg
Required by production	6,570	5,790	5,310	5,430	23,100
Plus required closing inventory	2,605.50	2,389.50	2,443.50	2,011.50	2,011.50
Less opening inventory	−2,956.50	−2,605.50	−2,389.50	−2,443.50	−2,956.50
Material Purchases Budget	6,219	5,574	5,364	4,998	22,155
Value	£43,533	£39,018	£37,548	£34,986	£155,085

(b) If material A is in short supply during the coming year, X plc will need to source a different supplier or find a substitute material. If they are unable to do this, then they will have to make best use of the materials in scarce supply and focus their efforts on producing the product which maximises contribution per limiting factor. Rather than starting with the sales budget they will now need to start with the production budget due to the scarcity of material A as there will be a limit to how many units of output they can produce. The production budget therefore becomes the key budget factor which will drive the preparation of all budgets.

X plc could also review any wastage that may be occurring and aim to reduce this.

(c) Operating Statement

	Fixed Budget	Flexed Budget	Actual	Flexible Budget Variance
Activity	7,700	7,250	7,250	
Overheads	£	£	£	£
Variable	168,000	158,182	185,000	26,818 adverse
Fixed	112,000	112,000	105,000	7,000 favourable
Labour				
Skilled	462,000	435,000	568,750	133,750 adverse
Semi-skilled	415,800	391,500	332,400	59,100 favourable
	1,157,800	**1,096,682**	**1,191,150**	**94,468 adverse**

(d) Incremental budgeting builds in any inefficiency contained in the previous year's budget as it simply takes the previous year's budget or actual results and adjusts for anticipated changes. Incremental budgeting does not encourage building the budget from zero and justifying each item of cost. It also does not allow for the changing nature of the business environment as it is inward looking.

ZBB does require each cost element to be specifically justified, as though the activities to which the budget relates were being undertaken for the first time, thereby avoiding the problems encountered with incremental budgeting.

(e) A rolling budget system is particularly useful when future costs and/or activities cannot be forecast accurately. A rolling budget is continuously updated by adding a further accounting period (month or quarter) when the earliest accounting period has expired. This means that a company will always be looking 9 to 12 months ahead. Also, the first three quarters of the new budget are reviewed and revised to take account of any changed circumstances.

As X plc is experiencing an increase in competition in the market it will need to be able to react to this by adjusting selling price, sales volume and so on. Also, the changes in material and labour availability mean that it will need to be able to adjust budgets if these resources become limited and therefore expensive, or the opposite where it could possibly produce more and therefore increase its sales effort.

(f) The linear regression method determines mathematically the regression line of best fit. When forecasting sales a series of historical values for sales volume that vary over time would be plotted on a graph and a time series may then reveal a trend or relationship. This trend or relationship can then be adjusted for variations, for example cyclical, seasonal, long-term trend and random variations. Once the trend line has been adjusted for such variations a forecast of future sales can be made. However, it should be noted that linear regression analysis assumes that the past is an indication of what will happen in the future.

The linear regression method for sales forecasting may be useful to X plc in that it could provide a base from which other adjustments can be made according to the state of the market, availability and costs of material and labour.

 Solution 14

Answer to (a)

(i) Difference in standard wage rate = £1·20 per hour

Planning variance	(standard hours for actual output) × difference in wage rate
	680 × (900/600) × £1·20
	1,020 × £1·20
	£1,224 Adverse
Operational efficiency variance	(standard hours for actual output − actual hours) × revised wage rate
	(1,020 − 1,070) × £31·20
	50 × £31·20
	£1,560 Adverse

(ii) The major benefit of analysing the variances into planning and operational components is that the revised standard should provide a realistic standard against which to measure performance. Any variances should then be a result of operational management efficiencies and inefficiencies and not faulty planning.

Answer to (b)

The main limitations of standard costing in the modern business environment are as follows:

• The business environment in the past was more stable whereas the modern business environment is more dynamic and subject to change. As a result if a business environment is continuously changing standard costing is not a suitable method because standards cannot be established for a reasonable period of time.

- The focus of the modern business environment is on improving quality and customer care whereas the environment in the past was focused on minimising cost.
- The life cycle of products in the modern business environment is shorter and therefore standards become quickly out of date.
- The increase in automation in the modern business environment has resulted in less emphasis on labour cost variances.

Answer to (c)

The benefit of investigating a variance should never exceed the cost of investigation. However this can be difficult to ascertain and therefore a manager should decide to investigate a variance based on the following:

Size

Criteria will be laid down which state that variances which are of a certain amount or percentage will be investigated. This is an extremely simple method to apply but the cut off values can be subjective.

Controllable/Uncontrollable

There is little point in investigating a variance if it is uncontrollable. The cost in this situation would outweigh the benefits of investigation since there would be no benefit obtained.

Interrelationships

An adverse variance in one part of the business may result in a favourable variance elsewhere. These interdependencies must be considered when deciding on investigation. For example a favourable labour rate variance may result in an adverse efficiency variance where less skilled workers are employed, costing less, as a result the workers take longer to do the job and an adverse efficiency variance arises.

Type of standard

If a company sets an ideal standard this will usually lead to adverse variances. The manager will need to decide at what size of adverse variance an investigation should take place on such variances.

Answer to (d)

Firstly G Group must consider the transfer pricing system. The system must provide information that motivates divisional managers to make good economic decisions not just for themselves but for the company as a whole. It should also provide information that is useful for evaluating the managerial and economic performance of the divisions and should ensure that divisional autonomy is not undermined.

If there is unlimited demand for the output of the two divisions in the market then the transfer price should equal the market price less any savings as a result of internal transfer. This then allows the divisions to report a profit on the transfers and will not cause any issue for the calculation of the bonus.

However, if there is a limit on the amount that can be sold on the external market then the divisions would be transferring at marginal cost as there is no opportunity cost. In this case they will simply cover the marginal cost and have no contribution towards fixed costs or profit. This will mean that if the bonus is awarded on profit the divisional manager will not receive a bonus despite the fact that they have made internal supplies.

Therefore the company must ensure that in order for decisions to remain goal congruent the bonus scheme must allow for internal transfers that impact on the divisions' ability to earn bonuses.

Other areas to consider when implementing a bonus scheme include:

- It should be clearly understood by all personnel involved;
- There should be no delay between the awarding of the bonus and the subsequent payment of the bonus;
- It should motivate the personnel;
- It should not cause sub-optimal behaviour;
- Controllable and uncontrollable costs and revenues should be identified separately.

Answer to (e)

A manufacturing resource planning system involves the planning of raw materials, components, subassemblies and other input resources, such as machine capacity and labour, so that the system provides a fully integrated planning approach to the management of all the company's manufacturing resources. The quality of the data which sets the parameters within a manufacturing resource planning system drives the company's operations and determines the optimal production and purchasing plan.

In order to ensure that a manufacturing resource planning system operates effectively it is essential to have:

- A master production schedule, which specifies both the timing and quantity demanded of each of the top-level finished good items.
- A bill of materials file for each sub-assembly, component and part, containing details of the number of items on hand, scheduled receipts and items allocated to released orders but not yet drawn from inventories.
- A master parts file containing planned lead times of all items to be purchased and sub-assemblies and components to be produced internally.
- A master labour and machine capacity file which specifies both the timing and quantity demanded to achieve planned production levels.

The data identified above that is used to ensure the manufacturing resource planning system operates effectively can then be used in a standard costing system to set parameters for materials, labour and overhead capacity. These will then be used to measure performance through variance analysis.

Answer to (f)

Just-in-time is a system whose objective is to produce or procure products or components as they are required by a customer or for use, rather than for inventory. A just-in-time system is a 'pull system' which responds to demand, in contrast to a 'push system', in which inventories act as buffers between the different elements of the system, such as purchasing, production and sales.

The traditional business environment is a 'push system' in which one process supplies parts to the next process without regard to the ability to continue work on those parts.

This extends onto producing finished goods inventory ready for sale to customers. Work in progress, inventory of raw materials and finished goods inventory are an inherent part of such a traditional system.

On the other hand a just in time system is described as a philosophy, or approach to management, as it encompasses a commitment to continuous improvement and the pursuit of excellence in the design and operation of the production management system. A JIT system operates in such a way that production and resource acquisition should be pulled by customer demand rather than being pushed by a planning process. A JIT based production operation responds quickly to customer demand and resources are acquired and utilised only when needed. A JIT system operates with little or no inventories and in order to be able to operate in this manner, an organisation must achieve excellence in the following areas:

- Production scheduling
- Supplier relations
- Plant maintenance
- Information systems
- Quality controls
- Customer relations

 ## Solution 15

(a) The traditional management accounting performance measures are best suited to a stable environment, which is programmable. These measures include budgetary control and standard costing which relies upon the ability to be able to predict the future with some accuracy. Standards are frequently set based upon past performance, the assumption being that the past is a good predictor of the future.

With the increase in competition in world markets and the ever-increasing rate of change of technology, the manufacturing environment has had to become more flexible in order to meet customer needs. Rather than being able to have long batch runs of the same product the emphasis is on small batches and constant product innovation and a requirement to improve and monitor quality.

Traditional management accounting techniques to monitor performance, such as standard costing, are unable to provide the information required because of the need to constantly revise standards. The move to more mechanised and computerised processes has also made the traditional labour variances obsolete because of the insignificant proportion of direct labour in total product cost. Taking the specific example of small batch manufacture, traditional standard costing spreads the set-up costs across the batch so that each item within the batch has a share. With small batch manufacture, this cost becomes a much larger proportion of total cost. The traditional costing system also lays little emphasis on the cost of quality and hence the system is not able to provide the information required by management to control this important aspect of modern manufacture. It is, therefore, true to say that traditional management accounting performance measures are, at best, irrelevant and, at worst, misleading in the new manufacturing environment.

(b) There are a number of ways management accounting can adapt to the new environment. Traditional standard costing systems can be modified to allow for the flexibility required. If the industrial engineering schemes are mechanised so that standard times can be calculated for each batch, these can be multiplied by the standard cost rate to give the standard cost against which actual costs can be measured. The standard cost rate would not have labour as a separate part, but would consider it as part of variable overhead.

An alternative is to move to a system of actual costing using statistical control charts to monitor costs. This is where a confidence interval is set about the mean and any deviations outside this are investigated.

In both standard and actual costing the move away from labour as the cost driver has meant that other bases of charging costs to products have had to be found. Although such methods have been used for many years, particularly in the metals industry, it has been recently formalised into activity-based costing.

Non-financial performance measures are also being developed to complement or replace the traditional measures. This is particularly true in the area of quality where control is essential for long-term survival.

 ## Solution 16

(a)

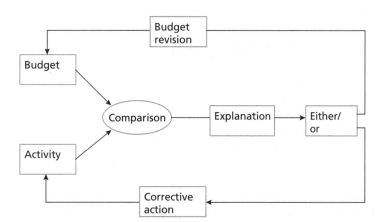

The classic control loop, shown above for a budgeting context, controls by setting an *ex ante* target (budget), measuring *ex post* performance (activity), making a comparison, seeking explanation for any significant variation and then taking one or both of two possible actions. Either action is taken to ensure that activity in future periods is in line with target, or in exceptional circumstances, the target is changed to conform with changes that have occurred since the target was set.

A major criticism of this approach is that it is reactive and backward looking. In other words, action is triggered by a report of variations from the set target or budget. One counter to this argument as the notion of 'feed-forward' control. The same procedures take place as in feedback control outlined above. However, it is argued that the fact that a comparison and explanation will take place in the future affects behaviour and thus managers act to ensure that when the comparison takes place, the actual performance will be in line with the set target. This results in control being forward looking and proactive.

(b)

The aim of total quality management (TQM) is that all goods and services produced can be relied upon to meet their specifications at all times. These specifications will include technical features and timing. The importance of TQM in a JIT environment includes the following:

1. JIT requires very precise planning that is only possible when goods can be relied upon.
2. JIT requires very low, or no, stocks to be held; thus, there must be total reliability that goods will perform to specification, as there will be no alternative stock if goods or services fail.

3. Where JIT is operated with a Kanban system for stock replacement, the stock re-order point is decided on the basis that all stock is usable and that replacement stock will be delivered in the specified and very short time period.
4. The consequences of poor quality are magnified in a JIT system and could cause considerable hold-ups in a process.

(c)

Some of the main advantages of participation in the setting of budgets include:

- Acceptance and commitment – where managers have taken part in the setting of the budget they are more likely to accept the resulting targets as relevant.
- Us v Them attitudes can be reduced when targets and budgets are set with participation, not simply imposed. If managers are involved in the budget-setting process, more knowledge is made available since the managers have considerable detailed knowledge of day-to-day operations.
- Better communication is achieved through participation, in particular communication is both upwards and downwards within the organisation.
- It is also generally accepted from research findings that participation will lead to:
  - increased job satisfaction;
  - decreased job-related tension;
  - improved job attitudes.

However, there are potential disadvantages to participation, including:

- Under some circumstances, participation may lead to setting less difficult targets – the creation of 'budget slack';
- Some personality types have been shown to react much better to an imposed budget, for example, 'externals under a locus of control' personality indicator;
- Increased need for training for non-financial managers – though this could also be argued as an advantage;
- The whole process may be more time-consuming

(d)

There are significant similarities between residual income (RI) and economic value added (EVA). In both, the basic measure is the profit for the division less an interest charge based on the net assets that have been invested in the division. This results in an absolute value, whereas Return on Investment yields a percentage or relative measure. There are considerable theoretical advantages for the absolute measure.

The major differences between the two are that EVA has a number of complications or developments from the simple RI. RI was developed in the early years of the last century, whereas EVA became popular in the early 1990s.

EVA adjusts the operating profit to bring 'accounting profit' in line with a measure of 'economic profit'. Thus, major long-term expenditure, such as R & D or marketing costs for a new product, can be capitalised over the expected useful life of the expenditure. More complex forms of depreciation are used, and taxation is treated in a more complex manner.

EVA also calculates the interest charge in a more complex manner than was traditionally the case for RI.

(e)
Controllability is defined by Horngren, Bhimani *et al.* as 'the degree of influence that a specific manager has over costs, revenues or other items in question'. Controllability refers to a specific manager – a superior may be able to control a cost, and for a period of time – all costs are controllable in the long run. The controllability principle is that managers should only be held responsible for costs that they have direct control over. So, for example, a divisional manager would not be held responsible for the allocation of central costs to her department if she has no control over the incurrence or magnitude of these costs. Under this principle, it would be held that dysfunctional consequences would arise if managers were held accountable for costs over which they have no control.

An alternative view argues that there are considerable advantages to be gained in holding managers responsible for costs even when they do not have any direct control over them. For example, it stops managers treating some costs as 'free goods' and thus stops them over-using these goods and services. Further, holding managers responsible for items outside their control may encourage them to become more involved with such issues and, as a result, the total cost may be reduced or the goods or services may be provided more efficiently.

There is no clear evidence as to which of these views will produce the best performance from a division or a division manager.

(f)
The basic analysis of transfer pricing assumes that one of the key objectives in setting such prices is that relevant divisions can be evaluated effectively, that is, that the transfer price will not distort the divisional performance evaluation. In practice, however, the existence of divisions in different countries, and particularly different systems of taxation, can add another objective. It may be valuable to the company to set transfer prices to minimise overall group tax liabilities and maximise overall group profits.

For example, profits could be reduced in a country with high taxation and increased in a country with low taxation, thus reducing the overall tax liability and increasing overall profits. If customs duties were based on the value of the goods, there would be an incentive to transfer the goods at a low transfer price to minimise customs duties. Some countries levy 'withholding taxes' on dividends paid outside the country. Here, it would be possible to set transfer prices for goods in or out of the country in such a manner that minimise the profits, and thus the dividends.

Most countries have tax legislation that limits the extent to which these practices can be used, but there is still considerable scope for using transfer prices to influence the incidence of profit and, through differing tax regimes, the overall amount of group profit. Where this occurs, the effectiveness of measuring divisional performance may have been substantially reduced.

✓ Solution 17

(a) (i) Kaplan & Norton devised the balanced scorecard (BSC) as a means to incorporate financial and non-financial performance measurement in a single document or process. Four perspectives are adopted to cover the main areas of a company's activity. These are: financial–shareholder perspective; customer perspective; internal business perspective; innovation and learning perspective.

   (ii) For a general insurance company, the following are examples of appropriate performance measures for each perspective. Two examples are given in this answer but only one was required in the actual exam.

Customer perspective

1. Percentage of repeat business as this indicates satisfaction with the policy and service received from the company.
2. Target data from customer satisfaction surveys such as response cards sent to new and renewal customers. This indicates customer satisfaction directly.

Internal business perspective

1. Percentage of policies and claims issued on time, that is, within the company's stated period, for example that all policies will be despatched within 5 working days. This is a measure of the firm's ability to efficiently organise its core activities.
2. Number of complaints received from policyholders in relation to claims they have made. Many complaints will have been caused by failures in the core processes, such as lost paperwork, or delays at some point in the process.

Innovation and learning perspective

1. The number of percentage of new insurance products issued per year which clearly indicates innovation. This would need to be compared with trends or benchmarked against competitors.
2. Amount of hours of staff training recorded as percentage of budget and/or last year. Although this is an input measure, such measures are frequently used to indicate staff development and learning.

Financial perspective

1. Meeting a key financial target such as Economic Value Added (EVA®). This is considered one of the best financial measures of overall performance.
2. Sales growth compared with previous period. Insurance companies are frequently concerned with market share and so sales growth is seen as a key financial measure.

(b) (i) EVA® attempts to modify accounting operating profit to become closer to an economic concept of income. To do this, many of the accounting conventions and adjustments are altered, for example:

- Goodwill will be amortised over its effective life
- R & D expenditure will be written off over its useful life
- Depreciation will model the decline in asset values
- Assets will be valued at current cost not historical cost

After this adjusted profit has been calculated, an interest rate charge is deducted to produce the EVA®. The interest rate used in EVA® is usually complex and it is usually based on the Capital Asset Pricing Model. All the above features require systems to be implemented so that the required data can be produced quickly and with minimum cost. For example, to compute EVA®, a separate depreciation calculation and separate records of assets are needed. The objective of EVA® is to better measure the true economic performance of a division.

(ii) It is argued that meeting an EVA® target will usually require managers to act in the best interests of the firm. In particular, EVA® is said to encourage long-term decision-making, rather than decisions that maximise short-run profits. EVA® proponents argue that it has strong motivational advantages because maximising EVA® will maximise shareholder value. Providing incentives for managers and workers to maximise value creation for shareholders has been recognised as a significant problem for decades; this claim for EVA® has made it popular.

The adjustments that are made to accounting profit to derive EVA® are designed to minimise any benefit that managers can obtain by manipulating accounting numbers. So, for example, there would be little gain to short-run profit from failing to invest in new machinery, and at least part of the cost of advertising would be deferred until the benefits arose.

Some companies set EVA® targets, and rewards are paid if these targets are reached. The adjustments to operating profit remove some of the accounting choices that can be used to manipulate profit, and so EVA® provides an incentive to produce more shareholder value.

(c) Four circumstances where participation is likely to contribute to *poor* performance include the following, although only three are required in an answer:

 (i) Strong evidence suggests that some personality types do not perform well in participatory systems and for these types, being given a budget may produce higher effort levels. For example, 'Externals' as defined on the basis of the 'locus of control' variable will usually respond well to imposed budgets.

 (ii) Whereas in conditions of uncertainty, participation has been shown to improve results, under conditions of stability participation may result in few or no benefits. It may result in more time and cost being expended for no benefits. This may be particularly relevant for cost centres within large organisations that have no direct link to market conditions.

 (iii) 'Pseudo-participation' – where there is a semblance of participation but no real participation – has been shown to produce very poor results. Individuals react strongly against this pretence at participation, and effort levels are significantly reduced.

 (iv) Participation may increase 'budget slack' and, thus, lead to lower targets and performance. Budget slack is where the budget is deliberately set at a level that is easier than could be achieved. There may be an increased incentive to build in budget slack if a bonus will be paid for meeting the budget.

(d) The Beyond Budgeting proposition is that many companies spend considerable resources on the budgeting process that are not justified by the benefits that accrue.

In particular, the levels of technological change and market uncertainty in modern business are such that it is inappropriate to set budgets 15 months or more before they will apply. This may produce a straight-jacket that inhibits companies from taking required actions, because 'it's not in the budget'.

W Limited is in an industry where there is considerable uncertainty and it would be very difficult to predict sales 3 years in advance. This may indicate that detailed long-term planning and budget-setting would be of limited value. The key question is how accurately W can predict 1 year in advance. If there is a high degree of accuracy in 1 year planning, then the current system, but with low emphasis on year 2 and 3 may be effective.

However, if the market situation is dynamic, then the 'beyond budgeting' arguments may indicate that budgetary control will not be effective; in fact, it may limit the ability that W has to respond to market changes. If W decides to abandon its current budgeting system, it will need other, more flexible, forms of control. These may include non-financial performance indicators, such as time to develop new games, gross margins on games, number of new games per year, market share and various cost control measures. W could decide to combine financial and non-financial measures into a Balanced Scorecard.

It is highly likely that some form of annual budgeting will still be needed. In particular, W will need a cash budget, capital expenditure budget, financing budget and some forecast for profit. Many firms in similar circumstances to W have kept their traditional form of budgeting, but with two major changes. First, the budget is in less detail, and it focuses on overall profits not on detailed lines within the budget. Second, the implementation of the budgetary control process must be flexible so that changes can be incorporated as the budget year progresses.

(e) The senior management of C plc states that the three divisions should see themselves as independent businesses as far as possible. However, the primary issue is that they are highly related and dependent on each other.

The WD sells approximately two-thirds of its output to the PD. Thus, the profits of WD and PD depend crucially on the cost-plus transfer price. Further, with only one third of output being sold to external customers, these internal transfers will significantly affect the ROI measure that is used to assess performance. This may lead to a variety of behavioural problems, including:

- attempts to manipulate internal pricing procedures, particularly by increasing costs;
- lack of effort and incentive to control costs;
- lack of effort in selling to external customers as the consequences may be small in relation to internal transfers;
- short-term decisions may be made at the expense of long-run profits.

PD must sell all its output to the TD and buy all its timber from WD. Thus, the problems mentioned for WD apply even more so to PD. It has little control over its business activities and, thus, cannot really be considered as an independent business. The additional behavioural consequences for PD include:

- The major emphasis for PD should be quality and technical efficiency. Control through ROI is likely to divert attention away from this, at best, and at worst, may conflict with this aim. For example, not replacing machinery because it would worsen ROI.
- PD needs to work very closely with WD and TD, and being structured as a separate profit centre may inhibit this (maybe a cost centre would be more appropriate?)

TD sells to the final market, and, thus, its sales revenue is not unduly affected by the structure of C. Its major costs are determined by internal transfers, so its ROI is not a good measure of performance, just as for the other two divisions. Other behavioural consequences include:

- problems with motivation if the transfer costs from PD mean that overall profit and ROI is low;
- frustration if the management of TD believes it could substantially increase sales and ROI by having a wider product range.

(f) In general, transfer prices should reflect market prices. There is much theory and evidence that such prices will minimise possible adverse behavioural consequences.

Where market-based prices are not possible, all transfer prices have potential problems. Many of the transfer price theories attempt to determine transfer prices that are similar to what a market price might be.

Transfer from PD to TD

Here there is a good case that PD is not actually a profit centre. It has no control over the volume of its output, and cannot buy or sell outside C plc. On pure economic criteria, PD should become a cost centre and transfer its output to TD at cost. In economic terms, there are theoretical arguments that this transfer price should be marginal cost. To achieve this, the performance measurement and reward system for PD would have to be changed, as marginal cost transfers will always produce 'losses' in the supplying division. In practice, it is more likely that the transfer would be at full cost or a standard cost. If this were the case, the performance target for PD would be to break even. TD would probably be receiving these products at below market price. This may lead to lower final prices and higher demand. Care would be needed as this higher output could lead to either increased or decreased profits.

It may be possible to accurately estimate a market-based price. If that were the case, it would be possible to operate the current structure. From the limited evidence, it is unlikely that market-based prices would be reliably available.

 ## Solution 18

The essential behavioural issue to be addressed in the establishment of standard costs is 'legitimacy'. The term relates to the acceptance by all parties that the standard cost is a meaningful and realistic figure which relates to things which are under the responsibility/control of the manager to whom it is attributed. A meaningful standard cost is one which has been arrived at through a proper allocation, apportionment and absorption of costs (or ABC equivalent) and where costs not under the control of the manager are either excluded or identified as such. It should be associated with realistic levels of planned activity and attainable levels of efficiency. A meaningful standard acts as a positive motivator and a proper measure of performance.

 ## Solution 19

The feedback of information relates to the reporting of things that have happened in the past. For example, a financial control report may state what costs have been incurred over the past quarter – this is feedback. The feed-forward of information relates to the reporting of things which are expected or forecast to happen in the future. For example, a financial control report may state what costs are currently forecast to be 'from now to year end' – this is feed-forward.

Solution 20

(a) (i) The main features of zero based budgeting (ZBB) include:
  - Each element of cost within the budget has to be explicitly justified each year; this is in contrast to adding an increment to the previous year's budget to allow for inflation;
  - ZBB forces judgements to be made on priorities as to whether expenditure should be included in the budget and at what level;
  - In practice, ZBB often forces an organisation to consider whether activities are best out-sourced or undertaken internally;
  - One method of implementing ZBB requires the activities of an organisation to be described as a set of decision packages. For example, in the case of a local government organisation, providing day-care for the elderly could be a decision package. All the decision packages are then ranked in priority order and resources are allocated accordingly;
  - ZBB seeks to act as a control to increase efficiency, and so, this approach is used particularly in the public sector where competitive markets do not provide a control on efficiency.

  (ii) There are problems in implementing this approach. Successful implementation of ZBB is extremely difficult. There are very few examples of 'successful' implementations of ZBB, and many disaster stories; it is high risk.
  - Implementation will only be effective if the staff of J are convinced of the value of undertaking ZBB. Thus, to effect the necessary 'culture change', additional problems may arise and additional expenditure is usually required.
  - Some of the judgements needed in the ZBB process are very sensitive, particularly regarding reducing indirect costs of J. These decisions can prove difficult to make and can be divisive.
  - It is usually expensive in terms of staff time; empirical evidence indicates this is frequently more so than expected. The business case for implementing ZBB prepared by the new owners of J must allow for this.
  - ZBB usually needs consultants to aid the implementation. This adds the further problems of managing consultants and may add substantial cost. The benefits of implementing ZBB must be substantial to outweigh these costs and difficulties.
  - Important aspects of work can be omitted from the activities included in the ZBB exercise, yet will still have to be undertaken.

(b) (i) 95% of outcomes will be within $\pm$ 1.96 standard deviations of the mean.
    Thus 95% of outcomes will be the range 90 kg $\pm$ (1.96 3 10 kg), that is, in the range 70.4–109.6 kg.
    The actual weight of this batch was 110 kg.
    Thus, this batch falls outside the 95% limit and the variance should be investigated.

  (ii) Other factors that should ideally be included in the decision include (only two needed):
  - Trend of past months – if there is a clear trend moving away from the mean, the company may wish to investigate before adverse variances go beyond the 95% limit;

- The cost of investigating the variance compared with the benefits of correcting it;
- The reliability of the standards set. Where standards are not reliable, there is a higher likelihood that an outcome outside the 95% limit is not worth investigating.

(c) 'McDonaldisation' is the phenomenon of producing large numbers of very similar products or services, such that they can be produced by repetitive processes, and with the minimum amount of variation. These processes would be well understood and would involve very low levels of uncertainty. The consequences for budgeting at UV are as follows:

- Standards can be set with a high degree of certainty and without great expense;
- Actual results are likely to be very close to budget if management perform well, thus budgetary control through comparison with variances is a reasonable strategy;
- For UV, the provision of set meals at events conforms to these characteristics. It should be possible to set accurate flexible budgets, and thus it would be possible to have published price schemes that will produce reliable profit margins;
- However, this only applies to part of the output of UV. The provision of specific meals to order for an event does not have the 'McDonaldisation' characteristics and thus budgeting for this output of the service provision will have to be different.

(d) Idle time variance is 10 hours at £60 per hour = £600 Adverse
The mix and efficiency variances are calculated excluding the idle time hours.

Actual hours at standard rate	Senior consultant	50 × £100	£5,000
	Junior consultant	45 × £60	£2,700
			£7,700

Thus, the labour efficiency variance is

$$£7,600 - £7,700 = £100 \text{ Adverse}$$

Labour mix variance:

	Actual hours	Standard mix		Mix variance hours	Rate per hour	£
Senior consultant	50	40%	38	12 Adverse	£100	1,200 Adverse
Junior consultant	45	60%	57	12 Favourable	£60	720
Favourable	95		95			480 Adverse

(e) (i) ERPS are integrated IT systems that include all aspects of the operations of a company and the financial accounting system. ERPS may affect the budget-setting process in the following ways:

- They are complex planning systems that will show the financial consequences of operational plans, and thus they can significantly improve efficiency in the budget-setting process;
- It is much easier with ERPS to conduct sensitivity analysis and budgets can be flexed with more precision;
- Some complex budget relationships are expensive to model and change, but this cost is reduced with effective ERPS;

- Some have argued that the budget-setting process almost disappears with an effective ERPS as the budget figures are a natural consequence of the planning process.
(ii) ERPS also has consequences for the budgetary control process, including:
    - Actual data can be calculated and compared with budget data within very short time; periods, in fact, virtually in real-time with some systems This can lead to intensification of the budgetary control process;
    - Far less resources are needed to operate a budgetary control system although vast resources may be needed to implement an ERPS;
    - Accountants may play a much reduced role, as much of the data required for budgetary control is automatically prepared by the ERPS that operational managers are using.
(f) The comment highlights the well-known issue of forecast versus motivation and control. When preparing the whole company's budget it is important to have a realistic forecast of what is likely to happen, particularly for cash, purchases, labour and capital budgets. However, for a budget to be effective for motivation, targets must be set that are challenging. It is also argued that for control purposes, the budget must be a realistic benchmark against which actual performance can be compared, that is, it must be close to a forecast.

The difficulty is that both of these objectives are valid and beneficial. Thus, the issue becomes whether one budget can do both tasks or whether companies need to choose which task the budget will be used for.

Virtually, all companies prepare one version of the budget that is a forecast. Some have two sets of budgets – one as a forecast and another as a motivating and controlling budget for managers. However, having two budgets can cause other problems. Some companies separate forecasting and motivation. Thus, they set a single budget as a forecast, but have an incentive scheme that rewards performance that exceeds budget, or they have separate incentive targets for motivation purposes.

Solution 21

The information reporting requirements of the four different types of business unit relate to the purpose that each serves within the organisation. A cost centre is typically a segment of the organisation where costs are incurred but to which it is not possible to attribute revenues. A workshop or assembly line may be a cost centre – and only costs incurred therein need be reported. A sales centre is a segment which is responsible for achieving sales but which does not itself incur significant costs. A regional sales office may be a sales centre – and only the sales achieved by that office need be reported regularly. Profit and investment centers tend to function more as small independent businesses and a full range of financial reporting may be required in these cases.

Solution 22

(a) (i) OAR = $12,800/2,000 = $6.40 per unit
Inventory is budgeted to increase, and therefore absorption costing profit will be higher than marginal costing profit.
Absorption costing profit = 5,700 + (600 × $6.40) = $9,540

(ii) Marginal costing focuses on contribution. This changes proportionally with sales volume, and therefore can be easily manipulated to help management with many aspects of planning, control and decision-making For example, 'what if' scenarios can be rapidly generated.

Note: Any two relevant situations would be accepted.

(b)

	£	£
Standard cost for 2-day procedure		1,165
Length of stay variances		
Nursing costs: 1 day × 0.75 × £320 per day	240	
Space and food costs: 1 day × £175 per day	175	
Hospital overheads	110	525
Standard cost for 3-day stay		1,690
Drug and specific cost variances		205
Nursing staffing variance: 3 days × (0.9 − 0.75) × £320		144
Actucal cost		2,039

Note: All variances are adverse.

(c)

		February	March	April
1	Standard cost of output (£)	132,000	61,200	109,200
2	Usage variance (£)	15,970	5,950	8,400
3	Standard cost of actual purchases (£)	147,970	67,150	117,600
4	Price variance (£)	12,300	4,500	6,200
	Usage % variance (2/1)	12.1%	9.7%	7.7%
	Price % variance (4/3)	8.3%	6.7%	5.3%

(d)

1. Standard costing and variance analysis is a post-mortem. Management needs 'real-time' information.
2. Standard costing variances tend to be on an aggregate basis – much more detailed information may be needed.
3. Standard costs can be viewed as the benchmark. In the modern business environment, the emphasis is on constant improvement.
4. In the modern business environment, flexibility and the rapid response to changing demands may be more of a measure of good performance than adherence to standard.
5. Product life cycles are shorter and hence standards will need to be constantly reviewed. This extra work may invalidate the worth of the standard-setting process.

Note: Any three relevant reasons would be accepted.

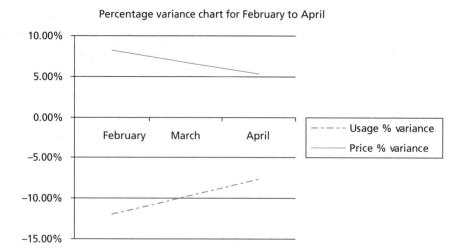

Percentage variance chart for February to April

(e) The underlying methodology is the same except that throughput accounting (TA) takes a more extreme view of contribution and regards direct materials as the only 'variable' cost.

Marginal costing (MC) is used in many situations including aspects of decision-making, planning and control.

MC and TA both focus on contribution (but because of their differing classification of variable costs, their definition of contribution will be different).

TA is based on the ideas of the 'Theory of Constraints' and seeks to maximise profits by maximising throughput by identifying and, where possible, removing bottlenecks. Maximising throughput on a bottleneck is similar to the MC idea of maximising contribution per unit of scarce resource.

(f) *Examiner's note:* There were many measures which candidates could have suggested. Candidates were expected to provide a justification of the measures suggested.

- *Detection of false claims.* Calculate the percentage of false claims to total claims. Compare this to previous periods. Obtain data from other similar organisations, trade journals and/or industry groups. The measure would highlight the effectiveness of the staff handling the claims and internal procedures and training.

- *Speed of processing claims.* log claims and record the time from receipt to settlement. Compare to previous periods. Register and investigate complaints from policyholders. Obtain data from other similar organisations, trade journals and/or industry groups. The measure would reflect internal efficiency and customer focus.

For both areas, every effort should be made to identify best practice and to use that to establish targets that are accepted.

Section C

 Solution 23

(a) Variances are significant if they materially affect the performance of a company. They may be positive, in which case the company performance is significantly better than planned; or negative, in which case the company's performance is significantly worse than expected. The level of significance will, therefore, depend upon the size of the company or department being considered.

There are a number of factors that determine whether a variance is significant or not. Its size relative to the budget is one measure of significance usually expressed as a percentage. This, however, is not sufficient on its own, as the size of the budget may be so small that a relatively large percentage may be insignificant in absolute terms. Also, a variance that always has the same sign, that is, positive or negative, is more significant than one that varies randomly. It is, therefore, necessary to monitor the cumulative variance, in addition to that for the current period.

(b) Significant variances can be identified in a number of ways. The simplest and most widely used method is that already described in (a) above where a percentage level is set, say 10%, outside of which all variances are investigated. A refinement of this is to only investigate those variances that are also above a predetermined level, say, £100. This is so that the cost of investigation does not outweigh the benefit, that is,

Cost of investigation < future cost saving × probability of successful
investigation

As noted in (a), such criteria should be applied to both the period and cumulative variances. A refinement of the above is to set control limits using statistical techniques. Previous data is analysed, assuming normal distribution, and the standard deviation is calculated. A control chart is then drawn showing results against control intervals of one, two or even three standard deviations from the expected value, in effect confidence intervals for the actual results against budget.

 Solution 24

(a) Standard cost of materials

$$0.65 \times £4 + 0.3 \times £6 + 0.2 \times £2.50 = £490 \text{ kg of FDN}$$

Standard cost of overheads

£3 kg of FDN

Standard cost of actual output

	£
Materials: 4,200 × 4.90	20,580
Overheads: 4,200 × 3	12,600
	33,180

Actual cost of actual output

	£
Materials	20,380
Overheads	12,600
	32,980

Variance analysis

	£	
Cost variances		
Materials	200	(F)
Overheads	–	

Standard overhead cost of output

		£
Deliveries: $(4,200/4,000) \times 10 \times 400 = 10.5 \times 400$		4,200
Despatches: $(4,200/4,000) \times 40 \times 200 = 42 \times 200$		8,400
		12,600

	£	
Activity variances		
Deliveries: $(12 - 10.5) \times 400$	600	(A)
Despatches: $(38 - 42) \times 200$	800	(F)
Expenditure variances		
Deliveries: $4,800 - (12 \times 400)$	–	
Despatches: $7,800 - (200 \times 38)$	200	(A)
Total	–	

(c) The main characteristic of an ABC system is that it is structured around the outputs of the operation, rather than the inputs. In designing an ABC system, one is not concerned primarily with the nature of the costs, but rather with their purpose. The information given in the question suggests that overhead costs are associated with the activities of receiving consignments and sending out orders. The cost drivers in this case appear to be the number of deliveries received and orders despatched.

The best approach to identifying appropriate activities and cost drivers is to interview a representative sample of employees, carrying out the support services at all levels in the organisation, and invite them to identify the relevant factors. If a clear and consistent view emerges, then this may be adopted; if not, a detailed analysis of the activity patterns of these employees may be required.

 Solution 25

(a)

Operating Statement

	£	
Budgeted profit	586,000	
Sales volume contribution variance	84,240	Favourable
	670,240	

Variance	£	
Sales price	129,710	Favourable
Material price		
A	43,000	Adverse
B	18,500	Favourable
C	5,875	Adverse
Material mix		
A	30,000	Favourable
B	8,000	Adverse
C	4,000	Adverse
Material yield	222,300	Favourable
Fixed production overheads expenditure	£35,000	Adverse
Total variances	304,635	Favourable
Actual profit	**974,875**	

Workings

Mix variance

	A	B	C	Total
	kg	kg	kg	kg
Actual materials in standard mix	45,000	36,000	22,500	103,500
Actual materials in actual mix	43,000	37,000	23,500	103,500
Difference	2,000	−1,000	−1,000	
Standard price	£15	£8	£4	
Variance	£30,000	£8,000	£4,000	£18,000
	favourable	adverse	adverse	favourable

Yield variance

Standard output from material input (103,500/23)	4,500 units
Actual output	5,450 units
Yield	950 units
	×£234
	£222,300 favourable

Material price variance

	A	B	C	
Standard price per kg	£15.00	£8.00	£4.00	
Actual price per kg	£16.00	£7.50	£4.25	
	−£1.00	£0.50	−£0.25	
	43,000	37,000	23,500	
×no of kg	£43,000	£18,500	£5,875	£30,375
	adverse	favourable	adverse	adverse

(b)   **Report**

To: Production Manager

From: Management Accountant

Date: 21 November 2006

Title: Material Price, Mix and Yield Variances

This report interprets the material price, mix and yield variances and also discusses the advantages and disadvantages of calculating the materials mix and yield variances.

(i) The material price variance is adverse because materials A and C cost more than standard and more than offsetting the favourable variance on B. Material, mix and yield variances are inter-related and, as individual variances, they should not be interpreted in isolation. By changing the mix this has led to a favourable mix and yield variance. This indicates that the decision to use less of material A and more of B and C has worked in the company's favour. The mix was also more efficient than the standard mix because the yield variance was also favourable. It should be remembered that substitution of one material for another can only occur up to a point, otherwise the identity of the product or the quality of the product can be seriously impacted upon.

(ii) The material mix and yield variances are sub-divisions of the material usage variance. X Ltd produces an industrial component where a standard input mix is the norm, and recognisable individual components of input are combined during the production process to produce an output in which the individual items are no longer separately identifiable. X Ltd may have decided to vary the input mix because of a shortage of material and or in order to take advantage of an attractive input price on material B. Whether X Ltd's input mix is a standard or non-standard one, there is a possibility that the outcome from the process will differ from that which was expected, that is the yield, in this instance the yield has been favourable. By calculating the mix and yield variances, X Ltd highlights the different aspects of the production process and provides additional insights to help managers to attain the optimum combination of materials input. You should note that mix and yield variances are appropriate only to those production processes where managers have the discretion to vary the mix of materials and deviate from engineered input–output relationships.

If X Ltd had not calculated the mix and yield variances they would have just calculated material usage variances which demonstrates how much of the direct material total variance was caused by using a different quantity of a material, compared with the standard allowance for the production achieved. The usage variance does not consider how a mix of different materials would have impacted on the yield and would not provide managers with an insight to attain the optimum combination.

Should you require any further information, please do not hesitate to contact me.

Solution 26

(a) Calculation of equivalent units (EU)

BM = base materials; FC = further chemicals; CC = conversion costs; WIP = work in process

	BM	FC	CC
Opening work in process	(40)	–	(10)
Finished	65	65	65
Abnormal loss	5	5	4
Closing work in process	50	50	45
Total	80	120	104
October's costs	$3,400	$7,200	$6,864
Cost per EU	$42.50	$60.00	$66.00

Calculation of costs

	BM $	FC $	CC $	Total $
Opening WIP (40 kg)	1,550.00	–	720.00	
Completion	–	2,400.00	1,980.00	
Total cost	1,550.00	2,400.00	2,700.00	6,650.00
Started and completed (25 kg)	1,062.50	1,500.00	1,650.00	4,212.50
Abnormal loss (5 kg)	212.50	300.00	264.00	776.50
Closing WIP (50 kg)	2,125.00	3,000.00	2,970.00	8,095.00
Total cost	4,950.00	7,200.00	7,584.00	19,734.00

Process account for October

	kg	$		kg	$
Opening inventory	40	2,270.00	Transfer to finished goods	65	10,862.50
Base materials	80	3,400.00	Abnormal loss	5	776.50
Further chemicals		7,200.00	Closing inventory	50	8,095.00
Conversion costs		6,864.00			
	120	19,734.00		120	19,734.00

(b) The following points could be made to the Managing Director (MD).
1. These accounts are no more complex than the reality, and are intended to show the true position (which is that this month's costs reflect this month's activity, not just the output actually completed). Treating the WIP as having zero value is not even true in financial accounting terms.
2. The appropriate comparison is thus between target cost and the actual cost per EU: (BM $40.00 v $42.50, CC $70.00 v $66.00, FC $60.00 v $60.00). These differences are small, and would be explained by a variance analysis in most companies.
3. The differences between the unit costs in the Process Account and the MD's short cut are caused by the large change in the volume of WIP: if this change is normally very small, the MD may have a point.
4. The MD has not taken into account the abnormal loss. This is a cause for concern, but he is comparing inputs for 70 kg with output of 65 kg.
5. The conversion costs normally include arbitrary overhead costs. Thus, the data from the Process Account is not suitable for comparing with the target cost as a means of control.
6. The MD's comments indicate that he has not grasped the nature of the process account. Production efficiency is probably much better assessed by measures of physical usage compared with targets or standards.

Solution 27

(a)

Summary Statement for 6 months to 30 September 2003

	Cumulative actual to date £	Cumulative budget to date £	Total variance £	Price-spending variance £	Efficiency volume £
Production	29,600	30,000	400		
Costs	£	£	£	£	£
Materials	1,207,100	1,184,000	(23,100)	(1,100)	(22,000)
Labour	846,129	976,800	130,671	130,671	0
Variable overheads	455,000	444,000	(11,000)	(11,000)	0
Fixed overheads	738,000	710,400	(27,600)	(18,000)	(9,600)
Total costs	3,246,229	3,315,200	68,971	100,571	(31,600)

( ) = Adverse variance
Note: Alternative statements that summarise the performance of the Service Department would be acceptable.

(b)

Report to the Operations Director of Marshall Limited

Re: Performance of the Service Department for the 6 months to 30 September 2003
A summary performance statement is attached to this report. The main features are set out below, along with issues that require further explanation or information.

- There has been a rise, then fall in volumes. Is this seasonal variation, such as less services required during the summer, or the result of other factors, such as action from competitors in months 4 to 6? If the trend in the last 3 months continues, this could be a serious problem that needs to be addressed promptly.

- A favourable material usage variance, as occurred in month 2 must mean that some parts were not replaced during the service. Is this acceptable? There seems to be a general inefficiency in material usage. Is this caused by a lack of care by service engineers or by poor quality sets? The price variance – see below – does not indicate cheap parts are being purchased.
- Material prices are on a general upward path. Is there a general drift in material places? Is there a material shortage? Are there other suppliers offering a better price?
- Labour price is massively out of line with budget yielding large favourable variances. Is this caused by a mistake in the budget or an unexpected change in the price, for example using different grades/mix of labour? This variance is more than 13% of budgeted cost and thus must be investigated quickly and thoroughly.
- Labour efficiency gets seriously worse after month 4. Has something unusual happened to labour during this month, perhaps a dispute? Is this significantly worse labour efficiency linked to the fall in output over the same months?
- Month 4 is significantly out of line with other months. What happened? Was production disrupted; was there a labour dispute or supplier problems or did another factor affect the result? It is important to find satisfactory explanations for the results in this month and attempt to ensure this performance is not repeated.
- Only total variable overhead variance has meaning and reveals a worsening position after the disaster in month 4, giving further evidence for some unusual circumstances.
- Fixed overhead spending seems to come under control from month 5, but what caused the problems in the early months? Has management acted to remedy matters?
- The fixed overhead volume variance is purely technical and represents differences between planned and actual production.
- Overall costs are 2% below budget, but this apparently satisfactory position masks considerable variation. Nevertheless, the general performance of the Service Department has been close to budget.

 Solution 28

(a)

Process 2 Account

	Litres	£		Litres	£
Opening work-in-process	1,200	7,640	Normal waste	920	nil
XP1	5,000	15,679	By-product Z	460	920
P2A	1,200	6,000	XP2	7,850	51,450
P2B	3,000	4,500			
Conversion cost		22,800			
			Closing work-in-process	1,450	6,002
Abnormal gain	280	1,753			
	10,680	58,372		10,680	58,372

Solution workings:

Equivalent units table	Process 1 and materials added	Conversion
Output		
Started and finished this period	6,650	6,650
Completion of opening work in process	nil	720
Abnormal gain	(280)	(280)
Closing work in process	1,450	435
	7,820	7,525
	£	£
Period costs	26,179	22,800
By-product value	(920)	
	25,259	22,800
Cost per equivalent unit	£3.23	£3.03

(b)

Valuation statement

		£
Finished output		
Started and finished 6,650 litres × (£3.23 + £3.03)	=	41,629
Opening work in process		
Cost brought forward	=	7,640
Cost of completion 720 litres × £3.03	=	2,181
		51,450
Abnormal gain		
280 litres × (£3.23 + £3.03)	=	£1,753
Closing work in process:		
1,450 litres × £3.23	=	£4,684
435 litres × £3.03	=	£1,318
		£6,002

 Solution 29

(a)

Income Statements

	Division X	Division Y
	£	£
Sales	100,000	270,000
Variable Costs	50,000	144,000
Contribution	50,000	126,000
Fixed Costs	15,000	100,000
Profit	**35,000**	**26,000**
Profit	35,000	26,000
Less cost of capital charge	6,000	11,000
Residual Income	**29,000**	**15,000**
Return on capital employed	**58.33%**	**23.64%**
Operating Profit Margin	**35.00%**	**9.63%**
Asset Turnover	**1.67**	**2.46**

(b)

	Division X Current Transfer Price is Marginal Cost	Division X Transfer Price is Market Price	Division Y Current Transfer Price is Marginal Cost	Division Y Transfer Price is Market Price
Residual Income	−£1,000	£29,000	£45,000	£15,000
Return on capital employed	8.33%	58.33%	50.91%	23.64%
Operating Profit Margin	7.14%	35.00%	20.74%	9.63%
Asset Turnover	1.17	1.67	2.46	2.46

The residual income for Division X has increased by £30 k and for Division Y it has decreased by £30 k. This is due to the transfer price being set at market price. Division X's revenue has increased by £10 per component transferred (3,000 transferred − £30,000) and Division Y's marginal cost has increased by £10 per component received (3,000 received − £30,000).

The ROCE for Division X has increased to 58.33%, that is by seven times as the operating profit has increased sevenfold (£5 k to £35 k). Division Y's ROCE has decreased from 50.91% to 23.64%, that is, by approximately 54% because profit has reduced by 54%, that is from £56 k to £26 k.

The operating profit margin for Division X has increased by approximately five times as profit has increased by seven times, and sales have increased by approximately 43%. For Division Y the operating profit margin has decreased by approximately 54% due to profit decreasing by approximately 54% and the sales remaining the same.

The asset turnover ratio for Division X has increased to 1.67 due to an extra £30 k sales being generated in relation to the same capital employed. Whereas for Division Y, the asset turnover ratio has remained unchanged as there has been no change to the turnover generated in relation to the capital employed.

Therefore in all of the above cases Division X's performance has improved whereas Division Y's performance has deteriorated with the exception of the asset turnover ratio which remains unchanged. The manager of Division X will be happy to set a transfer price equal to market price and Division Y will not be willing to pay the market price due to the impact on performance. Division Y will either wish to negotiate a lower transfer price or alternatively source the component externally at perhaps a more competitive price.

(c) (i) If ZZ Group relaxes the imposed transfer pricing system and the divisional managers of X and Y negotiate the transfer price instead, the manager of Division X will want to set a transfer price equal to the market price and the manager of Division Y will wish to retain the current transfer price equal to marginal cost, due to the impact on the performance ratios. This will mean that Division Y will either need to negotiate a lower transfer price with Division X or alternatively source the component externally at perhaps a more competitive price.

If the managers of Division X and Division Y negotiate a transfer price it should be acceptable to both divisions since both managers have been responsible for the negotiations. However, there are disadvantages to the use of negotiated transfer prices:

- The negotiations may be protracted and time consuming;
- The managers may find it impossible to reach agreement and then central management may need to intervene which would negate the objective of giving autonomy to divisions;
- The managers may not be negotiating from an equal basis, that is one may be more experienced than another and achieve a better result. This could lead to poor motivation and behavioural problems.

If negotiations fail and ZZ Group do not intervene, then Division Y may source the component externally. If the components are sourced externally this will result in spare capacity of 2,000 components for Division X as there is only an external market for an additional 1,000 components. Assuming Division X's fixed costs remain constant and they cannot use the spare capacity to generate further profits for the group, this will have a negative impact on the overall profit for the ZZ Group.

(ii) One of the main problems identified in C(i) is that Division X will want to set a transfer price equal to the market place and that the manager of Division Y will wish to retain the current transfer price equal to marginal cost, due to the impact on performance ratios. A recommended resolution to the problem could be a two-part tariff or dual pricing transfer pricing system. A two-part tariff works where the transfer is at marginal cost and a fixed fee is credited to Division X to compensate them for the lost additional contribution and the subsequent reduction in the performance ratios. Alternatively a dual pricing system could be used where the transfer is recorded in Division Y at marginal cost and in Division X at market price and the discrepancy between the two prices is recorded in an account at head office. Either of these methods would allow the divisions to remain autonomous and ZZ Group to protect group profits. The Group could continue to measure performance based on the four key ratios and still motivate the divisional managers to improve their performance.

The other issues are identified when managers are negotiating a transfer price, that is negotiations becoming protracted and time consuming; difficulty in reaching an agreement and the possibility that one manager may be more skilled than another in such negotiations could be overcome by head office appointing an arbitrator to assist the managers in arriving at a fair transfer price.

If the divisional managers fail to negotiate a transfer price, then central management will have to intervene to avoid a reduction in group profit if Division Y sources the component externally.

✓ Solution 30

(a) DL Hospital Trust: Unit H budget – actual reconciliation – November 20X3

	£	£	£
Original budgeted cost			
Direct labour (20 × £2,000)			40,000
Variable overhead			25,000
Budgeted variable cost			65,000
Fixed overhead			35,000
			100,000
Flexed to actual activity level (£65,000 × 2/20)			6,500
Flexed budget cost (see note below)			106,500
	(F)	(A)	
Surgical team fees rate variance	2,600		
Surgical team efficiency variance		3,000	
Variable overhead expenditure variance	725		
Variable overhead efficiency variance		1,875	
Fixed overhead expenditure variance		1,950	
	3,325	6,825	3,500 (A)
Actual cost			110,000

Note: A solution might alternatively show an activity adjustment to budgeted cost of £10,000 combined with a fixed overhead volume variance of £3,500(F).

Surgical team fees rate variance

> Actual cost − actual hours at standard cost per hour
> £44,400 − (235 × £200) = £2,600(F)

Efficiency variable

> Actual hours at standard cost per hour − standard cost of operations performed
> £47,000 − (£2,000 × 22) = £3,000(A)

Variable overhead − expenditure variance

> Actual cost − budgeted cost
> £28,650 − (£200 × 235 × 0.625) = £725(F)

Efficiency variance

> Budgeted cost − standard cost of operations performed
> £29,375 − (£2,000 × 0.625 × 22) = £1,875(A)

Fixed overhead expenditure variance

> Actual fixed overhead − budgeted fixed overhead
> £36,950 − (£2,000 × 0.875 × 20) = £1,950(A)

(b) *To*:   Finance director
    From: Management account
    Date:
    Subject: Absorbing overheads on a labour base

Overheads, in the context of the hospital, can be attributed to surgical operations on a labour cost basis on the grounds that it is an economic method to operate, it is a widely understood method of dealing with overheads cost, and as long as the mix of staff involved in surgical procedures does not vary too much, a labour cost-based system may be acceptable. There are, however, some potentially serious problems associated with this system.

It assumes that labour cost behaviour is reasonably closely related to overhead behaviour. In reality, there may be a number of 'drivers' of different elements of overhead cost.

As indicated above, if the mix of specialisms (with different levels of remuneration) change, there will be an impact upon the overhead charge to particular operations.

The use of labour cost as a basis for attributing overhead cost to operations therefore begs the question, why? If all that is required is a system that is both easy and cheap to operate, it may prove adequate; but if there is to be any managerial use made of the information assembled, then it is unlikely that this method will provide an acceptable quality of information, and therefore a study of the alternatives (focusing, in particular, on the identification of the causes of different elements of cost and on the possibility of using multiple absorption bases) should be considered.

Singed: Management accountant

Solution 31

Report

To: The board
From: Management account
Date: 26 November 20X9
Re: Proposed changes in budget preparation

I have prepared the following report, which you requested, in the temporary absence of the group finance director and on his behalf.

Discussion and recommendation

In preparing a budget for the following year, there are two issues that tend to pull in opposite directions: having a budget that is as up to date as possible while, at the same time, creating enough space for adequate manager involvement and negotiation. Because the budget is an important planning tool, in terms of target-setting and resource allocation, it is important that it should be accurate. It is also a management control technique, in terms of tracking financial performance, and therefore needs to be realistic.

Realistic budgets infer that the budget preparation process should probably be left as late as possible in the year preceding the new budget in order that information is as up to date as possible.

On the other hand, if budget preparation is left too late, then problems are likely to occur such as:

- insufficient time allowed to evaluate the current position and gather relevant data;
- insufficient time for managers to be involved in budget planning and resource allocation negotiations.

The danger is, then, that budgeting may be perceived by operating managers as a rushed exercise, primarily for financial planning purposes, and the use of budgets as a motivational device will be lessened.

Accordingly, the group finance director's proposal to commence budget preparation after the half-year results are available has the merit of allowing a broader discussion of issues than may be feasible with a tight time constraint. Managers are likely to feel more involved in managing their parts of the business, leading to greater accountability and hopefully more realistic budgets (subject to senior managers' efforts to minimise the impact of budget padding!).

Specific Problems

Division A. The difficulty here is that if the group finance director's proposal is accepted, then the budget for Division A will in effect be negotiated by the divisional finance director, who is acting managing director. There could be some conflict of interest – who is the divisional finance director's line manager? The new divisional managing director will inherit a plan over which he/she has had no input. On this basis, it may appear better to wait as long as possible before starting budget preparation. On the other hand, and in support of the group finance director's proposal, the budget for the next year could be agreed using the current year's budget and longer-term plans, despite the first quarter's disappointing results. Some form of contingency planning should be made in the event of continuing poor performance in the division, reviewed after the second-quarter results are available.

The new managing director should not be held accountable for the divisional budget if he/she is appointed after the group has approved it.

Division B. It would appear a little early to judge the impact of the new product/market strategy on next year's budget. The significance will depend upon the importance of the new market strategy in terms of the overall volume of activity and profitability in the division. If budget preparation is to be started earlier (after the half-year results), then some form of contingency planning should be considered for planning purposes. For example, if the new marketing strategy could have a significant impact on both divisional and group profits, then budgets based on pessimistic and optimistic forecasts could be prepared as well as for realistic forecasts. At the end of the day, Division B is accountable for its performance and has to make informed judgement. Presumably, for control purposes, the budget for next year can be flexed for actual activity in the division to separate out the impact of planning and operating variances.

Division C. This is a tougher issue than for the other two divisions discussed. The timescale for successful operation of the new plant is the third quarter of the current year, and this may well slip back. Product costings appear uncertain and there appears to be doubt as to whether customer quality can be achieved. A review of the situation after the second-quarter results are out should be undertaken. As with Division B, there is an issue of materiality in terms of the impact of the new plant on Division C's financial performance. If it is expected to be significant, then budget planning halfway through the current financial year is rather difficult. The budget for next year will, therefore, have to be prepared on assumptions agreed between divisional and group managers. As with Division B, contingency plans should be prepared for worse than expected performance next year that could affect group cash flows and profitability, and that may be harmful to the longer-term plans of the group. However, unless definite changes become necessary before the group budget is agreed, it may be better to budget for the new plant in line with its original capital investment justification proposal.

Other anticipated difficulties

Operating managers may not want the change in planning timetables and may have to be convinced of the benefits. The implication is that managers will be expected to put more effort (and time) into the budget-planning process and they may resent this.

As budget performance may well affect divisional managers' bonuses, then they may argue that more realistic budgets will be achieved by leaving preparation until later in the year, as is current practice. One way around this is to demonstrate that the current year's budgets are not that useful (according to the group finance director) and, possibly, to change the emphasis in divisional performance to a broader range of measures of which budget performance is only one element.

Signed: Management accountant

 Solution 32

(a) (i) Current system

£880,000/£8 m = 11% of list price of drugs supplied

Thus, Order A will have a charge of £1,200 × 0.11 = £132

Order B will have a charge of £900 × 0.11 = £99

(ii) Proposed system
Cost driver rates

Invoice costs
Charge per invoice = £70,000/8,000=   £8.75 per invoice
Charge per invoice line = £210,000/28,000=   £7.50 per line
Delivery costs
Charge per delivery trip = £40,000/1,000=   £40 per trip
So, for large package = £40/6=   £6.67
For small package = £40/12=   £3.33
Charge per delivery mile = £140,000/350,000=   £0.40 per mile
Other overheads allocated by orders (this is not a genuine cost driver)
£200,000/8,000=   £25 per order

Overhead costs	*Order A*	£	*Order B*	£
Invoice costs	1 × £8.75=	8.75	1 × £8.75 =	8.75
	2 × £7.50=	15.00	8 × £7.50 =	60.00
Packing		25.00		32.00
Delivery	1 × £3.33=	3.33	1 × £6.67 =	6.67
	8 × £0.40=	3.20	40 × £0.40=	16.00
Other overhead costs		25.00		25.00
Total charge for overheads		80.28		148.42

(b)

Report to the management of F plc on the implications of implementing an
activity-based costing approach

From: Management Accountant
Date: May 2005

This report covers two issues: (i) an assessment of the strengths and weaknesses of the proposed activity-based costing approach; and (ii) recommendations for action, the Management of F pic might take.

(i) All budgeting systems have strengths and weaknesses, and these are in part related to the specific circumstances of the company. For F the following are relevant.

Strengths include:

• Better understanding of the cost structure and what is driving costs.
• Ability to set prices that relate to the actual resources consumed, which should result in few or no loss-making orders being accepted.
• Highlights where costs are being incurred which should lead to action to reduce activities that have high costs.
• Prices could be defended if challenged by customers.
• Out-sourcing decisions can be analysed more easily.

Weaknesses might include:

• The costs may exceed benefits.
• The activity data is still very aggregated and may not be detailed enough to reveal important cost behaviour, for example the high cost of the longest distance category might be distorted by some very long deliveries.
• There are still arbitrary elements in the ABC system, particularly other overhead costs which means care must be taken with the data.

(ii) The following recommendations could be made to the directors of F plc.

The present policy is cost based. This approach is simple and relatively cheap to operate. However, such a policy is unlikely to be optimal, and will only be viable where the company is able to sell all its output. Thus, assuming that price is not closely linked to demand, a pricing policy that does no more than simply recover overheads and produce a profit may be deemed satisfactory. In this case, although the current charge for overheads is simple and cheap to calculate, it does not reflect the actual costs incurred by each order.

The new activity-based costing (ABC) system produces a measure of cost that better reflects the resources that have been used. This new ABC system produces very different costs to the previous system. However, the new costing system used, although a very simple version of ABC, is probably too complex for a pricing system.

As the first step in a review, it would be instructive to check whether some orders are actually losing money. The activity-based cost analysis indicates that orders with many different products and those delivered over a long distance are expensive, in comparison with orders for a larger volume of few products with shorter delivery distances.

F will need to develop a pricing structure that would enable some of the key cost drivers to be reflected in the prices charged, and to let customers know the charge in advance.

Another possible strategy would be to stop accepting long distance orders by imposing a distance limit. It might be possible to out-source long distance deliveries, possibly along with a high charge for the long distance band in the charging table, as mentioned above.

The costs based on the number of items on the invoice become very high when multiple products are ordered. This needs careful review. Would better systems using newer technology reduce these invoice costs – this is highly likely.

Solution 33

(a) Production Planning and Development: operating statement for period ended 30 November 20X1 (traditional expense-based analysis)

	Budget £'000	Actual £'000	Variance £'000
Salaries	600	667.8	67.8 (A)
Supplies	60	53.0	7.0 (F)
Travel cost	120	127.2	7.2 (A)
Technology cost	100	74.2	25.8 (F)
Occupancy cost	120	137.8	17.8 (A)
Total	1,000	1,060.0	60.0 (A)

Production planning and Development: operating statement for period ended 30 November 20X1 (activity-based analysis)

	Budget £'000	Actual £'000	Variance £'000
Routeing/scheduling – new products	200	169.6	30.4 (F)
Routeing/scheduling – existing products	400	360.4	39.6 (F)
Remedial rerouteing/scheduling	50	127.2	77.2 (A)
Special studies – specific orders	100	84.8	15.2 (F)
Training	100	159.0	59.0 (A)
Management and administration	150	159.0	9.0 (A)
Total	1,000	1,060.0	60.0 (A)

(b) Advantages claimed for the use of activity-based budgeting may include the following:
- Resource allocation is linked to a strategic plan for the future, prepared after considering alternative strategies.
- Traditional budgets tend to focus on resources and inputs rather than on objectives and alternatives. In the question, the traditional budget focuses on overall expenditure on resources such as salaries and the overall expenditure variance.
- New high-priority activities are encouraged rather than focusing on the existing planning model. Activity-based budgeting focuses on activities. This allows the identification of the cost of each activity, for example, special studies. It facilitates focus on control of the resources required to provide the activity. It will also help where financial constraints exist, in that activities may be ranked and their importance considered, rather than arbitrary cuts being made in areas such as production planning and development.
- There is more focus on efficiency and effectiveness and the alternative methods by which they may be achieved. Activity-based budgeting assists in the operation of a total quality philosophy. Focus within individual activities can be on areas such as waste reduction, inefficiency removal and innovation in methods.
- It avoids arbitrary cuts in specific budget areas in order to meet overall financial targets. Activities 1, 2 and 4 in the budget in (i) are primary activities that add value to products. Activity 3 (remedial rescheduling) is a non-value-added activity that should be eliminated. Activities 5 and 6 (training and management) are secondary activities that support the primary activities. Efforts should be made to ensure that their objectives are achieved in an efficient manner at minimum cost.
- It tends to lead to increased management commitment to the budget process. This should be achieved since the activity analysis enables management to focus on the objectives of each activity. Identification of primary, secondary and non-value-added activities should also help in motivating management in activity planning control.

(c) The statement in (i) shows the budget *vs.* actual cost comparison for each activity. This indicates that cost has fallen in all three primary activities – development of routeing, existing routeing and special studies. Remedial rerouteing is double the budget level, which must be investigated since it is a non-value-added activity. Training cost has increased by 50% from budget. This may be related to the high level of remedial rerouteing where staff under training have not been performing efficiently.

For each activity, it is also possible to prepare a cost analysis that compares budget *vs.* actual resources for salaries, and so on, in a similar way to the overall traditional budget statement given in the question. This will enable investigation of factors such as why salary costs for the activity exceed budget by £*x* or why supplies are below budget by £*y*.

The cost information does not specify the cost driver for each activity and the budget *vs.* actual comparison of these. For example, staff hours are likely to be the cost driver for an activity such as routeing/scheduling, whereas for training the cost driver may be number of staff trained. It is also necessary to determine the efficient cost-driver level, for example, staff hours per individual route development for a new product. How does this compare with the actual staff hours per individual route development? Again, a comparison of budget cost *vs.* actual cost per staff member trained will give an indication of efficiency of provision of the activity.

A further aspect of performance measurement is to determine the 'root cause' of each cost driver. For example, the staff hours required per route designed may be linked to the level of technology and software systems used. The root cause of employee training may be high labour turnover due to poor career prospects or a stressful work environment. It is important that such root causes are identified, since continuous improvement of the provision of an activity will only be achieved through improvement in the factors that influence its incidence.

Solution 34

(a) Material Handling Department: budget vs. actual cost statement period ended 28 November 20X1

	Flexed	Actual	Variance
Total forklift truck running hours	15,360	15,360	
	£	£	£
Variable costs			
Drivers' bonuses	7,680	7,400	1,280(F)
Battery power cost	23,040	21,800	1,240(F)
Fixed costs			
Drivers' salaries	80,000	81,600	1,600(A)
Maintenance	4,800	6,000	1,200(A)
Depreciation	16,000	16,000	–
	131,520	132,800	1,280(A)
Charge to user departments:		135,905	
Overabsorption of cost		3,105	

Workings

Forklift truck running hours

$$4 \times 120 \times 4 \times 80\% = 15,360$$

Flexed budget costs

Driver's bonues 15,360 hours $\times 10 \text{ m}^3 \times 5\text{p} = £7,680$

Driver's salaries $\dfrac{40 \times £26,000}{13} = £80,000$

Power 15,360 $\times$ £1.50 = £23,040

Maintenance 40 $\times$ £120 = £4,800

Depreciation $\dfrac{40 \times £26,000}{5 \times 13} = £16,000$

Charge to user departments

For fixed costs, this is based on the original budgeted running hours:

$$40 \times 115 \times 4 \times 80\% = 14,720 \text{ hours}$$

Charge per forklift truck running hours

For variable costs $= \dfrac{£7,680 + £23,040}{15,360} = £2.00$

For fixed costs $= \dfrac{£80,000 + £4,800 + £16,000}{14,720} = £6.848$

Hence, total charge per forklift truck hour = £2 + £6.848 = £8.848

Total charge to user departments = 15,360 hours $\times$ £8.848 = £135,905

(b) Various advantages may be claimed for the use of a budgeted charge rate both at the point of provision of the service and at the point of use. These follow on logically from the use of predetermined overhead absorption rates.

It should assist in the control of the provision of the service. Any excess costs caused by expenditure in excess of that budgeted for the materials handling department or caused by a reduction in the efficiency of operation of the trucks will be reported at the point of incidence, that is, in the materials handling department. Excess cost or reduced efficiency of operation cannot simply be passed on to the user departments by charging an increased charge rate based on actual expenditure.

It should also assist in control at the point of use. The user department will be charged for the number of hours of handling work that it requests, charged at the predetermined rate per forklift truck hour. This means that any variance reported in the operating statement of the user department will reflect any change in the quantity of forklift truck time used. The manager of the user department can investigate possible reasons for any increased level of requirement. It will not include any cost increases in the provision of the forklift truck service. Such cost increases will be monitored and explained at the point of provision, that is, in the materials handling department.

It also facilitates an equitable distribution of costs between departments. The transfer price charged will not reflect random variations in activity and usage throughout the whole organisation. A temporary shutdown due to a stock-out in department A will not impact on the level of transfer charges made to departments B and C.

 ## Solution 35

(a)

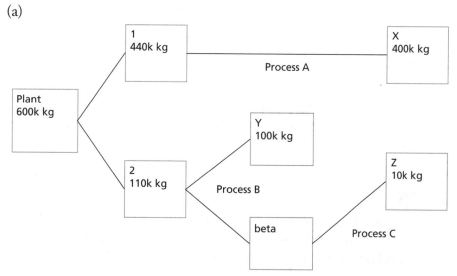

(b) (i) Units allocation

£	Product X		Product Y		Notes
	Total	CPU	Total	CPU	
Joint costs	440,000	1.100	110,000	1.100	(a)
Processing costs	410,000	1.025	135,000	1.350	
By-product net revenues			−5,000	−0.050	(b)
Total	850,000	2.125	240,000	2.400	
Revenues	970,000		450,000		
Profit	120,000		210,000		

Notes:
(a) Joint costs to X £550,000/(400 × 500)kg
(b) Net revs from Z £15,000 − £10,000

(ii) NRV allocation

£	Product X Total	CPU	Product Y Total	CPU	Notes
Joint costs	350,000	0.875	200,000	2.000	(a)
Processing costs	410,000	1.025	135,000	1.350	
By-product net revenues			−5,000	−0.050	(b)
Total	760,000	1.9	330,000	3.300	
Revenues	970,000		450,000		
Profit	210,000		120,000		

Notes:
(a) Joint costs to X £550,000/£ (560/880).
(b) Net revs from Z £15,000 − £10,000.

(c) In isolation, the impact of the extra sales of Y would be:

Incremental impact	£
10% variable plant costs	50,000
10% B variable costs	13,000
10% Z net revenues	800
Sales of extra Y	40,000
Total	−22,200

The proposed sale is not viable. However, stepping up production in the plant by 10% would allow a 10% increase in sales of X. If it is possible to sell the extra X at the usual price, then the impact would be:

Incremental impact	£
10% A variable costs	38,500
Sales of extra X	97,000
Total	58,500

Provided the extra X can be sold at the usual price, then the proposed extra sale of Y is viable. However, it all depends on circumstances. One can manipulate the data to provide a variety of breakeven points relating to volume sales or unit selling prices. The general point is that a business decision can only be made with an understanding of the full context in which it is posed.

 Solution 36

When you are calculating the standard allowances for the actual production in part (b) you will need to use the concept of equivalent units for job 109. Since the job is 60% complete as regards labour, the standard labour hours for variance calculations will be 60% of the original standard hours forecast for the job.

(a) Most organisations are required to set the price of their goods or services in advance of manufacturing and/or supplying them. The pricing policy for a product must be developed taking full account of the anticipated market conditions. As part of this decision-making process it is necessary to estimate all the costs involved to determine the profit generated by the forecast sales. This requires the use of a predetermined overhead absorption rate (OAR).

The timeframe used for calculating the OAR is usually the next budget year. Taking such a timescale will tend to even out seasonal or market fluctuations in demand.

For example, a gas supply company making monthly calculations of OAR would have a much lower OAR in the winter months than in the summer. These short-term OARs send the wrong pricing signals, suggesting that one might reduce price when demand is high and increase price when demand is low. Alternatively, if the price is held constant, the profit per unit will fluctuate with the seasons. The use of predetermined OARs will almost certainly result in over- or under-absorption. This is shown in variance analysis as the fixed overhead volume variance.

(b)

PSA Ltd – Cost control report for April

	Standard cost £	Actual cost £	Variance £
Labour	21,714	24,500	2,786 (A)
Hardwood	26,180	28,600	2,420 (A)
Softwood	8,640	9,200	560 (A)
Fixed overhead	8,272	7,800	472 (F)
Variable overheads	6,204	6,900	696 (A)
	71,010	77,000	5,990 (A)

Labour variances

	£	£
Operational efficiency (W1)	483 (A)	
Operational rate (W2)	1,400 (A)	
Planning (W3)	903 (A)	
	2,786 (A)	2,786

Hardwood variances

	£	£
Operational usage (W4)	1,045 (A)	
Price (W5)	0	
Planning (W6)	1,375 (A)	
	2,420 (A)	5,206

Softwood variances

	£	£
Operational usage (W7)	1,120 (A)	
Price (W8)	400 (A)	
Planning (W9)	960 (F)	
	560 (A)	5,766

Overhead variances

	£	£
Variable overhead (W10)	696 (A)	
Fixed overhead volume (W11)	272 (F)	
Fixed overhead expenditure (W12)	200 (F)	
	224 (A)	5,990

Workings
Labour
Std hours = 1,000 + 600 + (780 × 60%) = 2,068, actual hours = 2,200
Actual cost per hour £11.136
Revised std hours 2,068/0.96 = 2,154

(W1) $(2,154 - 2,200) \times 10.5 = 483$ (A)
(W2) $2,200 \times (11.136 - 10.5) = 1,400$ (A)
(W3) $(2,068 - 2,154) \times 10.5 = 903$ (A)

Hardwood

Std volume $= 200 + 180 + (120 \times 80\%) = 476$, actual volume $= 520$

Actual price $28,600/520 = £55$ per cu.m.

Revised std volume $476/0.95 = 501$

(W4) $(501 - 520) \times 55 = 1,045$ (A)
(W5) $(55 - 55) \times 520 = 0$
(W6) $(476 - 501) \times 55 = 1,375$ (A)

Softwood

Std use $= 320 + 400 + (300 \times 80\%) = 960$ cu. m., actual use $= 1,100$ cu. m.

Actual price $9,200/1,100 = £8.364$ cu. m.

(W7) $(960 - 1,100) \times 8 = 1,120$ (A)
(W8) $(8.00 - 8.364) \times 1,100 = 400$ (A)
(W9) $960 \times (9 - 8) = 960$ (F)

Overheads

'The OARs are £3 per hour for variable O/Hs (that is, £72,000/24,000 hours) and £4 per hour for fixed O/Hs (that is £96,000/24,000 hours). Consequently:

(W10) Variable O/H variance is $(2,068 \text{ hours} \times £3) - £6,900 = £696$ (A)
(W11) Fixed O/H volume variance is $(2,068 \times £4) - £8,000 = £272$ (F)
(W12) Fixed O/H expenditure variance is $£8,000 - £7,800 = £200$ (F)

Note: it is possible to undertake more detailed analysis on both the variable O/H variance and the fixed O/H volume variance – but the requirement does not specify this.'

(c) The traditional accounting system presently used by PSA Ltd follows all the costs as they are incurred for each product type, job or unit produced. These costs are classified and recorded forming an extensive database, which allows tight financial control to be exercised on the production process.

Specifically, PSA Ltd prepares a detailed monthly variance analysis as part of its control procedures. Its existing system is both flexible and powerful in that it incorporates adjustable standards to cater for external influences outside the control of PSA Ltd, for example the quality of labour or materials. The disadvantage of this system is that it is time-consuming and expensive to enter and manipulate the vast amount of data involved. In a modern AMT/JIT environment it may not be necessary to use such a complex system if

- all forms of stock inventory (raw materials, WIP and finished products) are kept at very low levels;
- production is highly automated and reliable, leading to low labour costs and efficient use of labour time;
- long-term relationships with suppliers ensure reliable delivery and fixed price and quality specifications.

Under these conditions, there will be little variation of input prices or efficiencies and therefore insignificant cost variations. Thus, there would be no need to use the traditional accounting technique, and backflush accounting may be used instead. The CIMA *Official Terminology* defines backflush accounting as 'a method of costing, associated with a JIT production system, which applies cost to the output of a process. Costs do not mirror the flow of products through the production process, but are attached to output produced (finished goods stock and cost of sales), on the assumption that such back-flushed costs are a realistic measure of the actual costs incurred.' Thus, conversion costs are only attached to products when they are completed. This system only uses raw, in-process and finished goods accounts, which saves costs by reducing the amount of data required and the frequency of data entry, for example data on materials used only enters the system when a piece of work is completed. However, this system does not enable the valuation of WIP nor any variance analysis.

The variances for PSA Ltd are significant for efficiency of inputs (labour and materials) and there is also a noticeable change in WIP, and the price of inputs. If this is typical, then the proposal should be rejected, as backflush accounting is unsuitable. Rapier, like many consultants, may be too concerned with selling its services than with truly serving its customers.

 Solution 37

When calculating your absorption rates, do not forget to include the data for 'other products' in your total figures.

(a) (i) Unit costs using traditional absorption costing
Material-related overhead cost (40% of £1.5m) = £600,000

$$\text{Overhead absorption rate } \frac{£600,000}{£2,400,000} \times 100 = 25\% \text{ of direct material cost}$$

Labour-related overhead cost (60% of £1.5m) = £900,000

$$\text{Overhead absorption rate } \frac{£900,000}{£800,000} \times 100 = 112.5\% \text{ of direct labour cost}$$

	Alpha £	*Beta* £
Direct materials	16	30
Direct labour	8	10
Prime cost	24	40
Material related overhead (25%)	4	7.5
Labour related overheads (112.5%)	9	11.25
Total variable costs	37	58.75

(ii) Unit costs based on activity-based costing

	Alpha	*Beta*	*Other*
Production units	5,000	10,000	40,000
Weight of direct material (kg)	4	1	1.5
Total weight of material (kg)	20,000	10,000	60,000

$$\text{Material-related overhead/kg } \frac{£600,000}{20,000 + 10,000 + 60,000} = £6.67/\text{kg}$$

	Alpha	Beta	Other
Production units	5,000	10,000	40,000
Labour operations/unit	6	1	2
Total operations	30,000	10,000	80,000

$$\text{Labour-related overheads/op } \frac{£900,000}{30,000 + 10,000 + 80,000} = £7.50 \text{ per operation}$$

Unit costs based on ABC	Alpha £	Beta £
Direct materials	16	30
Direct labour	8	10
Prime cost	24	40
Material related overhead	26.68	6.67
Labour related overheads	45	7.50
Total variable costs	95.68	54.17

(b)

	Alpha Traditional £	Alpha ABC £	Beta Traditional £	Beta ABC £
Direct material	16	16	30	30
Direct labour	8	8	10	10
Material-related overhead	4	26.68	7.50	6.67
Labour-related overhead	9	45	11.25	7.50
Total variable cost	37	95.68	58.75	54.17
Selling price	75	75.00	95.00	95.00
Contribution/unit	38	(20.68)	36.25	40.83
C/S ratio	51%	(28)%	38%	43%

Apollo plc require a minimum C/S ratio of 40%. If product costs are determined using the traditional methods Apollo would decide to proceed with the production of Alpha (C/S ratio of 51%) and reject Beta which has a C/S just below the required 40%.

If ABC is used the decision will be reversed. Alpha will be rejected on the basis of a negative C/S ratio and Apollo will proceed with Beta which has a C/S ratio of 43%.

ABC provides a more accurate cost of products unlike the traditional method used, which is a broad-based averaging of costs. ABC attempts to reflect the true consumption of resources.

(c) The use of target costing in conjunction with ABC will enable Apollo to find ways of reducing the costs of Alpha to arrive at a target cost. Cost reduction methods such as value analysis and value engineering could be used to achieve this. Though Beta just meets the required 40% C/S ratio, Apollo could decide to increase margins further by carrying out a similar exercise on Beta. Target costing should also be used to identify selling prices for specific markets.

Solution 38

(a) *Report to the operations manager of S Limited on performance for the period September to December*

From: Management Accountant
Date: December 2004

Four months is not a long period to recognise trends, but it is much better than a single month. The trends and significant features for this period include:

Output has fallen distinctly during the period. There are probably seasonal factors here. It is likely that more of these systems will be sold in Summer than in early Winter. It is also possible these differences are expected variations around the 1000 units per month budget? Were there some especially large contracts in September and October? This is not directly the responsibility of the operations manager but it will affect the operating results.

Material usage (efficiency) has varied over the 4 months, with October and December being poor. This is not related to volume, and so other explanations must be sought. One batch of systems has been more difficult to install and sometimes require additional or replacement parts. It would be important to ascertain whether other problems of material efficiency are linked to certain systems, certain fitters or specific stages of the installation process.

Material price – the buying in cost of the basic systems has risen over the 4 months. It appears that part of this increase has been the result of exchange movements. It would be important to quantify this effect. It would also be important to ascertain whether there are alternative sources. Have purchasing staff been active in seeking alternative sources? It might be possible to increase prices to reflect the rising cost, although this may be limited by its competitors or the firm's strategy, for example, to keep prices competitive to build market share.

The labour rate is higher than standard for all months and is deteriorating further. This clearly needs investigation. The most likely cause appears to be problems with keeping skilled staff and average labour rates may have risen to help retain staff. This may also have been caused by bad budgeting, or there may have been unexpected pay rises. As volumes have fallen during the months when hourly labour rates have risen, this rise is unlikely to have been caused by overtime payments.

More worrying than the rate variances are the labour efficiency variances that are also deteriorating. This may indicate that the cause of the higher wage rates is not the use of a higher proportion of skilled workers at higher wage rates. The problems with high staff turnover may have resulted in more staff learning the job and taking more time. Another possible cause is that fitters are taking longer on each vehicle as the monthly volumes are decreasing. This would indicate that labour is not actually a variable cost, although standard costing systems usually assume that it will be. Another explanation to be explored is whether the batch with the incorrect adapters has led to increased labour time being used. It might be that the average labour time is not as expected, purely as a consequence of the 25% variation that is known to occur.

For variable overheads only the total variable overhead variance has any real meaning. This also shows poor performance in November and December. This might indicate that variable overheads are not fully variable and as volumes fall, the variable overheads fall proportionately less.

A similar deteriorating pattern is seen with the fixed overhead spending variance. It is usually impossible to ascertain the causes of this without detailed investigation, as many different items of cost are included in this category. In this case it is clear that some of the main fixed costs have risen during the period, and these increases may not have been budgeted. It is important to enquire whether there has been effective control of costs by the department managers, although it also important to distinguish those costs where these managers have little control, such as rent, rates and insurance.

Overall there seems to be a worsening of operating performance in November and December, with no obvious cause apparent in the data. The total adverse variance is only 4.4% of the total standard cost and may not in itself require detailed investigation. However, this total includes some individual variances that are much larger in percentage terms, and these do need investigation. There are hints that lower volumes may be playing a part, and also hints that cost control needs to be tighter. As always, detailed questions will have to be asked to ensure that the causes of rising costs are understood. It may then be possible to manage these costs and reduce future costs.

The points above mention detailed additional information that would be helpful in assessing the performance for this period. There is other more general further information that would be helpful, including departmental information, market data, operating and quality data in physical units and details of the nature of the standards.

(b)
Report to the operations manager

Subject: Ways to increase motivation and improve performance
From: Management Accountant
Date: December 2004

Motivation and performance improvement are complex subjects. Many aspects of the firm interact to produce the overall motivation for each individual employee. It is possible to use the budgeting system to increase motivation and improve performance. The following are possible means to achieve this in S Limited:

- Set budgets with the participation of managers. It may be possible do this in conjunction with an initiative to establish teams of fitters that have some autonomy over how they organise their work. There is evidence that this approach frequently produces improved results, but this is not guaranteed.
- Attempt to achieve acceptance of the standards in the budget. Participation is seen as one way to do this. Other approaches are through consultation and clear explanation to staff.
- Give clear and rapid feedback to the first-line managers and supervisors/team leaders. There is strong evidence that this improves motivation as people are keen to know how well they are doing and this reinforces any motivation to perform well.
- Link with appropriate incentives. It may be beneficial to introduce some incentive scheme linked to achieving the budget, but note that too strong a link will lead to gaming behaviour. There is good evidence that incentives can improve performance, but also much evidence that where this emphasis is strong obtaining the reward becomes the objective and this may be achieved without making overall long run improvements in performance. For S Limited it would be very damaging for budgets to be met at the cost of damaging customer satisfaction.
- Encourage interchange between departments and teams, possibly by company-wide incentives not department-based incentives. This is particularly important where real improvements can best be achieved through improved cooperation.

- It may be important to note clearly the controllable and non-controllable elements within the budget. For example, the batch of systems that were difficult to fit was not the result of a decision by the fitters. There are strong arguments that managers should only be held responsible for performance where they have control, and that holding managers responsible for non-controllable results can be demotivating.

☑ Solution 39

For each proposal, calculate a revised operating profit figure and a revised figure for year-end assets. In part (b) the finance charge for the residual income is calculated as 12% of the net assets figure.

(a) The proposal to defer payment would have the following effects:
- 20X1   Net assets at year end will be reduced to £4,310,000 and operating profit will be reduced by the late payment penalty of £2,000. Therefore,

$$\text{ROCE} = \frac{647,000}{4,310,000} \times 100 = 15.01\%$$

This meets the target, so management will adopt this proposal and receive their bonuses.
- 20X2   No effect. The proposal to delay payment incurs expensive finance costs:

$$\frac{2,000}{90,000} \times 100 = 12.2\% \text{ for 12 days (or 1/30.4 of a year)}$$

which is an annual rate of $((1.022)^{30.4} - 1) \times 100$: that is approximately 94%. The proposal to replace the oldest machine tools would have the following effects.
- 20X1   Net assets at year end increased by £320,000 and no effect upon operating profit. Therefore,

$$\text{ROCE} = \frac{649,000}{4,720,000} \times 100 = 13.75\%$$
- 20X2   Extra depreciation charges £40,000 and operation saving £76,000. Therefore,

$$\text{The ROCE for the proposed is } \frac{36,000}{280,000} \times 100 = 12.9\%$$

This will not help to achieve an overall divisional ROCE of 15%.

The proposal to replace old assets will not increase the divisional ROCE in the short term. However, as the asset value of this new machinery declines, eventually the ROCE for this project will rise and assist in meeting the division's target. This illustrates the major weakness of ROCE as a measure of performance in that the ROCE increases over the life of the asset and the initial low values may discourage divisional managers from making necessary profitable investments.

This proposal has an internal rate of return of 17% (see working) which denotes a relatively attractive proposal. However, with the emphasis on short-term ROCE figures, this proposal is likely to be rejected.

(b) Both performance indicators compare the profit generated with the assets used to produce them. ROCE is a ratio which may be used to compare operations irrespective of the scale of operations. Residual income (RI) is an absolute value that is dependent upon the scale of operation.

If the two divisions are reassessed using RI, we have the following.

Division	Operating profit £	Finance charge £	RI £
K	649,000	528,000	121,000
D	120,000	58,000	62,000

In this analysis, Division K has a better residual income, twice that of Division D, but this has required nine times the assets to achieve this result. Thus, it would not be appropriate to set the same target RI for divisions that have significantly different asset values.

Residual income, like ROCE, tends to increase over the life of an asset. That is, as the asset is depreciated, the finance charge decreases. However, so long as a new investment generates profit at a rate above the company's cost of capital, it will increase the total RI of the division. Thus, it is less likely to discourage new investment.

The advantage of the ROCE ratio is that 1 year's one company's result is comparable with another result. The RI may vary from year to year, or from company to company, as the market interest rate or company cost of capital varies.

Both performance indicators value the assets at net book value, but this may not reflect technological obsolescence compared with the organisation's competitors. Many other factors may affect the division's profitability, for example calibre of management, degree of competition in the market place and so on. Thus, neither ROCE nor RI can be used on its own to measure how successfully a division has performed.

Thus, I disagree with the financial controller's proposal to merely replace one key indicator with another; a mixture of indicators is required.

Working

$$\text{IRR, investmen inflow ratio } \frac{£320,000}{£76,000} = 4.21$$

From annuity tables the sum of discount factors over 8 years that equals 4.208 is for 17%. Therefore IRR = 17%.

 ## Solution 40

(a)

ROI	Y £m	Z £m
Monthly net income	0.122	0.021
Annualised net income	1.464	0.252
Divisional net assets	9.76	1.26
ROI	15%	20%

The following comments can be made regarding the relative performance of the two divisions:

- On pure ROI, division Z is performing better than division Y;
- Division Y is earning a larger absolute amount by more than five times, and is exceeding the target return on capital, thus Y is increasing the wealth of the company more than Z, but this is not reflected in the ROI figures;
- The availability of capital and other projects are critical to the assessment of relative performance. If there is (virtually) unlimited availability of capital, then any division earning more than the target rate of return is increasing the company's wealth and both divisions are making a positive contribution. If division Z could repeat its performance by adding similar projects, then it should be allocated more funds as its rate of return is higher;
- If there is a chance that the target rate of return will have to be raised, then division Y is at greater risk as its actual return is much closer to the current target;
- Controllable income return on sales is 51% (460/900) for division Y and 36% (201/555) for division Z. This indicates that the operations of division Y are producing income at a higher rate per £ of sales than division Z;
- The controllable income return on net assets is 57% for division Y and 191% for division Z. Thus division Z is earning its income with much less use of divisional net assets – it could be argued that it is being more efficient;
- The net income figures are being strongly influenced by the apportionment of central costs. More needs to be known about the basis of the apportionment before a more definite evaluation can be made.

(b)

RI	Y	Z
	£m	£m
Annualised net income	1.464	0.252
Interest charge at 12% of Divisional Net Assets	1.171	0.151
Residual Income	0.293	0.101

The following points could be made regarding the performance of the two divisions in the light of the RI calculations:

- If capital is freely available, then the higher RI indicates the division that is contributing most to the company as a whole. Thus division Y is contributing more. This is the opposite conclusion to that indicated by ROI;
- The comments above concerning availability of capital and projects also apply;
- Overall the issue is that Y earns more income, but Z earns its income at a better rate.

(c) Strengths and weaknesses of ROI and RI can include the following:

- ROI gives a percentage result that is often considered to have intuitive appeal;
- ROI as a percentage is said to make comparison easier;
- ROI does not require a cost of capital to be specified;
- ROI has significant behavioural consequences that appear to make optimal decision-making less likely;
- Maximising RI leads to maximising company wealth in most cases;

- Both ROI and RI can be affected by the age of assets and the method of asset valuation, resulting in a similar performance by two companies showing different values for ROI and RI if the assets are valued on a different basis.
- Different interest rates can be used in the calculation of RI for each division, to reflect the different risk characteristics of each division.

Other methods of assessment that could be used alongside either ROI or RI include

- Economic Value Added® which is an adaption of RI;
- Balanced scorecards and other non-financial measures of divisional performance;
- Controllable profit, or other pure profit measures;
- Cash generated.

 Solution 41

(a)

	Original Budget	Flexed Budget	Actual	Variance	
Assembly labour hours	6,400	7,140	7,140		
Variable costs	$	$	$	$	
Assembly labour	49,920	55,692	56,177	485	(A)
Furniture packs	224,000	249,900	205,000	44,900	(F)
Other materials	23,040	25,704	24,100	1,604	(F)
Variable Overheads	34,560	38,556	76,340	37,784	(A)
Total Variable costs	331,520	369,852	361,617	8,235	(F)
Departmental Fixed costs					
Manager	2,050	2,050	2,050	–	
Overheads	18,500	27,000	27,000	–	
Total Departmental Fixed costs	20,550	29,050	29,050	–	
Central costs	9,000	9,000	9,000	–	
	361,070	407,902	399,667	8,235	(F)

Note: The variable costs have been flexed in relation to the number of assembly hours worked.

(b)

(i) The revised format of the statement is more helpful to the management and managers of M plc for performance measurement because
- it presents the information in a marginal format;
- it compares like with like', that is it is flexed to the actual level of activity and therefore an equitable comparison can be made;
- it separates controllable and uncontrollable items to facilitate responsibility accounting.

(ii) The company assumes that costs vary in line with labour hours but the furniture, and therefore it would follow that the assembly and fitting 'varies considerably in size, complexity and value'. This is evidenced by the cost of furniture assembled being less than budgeted but the hours used being more complex, time-consuming jobs could have been done this month. Consequently, the company should investigate other ways of setting and flexing the budget by determining what causes the variations in costs. It should identify the activities which drive costs. This would lead to activity-based budgeting.

(c) Benefits of participative budgeting for M plc:
- Improved communication;
- Provides a vehicle for training;
- Fosters acceptance of the accounting system and thereby reduces the possibility of dysfunctional behaviour;
- Departmental managers have areas of expertise that can be incorporated into the budget; for example, the Assembly Department Manager will be aware of what drives the costs in his department;
- Agreed budgets and targets provide a realistic target.

However, a participative approach is not always appropriate: many managers perform better within a given framework. The needs, styles and experiences of individual managers should be considered. For example, the manager of the Assembly Department may need a lot of training before he can play a role in a participative system. Another disadvantage of participative budgeting is that there is an increased likelihood of budget padding and the introduction of budgetary slack.

 Solution 42

(a)

	Division TM		Division FD	
Current situation	£'000	£'000	£'000	£'000
Sales				
Internal				990
External		7,500		400
		7,500		1,390
Less				
Variable costs				
Production	5,490		800	
Selling and distribution	375	5,865	20	820
Contribution		1,635		570
Less				
Fixed costs				
Production overheads		900		400
Administration overheads		375		80
Net profit		360		90
Less				
Imputed interest charge		180		90
Residual income		180		Nil
Target residual income		105		85
Bonus awarded		£9,000		Nil

Comment
- The manager of Division TM is happy as he has exceeded the target residual income and earned a bonus of £9,000.

- The manager of Division FD is unhappy as he has not achieved the residual income target and therefore has been awarded no bonus.
- This situation may result in demotivation in Division FD, which will impart on efficiency levels and the quality of the product. This, in turn, can lead to high staff turnover, dissatisfied customers and so on, which will incur additional costs for the group as a whole.
- The current situation is clearly not acceptable and a resolution must be achieved.

(b) (i) The transfer price per unit which Division TM will be willing to pay in order to achieve the 5% bonus is calculated as follows:

	£'000
Current residual income	180
Target residual income	105
Decrease acceptable	75

Division TM could suffer a decrease of £75,000 in residual income and the manager could still achieve the bonus. This would be shared over 15,000 units transferred. Therefore, the price of each unit could rise by £5 (£75,000/15,000) to £71.

(ii) The transfer price per unit which Division FD will want to charge in order to achieve the 5% bonus is calculated as follows:

	£'000
Current residual income	Nil
Target residual income	85
Increase required	85

Division FD needs an increase of £85,000 in residual income so that the manager can achieve the bonus. This would be gained from the 15,000 units transferred. Therefore, the transfer price of each unit would rise to £71.67 [(£85,000/15,000) + £66].

(c) **Report**

To: Management
From: Management Accountant
Re: Recommended Transfer Prices
Date: 20 November 2002

The transfer price should be set at marginal cost plus the opportunity cost to the company as a whole of supplying the unit internally.

For up to 20,000 mouldings the opportunity cost is zero as FD Division has spare capacity. The transfer price should therefore be set at £40.00, that is the marginal cost. TM Division would only wish to purchase externally at a price of less than £40.00, which would not be a sub-optimal decision for the group.

Therefore, if FD Division' external customer demand increased from 5,000 mouldings to 10,000 mouldings, then the transfer price should be set at £40 per moulding as no opportunity cost arises due to the level of spare capacity. However, if FD Division's external customer demand exceeded 10,000 mouldings, then the transfer price would be set at £80 for each moulding which displaces an external sale. This is because in order to satisfy the internal transfers to TM Division, FD Division would have to forgo external sales.

However, if the price is set at £71.67, a sub-optimal situation could arise if TM Division discovers a source of external supply of mouldings at a price which is between £40.00 and £71.67. Unless TM Division is obliged to purchase internally, a sub-optimal decision would result because TM Division would be paying more for each component than it costs to manufacture internally within the group.

It would be unsatisfactory for Division FD to use a transfer price equal to marginal cost, that is £40.00, as they would not cover their fixed costs. A transfer price of £40.00 will also not allow the manager to achieve their residual income target and therefore their bonus. Division FD may take the view that they will only sell externally because to transfer internally at variable costs will not rewarded them any profit.

If Division FD took this view and Division TM could not source the mouldings externally, they would make no sales. This would be unsatisfactory for the company as a whole, as it would cause a large fall in profit. Division TM would achieve their residual income target if the transfer price were £71, that is £0.67 less than the desired transfer price for Division FD.

Therefore, a conflict exists between the objectives of the two divisions and a solution will need to be found that rewards both divisions and eliminates this sub-optimal situation. The company could opt for one of the following solutions:

1. *Dual Pricing System*

   This is where the transfer price is at marginal cost, that is £40 per moulding and at the end of the period a proportion of the overall profit arising from the final sales of the 'TX' is credited to Division FD. The disadvantage of this system is that the proportion of profit to '… be credited to Division FD is determined centrally and this therefore undermines divisional autonomy. A variation of this system is where Division FD transfers at market price, that is £80, and Division TM accounts for the transfers at marginal cost, that is £40, and a discrepancy account is held in head office records. This avoids sub-optimal decision making but it can be administratively cumbersome. However, this method questions the objectivity of residual income as a basis of performance measurement.

2. *Two-Part Tariff System*

   This is where the transfer price is at marginal cost, that is £40 per moulding, and at the end of the period a fixed fee is credited to Division FD which represents an allowance for fixed costs. The disadvantage of this system is that the fixed cost fee to be credited to Division FD is determined centrally and this therefore undermines divisional autonomy.

3. *Negotiated Transfer Price*

   Perhaps Division FD and Division TM can negotiate a transfer price which is acceptable to both. This will depend on the ability of the divisional managers to compromise and also the divisional politics involved. A problem that may be encountered with this method is that if two divisional managers cannot agree, they may then have to seek a decision from central management on what transfer price to charge. If this is the case, then it undermines the main criterion set out for transfer prices, that is, that the divisions should remain as autonomous decision making units.

   If no agreement can be found between Division FD and Division TM, then head office may impose a transfer price which maximises the profit of the company as a whole. If this method is used, then it undermines divisional autonomy and can be demotivating for the managers involved.

Signed: Management Accountant

Solution 43

(a) Increased competition and technology changes like computer-aided design (CAD), flexible-manufacturing systems (FMS) and computer-integrated manufacturing (CIM), along with the TQM philosophy and JIT manufacturing systems, will dramatically change the manufacturing environment for X Ltd.

To respond to these changes, many new costing systems, for example target costing, have been introduced and other more traditional costing systems have been adapted. One of the more traditional costing systems is standard costing which X Ltd is currently using. This is a control technique which compares standard costs and revenues with actual results to obtain variances which are used to stimulate control action to achieve improved performance.

The use of standard costing in today's manufacturing environment is criticised and as a result X Ltd may have to adapt it to cope with the changing nature of their business. Such criticisms and how they have been remedied are discussed below:

The changing nature of product cost structures has affected the application of standard costing in that overhead costs have become a more significant element of total cost and direct labour cost has decreased considerably. This is as a result of the large-scale investment made in production equipment. As standard costing is focused on controlling direct costs and therefore variable costs its usefulness is now being questioned where there is a large amount of fixed costs and indirect costs.

However, research shows that variable costs are still a significant proportion of total costs, such as direct material costs and variable overheads and under these circumstances standard costing is an important cost accounting method.

Standard costing in the new manufacturing environment now places less emphasis on direct labour cost variances. This environment has developed other variances which focus on critical inputs to the production process, for example machine hours, direct material costs, variable overhead costs and product quality.

Standard costing is inconsistent with many of the modern management philosophies today. Many of today's manufacturing organisations have adopted techniques like TQM, ABC and ABM which focus on cost control, the elimination of rejects and the maintenance of high quality products which are delivered to the customer at the right price and at the right time.

Standard costing in some ways contradicts these modern techniques, as it requires managers to be responsible for their own variances which, in some cases, motivates managers to achieve favourable variances at the detriment of quality, for example purchasing poor quality materials at a lower price. The same issues arise in relation to increasing actual volume above budgeted volume leading to favourable volume variances but increasing inventory levels. The emphasis is too much on cost minimisation rather than on the maintenance of product quality and customer care.

Standard costing has been adapted so that the cost driver analysis derived from an activity-based management system is now used to calculate variances beyond those traditionally calculated under standard costing. X Ltd's steps in introducing the ABC system will provide them with more useful variance information.

Traditionally, it was quite usual for variances to be reported on a monthly basis and this time delay in reporting is of little use to the control of day-to-day operations. Many manufacturing companies have implemented real-time information systems, which calculate the variances on a real-time basis and allow for corrective action to be taken sooner. CAD, for example, allows the control of production costs at the pre-production stage and can be used alongside target costing as a way of controlling costs before they are incurred and in a way which reflects market costs.

The variances calculated from a standard costing system are too aggregate, that is they are not normally specific to product lines or production batches and this makes it difficult for managers to determine their cause. Adapting the standard costing system to allow for a broader analysis has been undertaken by many manufacturing organisations.

Traditionally, one of the crucial factors of standard costing was a stable production process. Today's manufacturing environment has less stable production processes in that many different products are produced on the same production lines. It is, therefore, important that standard costing is customised to reflect this.

Shorter product life cycles mean that standard costing information can quickly become out of date and therefore needs to be regularly updated, otherwise its application will be very limited. The modern manufacturing environment has embraced the need to keep the standard cost data up-to-date.

The majority of manufacturing organisations still use standard costing and it is therefore unlikely that it will ever be completely abandoned. It has, however, become an integral part of the cost management systems in today's manufacturing environment and tends to be broadened to provide whatever variance information the organisation may need from time to time. So even if standard costing were to be abandoned for cost control and performance evaluation purposes, it will still have a specific use for inventory valuation, profit measurement and decision-making.

(b) *Fixed overhead expenditure variance – $2,300(A)*

This variance represents the difference between the fixed production overhead that should have been incurred in the period and that which was incurred. The adverse variance indicates that actual fixed production overhead incurred was more than budgeted for the period.

The total fixed overhead expenditure variance does not pinpoint the precise reason for the variance occurring as any difference will be the result of a combination of reasons. Therefore, it would be more appropriate to detail the actual fixed production overhead costs compared to that budgeted for each individual item. Without this level of detail, this variance would be difficult to use for decision-making purposes, for example the identification of specific fixed costs that would arise as a result of a decision being made.

Fixed overhead capacity variance – $10,000(F)

This variance represents the over-or under-absorption of fixed production overhead costs, caused by the actual hours worked differing from the hours originally budgeted to be worked. It appears that X Ltd has managed to increase its capacity by 1,000 hours resulting in this favourable variance.

Fixed overhead efficiency variance – $5,000(A)

This variance represents the over-or under-absorption of fixed production overhead costs caused by actual labour efficiency differing from the standard level of labour efficiency. While the capacity was favourable, this variance indicates that labour did not work efficiently, using 1,000 extra actual hours to produce only 5,000 extra diaries, rather than the standard output of 10,000 diaries.

The purpose of the fixed overhead efficiency and capacity variances is to assist management's understanding of the causes of the variances. The use of these variances is limited in that it is only possible to calculate them under an absorption costing system. With an absorption costing system it is sometimes difficult to decide which costs are really fixed in nature. Also the usefulness of attaching a value for fixed overheads is questionable as fixed overheads often represent sunk costs and such costs are not appropriate for decision-making purposes. Perhaps it would be more appropriate to measure this variance in terms of lost contribution arising from lost sales. Also the use of labour hours as a driver of fixed costs may not be meaningful in the modern manufacturing environment in which X Ltd currently operates.

(c) (i) *Overhead expenditure variances*

These variances measure the difference between the actual production overhead costs and those in a budget flexed on the actual number of orders executed and the number of production runs.

Material handling has a $2,200 favourable variance indicating that the actual production overhead costs were less than the budget flexed on the actual number of orders executed.

This would be calculated as follows:

Material handling	$
Standard cost ($30,000/5,000 × 5,500)	33,000
Actual cost	30,800
Variance	2,200 (F)

The set up cost has a $6,500 adverse variance indicating that the actual production overhead costs were more than the budget flexed on the actual number of production runs.

This would be calculated as follows:

Set ups	$
Standard cost ($70,000/2,800 × 2,600)	65,000
Actual cost	71,500
Variance	6,500 (A)

These variances provide useful information as they compare each individual item of overhead expenditure against the budget.

Overhead efficiency variances

These variances measure the difference between the overhead cost budget flexed on the actual number of orders executed and the actual number of production runs and the overhead cost absorbed by the activity achieved.

Material handling – $ 1,500(A)

This variance indicates that the actual number of orders executed was more than expected for the output achieved resulting in this adverse variance.

This would be calculated as follows:

Material handling	
Standard orders executed	
(5,000/100,000 × 105,000)	5,250
Actual orders executed	5,500
Variance	250 × $6 = $1,500 (A)

Set up – $8,500(F)

This variance indicates that the actual number of production runs was less than expected for the output achieved resulting in this favourable variance.

This would be calculated as follows:

Set ups		
Standard production runs		
(2,800/100,00 × 105,000)	2,940	
Actual production runs	2,600	
Variance	340	× $25 = $8,500 (F)

(ii) When X Ltd implemented ABC the first stage in the process will have been to identify the major activities involved in the manufacturing of the electronic diaries. Examples of such activities are machine-related activities, direct labour-related activities and various support activities (ordering, receiving and so on). They will have identified the factors that influenced the cost of these activities, that is the cost drivers and a cost pool will then have been established for each activity and these costs will then have been traced to the electronic diaries based on the consumption estimates of these activities during the manufacturing process.

By implementing the ABC system it has become apparent that the traditional volume-based cost variances are replaced with activity-based cost driver variances which will provide more useful information as to the cause of such variances as these more accurately reflect the cause of resource consumption. So instead of aggregating all of the overhead costs as in the standard costing system, such overhead costs under an ABC system will be broken down based on the resources consuming those costs. The extent to which it leads to more accurate costing will depend on the analysis undertaken when determining the cost drivers.

The more detailed variances reported under the ABC system will allow the managers of X Ltd to gain better control of these areas and will assist in future planning and decision-making.

✅ Solution 44

(a)

	£ per repair	£ total repairs
Parts	54	
Labour	45	
Variable overhead	30	
Marginal cost	129	64,500
Fixed overhead	66	33,000
Total cost	195	97,500
Mark-up	78	39,000
Selling Price	273	136,500

(i) Transfers at 40% mark-up

	Sales	Service	FP
	£	£	£
Sales	120,000	136,500	120,000
Costs	136,500	97,500	97,500
Profit	(16,500)	39,000	22,500

(ii) Transfers at marginal cost

	Sales	*Service*	*FP*
	£	£	£
Sales	120,000	64,500	120,000
Costs	64,500	97,500	97,500
Profit	55,500	(33,000)	22,500

(iii) Repairs carried out by RS

	Sales	*Service*	*FP*
	£	£	£
Sales	120,000	0	120,000
Costs	90,000	33,000	123,000
Profit	30,000	(33,000)	(3,000)

(b)

(i) Full cost plus may not be appropriate
  - Are the fixed costs committed?
  - Why is the quote by RS lower than the cost of the Service Department?
  - Full cost would build in any inefficiencies in the Service Department;
  - Full cost would lead to implied poor performance by the Sales Department. The performance measures and reward system would lead to a sub-optimal decision by the manager of the Sales Department.

(ii) Issues to consider include
  - The quality of the repairs by RS;
  - Is the offer by RS a short-term offer? Would the price rise in the longer term?
  - Why are the costs of the Service Department higher than the price charged by RS?
  - Are the fixed costs avoidable?
  - Can the Service Department find other work to take up the capacity released if RS does the guarantee repairs?

(c)

Candidates should structure their discussion around the following themes:

Advantages
  - Improved decision-making – local knowledge;
  - Motivation;
  - Autonomy;
  - Allow senior management to focus on strategic issues;
  - Good training ground;
  - Reduce bureaucracy.

Disadvantages
  - Possible loss of control by senior management;
  - Dysfunctional decision-making;
  - Possible duplication of functions and costs.

Solution 45

(a) Total production cost:

Car X = $40,000 (standard unit cost from the table showing information for the cost of sales)

Car Y = $47,000

Fixed production overhead = $35,000,000

Budgeted machine hours = (1,100 × 200) + (1,600 × 300) = 700,000 machine hours

Fixed production overhead absorption rate = $35,000,000/700,000 = $50 per machine hour.

	Car X $ per car	Car Y $ per car
Total production cost	40,000	47,000
Fixed overhead absorbed	10,000	15,000
Variable production cost per car	30,000	32,000

Marginal costing operating statement – year ending 30 June 2008

	Car X $000	Car Y $000	Total $000
Sales	52,500	105,000	157,500
Variable production costs	30,000	56,000	86,000
Variable administration costs	6,300	12,600	18,900
Contribution	16,200	36,400	52,600
Specific fixed costs			
Marketing	2,000	4,000	6,000
Contribution to general fixed costs	14,200	32,400	46,600
General fixed costs			
Production			35,000
Administration			10,000
Profit			**1,600**

(b) The difference in the profit figures will be caused by the fixed production overheads that are absorbed into closing inventories. Changes in inventory levels will determine the amount of fixed production overheads that are 'moved' into the next accounting period and not charged in this period. If inventory levels increase, the absorption costing profit will be higher than the profit calculated using marginal costing.

	Car X	Car Y
Opening inventory (units)	200	250
Closing inventory (units)	300	100
Change in inventory (units)	+100	−150
Marginal profit will be	lower	higher
Fixed production overhead per car	$10,000	$15,000
Total difference in profits	$1,000,000	$2,250,000

Reconciliation

	$000
Absorption costing profit	350
Car X: inventory impact	(1,000)
Car Y: inventory impact	2,250
Marginal costing profit	1,600

(c)

Activity	Cost Driver	Calculation of drivers	Drivers
Machining costs	Machine hours	700,000	700,000
Set up costs	No. of production runs	(1,100/10) + (1,600/40)	150
Quality inspections	No. of inspections	(110 × 20) + (40 × 80)	5,400
Stores receiving	No. of deliveries	492 + 900	1,392
Stores issues	No. of issues	4,000 + 7,000	11,000

Activity	$000	Driver	Cost per driver
Machining costs	7,000	700,000	$10 per machine hour
Set up costs	12,000	150	$80,000 per set up
Quality inspections	7,020	5,400	$1,300 per inspection
Stores receiving	3,480	1,392	$2,500 per delivery
Stores issues	5,500	11,000	$500 per issue

	Car X		Car Y	
	Driver	$000	Driver	$000
Machining costs	220,000	2,200	480,000	4,800
Set up costs	110	8,800	40	3,200
Quality inspections	2,200	2,860	3,200	4,160
Stores receiving	492	1,230	900	2,250
Stores issues	4,000	2,000	7,000	3,500
Total overhead		17,090		17,910
Direct costs		33,000		51,200
Total production costs		50,090		69,110
Cars produced		1,100		1,600
Cost per car		**$45,536**		**$43,194**

(d)

Report

To: Production Director
From: Management Accountant
Date: 22 May 2007

Subject: Activity Based Budgeting – Performance Evaluation

As you are aware we are considering the implementation of an activity based costing system and moving away from the traditional absorption costing system which we currently operate.

There are many potential benefits associated with implementing activity based budgeting (ABB) for performance evaluation. Please find below an outline of some of the benefits that can be achieved from ABB.

Preparing budgets using a traditional absorption costing approach involves presenting costs under functional headings, that is, costs are presented in a manner that emphasises their nature. The weakness of this approach is that it gives little indication of the link between the level of activity of the department and the cost incurred. In contrast, activity based budgeting provides a clear framework for understanding the link between costs and the level of activity. This would allow us to evaluate performance based on the activity that drives the cost.

The modern business environment has a high proportion of costs that are indirect and the only meaningful way of attributing these costs to individual products is to find the root cause of such costs, that is, what activity is driving these costs. The traditional absorption costing approach does not provide this level of detail as costs under this system are attributed to individual products using a volume related measure. For our company this is machine hours which results in an arbitrary product cost. This makes it difficult to hold individual managers accountable for variances that arise. Whereas with an activity based costing approach responsibility can be broken down and assigned accordingly and individual managers can provide input into the budgeting process and subsequently be held responsible for the variances arising.

There is greater transparency with an ABB system due to the level of detail behind the costs. The traditional absorption costing approach combines all of the overheads together using a machine hour basis to calculate an overhead absorption rate and uses this rate to attribute overheads to products. ABB will drill down in much more detail examining the cost and the driver of such costs and calculates a cost driver rate which will be used to assign overheads to products. Therefore ABB has greater transparency than absorption costing and allows for much more detailed information on overhead consumption and so on. This then lends itself to better performance evaluation.

I would like to conclude that the traditional absorption costing approach to product costing does not enable us to provide a satisfactory explanation for the behaviour of costs. In contrast ABB will provide such details which will allow us to have better cost control, improved performance evaluation and greater manager accountability.

If you require any further information please do not hesitate to contact me.

 Solution 46

(a)

Cash Budget	Month 1	Month 2	Month 3	Total
	£	£	£	£
Sales receipts	2,940	10,180	15,545	28,665
Capital injection	16,250			16,250
Total receipts	**19,190**	**10,180**	**15,545**	**44,915**
Outflow				
Materials	0	3,515	3,420	6,935
Labour	6,105	5,940	6,666	18,711
Variable overhead	1,332	2,184	2,318	5,834
Fixed overhead	3,750	5,625	5,625	15,000
Total Outflow	**11,187**	**17,264**	**18,029**	**46,480**
Inflow-Outflow	8,003	(7,084)	(2,484)	(1,565)
Bal b/fwd	0	8,003	919	0
Bal c/fwd	8,003	919	(1,565)	(1,565)

Workings			
Sales receipts	**1**	**2**	**3**
Sales units	1,500	1,750	2,000
	£	£	£
Selling price	10	10	10
Sales	15,000	17,500	20,000
Paid in month – 20%	3,000	3,500	4,000
Discount paid in month 2%	−60	−70	−80
45% in the following month		6,750	7,875
25% in 3rd month			3,750
Receipts	**2,940**	**10,180**	**15,545**

Production	**1**	**2**	**3**	**4**
	units	*units*	*units*	*units*
Required by sales	1,500	1,750	2,000	2,100
Opening inventory		(350)	(400)	
	1,500	1,499	1,600	
Closing inventory	350	400	420	
Production	1,850	1,800	2,020	
Material price	£1·90	£1·90	£1·90	
Material cost	£3,515	£3,420	£3,838	
Payment		**£3,515**	**£3,420**	
Labour				
Production units	1,850	1,800	2,020	
Rate per unit	£3·30	£3·30	£3·30	
Payment	£6,105	£5,940	£6,666	
Variable Overhead				
Production units	1,850	1,800	2,020	
Rate per unit	£1·20	£1·20	£1·20	
Variable overhead cost	£2,220	£2,160	£2,424	
Payment	£	£	£	
60% in month	1,332	1,296	1,454	
40% in following month		888	864	
Payment	**1,332**	**2,184**	**2,318**	
Fixed overhead	6,250	6,250	6,250	
Payment				
60% in month	3,750	3,750	3,750	
30% in following month		1,875	1,875	
Payment	**3,750**	**5,625**	**5,625**	

(b) (i)

	Month 1	Month 2	Month 3
£1·50			
£1·50 − £1·90	£0·40	£0·40	£0·40
Production units	1,850	1,800	2,020
Saving	£740	£720	£808
Saving		£740	£720
Total cash benefit	£1,460		
Current cash flow at £1·90	£(1,565)		
Revised cash flow at £1·50	**£(105)**		

(ii)

	Month 1	Month 2	Month 3
£2·20			
£2·20 − £1·90	£0·30	£0·30	£0·30
Production units	1,850	1,800	2,020
Additional cost	£555	£540	£606
Payment		£555	£540
Total additional payment	£1.095		
Current cash flow at £1·90	£(1,565)		
Revised cash flow at £2·20	**£(2,660)**		

(c)

To:	Management
From:	Management Accountant
Date:	22 May 2007
Subject:	'What if' analysis and cash budgets

This report addresses the benefits or otherwise of 'what if' analysis in relation to cash budgets. When there is a degree of uncertainty concerning elements incorporated within a budget 'what if' analysis allows us to revise the budgets on the basis of a series of varied assumptions.

In preparing the cash budgets we have identified that there is a degree of uncertainty concerning the direct material cost. We have used assumptions in part (b) to perform some calculations to estimate the effect of this uncertainty on the budgeted cash flow. The results were as follows:

Direct material cost per component	Increase/(decrease) in cash flow	Budgeted cash flow
£2·20	(£1,095)	(£2,660)
£1·50	£1,460	(£105)
£1·90		(£1,565)

If we perform some 'what if' analysis around these figures we can determine that a direct material cost of £2·20, that is, a 16% increase in material cost, results in a negative cash flow of −£2,660. This is a 70% increase in the closing cash negative balance. A direct material cost of £1·50, that is, a 21% decrease in direct material cost, results in a revised cashflow of −£105. This is a 93% reduction in the closing cash negative balance. The benefits of 'what if' analysis are that it allows us to:

- assess how responsive the cash flow is to changes in variables. Therefore we can assess how sensitive the variable is to changing conditions. From our calculations above obviously if the material cost increases it has a significant impact on the closing cash position;
- review critical variables to assess whether or not there is a strong possibility of the event occurring which leads to a negative cash flow;
- assess the variables that are most sensitive. These are the variables which cause the greatest variation with the lowest percentage change. It is important for the founders to pay particular attention to such variables and carefully monitor them.

It should however be noted that there are serious limitations when using 'what if' analysis'. Two of the major ones are as follows.

- The changes in key variables are isolated whereas the management will be more interested in the effect on the cash flow of two or more key variables changing;
- There is no indication of the likelihood of a key variable changing and therefore the use of 'what if' analysis is limited.

Should you require any further analysis or information please do not hesitate to contact me.

November 2007
Examinations

November 2007 Examinations

Managerial Level

Paper P1 – Management Accounting – Performance Evaluation

The answers published here have been written by the Examiner and should provide a helpful guide for both tutors and students.

Published separately on the CIMA website (www.cimaglobal.com/students) from mid-February 2008 is a Post Examination Guide for this paper, which provides much valuable and complementary material including indicative mark information.

CIMA

Management Accounting Pillar

Managerial Level Paper

P1 – Management Accounting – Performance Evaluation

20 November 2007 – Tuesday Morning Session

Instructions to candidates

You are allowed three hours to answer this question paper.
You are allowed 20 minutes reading time **before the examination begins** during which you should read the question paper and, if you wish, highlight and/or make notes on the question paper. However, you will **not** be allowed, **under any circumstances**, to open the answer book and start writing or use your calculator during the reading time.
You are strongly advised to carefully read ALL the question requirements before attempting the question concerned (that is, all parts and/or sub-questions). The requirements for the questions in Section C are contained in a dotted box.
ALL answers must be written in the answer book. Answers or notes written on the question paper will **not** be submitted for marking.
Answer the ONE compulsory question in Section A. This has 16 sub-questions and is on pages 591 to 595.
Answer ALL SIX compulsory sub-questions in Section B on pages 591 and 595.
Answer ONE of the two questions in Section C on pages 596 to 597.
Maths Tables and Formulae are provided on pages 598 to 600.
The list of verbs as published in the syllabus is given for reference on the inside back cover of this question paper.
Write your candidate number, the paper number and examination subject title in the spaces provided on the front of the answer book. Also write your contact ID and name in the space provided in the right hand margin and seal to close.
Tick the appropriate boxes on the front of the answer book to indicate which questions you have answered.

SECTION A – 40 MARKS

[the indicative time for answering this section is 72 minutes]

ANSWER *ALL* SIXTEEN SUB-QUESTIONS

Instructions for answering Section A:

The answers to the sixteen sub-questions in Section A should ALL be written in your answer book.

Your answers should be clearly numbered with the sub-question number then ruled off, so that the markers know which sub-question you are answering. **For multiple choice questions, you need only write the sub-question number and the letter of the answer option you have chosen**. You do not need to start a new page for each sub-question.

For sub-questions **1.11 to 1.16** you should show your workings as marks are available for the method you use to answer these sub-questions.

Question One

1.1 T Ltd uses a standard labour hour rate to charge its overheads to its clients' work. During the last annual reporting period production overheads were under-absorbed by £19,250. The anticipated standard labour hours for the period were 38,000 hours while the standard hours actually charged to clients were 38,500. The actual production overheads incurred in the period were £481,250.

The budgeted production overheads for the period were

(A) £456,000
(B) £462,000
(C) £475,000
(D) None of the above.   **(2 marks)**

1.2 Operation B, in a factory, has a standard time of 15 minutes. The standard rate of pay for operatives is £10 per hour. The budget for a period was based on carrying out the operation 350 times. It was subsequently realised that the standard time for Operation B included in the budget did not incorporate expected time savings from the use of new machinery from the start of the period. The standard time should have been reduced to 12 minutes.

Operation B was actually carried out 370 times in the period in a total of 80 hours. The operatives were paid £850.

The operational labour efficiency variance was

(A) £60 adverse
(B) £75 favourable
(C) £100 adverse
(D) £125 adverse   **(2 marks)**

1.3 JP manufactures two joint products X and Y, and a by-product Z, in a single continuous process. The following information is available for period 3:

Raw materials input	20,000 litres
Raw material costs	$52,000
Conversion costs	$56,000
Outputs	10,000 litres of X, selling price $8 per litre
	8,000 litres of Y, selling price $6 per litre
	2,000 litres of Z, selling price $1 per litre

Process costs are apportioned on a sales value basis. There was no opening and closing inventory of raw materials. The revenue from the by-product is used to reduce the process costs.

What was the cost per litre of joint product X?

(A) $5.889
(B) $6.523
(C) $6.625
(D) $6.646   **(2 marks)**

1.4 A company has budgeted breakeven sales revenue of £800,000 and fixed costs of £320,000 for the next period.

The sales revenue needed to achieve a profit of £50,000 in the period would be

(A) £850,000
(B) £925,000
(C) £1,120,000
(D) £1,200,000   **(2 marks)**

1.5 The production volume ratio in a period was 95%.

Which statement will always be true?

(A) Actual hours worked exceeded the budgeted hours.
(B) Actual hours worked exceeded the standard hours of output.
(C) Budgeted hours exceeded the standard hours of output.
(D) Budgeted output was less than the actual output.   **(2 marks)**

1.6 Two CIMA definitions follow:

1. A system that converts a production schedule into a listing of the materials and components required to meet that schedule so that adequate stock levels are maintained and items are available when needed.
2. An accounting oriented information system, generally software driven, which aids in identifying and planning the enterprise-wide resources needed to resource, make, account for and deliver customer orders.

Which of the following pairs of terms matches the definitions?

Definition 1	*Definition 2*
(A) Material requirements planning	Enterprise resource planning
(B) Manufacturing resource planning	Material requirements planning
(C) Material requirements planning	Manufacturing resource planning
(D) Manufacturing resource planning	Enterprise resource planning

(2 marks)

1.7   The fixed overhead volume variance is defined as

(A)   the difference between the budgeted value of the fixed overheads and the standard fixed overheads absorbed by actual production;

(B)   the difference between the standard fixed overhead cost specified for the production achieved, and the actual fixed overhead cost incurred;

(C)   the difference between budgeted and actual fixed overhead expenditure;

(D)   the difference between the standard fixed overhead cost specified in the original budget and the same volume of fixed overheads, but at the actual prices incurred;   **(2 marks)**

1.8   Overheads will always be over-absorbed when

(A)   actual output is higher than budgeted output;

(B)   actual overheads incurred are higher than the amount absorbed;

(C)   actual overheads incurred are lower than the amount absorbed;

(D)   budgeted overheads are lower than the overheads absorbed;   **(2 marks)**

The following data are given for sub-questions 1.9 and 1.10 below.

A manufacturing company recorded the following costs in October for Product X:

	$
Direct materials	20,000
Direct labour	6,300
Variable production overhead	4,700
Fixed production overhead	19,750
Variable selling costs	4,500
Fixed distribution costs	16,800
Total costs incurred for Product X	72,050

During October 4,000 units of Product X were produced but only 3,600 units were sold. At the beginning of October there was no inventory.

1.9   The value of the inventory of Product X at the end of October using marginal costing was:

(A) $3,080

(B) $3,100

(C) $3,550

(D) $5,075   **(2 marks)**

1.10 The value of the inventory of Product X at the end of October using throughput accounting was

(A) $630
(B) $1,080
(C) $1,100
(D) $2,000

(2 marks)

1.11 A company has the following budgeted sales figures:

Month 1	£90,000
Month 2	£105,000
Month 3	£120,000
Month 4	£108,000

80% of sales are on credit and the remainder are paid in cash. Credit customers paying within 1 month are given a discount of 1.5%. Credit customers normally pay within the following time frame:

Within 1 month	40% of credit sales
Within 2 months	70% of credit sales
Within 3 months	98% of credit sales

There is an expectation that 2% of credit sales will become bad debts.

Outstanding receivables at the beginning of month 1 includes £6,000 expected to be received in month 4.

Calculate the total receipts expected in month 4. **(4 marks)**

1.12 The budgeted total costs for two levels of output are as shown below:

Output	25,000 units	40,000 units
Total cost	£143,500	£194,000

Within this range of output it is known that the variable cost per unit is constant but fixed costs rise by £10,000 when output exceeds 35,000 units.

Calculate for a budgeted output of 36,000 units:

(i) the variable cost per unit;
(ii) the total fixed costs. **(3 marks)**

1.13 A company can produce many types of product but is currently restricted by the number of labour hours available on a particular machine. At present this limitation is set at 12,000 hours per annum. One type of product requires materials costing $5 which are then converted to a final product which sells for $12. Each unit of this product takes 45 minutes to produce on the machine. The conversion costs for the factory are estimated to be $144,000 per annum.

Calculate the throughput accounting ratio for this product and state the significance of the result. **(3 marks)**

1.14 A company manufactures three joint products in a continuous single process. Normal losses are 10% of inputs and do not have any value. Budget data is available for the month of January as follows:

Opening and closing work in progress	NIL
Direct materials input	20,000 kg at a cost of £36,000
Direct labour costs	3,000 hours @ £6 per hour
Variable production overheads	3,000 hours @ £1 per hour

Fixed production overheads are absorbed at a rate of £8 per direct labour hour.

	Expected outputs	Selling price per kg
Joint product A	9,000 kg	£8
Joint product B	6,000 kg	£6
Joint product C	3,000 kg	£4

Joint costs are apportioned on a physical unit basis.
Calculate the gross profit margin for each of the joint products.   **(3 marks)**

1.15 A company has the following balance sheet totals at the end of its most recent financial year:

	£ million
Non-current assets	3.64
Current assets	0.42
Share capital and reserves*	2.69
Long term debt	1.00
Current liabilities	0.37

*Includes retained profit for the year of 320,000 after deducting:

Ordinary share dividends	£200,000
Interest on long-term debt	£100,000
Taxation	£70,000

Calculate the return on investment (ROI) of the company for the year (using end year balance sheet values for investment).   **(3 marks)**

1.16 A division is considering the purchase of a new machine which costs $1,500,000 and is expected to generate cost savings of $450,000 a year. The asset is expected to have a useful life of 5 years with no residual value. Depreciation is charged on a straight line basis. Divisional performance is evaluated on residual income (RI). The division's cost of capital is 10%.

Calculate for this machine for each of the 5 years:

(i) the residual income (RI);
(ii) the return on investment (ROI).

Note: When calculating performance measures the division always uses capital values as at the start of the year.   **(4 marks)**

(Total for Section A = 40 marks)

SECTION B – 30 MARKS

[the indicative time for answering this section is 54 minutes]

ANSWER *ALL* SIX SUB-QUESTIONS. EACH SUB-QUESTION IS WORTH 5 MARKS

? Question Two

The following data are given for sub-questions 2(a) and 2(b) below:

QBQ produces one type of product. Details of the budgeted sales and production are given below.

Selling Price and Costs per unit

	£
Selling price	40
Material FX: 1.5 kg @ £6 per kg	9
Conversion costs (variable)	8
Fixed production overheads	15

The fixed production overhead absorption rate is based on annual production overheads of £720,000 and budgeted annual output of 48,000 units. The fixed overheads will be incurred evenly throughout the year.

The company also incurs fixed costs for administration of £200,000 per year.

Budgeted Sales

Quarter	Units
1	10,000
2	12,000
3	14,000
4	12,000

Inventory

It has been decided that inventory levels are to be reduced. Details are as follows:

Finished goods: 5,500 units are currently held but it has been decided that the closing inventories for Quarters 1, 2 and 3 will be 45%, 40% and 35% of the following quarter's sales respectively.

Raw materials: 4,500 kg are currently held but it has been decided that the closing inventories for Quarters 1 and 2 will be 25% and 20% of the following quarter's production requirements respectively.

(a) Prepare a materials purchase budget for Quarter 1. **(5 marks)**

(b) In Quarter 3 the opening and closing inventories of finished goods will be 5,600 units and 4,200 units respectively. QBQ adjusts for any under- or over-absorption of overheads at the end of each quarter.

Assume that production and sales volumes were as budgeted and that inventory levels were as planned. Also assume that all costs and revenues were as budgeted.

   (i) Calculate using marginal costing the profit for Quarter 3.
   (ii) Calculate using absorption costing the profit for Quarter 3.
   (iii) Explain the difference, if any, in the profits you have calculated.   **(5 marks)**

(c) Explain, giving examples, how budgets can be used for feedback control and feed-forward control.   **(5 marks)**

(d) Briefly explain **three** reasons why budgetary planning and control might be inappropriate in a rapidly changing business environment.   **(5 marks)**

(e) Briefly explain Just-in-Time (JIT) and **two** major requirements for the successful operation of a JIT system.   **(5 marks)**

(f) A nursing home uses incremental budgeting. The previous period's budget is adjusted by reference to a set of indices. It is adjusted firstly for 'volume changes' and then for changes in the cost of resources. The indices are referenced to the previous period's budget by using that budget as the base index number of 100. The index numbers to be used to prepare Period 3's budget from that of Period 2 are as follows:

	Index
Patient days	90
House-keeping costs	106
Nursing costs	105
Administration costs	104

The budget for Period 2 was:

	£
House-keeping costs (all variable)	125,000
Nursing costs (see below)	324,000
Administration costs (all fixed)	100,000

Nursing costs are semi-variable. The nursing costs for Period 2 were adjusted from the total nursing costs of £280,000 for Period 1 by using a Patient days index of 125 and a Nursing costs index of 108.

Prepare the budget for Period 3.   **(5 marks)**
(Total for Question Two = 30 marks)
(Total for Section B = 30 marks)

SECTION C – 30 MARKS

[the indicative time for answering this section is 54 minutes]

ANSWER *ONE* OF THE TWO QUESTIONS

? Question Three

WC is a company that installs kitchens and bathrooms for customers who are renovating their houses. The installations are either pre-designed 'off the shelf' packages or highly customised designs for specific jobs.

The company operates with three divisions: Kitchens, Bathrooms and Central Services. The Kitchens and Bathrooms divisions are profit centres but the Central Services division is a cost centre. The costs of the Central Services division, which are thought to be predominantly fixed, include those incurred by the design, administration and finance departments. The Central Services costs are charged to the other divisions based on the budgeted Central Services costs and the budgeted number of jobs to be undertaken by the other two divisions.

The budgeting and reporting system of WC is not very sophisticated and does not provide much detail for the Directors of the company.

Budget details

The budgeted details for last year were:

	Kitchens	Bathrooms
Number of jobs	4,000	2,000
	$	$
Average price per job	10,000	7,000
Average direct costs per job	5,500	3,000
Central Services recharge per job	2,500	2,000
Average profit per job	2,000	1,500

Actual details

The actual results were as follows:

	Kitchens	Bathrooms
Number of jobs	2,600	2,500
	$	$
Average price per job	13,000	6,100
Average direct costs per job	8,000	2,700
Central Services recharge per job	2,500	2,500
Average profit per job	2,500	900

The actual costs for the Central Services division were $17.5 million.

Required:

(a) Calculate the budgeted and actual profits for each of the profit centres and for the whole company for the year.   **(4 marks)**

(b) Calculate the sales price variances and the sales mix profit and sales quantity profit variances.   **(6 marks)**

(c) Prepare a statement that reconciles the budgeted and actual profits and shows appropriate variances in as much detail as possible.   **(10 marks)**

(d) Using the statement that you prepared in part (c) above, discuss

    (i) the performance of the company for the year; and

    (ii) potential changes to the budgeting and reporting system that would improve performance evaluation within the company.   **(10 marks)**

(Total for Question Three = 30 marks)

 ## Question Four

A multinational computer manufacturer has a number of autonomous subsidiaries throughout the world. Two of the group's subsidiaries are in America and Europe. The American subsidiary assembles computers using chips that it purchases from local companies. The European subsidiary manufactures exactly the same chips that are used by the American subsidiary but currently only sells them to numerous external companies throughout Europe. Details of the two subsidiaries are given below.

America

The American subsidiary buys the chips that it needs from a local supplier. It has negotiated a price of $90 per chip. The production budget shows that 300,000 chips will be needed next year.

Europe

The chip production subsidiary in Europe has a capacity of 800,000 chips per year. Details of the budget for the forthcoming year are as follows:

Sales	600,000 chips
	$ per chip
Selling price	105
Variable costs	60

The fixed costs of the subsidiary at the budgeted output of 600,000 chips are $20 million per year but they would rise to $26 million if output exceeds 625,000 chips.

Note: The maximum external demand is 600,000 chips per year and the subsidiary has no other uses for the current spare capacity.

Group Directive

The Managing Director of the group has reviewed the budgets of the subsidiaries and has decided that in order to improve the profitability of the group the European subsidiary should supply chips to the American subsidiary. She is also thinking of linking the salaries of the subsidiary managers to the performance of their subsidiaries but is unsure which performance measure to use. Two measures that she is considering are 'profit' and the 'return on assets consumed' (where the annual fixed costs would be used as the 'assets consumed').

The Manager of the European subsidiary has offered to supply the chips at a price of $95 each. He has offered this price because it would earn the same contribution per chip that would be earned on external sales (this is after adjusting for increased distribution costs and reduced customer servicing costs).

Required:

(a) Assume that the 300,000 chips are supplied by the European subsidiary at a transfer price of $95 per chip. Calculate the impact of the profits on each of the subsidiaries and the group. **(5 marks)**

(b) Calculate the minimum unit price at which the European subsidiary would be willing to transfer the 300,000 chips to the American subsidiary if the performance and salary of the Manager of the subsidiary is to be based on

  (i) the profit of the subsidiary (currently $7 million);
  (ii) the return on assets consumed by the subsidiary (currently 35%).

(9 marks)

(c) Write a report to the Managing Director of the group that discusses issues raised by the directive and the introduction of performance measures. (You should use your answers to parts (a) and (b), where appropriate, to illustrate points in your report). **(10 marks)**

(d) Briefly explain how multinational companies can use transfer pricing to reduce their overall tax charge and the steps that national tax authorities have taken to discourage the manipulation of transfer prices. **(6 marks)**

(Total for Question Four = 30 marks)
(Total for Section C = 30 marks)

Area Under the Normal Curve

This table gives the area under the normal curve between the mean and a point Z standard deviations above the mean. The corresponding area for deviations below the mean can be found by symmetry.

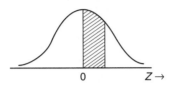

$Z = \dfrac{(x - \mu)}{\sigma}$	0.00	0.01	0.02	0.03	0.04	0.05	0.06	0.07	0.08	0.09
0.0	.0000	.0040	.0080	.0120	.0159	.0199	.0239	.0279	.0319	.0359
0.1	.0398	.0438	.0478	.0517	.0557	.0596	.0636	.0675	.0714	.0753
0.2	.0793	.0832	.0871	.0910	.0948	.0987	.1026	.1064	.1103	.1141
0.3	.1179	.1217	.1255	.1293	.1331	.1368	.1406	.1443	.1480	.1517
0.4	.1554	.1591	.1628	.1664	.1700	.1736	.1772	.1808	.1844	.1879
0.5	.1915	.1950	.1985	.2019	.2054	.2088	.2123	.2157	.2190	.2224
0.6	.2257	.2291	.2324	.2357	.2389	.2422	.2454	.2486	.2518	.2549
0.7	.2580	.2611	.2642	.2673	.2704	.2734	.2764	.2794	.2823	.2852
0.8	.2881	.2910	.2939	.2967	.2995	.3023	.3051	.3078	.3106	.3133
0.9	.3159	.3186	.3212	.3238	.3264	.3289	.3315	.3340	.3365	.3389
1.0	.3413	.3438	.3461	.3485	.3508	.3531	.3554	.3577	.3599	.3621
1.1	.3643	.3665	.3686	.3708	.3729	.3749	.3770	.3790	.3810	.3830
1.2	.3849	.3869	.3888	.3907	.3925	.3944	.3962	.3980	.3997	.4015
1.3	.4032	.4049	.4066	.4082	.4099	.4115	.4131	.4147	.4162	.4177
1.4	.4192	.4207	.4222	.4236	.4251	.4265	.4279	.4292	.4306	.4319
1.5	.4332	.4345	.4357	.4370	.4382	.4394	.4406	.4418	.4430	.4441
1.6	.4452	.4463	.4474	.4485	.4495	.4505	.4515	.4525	.4535	.4545
1.7	.4554	.4564	.4573	.4582	.4591	.4599	.4608	.4616	.4625	.4633
1.8	.4641	.4649	.4656	.4664	.4671	.4678	.4686	.4693	.4699	.4706
1.9	.4713	.4719	.4726	.4732	.4738	.4744	.4750	.4756	.4762	.4767
2.0	.4772	.4778	.4783	.4788	.4793	.4798	.4803	.4808	.4812	.4817
2.1	.4821	.4826	.4830	.4834	.4838	.4842	.4846	.4850	.4854	.4857
2.2	.4861	.4865	.4868	.4871	.4875	.4878	.4881	.4884	.4887	.4890
2.3	.4893	.4896	.4898	.4901	.4904	.4906	.4909	.4911	.4913	.4916
2.4	.4918	.4920	.4922	.4925	.4927	.4929	.4931	.4932	.4934	.4936
2.5	.4938	.4940	.4941	.4943	.4945	.4946	.4948	.4949	.4951	.4952
2.6	.4953	.4955	.4956	.4957	.4959	.4960	.4961	.4962	.4963	.4964
2.7	.4965	.4966	.4967	.4968	.4969	.4970	.4971	.4972	.4973	.4974
2.8	.4974	.4975	.4976	.4977	.4977	.4978	.4979	.4980	.4980	.4981
2.9	.4981	.4982	.4983	.4983	.4984	.4984	.4985	.4985	.4986	.4986
3.0	**.49865**	.4987	.4987	.4988	.4988	.4989	.4989	.4989	.4990	.4990
3.1	**.49903**	.4991	.4991	.4991	.4992	.4992	.4992	.4992	.4993	.4993
3.2	**.49931**	.4993	.4994	.4994	.4994	.4994	.4994	.4995	.4995	.4995
3.3	**.49952**	.4995	.4995	.4996	.4996	.4996	.4996	.4996	.4996	.4997
3.4	**.49966**	.4997	.4997	.4997	.4997	.4997	.4997	.4997	.4997	.4998
3.5	**.49977**									

Present Value Table

Present value of $1, that is $(1 + r)^{-n}$ where $r =$ interest rate; $n =$ number of periods until payment or receipt.

Periods (n)	Interest rates (r)									
	1%	2%	3%	4%	5%	6%	7%	8%	9%	10%
1	0.990	0.980	0.971	0.962	0.952	0.943	0.935	0.926	0.917	0.909
2	0.980	0.961	0.943	0.925	0.907	0.890	0.873	0.857	0.842	0.826
3	0.971	0.942	0.915	0.889	0.864	0.840	0.816	0.794	0.772	0.751
4	0.961	0.924	0.888	0.855	0.823	0.792	0.763	0.735	0.708	0.683
5	0.951	0.906	0.863	0.822	0.784	0.747	0.713	0.681	0.650	0.621
6	0.942	0.888	0.837	0.790	0.746	0.705	0.666	0.630	0.596	0.564
7	0.933	0.871	0.813	0.760	0.711	0.665	0.623	0.583	0.547	0.513
8	0.923	0.853	0.789	0.731	0.677	0.627	0.582	0.540	0.502	0.467
9	0.914	0.837	0.766	0.703	0.645	0.592	0.544	0.500	0.460	0.424
10	0.905	0.820	0.744	0.676	0.614	0.558	0.508	0.463	0.422	0.386
11	0.896	0.804	0.722	0.650	0.585	0.527	0.475	0.429	0.388	0.350
12	0.887	0.788	0.701	0.625	0.557	0.497	0.444	0.397	0.356	0.319
13	0.879	0.773	0.681	0.601	0.530	0.469	0.415	0.368	0.326	0.290
14	0.870	0.758	0.661	0.577	0.505	0.442	0.388	0.340	0.299	0.263
15	0.861	0.743	0.642	0.555	0.481	0.417	0.362	0.315	0.275	0.239
16	0.853	0.728	0.623	0.534	0.458	0.394	0.339	0.292	0.252	0.218
17	0.844	0.714	0.605	0.513	0.436	0.371	0.317	0.270	0.231	0.198
18	0.836	0.700	0.587	0.494	0.416	0.350	0.296	0.250	0.212	0.180
19	0.828	0.686	0.570	0.475	0.396	0.331	0.277	0.232	0.194	0.164
20	0.820	0.673	0.554	0.456	0.377	0.312	0.258	0.215	0.178	0.149

Periods (n)	Interest rates (r)									
	11%	12%	13%	14%	15%	16%	17%	18%	19%	20%
1	0.901	0.893	0.885	0.877	0.870	0.862	0.855	0.847	0.840	0.833
2	0.812	0.797	0.783	0.769	0.756	0.743	0.731	0.718	0.706	0.694
3	0.731	0.712	0.693	0.675	0.658	0.641	0.624	0.609	0.593	0.579
4	0.659	0.636	0.613	0.592	0.572	0.552	0.534	0.516	0.499	0.482
5	0.593	0.567	0.543	0.519	0.497	0.476	0.456	0.437	0.419	0.402
6	0.535	0.507	0.480	0.456	0.432	0.410	0.390	0.370	0.352	0.335
7	0.482	0.452	0.425	0.400	0.376	0.354	0.333	0.314	0.296	0.279
8	0.434	0.404	0.376	0.351	0.327	0.305	0.285	0.266	0.249	0.233
9	0.391	0.361	0.333	0.308	0.284	0.263	0.243	0.225	0.209	0.194
10	0.352	0.322	0.295	0.270	0.247	0.227	0.208	0.191	0.176	0.162
11	0.317	0.287	0.261	0.237	0.215	0.195	0.178	0.162	0.148	0.135
12	0.286	0.257	0.231	0.208	0.187	0.168	0.152	0.137	0.124	0.112
13	0.258	0.229	0.204	0.182	0.163	0.145	0.130	0.116	0.104	0.093
14	0.232	0.205	0.181	0.160	0.141	0.125	0.111	0.099	0.088	0.078
15	0.209	0.183	0.160	0.140	0.123	0.108	0.095	0.084	0.079	0.065
16	0.188	0.163	0.141	0.123	0.107	0.093	0.081	0.071	0.062	0.054
17	0.170	0.146	0.125	0.108	0.093	0.080	0.069	0.060	0.052	0.045
18	0.153	0.130	0.111	0.095	0.081	0.069	0.059	0.051	0.044	0.038
19	0.138	0.116	0.098	0.083	0.070	0.060	0.051	0.043	0.037	0.031
20	0.124	0.104	0.087	0.073	0.061	0.051	0.043	0.037	0.031	0.026

Cumulative present value of $1 per annum, Receivable or Payable at the end of each year for n years $\dfrac{1-(1+r)^{-n}}{r}$

Periods (n)	Interest rates (r)									
	1%	**2%**	**3%**	**4%**	**5%**	**6%**	**7%**	**8%**	**9%**	**10%**
1	0.990	0.980	0.971	0.962	0.952	0.943	0.935	0.926	0.917	0.909
2	1.970	1.942	1.913	1.886	1.859	1.833	1.808	1.783	1.759	1.736
3	2.941	2.884	2.829	2.775	2.723	2.673	2.624	2.577	2.531	2.487
4	3.902	3.808	3.717	3.630	3.546	3.465	3.387	3.312	3.240	3.170
5	4.853	4.713	4.580	4.452	4.329	4.212	4.100	3.993	3.890	3.791
6	5.795	5.601	5.417	5.242	5.076	4.917	4.767	4.623	4.486	4.355
7	6.728	6.472	6.230	6.002	5.786	5.582	5.389	5.206	5.033	4.868
8	7.652	7.325	7.020	6.733	6.463	6.210	5.971	5.747	5.535	5.335
9	8.566	8.162	7.786	7.435	7.108	6.802	6.515	6.247	5.995	5.759
10	9.471	8.983	8.530	8.111	7.722	7.360	7.024	6.710	6.418	6.145
11	10.368	9.787	9.253	8.760	8.306	7.887	7.499	7.139	6.805	6.495
12	11.255	10.575	9.954	9.385	8.863	8.384	7.943	7.536	7.161	6.814
13	12.134	11.348	10.635	9.986	9.394	8.853	8.358	7.904	7.487	7.103
14	13.004	12.106	11.296	10.563	9.899	9.295	8.745	8.244	7.786	7.367
15	13.865	12.849	11.938	11.118	10.380	9.712	9.108	8.559	8.061	7.606
16	14.718	13.578	12.561	11.652	10.838	10.106	9.447	8.851	8.313	7.824
17	15.562	14.292	13.166	12.166	11.274	10.477	9.763	9.122	8.544	8.022
18	16.398	14.992	13.754	12.659	11.690	10.828	10.059	9.372	8.756	8.201
19	17.226	15.679	14.324	13.134	12.085	11.158	10.336	9.604	8.950	8.365
20	18.046	16.351	14.878	13.590	12.462	11.470	10.594	9.818	9.129	8.514

Periods (n)	Interest rates (r)									
	11%	**12%**	**13%**	**14%**	**15%**	**16%**	**17%**	**18%**	**19%**	**20%**
1	0.901	0.893	0.885	0.877	0.870	0.862	0.855	0.847	0.840	0.833
2	1.713	1.690	1.668	1.647	1.626	1.605	1.585	1.566	1.547	1.528
3	2.444	2.402	2.361	2.322	2.283	2.246	2.210	2.174	2.140	2.106
4	3.102	3.037	2.974	2.914	2.855	2.798	2.743	2.690	2.639	2.589
5	3.696	3.605	3.517	3.433	3.352	3.274	3.199	3.127	3.058	2.991
6	4.231	4.111	3.998	3.889	3.784	3.685	3.589	3.498	3.410	3.326
7	4.712	4.564	4.423	4.288	4.160	4.039	3.922	3.812	3.706	3.605
8	5.146	4.968	4.799	4.639	4.487	4.344	4.207	4.078	3.954	3.837
9	5.537	5.328	5.132	4.946	4.772	4.607	4.451	4.303	4.163	4.031
10	5.889	5.650	5.426	5.216	5.019	4.833	4.659	4.494	4.339	4.192
11	6.207	5.938	5.687	5.453	5.234	5.029	4.836	4.656	4.486	4.327
12	6.492	6.194	5.918	5.660	5.421	5.197	4.988	7.793	4.611	4.439
13	6.750	6.424	6.122	5.842	5.583	5.342	5.118	4.910	4.715	4.533
14	6.982	6.628	6.302	6.002	5.724	5.468	5.229	5.008	4.802	4.611
15	7.191	6.811	6.462	6.142	5.847	5.575	5.324	5.092	4.876	4.675
16	7.379	6.974	6.604	6.265	5.954	5.668	5.405	5.162	4.938	4.730
17	7.549	7.120	6.729	6.373	6.047	5.749	5.475	5.222	4.990	4.775
18	7.702	7.250	6.840	6.467	6.128	5.818	5.534	5.273	5.033	4.812
19	7.839	7.366	6.938	6.550	6.198	5.877	5.584	5.316	5.070	4.843
20	7.963	7.469	7.025	6.623	6.259	5.929	5.628	5.353	5.101	4.870

Formulae

PROBABILITY

$A \cup B = \textbf{\textit{A} or \textit{B}}$. $A \cap B = \textbf{\textit{A} and \textit{B}}$ (overlap).
$P(B \mid A)$ = probability of B, **given** A.

Rules of Addition
If A and B are mutually exclusive: $P(A \cup B) = P(A) + P(B)$
If A and B are **not** mutually exclusive: $P(A \cup B) = P(A) + P(B) - P(A \cap B)$

Rules of Multiplication
If A and B are *independent*: $P(A \cap B) = P(A) \times P(B)$
If A and B are **not** *independent*: $P(A \cap B) = P(A) \times P(B \mid A)$
$E(X) = \Sigma(\text{probability} \times \text{payoff})$

Quadratic Equations
If $aX^2 + bX + c = 0$ is the general quadratic equation, the two solutions (roots) are given by:

$$X = \frac{-b \pm \sqrt{b^2 - 4ac}}{2a}$$

DESCRIPTIVE STATISTICS

Arithmetic Mean

$$\bar{x} = \frac{\Sigma x}{n} \quad \bar{x} = \frac{\Sigma fx}{\Sigma f} \text{ (frequency distribution)}$$

Standard Deviation

$$SD = \sqrt{\frac{\Sigma(x - \bar{x})^2}{n}} \quad SD = \sqrt{\frac{\Sigma fx^2}{\Sigma f} - \bar{x}^2} \text{ (frequency distribution)}$$

INDEX NUMBERS

Price relative $= 100 \times P_1/P_0$ Quantity relative $= 100 \times Q_1/Q_0$

Price:
$$\frac{\Sigma w \times \left(\dfrac{P_1}{P_0} \right)}{\Sigma w} \times 100$$

Quantity:
$$\frac{\Sigma w \times \left(\dfrac{Q_1}{Q_0} \right)}{\Sigma w} \times 100$$

TIME SERIES

Additive Model

Series = Trend + Seasonal + Random

Multiplicative Model

Series = Trend $\times$ Seasonal $\times$ Random

LINEAR REGRESSION AND CORRELATION

The linear regression equation of Y on X is given by:

$$Y = a + bX \ \text{ or } \ Y - \bar{Y} = b(X - \bar{X})$$

where

$$b = \frac{\text{Covariance } (XY)}{\text{Variance } (X)} = \frac{n\,\Sigma XY - (\Sigma X)(\Sigma Y)}{n\,\Sigma X^2 - (\Sigma X)^2}$$

and $a = \bar{Y} - b\bar{X}$

or solve

$$\Sigma Y = na + b\Sigma X$$
$$\Sigma XY = a\Sigma X + b\Sigma X^2$$

Coefficient of correlation

$$r = \frac{\text{Covariance } (XY)}{\sqrt{\text{Var}(X).\text{Var}(Y)}} = \frac{n\,\Sigma XY - (\Sigma X)(\Sigma Y)}{\sqrt{\left\{n\,\Sigma X^2 - (\Sigma X)^2\right\}\left\{n\Sigma Y^2 - (\Sigma Y)^2\right\}}}$$

$$R(\text{rank}) = 1 - \frac{6\,\Sigma d^2}{n(n^2 - 1)}$$

FINANCIAL MATHEMATICS

Compound Interest (Values and Sums)

Future Value S, of a sum of X, invested for n periods, compounded at $r\%$ interest

$$S = X[1 + r]^n$$

Annuity

Present value of an annuity of £1 per annum receivable or payable for n years, commencing in 1 year, discounted at $r\%$ per annum:

$$PV = \frac{1}{r}\left[1 - \frac{1}{[1 + r]^n}\right]$$

Perpetuity

Present value of £1 per annum, payable or receivable in perpetuity, commencing in 1 year, discounted at $r\%$ per annum:

$$PV = \frac{1}{r}$$

LIST OF VERBS USED IN THE QUESTION REQUIREMENTS

A list of the learning objectives and verbs that appear in the syllabus and in the question requirements for each question in this paper.

It is important that you answer the question according to the definition of the verb.

LEARNING OBJECTIVE	VERBS USED	DEFINITION
1 KNOWLEDGE		
What you are expected to know.	List	Make a list of
	State	Express, fully or clearly, the details of/facts of
	Define	Give the exact meaning of
2 COMPREHENSION		
What you are expected to understand.	Describe	Communicate the key features
	Distinguish	Highlight the differences between
	Explain	Make clear or intelligible/state the meaning of
	Identify	Recognise, establish or select after consideration
	Illustrate	Use an example to describe or explain something
3 APPLICATION		
How you are expected to apply your knowledge.	Apply	To put to practical use
	Calculate/compute	To ascertain or reckon mathematically
	Demonstrate	To prove with certainty or to exhibit by practical means
	Prepare	To make or get ready for use
	Reconcile	To make or prove consistent/compatible
	Solve	Find an answer to
	Tabulate	Arrange in a table
4 ANALYSIS		
How you are expected to analyse the detail of what you have learned.	Analyse	Examine in detail the structure of
	Categorise	Place into a defined class or division
	Compare and contrast	Show the similarities and/or differences between
	Construct	To build up or compile
	Discuss	To examine in detail by argument
	Interpret	To translate into intelligible or familiar terms
	Produce	To create or bring into existence
5 EVALUATION		
How you are expected to use your learning to evaluate, make decisions or recommendations.	Advise	To counsel, inform or notify
	Evaluate	To appraise or assess the value of
	Recommend	To advise on a course of action

The Examiner for Management Accounting – Performance Evaluation offers to future candidates and to tutors using this booklet for study purposes, the following background and guidance on the questions included in this examination paper.

Section A – Question One – Compulsory

Question One consists of 16 objective test sub-questions. These are drawn from all sections of the syllabus. They are designed to examine breadth across the syllabus and thus cover many learning outcomes.

Section B – Question Two – Compulsory

Question Two has six sub-questions.

(a) Covers learning outcome C(iii) – *Calculate projected revenues and costs based on product/ service volumes, pricing strategies and cost structures.*

(b) Covers learning outcome A(i) – *Compare and contrast marginal and absorption costing methods in respect of profit reporting and stock valuation.*

(c) Covers learning outcome C(x) – *Explain the ideas of feedback and feed-forward control and their application in the use of budgets for control.*

(d) Covers learning outcome C(xiv) – *Evaluate the criticisms of budgeting particularly from the advocates of techniques that are 'beyond budgeting'.*

(e) Covers learning outcome A(viii) – *Evaluate the impact of just-in-time manufacturing methods on cost accounting and the use of 'back-flush accounting' when work in progress stock is minimal.*

(f) Covers learning outcome C(ii) – *Calculate projected product/service volumes employing appropriate forecasting techniques.*

Section C – answer one of two questions

Question Three has four parts.

(a) Covers learning outcome A(v) – *Apply standard costing methods within costing systems and demonstrate the reconciliation of budgeted and actual profit margins.*

(b) Covers learning outcome B(ii) – *Calculate and interpret material, labour, variable overhead, fixed overhead and sales variances.*

(c) Covers learning outcome B(iii) – *Prepare and discuss a report which reconciles budget and actual profit using absorption and/or marginal costing principles.*

(d) Covers learning outcome C(ix) – *Identify controllable and uncontrollable costs in the context of responsibility accounting and explain why 'uncontrollable' costs may or may not be allocated to responsibility centres.*

Question Four has four parts.

(a) Covers learning outcome D(iii) – *Prepare revenue and cost information in appropriate formats for profit and investment centre managers, taking due account of cost variability, attributable costs, controllable costs and identification of appropriate measures of profit centre 'contribution'.*

(b) Covers learning outcome D(iv) – *Calculate and apply measures of performance for investment centres (often 'strategic business units' or divisions of larger groups).*

(c) Covers learning outcome D(v) – *Discuss the likely behavioural consequences of the use of performance metrics in managing cost, profit and investment centres.*

(d) Covers learning outcome D(vii) – *Identify the likely consequences of different approaches to transfer pricing for divisional decision-making, divisional and group profitability, the motivation of divisional management and the autonomy of individual divisions.*

Managerial Level Paper

P1 – Management Accounting – Performance Evaluation

Examiner's Answers

SECTION A

Answer to Question One

1.1

	£
Under-absorbed	−19,250
Actual	481,250
Charged to clients	462,000

Overhead rate £462,000/38,500 = £12 per hour
Budgeted overheads = 38,000 × £12 = £456,000

The correct answer is A

1.2 Actual time for 370 operations was 80 hours
Revised standard time per operation = 12 minutes = 0.2 hours
Revised expected time for actual operations = 370 × 0.2 = 74 hours
Operational labour efficiency variance = (80 − 74) × £10 = £60 adverse

The correct answer is A

1.3 $52,000 + $56,000 − $2,000 = $106,000

	Sales Value		Costs
X	$80,000	62.5%	$66,250
Y	$48,000	37.5%	$39,750
	$128,000		$106,000

$66,250/10,000 = $6.625

The correct answer is C

1.4   At breakeven total contribution equals fixed costs which equal £320,000. C/S ratio = £320,000 ÷ 800,000 = 0.4

Revenue needed to earn £50,000 profit = [(320,000 + 50,000) ÷ (320,000 ÷ 800,000)]

The correct answer is B

1.5   The correct answer is C

1.6   The correct answer is A

1.7   The correct answer is A

1.8   The correct answer is C

1.9   Marginal cost is the total of variable production costs. One tenth of the production is inventory at the end of the month and therefore the valuation is:

$(20,000 + 6,300 + 4,700)/10 = \$3,100$

The correct answer is B

1.10   Throughput accounting values inventory at direct materials cost only:

$\$20,000/10 = \$2,000$

The correct answer is D

1.11

	Month 4	£
Cash sales	(108,000 × 0.2)	21,600
From month 3	(120,000 × 0.8 × 0.4 × 0.985)	37,824
From month 2	(105,000 × 0.8 × 0.3)	25,200
From month 1	(90,000 × 0.8 × 0.28)	20,160
From previous budget period		6,000
		110,784

1.12   (i)   Variable cost per unit

[(£194,000 − £10,000 − £143,500) ÷ (40,000 − 25,000 units)] = **£2.70 per unit**

(ii)   Total fixed costs

[£194,000 − (40,000 units × £2.70 per unit)] = **£86,000**

1.13   Where: $\text{Return per factory hour} = \dfrac{\text{Sales price} - \text{Material cost}}{\text{Total time on key resource}}$

$= (12 - 5)/0.75 = \$9.33 \text{ per hour}$

And: $\text{Cost per factory hour} = \dfrac{\text{Total factory cost}}{\text{Total time on key resource}}$

$= 144,000/12,000 = \$12 \text{ per hour}$

$\text{Throughput accounting (TA) ratio} = \dfrac{\text{Return per factory hour}}{\text{Cost per factory hour}}$

$9.33/12 = 0.78$

As the throughput accounting ratio is less than 1, the product should not be produced.

1.14 Total production costs:

Direct materials	£36,000
Direct labour	£18,000
Variable production overheads	£3,000
Fixed production overheads	£24,000
	£81,000

Cost per unit of output £81,000/18,000 = £4.50

	Product A	Product B	Product C
Selling price	£8	£6	£4
Production cost	£4.50	£4.50	£4.50
Gross profit	£3.50	£1.50	(£0.50)
Gross profit %	43.75%	25%	(12.5%)

1.15 Return = £320,000 + £200,000 + £100,000 + £70,000 = £690,000

Investment = £3.64 million + £0.42 million − £0.37 million = £3.69 million
[(690,000 ÷ 3,690,000) × 100] = 18.7%

1.16

	Year 1($)	Year 2 ($)	Year 3 ($)	Year 4($)	Year 5 ($)
Cost savings	450,000	450,000	450,000	450,000	450,000
Depreciation	300,000	300,000	300,000	300,000	300,000
Profit	150,000	150,000	150,000	150,000	150,000
Cost of capital	150,000	120,000	90,000	60,000	30,000
RI	Nil	30,000	60,000	90,000	120,000
ROI	10%	12.5%	16.7%	25%	50%
Capital value	1.5	1.2	0.9	0.6	0.3

SECTION B

Answer to (a)

	Q1	Q2
Production Budget:		
For sales	10,000	12,000
Add closing inventory	5,400	5,600
	(12,000 × 45%)	(14,000 × 40%)
Less opening inventory	−5,500	−5,400
Production units	9,900	12,200
Material Purchases Budget	*kg*	
For production	14,850	
	(9,900 × 1.5)	
Add closing inventory	4,575	
	(18,300 × 25%)	
Less opening inventory	−4,500	
Purchases (kg)	14,925	
Purchases £ (at £6 per kg)	£89,550	

Answer to (b)

Workings:	Q3
	£ per unit
Marginal cost £9 + £8	17
Production overheads	15
Absorption cost	32

(i)
Calculation of profit by marginal costing for quarter 3

	£
Sales (14,000 × £40)	560,000
Variable costs (14,000 × £17)	238,000
Contribution	322,000
Fixed costs (Production and others)	230,000
Profit	92,000

(ii)
Calculation of profit by absorption costing for quarter 3

	£
Sales	560,000
Absorption cost of sales (14,000 × £32)	(448,000)
Over-absorbed overhead £180,000 − (12,600 × £15)	9,000
Other fixed costs	(50,000)
Profit	71,000

Workings:

The inventory of finished goods has fallen during the month and therefore the number of units produced will be less than the number sold. Production = sales − inventory change = 14,000 − 1,400 = 12,600 units.

(iii)

The difference is caused by the fixed production overheads included in the unit valuations under absorption costing.

During Quarter 3 the inventory fell and therefore the profit calculated by absorption costing will be lower than that calculated by marginal costing by £21,000 (calculated as 1,400 units × £15).

Reconciliation: £92,000 − £21,000 = £71,000.

Answer to (c)

Feedback control relates to information about past events. Actual results should be compared to planned or budgeted results as part of the control mechanism. Variance analysis is a good example of feedback control. The feedback should be used to revise future actions as appropriate and to learn from budgeting or operational errors.

Feed-forward control is a system where deviations from a plan are anticipated and corrective action is taken in advance. An example is a cash flow projection which for example can highlight in advance any shortages of cash and therefore action can be taken before the event to avoid any problems this may bring.

Answer to (d)

Budgets are often thought of as being bureaucratic and time consuming to produce. Consequently they are not updated on a regular basis and therefore in a dynamic environment budgets can quickly become out of date.

Budgets are often seen as constraints on responsiveness and as such stifle the ability of managers to react rapidly to change.

Budgets replicate vertical command and control structures and reinforce departmental barriers. Such rigid structures may not suit the organisation culture of companies operating in a rapidly changing environment.

Budgets have been criticised for being too inward looking and as such they pay little attention to the external environment. This is even more inappropriate if the environment is changing rapidly.

Answer to (e)

JIT is a commitment to continuous improvement and the pursuit of excellence in the design and operation of the production management system. Under this system, production and resource acquisition is pulled through the system by customer demand and therefore the JIT production system must be able to respond quickly to customer demand and resources are only acquired when needed. In order to be able to operate in this manner, an organisation must achieve excellence in all areas of management.

Operating on a JIT basis with low inventories requires excellence in:

- Production scheduling
- Supplier relations
- Plant maintenance
- Information systems
- Quality controls
- Customer relations.

Candidates were required to explain two requirements. For example as shown below.

Production scheduling
Under JIT it is thought that only the actual production time adds value to the product and that all other activities (inspection, move and storage times) do not add value but they do add cost. JIT aims to reduce and eliminate non-value adding activities.

Supplier relations
Under a JIT system a company would move towards having fewer suppliers and would build long-term relationships with them. The ability to work with the minimum level of inventory will be dependent on having a guaranteed supply of quality resources. Consequently the selection of suppliers will tend not to be based on price alone.

Answer to (f)

		£
House-keeping	£125,000 × 90% × 106%	119,250
Nursing: variable	£80,000 × 125% × 90% × 108% × 105%	102,060
Nursing: fixed	£200,000 × 108% × 105%	226,800
Administration	£100,000 × 104%	104,000

Workings:
Period 2's nursing costs included an uplift of 108% for cost changes. Stripping out the cost change for Period 2 gives an equivalent cost of £300,000 to be used in comparison with Period 1. The total cost rise of £20,000 from Period 1 was caused by the volume change on the variable costs. The volume change was 25% and therefore the variable costs in Period 1 were £80,000.

SECTION C

Answer to Question Three

Requirement (a)

Budget

	Kitchens	Bathrooms	Group
Profit	**$8 m**	**$3 m**	**$11 m**
	4,000 × 2,000	2,000 × 1,500	

Actual

	Kitchens	Bathrooms	Group
Profit	**$6.5 m**	**$2.25 m**	$8.75 m
	2,600 × 2,500	2,500 × 900	
	Under-absorbed		$4.75 m
			$4.00 m

Absorbed	12.75 m (2.6 × 2.5 + 2.5 × 2.5)
Actual	17.5 m
Under-absorbed	4.75 m

Requirement (b)

Sales Price Variances

Kitchens: 2,600 × (13,000 − 10,000) = $7.8 m favourable

Bathrooms: 2,500 × (6,100 − 7,000) = $2.25 m adverse

Total sales price variance = $5.55 m favourable

Sales Mix Profit Variances

Kitchens: (2,600 − 3,400) × $2,000 = $1.6 m adverse

Bathrooms: (2,500 − 1,700) × $1,500 = $1.2 m favourable

Total sales mix profit variance = $0.4 m adverse

Note: alternative calculations of $0.1333 m adverse and $0.2666 m adverse would also be accepted.

Sales Quantity Profit variances

Kitchens: (3,400 − 4,000) × 2,000 = $1.2 m adverse

Bathrooms: (1,700 − 2,000) × 1,500 = $0.45 m adverse

Total sales quantity profit variance = $1.65 m adverse

Note: alternative calculations of $1.1 m adverse and $0.55 adverse would also be accepted.

Requirement (c)

	Kitchens $m		Bathrooms $m		Group $m	
Budgeted Profit	**8.00**		**3.00**		**11.00**	
Sales mix	1.60	adv	1.20	fav	0.40	adv
Sales quantity	1.20	adv	0.45	adv	1.65	adv
Expected profit on actual sales	5.20		3.75		8.95	
Sales price variances	7.80	fav	2.25	adv	5.55	fav
					14.50	
Direct costs	6.50	adv	0.75	fav	5.75	adv
Central services expenditure					2.50	adv
Central services volume					2.25	adv
Actual profit	6.50		2.25		**4.00**	

Requirement (d)

To:	Managing Director of WC
From:	Management Accountant
Date:	November 2007
Terms of Reference:	Review of performance and changes to the system

Introduction

It is clear to see that the group did not achieve the budgeted profit but the budgeting and reporting system does not currently provide enough information for a full review of performance to take place. A major problem contributing to the lack of clarity within the system is the treatment of the costs incurred by the Central Services division.

Performance review and suggestions

Profit

The profit for the group is a lot lower than budgeted even though the system would show that the profits of each of the divisions are not as severely affected. This is caused by the treatment of the recharge for the Central Services division. The Central Services costs are under-absorbed as a result of the volume of jobs and the increased expenditure.

Sales

Sales volume, in terms of individual jobs was lower than budget for the Kitchens division but higher than budget for the Bathrooms division. This is reflected in the sales mix and quantity profit variances. The sales price variances show that the average price per kitchen was higher than budgeted and the average price per bathroom was lower than budgeted. Perhaps the Kitchens division undertook more customised jobs, and the reverse for the Bathrooms division.

The current level of information that the system provides does not reveal the type of jobs undertaken. Although the system tries to be 'sophisticated' by calculating mix and quantity variances for the sales of kitchens and bathrooms it is questionable how meaningful this information is. A better analysis of sales would be to look within each division. For example better management information could be provided by analysing the sales into 'customised' and 'off the shelf' jobs.

Direct costs

The average costs per job also point to the sales mix within each division. Again more detail is needed. As a minimum the system should record details to enable the calculation of price, rate, usage and efficiency variances for the differing types of job.

The reported variances appear to be as a result of the balance of the installations performed by the divisions. For example, the higher direct costs in the Kitchens division is likely to be interrelated with the higher average selling price

Central services recharge

The current treatment of the charges for the Central Services division can lead to many problems within the group. The Central Services include design, administration and finance and therefore it would seem inappropriate to use one blanket rate to cover the use of these three services.

The charge per job does not reflect the demands placed on the Central Services by the division. For example the costs of the designers will be driven by the number of designs that they do. Consequently if there are a lot of customised jobs the workload, and therefore costs, of the designing team will increase. The Kitchens and Bathrooms divisions do not face any financial penalty for the demands they place on Central Services. One way to improve the situation could be to set up a Design Division and to make it a profit centre: the divisions would be charged individually for each job based on the specific work undertaken.

Answer to Question Four
Requirement (a)

Europe		
Increased contribution 200,000 × $45		$9 m
Increased fixed costs		$6 m
Net increase in profit		$3 m

America: Extra cost of chips of 300,000 × $5 = $1.5 m reduction in profit
Group Profit = $3 m − $1.5 m = $1.5 m increase in profit

Requirement (b) (i)
The sales would need to cover the lost contribution from the external sales of $4.5 m (100,000 × $45) and the increased fixed costs of $6 m.
Total contribution needed = $10.5 m. This is from 300,000 chips and therefore the contribution per chip is $35.
The variable cost of selling to America is $95 − $45 = $50 per chip
Minimum price = $85 per chip

Requirement (b) (ii)
Need to cover the lost contribution of $4.5 m and generate a return of $8.1 m (calculated as 135% on the increased fixed costs of $6 m). This totals $12.6 m.
Contribution per chip = $12.6 m/300,000 = $42
Minimum price = $92 per chip

Requirement (c)

To:	Group Managing Director
From:	Management Accountant
Date:	November 2007
Terms of Reference:	Issues surrounding internal transfers and performance measures

Introduction

By issuing the directive that the American subsidiary must source its components from the European subsidiary you will be immediately taking away some of the autonomy of the managers. This could have a major impact on the behaviour and attitude of the managers. This will be compounded by issues surrounding the price of the transfers and this in turn is further complicated by the impact of a performance measurement system.

Transfer Pricing

It is evident from the calculations that it is in the group's best interest for the chips to be supplied from Europe; the group's profit would increase by $1.5 m. There is also the possibility that a lower price for the chips could allow the American subsidiary to lower the price of the assembled computer and increase its sales volume and thereby earn even more profits.

However the price quoted of $95 per chip by the European manager is clearly not acceptable to the American subsidiary as they can be bought locally for $90. This should be the maximum level of the transfer price.

The minimum transfer price should be the sum of the selling division's marginal cost and the opportunity cost. If output was restricted to 600,000 units this would be $105 but output can be raised above the current maximum demand and consequently the chip plant has some spare capacity. This will allow a price of $85 per chip.

Transfer pricing is a tricky area. If you impose a transfer price on the managers then it will take away some of their autonomy and consequently it will be better if the managers are allowed, if possible, to come to a mutually agreeable price. The price that is used should encourage goal congruence, motivate the managers and facilitate performance measurement.

Performance Measures

Performance measures should encourage goal congruence. If an unsuitable measure is chosen it is possible that managers will be encouraged to act in a way that does not lead to the optimal performance for the group. You have suggested two measures but careful thought should be given before you implement them.

Using 'profit' as a measure will allow the manager of the European plant to set a transfer price that will enhance the group's profits. However the manager may be reluctant to do so: at a price of $85 he will have to manage and control additional fixed costs of $6 m and the production of an extra 200,000 chips which will take the plant up to its maximum capacity.

Using your idea of 'return on assets consumed' will not promote goal congruence. The price needed by the European manager of $92 per chip does not satisfy the requirements. It is also higher than the price that can be paid in the open market.

Problems can arise when managers react to a single measure of performance, especially if it is a financial measure. An effective performance measurement system should emphasise both financial and non-financial measures and encourage behaviour that is in line with the group's objectives. One way to overcome these problems is to use a series of financial and non-financial measures in a balanced scorecard.

Requirement (d)

If the taxation rates are different in the countries in which the subsidiaries are based it is possible to set the transfer price to reduce the overall tax paid by the group. The objective will be to maximise the profit in the country that has the lowest tax rate. For example, in this case, if the tax rate is lower in America than in Europe, a low transfer price would be charged in order to produce a higher profit in America and a lower profit in Europe.

Transfer prices are monitored by taxation authorities and they will penalise companies they think are manipulating transfer prices. Guidelines were drawn up in 1995 by the Organisation for Economic Co-operation and Development (OECD) to standardise national approaches to transfer pricing. The guidelines were based on using an 'arm's length price.' In the USA companies are required to provide evidence to justify the transfer price being charged.

Index

Index

ELSEVIER

PUBLISHING

May 08 Q&A

To access the May 08 Q&A for the book you have bought
please follow these instructions:

Go to
http://cimapublishing.com/QandA

- Follow the step-by-step instructions on the site

- Fill in the registration form

- Download the PDF for immediate access to Q&As

Get **10% Discount**
off your next order

Quote ATP8 when ordering or
add it to the offer code box online.

Order Form

For CIMA Official Study Materials for 2008 Exams

QTY	PAPER	TITLE	ISBN-13	PRICE	TOTAL
CIMA Official *Learning Systems*					
	P1	Performance Evaluation	978-0-7506-8688-4	£35.00	
	P2	Decision Management	978-0-7506-8958-8	£35.00	
	P3	Risk and Control Strategy	978-0-7506-8713-3	£35.00	
	P4	Organisational Management & Information Systems	978-0-7506-8689-1	£35.00	
	P5	Integrated Management	978-0-7506-8769-0	£35.00	
	P6	Business Strategy	978-0-7506-8906-9	£35.00	
	P7	Financial Accounting and Tax Principles	978-0-7506-8700-3	£35.00	
	P8	Financial Analysis	978-0-7506-8691-4	£35.00	
	P9	Financial Strategy	978-0-7506-8715-7	£35.00	
	P10	TOPCIMA	978-0-7506-8770-6	£35.00	
CIMA Official *Exam Practice Kits*					
	P1	Performance Evaluation	978-0-7506-8669-3	£14.99	
	P2	Decision Management	978-0-7506-8676-1	£14.99	
	P3	Risk and Control Strategy	978-0-7506-8677-8	£14.99	
	P4	Organisational Management & Information Systems	978-0-7506-8681-5	£14.99	
	P5	Integrated Management	978-0-7506-8675-4	£14.99	
	P6	Business Strategy	978-0-7506-8678-5	£14.99	
	P7	Financial Accounting and Tax Principles	978-0-7506-8690-7	£14.99	
	P8	Financial Analysis	978-0-7506-8674-7	£14.99	
	P9	Financial Strategy	978-0-7506-8679-2	£14.99	
	P10	TOPCIMA	978-0-7506-8680-8	£14.99	
CIMA Official *Revision Cards*					
	P1	Performance Evaluation	978-0-7506-8123-0	£8.99	
	P2	Decision Management	978-0-7506-8124-7	£8.99	
	P3	Risk and Control Strategy	978-0-7506-8120-9	£8.99	
	P4	Organisational Management & Information Systems	978-0-7506-8121-6	£8.99	
	P5	Integrated Management	978-0-7506-8122-3	£8.99	
	P6	Business Strategy	978-0-7506-8119-3	£8.99	
	P7	Financial Accounting and Tax Principles	978-0-7506-8126-1	£8.99	
	P8	Financial Analysis	978-0-7506-8125-4	£8.99	
	P9	Financial Strategy	978-0-7506-8118-6	£8.99	
Books					
		Principles of Business Taxation	978-0-7506-8457-6	£49.99	
		CIMA: Pass First Time!	978-0-7506-8396-8	£12.99	
		Better Exam Results	978-0-7506-6357-1	£12.99	
			Postage and packing		£2.95
			TOTAL		

Elsevier Ltd, Science & Technology Books, retains certain personal information about you in hard copy and on computer.
It will be used to inform you about goods and services available from Elsevier Ltd and its offices worldwide in which you
may be interested.

Please tick the box if you do NOT wish to receive this information. ☐

Post this form to:

CIMA Publishing Customer Services
Elsevier
FREEPOST (OF 1639)
Linacre House, Jordan Hill
OXFORD, OX2 8DP, UK

Or **FAX**   +44 (0)1865 314 572
Or **PHONE**   +44 (0)1865 474 014
Email: cimaorders@elsevier.com
          www.cimapublishing.com

Name: _____

Organisation: _____

Invoice Address: _____

_____

_____

_____

Postcode: _____

Phone number: _____

Email: _____

Delivery Address if different:

FAO _____

Address _____

_____

_____

_____

Postcode _____

Please note that all deliveries must be signed for

1. Cheques payable to Elsevier.

2. Please charge my:

☐ Visa/Barclaycard   ☐ Access/Mastercard

☐ American Express   ☐ Diners Card

☐ Switch   Issue No._____

Card No. _____

Expiry Date _____

Cardholder Name: _____

Signature: _____

Date: _____

Get **10% Discount**

off your next order

Quote ATP8 when ordering or
add it to the offer code box online.

Order Form

For CIMA Official Study Materials for 2008 Exams

QTY	PAPER	TITLE	ISBN-13	PRICE	TOTAL
		CIMA Official *Learning Systems*			
	C1	Fundamentals of Management Accounting	978-0-7506-8955-7	£35.00	
	C2	Fundamentals of Financial Accounting	978-0-7506-8696-9	£35.00	
	C3	Fundamentals of Business Maths	978-0-7506-8957-1	£35.00	
	C4	Fundamentals of Business Economics	978-0-7506-8698-3	£35.00	
	C5	Fundamentals of Ethics, Corporate Governance and Business Law	978-0-7506-8956-4	£35.00	
		CIMA Official *Exam Practice Kits*			
	C1	Fundamentals of Management Accounting	978-0-7506-8717-1	£14.99	
	C2	Fundamentals of Financial Accounting	978-0-7506-8716-4	£14.99	
	C3	Fundamentals of Business Maths	978-0-7506-8718-8	£14.99	
	C4	Fundamentals of Business Economics	978-0-7506-8749-2	£14.99	
	C5	Fundamentals of Ethics, Corporate Governance and Business Law	978-0-7506-8714-0	£14.99	
		CIMA Official *Revision Cards*			
	C1	Fundamentals of Management Accounting	978-0-7506-8699-0	£8.99	
	C2	Fundamentals of Financial Accounting	978-0-7506-8722-5	£8.99	
	C3	Fundamentals of Business Maths	978-0-7506-8950-2	£8.99	
	C4	Fundamentals of Business Economics	978-0-7506-8697-6	£8.99	
	C5	Fundamentals of Ethics, Corporate Governance and Business Law	978-0-7506-8748-5	£8.99	
		eSuccess CDs			
	C1	CIMA eSuccess Fundamentals of Management Accounting	978-0-7506-8181-0	£24.99	
	C2	CIMA eSuccess Fundamentals of Financial Accounting	978-0-7506-8180-3	£24.99	
	C3	CIMA eSuccess Fundamentals of Business Maths	978-0-7506-8178-0	£24.99	
	C4	CIMA eSuccess Fundamentals of Business Economics	978-0-7506-8182-7	£24.99	
	C5	CIMA eSuccess Fundamentals of Ethics, CG and Law	978-0-7506-8179-7	£24.99	
		Complete eSuccess CD	978-0-7506-8183-4	£99.99	
		Books			
		Principles of Business Taxation	978-0-7506-8457-6	£49.99	
		CIMA: Pass First Time!	978-0-7506-8396-8	£12.99	
		Better Exam Results	978-0-7506-6357-1	£12.99	
			Postage and packing	£2.95	
			TOTAL		

Elsevier Ltd, Science & Technology Books, retains certain personal information about you in hard copy and on computer.
It will be used to inform you about goods and services available from Elsevier Ltd and its offices worldwide in which you
may be interested.

Please tick the box if you do NOT wish to receive this information. ☐

Post this form to:

CIMA Publishing Customer Services
Elsevier
FREEPOST (OF 1639)
Linacre House, Jordan Hill
OXFORD, OX2 8DP, UK

Or **FAX**   +44 (0)1865 314 572
Or **PHONE**   +44 (0)1865 474 014
Email: cimaorders@elsevier.com
                www.cimapublishing.com

Name:

Organisation:

Invoice Address:

Postcode:

Phone number:

Email:

Delivery Address if different:

FAO

Address

Postcode

Please note that all deliveries must be signed for

1. Cheques payable to Elsevier.

2. Please charge my:

☐ Visa/Barclaycard   ☐ Access/Mastercard
☐ American Express   ☐ Diners Card
☐ Switch   Issue No._____

Card No.

Expiry Date

Cardholder Name:

Signature:

Date:

CIMA Official *Exam Practice Kits*

Supplement the Learning Systems with a bank of additional questions focusing purely on applying what has been learnt to passing the exam. Ideal for independent study or tutored revision courses. Prepare with confidence for exam day, and pass the new syllabus first time.

- Avoid common pitfalls with fully worked model answers
- Type and weighting of questions match the format of the exam by paper, helping you prepare by giving you the closest available preview of the exam
- Summaries of key theory

CIMA Official *Revision Cards*

- Pocket-sized books for learning all the key points – especially for students on the move
- Relevant, succinct and compact reminders of all the bullet points and diagrams needed for the new CIMA exams
- Break down the syllabus into memorable bite-size chunks

Better Exam Results
A Guide for Business and
Accounting Students
2nd Edition
Sam Malone

- Shows CIMA students how to make the best use of valuable study time to pass exams first time
- Explains how to organise study, make notes, read faster and more effectively and improve your memory for maximising performance in the exam room
- Leading training consultant provides study and exam tips for success, particularly in CIMA exams but also for wider business exams and lifelong learning

ISBN-13: 978 07506 63571 : Price:£12.99

CIMA: Pass First Time!
David Harris

- Get the most out of your study time, and maximum marks at exam time – this book shows you how to work smarter, not harder
- Written by a CIMA Examiner and Tutor, this study buddy shows you exactly what the examiner is looking for
- Illustrations, mind-maps and cartoons cool your nerves and show you how to plan and write your answer succinctly and successfully

ISBN-13: 978 07506 83968 : Price:£12.99

Science & Technology Books, Elsevier Ltd.
Registered Office: The Boulevard, Langford Lane, Kidlington, OXON, OX5 1GB
Registered in England: 1982084

Give CIMA Publishing Your Feedback and Win a Prize

Win your choice of 3 further *Learning Systems* or an iPod

Help us to improve our product for next year by telling us of your experience using this product. All feedback forms returned will be entered into a prize draw. The first three forms drawn on 30 November 2008 will receive either three *Learning Systems* of their choice or an 2Gb iPod Nano. The winners will be notified by email.

Feedback form:

CIMA Official *Learning Systems* 2008 Editions

Name: _____

Address: _____

_____

Email: _____

■ **How did you use your CIMA Official *Learning System*?**

☐ Self-study (book only)

☐ On a full course?
How long was the course? _____
Which college did you attend? _____
_____

☐ On a revision course?
Which college did you attend? _____
_____

☐ Other _____
_____

Additional comments: _____
_____
_____
_____
_____
_____

■ **How did you order your CIMA Official *Learning System*?**

☐ Carrier sheet from CIMA Financial Management magazine

☐ CIMA Publishing catalogue found in Financial Management magazine

☐ Order form from the back of a previous *Learning System*

☐ www.cimapublishing.com website

☐ Bookshop
Name _____
Branch _____

☐ Other _____
_____

Additional comments: _____
_____
_____
_____
_____
_____

Your ratings and comments would be appreciated on the following aspects. Please circle your response, where one indicates an excellent rating and four a poor rating.

	Excellent		Poor	
☐ Topic coverage	1	2	3	4
☐ Accuracy	1	2	3	4
☐ Readings	1	2	3	4
☐ End of chapter				
questions and solutions	1	2	3	4
☐ Revision section	1	2	3	4
☐ Layout/Presentation	1	2	3	4
☐ Overall opinion of this study system	1	2	3	4

Additional comments:

_____

_____

_____

_____

■ Would you recommend CIMA Official *Learning Systems* to other students?

Please circle: Yes   No

Additional comments:

_____

_____

_____

_____

■ Which CIMA Publishing products have you used?
☐ CIMA Official *Learning Systems*
☐ Q&As
☐ CIMA eSuccess CDs
☐ CIMA Revision Cards
☐ CIMA Exam Practice Kits

Additional comments:

_____

_____

_____

_____

■ Are there any related products you would like to see from CIMA Publishing? If so, please elaborate below.

_____

_____

_____

_____

_____

_____

_____

■ Please note any further comments or errors found in the space below.

_____

_____

_____

_____

_____

_____

_____

_____

_____

_____

_____

Thank you for your time in completing this questionnaire. We wish you good luck in your exam.

Please return to:
CIMA Marketing
CIMA Publishing
FREEPOST – SCE 5435
Linacre House
Jordan Hill
Oxford, OX2 8DP, UK

ELSEVIER · CIMA PUBLISHING

Revision Resource on CD

- The only CBA preparation software and question bank endorsed by CIMA

- Questions written by the CIMA Faculty

- Assess your readiness for the CBA

- Identify areas you need to prioritise in your revision

- Increase your mark with the e-tutorials and feedback

C1	CIMA eSuccess Fundamentals of Management Accounting	978 0 7506 8181 0	£24.99
C2	CIMA eSuccess Fundamentals of Financial Accounting	978 0 7506 8180 3	£24.99
C3	CIMA eSuccess Fundamentals of Business Maths	978 0 7506 8178 0	£24.99
C4	CIMA eSuccess Fundamentals of Business Economics	978 0 7506 8182 7	£24.99
C5	CIMA eSuccess Fundamentals of Ethics, CG and Law	978 0 7506 8179 7	£24.99
Complete eSuccess CD		978 0 7506 8183 4	£99.99

1 Self Review Mode
Progress questions to help you test and develop your knowledge. Receive immediate marking on your answer, with full workings to explain the correct one

2 Self Test Mode
A timed test to simulate the CBA. At the end you will receive a report showing your overall mark and areas of strength and weakness

www.cimapublishing.com/esuccess